DATE DUE

DEMCO 38-296

FACTS ABOUT THE CONGRESS

By *Stephen G. Christianson*

With an introduction by Richard Allan Baker,
Historian for the United States Senate

THE H.W. WILSON COMPANY
NEW YORK AND DUBLIN

A New England Publishing Associates Book
1996

NEW ENGLAND
PUBLISHING
ASSOCIATES

Copy-Editing: Karen Storo
Design and Page Composition: Teri Prestash
Editorial Administration: Dave Voytek
Proofreading: Margaret Heinrich Hand
Indexing: Miccinello Associates

Library of Congress Cataloging-in-Publication Data
    Christianson, Stephen G.
    Facts about the Congress / by Stephen G. Christianson.
    p. cm.
    Includes biographical references (p.   ) and index.
    ISBN 0-8242-0883-8
    1. United States. Congress—History, I. Title.
    JK1021.C48   1996
    328.73'07'09   dc20   95-53691
                                                  CIP

Printed in the United States of America

DEDICATION

This book is dedicated to two people. First, to my father, who recently retired as a congressional staff director and who helped make this book possible. His life of quiet dedication to his country and his family are an inspiration to his sons. Second, to Jeannette Rankin, the first woman ever elected to Congress. Rankin was not only a Progressive and a leader in the women's rights movement, she was also passionately antiwar. She served only two terms in the House, but those terms coincided with the U.S. entry into World Wars I and II, and thus she has the distinction of being the only member of Congress to vote against both wars. Even when she was in her late eighties, this remarkable woman was leading protest marches against the Vietnam War.

CONTENTS

LIST OF ILLUSTRATIONS

All photos obtained with assistance of the Senate Historical Office.

PREFACE

This book is the first comprehensive treatment of the major achievements of, and the major developments in, the United States Congress from 1789 to the present. The objective is to present a reference guide to the history of the United States Congress for students and other researchers. Therefore, all of the important information is presented chronologically by Congress. Although there are many very fine sources on Congress for the post World War II period, this book is the only concise reference source covering the entire two hundred plus years of congressional history. This book is organized in chapters beginning with the First Congress, which lasted from 1789 to 1791, and ending with the first session of the 104th Congress, which began in 1995.

Although there are some cross-references between them, each chapter covers a single Congress and is intended to stand alone. While this results in some duplication of information, the author and publisher believe this will best suit the needs of researchers interested in a single Congress. There are also a series of notes to the text (found on page xxix) that contain information that would otherwise have to be repeated in nearly every Congress.

Each chapter contains the following information organized in a consistent structure and written in nontechnical language suitable for the general reader:
- Dates on which the sessions of Congress met.
- The gains and losses by the major parties in both the House and the Senate.
- A background summary of contemporary events.
- A detailed roster of the party leadership in the House and the Senate, including the chairmen of major committees and other important leaders in Congress when relevant.
- Important changes in Congress's organization and administration.
- A chronology of important dates for the Congress.
- Major legislation passed.
- A summary of important proposed legislation that failed to pass.
- Relations between the Congress and the president, with statistics on presidential vetoes.
- Statistics on presidential nominations, appointments, and confirmations for the judicial and executive branches.
- Information on impeachments of executive officials, if any.
- Information on the approval or rejection of constitutional amendments.
- A table of key votes for the Congress. (After World War II, when this information becomes readily and consistently available, the votes also are broken down by party.)
- Important scandals, if any.

- A bibliography for the reader who wishes to obtain further information on matters relevant to that historical time period. (A general bibliography on the history of Congress is included at the end of this book.)

In researching and compiling a reference work of such chronological scope, an author encounters surprising gaps in the historical record and numerous obstacles. For example, to research the period prior to World War II, the author spent two years searching through sources within the private libraries of Congress on Capitol Hill to find the facts needed. With the post-World War II period, the obstacle was too much rather than too little information. Material that covers hundreds of thousands of pages in the Congressional Record and other sources had to be sifted and condensed into a readable and useful format. The result is, I hope, an authoritative and concise reference work for the student, historian, and casual reader alike.

My thanks to Dr. Richard Baker, Historian of the Senate, for his invaluable help and for agreeing to be the consulting editor of this book. My thanks also to Gregory Harness and the staff of the Senate Library, who were kind enough to let me roam at will among the stacks. Finally, special thanks to my agent Edward Knappman and the staff at New England Publishing Associates, who were the genesis of this book and who have tolerated my computer illiteracy with good humor.

This book covers more than two hundred years of American history, a wide range of subject matter, and many academic and historical disciplines. With future editions in mind, if any reader believes that some matter has been missed or inadequately discussed, I would be interested in hearing from him or her. Inquiries and suggestions should be sent to me in care of the publisher. I will respond as soon as possible, but it may take some time for me to receive your inquiries or comments.

CONGRESS
HOW IT WORKS AND ITS ROLE IN AMERICAN GOVERNMENT

1. THE FEDERAL NATURE OF AMERICAN GOVERNMENT

Under the federal system, there are two overlapping types of government in the United States:

(1) The federal government with its bureaucracy and various agencies, centralized since the early 19th century in Washington, D.C., the nation's capital.

(2) The local state governments, with their state bureaucracies and agencies, located in the 50 state capitals around the country.

In a nutshell, the Constitution [See Appendix A for text] gives the federal government the necessary powers for effective national government, but leaves most local matters in the hands of the state governments. Today most Americans assume that the federal government and Congress can do essentially what they want, within constitutional boundaries, and that state governments have only as much power as the federal government allows. This is not true today, and historically was far from true. Before the Civil War the federal government was very small, and the states controlled most domestic social and economic matters. Southern states were particularly jealous of their prerogatives, since the South with its slave-based economy was losing political and economic power to the North with its wage-based industrial economy. A series of slavery and secession crises ultimately led to the Civil War. [See the background section of each Congress for further information.] After four years of Civil War, the federal government was unquestionably the stronger party in the federal-state relationship, but it continued to take a very limited role in such domestic matters as public works, poverty

relief, social reform, etc. Furthermore, a series of Supreme Court rulings restricted federal powers, such as the federal power to regulate interstate commerce. The balance of federal and state power changed in the 1930s, however, with the New Deal. The Supreme Court ended its restrictive attitude toward the exercise of federal powers, and Congress greatly expanded the federal role in domestic economic and social matters. World War II increased the size of the federal government again, particularly with the increase in federal taxes and expenditures to support a large and ultimately permanent military establishment. By the 1960s, when congressional legislation on civil rights was causing tensions in the South, the federal government occasionally was forced to use troops to enforce desegregation. However, unlike during the Civil War period, there was no serious state resistance to federal action. In the 1990s, the Republicans in Congress have sought to return many federal powers and programs to the states, but whether the balance of power will tilt by any considerable measure back toward the states remains debatable.

2. THE SEPARATION OF POWERS WITHIN THE FEDERAL GOVERNMENT

The framers of the Constitution deliberately separated the executive, legislative, and judicial functions of the federal government, so that each branch of government would act as a check on the other and no one branch would become too powerful.

The president and the federal bureaucracy (Department of State, Department of Defense, etc.), which the president controls, constitute the executive branch. The executive branch carries out the actions of government and enforces the laws passed by Congress. [See *Facts About the Presidents* for further information about the presidents.] Congress, with its two chambers, the Senate and the House of Representatives, is the legislative branch. The legislative branch passes the laws that the executive branch enforces and provides the funding for executive branch agencies and programs. The judicial branch consists of the Supreme Court, which was created by the Constitution as the highest court in the land, and the system of lower federal courts. Funded by Congress, the judicial branch interprets the laws and the Constitution and can nullify unconstitutional legislation passed by Congress or stop unconstitutional actions by the executive branch. [See *Facts About the Supreme Court* for further information about the Supreme Court.]

Although the executive, legislative, and judicial branches are intended to be equal in power, there have been periods during which one branch has been stronger or weaker than the others. Between Congress and the presidency, the power relationship waxes and wanes depending on how strong the president is, whether the president's political party controls Congress, and how determined and united congressional leaders are. For example, President Lyndon Johnson was decidedly the stronger party in dealing with Congress. His fellow Democrats had large majorities in both the House and the Senate, and as a former Senate majority leader, Johnson knew how to deal with his old colleagues. Conversely, President Andrew Johnson, who became president in 1865 when Abraham Lincoln was assassinated, was decidedly the weaker party in dealing with Congress. Johnson got along badly with the Republicans who dominated Congress, and was so unpopular personally that he ultimately faced impeachment and barely escaped removal from office. A more contemporary example of the shifting balance of power in the federal government is the Clinton administration. In the 103rd Congress President Clinton's legislative agenda had considerable support, since his fellow Democrats controlled Congress. However, the Republican opposition

rallied to defeat the administration's complex health care reform plan and won majorities in both chambers in the November 1994 elections. With the Republicans becoming the majority party in the 104th Congress, the legislative initiative shifted to Congress, forcing Clinton to use his veto power for the first time.

3. THE TWO CHAMBERS OF CONGRESS

House of Representatives: The House was designed by the Constitution to be closely in touch with the people and the concerns of the electorate. Thus, representatives are elected for two-year terms so that the entire House is up for reelection every other November. Their short terms force representatives to be constantly mindful of the popularity or unpopularity of their actions. If their actions are unpopular with the voters they may be defeated in the upcoming election. Unlike senators, representatives are distributed across the country on the basis of each state's population. When Congress first met in 1789, each representative's congressional district had approximately 30,000 people. Since that time, the population has grown rapidly, and as of 1990 nearly all congressional districts contain more than 600,000 people. (The size of the House was capped at 435 representatives in the early 20th century so that the House would not become too large to be efficient.) The Constitution stipulated that every 10 years a national census be undertaken to tally the nation's population and determine how many people live in each state. Each new census — the first one was in 1790 — is the basis for determining how many representatives each state will have, a process called *apportionment*. States with large populations are apportioned many representatives: California, the most populous state, has 52 representatives. States with small populations are guaranteed at least one representative by the Constitution: Wyoming, which has the lowest population of any state, some 450,000 people, has one representative and its single congressional district covers the whole state.

Between 10-year censuses, some states increase

in population while others stay the same or even lose population. With each new census, representatives are reapportioned among the states, but with the total number of representatives always staying at 435. [See the Table of Apportionments by Census at Appendix F for further information.]

Finally, in keeping with its role as the chamber closest to the people, the minimum age requirement for members of the House is only 25, lower than for senators (who must be at least 30 years old) and for the president (who must be at least 35 years old).

Since the House is supposed to be the branch that is most in touch with the electorate, the Constitution gives it certain powers that the Senate does not share.

• All tax legislation must originate in the House. This is a deliberate exception to the general rule in Congress that legislation can originate in either chamber. The reasoning behind this exception is that the House, being especially sensitive to electoral discontent, is unlikely to enact any really unpopular tax. Of course, any tax legislation passed by the House must also be passed by the Senate, where amendments can be proposed and passed, changing the House bill.

• For Congress to impeach the president or another federal official, such as a Supreme Court justice, the process must begin in the House, where a favorable vote is required to proceed. Although the impeachment trial is conducted in the Senate, there cannot be a trial if the House does not first vote for impeachment.

• If there is no clear electoral vote winner in a presidential election — which happened in the elections of 1800 and 1824 — the House can determine by its vote alone which of the candidates will be the next president.

Senate: The drafters of the Constitution also wanted a chamber of Congress composed of deliberative, experienced statesmen, who would be less susceptible to electoral mood swings, and who would act as a check on the House. The intent was to ensure that Congress as a whole acted more in accordance with the nation's long-term best interests than the politics of the moment. To make senators less subject to political mood swings, they are elected for six-year terms and only one-third are up for reelection at any one time.

To appease the states with small populations and small delegations to the House of Representatives, the Constitution gives every state, regardless of population, two senators. Since there were only 13 states in existence in 1789, there were 26 senators in the First Congress. Since there are now 50 states, there are 100 senators in the 104th Congress. Should the District of Columbia or another area become a state, there will be another two senators in Congress.

Originally, senators were not directly elected by a state's voters, but were chosen by the state legislature or the governor. Representatives, on the other hand, were from the beginning directly elected by those eligible to vote in their respective state's general election. The Seventeenth Amendment to the Constitution, ratified in 1913, abolished the system of indirect election and made senators directly elected by the people in the same congressional election process with representatives.

Senators must be at least 30 years old, a requirement meant to ensure that senators will be mature individuals. Accordingly, the Constitution gives to the Senate certain powers that the House does not enjoy:

• Only the Senate can approve treaties. Treaties must be approved by a two-thirds majority of the senators present at the vote.

• Only the Senate can approve presidential nominations to the Supreme Court, to cabinet positions (e.g. the secretary of defense), and to ambassadorships. Nominations must be approved by a simple majority of the senators present at the vote.

• Although only the House can vote for the impeachment of a federal official, only the Senate can conduct the actual impeachment trial. For someone to be removed from office, two-thirds of the senators present at the vote must vote in favor of impeachment.

4. CONGRESSIONAL LEADERSHIP

Congressional leadership is largely determined by which political party has the majority in the House and the Senate. In modern times the political affiliations of members of the House and the Senate have been very clear cut: almost everyone is either a Democrat or a Republican, although there is the occasional independent. During the 18th and 19th centuries, however, political affiliations often were much looser, and the historical records of the period are far from complete or clear on the question of party membership. For example, in the early Congresses it was not unusual for candidates to run for office on their own platform or on their own reputation without any tie to a political party. For those politicians, historical clues, such as their voting records in Congress, have to be analyzed in order to determine whether they can be categorized as Democratic-Republicans, Federalists, Whigs, or members of some other party. In this book, every effort has been made to provide readers with accurate breakdowns of party affiliations in both the House and the Senate, and to show the changes in party strength from Congress to Congress. However, readers should bear in mind the limitations of historical records, particularly in the period before the Civil War.

House of Representatives: The leader of the House is called the Speaker of the House. The Speaker is chosen by the political party with the most representatives in the House. The Speaker controls which bills come to the floor and when, presides during debates, and sets his party's legislative agenda in the House. By virtue of the power of the office, the Speaker is nearly always one of the most influential figures in American politics.

Below the Speaker, there are several levels of leadership for both the majority and minority parties:
- Majority Leader. The House majority leader works with the Speaker and is considered the second most powerful member.
- Majority Whip. The House majority whip is responsible for making sure that party members vote consistently with the party's agenda.
- Minority Leader. The leader of the political party in the minority is called the House minority leader.
- Minority Whip. The House minority whip is responsible for making sure that members of the minority party vote consistently with the party's agenda.

Senate Leadership: The Senate leadership is more complicated than that of the House. The Constitution provides that the vice president of the United States is also the president of the Senate. In fact, the vice president rarely exercises the right to preside over the Senate unless there is a tie vote on an important matter, in which case the vice president gets to cast the tie-breaking vote. In the absence of the vice president, which is most of the time, a president pro tempore presides over the Senate. The position of president pro tempore has no power to set the legislative agenda or influence the course of debate. It is the Senate majority leader, who leads the political party with the most senators, who is the effective leader of the Senate.

Other leaders:
- Majority Whip. The Senate majority whip is responsible for making sure that party members vote consistently with the party's agenda.
- Minority Leader. The leader of the political party in the minority is called the Senate minority leader.
- Minority Whip. The Senate minority whip is responsible for making sure that members of the minority party vote consistently with the party agenda.

5. THE LEGISLATIVE PROCESS

Here is a step-by-step description of the legislative process in Congress.

Step 1. Someone inside or outside of Congress may come up with an idea that requires federal legislation. This might be enacting a new law, repealing an old law, or changing an existing law. The idea must be written into a formal proposal called a bill. Because writing a proposed statute is something of an art, the actual writing is usually done by a lawyer or someone with legislative experience, generally an aide who works for a senator or representative.

Step 2. The bill is introduced in Congress. Although literally anyone can think of or write a bill, only senators and representatives can introduce a bill in Congress. A bill introduced in Congress by a senator starts in the Senate. A bill introduced by a representative starts in the House. Usually it does not matter in which chamber a bill is introduced except for tax legislation, which must originate in the House. Often, on important bills more than one senator or representative will jointly introduce, or sponsor, it. The bill is given an S number if introduced in the Senate and an HR number if introduced in the House. There may be several bills on the same topic introduced in the House, or the Senate, or both the House and the Senate. These different bills are considered, reconciled, or rejected during the rest of the legislative process.

Step 3. Once introduced, a bill is assigned to a committee. For example, a bill introduced in the Senate to increase aid to a foreign country would probably be assigned to the Senate Foreign Relations Committee. However, a bill may fall within the jurisdiction of more than one committee. For example, a Senate bill to increase aid to a foreign country by subsidizing military exports to that country could be heard by the Senate Foreign Relations Committee, or by the Senate Armed Services Committee, or by both committees. How a bill is assigned depends on its importance, political factors, committee workloads, the influence of the sponsor or sponsors, the power of committee chairmen, and so forth. Within each committee there are several subcommittees, one of which will probably be given the responsibility for working on the bill before it goes to the full committee. Most bills that are introduced travel no further in the legislative process because they simply do not have the political support to get past the subcommittee level.

Step 4. When subcommittee hearings begin, people from special interest groups, political organizations, think tanks, academic institutions, and the public at large may be invited to testify for or against the bill.

Step 5. The subcommittee meets to *mark up* the bill, which means to revise and amend it until it has sufficient support on the subcommittee, and can be reported favorably to the full committee.

Step 6. After deliberations, a subcommittee votes on whether to send the bill to the full committee. If it reports the bill favorably, the bill goes to the full committee for consideration. If the subcommittee does not report the bill favorably, the bill probably dies.

Step 7. The full committee considers the bill and may hold more hearings or make further revisions.

Step 8. The committee now votes on whether to report the bill favorably. If a House committee reports a bill favorably, it goes to the full House for a vote, and if a Senate committee reports a bill favorably it goes to the full Senate for a vote. If a committee does not report the bill favorably, the bill probably dies.

Step 9. Before the House or Senate votes on a bill reported favorably by one of its committees, time is set aside for debate. During the debate, there may be more amendments and revisions to the bill, each to be voted on before the bill as a whole is finally voted on. If a senator is interested in amending a bill, but is not a member of the relevant committee marking it up, he or she then can try to get the bill amended on the floor when the bill goes before the whole Senate.

Amendments always do not have to be relevant to a bill's purpose in order to be approved. For example, a member might ask that an agriculture bill be amended to include funding for a basketball program in the member's home state as the price for that member's support in getting the bill passed. In the Senate, but not in the House, a member can attempt to *filibuster* a bill. Under the Senate rules, a senator can speak for hours, even days, in order to delay or prevent a vote on a bill that a majority of senators favor. For example, during the civil rights turmoil of the 1960s, southern senators filibustered civil rights legislation, even reading from telephone books, in order to kill time. In order to end a filibuster, the Senate must *invoke cloture*, meaning to vote to cut off further debate. Under the current rules, it takes 60 votes in the Senate to invoke cloture. Thus, even if a majority of 51 out of the 100 senators support a bill, a filibuster can block a bill if at least nine more senators do not join in a vote to invoke cloture.

Step 10. If a bill passes one chamber, it then goes to the other for consideration. Frequently, the House and the Senate more or less simultaneously go through the whole process of committee hearings, floor debate, and amendment procedure on the same bill. In the case of most important legislation, the two chambers do not end up passing identical bills. When the House and Senate versions of the bill are different, a *conference committee* is formed by the House and Senate leaders to reconcile the differences between the bills. If the conference committee cannot reach an agreement, the bill probably dies.

If an agreement is reached, the conference committee version of the bill goes back to both chambers for final votes. [In the interests of clarity and practicality, in the Table of Key Votes for each Congress in this book, the dates and votes given refer to the first time the House and/or the Senate passed the measure, and not when a conference committee version of the bill was passed.]

Step 11. Once the House and the Senate have passed identical versions of the bill, the bill goes to the president. If the president signs the bill, it becomes law.

Step 12. If the president vetoes the bill, the bill goes back to Congress, where the two chambers can try to *override the veto*. If two-thirds of the House present and voting and two-thirds of the Senate present and voting vote to override a veto, the bill becomes law. If the required two-thirds majorities are not obtained in the House and the Senate, the veto stands and the bill dies. On the other hand, even if a veto is not overridden, there is nothing to prevent Congress from passing an identical bill in the future, which might or might not be vetoed again. As a practical matter, however, it is politically difficult for Congress to pass legislation that already has been vetoed if the override vote fails.

INTRODUCTION

Richard Allan Baker
Historian of the United States Senate

Article I, Section 1 of the United States Constitution states that "All legislative powers herein granted shall be vested in a Congress of the United States, which shall consist of a Senate and House of Representatives." For more than two centuries, this constitution, the world's oldest charter of government, has successfully sustained a system, unlike any other in human history, for sharing and dividing legislative, executive, and judicial powers.

The document's 55 framers met in secret during the hot spring and summer of 1787 at Philadelphia's Independence Hall. Their goal was to replace the ineffective 10-year-old Articles of Confederation with a system of representative government that more realistically met the new nation's needs. To remedy the defects of this earlier constitution, the framers gave Congress a series of specified powers, including the authority to raise revenue, declare war, provide for the nation's defense, regulate commerce, create executive branch agencies, and establish a system of courts below the Supreme Court. The convention completed its work on September 17, 1787. The necessary three-quarters of the states approved the Constitution as of June 1788, and the first federal Congress convened at New York City's Federal Hall on March 4, 1789.

Representation: The Constitution's framers realized that a more powerful national government was needed to protect the new nation against growing external threats from Great Britain and Spain, but also domestic conflicts like the recent Shay's Rebellion that could tear apart the fragile

union of states. However, the framers restrained the use of that additional governmental power by dividing Congress into two branches, or houses, each with a different basis of representation. Of the two congressional branches, the House of Representatives was intended to be more directly responsible to the people. Its members, who had to be at least 25 years old and to have been citizens of the United States for seven years, would be elected for two-year terms by the same voters — mainly landowners — who were eligible to vote for representatives in the lower house of their state legislatures. These brief terms required those seeking election to keep in close touch with the needs and opinions of their constituents. A state's voting power within the House depended on the size of its population; the Constitution called for one representative for every thirty thousand residents.

Unlike the House, the Senate was designed to be less influenced by public opinion. The framers provided that senators would not be elected directly by the voters but by state legislatures. With six-year terms, senators would be free to make decisions for which they would not be immediately accountable. (By the late 19th century, this form of election led to so many deadlocks between the two houses of the various state legislatures that the Seventeenth Amendment was added to the Constitution in 1913 providing that senators would be elected directly by the voters.) On the theory that age brings wisdom, the framers required senators to be at least 30 years old and to have been United States citizens for nine years. To balance turnover with the need for continuity, they also arranged that only one-third of the

Senate's seats would be subject to election during each two-year congressional election cycle.

Lawmaking: The enactment of a law, under the Constitution's guidelines, is a deceptively simple process that often leads to endless complications. When a member of either the House or Senate introduces a bill, the presiding officer of the member's chamber refers it to one or more committees for study and recommendations. A committee may refer the bill to a subcommittee for a more specialized review. After a committee "reports" (or approves) the bill either as introduced or in a modified form, the chamber as a whole votes to approve or rejects it. (Approval by either house requires a simple majority of those voting.) If approved, the measure then is sent to the other chamber where it is again referred, studied, reported, amended, and passed. If, as is highly likely, the measure emerges from the second house in a different form, it is sent to a "conference committee" made up of members from both houses whose task it is to resolve the differences. A compromise version is then returned to each house and, if both approve it, is sent to the president for final approval. If the president signs the measure, it becomes the law of the land, subject only to implementation by appropriate agencies of the executive branch. If the president vetoes the legislation, the measure can only become law if each house overrides his veto by a two-thirds majority. If the measure fails to gain that "super-majority," its sponsors may begin the lawmaking process all over again, typically by introducing a modified bill that the president is more likely to sign or that will attrack enough votes to override his veto. In each two-year session of Congress, members introduce some 10,000 bills and resolutions. Of that number, approximately 600 survive this difficult journey into law.

Congressional Operations: When the first Congress convened its first session on March 4, 1789, both chambers had to decide how they would operate. The Constitution itself provided many of the answers. For instance, while the House could elect anyone it wished—member or not—to be its presiding officer, the Senate had no choice but to recognize the vice president of the United States as its president, although a temporary replacement could be seated when the vice president was not available. Unlike the Speaker of the House, the Senate's president is not permitted to address that body without its permission and has only one formal duty—to cast tie-breaking votes. (The vice president routinely presided over most Senate sessions until the mid-20th century when the main focus of the office shifted from its few Capitol Hill duties to more important work at the White House.) The Constitution directs that Congress meet at least once each year. (The Twentieth Amendment in 1933 changed the meeting date from the first Monday in December to January 3.) Each house may determine its own operating rules, but the Constitution laid down an important stipulation—that a majority of eligible members must be present at a meeting in order to conduct business, although a smaller number present can vote to compel attendance and set penalties for those who refuse to appear. The Constitution also set disciplinary rules under which either house may expel a member (by a two-thirds) vote and may determine whether a newly elected member is qualified to serve (by simple majority vote). Long before the *Congressional Record* began publication in 1873 as the official account of House and Senate proceedings, the Constitution required each house to keep a "Journal of its Proceedings and from time to time to publish the same, excepting such Parts as may in their Judgment require Secrecy." From their service before 1787 in state legislatures and in the old Congress under the Articles of Confederation, most of the Constitution's framers had a great deal of experience with mischievous legislative behavior. Anticipating that there would be occasions when members might try to hide their votes, the framers included a requirement that the votes on any bill, whether in the House or Senate, must be published if demanded by one-fifth of those present. Since the approval of both houses is necessary for action to be taken, in order to prevent one house from blocking action by refusing to meet, the Constitution requires that neither house may adjourn for more than three days without the permission of the other. The framers found the issue of congressional salaries troublesome, so they left it to Congress to deal with it by providing that members "shall receive a Compensation for their Services, to be ascertained by Law, and paid out of the Treasury of the United States." Finally, the Constitution addressed the filling of vacancies between elections. For a House vacancy, the governor of the affected state must call an election, but for a Senate vacancy, the governor has the greater latitude to make a temporary appointment if the state legislature is not in session to fill the seat. (In addition to providing for direct popular election of senators, the Seventeenth Amendment allows state governors to fill vacancies until the next regular election if authorized to do so by state law.)

The Constitution gives to each house of Congress identical power to approve legislation. Unlike some nations' parliamentary bodies, such as the British Parliament, in which the house whose members are directly elected by the voters may overrule the actions of an indirectly appointed upper house, Congress cannot pass legislation in final form unless both chambers have agreed to it in identical language. While sharing fundamental legislative powers, each chamber also possesses unique prerogatives. The House of Representatives has sole responsibility for initiating revenue legislation and for deciding whether a federal officer should be impeached. In a presidential election, when no candidate receives a majority of electoral college votes, the House is given the sole power to select the president by voting for one of the three highest vote-getters (as it did in the elections of 1800 and 1824).

The framers modeled the Senate after the state senates of the time, most of which had evolved from advisory councils to colonial and state governors. The Senate was given the constitutional role of providing advice and giving consent to the president of the United States on such matters as presidential nominations to executive and judicial posts by requiring a simple majority vote for confirmation. A two-thirds vote is needed to approve treaties and to remove a federal officer who has been impeached by the House.

Amendments to the Constitution also require approval by a vote of at least two-thirds of each house of Congress and ratification by three-quarters of all states. Although thousands of constitutional amendments have been brought forward over the past two centuries, only 27 have been approved by Congress and then ratified by a sufficient number of states. Most of these amendments establish rights of citizens, as do the first 10—the Bill of Rights.

From their earliest days, the Senate and House of Representatives followed very different roads in their development as legislative institutions. The Senate of the First Congress began with only 22 members—a body the size of a single congressional committee in modern times. As there were so few members, they could speak on any subject for as long as they wished. This tradition of the right of unlimited debate continues today, although it is now possible, with great effort, to limit debate on a specific measure if 60 percent of all senators agree to do so. Like the Congress under the Articles of Confederation and the Constitutional Convention itself, the Senate originally met behind closed doors. (Within six years, however, the Senate relented to public pressure and permanently opened its doors, except for deliberations on nominations and treaties, which remained closed on most occasions until 1929.)

The House of Representatives grew in size much faster than the Senate. It began with 65 members in 1789. The nation's expanding population, as measured by the 1790 census, quickly increased the membership to 106 as of 1793. By 1823 more than 200 members jammed the House chamber. By the end of the 19th century that number would approach 400. (Following the 1910 census, Congress agreed to cap the number at 435, thus beginning the escalation of congressional district size from 30,000 inhabitants to the more than 600,000 voters today.) The growing numbers of House members had a major impact on House operations. For example, by the beginning of the 19th century, the House had developed strict rules to limit the amount of time an individual member could speak.

Committees: The Constitution's framers envisioned that the Senate would spend most of its time reviewing legislation crafted in the House of Representatives. When senators decided they needed to explore a complicated issue, whether in legislation sent from the House or in new legislation that a senator wished to introduce, they elected a temporary committee of from three to five members to explore the matter and draft the bill. Once the committee reported its draft legislation, it went out of existence. As similar issues came before the Senate, that body tended to select the same members to serve on successive temporary committees. When the president submitted his annual message to Congress, it was divided by subject and assigned to committees of specialists. In 1816 the Senate decided to establish permanent "standing" committees to avoid the inefficiency of constantly having to elect temporary "select" or "special" committees.

Members looked to committees as a substitute place for legislative discussions and, as a result, the much larger House, appreciating the value of these smaller forums, established permanent committees much earlier than the Senate. Prior to the Civil War, each permanent committee had the traditional legislative responsibility of deciding how much money a program or project deserved. The second major step in the legislative process— deciding how much revenue could actually be appropriated from available resources—was reserved in the House to the Ways and Means Committee, and in the Senate to the Finance Committee. In 1865 the House divided this fundamental process by creating a separate Committee on Appropriations. The Senate established its Appropriations Committee two years later.

Since the early 19th century, chairmen of major committees have exercised a great deal of power. In the House, the major struggle for control of the legislative agenda, which determines which bills will be brought up for a vote and when, traditionally has been framed as a battle between Speakers and committee chair-

men. This clash became increasingly more evident in the 20th century in both houses as holders of the newly created floor leader posts strengthened leadership's ability to resist challenges from senior chairmen. As early as the 1840s, Congress recognized the role of seniority as the basis for making committee assignments: by giving the chairmanship of a committee to the most senior eligible member, the House and Senate avoided exhausting battles for these positions. On occasion, particularly in the recent history of the House, the most senior member has been denied the promotion, but such rejections of the seniority system are still relatively rare. (In 1995 House Republicans agreed, for the first time in history, to limit service of committee chairmen to no more than three consecutive two-year terms.)

In the late 19th century, the number of committees escalated as increasingly busy members sought the office space and staff that these positions provided. In the 1880s Congress authorized construction, along the west side of the Capitol, of a terrace housing more than 100 small rooms. These rooms provided space for the multiplying number of minor committees, such as the Senate's Forest Reservation and Protection-of-Game Committee. From time to time Congress abolished these relatively useless panels, but pressure from members for space and staff inevitably led to the creation of others. To meet these needs, which reflected the growing role of the federal government in the nation's economic development, the House and Senate allowed members who did not chair committees to hire a small clerical staff. Both houses also authorized construction of permanent office buildings. These first two buildings, today named after House Speaker Joseph G. Cannon (Rep., Ill.) and Senator Richard B. Russell (Dem., Ga.), provided a private office for each member and for the major committees. Later in the 20th century the House and Senate each acquired two additional office buildings. The House buildings, completed in 1933 and 1965, were named after Speakers Nicholas Longworth (Rep., Ohio) and Sam Rayburn (Dem.,Tex.). The Senate buildings, completed in 1958 and 1982, were designated to honor Senators Everett McKinley Dirksen (Rep., Ill.) and Philip A. Hart (Dem., Mich.).

Political Parties: During the Constitutional Convention of 1787, delegates tended to form groupings based on their region, economic interests, and their view of government's proper role. In the First Congress, these groupings evolved into political parties—a development that the Constitution's framers had not anticipated. The two main parties were the Federalists and the Republicans, or Anti-Federalists. The former was led by Vice President John Adams and Treasury Secretary Alexander Hamilton and stood for an active, protective role for the national government, particularly to insure economic growth and a stable currency. The Republicans were led by Secretary of State Thomas Jefferson and Virginia Representative James Madison, who believed that the national government's powers should be limited, with most authority located at the state and local levels. These emerging political parties also disagreed over foreign policy, with the Federalists favoring Great Britain and the Jeffersonian Republicans siding with revolutionary France.

By 1815 the Federalist Party had lost its focus and ceased to be a significant political force. A second political party system took root in the 1820s around the leadership of Andrew Jackson. By the mid-1830s the nation was again in a position to choose between two actively contending political parties—Jackson's Democrats and Kentucky Senator Henry Clay's Whigs. The Whigs were unable to agree on a national platform of unifying principles, but nonetheless won the presidency and both houses of Congress in the election of 1840 and the presidency in 1848. The Whigs failed to develop a solid following, and the party disintegrated in the early 1850s over the issue of whether to allow slavery in the vast regions added to the nation in the 1840s as a result of the war with Mexico. Up to this time both parties had worked to keep the slavery issue out of the national spotlight, arguing that it was a matter for state rather than national decision.

As the two major parties began to fall apart over these sectional issues in the early 1850s, several splinter groups formed, including the Free-Soil Party and the Know-Nothing Party. From the chaos of this shattered party system emerged two reformed parties: the Republicans and the Democrats. The Civil War placed the Republicans in control of Congress as large numbers of southern Democratic members departed with their seceding states. That Republican dominance continued throughout most of the 50-year period from 1861 to 1911, with the Democrats controlling both houses of Congress during only four of those years. In periods of national political instability, third parties traditionally have arisen, such as the Anti-Masonic Party of the 1820s and 1830s, the Greenback Party of the 1870s, the People's Party of the 1890s, and the Progressives of the early 20th century.

Leadership: For most of its first century, Congress operated without much formal leadership beyond the committee chairmen. Senior members of each party met informally to decide on legislative priorities, and chairmen managed their committees' bills on the House and Senate floors. In the decades following the Civil War, however, as a flood of complex issues demanded federal government involvement, the political parties in Congress organized formal meetings of all their members, called caucuses, to determine a common legislative strategy and agenda. In 1880 the House created a permanent Committee on Rules and made the Speaker its chairman. In 1889 the House Republican majority elected Thomas B. Reed of Maine as Speaker. Reed, making the most of his role as Rules Committee chairman, developed the speakership into a powerful leadership post by, among other devices, expanding the use of "special rules" to set conditions under which specific bills would be scheduled for floor consideration. When, a generation later, rebellious House members curbed these powers in a revolt against the autocratic rule of a Reed successor, Joseph G. Cannon (Rep., Ill.), leadership in the crowded House chamber simply moved from the Speaker at the rostrum to the majority leader on the floor.

The lack of a formal, centralized leadership is one of the many features that has distinguished the Senate from the House of Representatives. In maintaining its tradition of unlimited debate, the Senate has denied the majority the crucial power to control proceedings by cutting off debate and calling for a vote. When, however, in 1913 the Democrats took control of the Senate for the first time in 20 years, they realized that they had a limited amount of time in which to enact the party's legislative agenda. Therefore, Senate Democrats designated a party floor leader, John W. Kern (Dem., Ind.), who served not only as liaison with committee chairmen but also with President Woodrow Wilson. In 1919, the Republicans regained control and followed suit by electing Senator Henry Cabot Lodge (Rep., Mass.) majority leader. Both parties in the Senate at this time also created the position of assistant leader, or "whip," to promote party discipline and to inform the floor leader how party members intended to vote on key issues. Still, despite the development of this formal leadership structure, the strength of a leader in the decades ahead came from the forcefulness of his personality rather than from institutional reinforcements. The only formal prerogative of office available to these Senate leaders is that the presiding officer must recognize them before all others wishing to obtain the floor. Nonetheless, this seemingly modest power, in skilled hands, has been used effectively to manage floor proceedings.

The Modern Congress: Three of the six office buildings that house the 535 members of Congress were constructed after World War II, a visual reminder of the major expansion of Congress in recent times. During the early 1940s, congressional leaders became increasingly concerned that President Franklin D. Roosevelt was using the wartime emergency to justify taking on more powers for the presidency at the expense of Congress. The president repeatedly told these Capitol Hill leaders that if they did not quickly provide the legislation he requested, "I shall accept the responsibility, and I shall act!" In 1945, the war ended, Roosevelt died, and Harry Truman suc-ceeded to the presidency. A year later, fearful of presidential dictatorship at home, Congress passed the Legislative Reorganization Act of 1946, the single most important law ever passed related to the operation of Congress.

That act served as the foundation for the Congress we know today. Its basic objective was to achieve a proper balance between the powers of Congress and those of the presidency. Its guiding principle was that Congress, as a co-equal branch of the national government, should have the same access to independent information and expertise as that available to the White House and the executive branch agencies. The act allowed committees and individual members, for the first time, to hire professional staff. The act also reduced the number of congressional committees, but in doing so triggered the expansion of subcommittees. These new legislative resources became available just as the United States took on new responsibilities for restoring and maintaining international economic and political order in the cold war era that followed the devastation of World War II. By the early 1950s, members came to view service in Congress as a career in itself. This reversed the traditional pattern of relatively short-term service by members who found more opportunities for personal development in the private sector or in public service at the state and local levels.

As the challenges confronting Congress and its members increased, so too did the size of the institution's legislative staff. By the mid-1960s, the House employed 600 committee staff members and 4,000 personal staff members. In the Senate, there were 500 committee staff members and 1,500 personal staff members. Over the next several decades, as committee and personal staffs continued to grow, both the House and Senate would continually implement modest reforms in their committee operations.

THE FOUR ERAS OF CONGRESS

There is much about Congress today that the members of the First Congress would recognize.

Among the most familiar enduring features of Congress has been its determined independence from the presidency, the Senate's tendency for deliberation over action, the House's tendency for action over deliberation, the deeply rooted suspicion and tension between the Senate and House, and the complexity of a seemingly simple legislative process. Although the nation's legislative system endured for more than two centuries without radical structural changes, four distinct eras of congressional history are evident.

THE FORMATIVE YEARS: 1789-1815

The First Congress has been called the "second session of the Constitutional Convention," for it did much to fill in the outline the framers had created. It passed legislation to provide funds to operate the government and establish its basic structure, including executive agencies and a federal court system; it established a temporary capital in Philadelphia and a permanent capital within a new federal district on the banks of the Potomac River; it confronted virtually an example of every problem that would arise to test the national government over the next two centuries, including taxation, sectionalism, acquisition and administration of public lands, threat of war, congressional salaries, immigration, tariff reform, and minority-group relations.

The new political system sustained rigorous tests during these formative years. When presidential candidates Thomas Jefferson and Aaron Burr received an identical number of electoral college votes in the 1800 election, the House of Representatives, after 36 ballots, peacefully resolved the contest in Jefferson's favor. When Supreme Court Justice Samuel Chase faced removal for political reasons in a Senate impeachment trial, senators decided that he should be acquitted, thereby protecting the High Court's members against reprisals for their decisions. By the end of the War of 1812, Congress had established its internal procedures, overcome temporarily the divisive influence of political parties, set the pattern of its relations with the exec-

utive and judicial branches, and had turned from a receding foreign threat to the challenges of developing the new nation.

NATIONAL GROWTH AND SECTIONAL CONFLICT: 1815-1877

Presidents Andrew Jackson and Abraham Lincoln followed in the tradition of Thomas Jefferson as assertive presidents who successfully battled the instincts of Congress to be the dominant branch of the national government. The other presidents of this era proved far less successful in their struggles with Congress. Even during Jackson's presidency, the Senate under Henry Clay—who earlier had elevated the position of House Speaker to one of great significance— managed to preserve congressional prerogatives. It was Congress and not the president that led in searching for temporary compromises over the issue of slavery's place in the new states formed from the Louisiana Purchase (1803) and the southwestern lands acquired from the 1840s war with Mexico. The Missouri Compromise of 1820 established the pattern of admitting slave and free states in balanced pairs. The Compromise of 1850 sought to preserve this delicate balance, but the 1854 Kansas-Nebraska Act destroyed it and paved a road straight to civil war.

During this period the original two parties— Federalists and Democratic-Republicans—were replaced by a Democratic Party that formed around the personality and beliefs of Andrew Jackson, and a Whig Party under Henry Clay's leadership. Reluctant to spell out their principles too clearly, the Whigs generally favored a national system of banks, transportation facilities, and protective tariffs, but by the early 1850s the Whigs had fragmented because of their inability to agree on the slavery question. By mid-decade a new northern-based Republican Party had formed to harness these issues. By 1860 efforts in Congress to fashion further compromises failed, and the largely Democratic southern states withdrew their members early in 1861, leaving the Republicans firmly in control of both houses. That new party quickly passed a great deal of legislation that long had been stalled because of sectional differences. Among the enduring legislative accomplishments of that era were the Homestead Act, providing cheap land to promote western settlement, the Pacific Railroad Act to build a transcontinental rail connection, the Legal Tender Act to centralize the nation's banking and currency system, and the Land Grant College Act to underwrite establishment of colleges promoting "agricultural and mechanical arts."

The end of the Civil War emergency and the death of Lincoln returned Congress to its accustomed dominance of the federal system. When President Andrew Johnson sought to follow a lenient reconstruction policy to return southern states to the Union, congressional radicals impeached him in the House of Representatives. Despite the Constitution's singular failure to prevent civil war, its moderating influence was most evident at Johnson's Senate impeachment trial, where a one-vote margin kept him in office. By 1877 the sectional crisis had abated with the return of southern states to the Union and a restored balance in Congress between the Republican and Democratic parties.

CONGRESS ENTERS THE MODERN ERA: 1877-1945

Over the seven decades from the end of Reconstruction through World War II, Congress developed into a complex modern institution with a clearly defined party leadership structure. Both houses revised their rules of procedure, reorganized their committee systems, and made greater use of their committees as investigators of wrongdoing in the executive branch, as well as in the economy and American life in general. A series of financial depressions, such as those of 1873 and 1893, through the remainder of the 19th century focused congressional attention on economic problems, resulting in legislation on currency and tariff reform, railroad regulation, and immigration restriction. The first 15 years of the 20th century brought a shift in public opinion in favor of sweeping reforms that led Congress to pass the Pure Food and Drug Act, regulate child labor,

and provide for the direct popular election of senators. During the same period, military emergencies, namely the Spanish American War and World War I, shifted the delicate legislative-executive power balance in the president's favor. Presidents Theodore Roosevelt and Woodrow Wilson took the first major steps in creating the "Imperial Presidency" of modern times. However, in 1919 the Senate, as a reassertion of congressional prerogatives against a weakened but stubborn President Wilson, rejected the war-ending Treaty of Versailles.

During the 1920s, Congress mirrored the nation's retreat from international entanglements and produced a weak legislative response to domestic issues. The Great Depression, beginning in 1929, reawakened debate on the role of the federal government in promoting and stabilizing the nation's economic well being. During its first 100 days in 1933, the 73rd Congress, in close association with the new administration of President Franklin Roosevelt, produced a vast outpouring of emergency relief legislation. The 74th Congress, under Roosevelt's determined leadership, left an equally rich legacy. By 1937, however, Roosevelt had overreached himself in his relations with Congress. His legislative proposal to "pack" the Supreme Court with justices sympathetic to his programs stimulated renewal of the ancient antagonisms between the legislative and executive branches. When the president set out to "purge" uncooperative Democrats in the 1938 congressional elections, a powerful coalition of southern Democrats and western Republicans formed to block presidents' progressive initiatives for the next quarter-century. Only the involvement of the United States in World War II allowed Roosevelt to maintain a dominant position in his relations with Congress.

CONGRESS SINCE 1945

While Roosevelt's death and the end of World War II often are seen as marking the beginning of a major new era in American history, the old struggle for dominance between Congress and the chief executive continued. Postwar reconstruction of Europe and the emerging cold war threat of the Soviet Union and Communist China shaped legislative priorities and led to a three-year-long military action in Korea and ultimately to a disastrous military engagement in Vietnam. During the late 1950s, a Democratic Congress sowed the seeds of major legislation that was harvested during the Great Society period of the 1960s, such as the Civil Rights Act of 1964. In the succeeding 89th Congress, the Senate and House agreed to fundamental legislation in support of education, Medicare, voting rights, water quality, transportation, and related social policy areas. This legislation greatly expanded the federal government's role in the daily lives of most Americans.

The war in Vietnam ended further significant advances in domestic social programs, destroyed the presidency of Lyndon Johnson, and brought the election of Richard Nixon. Nixon's aggressive use of powers available to him as president and his specific misconduct in the Watergate scandal resulted in his resignation to avoid certain impeachment by the House of Representatives. During the resulting power vacuum, Congress reasserted its authority, most notably with the controversial War Powers Resolution of 1973.

The story of Congress in these post-war decades is one of institutional expansion to keep pace with the rapid growth of the federal government. By the 1980s, however, many of the Democratic Party's New Deal and Great Society programs were coming under sharp review by a resurgent Republican Party. In the 20th century's final decade fundamental questions once again arose about the role of the national government in American society and the role of Congress within that system. The Republican framers of a new "Contract With America" argued that the federal government had become "too big, too intrusive, and too easy with the public's money." The Constitution's framers would likely appreciate this continuing tension between the Congress and the president, and between governments at the national and state levels. Against this tension, however, their document demonstrated its

flexibility and capacity to meet the challenges of a new era while maintaining the principles that have guided the nation, in good times and bad, for more than two centuries.

RESEARCHING CONGRESS

Unlike the presidency, with its focus on a single individual, Congress, with its hundreds of members and dozens of committees, presents a real challenge to those who wish to research its activities and accomplishments.

Original source material: The institution of Congress and its 11,000 individual members have created an abundance of original source material over the past two centuries. Although that record is richer and more accessible for the 20th century than for earlier times, it offers great rewards to the diligent researcher. The personal papers and office records of members are located in libraries and archives throughout the United States. As members have never been required to preserve their papers, some collections have been destroyed and others are incomplete. For information on the locations and extent of members' collections, consult the *Guide to Research Collections of Former United States Senators, 1789-1995* (Senate Document 103-35, 1995) and *A Guide to Research Collections of Former Members of the United States House of Representatives, 1789-1989* (House Document 100-171, 1988). The official records of the House and Senate, and their committees, are located in Washington at the National Archives, which has prepared two finding aids: *Guide to the Records of the United States Senate at the National Archives, 1789-1989* (Senate Document 100-42, 1989) and *Guide to the Records of the United States House of Representatives at the National Archives, 1789-1989* (House Document 100-245, 1989).

There is also a vast body of primary-sources documenting the work of congressional committees and the floor proceedings of both houses. Approximately 80,000 published and unpublished committee hearings and 350,000 reports and documents issued since the late 19th century are described in a series of publications produced by the Congressional Information Service, Inc. This series has revolutionized access to congressional source materials. For access to floor proceedings, there is no substitute for the *Congressional Record*, published by Congress since 1873. Its privately produced predecessors include the *Annals of Congress* (1789-1824), the *Register of Debates* (1824-1837), and the *Congressional Globe* (1833-1873).

Biographies: Many memoirs, autobiographies, and biographies illuminate the lives of those who have served in Congress. The best source of brief information is the *Biographical Directory of the United States Congress, 1774-1989* (Senate Document 100-34, 1989). This directory also includes citations to significant book-length biographies that may exist for individual members. A more detailed bibliography, which includes citations for approximately 1,100 of the more than 1,800 who have served in the Senate, is *Senators of the United States: A Historical Bibliography* (Senate Document 103-34, 1995).

Guides and Reference Books: Since 1945, Congressional Quarterly, Inc. has published a weekly journal that reports on congressional activity. That information is subsequently reorganized and published in annual almanacs, in reference volumes that cover a multi-year period, and in the *Guide to Congress*—a single-volume work that is updated periodically. Congressional Quarterly has also published a two-volume bibliography that includes citations to books and articles about Congress other than biographies (Robert U. Goehlert and John R. Sayre [1982] and Robert U. Goehlert and Fenton S. Martin [1995]).

The 1989 bicentennial of Congress stimulated publication of two major congressional encyclopedias. The four-volume *Encyclopedia of the United States Congress* offers 1,056 articles ranging from 250 to 6,000 words, with illustrations and bibliographical citations. *The Encyclopedia of the American Legislative System* offers, in three volumes, 91 chapter-length essays that cover Congress and state legislatures. To commemorate the Senate's 200th anniversary, Senator Robert C. Byrd (Dem., W.Va.) and the Senate Historical Office produced *The Senate, 1789-1989* (Senate Document 100-20, 1988-1994), a four-volume reference work that includes historical narratives (Volumes 1 and 2), classic speeches (Volume 3), and historical statistics (Volume 4).

Finally, the reader is directed to the pages that follow this introduction. *Facts About the Congress of the United States*, a pioneering work, is the first comprehensive reference source to offer consistently arranged information on each of the congressional sessions from the 1780s to the 1990s.

NOTES TO THE TEXT

1. After the 20th Amendment was ratified in 1933 [See 73rd Congress], Senate special sessions for this purpose became unnecessary.

2. Until the 17th Amendment was declared ratified on May 31, 1913 [See 63rd Congress], United States senators were elected by their respective state legislatures, and only the members of the House of Representatives were directly elected by the voters of their respective districts.

3. Gains or losses by the political parties in Congress do not necessarily match the gains or losses of the opposing party. This is due to such factors as resignations, deaths and other vacancies, special elections, reapportionments in the House after each 10-year census, the admission of new states to the Union, and the occasional third party or independent member of Congress.

4. In the 18th century and into the 19th century, the president pro tempore was frequently elected for only a specific occasion, and it was not until March 12, 1890 [See 51st Congress], that the president pro tempore continued to hold that office until otherwise ordered.

5. When an individual bill or other specific matter arose in the House or Senate, that body would choose a small group of its members to serve as a committee. When that legislation or other matter came to a conclusion, the committee was dissolved. Standing committees other than administrative ones first were established in the House in the Fourth Congress, and in the Senate in the 14th Congress. Prior to the 80th Congress, there are many gaps in the historical record. The committee structure was far less formal and organized, and committees often were created haphazardly, terminated, reorganized, split up, or combined.

Thus, the lists of key committee chairmen for the 1st through the 79th Congresses are confined to selected major standing committees which have historical continuity from the 79th Congress back to the Congress of their creation. There have been approximately two thousand committees throughout the history of Congress. However, the modern committee structure and the modern allocation of committee jurisdiction, seniority, and ranking minority member status was not established until after World War II [See 80th Congress and subsequent chapters].

6. In this book, legislation is referred to as having passed on the date that the Senate had its substantive vote approving legislation originating in the House, or the House had its substantive vote approving legislation originating in the Senate. When legislation becomes effective, however, depends on such matters as when the president signs it into law, if any veto is overridden, whether the legislation itself provides for a date on which it will become effective, and so forth.

7. Passed by voice vote refers to votes where members are asked to say "Yea" (Yes) or "Nay" (No), and there were more "Yeas" than "Nays," but the exact number of people for or against was not counted. Passage by voice vote was once a very common occurrence, but the voice vote is rarely used today for important votes.

8. Under the 20th Amendment, ratified in 1933 [See 73rd Congress], the terms of the president and vice president end at noon on January 20, but Congress must convene at noon on January 3. Thus, when a new vice president is elected, the previous vice president remains in offfice for the first 17 calendar days of the new Congress.

The First Congress

MARCH 4, 1789 – MARCH 3, 1791

First Session: March 4, 1789-September 29, 1789
Second Session: January 4, 1790-August 12, 1790
Third Session: December 6, 1790-March 3, 1791

After the 1788 elections for the First Congress, there were two parties in Congress, loosely identified as the Administration Party and the Opposition Party. They were not formally organized like modern political parties. The Administration Party held 17 seats in the Senate and the Opposition Party held 9 seats, for a total of 26 senators from 13 states. In the House, the Administration Party held 38 seats and the Opposition Party held 26 seats, for a total of 64 members. [See notes 2 and 3, p. xxix]

The First Congress met in New York City, then the capital, the only Congress to date to have done so.

BACKGROUND

On May 25, 1787, the Constitutional Convention met in Philadelphia, Pennsylvania, to discuss what form of government should replace the discredited and ineffective Articles of Confederation of 1781. The result was the Constitution of the United States of America, which was sent to the Confederation Congress on September 17, 1787, and ultimately to the states for submission to conventions of delegates.* Pursuant to Article VII of the Constitution, ratification became effective June 21, 1788, when New Hampshire became the ninth state of the thirteen states to ratify the Constitution and enter the Union.

When the First Congress convened, there was no president of the United States: George

Washington had been elected president on February 4, 1789 and the votes were counted on April 6, but he was not inaugurated until April 30. Only 9 of the 26 senators and 13 of the 64 representatives were present at the beginning of the first session. As more members arrived, Congress began setting up the basic framework of American government. The First Congress established the State Department, the War Department, the Treasury Department, and the first patent board. Other legislative firsts included the first immigration law, the first judiciary act, and the first copyright law.

The First Congress also sent twelve proposed amendments to the Constitution to the states for ratification, ten of which would be ratified and are known as The Bill of Rights. The census of 1790, which took place during the First Congress, revealed that the population of the United States was 3,929,214 as of August 2, 1790, resulting in a population density of 4.5 persons for each of the country's 864,746 square miles.

SENATE LEADERSHIP

Vice President: John Adams of Massachusetts had a long and distinguished political career that included being a member of the Continental Congress and a signer of the Declaration of Independence. He had proposed George Washington for general of the American army in 1775 and later served in diplomatic missions to France, Holland, and Great Britain. He would

---

* The Constitution of the United States is referred to in this book as the Constitution for convenience sake, although it should not be forgotten that the states have their own state constitutions as well. There is a copy of the Constitution at Appendix A, p. 559.

C H R O N O L O G Y

March 4, 1789:	The first session of the First Congress begins.
April 1, 1789:	Frederick Augustus Conrad Muhlenberg (Admin., Pa.) is elected the first Speaker of the House.
April 6, 1789:	John Langdon (Admin., N.H.) is elected the first president pro tempore of the Senate.
April 30, 1789:	President George Washington is inaugurated.
May 6, 1789:	Congress passes legislation concerning oaths.
July 20, 1789:	Congress passes legislation creating the State Department.
August 5, 1789:	Congress passes legislation creating the Treasury Department and the War Department.
September 9, 1789:	Congress sends 12 amendments to the Constitution—the first 10 known collectively as the Bill of Rights—to be ratified by the states.
September 11, 1789:	President Washington nominates Alexander Hamilton to be secretary of the Treasury and Henry Knox to be secretary of war. The Senate confirms Hamilton.
September 12, 1789:	The Senate confirms Knox.
September 17, 1789:	Congress passes legislation concerning the judiciary.
September 24, 1789:	President Washington nominates John Jay to be chief justice and John Blair Jr., William Cushing, Robert Harrison, John Rutledge, and James Wilson as associate justices.
September 25, 1789:	President Washington nominates Edmund Randolph to be attorney general and Thomas Jefferson to be secretary of state.
September 26, 1789:	The Senate confirms both Randolph and Jefferson.
September 26, 1789:	The Senate confirms Jay and all of the associate justices except Harrison.
September 29, 1789:	The first session ends.
January 4, 1790:	The second session begins.
February 8, 1790:	President Washington nominates James Iredell to the Supreme Court.
February 10, 1790:	The Senate confirms Iredell.
March 19, 1790:	Congress passes legislation concerning citizenship.
April 3, 1790:	Congress passes legislation concerning patents.
May 17, 1790:	Congress passes legislation concerning copyrights.
July 9, 1790:	Congress passes legislation creating the District of Columbia.
August 12, 1790:	The second session ends, and Congress leaves New York City.
December 6, 1790:	The third session begins, convening in Philadelphia, Pennsylvania.
January 28, 1791:	Congress passes legislation admitting Kentucky into the U.S.
February 14, 1791:	Congress passes legislation admitting Vermont into the U.S.
March 3, 1791:	The third session and First Congress end.

[See note 6, p. xxix]

become president after the Washington administration.

President Pro Tempore: John Langdon (Admin., N.H.) was elected the first president pro tempore on April 6, 1789, for the purpose of supervising the Senate's counting of the electoral vote in the presidential election of April 6, 1789. [See note 4, p. xxix] On April 6 Langdon wrote George Washington to officially notify him that he had been elected president.

Majority Leader, Majority Whip, Minority Leader, and Minority Whip: None. These functions did not evolve into formal Senate positions until the 62nd Congress (1911-1913).

Other Senate Leaders: Oliver Ellsworth (No definite party, Conn.) was one of the prominent members of the First Congress. He was a leading figure in getting the Bill of Rights and the Judiciary Act of 1789 passed, and was instrumental in drafting the Senate's rules of procedure.

Chairmen of Selected Key Committees: No entries for this Congress. [See Organization and Administration, below]

HOUSE LEADERSHIP

Speaker of the House: Frederick Augustus Conrad Muhlenberg (Admin., Pa.) was elected Speaker on April 1, 1789. Muhlenberg was a Lutheran minister from Pennsylvania who had been a member of the Continental Congress and a former Speaker of the Pennsylvania House of Representatives.

Majority Leader, Majority Whip, Minority Leader, and Minority Whip: None. These functions did not evolve into formal House positions until the 56th Congress (1899-1901).

Chairmen of Selected Key Committees: No entries for this Congress. [See Organization and Administration, below]

ORGANIZATION AND ADMINISTRATION

There was no permanent or standing committee structure in the first several Congresses, except for some committees overseeing administrative matters, such as the Joint Standing Committee on Enrolled Bills and the House Committee on Elections. Legislation was prepared by select or ad hoc committees. [See note 5, p. xxix]

MAJOR LEGISLATION PASSED

First Law Passed by Congress: The first legislation passed by the First Congress was titled "An Act to Regulate the Time and Manner of Administering Certain Oaths." This law required members of Congress, members of the state legislatures, and officers of the U.S. government to promise to support the Constitution.

Admission of Kentucky and Vermont as New States: Congress voted to admit Kentucky and Vermont into the United States. Although the votes to admit Kentucky occurred before the votes to admit Vermont, Vermont was formally admitted to the Union (on March 4, 1791) before Kentucky (on June 1, 1792) due to procedural differences in each legislation.

Citizenship: Termed a "Uniform Rule of Naturalization," this law enabled free white people to become citizens if they had resided in the United States for at least two years.

Copyrights: Congress exercised its power under Article I, Section 8, Clause 8 of the Constitution to establish the first system of federal protection for authors.

District of Columbia: Congress established the District of Columbia as the future capital of the United States, to take effect when the necessary federal buildings and facilities were constructed. Congress was not able to move to Washington, D.C. until the second session of the Sixth Congress.

Judiciary Act of 1789: Congress established the federal courts, and provided for a Supreme Court with a chief justice and five associate justices.

Patents: Congress exercised its power under Article I, Section 8, Clause 8 of the Constitution to establish the first system of federal protection for inventors.

TABLE OF KEY VOTES

Senate

Subject of Vote	Date of Vote	For	Against
Oaths	May 5, 1789	Passed by voice vote	
Judiciary Act	July 17, 1789	14	6
State Department	July 18, 1789	10	9
Treasury Department	July 31, 1789	Passed by voice vote	
War Department	August 4, 1789	Passed by voice vote	
Bill of Rights	September 9, 1789	Passed by voice vote	
Citizenship	March 19, 1790	Passed by voice vote	
Patents	March 30, 1790	Passed by voice vote	
Copyrights	May 14, 1790	Passed by voice vote	
District of Columbia	July 1, 1790	14	12
Admission of Kentucky to Union	January 12, 1791	Passed by voice vote	
Admission of Vermont to Union	February 12, 1791	Passed by voice vote	

House

Subject of Vote	Date of Vote	For	Against
Oaths	May 6, 1789	Passed by voice vote	
State Department	July 20, 1789	Passed by voice vote	
Treasury Department	August 5, 1789	Passed by voice vote	
War Department	August 5, 1789	Passed by voice vote	
Bill of Rights	August 24, 1789	Passed by voice vote	
Judiciary Act	September 17, 1789	Passed by voice vote	
Citizenship	March 4, 1790	Passed by voice vote	
Patents	April 3, 1790	Passed by voice vote	
Copyrights	May 17, 1790	Passed by voice vote	
District of Columbia	July 9, 1790	32	29
Admission of Kentucky to Union	January 28, 1791	Passed by voice vote	
Admission of Vermont to Union	February 14, 1791	Passed by voice vote	

[See note 7, p. xxix]

State Department: Congress established the Department of State to handle the foreign relations of the United States.

Treasury Department: Congress established the Department of the Treasury to handle the finances of the United States.

War Department: Congress established the Department of War to supervise the military forces of the United States.[†]

FAILED LEGISLATION

In addition to the ten amendments to the Constitution known as the Bill of Rights, Congress sent two other amendments to the states. One, which has never been ratified, was a lengthy amendment specifying how the number of members of the House of Representatives would be determined based on a mandatory apportionment formula. The other amendment simply stated that "No law varying the compensation for the services of the Senators and Representatives shall take effect, until an election of Representatives shall have intervened." The purpose of this amendment was to give Congress the power to raise or lower congressional salaries for future Congresses, but not the present Congress. This proposed amendment was largely forgotten for nearly two hundred years, but interest in it was revived in modern times in connection with the public debate over congressional pay raises. By the 1990s, three-fourths of the states had ratified it, and this historical relic of the 18th century became the Twenty-seventh Amendment effective May 7, 1992 [See 102nd Congress for further information].

RELATIONS WITH THE PRESIDENT

The first president of the United States was the popular commander in chief of the Continental army in the American Revolution, General George Washington. Perhaps luckily for the young Republic in a world still dominated by monarchies, Washington was a strict observer of the democratic principles of the Constitution. Washington had previously rejected suggestions that he become king of America. While most other heads of state were addressed with lofty titles, such as "Your Excellency," Washington was content with simply being "Mr. President." In the First Congress, Washington established an important principle: Presidents should not be physically present at congressional proceedings. In 1789 Washington had sat in on a few deliberations, but noting the tensions resulting from his presence, he decided that it was better for the president to be absent while Congress debated legislation. This principle has been observed by all subsequent presidents.

Washington vetoed no legislation during the First Congress.

NOMINATIONS, APPOINTMENTS, AND CONFIRMATIONS

The Judiciary: Pursuant to the Judiciary Act of 1789 [See Major Legislation], the Supreme Court initially consisted of a chief justice and five associate justices. On September 24, 1789, President George Washington nominated John Jay to be chief justice and John Blair Jr., William Cushing, Robert Harrison, John Rutledge, and James Wilson as associate justices. Jay and all of the associate justices except Harrison were confirmed by the Senate on September 26, 1789, without a vote. Harrison declined to serve on September 26, 1789, and Washington nominated James Iredell on February 8, 1790. The Senate confirmed Iredell on February 10, 1790, by voice vote.

The Executive Branch: On September 11, 1789, Washington nominated Alexander Hamilton to be secretary of the Treasury and Henry Knox to be secretary of war. That same day, the Senate confirmed Hamilton by voice vote, and on September 12 Knox, also by voice vote. On September 25, 1789, Washington nominated Edmund Randolph to be attorney general and Thomas Jefferson to be secretary of state. The next day, September 26, the Senate confirmed both Randolph and Jefferson by voice vote.

IMPEACHMENTS

None.

CONSTITUTIONAL AMENDMENTS

Congress authorized sending the first amendments to the Constitution to the states for ratification.

[†] Congress changed the Department of War's name to the Department of Defense after World War II.

The first ten amendments, known as the Bill of Rights, were ratified by the required three-fourths of the states effective December 15, 1791. The purpose of the Bill of Rights was to protect various individual freedoms that the Constitution did not address. [For the actual text of these first ten amendments, see the copy of the Constitution in Appendix A]

FURTHER READING

Adams, John. *The Adams Papers*. Cambridge, Mass.: Harvard University Press, 1961-present.

Bickford, Charlene and Kenneth R. Bowling. *Birth of the Nation: The First Federal Congress, 1789-1791*. Madison, Wis.: Madison House, 1989.

Bowen, Catherine Drinker. *Miracle at Philadelphia: The Story of the Constitutional Convention, May to September, 1787*.

Mayo, Lawrence. *John Langdon of New Hampshire*. New York: Kennikat Press, 1970.

Morris, Richard Brandon. *John Jay, the Nation, and the Court*. Boston: Boston University Press, 1967.

Wallace, Paul A.W. *The Muhlenbergs of Pennsylvania*. Freeport, N.Y.: Books for Libraries Press, 1970.

Washington, George. *The Papers of George Washington*. Charlottesville, Va.: The University Press of Virginia, 1983-present.

The Second Congress

MARCH 4, 1791 – MARCH 3, 1793

Special Senate Session: March 4, 1791
First Session: October 24, 1791-May 8, 1792
Second Session: November 5, 1792-March 2, 1793

The Senate held a special session on March 4, 1791, to vote on the confirmation of presidential appointees to various offices. [See note 1, p. xxix]

In the 1790 elections for the Second Congress, the new Federalist Party absorbed the Administration members of Congress and the new Democratic-Republican Party absorbed the Opposition members. The Federalist Party neither gained nor lost any seats in the Senate. The Democratic-Republican Party picked up 4 seats. However, the Federalists still held a majority with 17 of the 30 seats. Thirteen seats were held by the Democratic-Republicans. In the House, the Federalists lost 1 seat and the Democratic-Republicans gained 7 seats, for a total of 33, producing a Federalist majority of 37 out of a total of 70. [See notes 2 and 3, p. xxix]

BACKGROUND

The Second Congress met in Philadelphia, Pennsylvania. Vermont and Kentucky joined the United States during the Second Congress, for a total of 15 states. The Bill of Rights, passed and sent to the states by the First Congress, was ratified by the required number of states during the term of the Second Congress. George Washington was reelected president in the 1792 elections. Unlike the First Congress, whose members were somewhat loosely defined as being either Administration or Opposition, the Second Congress was dominated by two organized political parties. The first party,

the Federalist, was conservative, pro-British, and the forerunner of the modern Republican Party. The second party, the Democratic-Republican, was liberal, pro-French, and the forerunner of the modern Democratic Party. These two parties, periodically reorganized and renamed and with changing political agendas, established the bipolar nature of American politics — in general and in Congress particularly — that has persisted for two centuries.

SENATE LEADERSHIP

Vice President: John Adams of Massachusetts [See biographical note in First Congress]

President Pro Tempore: Richard Henry Lee (Dem-Rep., Va.) was elected on April 18, 1792. John Langdon (Fed., N.H.) was elected on November 5, 1792, and reelected on March 1, 1793. [See note 4, p. xxix]

Majority Leader, Majority Whip, Minority Leader, and Minority Whip: None. These functions did not evolve into formal Senate positions until the 62nd Congress (1911-1913).

Chairmen of Selected Key Committees: No entries for this Congress. [See Organization and Administration, below]

HOUSE LEADERSHIP

Speaker of the House: Jonathan Trumbull (Fed., Conn.) was elected Speaker on October 24, 1791. Trumbull was a former member and speaker of

CHRONOLOGY

March 4, 1791:	The Second Congress begins, and the Senate holds a special session.
March 5, 1791:	Supreme Court Justice John Rutledge resigns.
October 24, 1791:	The first session begins. Jonathan Trumbull (Fed., Conn.) is elected Speaker of the House.
October 31, 1791:	President Washington nominates Thomas Johnson to replace Rutledge.
November 7, 1791:	The Senate confirms Johnson.
February 21, 1792:	Congress passes legislation concerning presidential succession.
March 27, 1792:	Congress passes legislation establishing the Mint.
April 5, 1792:	President Washington uses the presidential veto for the first time in American history.
April 6, 1792:	The House fails to overturn the first veto.
May 8, 1792:	The first session ends.
November 5, 1792:	The second session begins.
February 5, 1793:	Congress passes legislation requiring federal and state officials to aid in the pursuit of fugitive slaves.
March 2, 1793:	The second session ends.
March 3, 1793:	The Second Congress ends.

[See note 6, p. xxix]

the House of the Connecticut legislature, and had served as President Washington's secretary and aide-de-camp in the American Revolution.

Majority Leader, Majority Whip, Minority Leader, and Minority Whip: None. These functions did not evolve into formal House positions until the 56th Congress (1899-1901).

Chairmen of Selected Key Committees: No entries for this Congress. [See Organization and Administration, below]

ORGANIZATION AND ADMINISTRATION

There was no permanent or standing committee structure in the first several Congresses, except for some committees overseeing administrative matters, such as the Joint Standing Committee on Enrolled Bills and the House Committee on Elections. Legislation was prepared by select or ad hoc committees. [See note 5, p. xxix]

MAJOR LEGISLATION PASSED

Fugitive Slaves: In the Fugitive Slave Act of 1793, Congress directed federal and state officials to assist slave owners in recapturing escaped slaves.

Mint: Congress established the first U.S. Mint, located in Philadelphia, Pennsylvania. In the same legislation, Congress established a decimal system of coinage, based on dollars, desimes, cents and milles.

Presidential Succession: In the Presidential Succession Act, Congress established a line of succession should the president and vice president both die, be removed, or resign. Next in line were the president pro tempore of the Senate and in his absence the Speaker of the House.

A contemporary print from when Congress was located in Philadelphia, Pennsylvania.

FAILED LEGISLATION

None of historical significance.

RELATIONS WITH THE PRESIDENT

In the Second Congress, the institution known as the cabinet, composed of senior executive branch officials, started to take shape. President Washington began to meet with the cabinet for advice on a regular basis. In his relations with Congress, Washington increasingly relied on Treasury Secretary Alexander Hamilton and Virginia Representative James Madison for advice. In this Congress, the first Congressional investigation involving the executive branch took place. On March 27, 1792 the House voted 44 to 10 to investigate Major General Arthur St. Clair's

defeat in an expedition into Indian country that cost 600 lives. Washington complied with the House's request for records, and St. Clair was ultimately cleared of any misconduct.

Also during the Second Congress, Washington exercised the presidential veto power for the first time. It was the only veto in this Congress. On April 5, 1792, Washington vetoed a bill which concerned the method for apportioning the members of the House of Representatives amongst the states. On April 6, 1792, the House sustained the veto by a vote of 28 in favor of overturning the veto to 33 against. Thus, there was no vote in the Senate.

NOMINATIONS, APPOINTMENTS, AND CONFIRMATIONS

The Judiciary: On March 5, 1791, Supreme Court Justice John Rutledge resigned. On October

TABLE OF KEY VOTES

Senate

Subject of Vote	Date of Vote	For	Against
Confirmation of Thomas Johnson to Supreme Court	November 7, 1791	Passed by voice vote	
Presidential Succession	February 20, 1792	Passed by voice vote	
Establishment of Mint	March 27, 1792	Passed by voice vote	
Fugitive Slaves	January 18, 1793	Passed by voice vote	

House

Subject of Vote	Date of Vote	For	Against
Presidential Succession	February 21, 1792	31	24
Establishment of Mint	March 26, 1792	32	22
To Overturn First Veto	April 6, 1792	28	33
Fugitive Slaves	February 5, 1793	48	7

[See note 7, p. xxix]

31, 1791, President George Washington nominated Thomas Johnson to replace Rutledge. The Senate confirmed Johnson on November 7, 1791, by voice vote. Johnson resigned on January 16, 1793, and would not be replaced until the Third Congress.

The Executive Branch: None of historical significance.

IMPEACHMENTS

None.

CONSTITUTIONAL AMENDMENTS

None.

FURTHER READING

Adams, John. *The Adams Papers.* Cambridge, Mass.: Harvard University Press, 1961-present.

Ifkovic, John. *Connecticut's Nationalist Revolutionary: Jonathan Trumbull, Jr.* Hartford, Conn.: American Revolution Bicentennial Commission of Connecticut, 1977.

The Third Congress

MARCH 4, 1793 – MARCH 3, 1795

Special Senate Session: *March 4, 1793*
First Session: *December 2, 1793-June 9, 1794*
Second Session: *November 3, 1794-March 3, 1795*

The Senate held a special session to vote on the confirmation of presidential appointees to various offices. [See note 1, p. xxix]

In the 1792 elections for the Third Congress, the Federalists neither gained nor lost any seats in the Senate, keeping their total at 17 of the 30 seats, and the Democratic-Republicans also continued to hold their seats from the Second Congress. Because of the 1790 census, the House was reapportioned and increased to 106 members. The Democratic-Republicans gained 24 seats for a majority of 57 and the Federalists gained nine seats for a total of 48, with one seat belonging to neither party.

BACKGROUND

The Third Congress met in Philadelphia, Pennsylvania. President George Washington was inaugurated for his second term on March 4, 1793. One of Washington's first actions was to issue a proclamation of neutrality on April 22, 1793, which stated that Americans should not aid either side in the war between Great Britain and the new revolutionary government of France. Washington was a Federalist, and Federalists believed that despite its having won the Revolutionary War against the British, the United States should protect its cultural and economic ties with that nation by becoming its ally. The Democratic-Republicans were pro-French, how-

ever, because the French had aided the colonies during the Revolution and the French Revolution was a revolt against monarchism. Washington decided that the best course for the United States with its limited financial and military resources was to stay out of the conflict entirely.

Domestically, the Whiskey Rebellion in western Pennsylvania began in July of 1794, triggered by the federal tax on whiskey. Washington called out the militia from four states and defeated the rebellion by November of 1794. There was also military action on the frontier, where on August 20, 1794, General Anthony Wayne defeated an Indian army on the Miami River in what is now Ohio. Wayne's victory opened the Northwest Territory to large-scale settlement. The Third Congress enacted some important immigration legislation, namely the Naturalization Act of 1795.

SENATE LEADERSHIP

Vice President: John Adams of Massachusetts [See biographical note in First Congress]

President Pro Tempore: Ralph Izard (Fed., S.C.) was elected on May 31, 1794; and Henry Tazewell (Dem-Rep., Va.) was elected on February 20, 1795, after Samuel Livermore (Fed., N.H.) was elected that day but declined to serve. [See note 4, p. xxix]

Majority Leader, Majority Whip, Minority Leader, and Minority Whip: None. These func-

CHRONOLOGY

March 4, 1793:	The Third Congress begins and the Senate holds a special session, during which it confirms William Paterson to the Supreme Court.
April 22, 1793:	President Washington issues a proclamation of neutrality.
December 2, 1793:	The first session begins, and Frederick Augustus Conrad Muhlenberg (Dem-Rep., Pa.) is elected Speaker of the House.
January 1, 1794:	President Washington nominates Edmund Randolph to be secretary of state.
January 2, 1794:	The Senate confirms Randolph.
January 24, 1794:	President Washington nominates William Bradford to be attorney general.
January 27, 1794:	The Senate confirms Bradford.
March 4, 1794:	Congress sends the 11th Amendment, reversing the Supreme Court's decision in *Chisholm v. Georgia* and limiting the jurisdiction of the federal courts, to the states for ratification.
March 19, 1794:	Congress passes legislation establishing the U.S. Navy.
June 9, 1794:	The first session ends.
November 3, 1794:	The second session begins.
January 2, 1795:	President Washington nominates, and the Senate confirms, Timothy Pickering to be secretary of war.
January 26, 1795:	Congress passes legislation requiring immigrants to reside in the United States for five years before they are eligible for citizenship.
February 2, 1795:	President Washington nominates Oliver Wolcott Jr. to be secretary of the Treasury.
February 3, 1795:	The Senate confirms Wolcott.
February 7, 1795:	The 11th Amendment, having been ratified by the required three-fourths of the states, becomes effective as of this date.
March 3, 1795:	The second session and the Third Congress end.

[See note 6, p. xxix]

tions did not evolve into formal Senate positions until the 62nd Congress (1911-1913).

Chairmen of Selected Key Committees: No entries for this Congress. [See Organization and Administration, p. 13]

HOUSE LEADERSHIP

Speaker of the House: Frederick Augustus Conrad Muhlenberg (Dem-Rep., Pa.) was elected on December 2, 1793. Muhlenberg was a Lutheran minister from Pennsylvania who had been a member of the Continental Congress and a former speaker of the Pennsylvania House of Representatives.

Majority Leader, Majority Whip, Minority Leader, and Minority Whip: None. These functions did not evolve into formal House positions until the 56th Congress (1899-1901).

Chairmen of Selected Key Committees: No entries for this Congress. [See Organization and Administration, p. 13]

TABLE OF KEY VOTES

Senate

Subject of Vote	Date of Vote	For	Against
Confirmation of William Paterson to Supreme Court	March 4, 1793	Passed by voice vote	
Confirmation of Edmund Randolph to be Secretary of State	January 2, 1794	Passed by voice vote	
11th Amendment	January 14, 1794	23	2
Confirmation of William Bradford to be Attorney General	January 27, 1794	Passed by voice vote	
Navy Established	March 19, 1794	Passed by voice vote	
Confirmation of Timothy Pickering to be Secretary of War	January 2, 1795	Passed by voice vote	
Immigrant Citizenship	January 26, 1795	Passed by voice vote	
Confirmation of Oliver Wolcott Jr. to be Secretary of the Treasury	February 3, 1795	Passed by voice vote	

House

Subject of Vote	Date of Vote	For	Against
Navy Established	February 21, 1794	43	41
11th Amendment	March 4, 1794	81	9
Immigrant Citizenship	January 8, 1795	Passed by voice vote	

[See note 7, p. xxix]

ORGANIZATION AND ADMINISTRATION

There was no permanent or standing committee structure in the first several Congresses, except for some committees overseeing administrative matters, such as the Joint Standing Committee on Enrolled Bills and the House Committee on Elections. Legislation was prepared by select or ad hoc committees. [See note 5, p. xxix]

MAJOR LEGISLATION PASSED

Immigration: In the Naturalization Act of 1795, Congress required aliens to reside in the United States for five years before they could obtain citizenship. In addition, aliens seeking citizenship had to renounce any allegiance to a foreign power.

Navy: Congress established the United States Navy and appropriated funds for the construction of six ships.

FAILED LEGISLATION

None of historical significance.

RELATIONS WITH THE PRESIDENT

President Washington's Neutrality Proclamation generated some criticism within Congress. The Federalists wanted the country to support Great Britain, while the Democratic-Republicans favored France. [See Background, p. 11] However, Congress took no action to overturn the Neutrality Proclamation.

Washington vetoed no legislation during the Third Congress.

NOMINATIONS, APPOINTMENTS, AND CONFIRMATIONS

The Judiciary: On January 16, 1793, Supreme Court Justice Thomas Johnson resigned. On March 4, 1873, during the special session of the Senate of the Third Congress, President George Washington nominated William Paterson as Johnson's successor. The Senate confirmed Paterson on the same day by voice vote.

The Executive Branch: On January 1, 1794, Washington nominated Edmund Randolph to be secretary of state, and the Senate confirmed him by voice vote the following day. On January 24, 1794, Washington nominated William Bradford to be attorney general, He was confirmed by the Senate on January 27, 1794, by voice vote. On January 2, 1795, Washington nominated, and the Senate confirmed by voice vote, Timothy Pickering to be secretary of war. On February 2, 1795, Washington nominated Oliver Wolcott Jr. to be secretary of the Treasury, and the Senate confirmed him by voice vote the next day.

IMPEACHMENTS

None.

CONSTITUTIONAL AMENDMENTS

On February 18, 1793, in the case of *Chisholm v. Georgia*, the Supreme Court held by a four-to-one vote that the federal courts had jurisdiction under the Constitution in cases brought against a state by citizens of another state. Thus, Chisholm, a citizen of South Carolina, could sue the state of Georgia in federal court. In response to *Chisholm v. Georgia*, Congress authorized the sending of the Eleventh Amendment to the states. The Eleventh Amendment, which eliminated this particular aspect of federal court jurisdiction and reversed the Chisholm decision, was ratified by the required three-fourths of the states effective February 7, 1795. [For the actual text of the Eleventh Amendment, see the copy of the Constitution at Appendix A]

FURTHER READING

Adams, John. *The Adams Papers*. Cambridge, Mass.: Harvard University Press, 1961-present.

O'Connor, John E. *William Paterson, Lawyer and Statesman, 1745-1806*. New Brunswick, N.J.: Rutgers University Press, 1979.

Wallace, Paul A.W. *The Muhlenbergs of Pennsylvania*. Freeport, N.Y.: Books for Libraries Press, 1970.

The Fourth Congress

MARCH 4, 1795-MARCH 3, 1797

Special Senate Session: June 8, 1795-June 26, 1795
First Session: December 7, 1795-June 1, 1796
Second Session: December 5, 1796-March 3, 1797

The Senate held a special session to vote on the Jay Treaty. [See Major Legislation, p. 17] [See note 1, p. xxix]

In the 1794 elections for the Fourth Congress, the Federalists gained 2 seats in the Senate, raising their total from 17 to 19 of the 32, while the Democratic-Republicans continued to hold 13 seats. In the House, the Federalists gained 6 seats for a majority of 54 of the 106 and the Democratic-Republicans lost 5 seats for a total of 52.

BACKGROUND

The Fourth Congress met in Philadelphia, Pennsylvania. Tennessee joined the Union on June 1, 1796, raising the number of states to 16. The major event of the period was President Washington's Farewell Address to the people of the United States on September 17, 1796, in which he stressed that America should stay out of foreign wars and preserve its resources for domestic matters. The address established an important precedent for the political viewpoint known as isolationism, which has been influential and at times even dominant in American foreign policy. Domestically, the Yazoo land fraud created a major scandal in the South, when a corrupt Georgia state legislature made, and then refused to honor, a grant of 35 million acres of frontier land to four companies.

SENATE LEADERSHIP

Vice President: John Adams of Massachusetts [See biographical note in First Congress]

President Pro Tempore: Henry Tazewell (Dem-Rep., Va.) was elected on December 7, 1795; Samuel Livermore (Fed., N.H.) was elected on May 6, 1796; and William Bingham (Fed., Pa.) was elected on February 16, 1797. [See note 4, p. xxix]

Majority Leader, Majority Whip, Minority Leader, and Minority Whip: None. These functions did not evolve into formal Senate positions until the 62nd Congress (1911-1913).

Chairmen of Selected Key Committees: No entries for this Congress. [See Organization and Administration, p. 16]

HOUSE LEADERSHIP

Speaker of the House: Jonathan Dayton (Fed., N.J.) was elected Speaker on December 7, 1795. Dayton was a former member and Speaker of the New Jersey General Assembly and was a delegate to the Constitutional Convention.

Majority Leader, Majority Whip, Minority Leader, and Minority Whip: None. These functions did not evolve into formal House positions until the 56th Congress (1899-1901).

C H R O N O L O G Y

March 4, 1795:	The Fourth Congress begins.
June 8, 1795:	The special session of the Senate begins.
June 24, 1795:	The Senate approves Jay's Treaty.
June 26, 1795:	The special session of the Senate ends.
June 29, 1795:	Supreme Court Chief Justice John Jay resigns.
July 1, 1795:	President Washington nominates former Associate Justice John Rutledge as Jay's replacement.
October 25, 1795:	Justice John Blair resigns.
December 7, 1795:	The first session begins, and Jonathan Dayton (Fed., N.J.) is elected Speaker of the House.
December 9, 1795:	President Washington nominates Charles Lee to be attorney general and Timothy Pickering to be secretary of state.
December 10, 1795:	The Senate confirms both Lee and Pickering.
December 15, 1795:	The Senate refuses to confirm Rutledge.
January 26, 1796:	President Washington nominates Samuel Chase to be associate justice of the Supreme Court and James McHenry to be secretary of war.
January 27, 1796:	The Senate confirms Chase and McHenry.
March 2, 1796:	The Senate approves a Treaty with Algiers.
March 3, 1796:	The Senate approves the Treaty of San Lorenzo, and President Washington nominates Oliver Ellsworth to be chief justice of the United States.
March 4, 1796:	The Senate confirms Ellsworth.
April 20, 1796:	Congress passes legislation concerning seamen.
May 6, 1796:	Congress passes the Land Act.
May 14, 1796:	Congress passes legislation concerning Native American lands.
May 26, 1796:	Congress passes legislation admitting Tennessee into the Union.
June 1, 1796:	The first session ends.
September 17, 1796:	President Washington gives his Farewell Address.
December 5, 1796:	The second session begins.
March 3, 1797:	The second session and the Fourth Congress end.

[See note 6, p. xxix]

Chairmen of Selected Key Committees: [See also Organization and Administration, below]

Committee on Ways and Means: William L. Smith (Fed., S.C.).

ORGANIZATION AND ADMINISTRATION

There was no permanent or standing committee structure in the first several Congresses, except for

TABLE OF KEY VOTES

Senate

Subject of Vote	Date of Vote	For	Against
Jay's Treaty	June 24, 1795	20	10
Treaty with Algiers	March 2, 1796	27	0
Treaty of San Lorenzo	March 3, 1796	26	0
Seamen	April 20, 1796	Passed by voice vote	
Land Act	May 6, 1796	Passed by voice vote	
Native American Lands	May 14, 1796	17	8
Admission of Tennessee to Union	May 26, 1796	15	8

House

Subject of Vote	Date of Vote	For	Against
Seamen	March 28, 1796	77	13
Land Act	April 6, 1796	Passed by voice vote	
Native American Lands	April 13, 1796	Passed by voice vote	
Admission of Tennessee to Union	May 6, 1796	43	30

[See note 7, p. xxix]

some committees overseeing administrative matters, such as the Joint Standing Committee on Enrolled Bills and the House Committee on Elections. Legislation was prepared by select or ad hoc committees. [See note 5, p. xxix]

MAJOR LEGISLATION PASSED

Admission of Tennessee as a New State: Congress voted May 26, 1796 to admit Tennessee into the United States.

Foreign Policy: The Senate approved three major treaties during the Fourth Congress. First, it approved Jay's Treaty, which resolved a variety of military and trade disputes with Great Britain that otherwise might have led to war. Second, it approved a treaty with the Barbary pirates of Algiers providing a ransom of approximately $1 million in exchange for the release of 115 cap-

tured American sailors. Third, it approved the Treaty of San Lorenzo, also known as Pinckney's Treaty, which resolved the differences with Spain over commercial relations, boundaries, and Spanish possessions in North America bordering on the United States, principally Florida.

Native Americans: Congress unsuccessfully attempted to limit America's westward expansion by denying European Americans the right to trap, hunt, or fish on Native American lands. Congress was concerned that further expansion would result in conflict between the United States and Native American tribes or European powers like Spain or Great Britain with interests in North America.

Public Lands: The Land Act of 1796 provided for surveys and public auctions of federal lands in the old Northwest Territory, which roughly comprised the present-day midwestern and north-midwestern states east of the Mississippi.

Seamen: Concerned about foreign navies that were abducting American seamen and impressing them into their service, Congress authorized the president to investigate the problem.

FAILED LEGISLATION

None of historical significance.

RELATIONS WITH THE PRESIDENT

In the final Congress of his presidency, George Washington set two important precedents. First [See Background, p. 15], Washington advocated a policy of American neutrality in foreign affairs in his Farewell Address. [See the discussion of the Neutrality Proclamation in the Third Congress] Second, Washington declined to run for a third term as president. Although limiting the presidency to two terms was not a constitutional restriction, no president broke Washington's precedent by seeking more than two terms until Franklin D. Roosevelt who was elected for a third term (1940) and again for a fourth term (1944). The two-term restriction became constitutionally binding with the passage of the 22nd Amendment.

Washington fought with little success to curb the rise of factionalism in Congress. He was concerned about the split between the Federalists and the Democratic-Republicans and the increasing power of special interest groups representing planters, industrialists, and so forth, who attempted to influence legislation. Nevertheless, political parties and special interest groups became a permanent fixture in the nation's politics.

During the Fourth Congress, Washington vetoed one bill, which concerned amendments to certain military legislation.

NOMINATIONS, APPOINTMENTS, AND CONFIRMATIONS

The Judiciary: On June 29, 1795, Supreme Court Chief Justice John Jay resigned. President George Washington, on July 1, 1795, nominated former Associate Justice John Rutledge as Jay's replacement, but, on December 15, 1795, the Senate voted 14 to 10 not to confirm Rutledge. This was the first Supreme Court nomination rejected by the Senate. Meanwhile, Justice John Blair had resigned on October 25, 1795, leaving Washington with two vacancies to fill. On January 26, 1796, Washington nominated, and the Senate confirmed the next day by voice vote, Samuel Chase to replace Blair. Then, on March 3, 1796, Washington nominated Oliver Ellsworth to be chief justice, and the Senate confirmed him the next day, by a 21-to-1 vote.

The Executive Branch: On December 9, 1795, Washington nominated Charles Lee to be attorney general and Timothy Pickering to be secretary of state. The next day, December 10, the Senate confirmed both Lee and Pickering by voice vote. On January 26, 1796, Washington nominated James McHenry to be secretary of war, and on January 27 the Senate confirmed McHenry by voice vote.

IMPEACHMENTS

None.

CONSTITUTIONAL AMENDMENTS

None.

FURTHER READING

Adams, John. *The Adams Papers.*
  Cambridge, Mass.: Harvard University
  Press, 1961-present.
Brown, William Garrott. *A Continental
  Congressman: The Life of Oliver Ellsworth.*
  New York: DeCapo Press, 1970 (reprint of
  1905 original).

The Fifth Congress

MARCH 4, 1797-MARCH 3, 1799

First Session: May 15, 1797-July 10, 1797
Second Session: November 13, 1797-July 16, 1798
Third Session: December 3, 1798-March 3, 1799

In the 1796 elections for the Fifth Congress, the Federalists gained 1 seat in the Senate, raising their total from 19 to 20 of the 32 seats. The Democratic-Republicans lost 1 seat to hold a total of 12. In the House, the Federalists gained 4 seats for a majority of 58 of the 106 seats, and the Democratic-Republicans lost 4 seats to hold a total of 48. [See notes 2 and 3, p. xxix]

BACKGROUND

The Fifth Congress met in Philadelphia, Pennsylvania. President John Adams, a Federalist, had been elected the second president of the United States and was inaugurated on March 4, 1797. Later that year, the crisis known as the XYZ affair developed. Three agents (known as X,Y, and Z) of French foreign minister Talleyrand approached American representatives Elbridge Gerry, John Marshall, and Charles Cotesworth Pickney demanding a loan to France and a bribe for French officials. Pickney refused, responding, "not a sixpence." Adams sent the papers detailing the XYZ affair to Congress on April 3, 1798, fanning anti-French sentiment among the public. The incident triggered an undeclared two-year naval war between France and the United States.

Major legislation of the Fifth Congress included the Alien and Sedition Acts, consisting of four laws passed in June and July of 1798 that amended the Naturalization Act of 1795. [See Third Congress] The Alien and Sedition Acts toughened citizenship requirements, increased the government's powers over resident aliens, and attempted to curb sedition against the United States.

SENATE LEADERSHIP

Vice President: Thomas Jefferson, a future president and prominent Virginia politician, supervised the drafting of the Declaration of Independence, had been a member of the Continental Congress and a minister to France, and had served as George Washington's secretary of state. Jefferson, a Democratic-Republican, disagreed with the pro-British leanings and various other policies of President John Adams, who was a Federalist. During his term as vice-president, Jefferson wrote a *Manual of Parliamentary Practice for the Use of the Senate of the United States.* This manual is still used today.

President Pro Tempore: William Bradford (Fed., R.I.) was elected on July 6, 1797; Jacob Read (Fed., S.C.) was elected on November 22, 1797; Theodore Sedgwick (Fed., Mass.) was elected on June 27, 1798; John Laurance (Fed., N.Y.) was elected on December 6, 1798; and James Ross (Fed., Pa.) was elected on March 1, 1799. [See note 4, p. xxix]

Majority Leader, Majority Whip, Minority Leader, and Minority Whip: None. These functions did not evolve into formal Senate positions until the 62nd Congress (1911-1913).

C H R O N O L O G Y

March 4, 1797:	The Fifth Congress begins.
May 15, 1797:	The first session begins. Jonathan Dayton (Fed., N.J.) is reelected Speaker of the House.
July 7, 1797:	The House votes to impeach Senator William Blount for conspiring with British agents.
July 8, 1797:	The Senate votes 25 to 1 to expel Senator Blount.
July 10, 1797:	The first session ends.
November 13, 1797:	The second session begins.
April 3, 1798:	President Adams sends the papers detailing the XYZ affair to Congress.
April 26, 1798:	Congress passes legislation establishing the Department of the Navy.
May 18, 1798:	President Adams nominates Benjamin Stoddert for secretary of the Navy.
May 21, 1798:	The Senate confirms Stoddert.
June 12, 1798:	Congress passes legislation concerning naturalization.
June 21, 1798:	Congress passes the Alien Act.
July 3, 1798:	Congress passes the Alien Enemies Act.
July 6, 1798:	Congress passes legislation establishing the Marine Corps as a separate branch of the armed services.
July 10, 1798:	Congress passes the Sedition Act.
July 16, 1798:	The second session ends.
August 21, 1798:	Supreme Court Justice James Wilson dies.
December 3, 1798:	The third session begins.
December 19, 1798:	President Adams nominates Bushrod Washington as Wilson's replacement.
December 20, 1798:	The Senate confirms Washington.
January 11, 1799:	The Senate dismisses charges against ex-Senator Blount.
March 3, 1799:	The third session and the Fifth Congress end.

[See note 6, p. xxix]

Chairmen of Selected Key Committees: No entries for this Congress. [See Organization and Administration, p. 21]

HOUSE LEADERSHIP

Speaker of the House: Jonathan Dayton (Fed., N.J.) was reelected May 15, 1797. Dayton was a former member and Speaker of the New Jersey General Assembly and was a delegate to the Constitutional Convention. George Dent (Fed., Md.) was elected Speaker pro tempore for April 20, 1798, and May 28, 1798.

Majority Leader, Majority Whip, Minority Leader, and Minority Whip: None. These functions did not evolve into formal House positions until the 56th Congress (1899-1901).

Chairmen of Selected Key Committees: [See also Organization and Administration, p. 21]

Committee on Ways and Means: William L. Smith (Fed., S.C.) served until July 10, 1797, when he resigned to accept an appointment as minister to Portugal and Spain. Robert G. Harper (Fed., S.C.) became the new chairman.

TABLE OF KEY VOTES

Senate

Subject of Vote	Date of Vote	For	Against
Expulsion of Senator William Blount	July 8, 1797	25	1
Navy Act	April 16, 1798	19	6
Alien Act	June 8, 1798	16	7
Naturalization Act	June 12, 1798	13	8
Alien Enemies Act	July 3, 1798	Passed by voice vote	
Sedition Act	July 4, 1798	18	6
Marine Corps	July 6, 1798	Passed by voice vote	
Dismissing Charges Against Ex-Senator Blount	January 11, 1799	14	11

House

Subject of Vote	Date of Vote	For	Against
Impeachment of Senator Blount	July 7, 1797	Passed by voice vote	
Navy Act	April 26, 1798	Passed by voice vote	
Naturalization Act	May 22, 1798	Passed by voice vote	
Marine Corps	June 1, 1798	Passed by voice vote	
Alien Act	June 21, 1798	46	40
Alien Enemies Act	June 26, 1798	Passed by voice vote	
Sedition Act	July 10, 1798	44	41

[See note 7, p. xxix]

ORGANIZATION AND ADMINISTRATION

There was no permanent or standing committee structure in the first several Congresses, except for some committees overseeing administrative matters, such as the Joint Standing Committee on Enrolled Bills and the House Committee on Elections. Legislation was prepared by select or ad hoc committees. [See note 5, p. xxix]

MAJOR LEGISLATION PASSED

Alien and Sedition Acts: The Fifth Congress passed four laws, collectively and popularly known as the Alien and Sedition Acts, implementing reactionary restrictions on obtaining citizenship and expressing political dissent. First, Congress passed the Naturalization Act, which required applicants for citizenship to have at least 14 years of residence in the United States and at least 5 years of residence in the state where the application was submitted. Second, Congress passed the Alien Act, which gave the president the authority to deport "undesirable" aliens. Third, Congress passed the Alien Enemies Act, which gave the president the authority in wartime to expel classes of aliens en masse. Fourth, Congress passed the Sedition Act, which gave the government the power to arrest any citizen or alien for seditious acts. The scope of "sedition" under the Sedition Act was so broad that the legislatures of Virginia and Kentucky passed resolutions declaring the Sedition Act unconstitutional.

Marine Corps: Congress organized the Marines, who were formerly part of the navy, as a separate branch of the armed services with its own command structure.

Navy: Congress established the Department of the Navy, which took over some of the jurisdiction of the War Department, and made the secretary of the Navy a cabinet-level appointment.

FAILED LEGISLATION

None of historical significance.

RELATIONS WITH THE PRESIDENT

Like George Washington before him, President Adams sought to keep the United States out of the war between Great Britain and France, a task made more difficult by the XYZ affair [See Background, p. 19] and rising anti-French sentiment among the public and in Congress. Nevertheless, Adams successfully kept the U.S. out of the war.

Adams vetoed no legislation during the Fifth Congress.

NOMINATIONS, APPOINTMENTS, AND CONFIRMATIONS

The Judiciary: On August 21, 1798, Supreme Court Justice James Wilson died. On December 19, 1798, President John Adams nominated Bushrod Washington, George Washington's nephew, as Wilson's replacement. The next day, December 20, the Senate confirmed him by voice vote.

The Executive Branch: On May 18, 1798, President Adams nominated Benjamin Stoddert to be secretary of the Navy, and on May 21 the Senate confirmed Stoddert by voice vote. Adams did not replace the cabinet-level officials from the previous Washington administration, and no

Senate confirmation vote was required for continuing those appointments.

IMPEACHMENTS

Senator William Blount (Dem-Rep., Tenn.), who had a distinguished career of service to the young nation and was one of the signers of the Declaration of Independence, was also a traitor. He was the first Senator to ever be expelled from the Senate. During his term in Congress, Blount secretly conspired with the British to help them seize Spanish West Florida with help from frontiersmen, the Cherokee Nation, and the Creek tribe. On July 3, 1797, President Adams sent evidence of Blount's actions to the Senate. After the House voted by voice vote on July 7, 1797, to impeach Blount, the Senate expelled him the next day by a vote of 25 to 1. Expulsion is not the same as impeachment, however. The actual impeachment trial did not take place in the Senate until January 11, 1799. Since Blount was by then a private citizen, not serving in the federal government, the Senate voted 14 to 11 to dismiss the charges against him.

CONSTITUTIONAL AMENDMENTS

None.

FURTHER READING

Adams, John. *The Adams Papers.* Cambridge, Mass.: Harvard University Press, 1961-present.

Jefferson, Thomas. *The Papers of Thomas Jefferson.* Princeton, N. J.: Princeton University Press, 1950-present.

Masterson, William. *William Blount.* New York: Greenwood Press, 1969.

Shaw, Peter. *The Character of John Adams.* Chapel Hill, N.C.: University of North Carolina Press, 1976.

The Sixth Congress

MARCH 4, 1799-MARCH 3, 1801

First Session: December 2, 1799-May 14, 1800
Second Session: November 17, 1800-March 3, 1801

In the 1798 elections for the Sixth Congress, the Federalists lost 1 seat in the Senate, lowering their total from 20 to 19 of the 32 seats. The Democratic-Republicans gained 1 seat to hold a total of 13. In the House, the Federalists gained 6 seats for a majority of 64 of the 106 seats, and the Democratic-Republicans lost 6 seats to hold a total of 42. [See notes 2 and 3, p. xxix]

BACKGROUND

The first session of the Sixth Congress met in Philadelphia, Pennsylvania. From the beginning of the second session until the present day, Congress has met in Washington, D.C.

According to the census of 1800, the population of the United States as of August 4, 1800, was 5,308,483, resulting in a population density of 6.1 persons for each of the country's 864,746 square miles. This was a population increase of 35.1 percent over the 1790 census.

The major legislation of the Sixth Congress was the division in 1800 of the Northwest Territory into the Ohio Territory and the Indiana Territory. After yet another division in 1802, these territories would eventually become the midwestern states of Ohio (1803) and Indiana (1816). In the presidential elections of 1800, there was a tie vote in the electoral college between Thomas Jefferson

and Aaron Burr. Thus, the issue of who would become president went to the House of Representatives, where the voting was by states. On February 17, 1801, after 35 ballots in which neither candidate won a majority of the states, the House reached a decision on the 36th ballot. Ten of the 16 states voted for Jefferson, 4 for Burr and 2 were tied. The House declared Jefferson president and Burr vice president.

SENATE LEADERSHIP

Vice President: Thomas Jefferson [See biographical note in Fifth Congress]

President Pro Tempore: Samuel Livermore (Fed., N.H.) was elected on December 2, 1799; Uriah Tracy (Fed., Conn.) was elected on May 14, 1800; John Eager Howard (Fed., Md.) was elected on November 21, 1800; and James Hillhouse (Fed., Conn.) was elected on February 28, 1801. [See note 4, p. xxix]

Majority Leader, Majority Whip, Minority Leader, and Minority Whip: None. These functions did not evolve into formal Senate positions until the 62nd Congress (1911-1913).

Chairmen of Selected Key Committees: No entries for this Congress. [See Organization and Administration, p. 25]

C H R O N O L O G Y

March 4, 1799:	The Sixth Congress begins.
October 20, 1799:	Supreme Court Justice James Iredell dies.
December 2, 1799:	The first session begins, and Theodore Sedgwick (Fed., Mass.) is elected Speaker of the House.
December 4, 1799:	President Adams nominates Alfred Moore to replace Iredell.
December 10, 1799:	The Senate confirms Moore.
March 28, 1800:	Congress passes the Bankruptcy Act.
April 21, 1800:	Congress passes legislation establishing the territories of Ohio and Indiana.
April 22, 1800:	Congress passes legislation to move the government to the District of Columbia.
May 12, 1800:	President Adams nominates John Marshall to be secretary of state and Samuel Dexter to be secretary of war.
May 13, 1800:	The Senate confirms Marshall and Dexter.
May 14, 1800:	The first session ends.
November 17, 1800:	The second session begins.
December 15, 1800:	Chief Justice Oliver Ellsworth resigns.
December 30, 1800:	President Adams nominates Samuel Dexter to be secretary of the Treasury.
December 31, 1800:	The Senate confirms Dexter.
January 20, 1801:	President Adams nominates Secretary of State John Marshall to replace Ellsworth as chief justice.
January 27, 1801:	The Senate confirms Marshall.
January 29, 1801:	President Adams nominates Roger Griswold to be secretary of war to replace Dexter.
February 3, 1801:	The Senate confirms Griswold.
February 17, 1801:	The House declares Thomas Jefferson president and Aaron Burr vice president after the presidential election of 1800.
March 3, 1801:	The second session and the Sixth Congress end.

[See note 6, p. xxix]

HOUSE LEADERSHIP

Speaker of the House: Theodore Sedgwick (Fed., Mass.) was elected on December 2, 1799. Sedgwick was a former member and Speaker of the Massachusetts House of Representatives.

Majority Leader, Majority Whip, Minority Leader, and Minority Whip: None. These func-

tions did not evolve into formal House positions until the 56th Congress (1899-1901).

Chairmen of Selected Key Committees: [See also Organization and Administration, p. 25]

Committee on Ways and Means: Robert G. Harper (Fed., S.C.) and Roger Griswold (Dem-Rep., Conn.)

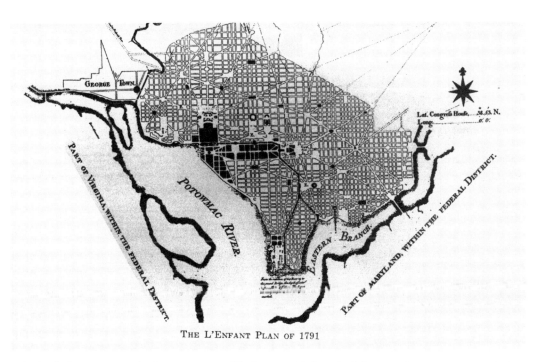

THE L'ENFANT PLAN OF 1791

The Sixth Congress was the first to move to Washington, D.C., which became the permanent capital of the United States.

ORGANIZATION AND ADMINISTRATION

There was no permanent or standing committee structure in the first several Congresses, except for some committees overseeing administrative matters, such as the Joint Standing Committee on Enrolled Bills and the House Committee on Elections. Legislation was prepared by select or ad hoc committees. [See note 5, p. xxix]

MAJOR LEGISLATION PASSED

Bankruptcy: Congress established the nation's first uniform bankruptcy code, although it was limited in scope to traders and merchants.

District of Columbia: The First Congress passed legislation creating the District of Columbia as the capital of the United States. By the second session of the Sixth Congress, the necessary buildings had been constructed. Congress passed legislation finalizing the move from Philadelphia, Pennsylvania, to Washington, D.C., where Congress has remained ever since.

Northwest Territory Division: Congress divided the Northwest Territory into the Ohio Territory and the Indiana Territory, which roughly comprised the present-day midwestern and north-midwestern states east of the Mississippi.

FAILED LEGISLATION

None of historical significance.

RELATIONS WITH THE PRESIDENT

Adams was a one-term president, and the Sixth Congress was his last Congress. He continued his policy of keeping the United States unaligned with either Great Britain or France, the two dominant and antagonistic European powers. This policy caused tensions with some of Adams' fellow Federalists in Congress, who were mostly pro-

TABLE OF KEY VOTES

Senate

Subject of Vote	Date of Vote	For	Against
Confirmation of Alfred Moore to Supreme Court	December 10, 1799	Passed by voice vote	
Bankruptcy Act	March 28, 1800	16	12
District of Columbia	April 17, 1800	18	10
Northwest Territory	April 21, 1800	Passed by voice vote	
Confirmations of Marshall and Dexter	May 13, 1800	Passed by voice vote	
Confirmation of Samuel Dexter for Secretary of the Treasury	December 31, 1800	Passed by voice vote	
Confirmation of John Marshall to Supreme Court	January 27, 1801	Passed by voice vote	
Confirmation of Roger Griswold for Secretary of War	February 3, 1801	25	5

House

Subject of Vote	Date of Vote	For	Against
Bankruptcy Act	February 21, 1800	49	48
Northwest Territory	March 31, 1800	Passed by voice vote	
District of Columbia	April 22, 1800	Passed by voice vote	

[See note 7, p. xxix]

British, as did Adams' policy of giving government jobs to the most qualified individuals regardless of whether they were Federalists or not. Adams vetoed no legislation during the Sixth Congress.

NOMINATIONS, APPOINTMENTS, AND CONFIRMATIONS

The Judiciary: Supreme Court Justice James Iredell died on October 20, 1799. On December 4, 1799, President Adams nominated Alfred Moore to replace Iredell, and the Senate confirmed Moore on December 10, 1799, by voice vote. On December 15, 1800, Chief Justice Oliver Ellsworth resigned, and on January 20, 1801, President Adams nominated Secretary of State John Marshall to replace Ellsworth. The Senate confirmed Marshall on January 27, 1801, by voice vote.

The Executive Branch: On May 12, 1800, Adams nominated John Marshall to be secretary of state and Samuel Dexter to be secretary of war. The next day, May 13, the Senate confirmed Marshall and Dexter by voice vote. Adams did not nominate anyone to replace Marshall at the State Department after Marshall became chief justice of the United States. On December 30, 1800, Adams nominated Dexter to be secretary of the Treasury, and the Senate confirmed him the next day by voice vote. To fill the vacant position of secretary of war, Adams nominated Lucius Stockton on January 15, 1801, but Stockton's nomination was withdrawn on January 29, 1801. On the same day, January 29, Adams nominated Roger Griswold for the post. Griswold was confirmed by the Senate on February 3, 1801, by a 25 to 5 vote. On February 18, 1801, Adams nominated Theophilus Parsons to be attorney general to replace Charles Lee, who had been continued from the Washington administration and thus had not required Senate confirmation. On February 20, 1801, Parsons declined to serve.

IMPEACHMENTS

None.

CONSTITUTIONAL AMENDMENTS

None.

FURTHER READING

Adams, John. *The Adams Papers*. Cambridge, Mass.: Harvard University Press, 1961-present.

Baker, Leonard. *John Marshall: A Life in Law*. New York: Macmillan, 1974.

Jefferson, Thomas. *The Papers of Thomas Jefferson*. Princeton: Princeton University Press, 1950-present.

Shaw, Peter. *The Character of John Adams*. Chapel Hill, N.C.: University of North Carolina Press, 1976.

Welch, Richard. *Theodore Sedgwick, Federalist: A Political Portrait*. Middletown, Conn.: Wesleyan University Press, 1965.

The Seventh Congress

MARCH 4, 1801-MARCH 3, 1803

Special Senate Session: *March 4, 1801-March 5, 1801*
First Session: *December 7, 1801-May 3, 1802*
Second Session: *December 6, 1802-March 3, 1802*

The Senate held a special session to vote on the confirmation of presidential appointees to various offices. [See note 1, p. xxix]

In the 1800 elections for the Seventh Congress, the Federalists lost 6 seats in the Senate, lowering their total from 19 to 13 of the 31 seats. The Democratic-Republicans gained 5 seats to hold a new majority of 18. In the House, the Democratic-Republicans won a sweeping victory, gaining 27 seats to give them a new majority of 69 out of the 106 seats. The Federalists lost 28 seats, leaving them with 36. One House seat belonged to neither party. [See notes 2 and 3, p. xxix]

BACKGROUND

Thomas Jefferson was inaugurated as the third president of the United States on March 4, 1801. In 1802 Jefferson discovered that France had acquired the Louisiana Territory from Spain by means of the secret treaty of San Ildefonso, executed in 1800. There was great public outcry over this development because American settlers in the Ohio and Indiana Territories were economically dependent on the Mississippi River. The Mississippi and its tributaries were the primary conduit for trade and the transportation of goods, but the mouth of the river at the Gulf of Mexico was controlled by the city of New Orleans, which was now French territory.

The Seventh Congress acted to establish the United States Military Academy at West Point, New York, and passed statehood legislation for the Ohio Territory. Ohio became the 17th state of the Union on February 19, 1803.

SENATE LEADERSHIP

Vice President: Aaron Burr was declared vice president by the House of Representatives after there was a tie in the electoral college between Burr and Thomas Jefferson in the presidential election of 1800. [See Sixth Congress] Burr was an erratic individual, who would later try, with British aid, to set up his own independent nation on the American frontier, an endeavor which ended in Burr's trial for treason. [See Ninth Congress]

President Pro Tempore: Abraham Baldwin (Dem-Rep., Ga.) was elected on December 7, 1801, and April 17, 1802; Stephen Row Bradley (Dem-Rep., Vt.) was elected on December 14, 1802, February 25, 1803, and March 2, 1803. [See note 4, p. xxix]

Majority Leader, Majority Whip, Minority Leader, and Minority Whip: None. These functions did not evolve into formal Senate positions until the 62nd Congress (1911-1913).

Chairmen of Selected Key Committees: No entries for this Congress. [See Organization and Administration, p. 29]

C H R O N O L O G Y

March 4, 1801:	The Seventh Congress begins, and the Senate begins a special session.
March 5, 1801:	President Jefferson nominates, and the Senate confirms, Levi Lincoln to be attorney general, James Madison to be secretary of state, and Henry Dearborn to be secretary of war. The Senate special session ends.
December 7, 1801:	The first session begins, and Nathaniel Macon (Dem-Rep., N.C.) is elected Speaker of the House.
December 19, 1801:	The Senate approves a treaty with France.
January 6, 1802:	President Jefferson nominates Robert Smith to be secretary of the Navy and Albert Gallatin to be secretary of the Treasury.
January 26, 1802:	The Senate confirms both Smith and Gallatin.
March 5, 1802:	Congress establishes West Point.
April 28, 1802:	Congress passes legislation to admit Ohio into the Union.
May 3, 1802:	The first session ends.
December 6, 1802:	The second session begins.
March 2, 1803:	The House votes to impeach Judge John Pickering.
March 3, 1803:	The second session and the Seventh Congress end.

[See note 6, p. xxix]

HOUSE LEADERSHIP

Speaker of the House: Nathaniel Macon (Dem-Rep., N.C.) was elected Speaker on December 7, 1801. Macon was first elected to the House in the Second Congress and was reelected 12 times until he left the House to serve in the Senate

Majority Leader, Majority Whip, Minority Leader, and Minority Whip: None. These functions did not evolve into formal House positions until the 56th Congress (1899-1901).

Chairmen of Selected Key Committees: [See also Organization and Administration, below.]

Committee on Ways and Means: John Randolph (Dem-Rep., Va.)

ORGANIZATION AND ADMINISTRATION

There was no permanent or standing committee structure in the first several Congresses, except for some committees overseeing administrative matters, such as the Joint Standing Committee on Enrolled Bills and the House Committee on Elections. Legislation was prepared by select or ad hoc committees. [See note 5, p. xxix]

MAJOR LEGISLATION PASSED

Admission of Ohio as a New State: Congress voted to admit Ohio into the United States.

Foreign Policy: The Senate approved the Treaty of Monfontaine with France. The treaty released France from certain American claims for inter-

TABLE OF KEY VOTES

Senate

Subject of Vote	Date of Vote	For	Against
Confirmation of Lincoln, Madison and Dearborn	March 5, 1801	Passed by voice vote	
Treaty with France	December 19, 1801	22	4
Confirmation of Smith and Gallatin	January 26, 1802	Passed by voice vote	
Establishment of West Point	March 5, 1802	15	10
Admission of Ohio as a State	April 28, 1802	16	6

House

Subject of Vote	Date of Vote	For	Against
Establishment of West Point	January 21, 1802	77	12
Admission of Ohio as a State	April 9, 1802	47	29
Impeachment of Judge John Pickering	March 2, 1803	45	8

[See note 7, p. xxix]

ference with shipping, and released America from its obligations to France under the 1778 Treaty of Alliance (executed by the colonies during the Revolutionary War in order to obtain French military aid). The Treaty effectively ended the undeclared naval war between France and the United States.

West Point: Congress established the United States Military Academy at West Point, New York, for the training of military officers.

FAILED LEGISLATION

None of historical significance.

RELATIONS WITH THE PRESIDENT

After the election of 1800, President Thomas Jefferson's Democratic-Republicans held new and large majorities in both the House and the Senate. Despite these majorities, however, Jefferson's legislative initiatives and accomplishments in the Seventh Congress were very modest. [See Major Legislation passed, above] Jefferson vetoed no legislation during the Seventh Congress.

NOMINATIONS, APPOINTMENTS, AND CONFIRMATIONS

The Judiciary: There were no significant nominations, appointments, or confirmations for the judiciary during the Seventh Congress.

The Executive Branch: On March 5, 1801, President Jefferson nominated, and the Senate confirmed by voice vote, Levi Lincoln to be attorney general, James Madison to be secretary of state, and Henry Dearborn to be secretary of war.

On January 6, 1802, Jefferson nominated Robert Smith to be secretary of the Navy and Albert Gallatin to be secretary of the Treasury. On January 26, 1802, the Senate confirmed both Smith and Gallatin by voice vote.

IMPEACHMENTS

On March 2, 1803, the House voted 45 to 8 to impeach federal Judge John Pickering. The impeachment trial, and its background, are discussed in the chapter on the Eighth Congress.

CONSTITUTIONAL AMENDMENTS

None.

FURTHER READING

Dodd, William E. *The Life of Nathaniel Macon*. Raleigh, N.C.: Edwards and Broughton, 1903.

Ellis, Richard E. *The Jeffersonian Crisis; Courts and Politics in the Young Republic*. New York: Oxford University Press, 1971.

Parmet, Herbert S. and Marie Hecht. *Aaron Burr: Portrait of an Ambitious Man*. New York: Macmillan, 1967.

The Eighth Congress

MARCH 4, 1803-MARCH 3, 1805

First Session: *October 17, 1803-March 27, 1804*
Second Session: *November 5, 1804-March 3, 1805*

I n the 1802 elections for the Eighth Congress, the Democratic-Republicans gained 7 seats in the Senate, raising their majority from 18 to 25 of the 34 seats. The Federalists lost 4 seats, leaving them with only 9 Senate seats. Because of the 1800 census [See Sixth Congress], the House was reapportioned and increased to 142 members, with the Democratic-Republicans gaining 33 seats for a majority of 102 and the Federalists gaining 3 seats to hold a total of 39. One seat belonged to neither party. [See notes 2 and 3, p. xxix]

BACKGROUND

In 1803 American concern over French ownership of the Louisiana Territory was resolved when President Jefferson negotiated the Louisiana Purchase. For $15 million, the United States acquired approximately 828,000 square miles of frontier territory. Out of this area would be carved the states of Arkansas, Iowa, Missouri, Nebraska, and North and South Dakota, as well as parts of Colorado, Kansas, Louisiana, Minnesota, Montana, Oklahoma, and Wyoming. Also during 1803, the Supreme Court issued its decision in *Marbury v. Madison*, which firmly established the principle of judicial review, giving the Supreme Court the power to declare acts of Congress unconstitutional and void. In foreign affairs, the United States's naval action against Yusuf Karamanli, the pasha of Tripoli, was escalating.

Jefferson sent a squadron of ships against Tripoli on May 23, 1803 in an effort to surpress the Barbary Coast pirates.

In 1804 Jefferson sent Merriwether Lewis and William Clark on an exploration expedition into the Louisiana Territory. The Lewis and Clark Expedition left St. Louis, Missouri, on May 14, 1804, and returned to St. Louis on September 23, 1806, with a wealth of information on the country's new possessions. During 1804 the 12th Amendment to the Constitution was ratified, which provides for a more specific procedure by which the electoral vote for president and vice president is balloted and counted, and ensures that both candidates would run on the same ticket. [See U.S. Constitution in Appendix A]

SENATE LEADERSHIP

Vice President: Aaron Burr was declared vice president by the House of Representatives after he and Thomas Jefferson tied in the presidential election of 1800. [See Sixth Congress] Burr was an erratic individual, who would later try, with British aid, to establish his own independent nation on the American frontier, an endeavor which ended in Burr's trial for treason. [See Ninth Congress] During this Congress, Burr quarreled with Alexander Hamilton, the famous secretary of the Treasury under President George Washington, and killed Hamilton in a duel on July 11, 1804, in Weehawken, New Jersey. Burr

C H R O N O L O G Y

March 4, 1803:	The Eighth Congress begins.
October 17, 1803:	The first session begins and Nathaniel Macon (Dem-Rep., N.C.) is reelected Speaker of the House.
October 20, 1803:	The Senate confirms the Louisiana Purchase Treaty.
October 28, 1803:	Congress passes legislation enabling President Jefferson to take control of the Louisiana Territory.
December 2, 1803:	Congress sends the 12th Amendment to the states for ratification.
January 26, 1804:	Supreme Court Justice Alfred Moore resigns.
March 12, 1804:	The House votes to impeach Justice Samuel Chase. The Senate holds the impeachment trial of Judge Pickering and removes him by a 20 to 6 vote.
March 22, 1804:	President Jefferson nominates William Johnson as Moore's replacement on the Supreme Court.
March 24, 1804:	The Senate confirms Johnson.
March 27, 1804:	The first session ends.
June 15, 1804:	The 12th Amendment is ratified by the required three-fourths of the states effective as of this date.
November 5, 1804:	The second session begins.
March 1, 1805:	Senate fails to convict Justice Chase at his impeachment trial.
March 2, 1805:	President Jefferson nominates Robert Smith to be attorney general and Jacob Crowninshield to be secretary of the Navy, but that same day both men decline to serve.
March 3, 1805:	The second session and the Eighth Congress end.

[See note 6, p. xxix]

fled to South Carolina to avoid a murder charge, then returned to Washington, D.C., to serve out his term as vice president. Jefferson did not choose Burr as his running mate in the presidential election of 1804.

President Pro Tempore: John Brown (Dem-Rep., Ky.) was elected on October 17, 1803, and January 23, 1804; Jesse Franklin (Dem-Rep., N.C.) was elected on March 10, 1804; and Joseph Anderson (Dem-Rep., Tenn.) was elected on January 15, 1805, February 28, 1805, and March 2, 1805. [See note 4, p. xxix]

Majority Leader, Majority Whip, Minority Leader, and Minority Whip: None. These functions did not evolve into formal Senate positions until the 62nd Congress (1911-1913).

Chairmen of Selected Key Committees: No entries for this Congress. [See Organization and Administration, p. 34]

HOUSE LEADERSHIP

Speaker of the House: Nathaniel Macon (Dem-Rep., N.C.) was reelected on October 17, 1803. Macon was first elected to the House in the Second Congress and was reelected 12 times until he left the House to serve in the Senate.

Majority Leader, Majority Whip, Minority Leader, and Minority Whip: None. These functions did not evolve into formal House positions

TABLE OF KEY VOTES

Senate

Subject of Vote	Date of Vote	For	Against
Louisiana Purchase Treaty	October 20, 1803	24	7
Louisiana Territory Enabling Legislation	October 26, 1803	26	6
12th Amendment	December 2, 1803	22	10
Impeachment of Judge Pickering	March 12, 1804	20	6
Confirmation of William Johnson to Supreme Court	March 24, 1804	Passed by voice vote	
Impeachment of Justice Samuel Chase	March 1, 1805	16-18, 10-24, 18-16 18-16, 0-34, 4-30, 10-24 and 19-15*	

House

Subject of Vote	Date of Vote	For	Against
Louisiana Territory Enabling Legislation	October 28, 1803	89	23
12th Amendment	October 28, 1803	88	31
Impeachment of Justice Samuel Chase	March 12, 1804	73	32

[See note 7, p. xxix]

until the 56th Congress (1899-1901).

Chairmen of Selected Key Committees: [See also Organization and Administration, below]

Committee on Ways and Means: John Randolph (Dem-Rep., Va.)

ORGANIZATION AND ADMINISTRATION

There was no permanent or standing committee structure in the first several Congresses, except for some committees overseeing administrative matters, such as the Joint Standing Committee on Enrolled Bills and the House Committee on Elections. Legislation was prepared by select or ad hoc committees. [See note 5, p. xxix]

MAJOR LEGISLATION PASSED

Foreign Policy: The Senate approved the Louisiana Purchase Treaty. Shortly thereafter, Congress passed legislation to implement the Louisiana Purchase by authorizing President Jefferson to take possession of the Louisiana Territory in the name of the United States.

FAILED LEGISLATION

None of historical significance.

RELATIONS WITH THE PRESIDENT

President Jefferson and his fellow Democratic-Republicans, who held large majorities in both

---

*There were 8 separate votes on motions to find Chase guilty, all of which failed to gain the necessary two-thirds majority.

houses of Congress, were united in their determination to break the Federalist domination of the judiciary. [See Impeachments, below] Jefferson and the Democratic-Republicans were also wary of the Supreme Court's assertion of the power of judicial review in *Marbury v. Madison*. [See Background, p. 32] There were some threats that Congress would limit the Court's jurisdiction through a constitutional amendment or through revisions to the statutes defining the Court's jurisdiction in certain federal cases, but none of these threats were realized. Jefferson vetoed no legislation during the Eighth Congress.

NOMINATIONS, APPOINTMENTS, AND CONFIRMATIONS

The Judiciary: On January 26, 1804, Supreme Court Justice Alfred Moore resigned. President Thomas Jefferson nominated William Johnson as Moore's replacement on March 22, 1804, and the Senate confirmed Johnson on March 24, 1804, by voice vote.

The Executive Branch: President Jefferson on March 2, 1805, nominated Robert Smith to be attorney general and Jacob Crowninshield to be secretary of the Navy. That same day, however, both men declined to serve.

IMPEACHMENTS

Near the end of the Seventh Congress, the House voted to impeach federal Judge John Pickering. There was evidence that Pickering was mentally ill and possibly an alcoholic, but there were political motivations as well: President Jefferson was a Democratic-Republican, and his party wanted to crack the Federalist control of the judiciary. Pickering, who was a Federalist, was an easy test case. He refused to attend his impeachment trial in the Senate, and even challenged Jefferson to a duel. On March 12, 1804, the Senate removed Pickering from office by a vote of 20 to 6. Emboldened by their success with Pickering, the Democratic-Republicans tried to impeach Supreme Court Justice Samuel Chase. Chase, openly pro-Federalist, was a competent jurist, and

did not deserve impeachment. On March 12, 1804, the House voted 73 to 32 to impeach Chase, but the Senate on March 1, 1805, failed to convict him. There were 8 separate votes that day [see Table of Key Votes, p. 34], none of which produced the two-thirds majority necessary to find Chase guilty.

CONSTITUTIONAL AMENDMENTS

Congress sent the Twelfth Amendment, which provides for a more specific procedure by which the electoral college vote for president and vice president is balloted and counted, to the states for ratification. The amendment also provides for the candidates to run on the same ticket, eliminating the possibility of having a president and vice president of opposing parties serving together, as happened when President Adams and Vice President Jefferson had been elected in 1796. The Twelfth Amendment was ratified by the required three-fourths of the states effective June 15, 1804. [For the text of the Twelfth Amendment, see the copy of the Constitution in Appendix A]

FURTHER READING

Christianson, Stephen G. "Samuel Chase Impeachment." In *Great American Trials*, edited by Edward W. Knappman. Detroit: Gale Research, 1994.

Dodd, William E. *The Life of Nathaniel Macon*. Raleigh, N.C.: Edwards and Broughton, 1903.

Morgan, Donald Grant. *Justice William Johnson, the First Dissenter: The Career and Constitutional Philosophy of a Jeffersonian Judge*. Columbia, S.C.: University of South Carolina Press, 1954.

Parmet, Herbert S. and Marie Hecht. *Aaron Burr: Portrait of an Ambitious Man*. New York: Macmillan Press, 1967.

The Ninth Congress

MARCH 4, 1805 - MARCH 3, 1807

First Session: December 2, 1805-April 21, 1806
Second Session: December 1, 1806-March 3, 1807

In the 1804 elections for the Ninth Congress, the Democratic-Republicans gained 2 seats in the Senate, raising their majority from 25 to 27 of the 34 seats. The Federalists lost 2 seats, reducing their total to 7 seats. In the House, the Democratic-Republicans gained 14 seats, giving them a majority of 116 of the 142 seats. The Federalists lost 14 seats, leaving them with a total of 25 seats. One seat was held by neither party. [See notes 2 and 3, p. xxix]

BACKGROUND

On March 4, 1805, when the Ninth Congress began, President Thomas Jefferson was inaugurated for his second term as the third president of the United States. George Clinton, not Aaron Burr, was Jefferson's vice president this term. On April 27, 1805, the United States won a major victory in its naval action against Tripoli when a small force of Marines supported by offshore warships captured the Tripoli port of Derna. On June 4, 1805, Tripoli agreed to stop halting and collecting tribute from U.S. merchant vessels in the Mediterranean. The British, however, continued to harass American ships with their policy of stopping American ships and impressing the seamen into service on the grounds that they were actually British subjects. Congress retaliated by placing an import embargo on British imports.

Domestically, the most significant event during the Ninth Congress was the ill-fated attempt by former Vice President Aaron Burr to establish, with British aid, his own independent nation on the American frontier. This endeavor ended in Burr's capture and trial for treason. Shortly before the Ninth Congress ended in 1807, Congress outlawed the importation of slaves into the U.S. after January 1, 1808.

SENATE LEADERSHIP

Vice President: George Clinton was elected vice president on Thomas Jefferson's ticket in the election of 1804. He had been a member of the Continental Congress, a general in the American Revolution, and a governor of New York.

President Pro Tempore: Samuel Smith (Dem-Rep., Md.) was elected on December 2, 1805, March 18, 1806, and March 2, 1807. [See note 4, p. xxix]

Majority Leader, Majority Whip, Minority Leader, and Minority Whip: None. These functions did not evolve into formal Senate positions until the 62nd Congress (1911-1913).

Chairmen of Selected Key Committees: No entries for this Congress. [See Organization and Administration, p. 37]

HOUSE LEADERSHIP

Speaker of the House: Nathaniel Macon (Dem-Rep., N.C.) was reelected on December 2, 1805. Macon was first elected to the House in the Second Congress and was reelected 12 times until he left the House to serve in the Senate.

Former Vice President Aaron Burr

Henry Clay

Majority Leader, Majority Whip, Minority Leader, and Minority Whip: None. These positions did not evolve into formal House positions until the 56th Congress (1899-1901).

Chairmen of Selected Key Committees: [See also Organization and Administration, below]

Committee on Ways and Means: John Randolph (Dem-Rep., Va.) and Joseph Clay (Dem-Rep., Pa.)

ORGANIZATION AND ADMINISTRATION

There was no permanent or standing committee structure in the first several Congresses, except for some committees overseeing administrative matters, such as the Joint Standing Committee on Enrolled Bills and the House Committee on Elections. Legislation was prepared by select or ad hoc committees. [See note 5, p. xxix]

MAJOR LEGISLATION PASSED

Cumberland Road: The Cumberland Road Act began the construction of a road from Cumberland, Maryland to Wheeling, Virginia (later West Virginia). Congress saw the Cumberland Road as a potentially important means of transportation from the East Coast to the Ohio River.

Judiciary: The Judiciary Act of 1807 increased the size of the Supreme Court from six justices to seven justices.

Slavery: The Constitution gave Congress the power to abolish the slave trade, but as a concession to Southern states this power was not made effective until 1808. Shortly before the Ninth Congress ended in 1807, Congress passed the Slave Trade Prohibition Act, which outlawed the importation of slaves into the United States after January 1, 1808.

Trade: The Non-Importation Act placed an import embargo on various British products in retaliation for British harassment of American shipping.

FAILED LEGISLATION

None of historical significance.

RELATIONS WITH THE PRESIDENT

President Jefferson and his fellow Democratic-Republicans, who controlled both houses of Congress by large majorities, were beginning to move from a policy of official neutrality to a more assertive position with the European powers who harassed American shipping, as embodied in the

C H R O N O L O G Y

March 4, 1805: The Ninth Congress begins.

December 2, 1805: The first session begins and Nathaniel Macon (Dem-Rep., N.C.) is reelected Speaker of the House.

March 24, 1806: Congress passes legislation to begin construction of the Cumberland Road.

April 15, 1806: Congress passes the Non-Importation Act.

April 21, 1806: The first session ends.

September 9, 1806: Supreme Court Justice William Paterson dies.

December 1, 1806: The second session begins.

December 13, 1806: President Jefferson nominates Brockholst Livingston to replace Paterson.

December 17, 1806: The Senate confirms Livingston.

February 13, 1807: Congress passes legislation barring the importation of slaves after January 1, 1808.

February 16, 1807: Congress passes the Judiciary Act, increasing the size of the Supreme Court from six to seven justices.

February 28, 1807: President Jefferson nominates Thomas Todd to fill a new position on the Supreme Court.

March 3, 1807: The Senate confirms Todd. The second session and the Ninth Congress end.

[See note 6, p. xxix]

Non-Importation Act. [See Major Legislation, above] New England, the center of American commerce and shipping at this time, suffered the most from the new policies. Some members of Congress from New England criticized Jefferson, who was from largely agricultural Virginia. Jefferson vetoed no legislation during the Ninth Congress.

NOMINATIONS, APPOINTMENTS, AND CONFIRMATIONS

The Judiciary: On September 9, 1806, Supreme Court Justice William Paterson died. President Jefferson on December 13, 1806, nominated Brockholst Livingston to replace Paterson, and the Senate confirmed Livingston on December 17, 1806, by voice vote. The Supreme Court was increased to seven members in 1807, and on February 28, 1807, President Jefferson nominated

Thomas Todd to fill the new position. The Senate confirmed Todd on March 3, 1807, by voice vote.

The Executive Branch: On December 20, 1805, President Jefferson nominated John Breckinridge to be attorney general, and on December 23 the Senate confirmed Breckinridge by voice vote. On January 15, 1807, Jefferson nominated Caesar A. Rodney to replace Breckinridge as attorney general, and on January 20 the Senate confirmed Rodney by voice vote.

IMPEACHMENTS

None.

CONSTITUTIONAL AMENDMENTS

None.

TABLE OF KEY VOTES

Senate

Subject of Vote	Date of Vote	For	Against
Confirmation of John Breckinridge for Attorney General	December 23, 1805	Passed by voice vote	
Cumberland Road Act	December 27, 1805	Passed by voice vote	
Non-Importation Act	April 15, 1806	19	9
Confirmation of Brockholst Livingston to Supreme Court	December 17, 1806	Passed by voice vote	
Confirmation of Caesar A. Rodney for Attorney General	January 15, 1807	Passed by voice vote	
Judiciary Act	January 26, 1807	Passed by voice vote	
Slave Importation Ban	January 27, 1807	Passed by voice vote	
Confirmation of Thomas Todd to Supreme Court	March 3, 1807	Passed by voice vote	

House

Subject of Vote	Date of Vote	For	Against
Cumberland Road Act	March 24, 1806	66	50
Non-Importation Act	March 26, 1806	93	32
Slave Importation Ban	February 13, 1807	113	5
Judiciary Act	February 16, 1807	82	7

[See note 7, p. xxix]

FURTHER READING

Cassell, Frank A. *Merchant Congressman in the Young Republic: Samuel Smith of Maryland, 1752-1839*. Madison, Wis.: University of Wisconsin Press, 1971.

Christianson, Stephen G. "Aaron Burr Trial." In *Great American Trials*, edited by Edward W. Knappman. Detroit: Gale Research, 1994.

Dodd, William E. *The Life of Nathaniel Macon*. Raleigh, N.C.: Edwards and Broughton, 1903.

Kaminski, John P. *George Clinton: Yeoman Politician of the New Republic*. Madison, Wis.: Madison House, 1993.

Wilder, Spaulding E. *His Excellency, George Clinton: Critic of the Constitution*. Port Washington, N.Y.: I.J. Friedman, 1964.

The Tenth Congress

MARCH 4, 1807-MARCH 3, 1809

First Session: October 26, 1807-April 25, 1808
Second Session: November 7, 1808-March 3, 1809

In the 1806 elections for the Tenth Congress, the Democratic-Republicans gained 1 seat in the Senate, raising their majority from 27 to 28 of the 34 seats. The Federalists lost 1 seat, reducing their total to 6 Senate seats. In the House, the Democratic-Republicans gained 2 seats, giving them a majority of 118 of the 142, and the Federalists lost 1 seat, reducing their total to 24 House seats. [See notes 2 and 3, p. xxix]

BACKGROUND

During the Tenth Congress, the primary concern was the continuing deterioration of relations with Great Britain and Napoleonic France over interference with American shipping. Britain and France were struggling for domination of Europe in the Napoleonic Wars, and both sides refused to recognize United States merchant vessels as neutral and free to trade with the other side. The American navy was not strong enough to prevent British and French harassment of American shipping, and so, at President Thomas Jefferson's request, Congress passed the Embargo Act, which forbade any American exports to either Britain or France. The Embargo Act backfired. Instead of forcing the British and French to stop harassing American trade, the British and French simply turned to other suppliers and relied on Americans willing to violate the act. The American economy suffered from the loss of these important export markets. To make matters worse, on April 17,

1808, the French emperor Napoleon took advantage of the embargo by issuing his Bayonne Decree, which ordered the seizure of all American merchant ships found in French-occupied ports, meaning most of continental Europe. The French justified their action in seizing millions of dollars of property by stating that under American law, the ships were there illegally. Ultimately, at the urging of Senator Timothy Pickering (Fed., Mass.), the Tenth Congress repealed the embargo legislation, and replaced it with the milder Non-Intercourse Act, which forbade British and French imports into the U.S. until the harassment of American trade ended.

SENATE LEADERSHIP

Vice President: George Clinton was elected vice president on Thomas Jefferson's ticket in the election of 1804. He had been a member of the Continental Congress, a general in the American Revolution, and a governor of New York.

President Pro Tempore: Samuel Smith (Dem-Rep., Md.) was elected on April 16, 1808; Stephen Row Bradley (Dem-Rep., Vt.) was elected on December 28, 1808; and John Milledge (Dem-Rep., Ga.) was elected on January 30, 1809. [See note 4, p. xxix]

Majority Leader, Majority Whip, Minority Leader, and Minority Whip: None. These functions did not evolve into formal Senate positions

C H R O N O L O G Y

March 4, 1807:	The Tenth Congress begins.
October 26, 1807:	The first session begins, and Joseph Bradley Varnum (Dem-Rep., Mass.) is elected Speaker of the House.
December 21, 1807:	Congress passes the Embargo Act.
April 25, 1808:	The first session ends.
November 7, 1808:	The second session begins.
February 27, 1809:	Congress passes the Non-Intercourse Act.
March 3, 1809:	The second session and the Tenth Congress end.

[See note 6, p. xxix]

until the 62nd Congress (1911-1913).

Other Senate Leaders: Senator Timothy Pickering (Fed., Mass.) who had served as secretary of war and secretary of state in the Washington administration, was an influential member of the Senate. He successfully led the effort by the New England states, who were economically dependent on trade and shipping, to repeal the embargo legislation. The embargo was replaced with the less restrictive Non-Intercourse Act.

Chairmen of Selected Key Committees: No entries for this Congress. [See Organization and Administration, below]

HOUSE LEADERSHIP

Speaker of the House: Joseph Bradley Varnum (Dem-Rep., Mass.) was elected Speaker on October 26, 1807. Varnum was a former member of the Massachusetts legislature and a state judge. He was first elected to the House in the Fourth Congress and was reelected eight times.

Majority Leader, Majority Whip, Minority Leader, and Minority Whip: None. These positions did not evolve into formal House positions until the 56th Congress (1899-1901).

Chairmen of Selected Key Committees: [See also Organization and Administration, below]

Committee on Ways and Means: George W. Campbell (Dem-Rep., Tenn.)

ORGANIZATION AND ADMINISTRATION

There was no permanent or standing committee structure in the first several Congresses, except for some committees overseeing administrative matters, such as the Joint Standing Committee on Enrolled Bills and the House Committee on Elections. Legislation was prepared by select or ad hoc committees. [See note 5, p. xxix]

MAJOR LEGISLATION PASSED

International Trade: The Tenth Congress's major legislative acts concerned trade with Great Britain and France. Congress passed the Embargo Act, which outlawed trade with both Britain and France. The Embargo Act was an economic disaster, and Congress repealed it. Congress then enacted the milder Non-Intercourse Act, which forbade British and French imports into the United States until the harassment of American trade ended.

FAILED LEGISLATION

None of historical significance.

TABLE OF KEY VOTES

Senate

Subject of Vote	Date of Vote	For	Against
Embargo Act	December 18, 1807	22	6
Non-Intercourse Act	February 21, 1809	21	12

House

Subject of Vote	Date of Vote	For	Against
Embargo Act	December 21, 1807	82	44
Non-Intercourse Act	February 27, 1809	81	40

[See note 7, p. xxix]

RELATIONS WITH THE PRESIDENT

As in the Ninth Congress, President Thomas Jefferson and his fellow Democratic-Republicans, who dominated both houses of Congress, moved towards a more assertive position with the European powers who were harassing American trade. This new policy included retaliation against the French [See Major Legislation, above], who had previously been favored by the Democratic-Republicans. Jefferson vetoed no legislation during the Tenth Congress.

NOMINATIONS, APPOINTMENTS, AND CONFIRMATIONS

There were no significant nominations, appointments, or confirmations in the federal judiciary or in the executive branch during the Tenth Congress.

IMPEACHMENTS

None.

CONSTITUTIONAL AMENDMENTS

None.

FURTHER READING

Clarfield, Gerald. *Timothy Pickering and the American Republic*. Pittsburgh: University of Pittsburgh Press, 1980.

Kaminski, John P. *George Clinton: Yeoman Politician of the New Republic*. Madison, Wis.: Madison House, 1993.

Varnum, Joseph. "Autobiography of General Joseph B. Varnum." *Magazine of American History*. 20 (November 1888); pp. 405-414.

Wilder, Spaulding E. *His Excellency, George Clinton: Critic of the Constitution*. Port Washington, N.Y.: I.J. Friedman, 1964.

The 11th Congress

MARCH 4, 1809 - MARCH 3, 1811

Special Senate Session: March 4, 1809-March 7, 1809
First Session: May 22, 1809-June 28, 1809
Second Session: November 27, 1809-May 1, 1810
Third Session: December 3, 1810-March 3, 1811

The Senate held a special session to vote on the confirmation of presidential appointees to various offices. [See note 1, p. xxix] The 1808 elections for the 11th Congress produced no change in the party balance in the Senate; the Democratic-Republicans continued to hold 28 seats in the Senate out of 34, and the Federalists continued to hold their 6 seats. In the House, the Democratic-Republicans lost 24 seats and yet still held a majority of 94 out of the 142 House seats. The Federalists gained 24 seats for a total of 48. [See notes 2 and 3, p. xxix]

BACKGROUND

James Madison, the fourth president of the United States, was inaugurated on March 4, 1809. According to the census of 1810, the population of the United States as of August 6, 1810,was 7,239,881, resulting in a population density of 4.3 persons for each of the country's 1,681,828 square miles. This was a population increase of 36.4 percent over the 1800 census. The population density of the 1810 census is the lowest in American history, because the Louisiana Purchase of 1803 nearly doubled the territory of the United States. [See Eighth Congress]

The United States acquired more territory in 1810 when American settlers in the territory known as West Florida stormed the Spanish fort at Baton Rouge (in present-day Louisiana) and declared their independence. On October 27, 1810, President Madison declared that West Florida was part of the U.S., and annexed it to the Orleans Territory of the Louisiana Purchase.

Madison's actions were less successful with respect to the British, who continued to harass American merchant and naval vessels. Congress passed Macon's Bill Number Two, named after its sponsor Representative Nathaniel Macon (Dem-Rep., N.C.). The bill offered to restore trade with Great Britain or France if one or both ceased their maritime harassment, but would eliminate all trade with the nation that refused. The French emperor Napoleon took the initiative on August 5, 1810, when he offered to stop his nation's confiscation of U.S. merchant shipping. Great Britain refused to reciprocate, and on February 11, 1811, Madison ordered the cessation of all American trade with Britain. By the end of the 11th Congress, the U.S. and Great Britain were drifting toward the War of 1812.

SENATE LEADERSHIP

Vice President: George Clinton had been vice president under former President Thomas Jefferson. He also had been a member of the Continental Congress; a general in the American Revolution; and a governor of New York.

President Pro Tempore: Andrew Gregg (Dem-Rep., Pa.) was elected on June 26, 1809; John Gaillard (Dem-Rep., S.C.) was elected on

CHRONOLOGY

March 4, 1809:	The 11th Congress and a special Senate session begin.
March 6, 1809:	President Madison nominates, and the Senate confirms, William Eustis to be secretary of war and Robert Smith to be secretary of state.
March 7, 1809:	President Madison nominates, and the Senate confirms, Paul Hamilton to be secretary of the Navy. The special session of the Senate ends.
May 22, 1809:	The first session begins, and Joseph Bradley Varnum (Dem-Rep., Mass.) is reelected Speaker of the House.
June 28, 1809:	The first session ends.
November 27, 1809:	The second session begins.
April 28, 1810:	Congress passes Macon's Bill Number Two.
May 1, 1810:	The second session ends.
September 13, 1810:	Supreme Court Justice William Cushing dies.
October 27, 1810:	President Madison declares that West Florida is part of the U.S., and annexes it to the Orleans Territory of the Louisiana Purchase.
December 3, 1810:	The third session begins.
February 4, 1811:	President Madison nominates Alexander Wolcott to replace Cushing on the Supreme Court.
February 7, 1811:	Congress passes legislation to admit Louisiana as a state.
February 13, 1811:	The Senate votes not to confirm Wolcott.
March 3, 1811:	The third session and the 11th Congress end.

[See note 6, p. xxix]

February 28, 1810, and April 17, 1810; and John Pope (Dem-Rep., Ky.) was elected on February 23, 1811. [See note 4, p. xxix]

Majority Leader, Majority Whip, Minority Leader, and Minority Whip: None. These functions did not evolve into formal Senate positions until the 62nd Congress (1911-1913).

Chairmen of Selected Key Committees: No entries for this Congress. [See Organization and Administration, p. 45]

HOUSE LEADERSHIP

Speaker of the House: Joseph Bradley Varnum (Dem-Rep., Mass.) was reelected Speaker on May 22, 1809. [See biographical note in Tenth Congress]

Majority Leader, Majority Whip, Minority Leader, and Minority Whip: None. These functions did not evolve into formal House positions until the 56th Congress (1899-1901).

Other House Leaders: Representative Nathaniel Macon (Dem-Rep., N.C.) had been in the House since the Second Congress and had served as Speaker in the Seventh, Eighth and Ninth Congresses. He introduced legislation, known as Macon's Bill Number Two, that replaced the Non-Intercourse Act. [See Major Legislation, p. 45]

Chairmen of Selected Key Committees: [See Organization and Administration, p. 45]

Committee on Ways and Means: John W. Eppes (Dem-Rep., Va.)

John Quincy Adams, future president of the United States.

ORGANIZATION AND ADMINISTRATION

There was no permanent or standing committee structure in the first several Congresses, except for some committees overseeing administrative matters, such as the Joint Standing Committee on Enrolled Bills and the House Committee on Elections. Legislation was prepared by select or ad hoc committees. [See note 5, p. xxix]

MAJOR LEGISLATION PASSED

Admission of Louisiana as a New State: Congress voted to admit Louisiana into the United States.

International Trade: The Tenth Congress enacted the Non-Intercourse Act, which forbade British and French imports into the U.S. until their harassment of American trade in connection with the

TABLE OF KEY VOTES

Senate

Subject of Vote	Date of Vote	For	Against
Confirmation of Eustis and Smith	March 6, 1809	Passed by voice vote	
Confirmation of Paul Hamilton for Secretary of the Navy	March 7, 1809	Passed by voice vote	
Macon's Bill Number Two	April 28, 1810	Passed by voice vote	
Admission of Louisiana as a State	February 7, 1811	22	10
Confirmation of Alexander Wolcott to Supreme Court	February 13, 1811	9	24

House

Subject of Vote	Date of Vote	For	Against
Macon's Bill Number Two	April 19, 1810	61	40
Admission of Louisiana as a State	January 15, 1811	77	36

[See note 7, p. xxix]

Napoleonic Wars ended. The 11th Congress replaced the Non-Intercourse Act with new legislation, called Macon's Bill Number Two named after its sponsor Representative Nathaniel Macon (Dem-Rep., N.C.), The bill offered to restore trade with Great Britain or France if one or both ceased their maritime harassment, but would eliminate all trade with the nation that refused. [See Background, p. 43, for further discussion]

FAILED LEGISLATION

None of historical significance.

RELATIONS WITH THE PRESIDENT

President Madison and his fellow Democratic-Republicans still controlled both houses of Congress, even though they lost 24 seats in the House of Representatives during the 1808 elections. Madison vetoed two bills during the 11th Congress. Both were minor pieces of legislation.

NOMINATIONS, APPOINTMENTS, AND CONFIRMATIONS

The Judiciary: On September 13, 1810, Supreme Court Justice William Cushing died. President James Madison tried unsuccessfully during the 11th Congress to replace Cushing. First, Madison nominated Levi Lincoln on January 2, 1811, but Lincoln declined on the following day. Next, on February 4, 1811, Madison nominated Alexander Wolcott, but the Senate voted not to confirm Wolcott on February 13, 1811, by a 24 to 9 vote. Finally, Madison nominated John Quincy Adams on February 21, 1811, but the next day Adams declined. Madison would not be able to successfully fill Cushing's seat on the Court until the 12th Congress.

The Executive Branch: On March 6, 1809, Madison nominated, and the Senate confirmed by voice vote, William Eustis to be secretary of war and Robert Smith to be secretary of state. The next day, March 7, Madison nominated, and the Senate confirmed by voice vote, Paul Hamilton to be secretary of the Navy.

IMPEACHMENTS

None.

CONSTITUTIONAL AMENDMENTS

None.

FURTHER READING

Brant, Irving. *James Madison*. Indianapolis: Bobbs-Merrill, 1948-1961 (six volumes).

Dodd, William E. *The Life of Nathaniel Macon*. Raleigh, N.C.: Edwards and Broughton, 1903.

Kaminski, John P. *George Clinton: Yeoman Politician of the New Republic*. Madison, Wis.: Madison House, 1993.

Rutland, Robert Allen. *James Madison: The Founding Father*. New York: Macmillan, 1987.

Wilder, Spaulding E. *His Excellency, George Clinton: Critic of the Constitution*. Port Washington, N.Y.: I.J. Friedman, 1964.

The 12th Congress

MARCH 4, 1811 - MARCH 3, 1813

First Session: *November 4, 1811-July 6, 1812*
Second Session: *November 2, 1812-March 3, 1813*

In the 1810 elections for the 12th Congress, the Democratic-Republicans gained 2 seats in the Senate, raising their majority from 28 to 30 of the 36 seats. The Federalists continued to hold 6 Senate seats. In the House, the Democratic-Republicans gained 14 seats for a majority of 108 out of the 144 seats. The Federalists lost 12 seats, reducing their total to 36 House seats. [See notes 2 and 3, p. xxix]

BACKGROUND

In 1811 the United States and Great Britain continued to spar at sea over whether American ships could travel and trade without British interference. On May 1, 1811, and again on May 16 there were incidents between American and British ships off the coast of the state of New York. In the second incident, a 44-gun U.S.frigate fired on a British corvette suspected of impressing American seamen, killing 9 and wounding 23 of the British vessel's crew. Madison's administration proposed a settlement of the matter on November 1, 1811, but the British were unwilling to make concessions, leaving relations tense between the two countries. Meanwhile, the first American colonists had reached the Pacific Ocean, and on April 12, 1811, established Astoria in present-day Oregon. On November 7, 1811, future President, William Henry Harrison won a major victory over an Indian force at the Tippecanoe River in present-day Indiana. The next year, on

April 30, 1812, Louisiana was admitted to the Union as the 18th state.

The War of 1812 began on June 18, 1812, when Congress declared war against Great Britain. Only five days later, on June 23, while still unaware of the American declaration of war, Great Britain rescinded the maritime policies that had caused the conflict. Throughout the rest of 1812 and into 1813, the Americans and British fought sporadically, with the Americans winning several naval engagements but losing some battles on the frontier.

SENATE LEADERSHIP

Vice President: George Clinton, who had been elected vice president on James Madison's ticket in the election of 1808, died on April 20, 1812. Until the Twenty-fifth Amendment was ratified on February 10, 1967 [See 90th Congress], there was no mechanism for filling vacancies in the office of vice president. Clinton had been vice president under former President Thomas Jefferson. Clinton was also a former member of the Continental Congress, a general in the American Revolution, and a former governor of New York.

President Pro Tempore: William Harris Crawford (Dem-Rep., Ga.) was elected on March 24, 1812. [See note 4, p. xxix]

Majority Leader, Majority Whip, Minority Leader, and Minority Whip: None. These func-

C H R O N O L O G Y

March 4, 1811:	The 12th Congress begins.
June 19, 1811:	Supreme Court Justice Samuel Chase dies.
November 4, 1811:	The first session begins, and Henry Clay (Dem-Rep., Ky.) is elected Speaker of the House.
November 13, 1811:	President Madison nominates James Monroe to be secretary of state.
November 15, 1811:	President Madison nominates Joseph Story and Gabriel Duvall to the Supreme Court to fill the two vacancies created by the deaths of Justices William Cushing and Samuel Chase.
November 18, 1811:	The Senate confirms both Story and Duvall.
November 25, 1811:	The Senate confirms Monroe.
December 10, 1811:	President Madison nominates William Pinckney to be attorney general.
December 11, 1811:	The Senate confirms Pinckney.
April 10, 1812:	Congress passes legislation expanding the size of the state of Louisiana.
April 20, 1812:	Vice President George Clinton dies.
May 11, 1812:	Congress passes legislation expanding the size of the Mississippi Territory.
June 17, 1812:	Congress votes to declare war against Great Britain.
July 6, 1812:	The first session ends.
November 2, 1812:	The second session begins.
January 8, 1813:	President Madison nominates William Jones to be secretary of the Navy and John Armstrong to be secretary of war.
January 12, 1813:	The Senate confirms Jones.
January 13, 1813:	The Senate confirms Armstrong.
March 3, 1813:	The second session and the 12th Congress end.

[See note 6, p. xxix]

tions did not evolve into formal Senate positions until the 62nd Congress (1911-1913).

Chairmen of Selected Key Committees: No entries for this Congress. [See Organization and Administration, p. 49.]

HOUSE LEADERSHIP

Speaker of the House: Henry Clay (Dem-Rep., Ky.) was elected on November 4, 1811, his first day in the House. Clay was a powerful figure in American politics, not only as Speaker, but also as a senator and presidential candidate. Clay was first elected to the House in the 12th Congress, and was Speaker of the House in six Congresses.

Majority Leader, Majority Whip, Minority Leader and Minority Whip: None. These positions did not evolve into formal House positions until the 56th Congress (1899-1901).

Chairmen of Selected Key Committees: [See also Organization and Administration, p. 49]

TABLE OF KEY VOTES

Senate

Subject of Vote	Date of Vote	For	Against
Confirmation of Story and Duval to Supreme Court	November 18, 1811	Passed by voice vote	
Confirmation of James Monroe to be Secretary of State	November 25, 1811	30	0
Confirmation of William Pinkney to be Attorney General	December 10, 1811	Passed by voice vote	
Louisiana Expansion Act	April 8, 1812	21	5
Mississippi Expansion Act	May 11, 1812	Passed by voice vote	
Declaration of War Against Britain	June 17, 1812	19	13
Confirmation of William Jones to be Secretary of the Navy	January 12, 1813	Passed by voice vote	
Confirmation of John Armstrong to be Secretary of War	January 13, 1813	18	15

House

Subject of Vote	Date of Vote	For	Against
Louisiana Expansion Act	April 10, 1812	Passed by voice vote	
Mississippi Expansion Act	May 5, 1812	Passed by voice vote	
Declaration of War Against Britain	June 4, 1812	79	49

[See note 7, p. xxix]

Committee on Ways and Means: Ezekiel Bacon (Dem-Rep., Mass.) and Langdon Cheves (Dem-Rep., S.C.)

ORGANIZATION AND ADMINISTRATION

There was no permanent or standing committee structure in the first several Congresses, except for some committees overseeing administrative matters, such as the Joint Standing Committee on Enrolled Bills and the House Committee on Elections. Legislation was prepared by select or ad hoc committees. [See note 5, p. xxix]

MAJOR LEGISLATION PASSED

Louisiana: Congress enlarged the state of Louisiana by giving it territory in West Florida that had been seized from Spain during the 11th Congress.

Mississippi Territory: Congress enlarged the Mississippi Territory, which had not yet achieved statehood, by giving it territory in West Florida that had been seized from Spain during the 11th Congress.

War of 1812: Congress declared war against Great Britain, starting the War of 1812.

FAILED LEGISLATION

None of historical significance.

RELATIONS WITH THE PRESIDENT

President Madison and his fellow Democratic-Republicans, who dominated both houses of Congress, have sometimes been characterized as stumbling into the War of 1812, which might have been avoided. The conflict was derided by some contemporaries as "Mr. Madison's War."

Madison vetoed two bills during the 12th Congress. Neither was historically significant.

NOMINATIONS, APPOINTMENTS, AND CONFIRMATIONS

The Judiciary: Supreme Court Justice William Cushing had died on September 13, 1810, during the 11th Congress, but President Madison was unable to fill the vacancy during that Congress. On June 19,1811, Justice Samuel Chase also died, leaving Madison with two seats to fill on the Court. Madison nominated Joseph Story and Gabriel Duval to the Court on November 15, 1811, and the Senate confirmed both on November 18 by voice vote.

The Executive Branch: On November 13, 1811, President Madison nominated James Monroe to be secretary of state, and on November 25, the Senate confirmed Monroe by a vote of 30 to 0. On December 10, 1811, President Madison nominated William Pinckney to be attorney general

and the next day, the Senate confirmed him by voice vote. On January 8, 1813, Madison nominated William Jones to be secretary of the Navy and John Armstrong to be secretary of war. The Senate confirmed Jones by voice vote on January 12 and Armstrong on January 13 by a vote of 18 to 15.

IMPEACHMENTS

None.

CONSTITUTIONAL AMENDMENTS

None.

FURTHER READING

Brant, Irving. *James Madison.* Indianapolis: Bobbs-Merrill, 1948-1961 (six volumes).

Kaminski, John P. *George Clinton: Yeoman Politician of the New Republic.* Madison, Wis.: Madison House, 1993.

Remini, Robert V. *Henry Clay: Statesman for the Union.* New York: Norton, 1991.

Rutland, Robert Allen. *James Madison: The Founding Father.* New York: Macmillan, 1987.

Wilder, Spaulding E. *His Excellency, George Clinton: Critic of the Constitution.* Port Washington, N.Y.: I.J. Friedman, 1964.

The 13th Congress

MARCH 4, 1813 - MARCH 3, 1815

First Session: *May 24, 1813-August 2, 1813*
Second Session: *December 6, 1813-April 18, 1814*
Third Session: *September 19, 1814-March 3, 1815*

In the 1812 elections for the 13th Congress, the Democratic-Republicans lost 3 seats in the Senate, lowering their majority from 30 to 27 of the 36 seats. The Federalists gained 3 seats for a total of 9. Because of the 1810 census [See 11th Congress], the House was reapportioned and increased to 186 seats. The Democratic-Republicans gained 4 seats for a majority of 112. The Federalists gained 32 seats for a total of 68. Six seats were held by neither party. [See notes 2 and 3, p. xxix]

BACKGROUND

President James Madison, the fourth president of the United States, was inaugurated on March 4, 1813 for his second term. The U.S. was fighting the War of 1812 against Great Britain, which in 1813 saw an American naval victory at the Battle of Lake Erie on September 10 and a land victory in Canada at the Battle of the Thames on October 5. In the South, Madison suppressed an uprising by the Creek Indians of Alabama and Georgia. In 1814, however, the British seemed to gain the upper hand, sacking Washington, D.C., on August 24, 1814, and setting most government buildings on fire. The war ended on December 24, 1814 with the signing of the Treaty of Ghent, which the Senate ratified on February 16, 1815. The treaty provided for the return of conquered territory by both sides and the establishment of a boundary commission to delineate the border between the U.S. and Canada.

Ironically, the most significant American victory of the war came after the peace treaty between armies unaware of the cessation of hostilities. On January 8, 1815, in the Battle of New Orleans, General Andrew Jackson, future president, defeated an army of British veterans nearly twice as large as his force, thanks in large part to the technologically superior long rifle developed on the frontier and used by Jackson's soldiers. The United States was not long at peace, however. Just before the 13th Congress ended in 1815, Congress declared war against the Bey of Algiers for acts of piracy on American shipping.

SENATE LEADERSHIP

Vice President: Elbridge Gerry, elected in 1812 as vice president for Madison's second term, had been a member of the Continental Congress, had signed the Declaration of Independence, and had served as a governor of Massachusetts. Gerry died on November 23, 1814, the second vice president to die in office while serving under President Madison. [See 12th Congress] Until the Twenty-fifth Amendment was ratified on February 10, 1967 [See 90th Congress], there was no mechanism for filling vacancies in the office of vice president.

President Pro Tempore: Joseph Bradley Varnum (Dem-Rep., Mass.) was elected on December 6, 1813; John Gaillard (Dem-Rep., S.C.) was elected on April 18,1814, and again after Gerry's death,

CHRONOLOGY

March 4, 1813:	The 13th Congress begins.
May 24, 1813:	The first session begins, and Henry Clay (Dem.-Rep., Ky.) is reelected Speaker of the House.
August 2, 1813:	The first session ends.
December 6, 1813:	The second session begins.
February 8, 1814:	President Madison nominates Richard Rush to be attorney general and George W. Campbell to be secretary of the Treasury.
February 9, 1814:	The Senate confirms Campbell.
February 10, 1814:	The Senate confirms Rush.
April 18, 1814:	The second session ends.
August 24, 1814:	The British reach Washington, D.C. and set most government buildings on fire.
September 19, 1814:	The third session begins.
September 26, 1814:	President Madison nominates James Monroe for secretary of war.
September 27, 1814:	The Senate confirms Monroe.
October 5, 1814:	President Madison nominates Alexander J. Dallas to succeed Campbell as secretary of the Treasury.
October 6, 1814:	The Senate confirms Dallas.
November 23, 1814:	Vice President Elbridge Gerry dies.
December 15, 1814:	President Madison nominates Benjamin W. Crowninshield to be secretary of the Navy.
December 19, 1814:	The Senate confirms Crowninshield.
December 24, 1814:	Hostilities between Great Britain and the United States cease with the signing of the Treaty of Ghent.
February 2, 1815:	Congress fails to override the president's veto of the Bank of the United States legislation.
February 16, 1815:	The Senate approves the Treaty of Ghent, which had already been signed.
February 27, 1815:	President Madison nominates James Monroe for secretary of state.
February 28, 1815:	The Senate confirms Monroe.
March 2, 1815:	Congress approves a declaration of war against Algiers. President Madison nominates William H. Crawford to be secretary of war.
March 3, 1815:	The Senate confirms Crawford and the third session and 13th Congress end.

[See note 6, p. xxix]

on November 25, 1814. [See note 4, p. xxix]

Majority Leader, Majority Whip, Minority Leader, and Minority Whip: None. These functions did not evolve into formal Senate positions

until the 62nd Congress (1911-1913).

Chairmen of Selected Key Committees: No entries for this Congress. [See Organization and Administration, p. 53]

The chambers of Congress, after being burnt by the British in 1814.

HOUSE LEADERSHIP

Speaker of the House: Henry Clay (Dem-Rep., Ky.) was reelected on May 24, 1813. Clay was a powerful figure in American politics, not only as Speaker, but also as a senator and presidential candidate. Clay was first elected to the House in the 12th Congress, and was Speaker of the House in six Congresses. Clay resigned from Congress on January 19, 1814, and became one of the commissioners who negotiated an end to the War of 1812 with Great Britain. Also, on January 19,1814, Langdon Cheves (Dem-Rep., S.C.) was elected Speaker to replace Clay.

Majority Leader, Majority Whip, Minority Leader, and Minority Whip: None. These functions did not evolve into formal House positions until the 56th Congress (1899-1901).

Chairmen of Selected Key Committees: [See also Organization and Administration, below]

Committee on Ways and Means: John W. Eppes (Dem-Rep., Va.)

ORGANIZATION AND ADMINISTRATION

There was no permanent or standing committee structure in the first several Congresses, except for some committees overseeing administrative matters, such as the Joint Standing Committee on Enrolled Bills and the House Committee on Elections. Legislation was prepared by select or ad hoc committees. [See note 5, p. xxix]

Speaker of the House Henry Clay (Dem-Rep., Ky.) is considered by many historians to be the first great Speaker, and the first Speaker to effectively use his power over committee appointments. Clay put loyal followers in charge of key committees, particularly the Ways and Means committee, which governed tax and budget matters.

MAJOR LEGISLATION PASSED

Treaty of Ghent: The Senate confirmed the Treaty of Ghent, which ended the War of 1812.

War with Algiers: Congress declared war against the pirate city-state of Algiers in North Africa, whose

TABLE OF KEY VOTES

Senate

Subject of Vote	Date of Vote	For	Against
Confirmation of George W. Campbell to be Secretary of the Treasury	February 9, 1814	Passed by voice vote	
Confirmation of Richard Rush to be Attorney General	February 10, 1814	23	6
Confirmation of James Monroe to be Secretary of War	September 27, 1814	24	2
Confirmation of Alexander J. Dallas to be Secretary of the Treasury	October 6, 1814	Passed by voice vote	
Confirmation of Benjamin W. Crowninshield to be Secretary of the Navy	December 19, 1814	18	9
Overriding Veto of Bank of the U.S. legislation	February 2, 1815	15	19
Treaty of Ghent	February 16, 1815	35	0
Confirmation of James Monroe to be Secretary of State	February 28, 1815	Passed by voice vote	
War with Algiers	March 2, 1815	27	2
Confirmation of William H. Crawford to be Secretary of War	March 3, 1815	Passed by voice vote	

House

Subject of Vote	Date of Vote	For	Against
War with Algiers	February 28, 1815	Passed by voice vote	

[See note 7, p. xxix]

pirates were once again harassing American ships.

FAILED LEGISLATION

Madison vetoed legislation which would have created a Bank of the United States. [See Relations with the President, below] Over the next several decades, the issue over whether there should be a Bank of the United States would periodically become an important political issue.

RELATIONS WITH THE PRESIDENT

The Congress and the president were preoccupied with the War of 1812, although the burning of Washington, D.C., and the stalemate in the conflict caused some critics to label the affair "Mr. Madison's War." Madison vetoed one bill during the 13th Congress, namely legislation which would have created a Bank of the United

States. On February 2, 1815, the Senate voted 15 in favor of overturning the veto and 19 against, which meant that the veto was sustained and was not voted upon by the House.

NOMINATIONS, APPOINTMENTS, AND CONFIRMATIONS

The Judiciary: There were no significant nominations, appointments, or confirmations in the federal judiciary during the 13th Congress.

The Executive Branch: On February 8, 1814, President Madison nominated Richard Rush to be attorney general and George W. Campbell to be secretary of the Treasury. On February 9, 1814, the Senate confirmed Campbell by voice vote, and on February 10, 1814, the Senate confirmed Rush by a vote of 23 to 6.

Madison nominated James Monroe to be secretary of war on September 26, 1814, and the Senate confirmed him the next day by a vote of 24 to 2.

On October 5, 1814, Madison nominated Alexander J. Dallas to succeed Campbell as secretary of the Treasury, and the next day the Senate confirmed him by voice vote.

Madison nominated Benjamin W. Crowninshield to be secretary of the Navy on December 15, 1814, and on December 19 the Senate confirmed him by a vote of 18 to 9. Madison decided to move James Monroe back into Monroe's previous position as secretary of state, and Madison officially nominated Monroe on February 27, 1815. The Senate confirmed Monroe by voice vote the following day. The next day, February 28, Madison nominated Henry Dearborn to succeed Monroe as secretary of war, but withdrew

Dearborn's nomination on March 2. Historical records indicate that the Senate may have voted to reject the nomination, but later erased the record of that vote in order to let Madison withdraw the nomination without embarassment. That same day, March 2, Madison then nominated William H. Crawford to be secretary of war, and the Senate confirmed Crawford by voice vote on March 3, 1815.

IMPEACHMENTS

None.

CONSTITUTIONAL AMENDMENTS

None.

FURTHER READING

Billias, George. *Elbridge Gerry, Founding Father and Republican Statesman.* New York: McGraw-Hill, 1976.

Brant, Irving. *James Madison.* Indianapolis: Bobbs-Merrill, 1948-1961 (six volumes).

Remini, Robert V. *Henry Clay: Statesman for the Union.* New York: W.W. Norton & Co., 1991.

Rutland, Robert Allen. *James Madison: The Founding Father.* New York: Macmillan, 1987.

The 14th Congress

MARCH 4, 1815 - MARCH 3, 1817

First Session: *December 4, 1815-April 30, 1816*
Second Session: *December 2, 1816-March 3, 1817*

In the 1814 elections for the 14th Congress, the Democratic-Republicans lost 2 seats in the Senate, reducing their majority from 27 to 25 of the 36 seats. The Federalists gained 2 seats for a total of 11. In the House, the Democratic-Republicans gained 5 seats, giving them a majority of 117 of the 186 seats. The Federalists lost 3 House seats, reducing their total to 65. Four seats were held by neither party. [See notes 2 and 3, p. xxix]

BACKGROUND

Shortly before the 14th Congress began, the 13th Congress had declared war against the Bey of Algiers for acts of piracy against U.S. shipping. The war also included the North African cities of Tripoli and Tunis, which together with Algiers comprised the stretch of Mediterranean pirate havens known as the Barbary Coast. After several months of successful U.S. naval attacks, the Barbary states capitulated and executed treaties requiring them to end piracy against American ships.

In 1816 Congress passed a tariff law designed to protect American manufacturers from foreign imports, and Indiana became the 19th state of the Union. During the 14th Congress, Congress authorized the establishment of a Bank of the United States.

SENATE LEADERSHIP

Vice President: None. [See 13th Congress] Elbridge Gerry died on November 23, 1814. Until the Twenty-fifth Amendment was ratified on February 10, 1967 [See 90th Congress], there was no mechanism for filling vacancies in the office of vice president.

President Pro Tempore: John Gaillard (Dem-Rep., S.C.) was a lawyer who served in the South Carolina state house of representatives and senate until he was elevated to the United States Senate on December 6, 1804, during the Eighth Congress to fill the vacancy left by the resignation of the previous senator. Gaillard was never defeated for reelection, and would serve in the Senate until his death on February 26, 1826. [See note 4, p. xxix]

Majority Leader, Majority Whip, Minority Leader, and Minority Whip: None. These functions did not evolve into formal Senate positions until the 62nd Congress (1911-1913).

Chairmen of Selected Key Committees: [See also Organization and Administration, p. 57]

Committee on Finance: George Campbell (Dem-Rep., Tenn.)

C H R O N O L O G Y

March 4, 1815:   The 14th Congress begins.

December 4, 1815:   The first session begins, and Henry Clay (Dem-Rep., Ky.) is elected Speaker of the House.

December 21, 1815:   The Senate ratifies a treaty with Algiers.

April 3, 1816:   Congress passes legislation to establish the Bank of the U.S.

April 13, 1816:   Congress passes legislation admitting Indiana into the Union.

April 20, 1816:   Congress passes legislation raising tariffs.

April 30, 1816:   The first session ends.

December 2, 1816:   The second session begins.

December 10, 1816:   The Senate creates eleven new standing committees.

March 3, 1817:   Congress passes legislation dividing the Mississippi Territory, and the House fails to override a presidential veto of certain road and canal legislation. The second session and the 14th Congress end.

[See note 6, p. xxix]

Committee on Foreign Relations: James Barbour (Dem-Rep., Va.)

Committee on the Judiciary: Dudley Chase (Dem-Rep., Vt.)

Committee on Military Affairs: John Williams (Dem-Rep., Tenn.)

Committee on Naval Affairs: Charles Tait (Dem-Rep., Ga.)

HOUSE LEADERSHIP

Speaker of the House: Henry Clay (Dem-Rep., Ky.) was elected Speaker on December 4, 1815. Clay was a powerful figure in American politics, not only as a Speaker, but also as a senator and presidential candidate. Clay was first elected to the House in the 12th Congress, and was Speaker of the House in six Congresses.

Majority Leader, Majority Whip, Minority Leader, and Minority Whip: None. These functions did not evolve into formal House positions until the 56th Congress (1899-1901).

Chairmen of Selected Key Committees: [See also Organization and Administration, below]

Committee on the Judiciary: Hugh Nelson (Dem-Rep., Va.)

Committee on Ways and Means: William Lowndes (Dem-Rep., S.C.)

ORGANIZATION AND ADMINISTRATION

There was no permanent or standing committee structure in the first several Congresses, except for some committees overseeing administrative matters, such as the Joint Standing Committee on Enrolled Bills and the House Committee on Elections. Legislation was prepared by select or ad hoc committees. [See note 5, p. xxix] In the Fourth Congress, the House began to create standing committees on matters other than internal affairs, and the Senate finally followed suit in this Congress on December 10, 1816, when it created 11 new standing committees: Claims; Commerce and Manufactures; Finance; Foreign Relations; Judiciary; Military Affairs; Militia; Naval Affairs; Pensions; Post Office and Post Roads; and Public Lands. In addition, at the beginning of this Congress, a standing Committee on the Judiciary became part of the House committee structure.

TABLE OF KEY VOTES

Senate

Subject of Vote	Date of Vote	For	Against
Treaty with Algier	December 21, 1815	25	1
Establishing Bank of the U.S.	April 3, 1816	22	12
Admission of Indiana as a State	April 13, 1816	Passed by voice vote	
Tariff Increase	April 20, 1816	Passed by voice vote	
Mississippi Territory Division	February 21, 1817	Passed by voice vote	

House

Subject of Vote	Date of Vote	For	Against
Establishing Bank of the U.S.	March 14, 1816	80	71
Admission of Indiana as a State	March 30, 1816	108	3
Tariff Increase	April 8, 1816	88	54
Mississippi Territory Division	March 3, 1817	Passed by voice vote	
Overriding Veto of Road and Canal Bill (veto sustained: not a two-thirds House majority).	March 3, 1817	60	56

[See note 7, p. xxix]

Speaker of the House Henry Clay (Dem-Rep., Ky.) is considered by many historians to be the first great Speaker, and the first Speaker to effectively use his power over committee appointments. Clay put loyal followers in charge of key committees, particularly the Ways and Means committee, which governed tax and budget matters.

MAJOR LEGISLATION PASSED

Admission of Indiana as a New State: Congress voted to admit Indiana into the United States.

Bank of the United States: Although previous efforts to create a Bank of the United States had been unpopular, and even resulted in President Madison's only veto of the 13th Congress, Congress made a controversial decision to revive the idea and created a new national Bank of the United States with $35 million in initial capital.

Mississippi Territory: Congress divided the Mississippi Territory into two smaller territories, the Mississippi Territory and the Alabama Territory.

Tariffs: Congress placed higher tariff duties on imports of manufactured goods and other products.

Treaty With Algiers: The Senate confirmed a peace treaty with Algiers that ended the war with the Barbary Coast pirates.

FAILED LEGISLATION

Representative John C. Calhoun (Dem-Rep., S.C.) introduced legislation to fund new road and canal projects that involved funds from the

Bank of the United States. President Madison supported the legislation in principle, but vetoed the bill [See Relations with the President, below] because he doubted whether the federal government had the constitutional authority to implement it.

RELATIONS WITH THE PRESIDENT

The military stalemate of the War of 1812, often derided as "Mr. Madison's War," was now over, and Madison's second presidential term came to a largely uneventful end. Madison vetoed two bills during the 14th Congress. One bill was historically insignificant. The other was the road and canal construction bill. [See Failed Legislation, above] Madison vetoed this bill on March 3, 1817, and that same day the House voted 60 in favor of overturning the veto to 56 against. Because the House vote was not a two-thirds majority, there was no vote in the Senate.

NOMINATIONS, APPOINTMENTS, AND CONFIRMATIONS

The Judiciary: There were no significant nominations, appointments, or confirmations in the federal judiciary during the 14th Congress. There was, however, a significant development which would affect the confirmation process in the future. The Senate Judiciary Committee was established in 1816 [See Organization and Administration, above] as one of the Senate standing committees, and in 1868 the Judiciary Committee would become the vehicle by which

presidential nominations for the federal judiciary would be processed in the Senate.

The Executive Branch: None of historical significance.

IMPEACHMENTS

None.

CONSTITUTIONAL AMENDMENTS

None.

FURTHER READING

Abraham, Henry Julian. *Justices and Presidents: A Political History of Appointments to the Supreme Court.* New York: Oxford University Press, 1992.

Brant, Irving. *James Madison.* Indianapolis: Bobbs-Merrill, 1948-1961 (six volumes).

Haynes, George H. *The Senate of the United States.* Boston: Houghton Mifflin, 1938.

Remini, Robert V. *Henry Clay: Statesman for the Union.* New York: W.W. Norton & Co., 1991.

Rutland, Robert Allen. *James Madison: The Founding Father.* New York: Macmillan, 1987.

The 15th Congress

MARCH 4, 1817-MARCH 3, 1819

Special Senate Session: March 4, 1817-March 6, 1817
First Session: December 1, 1817-April 20, 1818
Second Session: November 16, 1818-March 3, 1819

The Senate held a special session to vote upon the confirmation of presidential appointees to various offices. [See note 1, p. xxix]

In the 1816 elections for the 15th Congress, the Democratic-Republicans gained 9 seats in the Senate, raising their majority from 25 to 34 of the 44 seats. The Federalists lost 1 seat, leaving them with a total of 10. In the House, the Democratic-Republicans gained 24 seats, giving them a majority of 141 of the 186 seats. The Federalists lost 23 seats, reducing their total to 42. Three seats were not held by either party. [See notes 2 and 3, p. xxix]

BACKGROUND

On March 4, 1817, James Monroe was inaugurated as the fifth president of the United States. Later that year, a frontier war erupted in the South between the Seminole Indians and American settlers. On December 10, 1817, Mississippi was admitted to the Union as the 20th state, and on December 3, 1818, Illinois was admitted as the 21st state.

General Andrew Jackson, future president, pursued the Seminoles into the Spanish territory of East Florida in 1818, capturing Pensacola on May 24. U.S. pressure eventually caused Spain to cede the territory to the U.S.

In 1819 Congress experienced a significant dispute over slavery. On February 13, 1819, Representative James Tallmadge (Dem-Rep.,

N.Y.) proposed enacting a prerequisite to statehood for the Territory of Missouri that would effectively eliminate most slavery within Missouri. The Tallmadge proposal was dropped, and Missouri's admission into the Union was temporarily postponed.

SENATE LEADERSHIP

Vice President: Daniel D. Tompkins was elected a representative from New York in the Ninth Congress, but resigned to accept an appointment as an associate justice of the New York Supreme Court. Tompkins left the court in 1807 when he was elected governor of New York, and became James Monroe's running mate in the presidential election of 1816. Tompkins was vice president until Monroe left office in 1825.

President Pro Tempore: John Gaillard (Dem-Rep., S.C.) was elected on March 6, 1817, and again on March 31, 1818. James Barbour (Dem-Rep., Va.) was elected on February 15, 1819. [See note 4, p. xxix]

Majority Leader, Majority Whip, Minority Leader, and Minority Whip: None. These functions did not evolve into formal Senate positions until the 62nd Congress (1911-1913).

Chairmen of Selected Key Committees: [See also Organization and Administration, p. 62]

Committee on Finance: George Campbell (Dem-Rep., Tenn.) and John Eppes (Dem-Rep., Va.)

C H R O N O L O G Y

March 4, 1817:	The 15th Congress begins, and the Senate begins a special session.
March 5, 1817:	President Monroe nominates, and the Senate confirms, John Quincy Adams to be secretary of state, William H. Crawford to be secretary of the Treasury, and Isaac Shelby to be secretary of war.
March 6, 1817:	The Senate's special session ends.
December 1, 1817:	The first session begins, and Henry Clay (Dem-Rep., Ky.) is reelected Speaker of the House.
December 8, 1817:	Congress passes legislation admitting Mississippi into the Union.
December 12, 1817:	President Monroe nominates William Wirt to be attorney general and John C. Calhoun to succeed Shelby as secretary of war.
December 15, 1817:	The Senate confirms both Wirt and Calhoun.
March 31, 1818:	Congress passes legislation establishing the design of the U.S. flag.
April 14, 1818:	Congress passes legislation admitting Illinois into the Union.
April 16, 1818:	The Senate approves the Rush-Bagot Agreement between the U.S. and Britian.
April 20, 1818:	The first session ends.
November 16, 1818:	The second session begins.
November 27, 1818:	President Monroe nominates Smith Thompson to be secretary of the Navy.
November 30, 1818:	The Senate confirms Thompson.
February 4, 1819:	Congress passes legislation providing for registration of immigrants.
February 13, 1819:	Representative James Tallmadge (Dem-Rep., N.Y.) unsuccessfully proposes enacting a prerequisite to statehood for the Territory of Missouri that would effectively eliminate most slavery within Missouri.
February 19, 1819:	Congress passes legislation admitting Alabama into the Union.
March 3, 1819:	The second session and the 15th Congress end.

[See note 6, p. xxix]

Committee on Foreign Relations: James Barbour (Dem-Rep., Va.) and Nathaniel Macon (Dem-Rep., N.C.)

Committee on the Judiciary: John J. Crittenden (Dem-Rep., Ky.) and James Burrill, Jr. (Fed., R.I.)

Committee on Military Affairs: George M. Troup (Dem-Rep., Ga.) and John Williams (Dem-Rep., Tenn.)

Committee on Naval Affairs: Charles Tait (Dem-Rep., Ga.) and Nathan Sanford (Dem-Rep., N.Y.)

HOUSE LEADERSHIP

Speaker of the House: Henry Clay (Dem-Rep., Ky.) was reelected Speaker on December 1, 1817. [See biographical note in 14th Congress]

Majority Leader, Majority Whip, Minority Leader, and Minority Whip: None. These functions did not evolve into formal House positions until the 56th Congress (1899-1901).

Other House Leaders: Representative James Tallmadge (Dem-Rep., N.Y.) on February 13,

TABLE OF KEY VOTES

Senate

Subject of Vote	Date of Vote	For	Against
Confirmation of Adams	March 5, 1817	29	1
Confirmation of Crawford and Shelby	March 5, 1817	Passed by voice vote	
Admission of Mississippi to Union	December 3, 1817	Passed by voice vote	
Confirmation of Wirt and Calhoun	December 15, 1817	Passed by voice vote	
Flag Design Approved	March 31, 1818	Passed by voice vote	
Admission of Illinois to Union	April 14, 1818	Passed by voice vote	
Rush-Bagot Agreement Approved	April 16, 1818	30	0
Confirmation of Smith Thompson to be Secretary of the Navy	November 30, 1818	Passed by voice vote	
Admission of Alabama to Union	January 12, 1819	Passed by voice vote	
Immigrant Registration	February 4, 1819	Passed by voice vote	

House

Subject of Vote	Date of Vote	For	Against
Admission of Mississippi to Union	December 8, 1817	Passed by voice vote	
Flag Design Approved	March 25, 1818	Passed by voice vote	
Admission of Illinois to Union	April 6, 1818	Passed by voice vote	
Immigrant Registration	December 17, 1818	Passed by voice vote	
Admission of Alabama to Union	February 19, 1819	Passed by voice vote	

[See note 7, p. xxix]

1819, made a controversial and ultimately unsuccessful proposal to eliminate slavery in the Territory of Missouri prior to Missouri's admission into the United States. Tallmadge was a one-term congressman. He was first elected to the House in this Congress, and decided not to run for election to the 16th Congress.

Chairmen of Selected Key Committees: [See also Organization and Administration, below]

Committee on the Judiciary: Hugh Nelson (Dem-Rep., Va.)

Committee on Ways and Means: William Lowndes (Dem-Rep., S.C.) and Samuel Smith (Dem-Rep., Md.)

ORGANIZATION AND ADMINISTRATION

Speaker of the House Henry Clay (Dem-Rep., Ky.) is considered by many historians to be the first great Speaker, and the first Speaker to effectively use his power over committee appointments. Clay put loyal followers in charge of key committees, particularly the Ways and Means committee which governed tax and budget matters. [See note 5, p. xxix]

MAJOR LEGISLATION PASSED

Admission of Mississippi, Illinois and Alabama as New States: Congress voted to admit Mississippi, Illinois, and Alabama into the United States.

Flag Design: Establishing a principle that has lasted until the present day, Congress decided that the flag of the United States would consists of 13 stripes in honor of the original 13 colonies, and a field consisting of 1 star for each state.

Immigration: Congress instituted a policy of immigrant registration that made it possible for the first time to keep accurate records and statistics on the number of immigrants entering the U.S.

Rush-Bagot Agreement: As a follow-up to the Treaty of Ghent and the end of the War of 1812, the Senate confirmed the Rush-Bagot Agreement with Great Britain providing for naval disarmament on the Great Lakes and fixing the U.S.-Canada border.

FAILED LEGISLATION

None of historical significance.

RELATIONS WITH THE PRESIDENT

President Monroe's relations with Congress were generally unremarkable, except for the fact that his social gatherings and dealings with Congress were often criticized by contemporaries as being too formal and cold. This was perhaps a reaction to the more lively Washington social atmosphere encouraged by Dolley Madison, former President James Madison's wife, which was an unofficial but important part of the political life of Congress. Monroe vetoed no legislation during the 15th Congress.

NOMINATIONS, APPOINTMENTS, AND CONFIRMATIONS

The Judiciary: There were no significant nominations, appointments, or confirmations in the federal judiciary during the 15th Congress.

The Executive Branch: On March 5, 1817, President Monroe nominated John Quincy Adams to be secretary of state, William H. Crawford to be secretary of the Treasury, and Isaac Shelby to be secretary of war. On the same day, the Senate confirmed Adams by a vote of 29 to 1 and Crawford and Shelby by voice vote. On December 12, 1817, Monroe nominated William Wirt to be attorney general and John C. Calhoun to succeed Shelby as secretary of war. On December 15, 1817, the Senate confirmed both Wirt and Calhoun by voice vote. On November 27, 1818, Monroe nominated Smith Thompson to be secretary of the Navy, and on November 30 the Senate confirmed Thompson by voice vote.

IMPEACHMENTS

None.

CONSTITUTIONAL AMENDMENTS

None.

FURTHER READING

Ammon, Harry. *James Monroe. The Quest for National Identity.* New York: McGraw-Hill, 1971.

Irwin, Ray W. *Daniel D. Tompkins: Governor of New York and Vice President of the United States.* New York: New York Historical Society, 1968.

Remini, Robert V. *Henry Clay: Statesman for the Union.* New York: W.W. Norton & Co., 1991.

The 16th Congress

MARCH 4, 1819 - MARCH 3, 1821

First Session: *December 6, 1819 - May 15, 1820*
Second Session: *November 13, 1820 - March 3, 1821*

In the 1818 elections for the 16th Congress, the Democratic-Republicans gained 1 seat in the Senate, raising their majority to 35 of the 44 seats. The Federalists lost 3 seats, leaving them with a total of 7 seats. There were 2 seats that were not held by either party. In the House, the Democratic-Republicans gained 15 seats, giving them a majority of 156 of the 186. The Federalists lost 15 seats, leaving them only 27. There were 3 seats that were not held by either party. [See notes 2 and 3, p. xxix]

BACKGROUND

According to the census of 1820, the population of the United States as of August 7, 1820 was 9,638,453, resulting in a population density of 5.5 persons for each of the country's 1,749,462 square miles. This was a population increase of 33.1 percent over the 1810 census.

On December 14, 1819, Alabama was admitted to the Union as the 22nd state, which meant that there were 11 states where slavery was legal ("slave states") and 11 states where slavery was illegal ("free states"). Although this balance meant that the free states of the North and the slave states of the South would be equal in the Senate, the North's rapidly growing population gave it superiority in the House. Therefore, in order to preserve equality in the Senate and mollify southern fears of northern domination, Congress agreed to the Missouri Compromise on March 5, 1820. The Compromise provided for the admission of two states that were ready to become part of the Union: Maine and Missouri. Maine, a free state, was admitted on March 15, 1820, as the 23rd state, and Missouri, a slave state, became the 24th state on August 10, 1821. Further, the Missouri Compromise outlawed slavery in the Louisiana Purchase north of the latitude that ran east to west across the southern boundary of Missouri, except in Missouri itself.

SENATE LEADERSHIP

Vice President: Daniel D. Tompkins [See biographical note in 15th Congress]

Presidents Pro Tempore: James Barbour (Dem-Rep., Va.) and John Gaillard (Dem-Rep., S.C.) both served as president pro tempore on January 25, 1820. [See note 4, p. xxix]

Majority Leader, Majority Whip, Minority Leader, and Minority Whip: None. These functions did not evolve into formal Senate positions until the 62nd Congress (1911-1913).

Chairmen of Selected Key Committees: [See also Organization and Administration, p. 65]

Committee on Finance: Nathan Sanford (Dem-Rep., N.Y.)

Committee on Foreign Relations: James Brown (Dem-Rep., La.) and James Barbour (Dem-Rep., Va.)

Committee on the Judiciary: William Smith

C H R O N O L O G Y

March 4, 1819:	The 16th Congress begins.
December 6, 1819:	The first session begins, and Henry Clay (Dem-Rep., Ky.) is reelected Speaker of the House.
March 5, 1820:	Congress passes the Missouri Compromise.
May 15, 1820:	The first session ends.
October 28, 1820:	Clay resigns as Speaker.
November 13, 1820:	The second session begins.
November 15, 1820:	John W. Taylor (Dem-Rep., N.Y.) is elected the new Speaker of the House.
February 19, 1821:	The Senate ratifies a treaty with Spain under which the U.S. takes possession of Florida.
March 3, 1821:	The second session and the 16th Congress end.

[See note 6, p. xxix]

(Dem-Rep., S.C.)

Committee on Military Affairs: John Williams (Dem-Rep., Tenn.)

Committee on Naval Affairs: James Pleasants (Dem-Rep., Va.)

HOUSE LEADERSHIP

Speaker of the House: Henry Clay (Dem-Rep., Ky.) was reelected Speaker on December 6, 1819. [See biographical note in 14th Congress] Clay strongly supported the Missouri Compromise, and was instrumental in getting the Compromise passed in this Congress. On October 28, 1820, Clay resigned as Speaker. John W. Taylor (Dem-Rep., N.Y.) was elected as the new Speaker on November 15, 1820. Taylor was first elected to the House in the 13th Congress and was reelected nine times. Taylor would be elected Speaker again in the 19th Congress.

Majority Leader, Majority Whip, Minority Leader, and Minority Whip: None. These functions did not evolve into formal House positions until the 56th Congress (1899-1901).

Chairmen of Selected Key Committees: [See also Organization and Administration, below]

Committee on Agriculture: Thomas Forrest (No definite party, Pa.)

Committee on the Judiciary: John Sergeant (Fed., Pa.)

Committee on Ways and Means: Samuel Smith (Dem-Rep., Md.)

ORGANIZATION AND ADMINISTRATION

Speaker of the House Henry Clay (Dem-Rep., Ky.) is considered by many historians to be the first great Speaker. He was certainly the first to effectively use his power over committee appointments. Clay put loyal followers in charge of key committees, particularly the Ways and Means Committee, which governed tax and budget matters. During this Congress, the House Committee on Agriculture was established. [See note 5, p. xxix]

MAJOR LEGISLATION PASSED

Missouri Compromise: Congress voted to admit Maine and Missouri into the United States. Maine would be a free state, Missouri would be a slave

TABLE OF KEY VOTES

Senate

Subject of Vote	Date of Vote	For	Against
Missouri Compromise	March 5, 1820	Passed by voice vote	
Treaty with Spain	February 19, 1821	40	4

House

Subject of Vote	Date of Vote	For	Against
Missouri Compromise	March 5, 1820	Passed by voice vote	

[See note 7, p. xxix]

state, and slavery would be forbidden in the rest of the Louisiana Territory north of the latitude corresponding to the southern boundary of Missouri, except in Missouri itself.

Treaty with Spain: The Senate approved the Adams-Onis Treaty with Spain, whereby Spain ceded Florida and other remaining possessions in the Southeast to the United States, and renounced Spanish claims to the Oregon Territory.

FAILED LEGISLATION

None of historical significance.

RELATIONS WITH THE PRESIDENT

President Monroe's relations with Congress were generally unremarkable, except for the fact that his social gatherings and dealings with Congress were often criticized by contemporaries as being too formal and cold. This was perhaps a reaction to the more lively Washington social atmosphere encouraged by Dolley Madison, former President James Madison's wife, which was an unofficial but important part of the political life of Congress. The major legislative initiative of the 16th Congress, namely the Missouri Compromise, was largely the result of the leadership of Speaker of the House Henry Clay (Dem-Rep., Ky.). Monroe vetoed no legislation during the 16th Congress.

NOMINATIONS, APPOINTMENTS, AND CONFIRMATIONS

There were no significant nominations, appointments, or confirmations in the federal judiciary or in the executive branch during the 16th Congress.

IMPEACHMENTS

None.

CONSTITUTIONAL AMENDMENTS

None.

FURTHER READING

Ammon, Harry. *James Monroe: The Quest for National Identity.* New York: McGraw-Hill, 1971.

Irwin, Ray W. *Daniel D. Tompkins: Governor of New York and Vice President of the United States.* New York: New York Historical Society, 1968.

Remini, Robert V. *Henry Clay: Statesman for the Union.* New York: W.W. Norton, & Co. 1991.

The 17th Congress

MARCH 4, 1821 - MARCH 3, 1823

First Session: December 3, 1821 - May 8, 1822
Second Session: December 2, 1822 - March 3, 1823

In the 1820 elections for the 17th Congress, the Democratic-Republicans gained 9 seats in the Senate, raising their majority from 35 to 44 of the 48, and the Federalists lost 3 seats for a total of 4. In the House the Democratic-Republicans gained 2 seats for a majority of 158 of the 186, the Federalists lost 2 seats for a total of 25, and 3 seats were held by neither party.

BACKGROUND

On March 5, 1821, the day after the 17th Congress began, President James Monroe was inaugurated for a second term as the fifth president of the United States. Pursuant to the Missouri Compromise [See 16th Congress], Missouri, a slave state, became the 24th state on August 10, 1821.

On the frontier in 1821, the Seminole Indians were pushed into the inhospitable lands of central Florida, and Stephen Austin founded the first permanent American settlement in Texas. In 1822 a plot by a free black man named Denmark Vesey to lead a slave revolt in Charleston, South Carolina, was discovered. Although the plot was quickly and easily crushed, its existence increased Southern paranoia about the threat of slave rebellions. In foreign affairs, at Monroe's request, Congress provided for U.S. diplomatic recognition of Argentina, Brazil, Chile, Colombia, Mexico, Peru, and a federation of Central American states.

SENATE LEADERSHIP

Vice President: Daniel Tompkins, a former representative from New York in the Ninth Congress, an associate justice of the New York Supreme Court, and later governor of New York, became James Monroe's running mate in the presidential elections of 1816 and 1820. Tompkins was vice president until Monroe left office in 1825.

President Pro Tempore: John Gaillard (Dem-Rep., S.C.) was elected president pro tempore on February 1, 1822, and again on February 19, 1823. [See note 4, p. xxix]

Majority Leader, Majority Whip, Minority Leader, and Minority Whip: None. These functions did not evolve into formal Senate positions until the 62nd Congress (1911-1913).

Chairmen of Selected Key Committees: [See also Organization and Administration, p. 68]

Committee on Finance: John Holmes (Dem-Rep., Maine) and Walter Lowrie (Dem-Rep., Pa.)

Committee on Foreign Relations: Rufus King (Fed., N.Y.) and James Barbour (Dem-Rep., Va.)

Committee on the Judiciary: William Smith (Dem-Rep., S.C.)

Committee on Military Affairs: John Williams (Dem-Rep., Tenn.)

Committee on Naval Affairs: James Pleasants (Dem-Rep., Va.)

CHRONOLOGY

March 4, 1821:	The 17th Congress begins.
December 3, 1821:	The first session begins.
December 4, 1821:	Philip Pendleton Barbour (Dem-Rep., Va.) is elected Speaker of the House.
April 30, 1822:	Congress recognizes seven new nations in Latin America.
May 3, 1822:	Congress passes legislation to pay for the upkeep of the Cumberland Road.
May 4, 1822:	President Monroe vetoes the Cumberland Road legislation.
May 6, 1822:	The House fails to override the Cumberland Road veto.
May 8, 1822:	The first session ends.
December 2, 1822:	The second session begins.
March 3, 1823:	The second session and the 17th Congress end.

[See note 6, p. xxix]

HOUSE LEADERSHIP

Speaker of the House: Philip Pendleton Barbour (Dem-Rep., Va.) was elected Speaker on December 4, 1821. Barbour was a lawyer who had served in the Virginia House of Delegates and was first elected to the House in the 13th Congress. This was the only Congress in which he would serve as Speaker.

Majority Leader, Majority Whip, Minority Leader, and Minority Whip: None. These functions did not evolve into formal House positions until the 56th Congress (1899-1901).

Chairmen of Selected Key Committees: [See also Organization and Administration, below]

Committee on Agriculture: Josiah Butler (Dem-Rep., N.Y.)

Committee on Foreign Affairs: Jonathan Russell (Dem-Rep., Mass.)

Committee on the Judiciary: Hugh Nelson (Dem-Rep., Va.) and John Sergeant (Fed., Penn.)

Committee on Military Affairs: William Eustis (Dem-Rep., Mass.)

Committee on Naval Affairs: Timothy Fuller (Dem-Rep., Mass.) and Louis McLane (Fed., Del.)

Committee on Ways and Means: Samuel Smith (Dem-Rep., Md.) and Louis McLane (Fed., Del.)

ORGANIZATION AND ADMINISTRATION

In this Congress, the House established three more standing committees of historical significance: the Committees on Foreign Affairs, Military Affairs and Naval Affairs. [See note 5, p. xxix]

MAJOR LEGISLATION PASSED

Latin America: In the Latin American Republics Act, Congress gave U.S. diplomatic recognition to the newly independent nations of Argentina, Brazil, Chile, Colombia, Mexico, Peru, and a federation of Central American states.

FAILED LEGISLATION

Congress passed legislation to fund the preservation and repair of the Cumberland Road, which went from Cumberland, Maryland, to the Ohio River. For the first and only time in his presidency, President Monroe exercised his veto power and vetoed this legislation on May 4, 1822, claim-

TABLE OF KEY VOTES

Senate

Subject of Vote	Date of Vote	For	Against
Latin American Recognition	April 30, 1822	Passed by voice vote	
Cumberland Road Bill	May 3, 1822	29	7

House

Subject of Vote	Date of Vote	For	Against
Latin American Recognition	April 11, 1822	Passed by voice vote	
Cumberland Road Bill	April 29, 1822	87	68
Cumberland Road Bill Veto Override (Which Failed)	May 6, 1822	68	72

[See note 7, p. xxix]

ing that it contained provisions that unlawfully expanded federal authority. On May 6, 1822, the House voted 68 to override the veto and 72 against. There was no vote in the Senate, since the House vote had sustained the veto.

RELATIONS WITH THE PRESIDENT

President Monroe's relations with Congress were generally unremarkable, except for the fact that his social gatherings and dealings with Congress were often criticized by contemporaries as being too formal and cold. This was perhaps a reaction to the more lively social atmosphere—encouraged by Dolley Madison, former President James Madison's wife—which had been an unofficial but important part of the political life of Congress. Monroe vetoed only one bill in the 17th Congress. [See Failed Legislation, p. 68]

NOMINATIONS, APPOINTMENTS, AND CONFIRMATIONS

There were no significant nominations, appointments, or confirmations in the federal judiciary or in the executive branch during the 17th Congress.

IMPEACHMENTS

None.

CONSTITUTIONAL AMENDMENTS

None.

FURTHER READING

Ammon, Harry. *James Monroe: The Quest for National Identity.* New York: McGraw-Hill, 1971.

Irwin, Ray W. *Daniel D. Tompkins: Governor of New York and Vice President of the United States.* New York: New York Historical Society, 1968.

The 18th Congress

MARCH 4, 1823 - MARCH 3, 1825

First Session: *December 1, 1823 - May 27, 1824*
Second Session: *December 6, 1824 - March 3, 1825*

The 1822 elections for the 18th Congress resulted in no change in the party balance in the Senate, the Democratic-Republicans retaining their majority from the 17th Congress, of 44 seats out of the 48, and the Federalists keeping their 4 seats.

Because of the 1820 census [See 16th Congress], the House was increased to 213 seats. Here the Democratic-Republicans gained 29 seats, giving them a majority of 187, while the Federalists gained 1 seat for a total of 26. [See notes 2 and 3, p. xxix]

BACKGROUND

In the previous Congress, President Monroe had obtained from Congress diplomatic recognition of seven Latin American states. In the 18th Congress, on December 2, 1823, Monroe went further when he announced a policy that became known as the Monroe Doctrine. The Monroe Doctrine stated that the United States would not permit, or at least would view with great suspicion, any interference by a European power in the internal affairs of any nation in the New World. In return, the United States pledged its own noninterference in European affairs. In 1823 the United States had neither the power to establish the New World as its exclusive sphere of influence nor the power to assert itself in European affairs. However, the Monroe Doctrine as a statement of national intention would grow in importance in the future as American power and influence grew.

The most significant task the 18th Congress had to contend with was that of choosing the next president of the United States. Since no candidate received a majority of the electoral college votes in the presidential election of 1824 (Monroe, following George Washington's precedent, did not seek a third term), the House of Representatives, voting by state delegation, had the constitutional responsibility for electing a president. Andrew Jackson had received 99 electoral college votes, John Quincy Adams 84, Secretary of State William H. Crawford 41, and Henry Clay 37 votes. Although Jackson had received the most votes, Adams proved to be more adept at congressional politics. Clay's supporters agreed to back Adams, and on February 9, 1825, the House of Representatives elected Adams the sixth president of the United States. As a Westerner from Kentucky, which was then on the frontier, Clay was looked upon as a traitor and opportunist by Jackson's supporters. As a result, Clay's political career, which had seemed destined to take him to the White House, lost momentum.

SENATE LEADERSHIP

Vice President: Daniel D. Tompkins, a former representative from New York in the Ninth Congress, an associate justice of the New York Supreme Court, and later governor of New York, became James Monroe's running mate in the presidential elections of 1816 and 1820.

C H R O N O L O G Y

March 4, 1823: The 18th Congress begins.

March 18, 1823: Supreme Court Justice Brockholst Livingston dies.

December 1, 1823: The first session begins, and Henry Clay (Dem-Rep., Ky.) is elected Speaker of the House.

December 2, 1823: President Monroe announces the Monroe Doctrine.

December 5, 1823: President Monroe nominates Samuel L. Southard to be secretary of the Navy.

December 8, 1823: President Monroe nominates Smith Thompson to replace Livingston.

December 9, 1823: The Senate confirms Southard by voice vote.

December 19, 1823: The Senate confirms Thompson.

April 24, 1824: Congress passes legislation enabling the president to fund surveys and estimates for new roads and canals.

May 13, 1824: Congress passes legislation raising tariffs.

May 27, 1824: The first session ends.

December 6, 1824: The second session begins.

February 9, 1825: The House elects John Quincy Adams the next president of the United States.

March 3, 1825: The second session and the 18th Congress end.

[See note 6, p. xxix]

President Pro Tempore: John Gaillard (Dem-Rep., S.C.) was elected on May 21, 1824. [See note 4, p. xxix]

Majority Leader, Majority Whip, Minority Leader, and Minority Whip: None. These functions did not evolve into formal Senate positions until the 62nd Congress (1911-1913).

Chairmen of Selected Key Committees: [See also Organization and Administration, p. 72]

Committee on Finance: Samuel Smith (Dem-Rep., Md.)

Committee on Foreign Relations: James Barbour (Dem-Rep., Va.)

Committee on the Judiciary: Martin Van Buren (Dem-Rep., N.Y.)

Committee on Military Affairs: Andrew Jackson (Dem-Rep., N.Y.)

Committee on Naval Affairs: James Lloyd (presumably Dem-Rep., Mass.)

HOUSE LEADERSHIP

Speaker of the House: Henry Clay (Dem-Rep., Ky.), elected Speaker on December 1, 1823, was a powerful figure in American politics, not only as a Speaker, but also later as a senator and presidential candidate. Clay was first elected to the House in the 12th Congress, and was Speaker of the House in six Congresses.

Majority Leader, Majority Whip, Minority Leader, and Minority Whip: None. These functions did not evolve into formal House positions until the 56th Congress (1899-1901).

TABLE OF KEY VOTES

Senate

Subject of Vote	Date of Vote	For	Against
Confirmation of Samuel L. Southard to be Secretary of the Navy	December 9, 1823	Passed by voice vote	
Confirmation of Smith Thompson to Supreme Court	December 19, 1823	Passed by voice vote	
Road and Canal Survey Funding	April 24, 1824	24	18
Tariff Increase	May 13, 1824	25	21

House

Subject of Vote	Date of Vote	For	Against
Roads and Canals Survey Funding	February 11, 1824	Passed by voice vote	
Tariff Increase	April 16, 1824	107	102
Presidential Election	February 9, 1825	13 for John Quincy Adams, (balloting was by state) who therefore won, 7 for Andrew Jackson, and 4 for William Harris Crawford	

[See note 7, p. xxix]

Chairmen of Selected Key Committees: [See also Organization and Administration, below]

Committee on Agriculture: Stephen Van Rensselaer (No definite party, N.Y.)

Committee on Foreign Affairs: John Forsyth (Dem-Rep., Ga.)

Committee on the Judiciary: Daniel Webster (Fed., Mass.)

Committee on Military Affairs: James Hamilton Jr. (No definite party, S.C.)

Committee on Naval Affairs: Benjamin W. Crowninshield (Dem-Rep., Mass.)

Committee on Ways and Means: Louis McLane (Fed., Del.)

ORGANIZATION AND ADMINISTRATION

Speaker of the House Henry Clay (Dem-Rep., Ky.) is considered by many historians to be the first great Speaker and the first Speaker to make effective use of his power over committee appointments. Clay put loyal followers in charge of key committees, particularly the Ways and Means committee, which governed tax and budget matters. [See note 5, p. xxix]

MAJOR LEGISLATION PASSED

Roads and Canals: In the General Survey Act, Congress enabled the president to fund surveys and estimates concerning the construction and cost of potentially important new roads and canals.

Tariffs: In the Tariff Act of 1824, Congress raised tariffs on imported items such as iron, cotton goods, and wool.

FAILED LEGISLATION

None of historical significance.

RELATIONS WITH THE PRESIDENT

President Monroe's relations with Congress in this final Congress of his presidency were generally unremarkable, except for his Monroe Doctrine proclamation. Monroe vetoed no legislation during the 18th Congress.

NOMINATIONS, APPOINTMENTS, AND CONFIRMATIONS

The Judiciary: On March 18, 1823, Supreme Court Justice Brockholst Livingston died. On December 8, 1823, President Monroe nominated Smith Thompson to replace Livingston, and the Senate confirmed Thompson on December 19, 1823, by voice vote.

The Executive Branch: On December 5, 1823, President Monroe nominated Samuel L. Southard to be secretary of the Navy, and on December 9 the Senate confirmed Southard by voice vote.

IMPEACHMENTS

None.

CONSTITUTIONAL AMENDMENTS

None.

FURTHER READING

Ammon, Harry. *James Monroe: The Quest for National Identity.* New York: McGraw-Hill, 1971.

Irwin, Ray W. *Daniel D. Tompkins: Governor of New York and Vice President of the United States.* New York: New York Historical Society, 1968.

Roper, Donald Malcolm. *Mr. Justice Thompson and the Constitution.* New York: Garland, 1987.

Remini, Robert V. *Henry Clay: Statesman for the Union.* New York: W.W. Norton & Co., 1991.

The 19th Congress

MARCH 4, 1825 - MARCH 3, 1827

Special Senate Session: March 4, 1825 - March 9, 1825
First Session: December 5, 1825 - May 22, 1826
Second Session: December 4, 1826 - March 3, 1827

The Senate held a special session to vote on the confirmation of presidential appointees to various offices. [See note 1, p. xxix]

In the 1824 elections for the 19th Congress, the Democratic-Republicans became the Administration party, and lost 18 seats in the Senate, reducing their majority from 44 to 26 of the 48 seats. The Federalists were replaced by the Jacksonians as the primary opposition party, who were elected to 20 seats. Two seats were not held by either major party. In the House, the Administration party lost 82 seats to reduce their majority to 105 of the 213. The Jacksonians were elected to 97 seats. Eleven seats were not held by either major party. [See notes 2 and 3, p. xxix]

BACKGROUND

On March 4, 1825, John Quincy Adams was inaugurated the sixth president of the United States. In 1826 William Morgan, a Free Mason, was killed, allegedly for revealing the secrets of the secret society known as the Masons. Morgan's murder led to the founding of the Anti-Masonic Party, which achieved some notable successes attacking secret societies before the excitement subsided and the party was absorbed by the Whigs. (Many Anti-Masons later became leaders of the abolitionist movement.)

There was a dispute in the 19th Congress over whether to impose tariffs on imports of woolen products. The industrial North, which dominated the House of Representatives because of its large population, favored high tariffs in order to protect domestic industries from foreign competition. Thus, a tariff bill passed the House. The agrarian South, however, opposed tariffs because they would increase the cost of manufactured goods that the South needed. The South also feared that tariffs would upset foreign markets for southern exports. The North and the South were equal in voting strength in the Senate, and on February 28, 1827, Vice President John C. Calhoun from South Carolina cast his tie-breaking vote against the Woolens Bill.

On July 4, 1826, in an unusual coincidence, both John Adams and Thomas Jefferson died while the nation celebrated the 50th anniversary of the Declaration of Independence.

SENATE LEADERSHIP

Vice President: John Caldwell Calhoun, a famous representative and senator from South Carolina, became President Adams's vice president in 1824. He would be reelected vice president under President Andrew Jackson in the 1828 presidential election. Calhoun was one of the most vigorous spokesmen for the South and southern opposition to higher import tariffs.

President Pro Tempore: John Gaillard (Jacksonian, S.C.) was elected on March 9, 1825. Nathaniel Macon (Jacksonian, N.C.) was elected on May 20,

C H R O N O L O G Y

March 4, 1825: The 19th Congress begins, and a special session begins in the Senate.
March 5, 1825: President Adams nominates James Barbour to be secretary of war, Henry Clay to be secretary of state and Richard Rush to be secretary of the treasury.
March 7, 1825: The Senate confirms Barbour, Clay, and Rush.
March 9, 1825: The Senate's special session ends.
December 5, 1825: The first session begins, John W. Taylor (Admin., N.Y.) is elected Speaker of the House.
February 7, 1826: Supreme Court Justice Thomas Todd dies.
April 11, 1826: President John Quincy Adams nominates Robert Trimble to replace Todd.
May 3, 1826: Congress approves American participation in the Panama Conference.
May 9, 1826: The Senate confirms Trimble.
May 22, 1826: The first session ends.
July 4, 1826: Both John Adams and Thomas Jefferson die.
December 4, 1826: The second session begins.
February 28, 1827: The Woolens Bill fails to pass the Senate.
March 3, 1827: The second session and the 19th Congress end.

[See note 6, p. xxix]

1826, January 2, 1827, and March 2, 1827. [See note 4, p. xxix]

Majority Leader, Majority Whip, Minority Leader, and Minority Whip: None. These functions did not evolve into formal Senate positions until the 62nd Congress (1911-1913).

Chairmen of Selected Key Committees: [See also Organization and Administration, p. 76]

Committee on Finance: Samuel Smith (Jacksonian, Md.)

Committee on Foreign Relations: Nathaniel Macon (Jacksonian, N.C.) and Nathan Sanford (Admin., N.Y.)

Committee on the Judiciary: Martin Van Buren (Jacksonian, N.Y.)

Committee on Military Affairs: William Henry Harrison (Admin., Ohio.)

Committee on Naval Affairs: Robert Y. Hayne (Jacksonian, S.C.)

HOUSE LEADERSHIP

Speaker of the House: John W. Taylor (Admin., N.Y.) was elected Speaker on December 5, 1825. Taylor had been first elected to the House in the 13th Congress and was reelected nine times. Taylor had previously served as Speaker in the 16th Congress.

Majority Leader, Majority Whip, Minority Leader, and Minority Whip: None. These functions did not evolve into formal House positions until the 56th Congress (1899-1901).

Chairmen of Selected Key Committees: [See also Organization and Administration, p. 76]

Committee on Agriculture: Stephen Van Rensselaer (No definite party, N.Y.)

TABLE OF KEY VOTES

Senate

Subject of Vote	Date of Vote	For	Against
Confirmation of Barbour, Clay and Rush	March 7, 1825	27	14 (for Clay) Others passed by voice vote
Panama Conference	May 3, 1826	23	19
Confirmation of Robert Trimble to the Supreme Court	May 9, 1826	27	5

House

Subject of Vote	Date of Vote	For	Against
Panama Conference	April 22, 1826	134	60
Woolens Bill	February 10, 1827	106	95

[See note 7, p. xxix]

Committee on Foreign Affairs: John Forsyth (Admin., Ga.)

Committee on the Judiciary: Daniel Webster (Jacksonian, Mass.)

Committee on Military Affairs: James Hamilton Jr. (No definite party, S.C.) and Joseph Vance (Admin., Ohio.)

Committee on Naval Affairs: Henry R. Storrs (Jacksonian, N.Y.)

Committee on Ways and Means: Louis McLane (Jacksonian, Del.) and George McDuffie (Admin., S.C.)

ORGANIZATION AND ADMINISTRATION

In this Congress, the Senate created its first standing Committee on Agriculture. Unlike its House counterpart, however, the committee was terminated in 1857. Nevertheless, it was revived in 1863 and can be considered the ancestor of the modern Committee on Agriculture, Nutrition, and Forestry. [See note 5, p. xxix]

MAJOR LEGISLATION PASSED

Panama Conference: Congress approved sending American envoys to an international conference in Panama sponsored by revolutionary leader Simon Bolivar.

FAILED LEGISLATION

Woolens Bill: The House of Representatives approved tariff legislation concerning woolen products, but the South successfully blocked this legislation in the Senate. [See Background, p. 74]

RELATIONS WITH THE PRESIDENT

President Adams did not get along well with Congress, largely because of the rising power of the opposition party, the Jacksonians. Adams wanted the government to fund more road and canal projects, but was unable to get sufficient congressional support. Adams vetoed no legislation during the 19th Congress.

NOMINATIONS, APPOINTMENTS, AND CONFIRMATIONS

The Judiciary: On February 7, 1826, Supreme Court Justice Thomas Todd died. President John Quincy Adams, on April 11, 1826, nominated Robert Trimble to replace Todd, and the Senate confirmed Trimble on May 9, 1826, by a 27-to-5 vote.

The Executive Branch: On March 5, 1825, President Adams nominated James Barbour to be secretary of war, Henry Clay to be secretary of state and Richard Rush to be secretary of the Treasury. On March 7, 1825, the Senate confirmed Clay by a vote of 27 to 14 and confirmed Barbour and Rush by voice vote. Clay's nomination was controversial because the presidential election of 1824 had to be decided in the House of Representatives, where Clay threw his support to Adams, even though his fellow westerner Andrew Jackson had won a plurality of the popular vote. Many Jacksonians believed Clay had turned the votes of his supporters to Adams in exchange for a promise that Adams would make him secretary of state. Clay's career never fully recovered from what many of his colleagues regarded as an act of crass opportunism.

President Adams did not replace several other cabinet-level officials from the previous Monroe administration, and no Senate confirmation vote was required for continuing those appointments.

IMPEACHMENTS

None.

CONSTITUTIONAL AMENDMENTS

None.

SCANDALS

In 1826, Senator John Randolph (Jacksonian, Va.) verbally attacked Secretary of State Henry Clay, casting epithets at him and accusing him of corruption. Clay challenged Randolph to a duel to avenge his honor, and on April 8, 1826, Clay and Randolph met on a dueling field. In the first round of fire, both men missed. In the second round, Clay missed, and Randolph deliberately fired into the air in order to miss Clay. Randolph's gesture caused Clay to announce that his honor had been satisfied, and the two men ended the duel unhurt.

FURTHER READING

Bartlett, Irving H. *John Calhoun.* New York: W.W. Norton & Co., 1993.

Remini, Robert V. *Henry Clay: Statesman for the Union.* New York: W.W. Norton & Co., 1991.

Richards, Leonard. *The Life and Times of Congressman John Quincy Adams.* New York: Oxford University Press, 1986.

The 20th Congress

MARCH 4, 1827-MARCH 3, 1829

First Session: *December 3, 1827 - May 26, 1828*
Second Session: *December 1, 1828 - March 3, 1829*

In the 1826 elections for the 20th Congress, the Jacksonians gained 8 seats in the Senate, giving them a new majority of 28 out of the 48 seats, and the Administration party lost 6 seats, reducing their total to 20. In the House, the Jacksonians gained 22 seats, giving them a new majority of 119 of the 213, and the Administration party lost 11 seats, leaving them with 94. [See notes 2 and 3, p. xxix]

BACKGROUND

The 20th Congress passed tariff legislation, which had failed to pass in the Senate during the 19th Congress [See Background, The 19th Congress], that was quickly labeled the Tariff of Abominations by the South. By the end of 1828 the state legislatures of Georgia, Mississippi, South Carolina, and Virginia had declared the Tariff of Abominations to be illegal and unconstitutional. Vice President John C. Calhoun, from South Carolina, was particularly vocal in his opposition to the tariff and wrote a treatise in support of the southern position entitled "South Carolina Exposition and Protest."

On the frontier, more American settlers were heading for Texas due to the Mexican government's policy of giving Americans cheap land grants, and American explorers were exploring and mapping the Southwest.

SENATE LEADERSHIP

Vice President: John Caldwell Calhoun, a famous representative and senator from South Carolina, served as President Adams's vice president. He was reelected vice president under President Andrew Jackson in the 1828 presidential election. Calhoun was one of the most vigorous spokesmen for the South and southern opposition to higher import tariffs.

President Pro Tempore: Samuel Smith (Jacksonian, Md.) was elected on May 15, 1828. [See note 4, p. xxix]

Majority Leader, Majority Whip, Minority Leader, and Minority Whip: None. These functions did not evolve into formal Senate positions until the 62nd Congress (1911-1913).

Chairmen of Selected Key Committees: [See also Organization and Administration, p. 79]

Committee on Finance: Samuel Smith (Jacksonian, Md.)

Committee on Foreign Relations: Nathaniel Macon (Jacksonian, N.C.) and Littleton Tazewell (Jacksonian, Va.)

Committee on the Judiciary: Martin Van Buren (Jacksonian, N.Y.) and John Macpherson Berrien (Jacksonian, Ga.)

CHRONOLOGY

March 4, 1827: The 20th Congress begins.

December 3, 1827: The first session begins, and Andrew Stevenson (Jacksonian, Va.) is elected Speaker of the House.

May 13, 1828: Congress passes legislation nicknamed the "Tariff of Abominations" by Southerners.

May 24, 1828: President Adams nominates Peter B. Porter to succeed James Barbour as secretary of war.

May 26, 1828: The Senate confirms Porter, and the first session ends.

August 25, 1828: Supreme Court Justice Robert Trimble dies, but will not be replaced until the 21st Congress.

December 1, 1828: The second session begins.

March 3, 1829: The second session and the 20th Congress end.

[See note 6, p. xxix]

Committee on Military Affairs: William Henry Harrison (Admin., Ohio) and Thomas H. Benton (Jacksonian, Mo.)

Committee on Naval Affairs: Robert Y. Hayne (Jacksonian, S.C.).

HOUSE LEADERSHIP

Speaker of the House: Andrew Stevenson (Jacksonian, Va.), elected Speaker on December 3, 1827, was a lawyer who had served in the Virginia state legislature. He was elected to the House in the 17th Congress. He was Speaker of the House from the 20th Congress through the 23rd Congress, when he resigned to become minister to Great Britain.

Majority Leader, Majority Whip, Minority Leader, and Minority Whip: None. These functions did not evolve into formal House positions until the 56th Congress (1899-1901).

Chairmen of Selected Key Committees: [See also Organization and Administration, below]

Committee on Agriculture: Stephen Van Rensselaer (No definite party, N.Y.)

Committee on Foreign Affairs: Edward Everett (No definite party, Mass.)

Committee on the Judiciary: Philip P. Barbour (Jacksonian, Va)

Committee on Military Affairs: James Hamilton Jr. (No definite party, S.C.) and William Drayton (Jacksonian, S.C.)

Committee on Naval Affairs: Michael Hoffman (Jacksonian, N.Y.)

Committee on Ways and Means: George McDuffie (Jacksonian, S.C.) and John Randolph (Jacksonian, Va.)

ORGANIZATION AND ADMINISTRATION

There have been approximately two thousand committees throughout the history of Congress. However, the modern committee structure and the modern allocation of committee jurisdiction, seniority, and ranking minority member status was not established until after World War II. [See also note 5, p. xxix]

TABLE OF KEY VOTES

Senate

Subject of Vote	Date of Vote	For	Against
Tariff of Abominations	May 13, 1828	26	21
Confirmation of Peter B. Porter as Secretary of War	May 26, 1828	22	11

House

Subject of Vote	Date of Vote	For	Against
Tariff of Abominations	April 22, 1828	105	94

[See note 7, p. xxix]

MAJOR LEGISLATION PASSED

Tariffs: Congress passed legislation, which the South called the Tariff of Abominations, that raised tariffs up to 41 percent on woolen products and other imported manufactured goods.

FAILED LEGISLATION

None of historical significance.

RELATIONS WITH THE PRESIDENT

As was true during the 19th Congress, President Adams had poor relations with Congress, largely because of the rising power of the opposition party, the Jacksonians, who now dominated both houses of Congress. Adams wanted the government to fund more road and canal projects, but was unable to get sufficient congressional support. Adams vetoed no legislation during the 20th Congress.

NOMINATIONS, APPOINTMENTS, AND CONFIRMATIONS

The Judiciary: On August 25, 1828, Supreme Court Justice Robert Trimble died. The vacancy on the Court was not filled until the 21st Congress.

The Executive Branch: On May 24, 1828, President Adams nominated Peter B. Porter to succeed James Barbour as secretary of war, and on May 26 the Senate confirmed Porter by a vote of 22 to 11.

IMPEACHMENTS

None.

CONSTITUTIONAL AMENDMENTS

None.

FURTHER READING

Bartlett, Irving H. *John C. Calhoun.* New York: W.W. Norton & Co., 1993.

Richards, Leonard. *The Life and Times of Congressman John Quincy Adams.* New York: Oxford University Press, 1986.

Wayland, Francis Fry. *Andrew Stevenson, Democrat and Diplomat, 1785-1857.* Philadelphia: University of Pennsylvania Press, 1949.

The 21st Congress

MARCH 4, 1829 - MARCH 3, 1831

Special Senate Session: *March 4, 1829 - March 17, 1829*
First Session: *December 7, 1829 - May 31, 1830*
Second Session: *December 6, 1830 - March 3, 1831*

The Senate held a special session to vote on the confirmation of presidential appointees to various offices. [See note 1, p. xxix]

In the 1828 elections for the 21st Congress, the Jacksonians and the Administration Party were replaced by the Democratic Party and the National Republican Party. The new parties were formed by a realignment among the various political factions, notably the supporters of President Andrew Jackson (who dominated the Democrats) on one side, and the supporters of former President John Quincy Adams and Kentucky politician Henry Clay on the other. Therefore, to say that a party "gained" or "lost" seats from the previous Congress would be misleading. In the Senate, the Democrats were elected to a majority of 26 seats out of the 48. The National Republicans won 22 seats. In the House, Democrats were elected to 139 seats out of the 213, and National Republicans won 74 seats. [See notes 2 and 3, p. xxix]

BACKGROUND

According to the census of 1830, the population of the United States as of June 1, 1830, was 12,866,020, resulting in a population density of 7.4 persons for each of the country's 1,749,462 square miles. This was a population increase of 33.5 percent over the 1820 census.

On March 4, 1829, Andrew Jackson was inaugurated as the seventh president of the United States. Jackson's inauguration was widely seen as a triumph for democracy, after the machinations of the split presidential election of 1824, in which Jackson got the most votes but did not become president because Henry Clay threw his support to John Quincy Adams. [See 18th Congress] Tennessean Jackson was the first president from a frontier state and from a state that had not been one of the original 13 states, whereas four of the six previous presidents were from Virginia and the other two from Massachusetts. Jackson seemed to symbolize the democratic man who represented a new America that was no longer confined to the Atlantic seaboard, and his presidency is often referred to as the Jacksonian Era. Less admirable was his new "spoils system," by which choice government positions went to office-seekers as a reward for political support or a recognition of influence rather than because of their merit, a system which Jackson justified on the basis of the supposed ease and simplicity of government jobs.

In 1830 Congress passed the Indian Removal Act, which provided for the relocation of Indians living east of the Mississippi to new lands west of the river. On the frontier, Mexico reversed its liberal policy on American settlers in Texas and forbade any further immigration.

C H R O N O L O G Y

March 4, 1829:	The 21st Congress and a special session of the Senate begin.
March 6, 1829:	President Andrew Jackson nominates John McLean to a vacancy on the Supreme Court left unfilled at the end of the 20th Congress. President Jackson also nominates, and the Senate confirms, Martin Van Buren to be secretary of state and Samuel D. Ingham to be secretary of the Treasury.
March 7, 1829:	The Senate confirms McLean.
March 9, 1829:	Jackson nominates, and the Senate confirms, John M. Berrien to be attorney general, John Branch to be secretary of the Navy, and John H. Eaton to be secretary of war.
March 17, 1829:	The Senate special session ends.
November 26, 1829:	Supreme Court Associate Justice Bushrod Washington dies.
December 7, 1829:	The first session begins, and Andrew Stevenson (Dem., Va.) is reelected Speaker of the House.
January 4, 1830:	President Jackson nominates Henry Baldwin to replace Washington.
January 6, 1830:	The Senate confirms Baldwin as associate justice.
January 26, 1830:	Senator Daniel Webster (Nat. Rep., Mass.) gives his famous reply to a speech by Senator Robert Y. Hayne (Dem., S.C.).
April 24, 1830:	The House votes to impeach federal Judge James H. Peck.
May 26, 1830:	Congresses passes the Indian Removal Act.
May 29, 1830:	Congress passes legislation to establish free trade with certain British colonies if Great Britain reciprocates.
May 31, 1830:	The first session ends.
December 6, 1830:	The second session begins.
January 31, 1831:	The Senate impeachment trial of Judge Peck results in a vote of not guilty.
March 3, 1831:	The second session and the 21st Congress end.

[See note 6, p. xxix]

SENATE LEADERSHIP

Vice President: John Caldwell Calhoun was a famous representative and senator from South Carolina. He had also been vice president under previous President John Quincy Adams. Calhoun was one of the most vigorous spokesmen for the South and southern opposition to higher import tariffs.

President Pro Tempore: Samuel Smith (Dem., Md.) was elected on March 13, 1829, May 29, 1830, and March 1, 1831. [See note 4, p. xxix]

Majority Leader, Majority Whip, Minority Leader, and Minority Whip: None. These functions did not evolve into formal Senate positions until the 62nd Congress (1911-1913).

Other Senate Leaders: Daniel Webster (Nat. Rep., Mass.) was one of the greatest orators to

TABLE OF KEY VOTES

Senate

Subject of Vote	Date of Vote	For	Against
Native Americans Removed from Land East of Mississippi	April 26, 1830	Passed by voice vote	
Trade with Great Britain	May 29, 1830	Passed by voice vote	
Verdict in Impeachment Trial of Judge Peck	January 31, 1831	21	22

House

Subject of Vote	Date of Vote	For	Against
To Impeach Judge Peck	April 24, 1830	123	49
Native Americans Removed from Land East of Mississippi	May 26, 1830	102	97
Trade with Great Britain	May 27, 1830	105	28

[See note 7, p. xxix]

ever serve in the U.S. Senate. On January 25, 1830, when Senator Robert Y. Hayne (Dem., S.C.) made a speech attacking tariff legislation as unconstitutional, and asserting that the states could nullify federal laws that infringed on state interests, Webster responded the next day with a speech, lasting nearly three hours, that was a ringing defense of the Union and the principle of national government. Webster's reply is one of the most famous speeches in American history.

Chairmen of Selected Key Committees: [See also Organization and Administration, p. 84]

Committee on Finance: Samuel Smith (Dem., Md.)

Committee on Foreign Relations: Littleton Tazewell (Dem., Va.)

Committee on the Judiciary: John Rowan (Dem., Ky.)

Committee on Military Affairs: Thomas H. Benton (Dem., Mo.)

Committee on Naval Affairs: Robert Y. Hayne (Dem., S.C.)

HOUSE LEADERSHIP

Speaker of the House: Andrew Stevenson (Dem., Va.) was reelected Speaker on December 7, 1829. [See biographical note in 20th Congress]

Majority Leader, Majority Whip, Minority Leader, and Minority Whip: None. These functions did not evolve into formal House positions until the 56th Congress (1899-1901).

Chairmen of Selected Key Committees: [See also Organization and Administration, p. 84]

Committee on Agriculture: Ambrose Spencer (Dem., N.Y.)

Committee on Foreign Affairs: William S. Archer (Nat. Rep., Va.)

Committee on the Judiciary: James Buchanan (Dem., Pa.)

Committee on Military Affairs: William Drayton (Dem., S.C.)

Committee on Naval Affairs: Michael Hoffman (Dem., N.Y.)

Committee on Ways and Means: George McDuffie (Dem., S.C.)

ORGANIZATION AND ADMINISTRATION

There have been approximately two thousand committees throughout the history of Congress. However, the modern committee structure and the modern allocation of committee jurisdiction, seniority, and ranking minority member status was not established until after World War II. [See also note 5, p. xxix]

MAJOR LEGISLATION PASSED

Great Britain: Congress authorized the restoration of free trade with certain British colonies if the British would reciprocate.

Native Americans: In the Indian Removal Act, Congress appropriated one-half million dollars for the resettlement of all Indians still east of the Mississippi to new lands west of the Mississippi. President Jackson, a former Indian fighter, and his congressional supporters from the frontier states favored a harsh policy toward Native Americans, whom they believed could never assimilate into American society.

FAILED LEGISLATION

Four transportation improvement bills were vetoed by President Jackson [See Relations with the President, below]

RELATIONS WITH THE PRESIDENT

President Jackson was a firm supporter of the Union and strongly opposed the theory of "nul-lification," under which the states could supposedly declare federal legislation unconstitutional and thus unenforceable. However, Jackson also believed in limited government. Jackson vetoed four bills in the 21st Congress, all of which concerned roads, canals and other transportation improvements, because he considered this an unwarranted expansion of the federal government's role in national life.

NOMINATIONS, APPOINTMENTS, AND CONFIRMATIONS

The Judiciary: On August 25, 1828, during the 20th Congress, Supreme Court Justice Robert Trimble died. The vacancy was not filled until this Congress, when President Andrew Jackson nominated John McLean on March 6, 1829, and the Senate confirmed McLean the next day by voice vote. Justice Bushrod Washington died on November 26, 1829, and President Jackson nominated Henry Baldwin on January 4, 1830, to replace him. The Senate confirmed Baldwin on January 6, 1830 by a 41 to 2 vote.

The Executive Branch: On March 6, 1829, President Jackson nominated, and the Senate confirmed by voice vote, Martin Van Buren to be secretary of state and Samuel D. Ingham to be secretary of the Treasury. On March 9, 1829, Jackson nominated, and the Senate confirmed by voice vote, John M. Berrien to be attorney general, John Branch to be secretary of the Navy and John H. Eaton to be secretary of war.

IMPEACHMENTS

On April 24, 1830, the House voted 123 to 49 to impeach federal Judge James H. Peck. The trial on the impeachent charges was held in the Senate. On January 31, 1831, the Senate found Peck not guilty by a vote of 21 to 22.

CONSTITUTIONAL AMENDMENTS

None.

FURTHER READING

Bartlett, Irving H. *John C. Calhoun*. New York: W.W. Norton & Co., 1993.

Jackson, Andrew. *The Papers of Andrew Jackson*. Knoxville, Tenn.: University of Tennessee Press, 1980-present (two volumes to date).

Remini, Robert V. *Henry Clay: Statesman for the Union*. New York: W.W. Norton & Co., 1991.

Wayland, Francis Fry. *Andrew Stevenson, Democrat and Diplomat, 1785-1857*. Philadelphia: University of Pennsylvania Press, 1949.

The 22nd Congress

MARCH 4, 1831 - MARCH 3, 1833

First Session: December 5, 1831 - July 16, 1832
Second Session: December 3, 1832 - March 2, 1833

In the 1830 elections for the 22nd Congress, the Democratic party lost 1 seat in the Senate to lower their majority to 25 out of the 48, the National Republicans lost a seat for a total of 21, and 2 seats were held by a South Carolina party called the Nullifiers, who believed that a state could nullify federal legislation within its borders. In the House, the Democratic party gained 2 seats for a total of 58, and 14 seats were held by neither party. Four of these seats were held by the Nullifiers, and most of the other seats probably belonged to the Anti-Masonic Party.

BACKGROUND

In August 1831 a slave named Nat Turner led a slave revolt in Southampton County, Virginia, that resulted in the killing of some 55 white slave owners or members of their families. The rebellion was crushed within two months and was never a serious threat to the institution of slavery, but the incident led to harsher laws enforcing slavery and black submissiveness throughout the slave states. Further, the South began to blame northern abolitionists for slave rebellions, with Georgia going so far as to offer a bounty for the publisher of *The Liberator*, William Lloyd Garrison. In addition to slavery, the Tariff of Abominations [See 20th Congress] was widely resented throughout the South as a violation of states' rights and as a subsidy to northern manufacturers. On November 24, 1832, a crisis arose when South Carolina declared the federal tariffs null and void and threatened to secede if

President Jackson used the military to enforce them. Jackson responded on December 10, 1832, declaring that a state could not nullify a federal law and that to do so was rebellion. However, on March 2, 1833, which was the last day of the second session of the 22nd Congress, Jackson signed the Compromise Tariff of 1833 that in the next Congress would end the South Carolina crisis. The compromise capped tariffs at 20 percent effective in 1842.

Other significant events during the 22nd Congress include the Indian uprisings along the frontier in resistance to forced settlement, and Jackson's veto of the renewal of the Bank of the United States' charter.

SENATE LEADERSHIP

Vice President: John Caldwell Calhoun, a famous representative and senator from South Carolina, also had been vice president under the previous president, John Quincy Adams. Calhoun was one of the most vigorous spokesmen for the South and southern opposition to higher tariffs on imports. Calhoun resigned as vice president on December 28, 1832, having been elected to the Senate on December 12, 1832, to replace Robert Y. Hayne (Dem., S.C.), who left the Senate to become governor of South Carolina. Until the Twenty-fifth Amendment was ratified on February 10, 1967 [See 90th Congress], there was no mechanism other than an election for filling vacancies in the office of vice president, so for the remainer of the 22nd Congress's second session, there was

C H R O N O L O G Y

March 4, 1831:	The 22nd Congress begins.
December 5, 1831:	The first session begins, and Andrew Stevenson (Dem., Va.) is reelected Speaker of the House.
December 7, 1831:	President Jackson nominates Lewis Cass to be secretary of war, Edward Livingston to be secretary of state, Louis McLane to be secretary of the Treasury, Roger B. Taney to be attorney general, and Levi Woodbury to be secretary of the Navy.
December 27, 1831:	The Senate confirms Taney and Woodbury.
December 30, 1831:	The Senate confirms Cass.
January 12, 1832:	The Senate confirms Livingston.
January 13, 1832:	The Senate confirms McLane.
June 23, 1832:	The Senate rejects the Maine Boundary Treaty by one vote.
July 9, 1832:	Congress passes the Tariff Act of 1832.
July 10, 1832:	President Jackson vetoes legislation that would continue the Bank of the United States.
July 13, 1832:	The Senate fails to override President Jackson's veto of the Bank of the United States legislation.
July 16, 1832:	The first session ends.
November 24, 1832:	South Carolina declares that federal tariffs are null and void and threatens to secede if President Jackson uses the military to enforce the tariffs.
December 3, 1832:	The second session begins.
December 10, 1832:	President Jackson responds to South Carolina, declaring that a state cannot nullify a federal law and that to do so is rebellion.
December 12, 1832:	Vice President Calhoun is elected to the Senate to replace Robert Y. Hayne (Dem., S.C.), who left the Senate to become governor of South Carolina.
December 28, 1832:	Calhoun resigns as vice president to take his seat in the Senate.
March 1, 1833:	Congress passes the Compromise Tariff and the Force Bill, authorizing the president to use the armed forces to impose the tariff.
March 2, 1833:	The second session ends.
March 3, 1833:	The 22nd Congress ends.

[See note 6, p. xxix]

no vice president of the United States and therefore no president of the Senate.

President Pro Tempore: Littleton Waller Tazewell (Nat. Rep., Va.) was elected on July 9, 1832; and Hugh Lawson White (Nat. Rep., Tenn.) was elected on December 3, 1832. [See note 4, p. xxix]

Majority Leader, Majority Whip, Minority Leader, and Minority Whip: None. These functions did not evolve into formal Senate positions until the 62nd Congress (1911-1913).

Chairmen of Selected Key Committees: [See also Organization and Administration, p. 89]

TABLE OF KEY VOTES

Senate

Subject of Vote	Date of Vote	For	Against
Confirmation of Taney and Woodbury	December 27, 1831	Passed by a voice vote	
Confirmation of Lewis Cass to be Secretary of State	December 30, 1831	Passed by a voice vote	
Confirmation of Edward Livingston to be Secretary of State	January 12, 1832	Passed by a voice vote	
Confirmation of Louis McLane to be Secretary of the Treasury	January 13, 1832	Passed by a voice vote	
Maine Boundary Treaty	June 23, 1832	20	21
Tariff Act of 1832	July 9, 1832	32	16
Overriding Veto of Bank of the United States Legislation (veto sustained: not a two-thirds majority)	July 13, 1832	22	19
Force Bill	February 20, 1833	32	1
Compromise Tariff	March 1, 1833	29	16

House

Subject of Vote	Date of Vote	For	Against
Tariff Act of 1832	June 28, 1832	132	65
Compromise Tariff	February 26, 1833	119	85
Force Bill	March 1, 1833	149	47

[See note 7, p. xxix]

Committee on Finance: Samuel Smith (Dem., Md.)

Committee on Foreign Relations: Littleton Tazewell (Dem., Va.) and John Forsyth (Dem., Ga.)

Committee on the Judiciary: William Marcy (Dem., N.Y.) and William Wilkins (Dem., Pa.)

Committee on Military Affairs: Thomas H. Benton (Dem., Mo.)

Committee on Naval Affairs: Robert Y. Hayne (Dem., S.C.) and George M. Dallas (Dem., Pa.)

HOUSE LEADERSHIP

Speaker of the House: Andrew Stevenson (Dem., Va.) was reelected Speaker on December 5, 1831. [See biographical note in 20th Congress]

Majority Leader, Majority Whip, Minority Leader, and Minority Whip: None. These func-

tions did not evolve into formal House positions until the 56th Congress (1899-1901).

Chairmen of Selected Key Committees: [See also Organization and Administration, below]

Committee on Agriculture: Erastus Root (Dem., N.Y.)

Committee on Foreign Affairs: William S. Archer (Nat. Rep., Va.)

Committee on the Judiciary: Warren R. Davis (Dem., S.C.) and John Bell (Nat. Rep., Tenn.)

Committee on Military Affairs: William Drayton (Dem., S.C.) and Richard M. Johnson (Dem., Ky.)

Committee on Naval Affairs: Michael Hoffman (Dem., N.Y.) and John Anderson (Dem., Maine)

Committee on Ways and Means: George McDuffie (Dem., S.C.) and Gulian C. Verplanck (Dem., N.Y.)

ORGANIZATION AND ADMINISTRATION

There have been approximately two thousand committees throughout the history of Congress. However, the modern committee structure and the modern allocation of committee jurisdiction, seniority, and ranking minority member status was not established until after World War II. [See note 5, p. xxix]

MAJOR LEGISLATION PASSED

Foreign Policy: The United States and Great Britain had a long-standing dispute over the exact location of the boundary between Maine and the British colonies in Canada. Both sides agreed to submit the matter to the king of the Netherlands, a neutral party, who decided to split the disputed territory evenly. The settlers in Maine protested the decision, causing the Senate to reject — by a single vote — a treaty that would have accepted the king's decision. Eventually, on August 9, 1842, the United States and Great Britain settled their territorial disputes in the Webster-Ashburton Treaty. [See 27th Congress]

Tariffs: The Tariff of Abominations passed by the 20th Congress caused a political crisis when South Carolina threatened to secede from the United States. The Tariff Act of 1832 reduced tariffs slightly, but not enough to defuse the political crisis. The Compromise Tariff of 1833 lowered tariffs substantially, establishing a general tariff rate of 20 percent, and ended the crisis. Congress also passed legislation, known as the Force Bill, which authorized the president to use the armed forces to enforce the tariff laws. The purpose of the Force Bill was to impress upon the South that, although the North had agreed to the Compromise Tariff, it would not tolerate rebellion.

FAILED LEGISLATION

President Jackson vetoed legislation that would have continued the Bank of the United States, and Congress failed to overturn the veto. [See Relations with the President, below]

RELATIONS WITH THE PRESIDENT

President Jackson was a firm supporter of the Union, and strongly opposed the theory of "nullification", under which the states could supposedly declare federal legislation unconstitutional and thus unenforceable. However, Jackson also believed in limited government. Jackson vetoed four bills in the 22nd Congress, the most significant of which occurred on July 10, 1832, when he vetoed legislation that would have continued the Bank of the United States. On July 13, 1832, the Senate voted 22 to override the veto and 19 against, thus failing to achieve the two-thirds majority necessary to overturn the veto.

NOMINATIONS, APPOINTMENTS, AND CONFIRMATIONS

The Judiciary: There were no significant nominations, appointments, or confirmations in the federal judiciary during the 22nd Congress.

The Executive Branch: On December 7, 1831, President Jackson nominated Lewis Cass to be secretary of war, Edward Livingston to be secretary of state, Louis McLane to be secretary of the Treasury, Roger B. Taney to be attorney general, and Levi Woodbury to be secretary of the Navy. The Senate confirmed all five men by voice votes: Taney and Woodbury on December 27, 1831; Cass on December 30, 1831; Livingston on January 12, 1832; and McLane on January 13, 1832.

IMPEACHMENTS

None.

CONSTITUTIONAL AMENDMENTS

None.

FURTHER READING

Bartlett, Irving H. *John C. Calhoun*. New York: W.W. Norton & Co., 1993.

Jackson, Andrew. *The Papers of Andrew Jackson*. Knoxville, Tenn.: University of Tennessee Press, 1980-present (two volumes to date).

Wayland, Francis Fry. *Andrew Stevenson, Democrat and Diplomat, 1785-1857*. Philadelphia: University of Pennsylvania Press, 1949.

The 23rd Congress

MARCH 4, 1833 - MARCH 3, 1835

First Session: December 2, 1833 - June 30, 1834
Second Session: December 1, 1834 - March 3, 1835

In the 1832 elections for the 23rd Congress, the Democrats lost 5 seats in the Senate to lower their total to 20 seats out of the 48, which put them in a tie with the National Republicans, who lost a seat to lower their total to 20 as well. Of the remaining 8 seats, 2 were held by the Nullifiers and the other 6 generally leaned toward the Democrats. In the House, the membership was reapportioned because of the 1830 census (see 21st Congress) and increased to 242, although this theoretical limit was ignored in the 1830s when it was politically expedient to permit newly admitted states to send provisional representatives pending the 1840 census. The Democrats gained 6 seats and increased their majority to 147, while the National Republicans lost 5 seats for a total of 53, with an unprecedented 42 seats being held by members not aligned with either party. Nine of these seats were held by the Nullifiers, and most of the other seats were held by the Anti-Masonic Party.

BACKGROUND

On March 4, 1833, President Andrew Jackson was inaugurated for his second term as the seventh president of the United States. A crisis between the federal government and the state of South Carolina over tariffs on imports ended when Jackson agreed to compromise legislation at the end of the 22nd Congress and South Carolina withdrew its threat to nullify federal

tariffs. For the time being, the prospect of a southern secession also was ended.

In 1834 Jackson and the Senate, led by Henry Clay (Nat. Rep., Ky.), feuded constantly over Jackson's withdrawal of federal funds from the Bank of the United States, which Jackson was determined to destroy. On December 11, 1833, the Senate voted to order Jackson to turn over a document relating to this withdrawal of funds. Jackson refused, causing the Senate on March 28, 1834, to censure him. The censure gave the Senate a purely symbolic last word, but Jackson won the "Bank War" when the Bank's charter expired in 1836.

On the frontier, the last of the Seminole Indians were ordered out of Florida, but the Seminoles were able to fight back and resist resettlement for nearly a decade. American settlers established towns in Idaho, and continued to move toward the Pacific Ocean along what would become the Oregon Trail.

SENATE LEADERSHIP

Vice President: Martin Van Buren, President Jackson's 1828 running mate, was a former senator from, and governor of, New York. Van Buren also had served as secretary of state during President Jackson's first term and succeed Jackson as president in 1837.

Presidents Pro Tempore: In an unusual procedural move, the Senate elected two presidents pro tempore on June 28, 1834, namely, Hugh Lawson

C H R O N O L O G Y

March 4, 1833:	The 23rd Congress begins.
March 15, 1833:	The tariff crisis from the 22nd Congress ends when South Carolina withdraws its threat to nullify federal tariffs.
December 2, 1833:	The first session begins, and Andrew Stevenson (Dem., Va.) is reelected Speaker of the House.
December 11, 1833:	The Senate orders President Jackson to turn over a document relating to his withdrawl of funds from the Bank of the United States.
March 28, 1834:	The Senate censures President Jackson.
June 2, 1834:	Speaker of the House Andrew Stevenson (Dem., Va.) resigns and John Bell (Nat. Rep., Tenn.) is elected Speaker.
June 23, 1834:	President Jackson nominates Benjamin F. Butler to be attorney general and Roger B. Taney to be secretary of the Treasury.
June 24, 1834:	The Senate confirms Butler, but rejects Taney.
June 27, 1834:	President Jackson nominates, and the Senate confirms, John Forsyth to be secretary of state and Levi Woodbury to be secretary of the Treasury.
June 28, 1834:	Congress passes legislation establishing a Department of Indian Affairs. President Jackson nominates Mahlon Dickerson to be secretary of the Navy.
June 30, 1834:	The Senate confirms Dickerson by voice vote. The first session ends.
August 4, 1834:	Supreme Court Justice William Johnson dies.
December 1, 1834:	The second session begins.
January 6, 1835:	President Jackson nominates James Moore Wayne to replace Johnson.
January 9, 1835:	The Senate confirms Wayne.
January 14, 1835:	Justice Gabriel Duvall resigns. He will not be replaced until the 24th Congress.
March 3, 1835:	The second session and the 23rd Congress end.

[See note 6, p. xxix]

White (Nat. Rep., Tenn.) and George Poindexter (Dem., Miss). John Tyler (Dem., Va.) was elected on March 3, 1835. [See note 4, p. xxix]

Majority Leader, Majority Whip, Minority Leader, and Minority Whip: None. These functions did not evolve into formal Senate positions until the 62nd Congress (1911-1913).

Chairmen of Selected Key Committees: [See also Organization and Administration, p. 93]

Committee on Finance: Daniel Webster (Nat. Rep., Mass.)

Committee on Foreign Relations: William Wilkins (Dem., Pa.) and Henry Clay (Nat. Rep., Ky.)

Committee on the Judiciary: John Clayton (Nat. Rep., Del.)

Committee on Military Affairs: Thomas H. Benton (Dem., Mo.)

Committee on Naval Affairs: Samuel Southard (Nat. Rep., N.J.)

HOUSE LEADERSHIP

Speaker of the House: Andrew Stevenson (Dem., Va.) was reelected Speaker on December 2, 1833. [See biographical note in 20th Congress] Stevenson resigned on June 2, 1834, to become minister to Great Britain, and John Bell (Nat. Rep., Tenn.) was elected to replace him the same day. Bell was Speaker in only one Congress, the 23rd, but his political career was a long one. A former lawyer, he had served in the Tennessee state legislature, had first been elected to the House in the 20th Congress, and would later serve in the Senate, become President Benjamin Harrison's secretary of war, and run against Abraham Lincoln in the presidential election of 1860 as a third-party (Constitutional Union) candidate.

Majority Leader, Majority Whip, Minority Leader, and Minority Whip: None. These functions did not evolve into formal House positions until the 56th Congress (1899-1901).

Chairmen of Selected Key Committees: [See also Organization and Administration, below]

Committee on Agriculture: Abraham Bockee (Dem., N.Y.)

Committee on Foreign Affairs: William S. Archer (Nat. Rep., Va.), Churchill C. Cambreleng (Dem., N.Y.) and James M. Wayne (Dem., Ga.)

Committee on the Judiciary: John Bell (Nat. Rep., Tenn.), until he became Speaker of the House on June 2, 1834. [See House Leadership, above] Thomas F. Foster (Dem., Ga.) succeeded Bell as chairman.

Committee on Military Affairs: Richard M. Johnson (Dem., Ky.)

Committee on Naval Affairs: Campbell P. White (Dem., N.Y.)

Committee on Ways and Means: James K. Polk (Dem., Tenn.)

ORGANIZATION AND ADMINISTRATION

There have been approximately two thousand committees throughout the history of Congress. However, the modern committee structure and the modern allocation of committee jurisdiction, seniority, and ranking minority member status was not established until after World War II. [See note 5, p. xxix]

MAJOR LEGISLATION PASSED

Department of Indian Affairs: Congress established a Department of Indian Affairs within the Department of War.

FAILED LEGISLATION

None of historical significance.

RELATIONS WITH THE PRESIDENT

Relations between President Jackson and the Senate were very strained during the 23rd Congress. [See Background, p. 91] The Senate censured Jackson for refusing to turn over a document relating to his withdrawal of funds from the Bank of the United States, and rejected Jackson's nomination of Roger B. Taney to be secretary of the Treasury. Jackson vetoed two bills during the 23rd Congress. Both were minor pieces of legislation.

NOMINATIONS, APPOINTMENTS, AND CONFIRMATIONS

The Judiciary: On August 4, 1834, Supreme Court Justice William Johnson died. President Andrew Jackson nominated James Moore Wayne on January 6, 1835, to replace Johnson, and the Senate confirmed him on January 9, 1835, by voice vote. On January 14, 1835, Justice Gabriel Duvall resigned, and would not be replaced until the 24th Congress.

The Executive Branch: On June 23, 1834, President Jackson nominated Benjamin F. Butler to be attorney general and Roger B. Taney to be secretary of the Treasury. The next day, June 24, the

TABLE OF KEY VOTES

Senate

Subject of Vote	Date of Vote	For	Against
Ordering Jackson to Turn Over Document on Withdrawal of Funds from the Bank of the United States	December 11, 1833	23	18
Censure of Jackson	March 28, 1834	26	20
Confirmation of Benjamin F. Butler to be Attorney General	June 24, 1834	Passed by voice vote	
Taney Nomination to the treasury Rejected	June 24, 1834	18	28
Confirmation of Forsyth and Woodbury	June 27, 1834	Passed by voice vote	
Confirmation of Mahlon Dickerson to be Secretary of the Navy	June 30, 1834	Passed by voice vote	
Department of Indian Affairs Established	June 28, 1834	Passed by voice vote	
Confirmation of James Moore Wayne to Supreme Court	January 9, 1835	Passed by voice vote	

House

Subject of Vote	Date of Vote	For	Against
Department of Indian Affairs Established	June 26, 1834	Passed by voice vote	

[See note 7, p. xxix]

Senate confirmed Butler by voice vote, but rejected Taney; the vote was 18 for Taney and 28 against. This was the first Senate rejection of such a senior presidential nominee in American history.

On June 27, 1834, Jackson nominated, and the Senate confirmed by voice vote, John Forsyth to be secretary of state and Levi Woodbury to be secretary of the Treasury. On June 28, 1834, Jackson nominated Mahlon Dickerson to be sec-retary of the Navy, and on June 30, 1834, the Senate confirmed Dickerson by voice vote.

IMPEACHMENTS

None.

CONSTITUTIONAL AMENDMENTS

None.

FURTHER READING

Cole, Donald. *Martin Van Buren and the American Political System*. Princeton, N.J.: Princeton University Press, 1984.

Jackson, Andrew. *The Papers of Andrew Jackson*. Knoxville, Tenn.: University of Tennessee Press, 1980-present (two volumes to date).

Lawrence, Alexander A. *James Moore Wayne: Southern Unionist*. Chapel Hill, N.C.: University of North Carolina Press, 1943.

Parks, Joseph H. *John Bell of Tennessee*. Baton Rouge, La.: Louisiana State University Press, 1950.

Remini, Robert V. *Henry Clay: Statesman for the Union*. New York: W.W. Norton & Co., 1991.

Wayland, Francis Fry. *Andrew Stevenson, Democrat and Diplomat, 1785-1857*. Philadelphia: University of Pennsylvania Press, 1949.

The 24th Congress

MARCH 4, 1835 - MARCH 3, 1837

First Session: December 7, 1835 - July 4, 1836
Second Session: December 5, 1836 - March 3, 1837

In the 1834 elections for the 24th Congress, the Democrats gained 7 seats in the Senate, giving them a new, if bare, majority with 27 seats out of the 52. The National Republicans, now known as the Whigs, lost 5 Senate seats, leaving them with a total of 25. In the House, the total membership increased to 243. The Democrats lost 2 seats to reduce their majority to 145 of the 243 seats. The Whigs gained 45 seats for a total of 98. [See notes 2 and 3, p. xxix]

BACKGROUND

During the 24th Congress, the United States was engaged in a guerrilla war in Florida with the Seminole Indians, whom President Jackson was trying to resettle west of the Mississippi. In the North, groups such as the American Anti-Slavery Society were leading the growing public opposition to slavery.

On January 30, 1835, Richard Lawrence made the first attempt to assassinate a U.S. president when he tried to shoot President Jackson at a funeral. In 1836 Texas declared its independence from Mexico, establishing itself as the Republic of Texas. After Mexican troops massacred the occupants of the Alamo on March 6, 1836, Texas General Sam Houston defeated the Mexicans on April 21, 1836, at the decisive Battle of San Jacinto, and Texas won its war of independence. On June 15, 1836, Arkansas was admitted to the United States as the 25th state. On January 26, 1837, Michigan was admitted to the United States as the 26th state. Shortly before the end of the 24th Congress, Congress passed the Judiciary Act of 1837, which raised the number of Supreme Court justices from seven to nine.

SENATE LEADERSHIP

Vice President: Martin Van Buren was a former senator from, and governor of, New York and a former secretary of state in President Jackson's first term. He would become the eigth president, following Jackson's second term.

President Pro Tempore: William Rufus de Vane King (Dem., Ala.) was elected on July 1, 1836, and reelected on January 28, 1837. [See note 4, p. xxix]

Majority Leader, Majority Whip, Minority Leader, and Minority Whip: None. These functions did not evolve into formal Senate positions until the 62nd Congress (1911-1913).

Chairmen of Selected Key Committees: [See also Organization and Administration, p. 98]

Committee on Finance: Daniel Webster (Whig, Mass.) and Silas Wright Jr. (Dem., N.Y.)

Committee on Foreign Relations: Henry Clay (Whig, Ky.) and James Buchanan (Dem., Pa.)

Committee on the Judiciary: John Clayton (Whig, Del.) and Felix Grundy (Dem., Tenn.)

Committee on Military Affairs: Thomas H. Benton (Dem., Mo.)

Committee on Naval Affairs: Samuel Southard (Whig, N.J.) and William Rives (Dem., Va.)

C H R O N O L O G Y

March 4, 1835:	The 24th Congress begins.
July 6, 1835:	Chief Justice John Marshall dies.
December 7, 1835:	The first session begins, and James Knox Polk (Dem., Tenn.) is elected Speaker of the House.
December 28, 1835:	Jackson nominates Philip P. Barbour to fill a vacancy on the Supreme Court that occurred during the 23rd Congress, and Roger B. Taney to replace Marshall.
March 15, 1836:	The Senate confirms Barbour and Taney.
June 13, 1836:	Congress passes legislation admitting Arkansas and Michigan into the United States.
June 21, 1836:	Congress passes the Deposit Act.
July 4, 1836:	The first session ends.
December 5, 1836:	The second session begins.
January 16, 1837:	The Senate votes to remove the censure of President Jackson passed in the 23rd Congress.
March 3, 1837:	Congress passes the Judiciary Act of 1837. President Jackson nominates, and the Senate confirms, Benjamin F. Butler to be secretary of war. President Jackson nominates John Catron for one of the two new Supreme Court seats created by the Judiciary Act of 1837, but the Senate would not act on the nomination until the next Congress. The second session and the 24th Congress end.

[See note 6, p. xxix]

HOUSE LEADERSHIP

Speaker of the House: James Knox Polk (Dem., Tenn.) was elected Speaker on December 7, 1835. Polk had served in the Tennessee legislature and had been first elected to the House in the 19th Congress. He was a long-standing Jacksonian. After serving as Speaker in the 24th and 25th Congresses, Polk left Congress to become governor of Tennessee and eventually president of the United States.

Majority Leader, Majority Whip, Minority Leader, and Minority Whip: None. These functions did not evolve into formal House positions until the 56th Congress (1899-1901).

Chairmen of Selected Key Committees: [See also Organization and Administration, p. 98]

Committee on Agriculture: Abraham Bockee (Dem., N.Y.)

Committee on Foreign Affairs: John Y. Mason (Dem., Va.) and Benjamin C. Howard (Dem., Md.)

Committee on the Judiciary: Samuel Beardsley (Dem., N.Y.) and Francis Thomas (Dem., Md.)

Committee on Military Affairs: Richard M. Johnson (Dem., Ky.)

Committee on Naval Affairs: Leonard Jarvis (Dem., Maine)

Committee on Ways and Means: Churchill C. Cambreleng (Dem., N.Y.)

TABLE OF KEY VOTES

Senate

Subject of Vote	Date of Vote	For	Against
Confirmation of Philip P. Barbour to Supreme Court	March 15, 1836	30	11
Confirmation of Roger B. Taney to Supreme Court	March 15, 1836	29	15
Admission of Michigan to Union	April 2, 1836	24	18
Admission of Arkansas to Union	April 4, 1836	31	6
Federal Deposits Act	June 17, 1836	39	6
Removing Censure of President Jackson	January 16, 1837	24	19
1837 Judiciary Act	February 15, 1837	Passed by voice vote	
Confirmation of Benjamin F. Butler to be Secretary of War	March 3, 1837	Passed by voice vote	

House

Subject of Vote	Date of Vote	For	Against
Admission of Arkansas to Union	June 13, 1836	143	50
Admission of Michigan to Union	June 13, 1836	Passed by voice vote	
Federal Deposits Act	June 21, 1836	155	38
1837 Judiciary Act	March 3, 1837	Passed by voice vote	

[See note 7, p. xxix]

ORGANIZATION AND ADMINISTRATION

There have been approximately two thousand committees throughout the history of Congress. However, the modern committee structure and the modern allocation of committee jurisdiction, seniority, and ranking minority member status was not established until after World War II. [See note 5, p. xxix]

MAJOR LEGISLATION PASSED

Admission of Arkansas and Michigan as New States: Congress voted to admit Arkansas and Michigan into the United States. Although the final votes in the House to admit the two states occurred on the same day (June 13, 1836), Arkansas was formally admitted to the Union on June 15, 1836; and Michigan on January 26, 1837, due to procedural differences in the respective legislations.

Federal Funds: In the Deposit Act, Congress established a network of federal bank deposits in the states and territories of the United States.

Supreme Court: In the Judiciary Act of 1837, Congress increased the number of Supreme Court justices from seven to nine.

FAILED LEGISLATION

None of historical significance.

RELATIONS WITH THE PRESIDENT

In the 23rd Congress, President Jackson had refused to turn over to the Senate a document concerning his withdrawal of federal funds from the Bank of the United States, and the Senate officially censured him. Tensions between the president and the Senate were less serious in the 24th Congress, because Jackson's fellow Democrats were now in the majority. On January 16, 1837, shortly before the end of the 24th Congress and Jackson's presidency, the Senate voted 24 to 19 to remove the censure.

Jackson vetoed two bills during the 24th Congress. Both were minor pieces of legislation.

NOMINATIONS, APPOINTMENTS, AND CONFIRMATIONS

The Judiciary: On January 14, 1835, during the 23rd Congress, Justice Gabriel Duvall resigned and was not replaced until the 24th Congress. Chief Justice John Marshall died on July 6, 1835, and President Jackson thus had two vacancies to fill on the Court. On December 28, 1835, Jackson nominated Philip P. Barbour to replace Duvall and Roger B. Taney to replace Marshall. The Senate confirmed Barbour on March 15, 1836,

by a 30 to 11 vote, and confirmed Taney on the same day by a 29 to 15 vote.

The Supreme Court was increased to nine justices in 1837 before the end of the 24th Congress, but the two additional seats on the Court were not filled until the 25th Congress. On March 3, 1837, the last day of the 24th Congress, Jackson nominated John Catron for one of the Supreme Court seats, but the Senate would not act on the nomination until the next Congress.

The Executive Branch: On March 3, 1837, Jackson nominated, and the Senate confirmed by voice vote, Benjamin F. Butler to be secretary of war.

IMPEACHMENTS

None.

CONSTITUTIONAL AMENDMENTS

None.

FURTHER READING

Cole, Donald. *Martin Van Buren and the American Political System.* Princeton, N.J.: Princeton University Press, 1984.

Lewis, Walker. *Without Fear or Favor: A Biography of Chief Justice Roger Brooke Taney.* Boston: Houghton Mifflin, 1965.

Sellers, Charles G., Jr. *James K. Polk.* Princeton, N.J.: Princeton University Press, 1957-1966 (two volumes).

The 25th Congress

MARCH 4, 1837-MARCH 3, 1839

Special Senate Session: March 4, 1837 - March 10, 1837
First Session: September 4, 1837 - October 16, 1837
Second Session: December 4, 1837 - July 9, 1838

The Senate held a special session to vote on the confirmation of presidential appointees to various offices. [See note 1, p. xxix]

In the 1836 election for the 25th Congress, the Democrats gained 3 seats in the Senate to increase their total to 30 seats out of the 52 and the Whigs lost 7 seats for a total of 18, with 4 seats being held by neither party. In the House, the Democrats lost 37 seats to lower their majority to 108 of the 243, the Whigs gained 9 seats for a total of 107, and 28 seats were held by neither party. Six of these seats were held by the Nullifiers, and many of the other seats were held by the Anti-Masonic Party.

BACKGROUND

On March 4, 1837, Martin Van Buren was inaugurated as the eighth president of the United States, the first president born after the Declaration of Independence. On May 10, 1837, the panic of 1837 started. It was caused by excessive land speculation, an overextension of bank credit by New York banks without sufficient backing in gold and silver assets, and huge state debts piled up in the construction of canals and railroads. When the New York banks suspended specie (gold and silver) payments on May 10, 1837, the country was plunged into a deep depression that lasted until 1843. The economic collapse contributed to the resurgence of the Whigs in the 1840 elections.

The remaining Cherokees in Tennessee and Georgia were forced to move to reservation land on the Oklahoma frontier. Approximately 4,000 of the 14,000 Cherokees died during their forced march west, a journey called the Trail of Tears. Tensions between the United States and Canada flared on February 12, 1839, when a United States land agent was kidnapped in the disputed Aroostook territory between Maine and New Brunswick. War was averted when both sides agreed to resolve the matter before a boundary commission.

SENATE LEADERSHIP

Vice President: Richard Mentor Johnson was a former representative and senator from Kentucky who had first been elected to Congress in the Tenth Congress.

President Pro Tempore: William Rufus de Vane King (Dem., Ala.) was elected on March 7, 1837 and reelected on October 13, 1837, July 2, 1838 and February 25, 1839. [See note 4, p. xxix]

Majority Leader, Majority Whip, Minority Leader, and Minority Whip: None. These functions did not evolve into formal Senate positions until the 62nd Congress (1911-1913).

Chairmen of Selected Key Committees: [See also Organization and Administration, p. 102]

Committee on Finance: Silas Wright Jr. (Dem., N.Y.)

C H R O N O L O G Y

March 4, 1837:	The 25th Congress begins. A Special Senate Session begins.
March 7, 1837:	President Van Buren nominates, and the Senate confirms, Joel R. Poinsett to be secretary of war.
March 8, 1837:	The Senate confirms John Catron (nominated to the Supreme Court in the 24th Congress) to fill one of the two newly created seats on the Court.
March 10, 1837:	The special session of the Senate ends.
May 10, 1837:	The panic of 1837 starts.
September 4, 1837:	First session begins, and James K. Polk (Dem., Tenn.) is reelected Speaker of the House.
September 18, 1837:	President Van Buren nominates John McKinley to fill the remaining vacancy on the Supreme Court.
September 25, 1837:	The Senate confirms McKinley.
October 10, 1837:	Congress passes legislation to issue $10 million in notes to ease the panic of 1837.
October 16, 1837:	The first session ends.
December 4, 1837:	The second session begins.
June 15, 1838:	President Van Buren nominates James K. Paulding to be secretary of the Navy.
June 20, 1838:	The Senate confirms Paulding.
July 5, 1838:	President Van Buren nominates, and the Senate confirms, Felix Grundy to be attorney general.
July 9, 1838:	The second session ends.
December 3, 1838:	The third session begins.
March 3, 1839:	The third session and the 25th Congress end.

[See note 6, p. xxix]

Committee on Foreign Relations: James Buchanan (Dem., Pa.)

Committee on the Judiciary: Felix Grundy (Dem., Tenn.) and Garret D. Wall (Dem., N.J.)

Committee on Military Affairs: Thomas H. Benton (Dem., Mo.)

Committee on Naval Affairs: William Rives (Dem., Va.)

HOUSE LEADERSHIP

Speaker of the House: James K. Polk (Dem., Tenn.) was reelected Speaker on September 4, 1837. [See biographical note in 24th Congress]

Majority Leader, Majority Whip, Minority Leader, and Minority Whip: None. These functions did not evolve into formal House positions until the 56th Congress (1899-1901).

Chairmen of Selected Key Committees: [See also

TABLE OF KEY VOTES

Senate

Subject of Vote	Date of Vote	For	Against
Confirmation of Joel R. Poinsett to be Secretary of War	March 7, 1837	Passed by voice vote	
Confirmation of John Catron to Supreme Court	March 8, 1837	Passed by voice vote	
Confirmation of John McKinley to Supreme Court	September 25, 1837	Passed by voice vote	
Issuance of Treasury Notes to Ease Panic of 1837	October 10, 1837	35	6
Confirmation of James K. Paulding to be Secretary of the Navy	June 20, 1838	Passed by voice vote	
Confirmation of Felix Grundy to be Attorney General	July 5, 1838	Passed by voice vote	

House

Subject of Vote	Date of Vote	For	Against
Issuance of Treasury Notes to Ease Panic of 1837	October 10, 1837	Passed by voice vote	

[See note 7, p. xxix]

Organization and Administration, below]

Committee on Agriculture: Edmund Deberry (Whig, N.C.)

Committee on Foreign Affairs: Benjamin C. Howard (Dem., Md.)

Committee on the Judiciary: Francis Thomas (Dem., Md.)

Committee on Military Affairs: James I. McKay (Dem., N.C.)

Committee on Naval Affairs: Samuel Ingham (Dem., Conn.)

Committee on Ways and Means: Churchill C. Cambreleng (Dem., N.Y.)

ORGANIZATION AND ADMINISTRATION

There have been approximately two thousand committees throughout the history of Congress. However, the modern committee structure and the modern allocation of committee jurisdiction, seniority, and ranking minority member status was not established until after World War II. [See note 5, p. xxix]

MAJOR LEGISLATION PASSED

Panic of 1837: Congress authorized the issuance of $10 million in Treasury notes to help ease the financial crisis caused by the panic of 1837.

FAILED LEGISLATION

None of historical significance.

RELATIONS WITH
THE PRESIDENT

Martin Van Buren became president largely because he was the vice president in Andrew Jackson's second administration. The panic of 1837 took place almost immediately after Van Buren took office, hurting his popularity. Like many former vice presidents throughout American history, Van Buren found it hard to follow his successful predecessor. Van Buren would become a one-term president, with limited ambitions and achievements in Congress.

Van Buren vetoed one bill in the 25th Congress, which was a minor piece of legislation.

NOMINATIONS, APPOINTMENTS,
AND CONFIRMATIONS

The Judiciary: The Supreme Court was increased to nine justices in 1837 during the 24th Congress, but the two additional seats on the Court were not filled until the 25th Congress. President Andrew Jackson nominated John Catron on March 3, 1837, the last day of the 24th Congress. During its special session, the Senate confirmed Catron on March 8, 1837, by voice vote. President Van Buren nominated John McKinley on September 18, 1837, to fill the second remaining seat on the Court, and the Senate confirmed McKinley on September 25, 1837, by voice vote.

The Executive Branch: On March 7, 1837, President Van Buren nominated, and the Senate confirmed by voice vote, Joel R. Poinsett to be

secretary of war. On June 15, 1838, Van Buren nominated James K. Paulding to be secretary of the Navy, and on June 20, 1838, the Senate confirmed Paulding by voice vote. On July 5, 1838, Van Buren nominated, and the Senate confirmed by voice vote, Felix Grundy to be attorney general. President Van Buren did not replace several other cabinet-level officials from the previous Jackson administration, and no Senate confirmation vote was required for continuing those appointments.

IMPEACHMENTS

None.

CONSTITUTIONAL AMENDMENTS

None.

FURTHER READING

Cole, Donald. *Martin Van Buren and the American Political System.* Princeton, N.J.: Princeton University Press, 1984.

Meyer, Leland. *The Life and Times of Colonel Richard M. Johnson of Kentucky.* New York: AMS Press, 1967.

Sellers, Charles G., Jr. *James K. Polk.* Princeton, N.J.: Princeton University Press, 1957-1966 (two volumes).

The 26th Congress

MARCH 4, 1839 - MARCH 3, 1841

First Session: December 2, 1839-July 21, 1840
Second Session: December 7, 1840-March 3, 1841

In the 1838 elections for the 26th Congress, the Democrats lost 2 seats in the Senate to reduce their majority to 28 seats out of the 52. The Whigs gained 4 seats to raise their total to 22. Two seats were held by neither party. In the House, the Democrats gained 16 seats to increase their majority to 124 of the 243, and the Whigs gained 11 seats for a total of 118. One seat was not held by either party.

BACKGROUND

According to the census of 1840, the population of the United States as of June 1, 1840, was 17,069,453, resulting in a population density of 9.8 persons for each of the country's 1,749,462 square miles. This was a population increase of 32.7 percent over the 1830 census.

In 1839 the growing abolitionist movement won a victory in the nationally publicized case of the *Amistad*, a Spanish slave ship from Havana, Cuba. The slaves on board mutinied in June of 1839 and seized control of the ship. During their attempt to navigate the ship back to Africa, the slaves and the ship were seized by American authorities off Long Island, New York. The abolitionists successfully defended the slaves against attempts to return them to their masters, and by order of the Supreme Court the slaves were set free.

SENATE LEADERSHIP

Vice President: Richard Mentor Johnson, a former representative and senator from Kentucky, first had been elected to Congress in the Tenth Congress.

President Pro Tempore: William Rufus de Vane King (Dem., Ala.) was elected on July 3, 1840, and March 3, 1841.

Majority Leader, Majority Whip, Minority Leader, and Minority Whip: None. These functions did not evolve into formal Senate positions until the 62nd Congress (1911-1913).

Chairmen of Selected Key Committees: [See also Organization and Administration]

Committee on Finance: Silas Wright Jr. (Dem., N.Y.)

Committee on Foreign Relations: James Buchanan (Dem., Pa.)

Committee on the Judiciary: Garret D. Wall (Dem., N.J.)

Committee on Military Affairs: Thomas H. Benton (Dem., Mo.)

Committee on Naval Affairs: Reuel Williams (Dem., Maine)

C H R O N O L O G Y

March 4, 1839:	The 26th Congress begins.
December 2, 1839:	The first session begins.
December 16, 1839:	Robert Mercer Taliaferro Hunter (Dem., Va.) is elected Speaker of the House.
January 8, 1840:	President Van Buren nominates Henry D. Gilpin to be attorney general.
January 10, 1840:	The Senate confirms Gilpin.
June 30, 1840:	Congress passes the Independent Treasury Act of 1840.
July 21, 1840:	The first session ends.
December 7, 1840:	The second session begins.
February 25, 1841:	Supreme Court Justice Philip P. Barbour dies.
February 26, 1841:	President Van Buren nominates Peter V. Daniel to replace Barbour.
March 2, 1841:	The Senate confirms Daniel.
March 3, 1841:	The second session and the 26th Congress end.

[See note 6, p. xxix]

HOUSE LEADERSHIP

Speaker of the House: Robert Mercer Taliaferro Hunter (Dem., Va.) had been elected Speaker on December 16, 1839. Hunter was first elected to Congress in the 25th Congress, and during his political career represented the state of Virginia as both a representative and a senator. This was the only Congress in which Hunter was elected Speaker.

Majority Leader, Majority Whip, Minority Leader, and Minority Whip: None. These functions did not evolve into formal House positions until the 56th Congress (1899-1901).

Chairmen of Selected Key Committees: [See also Organization and Administration]

Committee on Agriculture: Edmund Deberry (Whig, N.C.)

Committee on Foreign Affairs: Francis W. Pickens (Dem., S.C.)

Committee on the Judiciary: John Sergeant (Whig, Pa.)

Committee on Military Affairs: Waddy Thompson Jr. (Whig, S.C.) and Cave Johnson (Dem., Tenn.)

Committee on Naval Affairs: Francis Thomas (Dem., Md.)

Committee on Ways and Means: John W. Jones (Dem., Va.)

ORGANIZATION AND ADMINISTRATION

There have been approximately two thousand committees throughout the history of Congress. However, the modern committee structure and the modern allocation of committee jurisdiction, seniority, and ranking minority member status was not established until after World War II. [See 80th Congress and subsequent chapters]

MAJOR LEGISLATION PASSED

Treasury: In the Independent Treasury Act of 1840, Congress reorganized the Treasury Department. The Treasury would now have its

TABLE OF KEY VOTES

Senate

Subject of Vote	Date of Vote	For	Against
Confirmation of Henry D. Gilpin to be Attorney General	January 10, 1840	Passed by voice vote	
Independent Treasury Act	January 24, 1840	24	18
Confirmation of Peter V. Daniel to Supreme Court	March 2, 1841	22	5

House

Subject of Vote	Date of Vote	For	Against
Independent Treasury Act	June 30, 1840	124	107

[See note 7, p. xxix]

own depository facilities, independent of state and private banks, and sub-treasuries were established in seven cities throughout the U.S. Further, all government payments were to be made in gold or silver after June 30, 1843.

FAILED LEGISLATION

None of historical significance.

RELATIONS WITH THE PRESIDENT

Martin Van Buren was elected president in 1836 largely because he was vice president in Jackson's second administration. The panic of 1837 took place almost immediately after Van Buren took office, hurting his popularity. Like many former vice presidents throughout American history, Van Buren found it hard to follow his successful predecessor and would be a one-term president, with limited ambitions and achievements in Congress. Van Buren

vetoed no legislation during the 26th Congress.

NOMINATIONS, APPOINTMENTS, AND CONFIRMATIONS

On February 25, 1841, Supreme Court Justice Philip P. Barbour died. The next day, February 26, President Van Buren nominated Peter V. Daniel to replace Barbour, and the Senate confirmed Daniel on March 2, 1841, by a 22 to 5 vote.

The Executive Branch: On January 8, 1840, President Van Buren nominated Henry D. Gilpin to be attorney general, and the Senate confirmed him by voice vote on January 10, 1840.

IMPEACHMENTS

None.

CONSTITUTIONAL AMENDMENTS

None.

FURTHER READING

Christianson, Stephen G. "U.S. v. Cinque." In *Great American Trials*, edited by Edward W. Knappman. Detroit: Gale Research, 1994.

Cole, Donald. *Martin Van Buren and the American Political System*. Princeton, N.J.: Princeton University Press, 1984.

Frank, John Paul. *Justice Daniel Dissenting: A Biography of Peter V. Daniel, 1784-1860*. Cambridge, Mass.: Harvard University Press, 1964.

Meyer, Leland. *The Life and Times of Colonel Richard M. Johnson of Kentucky*. New York: AMS Press, 1967.

The 27th Congress

MARCH 4, 1841 - MARCH 3, 1843

Special Senate Session: March 4, 1841-March 15, 1841
First Session: May 31, 1841-September 13, 1841
Second Session: December 6, 1841-August 31, 1842
Third Session: December 5, 1842-March 3, 1843

The Senate held a special session to vote on the confirmation of presidential appointees to various offices. [See note 1, p. xxix]

In the 1840 elections for the 27th Congress, the Whigs gained 6 seats in the Senate to create a new majority of 28 seats out of the 52, and the Democrats lost 6 seats reducing their total to 22. Two seats were not held by either party. In the House, the Whigs gained 15 seats to create a new majority of 133 of the 243 seats. The Democrats lost 22 seats, leaving them with a total of 102. Eight seats were not held by either party. [See notes 2 and 3, p. xxix]

BACKGROUND

On March 4, 1841, William Henry Harrison was inaugurated as the ninth president of the United States, but he caught pneumonia during the inauguration proceedings and died on April 4, 1841. Vice President John Tyler succeeded him and became the tenth president and the first vice president to take the office of president because of the incumbent's death. In 1841 Tyler vetoed two attempts by Congress to reestablish a Bank of the United States, causing everyone in Tyler's cabinet except Secretary of State Daniel Webster to resign on September 11, 1841. Also during 1841, the first American settlers reached California.

In 1842 John Fremont led an expedition to explore Wyoming and open up that area of the West for settlement. On August 9, 1842, the U.S. and Great Britain executed the Webster-Ashburton Treaty, settling a territorial dispute that had been lingering since the 22nd Congress between Maine and the Canadian province of New Brunswick. The most important legislation of the 27th Congress was a new tariff act in 1842 that raised tariff rates.

SENATE LEADERSHIP

Vice President: John Tyler served as vice president for just one month until April 4, 1841, when he became president upon the death of President William Henry Harrison, so for the remainder of the 27th Congress, there was no president of the Senate. (Until the Twenty-fifth Amendment was ratified on February 10, 1967 [See 90th Congress], there was no mechanism for filling vacancies in the office of the vice president.)

President Pro Tempore: William Rufus de Vane King (Dem., Ala.) was elected on March 4, 1841; Samuel Lewis Southard (Whig, N.J.) was elected on March 11, 1841; and Willie Person Mangum (Whig, N.C.) was elected on May 31, 1842. [See note 4, p. xxix]

Majority Leader, Majority Whip, Minority Leader, and Minority Whip: None. These func-

C H R O N O L O G Y

March 4, 1841:	The 27th Congress and a special session of the Senate begin.
March 5, 1841:	President Harrison nominates, and the Senate confirms, George E. Badger to be secretary of the Navy, John Bell to be secretary of war, John J. Crittenden to be attorney general, Thomas Ewing to be secretary of the Treasury, and Daniel Webster to be secretary of state.
March 15, 1841:	The special session of the Senate ends.
April 4, 1841:	Vice President John Tyler becomes president after the death of President William Henry Harrison.
May 31, 1841:	The first session begins and John White (Whig, Ky.) is elected Speaker of the House.
August 6, 1841:	Congress passes legislation establishing a Fiscal Bank of the United States.
August 9, 1841:	Congress repeals the Independent Treasury Act of 1840, enacted by the 26th Congress.
August 16, 1841:	President Tyler vetoes the legislation establishing a Fiscal Bank of the United States.
August 19, 1841:	The Senate fails to override President Tyler's veto of the Bank legislation.
September 3, 1841:	Congress passes legislation creating a Fiscal Corporation of the United States.
September 9, 1841:	President Tyler vetoes the Fiscal Corporation legislation.
September 11, 1841:	After President Tyler's two vetoes of legislation aimed at reestablishing a Bank of the United States, everyone in Tyler's cabinet except Secretary of State Daniel Webster resigns. President Tyler nominates Walter Forward to be secretary of the Treasury, Hugh S. Legare to be attorney general, and Abel P. Upshur to be secretary of the Navy. Tyler also nominates John McLean to be secretary of war, but McLean declines to serve.
September 13, 1841:	The Senate confirms Forward, Legare, and Upshur, and the first session ends.
December 6, 1841:	The second session begins.
December 13, 1841:	President Tyler nominates John C. Spencer to be secretary of war.
December 20, 1841:	The Senate confirms Spencer.
August 5, 1842:	Congress passes legislation raising tariffs.
August 17, 1842:	The House fails to override President Tyler's veto of the legislation establishing the Fiscal Corporation of the United States.
August 20, 1842:	The Senate ratifies the Webster-Ashburton Treaty.
August 31, 1842:	The second session ends.

(continued on page 110)

(continued from page 109)

December 5, 1842:	The third session begins.
March 2, 1843:	President Tyler nominates Caleb Cushing to be secretary of the Treasury.
March 3, 1843:	The Senate fails to confirm Cushing. President Tyler nominates, and the Senate confirms, John C. Spencer to be secretary of the Treasury. The third session and the 27th Congress end.

[See note 6, p. xxix]

tions did not evolve into formal Senate positions until the 62nd Congress (1911-1913).

Chairmen of Selected Key Committees: [See also Organization and Administration, below]

Committee on Finance: George Evans (Whig, Maine)

Committee on Foreign Relations: William C. Rives (Whig, Va.) and William Archer (Whig, Va.)

Committee on the Judiciary: John Macpherson Berrien (Whig, Ga.)

Committee on Military Affairs: William Preston (Whig, S.C.) and John J. Crittenden (Whig, Ky.)

Committee on Naval Affairs: Willie P. Mangum (Whig, N.C.) and Richard Bayard (Whig, Del.)

HOUSE LEADERSHIP

Speaker of the House: John White (Whig, Ky.) was elected Speaker on May 31, 1841. White was a lawyer who had served in the Kentucky legislature, and first had been elected to the House in the 24th Congress. The 27th Congress was the only Congress in which White was Speaker.

Majority Leader, Majority Whip, Minority Leader, and Minority Whip: None. These functions did not evolve into formal House positions until the 56th Congress (1899-1901).

Chairmen of Selected Key Committees: [See also Organization and Administration, below]

Committee on Agriculture: Edmund Deberry (Whig, N.C.)

Committee on Foreign Affairs: John Q. Adams (Whig, Mass.) and Caleb Cushing (Whig, Mass.)

Committee on the Judiciary: Daniel D. Barnard (Whig, N.Y.)

Committee on Military Affairs: William C. Dawson (Whig, Ga.) and Edward Stanly (Whig, N.C.)

Committee on Naval Affairs: Henry A. Wise (Whig, Va.)

Committee on Ways and Means: Millard Fillmore (Whig, N.Y.)

ORGANIZATION AND ADMINISTRATION

There have been approximately two thousand committees throughout the history of Congress. However, the modern committee structure and the modern allocation of committee jurisdiction, seniority, and ranking minority member status was not established until after World War II. [See note 5, p. xxix]

TABLE OF KEY VOTES

Senate

Subject of Vote	Date of Vote	For	Against
Treasury Legislation Repeal	June 9, 1841	29	18
Fiscal Bank (First Law)	July 28, 1841	26 (vetoed)	23
Overriding veto of First Fiscal Bank Law (veto sustained: not a two-thirds majority)	August 19, 1841	25	24
Fiscal Bank (Second Law)	September 3, 1841		voice vote (vetoed)
Tariff Increase	August 5, 1842	25	23
Webster-Ashburton Treaty	August 20, 1842	39	9

House

Subject of Vote	Date of Vote	For	Against
Fiscal Bank (First Law)	August 6, 1841	128	98
Treasury Legislation Repeal	August 9, 1841	134	87
Fiscal Bank (Second Law)	August 23, 1841	125	94
Tariff Increase	July 16, 1842	116	112
Overriding veto of Second Fiscal Bank Law (veto sustained: not a two-thirds majority)	August 17, 1842	92	87

[See note 7, p. xxix]

MAJOR LEGISLATION PASSED

Great Britain: The Senate confirmed the Webster-Ashburton Treaty with Great Britain [See Background, above] settling the boundary dispute between Maine and New Brunswick.

Tariffs: Congress raised tariffs on a variety of imported goods. High tariffs were popular in the North, where most American manufacturers were located and who did not want foreign competition. High tariffs were unpopular in the South, where there were few industries and higher tariffs only meant higher prices for goods.

Treasury: Congress repealed the Independent Treasury Act of 1840, enacted by the 26th Congress.

FAILED LEGISLATION

Bank of the United States: Tyler vetoed two attempts by Congress to reestablish a national bank. In the first legislative attempt, the bank would have been called the Fiscal Bank of the United States. Tyler vetoed this bill on August 16, 1841. On August 19, 1841, the Senate voted 25 in favor of overturning the veto to 24 against, thus failing to achieve the two-thirds majority necessary to overturn the veto. The failure of the override veto in the Senate made a vote in the House unnecessary. In the second legislative attempt, the name was changed to the Fiscal Corporation of the United States, but the concept was essentially the same. Tyler vetoed that bill on September 9, 1841. This time the veto was sustained in the House, where on August 17, 1842, the vote of 92 in favor of overturning the veto to 87 against similarly failed to achieve a two-thirds majority. The failure of the override vote in the House made a vote in the Senate unnecessary.

RELATIONS WITH THE PRESIDENT

President Tyler, a Whig, took office at the same time that the Whigs had won a majority in both houses of Congress. He proceeded to alienate most of his own party in Congress by opposing the Whig legislative agenda, notably the Bank of the United States. [See Failed Legislation, above] His predecessor, President Harrison vetoed no bills during his one-month presidency. During the balance of the 27th Congress, President Tyler vetoed seven bills, by far the most important of which were those on the Bank.

NOMINATIONS, APPOINTMENTS, AND CONFIRMATIONS

The Judiciary: There were no significant nominations, appointments, or confirmations to the federal judiciary during the 27th Congress.

The Executive Branch: On March 5, 1841, President Harrison nominated, and the Senate confirmed by voice vote, George E. Badger to be secretary of the Navy, John Bell to be secretary of war, John J. Crittenden to be attorney general, Thomas Ewing to be secretary of the Treasury, and Daniel Webster to be secretary of state.

After President Harrison died, the new president, John Tyler, was forced, when most of his cabinet members resigned, to reorganize the cabinet to protect his vetos of the Bank legislation. On September 11, 1841, Tyler nominated Walter Forward to be secretary of the Treasury, Hugh S. Legare to be attorney general, and Abel P. Upshur to be secretary of the Navy. Tyler also nominated John McLean to be secretary of war, but McLean declined to serve. On September 13, 1841, the Senate confirmed Upshur by vote of 23 to 5 and

Forward and Legare by a voice vote. On December 13, 1841, Tyler nominated John C. Spencer to be secretary of war, and on December 20, 1841, the Senate confirmed Spencer by voice vote.

On March 2, 1843, Tyler nominated Caleb Cushing to be secretary of the Treasury. On March 3, 1843, the Senate voted on Cushing's nomination three times, and each time Cushing failed to get Senate approval; the votes were 19 to 27, 10 to 27, and 2 to 29. Later that day, Tyler nominated John C. Spencer to the post, and within hours the Senate confirmed Spencer by a vote of 22 to 20.

IMPEACHMENTS

None

CONSTITUTIONAL AMENDMENTS

None

FURTHER READING

Cleaves, Feeman. *Old Tippecanoe: William Henry Harrison and His Time.* New York: C. Scribner's Sons, 1939.

Goebel, Dorothy. *William Henry Harrison: A Political Biography.* Philadelphia: Porcupine Press, 1974.

Miller, William Lee. *Arguing About Slavery: The Great Battle in the United States Congress.* New York: Alfred A. Knopf, 1996.

Seagar, Robert. *And Tyler Too: A Biography of John & Julia Gardiner Tyler.* Norwalk Conn.: Easton Press, 1989 (Reprint of 1963 ed.)

Tyler, Lyon. *The Letters and the Times of the Tylers.* New York: Da Capo Press, 1970 (three volumes).

The 28th Congress

MARCH 4, 1843 - MARCH 3, 1845

First Session: December 4, 1843-June 17, 1844
Second Session: December 2, 1844-March 3, 1845

In the 1842 elections for the 28th Congress, the Whigs neither gained nor lost any seats in the Senate and kept their majority of 28 seats out of the 54. The Democrats gained 3 seats, giving them a total of 25, and 1 seat was not held by either party.

Because of the 1840 census [See 26th Congress], the House was reapportioned. Due to a change in the method of apportionment, the number of members decreased to 232, but this limit was ignored when it was politically expedient to permit newly admitted states to send provisional representatives. The Democrats gained 40 seats to create a new majority of 142 of the 232 seats. The Whigs lost 54 seats, reducing their total to 79 seats. Eleven seats were not held by either party. Two of these seats were held by the Law and Order Party. [See notes 2 and 3, p. xxix]

BACKGROUND

Thanks to the expeditions of John Fremont and other government-sponsored explorers, American settlers were moving into the Pacific Northwest along the Oregon Trail and into the southwest over the Santa Fe and Mormon Trails.

The expansion of the country's boundaries was temporarily delayed on June 8, 1844, however, when the Senate refused to ratify the Texas Annexation Treaty, whereby the Republic of Texas would have become a U.S. territory. The next year President Tyler resubmitted the annex-

ation issue in the form of a joint resolution, which could be passed with a simple majority vote rather than the two-thirds necessary to ratify a treaty, and in 1845 Congress approved annexation. The abolitionists opposed Texas annexation, because it probably would become a slave state, while pro-annexation forces contended that the U.S. had to act in order to prevent the possibilities of European powers gaining influence over an independent Texas.

The 28th Congress also established the first Tuesday after the first Monday in November as the national election day for presidential elections.

SENATE LEADERSHIP

Vice President: There was no vice president because Vice President John Tyler had become president on April 4, 1841, after the death of President William Henry Harrison during the 27th Congress. (Until the Twenty-fifth Amendment was ratified on February 10, 1967 [See 90th Congress], there was no mechanism for filling vacancies in the office of the vice president.)

President Pro Tempore: Willie Person Mangum (Whig, N.C.) was a lawyer who had served as a North Carolina state legislator and state judge, and first had been elected to Congress in the 18th Congress. He was an also-ran in the presidential election of 1836, carrying only the state of South Carolina. [See note 4, p. xxix]

CHRONOLOGY

March 4, 1843:	The 28th Congress begins.
December 4, 1843:	The first session begins, and John Winston Jones (Dem., Va.) is elected Speaker of the House.
December 6, 1843:	President Tyler nominates David Henshaw to be secretary of the Navy, John Nelson to be attorney general, James M. Porter to be secretary of war, and Abel P. Upshur to be secretary of state.
December 18, 1843:	Supreme Court Associate Justice Smith Thompson dies.
January 2, 1844:	The Senate confirms Nelson and Upshur.
January 15, 1844:	The Senate rejects Henshaw.
January 30, 1844:	The Senate rejects Porter.
February 15, 1844:	President Tyler nominates, and the Senate confirms, Thomas W. Gilmer to be secretary of the Navy and William Wilkins to be secretary of war.
March 6, 1844:	President Tyler nominates, and the Senate confirms, John C. Calhoun to be secretary of state.
March 13, 1844:	President Tyler nominates John Y. Mason to be secretary of the Navy.
March 14, 1844:	The Senate confirms Mason.
April 21, 1844:	Supreme Court Associate Justice Henry Baldwin dies.
June 8, 1844:	The Senate rejects the Texas Annexation Treaty.
June 14, 1844:	President Tyler nominates James S. Green to be secretary of the Treasury.
June 15, 1844:	The Senate rejects Green. President Tyler nominates, and the Senate confirms, George M. Bibb for the position.
June 17, 1844:	The first session ends.
December 2, 1844:	The second session begins.
January 16, 1845:	Congress passes legislation fixing the date for presidential elections.
February 4, 1845:	President Tyler nominates Samuel Nelson to fill one of the two vacancies on the Supreme Court.
February 14, 1845:	The Senate confirms Nelson.
February 20, 1845:	President Tyler vetoes a bill blocking the construction of revenue cutters and steamers without prior congressional approval.
February 27, 1845:	Congress passes the Texas Annexation Resolution.
March 1, 1845:	Congress passes legislation admitting Florida and Iowa into the Union.
March 3, 1845:	For the first time in American history Congress overrides a presidential veto, and the bill on revenue cutters and steamers becomes law. The second session and the 28th Congress end.

[See note 6, p. xxix]

Majority Leader, Majority Whip, Minority Leader, and Minority Whip: None. These functions did not evolve into formal Senate positions until the 62nd Congress (1911-1913).

Chairmen of Selected Key Committees: [See also Organization and Administration, below]

Committee on Finance: George Evans (Whig, Maine)

Committee on Foreign Relations: William Archer (Whig, Va.)

Committee on the Judiciary: John Macpherson Berrien (Whig, Ga.)

Committee on Military Affairs: John J. Crittenden (Whig, Ky.)

Committee on Naval Affairs: Richard Bayard (Whig, Del.).

HOUSE LEADERSHIP

Speaker of the House: John Winston Jones (Dem., Va.) was elected Speaker on December 4, 1843. Jones was a former prosecutor who had been elected to Congress in the 24th Congress and would not seek reelection after being Speaker in this Congress.

Majority Leader, Majority Whip, Minority Leader, and Minority Whip: None. These functions did not evolve into formal House positions until the 56th Congress (1899-1901).

Chairmen of Selected Key Committees: [See also Organization and Administration, below]

Committee on Agriculture: Edmund Deberry (Whig, N.C.)

Committee on Foreign Affairs: Samuel W. Inge (Dem., Ala.)

Committee on the Judiciary: Romulus M. Saunders (Dem., N.C.) and William Wilkins (Dem., Pa.)

Committee on Military Affairs: Hugh A. Haralson (Dem., Ga.)

Committee on Naval Affairs: Henry A. Wise

(Dem., Va.), who left the Whig party after the 27th Congress to join the Democrats. Historical records indicate that William Parmenter (Dem., Mass.) also chaired the committee for a while.

Committee on Ways and Means: James I. McKay (Dem., N.C.)

ORGANIZATION AND ADMINISTRATION

There have been approximately two thousand committees throughout the history of Congress. However, the modern committee structure and the modern allocation of committee jurisdiction, seniority, and ranking minority member status was not established until after World War II [See note 5, p. xxix]

MAJOR LEGISLATION PASSED

Admission of Florida and Iowa as New States: In a combined piece of statehood legislation, Congress voted to admit both Florida and Iowa into the United States.

Elections: Congress voted to make the first Tuesday after the first Monday in November the national presidential election day.

Texas: Although the Senate rejected the Texas Annexation Treaty, Texas was ultimately admitted into the Union by means of a joint congressional resolution. [See Background, above]

FAILED LEGISLATION

None of historical significance.

RELATIONS WITH THE PRESIDENT

President Tyler, a Whig, had alienated most of his fellow party members in Congress during the 27th Congress, notably by vetoing efforts to reestablish a Bank of the United States. Tyler could not get the Texas Annexation Treaty passed in the Whig-dominated Senate, although he was subsequently able to get Texas admitted into the Union by other means. [See Background, above] Tyler vetoed three

TABLE OF KEY VOTES

Senate

Subject of Vote	Date of Vote	For	Against
Texas Annexation Treaty	June 8, 1844	16	35
Election Date	January 16, 1845	Passed by voice vote	
Texas Annexation Resolution	February 27, 1845	Passed by voice vote	
Admission of Florida and Iowa to Union	March 1, 1845	36	9
First Override of a Veto	March 3, 1845	41	1

House

Subject of Vote	Date of Vote	For	Against
Election Date	December 16, 1844	Passed by voice vote	
Texas Annexation Resolution	January 25, 1845	120	98
Admission of Florida and Iowa to Union	February 13, 1845	144	48
First Override of a Veto	March 3, 1845	127	30

[See note 7, p. xxix]

bills during the 28th Congress. Only his veto of February 20, 1845, of a bill "relating to revenue cutters and steamers" was notable and then only because it became the first presidential veto in American history to be overridden by Congress. The bill in question provided that no revenue cutter or steamer could be built unless Congress had first passed appropriations legislation funding such construction. Tyler vetoed the bill because two revenue cutters had already been contracted for, but Congress wished to assert its control over government spending and overrode the veto. On March 3, 1845, the Senate overrode the veto by a vote of 41 to 1, and the House followed suit later that day by a vote of 127 to 30.

NOMINATIONS, APPOINTMENTS, AND CONFIRMATIONS

The Judiciary: On December 18, 1843, Supreme Court Justice Smith Thompson died, and Justice Henry Baldwin died on April 21, 1844. President John Tyler only was able to nominate one justice during the 28th Congress, namely, Samuel Nelson on February 4, 1845. The Senate confirmed Nelson on February 14, 1845, by voice vote, leaving the remaining vacancy to be filled by the 29th Congress.

The Executive Branch: On December 6, 1843, President Tyler nominated David Henshaw to be secretary of the Navy, John Nelson to be attorney general, James M. Porter to be secretary of war, and Abel P. Upshur to be secretary of state. On January 2, 1844, the Senate confirmed Nelson and Upshur by voice vote, but the Senate rejected Henshaw on January 15, 1844, by a vote of 8 in favor of Henshaw's confirmation to 34 against. On January 30, 1844, the Senate also rejected Porter by a vote of 3 in favor of Porter's nomination to 38 against. On February 15, 1844, Tyler nominated, and the Senate confirmed by voice vote, Thomas W. Gilmer to be secretary of the Navy and William Wilkins to be secretary of war. In March 1844 Tyler chose a new secretary of state and secretary of the Navy. On March 6,

1844, Tyler nominated, and the Senate confirmed by voice vote, John C. Calhoun to be secretary of state. Then, on March 13, 1844, Tyler nominated John Y. Mason to be secretary of the Navy, and the next day the Senate confirmed Mason by voice vote. On June 14, 1844, Tyler nominated James S. Green to be secretary of the Treasury, but the Senate rejected Green on June 15, 1844, by voice vote. Later that day, Tyler nominated, and the Senate confirmed by voice vote, George M. Bibb to be secretary of the Treasury.

IMPEACHMENTS

None.

CONSTITUTIONAL AMENDMENTS

None.

FURTHER READING

Chitwood, Oliver Perry. *John Tyler: Champion of the Old South*. Newtown, Conn.: American Political Biography Press, 1990 (Reprint of 1939 ed.)

Seager, Robert. *And Tyler Too: A Biography of John & Julia Gardiner Tyler*. Norwalk, Conn.: Easton Press, 1989 (Reprint of 1963 ed.)

Tyler, Lyon. *The Letters and the Times of the Tylers*. New York: Da Capo Press, 1970 (three volumes).

The 29th Congress

MARCH 4, 1845 - MARCH 3, 1847

Special Senate Session: March 4, 1845-March 20, 1845
First Session: December 1, 1845-August 10, 1846
Second Session: December 7, 1846-March 3, 1847

The Senate held a special session to vote on the confirmation of presidential appointees to various offices. [See note 1, p. xxix]

In the 1844 elections for the 29th Congress, the Democrats gained 6 seats in the Senate giving them a new majority of 31 seats out of the 56. The Whigs lost 3 seats, reducing their total to 25. In the House, the Democrats gained 1 seat, increasing their majority to 143 of the 232 seats. The Whigs lost 2 seats leaving them with a total of 77 seats. Twelve seats were not held by either of the major parties. Six of these seats were held by the Know-Nothings, an anti-immigrant movement whose members were told to deny any knowledge about the organization, thus giving rise to the "Know-Nothing" label. [See notes 2 and 3, p. xxix]

BACKGROUND

On March 4, 1845, James K. Polk was inaugurated as the 11th president of the United States. Because the U.S. had approved the annexation of the Republic of Texas, which was awaiting the concurrence of the Texas legislature, Mexico severed diplomatic ties with the U.S. on March 28, 1845. On December 29, 1845, Texas was officially admitted as the 28th state of the Union. Meanwhile, revolutionary sentiment was growing amongst the American settlers in the California territory of Mexico. In May 1846, after hearing reports of Mexican military actions against Americans, Congress passed a declaration of war against Mexico. There already had been skirmishes in Texas and California. On February 23, 1847, close to the end of the 29th Congress, the U.S. Army under General Zachary Taylor won one of the decisive engagements of the war at the Battle of Buena Vista.

SENATE LEADERSHIP

Vice President: George Mifflin Dallas, a former senator from Pennsylvania and minister to Russia, served as President James Polk's vice president. Dallas later would serve as minister to Great Britain.

President Pro Tempore: Ambrose Hundley Sevier (Dem., Ark.) was elected on December 27, 1845, and David Rice Atchison (Dem., Mo.) was elected on August 8, 1846, January 11, 1847, and March 3, 1847. [See note 4, p. xxix]

Majority Leader, Majority Whip, Minority Leader, and Minority Whip: None. These functions did not evolve into formal Senate positions until the 62nd Congress (1911-1913).

Chairmen of Selected Key Committees: [See also Organization and Administration, below]

Committee on Finance: Dixon Lewis (Dem., Ala.)

Committee on Foreign Relations: William

C H R O N O L O G Y

March 4, 1845:	The 29th Congress begins, and a special session of the Senate begins.
March 5, 1845:	President Polk nominates George Bancroft to be secretary of the Navy, James Buchanan to be secretary of state, William L. Marcy to be secretary of war, John Y. Mason to be attorney general, and Robert J. Walker to be secretary of the Treasury. The Senate confirms all except Bancroft.
March 10, 1845:	The Senate confirms Bancroft.
March 20, 1845:	The special session of the Senate ends.
March 28, 1845:	Mexico severs diplomatic ties with the U.S. as the dispute over Texas grows.
September 10, 1845:	Supreme Court Justice Joseph Story dies. With a vacancy left over from the 28th Congress, there are now two vacancies on the Supreme Court.
December 1, 1845:	The first session begins, and John Wesley Davis (Dem., Ind.) is elected Speaker of the House.
December 23, 1845:	President Polk nominates Levi Woodbury to the Supreme Court.
December 29, 1845:	Texas is officially admitted as the 28th state.
January 3, 1846:	The Senate confirms Woodbury.
May 12, 1846:	Congress approves a declaration of war against Mexico.
June 18, 1846:	The Senate approves a treaty with Great Britain setting the boundary between the Oregon Territory and Canada.
July 28, 1846:	Congress passes the Walker Tariff Act.
August 3, 1846:	President Polk nominates Robert C. Grier for the remaining Supreme Court position.
August 4, 1846:	The Senate confirms Grier.
August 5, 1846:	Congress passes legislation admitting Wisconsin into the United States.
August 10, 1846:	The first session ends.
December 7, 1846:	The second session begins.
December 14, 1846:	President Polk nominates John Y. Mason to succeed George Bancroft as secretary of the Navy and Nathan Clifford to take over Mason's position as attorney general.
December 17, 1846:	The Senate confirms Mason.
December 23, 1846:	The Senate confirms Clifford.
March 3, 1847:	The second session and the 29th Congress end.

[See note 6, p. xxix]

Archer (Whig, Va.) and Ambrose Hundley Sevier (Dem., Ark.)

Committee on the Judiciary: Chester Ashley (Dem., Ark.)

Committee on Military Affairs: Thomas H. Benton (Dem., Mo.)

Committee on Naval Affairs: John Fairfield (Dem., Maine)

HOUSE LEADERSHIP

Speaker of the House: John Wesley Davis (Dem., Ind.) was elected Speaker on December 1, 1845. Davis had served as an Indiana state legislator and first had been elected to Congress in the 24th Congress. After the 29th Congress, Davis never ran for Congress again.

Majority Leader, Majority Whip, Minority Leader, and Minority Whip: None. These functions did not evolve into formal House positions until the 56th Congress (1899-1901).

Chairmen of Selected Key Committees: [See also Organization and Administration, below]

Committee on Agriculture: Joseph H. Anderson (Dem., N.Y)

Committee on Foreign Affairs: Samuel W. Inge (Dem., Ala.)

Committee on the Judiciary: George O. Rathbun (Dem., N.Y.)

Committee on Military Affairs: Hugh A. Haralson (Dem., Ga.)

Committee on Naval Affairs: Isaac E. Holmes (Dem., S.C.)

Committee on Ways and Means: James I. McKay (Dem., N.C.)

ORGANIZATION AND ADMINISTRATION

There have been approximately two thousand committees throughout the history of Congress. However, the modern committee structure and the modern allocation of committee jurisdiction, seniority, and ranking minority member status was not established until after World War II. [See note 5, p. xxix]

MAJOR LEGISLATION PASSED

Admission of Wisconsin as a New State: Congress voted to admit Wisconsin into the Union.

Declaration of War Against Mexico: Congress declared war against Mexico [See Background, above] and appropriated funds for the war effort.

Oregon: The Senate approved a treaty with Great Britain that set the 49th Parallel as the boundary line between American territory west of the Rocky Mountains and British Canada.

Tariffs: In the Walker Tariff Act, Congress reduced import duties roughly to the level of the Compromise Tariff of 1833. [See 22nd Congress]

FAILED LEGISLATION

None of historical significance.

RELATIONS WITH THE PRESIDENT

President James K. Polk came into office with two basic promises, and kept both. First, he promised to be aggressive in expanding America's frontiers, and kept that promise in this Congress by successfully pursuing the Mexican War and a treaty with Great Britain concerning Oregon. The second promise, namely, to serve only one term so that he would not be diverted by political considerations as president, would be carried out in the next Congress. Polk vetoed three bills in the 29th Congress. All were minor pieces of legislation.

NOMINATIONS, APPOINTMENTS, AND CONFIRMATIONS

The Judiciary: On September 10, 1845, Supreme Court Justice Joseph Story died, which now left two vacancies on the Supreme Court. [See 28th

TABLE OF KEY VOTES

Senate

Subject of Vote	Date of Vote	For	Against
Confirmation of Cabinet Nominees	March 5, 1845	Passed by voice vote	
Confirmation of George Bancroft to be Secretary of the Navy	March 10, 1845	Passed by voice vote	
Confirmation of Levi Woodbury to Supreme Court	January 3, 1846	Passed by voice vote	
War with Mexico	May 12, 1846	40	2
Oregon Treaty	June 18, 1846	41	14
Tariff Reduction	July 28, 1846	28	27
Confirmation of Robert C. Grier to Supreme Court	August 4, 1846	Passed by voice vote	
Admission of Wisconsin to Union	August 5, 1846	Passed by voice vote	
Confirmation of John Y. Mason to be Secretary of the Navy	December 17, 1846	Passed by voice vote	
Confirmation of Nathan Clifford to be Attorney General	December 23, 1846	Passed by voice vote	

House

Subject of Vote	Date of Vote	For	Against
War with Mexico	May 11, 1846	174	14
Admission of Wisconsin to Union	June 9, 1846	Passed by voice vote	
Tariff Reduction	July 3, 1846	114	95

[See note 7, p. xxix]

Congress] President Polk nominated Levi Woodbury on December 23, 1845, and the Senate confirmed Woodbury on January 3, 1846, by voice vote. Polk nominated Robert C. Grier for the remaining Court position on August 3, 1846, and the Senate confirmed him the next day by voice vote.

The Executive Branch: On March 5, 1845, President Polk nominated George Bancroft to be secretary of the Navy, James Buchanan to be secretary of state, William L. Marcy to be secretary of war, John Y. Mason to be attorney general, and Robert J. Walker to be secretary of the Treasury. That same day, the Senate confirmed by voice vote all of the nominees except Bancroft. Bancroft was confirmed by voice vote on March 10, 1845.

On December 14, 1846, Polk nominated John Y. Mason to succeed George Bancroft as secretary of the Navy and Nathan Clifford to take over Mason's position as attorney general. The Senate confirmed both men by voice vote, Mason on December 17, 1846, and Clifford on December 23, 1846.

IMPEACHMENTS

None.

CONSTITUTIONAL AMENDMENTS

None.

FURTHER READING

Belohlavek, John M. *George Mifflin Dallas: Jacksonian Patrician*. State College, Pa.: Pennsylvania State University Press, 1977.

Eisenhower, John S.D. *So Far From God: The U.S. War With Mexico, 1846-1848*. New York: Random House, 1989.

Sellers, Charles G. Jr. *James K. Polk*. Princeton, N.J.: Princeton University Press, 1957-1966 (two volumes).

The 30th Congress

MARCH 4, 1847-MARCH 3, 1849

First Session: December 6, 1847-August 14, 1848
Second Session: December 4, 1848-March 3, 1849

In the 1846 elections for the 30th Congress, the Democrats gained 5 seats in the Senate to increase their majority to 36 seats out of the 58. The Whigs lost 4 seats, leaving them with a total of 21. One seat was held by an "Independent Democrat." In the House, the Whigs gained 38 seats to create a new, if slim, majority of 115 of the 232 seats. The Democrats lost 35 seats, reducing their total to 108 seats. Nine seats were not held by either party. Two of these seats were held by Independent Democrats and 1 by a Know Nothing. [See notes 2 and 3, p. xxix]

BACKGROUND

As the 30th Congress began, the United States was at war with Mexico, a war triggered over America's annexation of the former Mexican territory and once independent Republic of Texas. On March 29, 1847, General Winfield Scott captured the fortifications at Vera Cruz on the gulf coast of Mexico and began to move on Mexico City, the capital. After several victories, General Scott's army and a force of Marines took Mexico City on September 14, 1847. In 1848 the Mexican War ended according to the terms of the Treaty of Guadalupe-Hidalgo, which provided for the massive Mexican cession of over one-half million square miles of territory to the U.S. In addition to most of the Southwest, the Mexican cession included California, where the discovery of gold in 1848 triggered a gold rush and spurred further settlement.

In July 1848 Susan B. Anthony and other pioneering feminists met to discuss women's rights at the famous Seneca Falls convention.

SENATE LEADERSHIP

Vice President: George Mifflin Dallas, a former senator from Pennsylvania and minister to Russia, served as President James K. Polk's vice president. Dallas would later serve as minister to Great Britain.

President Pro Tempore: David Rice Atchison (Dem., Mo.) was elected on February 2, 1848, June 1, 1848, June 26, 1848, July 29, 1848, December 26, 1848, and March 2, 1849. [See note 4, p. xxix]

Majority Leader, Majority Whip, Minority Leader, and Minority Whip: None. These functions did not evolve into formal Senate positions until the 62nd Congress (1911-1913).

Chairmen of Selected Key Committees: [See also Organization and Administration, below]

Committee on Finance: Charles Atherton (Dem., N.H.)

Committee on Foreign Relations: Edward Hannegan (Dem., Ind.)

Committee on the Judiciary: Andrew Butler (Dem., S.C.)

Committee on Military Affairs: Thomas H. Benton (Dem., Mo.)

C H R O N O L O G Y

March 4, 1847:	The 30th Congress begins.
December 6, 1847:	The first session begins, and Robert Charles Winthrop (Whig, Mass.) is elected Speaker of the House.
March 10, 1848:	The Senate ratifies the Treaty of Guadalupe-Hidalgo, ending the Mexican War.
June 3, 1848:	The Senate ratifies the Treaty of New Granada, giving the U.S. a right-of-way across the Isthmus of Panama.
June 15, 1848:	President Polk nominates Isaac Toucey to be attorney general.
June 21, 1848:	The Senate confirms Toucey.
August 10, 1848:	Congress passes legislation establishing a government in the Oregon Territory.
August 14, 1848:	The first session ends.
December 4, 1848:	The second session begins.
March 3, 1849:	Congress establishes the department of the Interior. The second session and the 30th Congress end.

[See note 6, p. xxix]

Committee on Naval Affairs: David Yulee (Dem., Fla.)

HOUSE LEADERSHIP

Speaker of the House: Robert Charles Winthrop (Whig, Mass.) was elected Speaker on December 6, 1847. He was a former member of the Massachusetts state legislature and first had been elected to Congress in the 26th Congress. The 30th Congress was his only Congress as Speaker.

Majority Leader, Majority Whip, Minority Leader, and Minority Whip: None. These functions did not evolve into formal House positions until the 56th Congress (1899-1901).

Chairmen of Selected Key Committees: [See also Organization and Administration, below]

Committee on Agriculture: Hugh White (Whig, N.Y.)

Committee on Foreign Affairs: Truman Smith (Whig, Conn.)

Committee on the Judiciary: Joseph R. Ingersoll (Whig, Pa.)

Committee on Military Affairs: John M. Botts (Whig, Va.)

Committee on Naval Affairs: Thomas Butler King (Whig, Ga.)

Committee on Ways and Means: Samuel F. Vinton (Whig, Ohio)

ORGANIZATION AND ADMINISTRATION

There have been approximately two thousand committees throughout the history of Congress. However, the modern committee structure and the modern allocation of committee jurisdiction,

TABLE OF KEY VOTES

Senate

Subject of Vote	Date of Vote	For	Against
Treaty of Guadalupe-Hidalgo	March 10, 1848	38	14
Panama Treaty	June 3, 1848	29	7
Confirmation of Isaac Toucey as Attorney General	June 21, 1848	Passed by voice vote	
Oregon Territory	August 10, 1848	Passed by voice vote	
Department of the Interior Established	March 3, 1849	31	25

House

Subject of Vote	Date of Vote	For	Against
Oregon Territory	August 2, 1848	128	71
Department of the Interior Established	February 15, 1849	112	78

[See note 7, p. xxix]

seniority, and ranking minority member status was not established until after World War II. [See note 5, p. xxix]

MAJOR LEGISLATION PASSED

Department of the Interior: Congress changed the name of the Home Department to the department of the Interior, and consolidated several other government agencies within that department.

Mexican War: The Senate confirmed the Treaty of Guadalupe-Hidalgo, which ended the Mexican War. [See Background, above]

Oregon: Congress established a government for the Territory of Oregon, and outlawed slavery within the territory.

Panama: The Senate confirmed the Treaty of New Granada, which gave the United States a right-of-way across the Isthmus of Panama.

FAILED LEGISLATION

None of historical significance.

RELATIONS WITH THE PRESIDENT

President Polk had been so successful in pursuing his 1844 campaign promise to expand America's frontiers at the expense of her neighbors that, when the Treaty of Guadalupe-Hidalgo went to the senate, he had to restrain his fellow Democrats from demanding the total annexation of Mexico. Polk succeeded in getting the Treaty ratified and, when the Congress came to a close, also kept his campaign pledge to not run for a second term. Polk vetoed no legislation during the 30th Congress.

NOMINATIONS, APPOINTMENTS, AND CONFIRMATIONS

The Judiciary: There were no significant nominations, appointments, or confirmations in the federal judiciary during the 30th Congress.

The Executive Branch: On June 15, 1848, President Polk nominated Isaac Toucey to succeed Nathan Clifford as attorney general. On June 21, 1848, the Senate confirmed Toucey by voice vote.

IMPEACHMENTS

None.

CONSTITUTIONAL AMENDMENTS

None.

FURTHER READING

Belohlavek, John M. *George Mifflin Dallas: Jacksonian Patrician.* State College, Pa.: Pennsylvania State University Press, 1977.

Eisenhower, John S.D. *So Far From God: The U.S. War With Mexico, 1846-1848.* New York: Random House, 1989.

Sellers, Charles G. Jr. *James K. Polk.* Princeton, N.J.: Princeton University Press, 1957 1966 (two volumes).

Winthrop, Robert Jr. *Memoir of Robert Charles Winthrop.* Boston: Little, Brown and Co., 1897.

The 31st Congress

MARCH 4, 1849 - MARCH 3, 1851

Special Senate Session: March 5, 1849-March 23, 1849
First Session: December 3, 1849-September 30, 1850
Second Session: December 2, 1850-March 3, 1851

The Senate held a special session to vote on the confirmation of presidential appointees to various offices. [See note 1, p. xxix]

In the 1848 elections for the 31st Congress, the Democrats lost 1 seat in the Senate to reduce their majority to 35 seats out of the 62. The Whigs gained 4 seats to give them a total of 25. Two seats were held by the Free Soil Party. In the House, the Democrats gained 4 seats to give them a new majority of 112 of the 232. The Whigs lost 6 seats leaving them with 109 seats. Eleven seats were not held by either of the major parties. Nine of these seats were held by the Free Soil Party, and 1 was held by a Know-Nothing. [See notes 2 and 3, p. xxix]

BACKGROUND

According to the census of 1850, the population of the United States as of June 1, 1850, was 23,191,876, resulting in a population density of 7.9 persons for each of the country's 2,940,042 square miles. This was a population increase of 35.9 percent over the 1840 census. Population density had decreased from the 9.8 persons per square mile of the 1840 census, however, because the Mexican land cession of 1848 increased the territory of the U.S. by 59.5 percent. [See 30th Congress] Zachary Taylor was inaugurated as the 12th president of the United States on March 5, 1849, and Millard Fillmore became the 13th pres-

ident when Taylor died on July 9, 1850.

In 1850 the number of settlers in the West was increasing rapidly, due to the new land available in the Mexican cession and the gold rush in California. There was a new North-South political crisis in Congress, however, due to the battle over whether newly admitted states in the Mexican cession region would be slave states or free states. The result was the Compromise of 1850, in which both sides won some victories. The North got the admission of California as a free state and the abolition of the slave trade in the District of Columbia. The South got a tough Fugitive Slave Law and legislation providing that New Mexico and Utah would, when Congress authorized their statehood, be admitted as free or slave states in accordance with their future state constitutions. The Fugitive Slave Law was extremely unpopular throughout the North, and many states passed legislation designed to help fugitive slaves circumvent the federal law.

SENATE LEADERSHIP

Vice President: Millard Fillmore was vice president until he became president after the July 9, 1850 death of President Zachary Taylor. (Until the Twenty-fifth Amendment was ratified on February 10, 1967, [See 90th Congress] there was no mechanism for filling vacancies in the office of the vice president, so there was no president of the Senate after Taylor's death.)

C H R O N O L O G Y

March 4, 1849:	The 31st Congress begins.
March 5, 1849:	A special session of the Senate begins.
March 6, 1849:	President Taylor nominates John M. Clayton to be secretary of state, George W. Crawford to be secretary of war, Thomas Ewing to be secretary of the Interior, Reverdy Johnson to be attorney general, William M. Meredith to be secretary of the Treasury and William B. Preston to be secretary of the Navy.
March 7, 1849:	The Senate confirms all six men.
March 23, 1849:	The special session of the Senate ends.
December 3, 1849:	The first session begins.
December 22, 1849:	Howell Cobb (Dem., Ga.) is elected Speaker of the House.
April 17, 1850:	Senators Thomas H. Benton (Dem., Mo.) and Henry Foote (Dem., Miss.) have a widely publicized confrontation in the Senate chamber.
May 22, 1850:	The Senate ratifies the Clayton-Bulwer Treaty with Great Britain providing for cooperation and joint control in the construction of a canal across Central America to link the Atlantic and Pacific Oceans.
July 9, 1850:	President Zachary Taylor dies and Vice President Millard Fillmore becomes the next president.
July 20, 1850:	President Fillmore nominates, and the Senate confirms, Thomas Corwin to be secretary of the Treasury, John J. Crittenden to be attorney general, William A. Graham to be secretary of the Navy, and Daniel Webster to be secretary of state.
August 15, 1850:	President Fillmore nominates, and the Senate confirms, Charles M. Conrad to be secretary of war and Thomas M. T. McKennon to be secretary of the Interior.
September 6, 1850:	Congress passes the Texas and New Mexico Act.
September 7, 1850:	Congress passes legislation admitting California into the United States as a state, and admitting Utah as a territory.
September 11, 1850:	President Fillmore nominates Alexander H. H. Stuart as the new secretary of the Interior.
September 12, 1850:	Congress passes the Fugitive Slave Act. The Senate confirms Stuart.
September 17, 1850:	Congress passes the District of Columbia Slave Trade Act.
September 30, 1850:	The first session ends.
December 2, 1850:	The second session begins.
March 3, 1851:	The second session and the 31st Congress end.

[See note 6, p. xxix]

President Pro Tempore: David Rice Atchison (Dem., Mo.) was elected on March 5, 1849, and March 16, 1849. William Rufus de Vane King (Dem., Ala.) was elected on May 6, 1850, and July 11, 1850. [See note 4, p. xxix]

Majority Leader, Majority Whip, Minority Leader, and Minority Whip: None. These functions did not evolve into formal Senate positions until the 62nd Congress (1911-1913).

Chairmen of Selected Key Committees: [See also Organization and Administration, below]

Committee on Finance: Daniel Dickinson (Dem., N.Y.) and Robert M. T. Hunter (Dem., Va.)

Committee on Foreign Relations: William R. King (Dem., Ala.) and Henry S. Foote (Dem., Miss.)

Committee on the Judiciary: Andrew Butler (Dem., S.C.)

Committee on Military Affairs: Jefferson Davis (Dem., Miss.)

Committee on Naval Affairs: David Yulee (Dem., Fla.)

HOUSE LEADERSHIP

Speaker of the House: Howell Cobb (Dem., Ga.) was elected Speaker on December 22, 1849. Cobb, a former lawyer, first was elected to Congress in the 28th Congress. After the 31st Congress, Cobb left Congress to become the governor of Georgia.

Majority Leader, Majority Whip, Minority Leader, and Minority Whip: None. These functions did not evolve into formal House positions until the 56th Congress (1899-1901).

Chairmen of Selected Key Committees: [See also Organization and Administration, below]

Committee on Agriculture: Nathaniel S. Littlefield (Dem., Maine)

Committee on Foreign Affairs: John A. McClernand (Dem., Ill.)

Committee on the Judiciary: Unknown.

Committee on Military Affairs: Armistead Burt (Dem., S.C.)

Committee on Naval Affairs: Frederick P. Stanton (Dem., Tenn.).

Committee on Ways and Means: Thomas H. Bayly (Dem., Va.)

ORGANIZATION AND ADMINISTRATION

There have been approximately two thousand committees throughout the history of Congress. However, the modern committee structure and the modern allocation of committee jurisdiction, seniority, and ranking minority member status was not established until after World War II. [See note 5, p. xxix]

MAJOR LEGISLATION PASSED

Compromise of 1850: The Compromise of 1850 [See Background, above] was composed of five pieces of legislation. First, California was admitted to the Union as a free state. Second, in the District of Columbia Slave Trade Act, Congress abolished the slave trade in the District of Columbia. Third, Congress passed a tough Fugitive Slave Act, which also made it a crime to harbor or assist fugitive slaves. Fourth, under the Utah Act, Utah was to be admitted to the Union as a territory, and its free or slave status would be determined by the voters of Utah when they enacted their state constitution. Fifth, under the Texas and New Mexico Act, Congress gave Texas $10 million as compensation for surrendering claims to territory in New Mexico, and admitted New Mexico to the Union as a territory with its free or slave status to be determined by the voters in their state constitution.

Foreign Policy: Congress approved the Clayton-Bulwer Treaty, which provided for mutual cooperation between the United States and Great Britain and joint control by the two countries in the construction of a canal through Central America linking the Atlantic and Pacific Oceans. The treaty was never implemented, however, and it would be decades before the Panama Canal was built.

TABLE OF KEY VOTES

Senate

Subject of Vote	Date of Vote	For	Against
Clayton-Bulwer Treaty	May 22, 1850	42	11
Admission of Utah as a territory	August 1, 1850	Passed by voice vote	
Texas and New Mexico Act	August 9, 1850	30	20
Admission of California to the Union	August 14, 1850	34	18
Fugitive Slave Act	August 26, 1850	Passed by voice vote	
District of Columbia Slave Trade Ban	September 16, 1850	33	19

House

Subject of Vote	Date of Vote	For	Against
Texas and New Mexico Act	September 6, 1850	108	97
Admission of California to the Union	September 7, 1850	150	56
Admission of Utah as a territory	September 7, 1850	97	85
Fugitive Slave Act	September 12, 1850	109	76
District of Columbia Slave Trade Ban	September 17, 1850	124	59

[See note 7, p. xxix]

FAILED LEGISLATION

None of historical significance.

RELATIONS WITH THE PRESIDENT

The 31st Congress coincided with the tenures of two of the most obscure presidents of American history, Zachary Taylor and Millard Fillmore. Taylor died after a little more than a year in office [See Background, above], and Vice President Fillmore became president. Fillmore supported the congressional legislation known as the Compromise of 1850. Neither Taylor nor Fillmore vetoed any legislation during the 31st Congress.

NOMINATIONS, APPOINTMENTS, AND CONFIRMATIONS

The Judiciary: There were no significant nominations, appointments, or confirmations in the federal judiciary during the 31st Congress.

The Executive Branch: President Taylor nominated his cabinet on March 6, 1849: John M. Clayton to be secretary of state, George W. Crawford to be secretary of war, Thomas Ewing to be secretary of the Interior, Reverdy Johnson to be attorney general, William M. Meredith to be secretary of the Treasury, and William B. Preston to be secretary of the Navy. On March 7, 1849, the Senate confirmed all six men by voice vote.

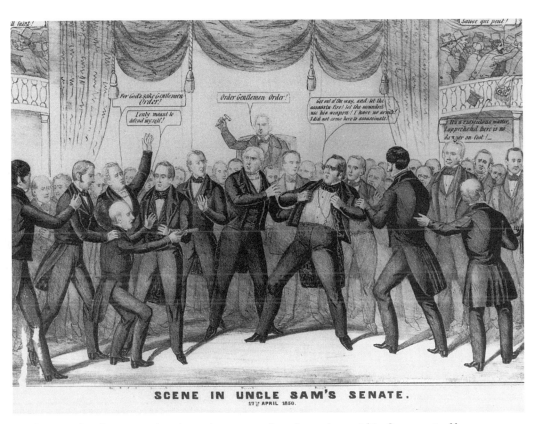

SCENE IN UNCLE SAM'S SENATE.
17th APRIL 1850.

North versus South tensions deteriorate into personal confrontations within Congress itself. See Scandals, below.

After Taylor died, President Fillmore reorganized the cabinet. On July 20, 1850, Fillmore nominated, and the Senate confirmed by voice vote, Thomas Corwin to be secretary of the Treasury, John J. Crittenden to be attorney general, William A. Graham to be secretary of the Navy, and Daniel Webster to be secretary of state. On August 15, 1850, Fillmore nominated, and the Senate confirmed by voice vote, Charles M. Conrad to be secretary of war and Thomas M. T. McKennon to be secretary of the Interior. On September 11, 1850, Fillmore nominated Alexander H. H. Stuart to succeed McKennon as secretary of the Interior, and on September 12, 1850, the Senate confirmed Stuart by voice vote.

IMPEACHMENTS

None.

CONSTITUTIONAL AMENDMENTS

None.

SCANDALS

The issue of slavery was raising tensions and causing personal quarrels in Congress. During the debates in Congress over the Compromise of 1850, Senators Thomas H. Benton (Dem., Mo.) and Henry Foote (Dem., Miss.) made increasingly hostile remarks toward each other. On April 17, 1850, Foote interrupted Benton during a speech, but stopped when Benton moved through the Senate chamber toward Foote. Foote retreated, and drew his pistol. Fortunately, several other senators were able to restrain Benton and Foote, and neither was hurt. Their confrontation was widely publicized in the press.

FURTHER READING

Grayson, Benson Lee. *The Unknown President: The Administration of President Millard Fillmore*. Washington, D.C.: University Press of America, 1981.

Hamilton, Holman. *Prologue to Conflict: The Crisis and Compromise of 1850*. Lexington, Ky.: University of Kentucky Press, 1964.

Simpson, John E. *Howell Cobb: The Politics of Ambition*. Chicago: Adams Press, 1973.

The 32nd Congress

MARCH 4, 1851 - MARCH 3, 1853

Special Senate Session: March 4, 1851-March 13, 1851
First Session: December 1, 1851-August 31, 1852
Second Session: December 6, 1852-March 3, 1853

The Senate held a special session to vote on the confirmation of presidential appointees to various offices. [See note 1, p. xxix]

In the 1850 elections for the 32nd Congress, the Democrats neither lost nor gained any seats in the Senate, and kept their majority of 35 seats out of the 62. The Whigs lost 1 seat, reducing their total to 24. Three seats were not held by either of the two major parties, and were held by the Free Soil Party. In the House, the membership increased to 233. The Democrats gained 28 seats to increase their majority to 140 of the 233. The Whigs lost 21 seats, which reduced their total to 88 seats. Five seats were not held by either party. Of these seats, 4 were held by the Free Soil Party. [See notes 2 and 3, p. xxix]

BACKGROUND

A fire broke out in the Library of Congress on December 24, 1851, that destroyed approximately two-thirds of the invaluable historic documents stored there. Also during the 32nd Congress, in response to the rapid American settlement of the West Coast, Congress formed the Washington Territory out of the Oregon Territory. Finally, Congress funded a survey to find the best route for a future transcontinental railroad.

SENATE LEADERSHIP

Vice President: None. Millard Fillmore had become president during the 31st Congress after the death on July 9, 1850, of President Zachary Taylor. (Until the Twenty-fifth Amendment was ratified on February 10, 1967 [See 90th Congress], there was no mechanism for filling vacancies in the office of the vice president, so there was no president of the Senate during the 32nd Congress.)

President Pro Tempore: William Rufus de Vane King (Dem., Ala.) served as a president pro tempore until December 20, 1852, when he resigned. King was a veteran in Congress. He first had been elected to Congress in the 12th Congress to represent North Carolina, but later moved to Alabama. After Alabama was admitted to the Union in 1819, King was elected to Congress again. David Rice Atchison (Dem., Mo.) was elected the new president pro tempore on the same day, December 20, that King resigned. Atchison had served in the Senate since 1843. [See note 4, p. xxix]

Majority Leader, Majority Whip, Minority Leader, and Minority Whip: None. These functions did not evolve into formal Senate positions until the 62nd Congress (1911-1913).

Chairmen of Selected Key Committees: [See also Organization and Administration, p. 135]

Committee on Finance: Robert M. T. Hunter (Dem., Va.)

Committee on Foreign Relations: James Mason (Dem., Va.)

CHRONOLOGY

March 4, 1851:	The 32nd Congress and a special session of the Senate begin.
March 13, 1851:	The special session of the Senate ends.
September 4, 1851:	Supreme Court Justice Levi Woodbury dies.
December 1, 1851:	The first session begins, and Linn Boyd (Dem., Ky.) is elected Speaker of the House.
December 11, 1851:	President Fillmore nominates Benjamin R. Curtis to replace Woodbury.
December 20, 1851:	The Senate confirms Curtis.
July 19, 1852:	Supreme Court Justice John McKinley dies and is not replaced until the 33rd Congress.
July 22, 1852:	President Fillmore nominates, and the Senate confirms, John P. Kennedy to be secretary of the Navy.
August 31, 1852:	The first session ends.
December 6, 1852:	The second session begins.
December 7, 1852:	President Fillmore nominates Edward Everett to be secretary of state.
December 9, 1852:	The Senate confirms Everett.
February 26, 1853:	Congress authorizes a transcontinental railroad survey.
March 2, 1853:	Congress creates the Washington Territory.
March 3, 1853:	The second session and the 32nd Congress end.

[See note 6, p. xxix]

Committee on the Judiciary: Andrew Butler (Dem., S.C.)

Committee on Military Affairs: James Shields (Dem., Ill.)

Committee on Naval Affairs: William Gwin (Dem., Cal.)

HOUSE LEADERSHIP

Speaker of the House: Linn Boyd (Dem., Ky.) was elected Speaker on December 1, 1851. Boyd first had been elected to Congress in the 24th Congress, and was Speaker in the 32nd and 33rd Congresses.

Majority Leader, Majority Whip, Minority Leader, and Minority Whip: None. These functions did not evolve into formal House positions until the 56th Congress (1899-1901).

Chairmen of Selected Key Committees: [See also Organization and Administration, p. 135]

Committee on Agriculture: John G. Floyd (Dem., N.Y.)

Committee on Foreign Affairs: Thomas H. Bayly (Dem., Va.)

Committee on the Judiciary: James Thompson (Dem., Pa.) and James X. McLanahan (Dem., Pa.)

Committee on Military Affairs: Armistead Burt (Dem., S.C.) and William H. Bissell (Dem., Ill.)

Committee on Naval Affairs: Frederick P. Stanton (Dem., Tenn.)

Committee on Ways and Means: George S. Houston (Dem., Ala.)

TABLE OF KEY VOTES

Senate

Subject of Vote	Date of Vote	For	Against
Confirmation of Benjamin R. Curtis to Supreme Court	December 20, 1851	Passed by voice vote	
Confirmation of John P. Kennedy to be Secretary of the Navy	July 22, 1852	Passed by voice vote	
Confirmation of Edward Everett to be Secretary of State	December 9, 1852	Passed by voice vote	
Transcontinental Railroad Survey	February 26, 1853	Passed by voice vote	
Washington Territory Act	March 2, 1853	Passed by voice vote	

House

Subject of Vote	Date of Vote	For	Against
Washington Territory Act	February 10, 1853	129	29
Transcontinental Railroad Survey	February 11, 1853	Passed by voice vote	

[See note 7, p. xxix]

ORGANIZATION AND ADMINISTRATION

There have been approximately two thousand committees throughout the history of Congress. However, the modern committee structure and the modern allocation of committee jurisdiction, seniority, and ranking minority member status was not established until after World War II. [See note 5, p. xxix]

MAJOR LEGISLATION PASSED

Transcontinental Railroad Survey: Congress funded a survey to find the best route for a potential transcontinental railroad.

Washington Territory: Congress formed a separate Washington Territory out of the Oregon Territory.

FAILED LEGISLATION

None of historical significance.

RELATIONS WITH THE PRESIDENT

This was the last Congress of President Millard Fillmore, a one-term president who had become president during the previous Congress because he was the vice president when President Zachary Taylor died. He was not renominated by his party in the presidential election of 1852. Given the limited legislative activity of the 32nd Congress, relations between Fillmore and the 32nd Congress were neither good nor bad. Fillmore vetoed no legislation during the 32nd Congress.

NOMINATIONS, APPOINTMENTS, AND CONFIRMATIONS

The Judiciary: On September 4, 1851, Supreme Court Justice Levi Woodbury died. President Millard Fillmore nominated Benjamin R. Curtis on December 11, 1851, to replace Woodbury, and on December 20, 1851, the Senate confirmed him by voice vote. On July 19, 1852, Justice John McKinley died, and was not replaced until the 33rd Congress.

The Executive Branch: On July 22, 1852, President Fillmore nominated, and the Senate confirmed, John P. Kennedy to be secretary of the Navy. On December 7, 1852, Fillmore nominated Edward Everett to be secretary of state, and on December 9, 1852, the Senate confirmed him by voice vote.

IMPEACHMENTS

None.

CONSTITUTIONAL AMENDMENTS

None.

FURTHER READING

Grayson, Benson Lee. *The Unknown President: The Administration of President Millard Fillmore*. Washington, D.C.: University Press of America, 1981.

Rayback, Robert J. *Millard Fillmore: Biography of a President*. Norwalk, Conn.: Easton Press, 1989 (Reprint of 1959 ed.)

Scarry, Robert J. *Millard Fillmore, 13th President of the United States*. Moravia, N.Y.: R. J. Scarry, 1982.

Smith, Elbert B. *The Presidencies of Zachary Taylor & Millard Fillmore*. Lawrence, Kan.: University Press of Kansas, 1988.

The 33rd Congress

MARCH 4, 1853 - MARCH 3, 1855

Special Senate Session: *March 4, 1853-April 11, 1853*
First Session: *December 5, 1853-August 7, 1854*
Second Session: *December 4, 1854-March 3, 1855*

The Senate held a special session to vote on the confirmation of presidential appointees to various offices. [See note 1, p. xxix]

In the 1852 elections for the 33rd Congress, the Democrats gained 3 seats in the Senate, increasing their majority to 38 seats out of the 62. The Whigs lost 2 seats, reducing their total to 22. Two seats were held by the Free Soil Party. Because of the 1850 census [See 31st Congress], the House was reapportioned, and the membership increased to 237. The Democrats gained 19 seats to increase their majority to 159 of the 237. The Whigs lost 17 seats, leaving them with a total of 71 seats. Seven seats were not held by either of the two major parties. Of these seats, 4 were held by the Free Soil Party. [See notes 2 and 3, p. xxix]

BACKGROUND

On March 4, 1853, Franklin Pierce was inaugurated as the 14th president of the United States. American explorers now were crossing the world. The second Arctic expedition in four years left on May 31, 1853, and Commodore Matthew Perry entered Tokyo harbor on July 8, 1853, with a squadron of ships. Congress's interest in a transcontinental railroad, first expressed in the 32nd Congress, led to the Gadsden Purchase Treaty. The treaty was negotiated by U.S. envoy James Gadsden and led to the purchase from Mexico of 29,644 square miles of land that today comprises the southern portion of Arizona and New Mexico. The territory was considered a desirable route for the Southern Pacific Railroad.

In 1854 the Kansas-Nebraska Act, which provided that the residents of the Kansas and Nebraska territories could decide for themselves the question of free or slave state status, was passed, leading to years of violence. In "Bleeding Kansas," the fighting between pro and antislavery factions was particularly fierce and frequently led to murder. On July 6, 1854, the Republican Party was formed from the old Whig Party, northern Democrats, and various third-party groups. The Republicans backed abolition and opposed the Kansas-Nebraska Act.

SENATE LEADERSHIP

Vice President: William Rufus de Vane King served as vice president until his death on April 18, 1853, before the first session of the 33rd Congress began. (Until the Twenty-fifth Amendment was ratified on February 10, 1967 [See 90th Congress], there was no mechanism for filling vacancies in the office of the vice president, so there was no president of the Senate during the 33rd Congress.)

President Pro Tempore: David Rice Atchison (Dem., Mo.) was elected on March 4, 1853; Lewis Cass (Dem., Mich.) was elected on December 4, 1854; and Jesse David Bright (Dem., Ind.) was

C H R O N O L O G Y

March 4, 1853: The 33rd Congress and a special session of the Senate begin.

March 7, 1853: President Pierce nominates his cabinet, and the Senate confirms all of the nominees.

March 22, 1853: President Pierce nominates John A. Campbell to fill a vacancy on the Supreme Court left unfilled at the end of the 32nd Congress.

March 25, 1853: The Senate confirms Campbell.

April 11, 1853: The special session of the Senate ends.

April 18, 1853: Vice President William Rufus de Vane King dies.

December 5, 1853: The first session begins, and Linn Boyd (Dem., Ky.) is reelected Speaker of the House.

April 25, 1854: The Senate ratifies the Gadsden Treaty with Mexico.

May 25, 1854: Congress passes the Kansas-Nebraska Act.

July 15, 1854: The Senate ratifies the Treaty of Kanagawa, opening two Japanese ports to American shipping.

August 7, 1854: The first session ends.

December 4, 1854: The second session begins.

December 20, 1854: Congress passes the Citizenship Act.

February 23, 1855: Congress establishes the Court of Claims.

March 3, 1855: The second session and the 33rd Congress end.

[See note 6, p. xxix]

---

elected on December 5, 1854. [See note 4, p. xxix]

Majority Leader, Majority Whip, Minority Leader, and Minority Whip: None. These functions did not evolve into formal Senate positions until the 62nd Congress (1911-1913).

Chairmen of Selected Key Committees: [See also Organization and Administration, p. 139]

Committee on Finance: Robert M. T. Hunter (Dem., Va.)

Committee on Foreign Relations: James Mason (Dem., Va.)

Committee on the Judiciary: Andrew Butler (Dem., S.C.)

Committee on Military Affairs: James Shields (Dem., Ill.)

Committee on Naval Affairs: William Gwin (Dem., Cal.)

HOUSE LEADERSHIP

Speaker of the House: Linn Boyd (Dem., Ky.) was reelected Speaker on December 5, 1853. Boyd first had been elected to Congress in the 24th Congress, and was Speaker in the 32nd and 33rd Congresses.

Majority Leader, Majority Whip, Minority Leader, and Minority Whip: None. These functions did not evolve into formal House positions until the 56th Congress (1899-1901).

Chairmen of Selected Key Committees: [See also Organization and Administration, below]

Committee on Agriculture: John L. Dawson (Dem., Pa.)

TABLE OF KEY VOTES

Senate

Subject of Vote	Date of Vote	For	Against
Gadsden Treaty Ratification	April 25, 1854	33	13
Kansas-Nebraska Act	May 25, 1854	Passed by voice vote	
Treaty of Kanagawa Ratification	July 15, 1854	Unanimous voice vote	
Citizenship Act	December 20, 1854	Passed by voice vote	
Court of Claims Established	December 21, 1854	Passed by voice vote	

House

Subject of Vote	Date of Vote	For	Against
Citizenship Act	January 13, 1854	Passed by voice vote	
Kansas-Nebraska Act	May 22, 1854	113	100
Court of Claims Established	February 23, 1855	148	46

[See note 7, p. xxix]

Committee on Foreign Affairs: Thomas H. Bayly (Dem., Va.)

Committee on the Judiciary: Frederick P. Stanton (Dem., Tenn.)

Committee on Military Affairs: William H. Bissell (Dem., Ill.) and Thomas H. Benton (Dem., Mo.)

Committee on Naval Affairs: Thomas S. Bocock (Dem., Va.)

Committee on Ways and Means: George S. Houston (Dem., Ala.)

ORGANIZATION AND ADMINISTRATION

There have been approximately two thousand committees throughout the history of Congress. However, the modern committee structure and the modern allocation of committee jurisdiction, seniority, and ranking minority member status

was not established until after World War II. [See note 5, p. xxix]

MAJOR LEGISLATION PASSED

Citizenship: In the Citizenship Act, Congress gave United States citizenship to children born outside of the U.S. if their parents were U.S. citizens.

Court of Claims: Congress established the United States Court of Claims, with jurisdiction over lawsuits brought against the federal government.

Gadsden Purchase Treaty: The Senate approved a treaty with Mexico providing for the purchase of land in what today comprises southern Arizona and New Mexico.

Japan: The Senate approved the Treaty of Kanagawa, which opened two Japanese ports to American ships.

Kansas and Nebraska: Congress effectively repealed the Missouri Compromise of 1820. The Kansas-

Nebraska Act gave the residents of the Kansas Territory and the Nebraska Territory the right to determine for themselves whether they would enter the Union as a free state or a slave state.

FAILED LEGISLATION

None of historical significance.

RELATIONS WITH THE PRESIDENT

President Franklin Pierce was largely inactive in the congressional debate over slavery and the Kansas-Nebraska Act, preferring instead to concentrate on foreign policy objectives. The Gadsden Purchase Treaty and the Treaty of Kanagawa [See Major Legislation Passed, above] were largely Pierce's initiatives. Pierce vetoed four bills during the 33rd Congress, all of which concerned minor pieces of legislation.

NOMINATIONS, APPOINTMENTS, AND CONFIRMATIONS

The Judiciary: On July 19, 1852, during the 32nd Congress, Supreme Court Justice John McKinley died, and was not replaced until the 33rd Congress. President Franklin Pierce on March 22, 1853, nominated John A. Campbell to replace McKinley, and the Senate confirmed Campbell on March 25, 1853, by voice vote.

The Executive Branch: On March 7, 1853, President Pierce nominated his cabinet: Caleb Cushing to be attorney general, Jefferson Davis to be secretary of war, James C. Dobbin to be sec-

retary of the Navy, James Guthrie to be secretary of the Treasury, William L. Marcy to be secretary of state and Robert McClelland to be secretary of the Interior. That same day, the Senate confirmed all six men by voice vote.

IMPEACHMENTS

None.

CONSTITUTIONAL AMENDMENTS

None.

FURTHER READING

Bisson, Wilfred J. *Franklin Pierce: A Bibliography.* Westport, Conn.: Greenwood Press, 1993.

Gara, Larry. *The Presidency of Franklin Pierce.* Lawrence, Kan.: University Press of Kansas, 1991.

Gienapp, William E. *The Origins of the Republican Party, 1852-1856.* New York: Oxford, 1987.

Nichols, Roy. *Franklin Pierce: Young Hickory of the Granite Hills.* Philadelphia: University of Pennsylvania Press, 1958.

The 34th Congress

MARCH 4, 1855 - MARCH 3, 1857

First Session: December 3, 1855-August 18, 1856
Second Session: August 21, 1856-August 30, 1856
Third Session: December 1, 1856-March 3, 1857

In the 1854 elections for the 34th Congress, the Democrats gained 2 seats in the Senate, increasing their majority to 40 seats out of the 62. The Whigs became the Republican Party and lost 7 seats, leaving them with a total of 15. Seven seats were not held by either major party. One of these seats was held by a Know-Nothing, and the remaining 6 members generally leaned toward the Whigs. In the House, the Whigs-turned-Republicans gained 37 seats, giving them a total of 108 seats out of the 237. The Democrats lost 76 seats, leaving them with a total of 83 seats. Forty-six seats were not held by either of the two major parties. Virtually all of these 46 seats were held by the Know-Nothings. [See notes 2 and 3, p. xxix]

BACKGROUND

Throughout the 34th Congress, the violence in Kansas intensified, due to the passage in the 33rd Congress of the Kansas-Nebraska Act, which left the question of free state versus slave state status to the residents of the two territories. Free state and slave state factions battled constantly, with arms and assistance from their respective supporters in the North and the South, but neither side had yet gained the upper hand in "Bleeding Kansas." On May 22, 1856, the tensions in Congress between the North and South over slavery became personal, when Representative Preston S. Brooks (Dem., S.C.) used his cane to savagely beat Senator Charles Sumner (Rep., Mass.) for making an antislavery speech on the Senate floor. Members of Congress began to carry pistols and knives with them into the House and Senate for self-protection.

In 1857 Congress made American currency the only legitimate medium of exchange in the U.S. and lowered import tariffs.

SENATE LEADERSHIP

Vice President: None. William Rufus de Vane King had been vice president in the 33rd Congress, but he died on April 18, 1853. (Until the Twenty-fifth Amendment was ratified on February 10, 1967 [See 90th Congress], there was no mechanism for filling vacancies in the office of the vice president. Therefore, there was no president of the Senate during the 34th Congress.)

President Pro Tempore: Jesse David Bright (Dem., Ind.) was reelected on June 11, 1856. Charles Edward Stuart (Dem., Mich.) was elected president pro tempore for June 5, 1856, and June 9, 1856-June 11, 1856. James Murray Mason (Dem., Va.) was elected January 6, 1857. [See note 4, p. xxix]

Majority Leader, Majority Whip, Minority Leader, and Minority Whip: None. These functions did not evolve into formal Senate positions until the 62nd Congress (1911-1913).

CHRONOLOGY

March 4, 1855:	The 34th Congress begins.
December 3, 1855:	The first session begins.
February 2, 1856:	Nathaniel Prentice Banks (Rep., Mass.) is elected Speaker of the House.
May 22, 1856:	Representative Preston S. Brooks (Dem., S.C.) assaults Senator Charles Sumner (Rep., Mass.).
August 18, 1856:	The first session ends.
August 21, 1856:	The second session begins.
August 30, 1856:	The second session ends.
December 1, 1856:	The third session begins.
January 15, 1857:	Congress passes legislation barring the use of foreign coins as legal tender.
February 21, 1857:	Congress passes legislation admitting Minnesota into the United States.
March 3, 1857:	The third session and the 34th Congress end. Congress passes the Tariff Act of 1857, reducing import duties.

[See note 6, p. xxix]

Chairmen of Selected Key Committees: [See also Organization and Administration, below]

Committee on Finance: Robert M. T. Hunter (Dem., Va.)

Committee on Foreign Relations: James Mason (Dem., Va.)

Committee on the Judiciary: Andrew Butler (Dem., S.C.)

Committee on Military Affairs: John Weller (Dem., Cal.)

Committee on Naval Affairs: Stephen Mallory (Dem., Fla.)

HOUSE LEADERSHIP

Speaker of the House: Nathaniel Prentice Banks (Rep., Mass.) was elected on February 2, 1856.

Banks, a former Speaker in the Massachusetts legislature, first had been elected to Congress in the 33rd Congress. This was Banks's first and last Congress as Speaker.

Majority Leader, Majority Whip, Minority Leader, and Minority Whip: None. These functions did not evolve into formal House positions until the 56th Congress (1899-1901).

Chairmen of Selected Key Committees: [See also Organization and Administration, below]

Committee on Agriculture: David P. Holloway (Rep., Ind.)

Committee on Foreign Affairs: Alexander C. M. Pennington (Rep., N.J.)

Committee on the Judiciary: George A. Simmons (Rep., N.Y.)

TABLE OF KEY VOTES

Senate

Subject of Vote	Date of Vote	For	Against
Legal Tender Act	April 16, 1856	Passed by voice vote	
Admission of Minnesota to Union	February 21, 1857	41	1
Tariff Reduction	February 23, 1857	Passed by voice vote	

House

Subject of Vote	Date of Vote	For	Against
Legal Tender Act	January 15, 1857	Passed by voice vote	
Admission of Minnesota to Union	January 31, 1857	97	75
Tariff Reduction	March 3, 1857	Passed by voice vote	

[See note 7, p. xxix]

Committee on Military Affairs: John A. Quitman (Dem., Miss.)

Committee on Naval Affairs: Samuel P. Benson (Rep., Maine)

Committee on Ways and Means: Lewis D. Campbell (Rep., Ohio)

ORGANIZATION AND ADMINISTRATION

There have been approximately two thousand committees throughout the history of Congress. However, the modern committee structure and the modern allocation of committee jurisdiction, seniority, and ranking minority member status was not established until after World War II. [See note 5, p. xxix]

MAJOR LEGISLATION PASSED

Admission of Minnesota as a New State: Congress voted to admit Minnesota into the United States.

Legal Tender: Congress declared that foreign coins could no longer be used as legal tender in the United States.

Tariffs: The Tariff Act of 1857 reduced import duties.

FAILED LEGISLATION

None of historical significance.

RELATIONS WITH THE PRESIDENT

President Franklin Pierce was not a strong president, and his difficulty in controlling his fellow Democrats began to show as his first term neared its end. Pierce never had much respect within his party to begin with: in the 1852 Democratic convention, he was nominated only as a compromise candidate in the 49th ballot. This weakness manifested itself when the Democrats refused to renominate Pierce in 1856, and when Congress overrode all 5 of his vetoes in the 34th Congress. The vetoes were all of minor navigational dredging and other improvement projects that Pierce thought were unnecessary.

NOMINATIONS, APPOINTMENTS, AND CONFIRMATIONS

There were no significant nominations, appointments, or confirmations in the federal judiciary or in the executive branch during the 34th Congress.

IMPEACHMENTS

None.

CONSTITUTIONAL AMENDMENTS

None.

SCANDALS

As the debate in Congress and the nation over slavery grew, so did personal rivalries, such as the infamous incident on May 22, 1856, when Representative Preston S. Brooks (Dem., S.C.) physically assaulted Senator Charles Sumner (Rep., Mass.). [See Background, above, for details]

FURTHER READING

Bisson, Wilfred J. *Franklin Pierce: A Bibliography.* Westport, Conn.: Greenwood Press, 1993.

Donald, David H. *Charles Sumner and the Coming of the Civil War.* New York: Knopf, 1960.

Gara, Larry. *The Presidency of Franklin Pierce.* Lawrence, Kan.: University Press of Kansas, 1991.

Nichols, Roy. *Franklin Pierce: Young Hickory of the Granite Hills.* Philadelphia: University of Pennsylvania Press, 1958.

The 35th Congress

MARCH 4, 1857-MARCH 3, 1859

*Special Senate Sessions: March 4, 1857-March 14, 1857
and June 15, 1858-June 16, 1858
First Session: December 7, 1857-June 14, 1858
Second Session: December 6, 1858-March 3, 1859*

The Senate held special sessions in March and June of 1857 to vote on the confirmation of presidential appointees to various offices. [See note 1, p. xxix]

In the 1856 elections for the 35th Congress, the Democrats lost 4 seats in the Senate, reducing their majority to 36 seats out of the 64. The Republicans gained 5 seats, giving them a total of 20 seats. Eight seats were not held by either of the two major parties. Five of these seats were held by Know-Nothings. In the House, the Democrats gained 35 seats, giving them a total of 118 seats out of the 237. The Republicans lost 16 seats, reducing their total to 92 seats. Twenty-seven seats were not held by either of the two major parties. Fourteen of these seats were held by Know-Nothings. [See notes 2 and 3, p. xxix]

BACKGROUND

On March 4, 1857, James Buchanan was inaugurated as the 15th president of the United States. Two days later, the Supreme Court issued its decision in the case of *Dred Scott v. Sandford*, which effectively nullified most of Congress's power to prevent the spread of slavery. Between August 21, 1858, and October 15, 1858, historic debates over the issue of slavery took place in Illinois between incumbent Senator Stephen A. Douglas (Dem., Ill.) and Republican challenger Abraham Lincoln. Lincoln argued in favor of national abolition, while Douglas supported state self-determination. The Illinois legislature was controlled by Democrats and reelected Douglas, but the publicity made Lincoln a national figure.

SENATE LEADERSHIP

Vice President: John Cabell Breckinridge, a lawyer and Mexican War veteran from Kentucky, first had been elected to Congress in the 32nd Congress. His success in politics had been swift: he was only 36 years old when he was sworn in as vice president. Breckinridge was loyal to the South. After the Buchanan administration, he joined the Confederate army, where he rose to the rank of major general and served for a time as Confederate secretary of war.

President Pro Tempore: James Murray Mason (Dem., Va.) was elected on March 4, 1857; Thomas Jefferson Rusk (Dem., Tex.) was elected on March 14, 1857, and Benjamin Fitzpatrick (Dem., Ala.) was elected on December 7, 1857, March 29, 1858, June 14, 1858, and January 25, 1859. [See note 4, p. xxix]

Majority Leader, Majority Whip, Minority Leader, and Minority Whip: None. These functions did not evolve into formal Senate positions until the 62nd Congress (1911-1913).

Chairmen of Selected Key Committees: [See also Organization and Administration, p. 147]

CHRONOLOGY

March 4, 1857:	The 35th Congress and a special session of the Senate begin.
March 6, 1857:	President Buchanan nominates his cabinet. The Senate confirms all of the nominees.
March 14, 1857:	The special session of the Senate ends.
September 30, 1857:	Supreme Court Justice Benjamin Robbins Curtis resigns.
December 7, 1857:	The first session begins, and James Lawrence Orr (Dem., S.C.) is elected Speaker of the House.
December 9, 1857:	President Buchanan nominates Nathan Clifford to replace Curtis.
January 12, 1858:	The Senate confirms Clifford.
April 1, 1858:	Congress passes legislation admitting Kansas into the United States.
June 14, 1858:	The first session ends.
June 15, 1858:	A special session of the Senate begins.
June 16, 1858:	A special session of the Senate ends.
August 21, 1858:	The Lincoln-Douglas debates begin.
October 15, 1858:	The Lincoln-Douglas debates end.
December 6, 1858:	The second session begins.
February 12, 1859:	Congress passes legislation admitting Oregon into the United States.
March 3, 1859:	The second session and the 35th Congress end.

[See note 6, p. xxix]

Committee on Finance: Robert M. T. Hunter (Dem., Va.)

Committee on Foreign Relations: James Mason (Dem., Va.)

Committee on the Judiciary: James Bayard Jr. (Dem., Del.)

Committee on Military Affairs: Jefferson Davis (Dem., Miss.)

Committee on Naval Affairs: Stephen Mallory (Dem., Fla.)

HOUSE LEADERSHIP

Speaker of the House: James Lawrence Orr (Dem., S.C.) was elected Speaker on December 7, 1857. Orr had served in the South Carolina legislature and first had been elected to Congress in the 31st Congress. After serving as Speaker in the 35th Congress, Orr did not run for reelection in the congressional elections of 1858, and never served in Congress again. Like Vice President Breckinridge, Orr was loyal to the South. After the Buchanan administration, Orr was one of the three Confederate envoys sent in 1861 to demand the surrender of Fort Sumter in Charleston Harbor. He served in the Confederate army during the Civil War.

Majority Leader, Majority Whip, Minority Leader, and Minority Whip: None. These functions did not evolve into formal House positions until the 56th Congress (1899-1901).

Chairmen of Selected Key Committees: [See also Organization and Administration, below]

Committee on Agriculture: William G. Whitely (Dem., Del.)

Committee on Foreign Affairs: Thomas L.

TABLE OF KEY VOTES

Senate

Subject of Vote	Date of Vote	For	Against
Confirmation of Cabinet	March 6, 1857	Passed by voice vote	
Confirmation of Nathan Clifford to Supreme Court	January 12, 1858	26	23
Admission of Kansas to Union	March 23, 1858	33	25
Admission of Oregon to Union	May 18, 1858	35	17

House

Subject of Vote	Date of Vote	For	Against
Admission of Kansas to Union	April 1, 1858	120	112
Admission of Oregon to Union	February 12, 1859	114	103

[See note 7, p. xxix]

Clingman (Dem., N.C.) and George W. Hopkins (Dem., Va.)

Committee on the Judiciary: George S. Houston (Dem., Ala.)

Committee on Military Affairs: John A. Quitman (Dem., Miss.) and Charles J. Faulkner (Dem., Va.)

Committee on Naval Affairs: Thomas S. Bocock (Dem., Va.)

Committee on Ways and Means: John S. Phelps (Dem., Mo.) and J. Glancy Jones (Dem., Pa.)

ORGANIZATION AND ADMINISTRATION

There have been approximately two thousand committees throughout the history of Congress. However, the modern committee structure and the modern allocation of committee jurisdiction, seniority, and ranking minority member status was not established until after World War II. [See note 5, p. xxix]

MAJOR LEGISLATION PASSED

Admission of Oregon and Kansas as New States: Congress voted to admit Oregon and Kansas into the United States. Although the votes to admit Kansas occurred before the votes to admit Oregon, Oregon was formally admitted to the Union (on February 14, 1859), before Kansas (on January 29, 1861), due to procedural differences in the respective legislation.

FAILED LEGISLATION

None of historical significance.

RELATIONS WITH THE PRESIDENT

James Buchanan's presidency began with high expectations: His forty-years of public service included terms in the Senate and House, service to Great Britain and Russia, and secretary of state in President Polk's administration. However, Buchanan's one-term presidency proved to be mediocre at best. He did nothing to prevent the slavery issue from dividing Congress and the nation in the years leading up to the Civil War.

President Buchanan vetoed four bills in the 35th Congress, none of which historically was significant.

NOMINATIONS, APPOINTMENTS, AND CONFIRMATIONS

The Judiciary: On September 30, 1857, Supreme Court Justice Benjamin Robbins Curtis resigned. On December 9, 1857, President James Buchanan nominated Nathan Clifford to replace Curtis, and the Senate confirmed Clifford on January 12, 1858, by a 26 to 23 vote.

The Executive Branch: On March 6, 1857, President Buchanan nominated his cabinet: Jeremiah S. Black to be attorney general, Lewis Cass to be secretary of state, Howell Cobb to be secretary of the Treasury, John B. Floyd to be secretary of war, Jacob Thompson to be secretary of the Interior, and Isaac Toucey to be secretary of the Navy. That same day, March 6, the Senate confirmed all six men by voice vote.

IMPEACHMENTS

None.

CONSTITUTIONAL AMENDMENTS

None.

FURTHER READING

Clifford, Philip Greely. *Nathan Clifford, Democrat*. New York and London: G. P. Putnam's Sons, 1922.

Heck, Frank. *Proud Kentuckian, John C. Breckinridge, 1821-1875*. Lexington, Ky.: University Press of Kentucky, 1976.

Kein, Philip. *President James Buchanan: A Biography*. University Park, Pa.: Pennsylvania State University Press, 1962.

Leemhuis, Roger P. *James L. Orr and the Sectional Conflict*. Washington, D.C.: University Press of America, 1979.

The 36th Congress

MARCH 4, 1859 - MARCH 3, 1861

Special Senate Sessions: March 4, 1859-March 10, 1859
and June 26, 1860-June 28, 1860.
First Session: December 5, 1859-June 25, 1860
Second Session: December 3, 1860-March 3, 1861

The Senate held a special session in March 1859 to vote on the confirmation of presidential appointees to various offices. [See note 1, p. xxix] The Senate held another special session in June 1860 to decide whether to ratify various minor treaties proposed by President Buchanan.

In the 1858 elections for the 36th Congress, the Democrats neither gained nor lost any seats in the Senate and kept their majority of 36 seats out of the 66. The Republicans gained 6 seats, giving them a total of 26 seats. Four seats were not held by either of the two major parties. Two of these seats were held by Know-Nothings, and the other 2 members leaned toward the Democrats. In the House, the Republicans gained 22 seats, giving them a total of 114 seats out of the 237. The Democrats lost 26 seats reducing their total to 92 seats. Thirty-one seats were not held by either of the two major parties. Five of these seats were held by Know-Nothings, and most of the rest were held by splinter factions of the Democrats or members with Democratic sympathies. [See notes 2 and 3, p. xxix]

BACKGROUND

According to the census of 1860, the population of the United States as of June 1, 1860, was 31,443,321, resulting in a population density of 10.6 persons for each of the country's 2,969,640 square miles. This was a population increase of 35.6 percent over the 1850 census.

In 1859 the crisis in "Bleeding Kansas" over whether the territory should become a free state or a slave state ended, when on July 5 a Kansas state constitutional convention chose an anti-slavery constitution by a vote of nearly 2 to 1. On October 16, 1859, radical abolitionist John Brown led a raid on Harpers Ferry, Virginia, to free the slaves. The raid failed, and Brown was hanged on December 2, 1859, for treason against Virginia. However, to many in the North and in the abolition movement, Brown was a hero and a martyr.

The 1860 presidential election was dominated by the slavery issue. The Republicans were anti-slavery and strong in the North and West, but virtually had no support in the South. The Democrats were strong in the South, but very weak in the North, where Democrats were bitterly divided over abolition. Of the 33 states, Lincoln won in 17 of the 18 free states, but was not even on the ballot in some slave states. Lincoln received only 39.82 percent of the popular vote, but because of his victory in the heavily populated free states of the North, Lincoln easily won a majority of the electoral votes. Lincoln's victory made it impossible for the North and South to settle their differences concerning states' rights and slavery, as they previously had done with the Missouri Compromise and the Compromise of 1850. South Carolina, which during the 22nd Congress had threatened to secede over tariffs, actually seceded on December 20,

CHRONOLOGY

March 4, 1859:	The 36th Congress and a special session of the Senate begin.
March 10, 1859:	The special session of the Senate ends.
December 5, 1859:	The first session begins.
February 1, 1860:	William Pennington (Rep., N.J.) is elected Speaker of the House.
May 31, 1860:	Supreme Court Justice Peter Vivian Daniel dies.
June 25, 1860:	The first session ends.
June 26, 1860:	A special session of the Senate begins.
June 28, 1860:	The special session of the Senate ends.
December 3, 1860:	The second session begins.
December 10, 1860:	President Buchanan nominates Philip F. Thomas to be secretary of the Treasury.
December 12, 1860:	The Senate confirms Thomas.
December 16, 1860:	President Buchanan nominates Jeremiah S. Black to be secretary of state.
December 17, 1860:	The Senate confirms Black.
December 19, 1860:	President Buchanan nominates Edwin M. Stanton to be attorney general.
December 20, 1860:	The Senate confirms Stanton. South Carolina secedes from the United States.
January 11, 1861:	President Buchanan nominates, and the Senate confirms, John A. Dix to be secretary of the Treasury.
January 17, 1861:	President Buchanan nominates Joseph Holt to be secretary of war.
January 18, 1861:	The Senate confirms Holt.
February 5, 1861:	President Buchanan nominates Jeremiah S. Black to replace Daniel.
February 20, 1861:	Congress passes legislation raising tariffs.
February 21, 1861:	The Senate votes against Black's confirmation. The vacancy on the Court would not be filled until the 37th Congress.
March 3, 1861:	The second session and the 36th Congress end.

[See note 6, p. xxix]

1860, because of Lincoln's election. Six more southern states seceded before the end of the 36th Congress, while President Buchanan did nothing to hold the Union together.

SENATE LEADERSHIP

Vice President: John Cabell Breckinridge [See biographical note in 35th Congress]

President Pro Tempore: Benjamin Fitzpatrick (Dem., Ala.) was elected on March 9, 1859, December 19, 1859, February 20, 1860, and June 26, 1860. Jesse David Bright (Dem., Ind.) was elected on June 12, 1860, and Solomon Foot (Rep., Vt.) was elected on February 16, 1861. [See note 4, p. xxix]

Majority Leader, Majority Whip, Minority Leader, and Minority Whip: None. These functions did not evolve into formal Senate positions until the 62nd Congress (1911-1913).

TABLE OF KEY VOTES

Senate

Subject of Vote	Date of Vote	For	Against
Confirmation of Philip F. Thomas to be Secretary of the Treasury	December 12, 1860	Passed by voice vote	
Confirmation of Jeremiah S. Black to be Secretary of State	December 17, 1860	Passed by voice vote	
Confirmation of Edwin M. Stanton to be Attorney General	December 20, 1860	Passed by voice vote	
Confirmation of John A. Dix to be Secretary of the Treasury	January 11, 1861	Passed by voice vote	
Confirmation of Joseph Holt to be Secretary of War	January 18, 1861	38	13
Tariff Increase	February 20, 1861	25	14
Nomination of Jeremiah S. Black to Supreme Court	February 21, 1861	25	26

House

Subject of Vote	Date of Vote	For	Against
Tariff Increase	May 10, 1860	105	64

[See note 7, p. xxix]

Chairmen of Selected Key Committees: [See also Organization and Administration, below]

Committee on Finance: Robert M. T. Hunter (Dem., Va.)

Committee on Foreign Relations: James Mason (Dem., Va.)

Committee on the Judiciary: James Bayard Jr. (Dem., Del.)

Committee on Military Affairs: Jefferson Davis (Dem., Miss.)

Committee on Naval Affairs: Stephen Mallory (Dem., Fla.)

HOUSE LEADERSHIP

Speaker of the House: William Pennington (Rep., N.J.) was elected Speaker on February 1, 1860. Pennington's election as Speaker was somewhat of an historical fluke. He was a former governor of New Jersey, but had been largely inactive in politics since the end of his term as governor in 1843. Now in his sixties, Pennington was elected to his first and only term in Congress, as he was defeated in the 1860 congressional elections for the 37th Congress and died not long after.

Majority Leader, Majority Whip, Minority Leader, and Minority Whip: None. These func-

tions did not evolve into formal House positions until the 56th Congress (1899-1901).

Chairmen of Selected Key Committees: [See also Organization and Administration, below]

Committee on Agriculture: Martin Butterfield (Rep., N.Y.)

Committee on Foreign Affairs: Thomas Corwin (Rep., Ohio)

Committee on the Judiciary: John Hickman (Dem., Pa.)

Committee on Military Affairs: Benjamin Stanton (Rep., Ohio)

Committee on Naval Affairs: Freeman H. Morse (Rep., Maine)

Committee on Ways and Means: John Sherman (Rep., Ohio)

ORGANIZATION AND ADMINISTRATION

There have been approximately two thousand committees throughout the history of Congress. However, the modern committee structure and the modern allocation of committee jurisdiction, seniority, and ranking minority member status was not established until after World War II. [See note 5, p. xxix]

MAJOR LEGISLATION PASSED

Tariffs: Congress raised import duties on a variety of imported goods, particularly woolen and iron products.

FAILED LEGISLATION

None of historical significance.

RELATIONS WITH THE PRESIDENT

James Buchanan's presidency had begun with high expectations, given his long and distinguished career in public service. However, Buchanan's one-term presidency proved to have disasterous consequences, as he ignored the nation's slide toward division and civil war. Buchanan did nothing to prevent the southern states from seceding after the election of Abraham Lincoln in the 1860 presidential contest. President Buchanan vetoed three bills in the 36th Congress, none of which historically was significant.

NOMINATIONS, APPOINTMENTS, AND CONFIRMATIONS

The Judiciary: On May 31, 1860, Supreme Court Justice Peter Vivian Daniel died. On February 5, 1861, President James Buchanan nominated Jeremiah S. Black to replace Daniel, but the Senate voted against Black's confirmation on February 21, 1861, by a 26 to 25 vote. The vacancy on the Court would not be filled until the 37th Congress.

The Executive Branch: On December 10, 1860, President Buchanan nominated Philip F. Thomas to be secretary of the Treasury, and on December 12, 1860, the Senate confirmed Thomas by voice vote. Buchanan nominated Jeremiah S. Black to be secretary of state on December 16, 1860, and the Senate confirmed Black by voice vote the next day. Buchanan nominated Edwin M. Stanton to be attorney general on December 19, 1860, and the Senate confirmed Stanton by voice vote the next day. On January 11, 1861, Buchanan nominated, and the Senate confirmed by voice vote, John A. Dix to be secretary of the Treasury. On January 17, 1861, Buchanan nominated Joseph Holt to be secretary of war, and on January 18, 1861, the Senate confirmed Holt by a vote of 38 to 13.

IMPEACHMENTS

None.

CONSTITUTIONAL AMENDMENTS

None.

FURTHER READING

Christianson, Stephen G. "John Brown Trial." In *Great American Trials*, edited by Edward W. Knappman. Detroit: Gale Research, 1994.

Heck, Frank. *Proud Kentuckian, John C. Breckinridge, 1821-1875*. Lexington, Ky.: University Press of Kentucky, 1976.

Kein, Philip. *President James Buchanan: A Biography*. University Park, Pa.: Pennsylvania State University Press, 1962.

The 37th Congress

MARCH 4, 1861-MARCH 3, 1863

Senate Special Session: March 4, 1861-March 28, 1861
First Session: July 4, 1861-August 6, 1861
Second Session: December 2, 1861-July 17, 1862
Third Session: December 1, 1862-March 3, 1863

The Senate held a special session to vote on the confirmation of presidential appointees to various offices. [See note 1, p. xxix]

In the 1860 elections for the 37th Congress, the Republicans gained 5 seats in the Senate, giving them a total of 31 seats out of the 66. The Democrats lost 26 seats, leaving them with only 10 seats. Of the 25 remaining seats, 19 were vacant due to the secession of Southern states, and 6 seats were held by senators who were neither Republicans nor Democrats or were vacant for other reasons. In the House, the Republicans lost 9 seats, leaving them with a total of 105 out of the 237 seats. The Democrats lost 49 seats, reducing their total to 43 seats. Of the remaining 89 seats, 56 were vacant due to the secession of Southern states, and 33 seats were held by representatives who were neither Republicans nor Democrats or were vacant for other reasons. [See notes 2 and 3, p. xxix]

BACKGROUND

On March 4, 1861, Abraham Lincoln was inaugurated as the 16th president of the United States. In the previous Congress, seven southern states seceded when Lincoln won the presidential election of 1860 and formed the Confederate States of America. Unlike his predecessor, President James Buchanan, Lincoln was determined to preserve the Union. Lincoln told South Carolina, the first state to secede, that he intended to send a relief force to Fort Sumter in Charleston Harbor where federal forces were surrounded. On April 12, 1861, the Civil War began when the Confederates opened fire on Fort Sumter, which surrendered the next day. Lincoln began to organize the Union for war, while the rest of the southern states seceded to join the Confederacy.* In the summer of 1861 Congress imposed an income tax to finance the war effort.

In 1862, while the Civil War raged, Congress passed two important laws. The first, the Homestead Act, gave 160 acres of federal land in the West to anyone willing to settle and farm the land for five years, in order to encourage settlement. The second, the Morrill Act, gave federal land to the states still in the Union to be used in support of higher education, and was the basis of the land grant colleges of future years.

On September 22, 1862, following the September 17 Union victory at the Battle of Antietam, Lincoln issued the Emancipation Proclamation, which freed the slaves in the territory controlled by the Confederacy effective January 1, 1863. In 1863, shortly before the end of the 37th Congress, Congress passed the U.S.'s first draft law, which favored the rich by permitting exemptions in return for $300 or a substitute.

---

* The 11 states that seceded from the Union were Alabama, Arkansas, Florida, Georgia, Louisiana, Mississippi, North Carolina, South Carolina, Tennessee, Texas, and Virginia. Of the 22 senators from these 11 states, only 3 were left in Congress: Future president Andrew Johnson (Dem., Tenn.) stayed loyal to the Union and the two Virginia senators were from that part of the state that had stayed in the Union and would later become West Virginia. Two representatives from Louisiana, 3 from Tennessee and 5 from Virginia also remained, although they did not return to the 38th Congress.

C H R O N O L O G Y

March 4, 1861:	The 37th Congress and a special session of the Senate begin.
March 5, 1861:	President Lincoln nominates his cabinet, and the Senate confirms all of the nominees.
March 28, 1861:	The special session of the Senate ends.
April 4, 1861:	Justice John McLean dies.
April 12, 1861:	The Civil War begins when Confederate artillery batteries open fire on Fort Sumter in Charleston harbor.
April 30, 1861:	Justice John Archibald Campbell resigns, raising the number of Supreme Court vacancies to three. (There was one vacancy at the end of the 36th Congress.)
July 4, 1861:	The first session begins, and Galusha Aaron Grow (Rep., Pa.) is elected Speaker of the House.
July 30, 1861:	Congress passes legislation imposing the first federal income tax.
August 6, 1861:	The first session ends.
December 2, 1861:	The second session begins.
January 13, 1862:	President Lincoln nominates Edwin M. Stanton to succeed Simon Cameron as secretary of war.
January 15, 1862:	The Senate confirms Stanton.
January 22, 1862:	President Lincoln nominates Noah H. Swayne to the Supreme Court.
January 24, 1862:	The Senate confirms Swayne.
February 13, 1862:	Congress passes legislation authorizing the issuance of greenbacks.
May 6, 1862:	The House votes to impeach federal Judge West H. Humphreys. Congress passes the Homestead Act.
May 8, 1862:	Congress establishes the Department of Agriculture.
June 17, 1862:	Congress passes the Morrill Land Grant College Act.
June 20, 1862:	Congress passes the Pacific Railroad Act.
June 26, 1862:	The Senate removes Judge Humphreys from office and disqualifies him from holding any federal office in the future.
July 16, 1862:	President Lincoln nominates, and the Senate confirms, Samuel F. Miller to the Supreme Court.
July 17, 1862:	The second session ends.
September 22, 1862:	President Lincoln issues the Emancipation Proclamation.
December 1, 1862:	The third session begins, and President Lincoln nominates David Davis to the Supreme Court.
December 8, 1862:	The Senate confirms Davis.
December 10, 1862:	Congress passes legislation admitting West Virginia into the United States.
January 5, 1863:	President Lincoln nominates John P. Usher to succeed Caleb Smith as secretary of the Interior.

(continued on page 156)

(continued from page 155)

January 8, 1863: The Senate confirms Usher.
January 27, 1863: Congress passes the Habeas Corpus Act.
February 25, 1863: Congress passes draft legislation.
March 3, 1863: The third session and the 37th Congress end.

[See note 6, p. xxix]

SENATE LEADERSHIP

Vice President: Hannibal Hamlin, a former representative and senator from Maine, first had been elected to Congress in the 28th Congress. He played only a minor role during his four years as vice president. Lincoln would not run with Hamlin again, and in 1865 appointed Hamlin port collector for Boston harbor.

President Pro Tempore: Solomon Foot (Rep., Vt.) was elected on March 23, 1861, July 18, 1861, January 15, 1862, March 31, 1862, June 19,1862, and February 18, 1863. [See note 4, p. xxix]

Majority Leader, Majority Whip, Minority Leader, and Minority Whip: None. These functions did not evolve into formal Senate positions until the 62nd Congress (1911-1913).

Chairmen of Selected Key Committees: [See also Organization and Administration, p. 157]

Committee on Finance: William Fessenden (Rep., Maine)

Committee on Foreign Relations: Charles Sumner (Rep., Mass.)

Committee on the Judiciary: Lyman Trumbull (Rep., Ill.)

Committee on Military Affairs: Henry Wilson (Rep., Mass.)

Committee on Naval Affairs: John Hale (Rep., N.H.)

HOUSE LEADERSHIP

Speaker of the House: Galusha Aaron Grow (Rep., Pa.) was elected Speaker on July 4, 1861. Grow first had been elected to Congress in the 32nd Congress as a Democrat, but joined the Republicans in the 35th Congress. As Speaker, Grow was particularly active in getting the Homestead Act passed. [See Major Legislation, p. 158] This was Grow's one and only Congress as Speaker.

Majority Leader, Majority Whip, Minority Leader, and Minority Whip: None. These functions did not evolve into formal House positions until the 56th Congress (1899-1901).

Chairmen of Selected Key Committees: [See also Organization and Administration, p. 157]

Committee on Agriculture: Owen Lovejoy (Rep., Ill.)

Committee on Foreign Affairs: John J. Crittenden (Rep., Ky.)

Committee on the Judiciary: John Hickman (Rep., Pa.) was a Democrat in the 36th Congress, but became a Republican in the 37th Congress.

Committee on Military Affairs: Francis P. Blair Jr. (Rep., Mo.) resigned in July 1862 to accept a commission in the Union army. James Buffington (Rep., Mass.) became the next chairman.

Committee on Naval Affairs: Charles B. Sedgwick (Rep., N.Y.)

TABLE OF KEY VOTES

Senate

Subject of Vote	Date of Vote	For	Against
Income Tax Established	July 30, 1861	22	18
Greenback Legal Tender Act	February 13, 1862	30	7
Homestead Act	May 6, 1862	33	7
Department of Agriculture Established	May 8, 1862	25	13
Land Grant College Act	June 10, 1862	32	7
Pacific Railroad Act	June 20, 1862	35	5
Admission of West Virginia to Union	July 14, 1862	23	17
Suspension of Habeas Corpus Authorized	January 27, 1863	33	7
National Draft Established	February 16, 1863	Passed by voice vote	

House

Subject of Vote	Date of Vote	For	Against
Income Tax Established	July 18, 1861	Passed by voice vote	
Greenback Legal Tender Act	February 6, 1862	93	59
Department of Agriculture Established	February 17, 1862	122	7
Homestead Act	February 28, 1862	105	16
Pacific Railroad Act	May 6, 1862	79	49
Land Grant College Act	June 17, 1862	89	25
Suspension of Habeas Corpus Authorized	December 8, 1862	91	46
Admission of West Virginia to Union	December 10, 1862	96	57
National Draft Established	February 25, 1863	115	49

[See note 7, p. xxix]

Committee on Ways and Means: Thaddeus Stevens (Rep., Pa.)

ORGANIZATION AND ADMINISTRATION

There have been approximately two thousand committees throughout the history of Congress. However, the modern committee structure and the modern allocation of committee jurisdiction, seniority, and ranking minority member status was not established until after World War II. [See note 5, p. xxix]

MAJOR LEGISLATION PASSED

Admission of West Virginia as a New State: Congress voted to admit West Virginia into the United States. The new state is made up of pro-Union counties in what was formerly northwestern Virginia. They, in effect, seceded from Virginia when that state seceded from the Union.

Department of Agriculture: Congress established the Department of Agriculture to support and assist American farmers.

Draft: In the Conscription Act, Congress established a national draft system for all white men between the ages of 20 and 45 to raise armies for the Civil War.

Education: The Morrill Land Grant College Act gave federal land to states still in the Union to be used in support of higher education.

Greenbacks: In the Legal Tender Act, Congress authorized the printing of paper money known as "greenbacks" in order to pay off government debts.

Habeas Corpus: In the Habeas Corpus Act, Congress gave President Lincoln the power to suspend habeas corpus for people arrested by the government.

Homesteads: In the Homestead Act, Congress offered 160 acres of federal land in the West to anyone willing to settle and farm the land for five years.

Income Tax: Congress imposed the first federal income tax in American history to help finance the Civil War.

Railroads: In the Pacific Railroad Act, Congress subsidized the construction by the Central Pacific Railroad and the Union Pacific Railroad of a line linking the rest of the nation with California.

FAILED LEGISLATION

None of historical significance.

RELATIONS WITH THE PRESIDENT

Lincoln's presidency was dominated by the Civil War. Although the Confederate states were no longer represented in Congress and Lincoln was largely successful in getting the legislation and war powers he wanted, there were difficulties in Lincoln's relations with Congress. Four of the delegations were from slave states that were kept in the Union by force: Delaware, Kentucky, Maryland, and Missouri. The Democrats generally wanted to come to terms with the Confederacy, while many Republicans criticized Lincoln for not pursuing the war vigorously enough. There were few military successes for the Union during this Congress, and while Lincoln struggled to find competent generals for the Union armies, he had to resist efforts within Congress and his own cabinet to take over his control of the war. Further, Lincoln's wife, Mary Todd, was from an influential southern family in Kentucky and had several relatives in the Confederate army. Many members of Congress were suspicious of her, and some even accused her of being a spy.

Lincoln vetoed three bills during the 37th Congress, none of which was of historical significance.

NOMINATIONS, APPOINTMENTS, AND CONFIRMATIONS

The Judiciary: On May 31, 1860, Supreme Court Justice Peter Vivian Daniel died, leaving a vacancy on the Court that was not filled during the 36th Congress. On April 4, 1861, Justice John McLean died, and on April 30, 1861, Justice John Archibald Campbell resigned. Thus, President Lincoln had three vacancies to fill. First, Lincoln nominated Noah H. Swayne on January 22, 1862, and the Senate confirmed Swayne on January 24, 1862, by a 38 to 1 vote. Second, Lincoln nominated, and the Senate confirmed by voice vote, Samuel F. Miller on July 16, 1862. Third, Lincoln nominated David Davis on December 1, 1862, and the Senate confirmed him on December 8, 1862, by voice vote. In addition, the Court was increased from nine to ten justices before the 37th Congress ended in 1863, although this new position was not filled until the 38th Congress.

The Executive Branch: On March 5, 1861, President Lincoln nominated his cabinet: Edward Bates to be attorney general, Simon Cameron to be secretary of war, Salmon P. Chase to be secretary of the Treasury, William H. Seward to be secretary of state, Caleb B. Smith to be secretary of the Interior and Gideon Welles to be secretary of the Navy. That same day, the Senate confirmed Bates by a vote of 40 to 5 and confirmed the other five nominees by voice vote.

On January 13, 1862, Lincoln nominated Edwin M. Stanton to succeed Simon Cameron as secretary of war, and on January 15, 1862, the Senate confirmed Stanton by a vote of 38 to 2. On January 5, 1863, Lincoln nominated John P. Usher to succeed Smith as secretary of the Interior, and on January 8, 1863, the Senate confirmed Usher by voice vote.

IMPEACHMENTS

Congress impeached federal Judge West H. Humphreys: Humphreys supported the Confederacy, and left his post in Tennessee to become a Confederate judge. The House decided to remove him for supporting sucession, and voted to impeach Humphreys on May 6, 1862, by voice vote. On June 26, 1862, the Senate voted 38 to 0 to remove Humphreys from office, and voted 36 to 0 to disqualify Humphreys from holding any federal office in the future.

CONSTITUTIONAL AMENDMENTS

None.

FURTHER READING

Dubois, James T., and Gertrude S. Mathews. *Galusha A. Grow, Father of the Homestead Law*. Boston: Houghton Mifflin Company, 1917.

Fairman, Charles. *Mr. Justice Miller and the Supreme Court, 1862-1890*. Cambridge, Mass.: Harvard University Press, 1939.

Findley, Paul. A. *Lincoln: The Crucible of Congress*. New York: Crown Publishers, Inc., 1979.

Hunt, H. Draper. *Hannibal Hamlin: Lincoln's First Vice President*. Syracuse, N.Y.: Syracuse University Press, 1969.

King, Willard Leroy. *Lincoln's Manager David Davis*. Cambridge, Mass.: Harvard University Press, 1960.

Lincoln, Abraham. *The Collected Works of Abraham Lincoln*. New Brunswick, N.J.: Rutgers University Press, 1953 (eight volumes).

The 38th Congress

MARCH 4, 1863 - MARCH 3, 1865

Special Senate Session: *March 4, 1863-March 14, 1863*
First Session: *December 7, 1863-July 4, 1864*
Second Session: *December 5, 1864-March 3, 1865*

The Senate held a special session to vote on the confirmation of presidential appointees to various offices. [See note 1, p. xxix]

In the 1862 elections for the 38th Congress, the Republicans gained 5 seats in the Senate to increase their majority to 36 seats out of the 68. The Democrats lost 1 seat, reducing their total to 9 seats. Of the 23 remaining seats, 20 were vacant due to the secession of southern states, and 3 seats were held by senators who were neither Republicans or Democrats or were vacant for other reasons. *As a result of the 1860 census [see 36th Congress], the House was reapportioned and increased to 243 members. The Republicans lost 3 seats to reduce their majority to 102 out of the 243 seats. The Democrats gained 32 seats, giving them a total of 75 seats. Of the remaining 66 seats, 60 were vacant due to the secession of southern states, and 6 seats were held by representatives who were neither Republicans nor Democrats or were vacant for other reasons. [See notes 2 and 3, p. xxix]

BACKGROUND

When the 38th Congress began, the Civil War had been going on for two years. Until 1863 the conflict had been largely a stalemate between the North, which was numerically and industrially superior, and the South, which had superior military leadership. By the summer of 1863, how-ever, the Union was gaining the upper hand. Virginia's western counties seceded, and joined the Union as West Virginia, the 35th state. After several days of battle, in July 1863 the Union army under Generel George Meade defeated the Confederate forces under General Robert E. Lee at Gettysburg, Pennsylvania.

In 1864 President Lincoln won the presidential election, despite strong opposition from former Union general and now Democratic candidate George McClellan. Lincoln became the first leader in history to be democratically elected during a civil war. Shortly before the 38th Congress ended, Congress created the Freedmen's Bureau to assist the newly freed southern slaves.

SENATE LEADERSHIP

Vice President: Hannibal Hamlin [See biographical note in 37th Congress]

President Pro Tempore: Solomon Foot (Rep., Vt.) was elected on March 4, 1863, December 18, 1863, February 23, 1864, March 11, 1864, and April 11, 1864. Daniel Clark (Rep., N.H.) was elected on April 26, 1864, and February 9, 1865. [See note 4, p. xxix]

Majority Leader, Majority Whip, Minority Leader, and Minority Whip: None. These functions did not evolve into formal Senate positions until the 62nd Congress (1911-1913).

Chairmen of Selected Key Committees: [See also

---

*The 11 states that seceded from the Union were Alabama, Arkansas, Florida, Georgia, Louisiana, Mississippi, North Carolina, South Carolina, Tennessee, Texas and Virginia. None of these states had representatives in Congress, and only Virginia had senators. Of the two Virginia senators, John S. Carlile (Rep., Va.) was really from Clarksburg, West Virginia. West Virginia was now a state and sent its first senators to this Congress, but Carlile stayed on as a "Virginia" senator. The other senator, Lemuel J. Bowden (Rep., Va.) of Williamsburg, also was not loyal to the Confederacy and was not chosen by the legislature in Richmond. Carlile did not return to the 39th Congress, and Bowden died on January 2, 1864.

C H R O N O L O G Y

March 4, 1863:	The 38th Congress and a special session of the Senate begin.
March 6, 1863:	President Lincoln nominates Stephen J. Field to fill a newly created position on the Supreme Court.
March 10, 1863:	The Senate confirms Field.
March 14, 1863:	The special session of the Senate ends.
December 7, 1863:	The first session begins, and Schuyler Colfax (Rep., Ind.) is elected Speaker of the House.
March 17, 1864:	Congress passes legislation admitting Nevada into the United States.
April 14, 1864:	Congress passes legislation admitting Nebraska into the United States.
June 27, 1864:	Congress authorizes construction of the Northern Pacific Railroad.
July 1, 1864:	President Lincoln nominates, and the Senate confirms, William P. Fessenden to be secretary of the Treasury.
July 4, 1864:	The first session ends.
October 12, 1864:	Chief Justice Roger B. Taney dies.
December 5, 1864:	The second session begins. President Lincoln nominates James Speed to be attorney general.
December 6, 1864:	President Lincoln nominates, and the Senate confirms, Salmon P. Chase to replace Taney as chief justice.
December 12, 1864:	The Senate confirms Speed.
January 31, 1865:	Congress sends the 13th Amendment to the states for ratification.
March 1, 1865:	Congress establishes the Freedmen's Bureau.
March 3, 1865:	The second session and the 38th Congress end.

[See note 6, p. xxix]

Organization and Administration, p. 163]

Committee on Finance: William Fessenden (Rep., Maine) and John Sherman (Rep., Ohio)

Committee on Foreign Relations: Charles Sumner (Rep., Mass.)

Committee on the Judiciary: Lyman Trumbull (Rep., Ill.)

Committee on Military Affairs: Henry Wilson (Rep., Mass.)

Committee on Naval Affairs: John Hale (Rep., N.H.) and James Grimes (Rep., Iowa)

HOUSE LEADERSHIP

Speaker of the House: Schuyler Colfax (Rep., Ind.) was elected Speaker on December 7, 1863. Colfax first had been elected to Congress in the 34th Congress and soon proved to be a leader among his fellow Republicans. After a succession of one-term Speakers, Colfax would serve as Speaker from the 38th Congress through the 40th Congress, before leaving Congress to become President Grant's vice president after the presidential elections of 1868.

Majority Leader, Majority Whip, Minority Leader, and Minority Whip: None. These func-

TABLE OF KEY VOTES

Senate

Subject of Vote	Date of Vote	For	Against
Confirmation of Stephen J. Field to Supreme Court	March 10, 1863	Passed by voice vote	
Admission of Nevada	March 3, 1864	24	16
13th Amendment	April 8, 1864	38	6
Admission of Nebraska to the Union	April 14, 1864	Passed by voice vote	
Northern Pacific Railroad Authorization	June 27, 1864	Passed by voice vote	
Freedmen's Bureau Established	June 28, 1864	21	9
Confirmation of William P. Fessenden to be Secretary of the Treasury	July 1, 1864	Passed by voice vote	
Confirmation of Salmon P. Chase to Supreme Court	December 6, 1864	Passed by voice vote	
Confirmation of James Speed to be Attorney General	December 12, 1864	Passed by voice vote	

House

Subject of Vote	Date of Vote	For	Against
Admission of Nevada to the Union	March 17, 1864	Passed by voice vote	
Admission of Nebraska to the Union	March 17, 1864	Passed by voice vote	
Northern Pacific Railroad Authorization	May 31, 1864	74	50
13th Amendment	January 31, 1865	119	56
Freedmen's Bureau Established	March 1, 1865	69	67

[See note 7, p. xxix]

tions did not evolve into formal House positions until the 56th Congress (1899-1901).

Chairmen of Selected Key Committees: [See also Organization and Administration, p. 163]

Committee on Agriculture: Brutus J. Clay (Rep., Ky.)

Committee on Foreign Affairs: Henry Winter Davis (Rep., Md.)

The dome of the Capitol building was completed during the Civil War.

Committee on the Judiciary: James F. Wilson (Rep., Iowa)

Committee on Military Affairs: Robert C. Schenck (Rep., Ohio)

Committee on Naval Affairs: Alexander H. Rice (Rep., Mass.)

Committee on Ways and Means: Thaddeus Stevens (Rep., Pa.)

ORGANIZATION AND ADMINISTRATION

There have been approximately two thousand committees throughout the history of Congress. However, the modern committee structure and the modern allocation of committee jurisdiction, seniority, and ranking minority member status was not established until after World War II. [See note 5, p. xxix]

MAJOR LEGISLATION PASSED

Admission of Nevada and Nebraska as New States: Congress voted to admit Nevada and Nebraska into the United States.

Freedmen's Bureau: Congress established the Bureau of Refugees, Freedmen, and Abandoned Lands to assist the newly freed southern slaves. This bureau was known as the Freedmen's Bureau.

Northern Pacific Railroad: Congress authorized the Northern Pacific Railroad to construct a railroad from the Great Lakes to the city of Portland, Oregon, in the Pacific Northwest. Congress's authorization included a substantial subsidy in the form of land grants.

FAILED LEGISLATION

None of historical significance.

RELATIONS WITH THE PRESIDENT

Lincoln's presidency was dominated by the Civil War. Although the Confederate states were no longer represented in Congress and Lincoln was largely successful in getting the legislation and war powers he wanted, there were difficulties in his relations with Congress. The Democrats in Congress were mostly pro-southern. Within the Republican Party, the increasingly powerful faction called the Radical Republicans criticized Lincoln's plan for treating the South leniently after the war and resented Lincoln's opposition to their legislative initiatives that would have required harsher treatment. Further, Lincoln's wife, Mary Todd, was from an influential southern family in Kentucky and had several relatives in the Confederate army. Many members of Congress were suspicious of her, and some even accused her of being a spy.

Lincoln vetoed four bills during the 38th Congress. One veto was historically significant. The Radical Republicans, led by Senator Benjamin F. Wade (Rep., Ohio) and Representative Henry W. David (Rep., Md.), enacted legislation requiring a majority of the population of each southern state to swear allegiance to the federal government before that state could be readmitted to the Union. Lincoln pocket vetoed the bill, and Congress never took action to override.

NOMINATIONS, APPOINTMENTS, AND CONFIRMATIONS

The Judiciary: The Court was increased to ten justices before the 37th Congress ended in 1863, and on March 6, 1863, President Lincoln nominated Stephen J. Field to fill the newly created position. The Senate confirmed Field on March 10, 1863, by voice vote. On October 12, 1864, Chief Justice Roger B. Taney died. On December 6, 1864, Lincoln nominated, and the Senate confirmed by voice vote, Salmon P. Chase to replace Taney.

The Executive Branch: On July 1, 1864, President Lincoln nominated, and the Senate confirmed by voice vote, William P. Fessenden to be secretary of the Treasury. On December 5, 1864, Lincoln nominated James Speed to be attor-

ney general, and on December 12, 1864, the Senate confirmed Speed by voice vote.

IMPEACHMENTS

None.

CONSTITUTIONAL AMENDMENTS

Congress sent the Thirteenth Amendment, which abolished slavery, to the states for ratification. The amendment was ratified by the required three-fourths of the states effective December 6, 1865. [For the text of the Thirteenth Amendment, see the copy of the Constitution at Appendix A]

FURTHER READING

Findley, Paul. A. *Lincoln: The Crucible of Congress.* New York: Crown Publishers, Inc., 1979.

Hunt, H. Draper. *Hannibal Hamlin: Lincoln's First Vice President.* Syracuse, N.Y.: Syracuse University Press, 1969.

Lincoln, Abraham. *The Collected Works of Abraham Lincoln.* New Brunswick, N.J.: Rutgers University Press, 1953 (eight volumes).

Smith, Willard. *Schuyler Colfax: The Changing Fortunes of a Political Idol.* Indianapolis: Indiana Historical Bureau, 1952.

Swisher, Carl Brent. *Stephen J. Field, Craftsman of the Law.* Washington, D.C.: The Brookings Institution, 1930.

The 39th Congress

MARCH 4, 1865-MARCH 3, 1867

Special Senate Session: March 4, 1865-March 11, 1865
First Session: December 4, 1865-July 28, 1866
Second Session: December 3, 1866-March 3, 1867

The Senate held a special session to vote on the confirmation of presidential appointees to various offices. [See note 1, p. xxix]

In the 1864 elections for the 39th Congress, the Republicans gained 6 seats in the Senate to increase their majority to 42 seats out of the 72. The Democrats gained 1 seat giving them a total of 10 seats. All of the 20 remaining seats were vacant due to the secession of southern states.* In the House, the Republicans gained 47 seats to increase their majority to 149 of the 243 seats. The Democrats lost 33 seats leaving them with 42. Of the remaining 52 seats, 50 were vacant due to the secession of southern states, and 2 seats were held by representatives who were neither Republicans nor Democrats or were vacant for other reasons. [See notes 2 and 3, p. xxix]

BACKGROUND

On March 4, 1865, President Abraham Lincoln was inaugurated for his second term as the 16th president of the United States. The Civil War was all but over. Except for some scattered Confederate forces, General Lee surrendered the last major Confederate force on April 9, 1865, at Appomattox, Virginia. Five days later, on April 14, John Wilkes Booth assassinated Lincoln at Ford's Theatre in Washington, D.C. On April 15, Vice President Andrew Johnson was inaugurated as the 17th president of the U.S.

By the end of 1865 the Thirteenth Amendment to the Constitution abolishing slavery had been ratified by the states. In 1866 Congress passed the New Freedmen's Bureau Act and a Civil Rights Act over President Johnson's vetoes. In 1867 Congress passed the Tenure of Office Act, which prevented the president from unilaterally terminating government officials who had been appointed with the Senate's advice and consent.

SENATE LEADERSHIP

Vice President: Andrew Johnson was vice president until April 15, 1865, when he became president after the assassination of President Abraham Lincoln on April 14, 1865. (Until the Twenty-fifth Amendment was ratified on February 10, 1967 [See 90th Congress], there was no mechanism for filling vacancies in the office of the vice president. Therefore, there was no president of the Senate during the 39th Congress.)

President Pro Tempore: Lafayette Sabine Foster (Rep., Conn.) was elected on March 7, 1865, and Benjamin Franklin Wade (Rep., Ohio) was elected on March 2, 1867. [See note 4, p. xxix]

Majority Leader, Majority Whip, Minority Leader, and Minority Whip: None. These functions did not evolve into formal Senate positions until the 62nd Congress (1911-1913).

---

* The 11 states that seceded from the Union were Alabama, Arkansas, Florida, Georgia, Louisiana, Mississippi, North Carolina, South Carolina, Tennessee, Texas and Virginia. Tennessee, however, had been under Union occupation since 1862 and was once again permitted to send senators and representatives beginning with this Congress.

C H R O N O L O G Y

March 4, 1865:	The 39th Congress and a special session of the Senate begin.
March 6, 1865:	President Lincoln nominates Hugh McCulloch to be secretary of the Treasury.
March 7, 1865:	The Senate confirms McCulloch.
March 9, 1865:	President Lincoln nominates, and the Senate confirms, James Harlan to be secretary of the interior.
March 11, 1865:	The special session of the Senate ends.
April 9, 1865:	The last significant Confederate army surrenders at Appomattox, Virginia.
April 14, 1865:	John Wilkes Booth assassinates President Lincoln.
April 15, 1865:	Vice President Andrew Johnson is inaugurated as president.
May 30, 1865:	Supreme Court Justice John Catron dies, but is not replaced, due to a reduction in the size of the Supreme Court.
December 4, 1865:	The first session begins, and Schuyler Colfax (Rep., Ind.) is reelected Speaker of the House.
March 13, 1866:	Congress passes the Civil Rights Act of 1866.
March 27, 1866:	President Johnson vetoes the Civil Rights Act.
April 6, 1866:	The Senate votes to override Johnson's veto.
April 9, 1866:	The House also votes to override the Civil Rights Act veto.
June 8, 1866:	Congress sends the 14th Amendment to the states for ratification.
June 26, 1866:	Congress passes legislation continuing the Freedmen's Bureau.
July 16, 1866:	President Johnson vetoes the Freedmen's Bureau bill. Both the Senate and the House vote to override the veto.
July 20, 1866:	President Johnson nominates Henry Stanbery to be attorney general.
July 23, 1866:	The Senate confirms Stanbery.
July 27, 1866:	Johnson nominates, and the Senate confirms, Orville H. Browning to be secretary of the Interior.
July 28, 1866:	The first session ends.
December 3, 1866:	The second session begins.
February 2, 1867:	Congress passes the Tenure of Office Act.
March 3, 1867:	The second session and the 39th Congress end.

[See note 6, p. xxix]

Chairmen of Selected Key Committees: [See also Organization and Administration, p. 167]

Committee on Finance: William Fessenden (Rep., Maine)

Committee on Foreign Relations: Charles Sumner (Rep., Mass.)

Committee on the Judiciary: Lyman Trumbull (Rep., Ill.)

Committee on Military Affairs: Henry Wilson (Rep., Mass.)

Committee on Naval Affairs: James Grimes (Rep., Iowa)

HOUSE LEADERSHIP

Speaker of the House: Schuyler Colfax (Rep., Ind.) was reelected Speaker on December 4, 1865. [See biographical note in 38th Congress]

Majority Leader, Majority Whip, Minority Leader, and Minority Whip: None. These functions did not evolve into formal House positions until the 56th Congress (1899-1901).

Chairmen of Selected Key Committees: [See also Organization and Administration, below]

Committee on Agriculture: John Bidwell (Rep., Calif.)

Committee on Appropriations: Thaddeus Stevens (Rep., Pa.)

Committee on Banking, Finance, and Urban Affairs: Theodore M. Pomeroy (Rep., N.Y.)

Committee on Foreign Affairs: Nathaniel P. Banks (Rep., Mass.)

Committee on the Judiciary: James F. Wilson (Rep., Iowa)

Committee on Military Affairs: Robert C. Schenck (Rep., Ohio)

Committee on Naval Affairs: Alexander H. Rice (Rep., Mass.)

Committee on Ways and Means: Justin S. Morrill (Rep., Vt.)

ORGANIZATION AND ADMINISTRATION

In this Congress, the Committee on Appropriations and the Committee on Banking, Finance, and Urban Affairs became permanent standing committees in the House. They were spin-offs of the Committee on Ways and Means, which had become the largest committee in the House and had jurisdiction over financial matters from banking to tariffs and taxes. Thaddeus Stevens (Rep., Pa.), the chairman of Ways and Means in the 38th Congress, became the first chairman of the Appropriations Committee. [See note 5, p. xxix]

MAJOR LEGISLATION PASSED

Civil Rights: Congress enacted the Civil Rights Act of 1866, which gave U.S. citizenship and full civil rights to every person born in the United States, except Native Americans. In a variety of ways, Congress would attempt to protect the civil rights of the freed slaves in the military occupation districts of the South during the period known as Reconstruction.

Freedmen's Bureau: In the New Freedmen's Bureau Act, Congress continued the Freedmen's Bureau for another two years.

Government Officials: In the Tenure of Office Act, Congress stated that before the president could terminate government officials who had been appointed with the Senate's advice and consent, the president first had to get the Senate's approval.

FAILED LEGISLATION

None of historical significance.

RELATIONS WITH THE PRESIDENT

Lincoln's presidency during the 39th Congress was too short to characterize his relations with Congress. The new president, Andrew Johnson, never got along well with Congress. Johnson wanted to treat the states of the defeated Confederacy leniently, which helped to fan the animosity on Capitol Hill that would lead to impeachment proceedings in the next Congress.

Johnson vetoed 13 bills during the 39th Congress. Two major vetoes, concerning civil rights legislation and the Freedmen's Bureau, were overridden. Johnson vetoed the civil rights legislation on March 27, 1866; the Senate voted to override the veto by a 33-to-15 vote on April 6, 1866, and the House voted to override by a vote of 122 to 41 on April 9, 1866. Johnson vetoed a bill extending the life of the Freedmen's Bureau on July 16, 1866. On that same day, the House voted to override the veto by a vote of 103 to 33, and the Senate voted to override the veto by a vote of 33 to 12.

TABLE OF KEY VOTES

Senate

Subject of Vote	Date of Vote	For	Against
Civil Rights Act	February 2, 1866	33	12
Overriding Civil Rights Veto	April 6, 1866	33	15
14th Amendment	June 8, 1866	33	11
Freedmen's Bureau Extention	June 26, 1866	Passed by voice vote	
Overriding Freedmen's Bureau Veto	July 16, 1866	33	12
Tenure of Government Officials	January 19, 1867	29	9

House

Subject of Vote	Date of Vote	For	Against
Civil Rights Act	March 13, 1866	111	38
Overriding Civil Rights Veto	April 9, 1866	122	41
14th Amendment	May 10, 1866	128	37
Freedmen's Bureau Extension	May 29, 1866	96	32
Overriding Freedmen's Bureau Veto	July 16, 1866	103	33
Tenure of Government Officials	February 2, 1867	111	38

[See note 7, p. xxix]

NOMINATIONS, APPOINTMENTS, AND CONFIRMATIONS

The Judiciary: On May 30, 1865, Supreme Court Justice John Catron died. Catron was not replaced because the Supreme Court had been reduced from ten justices to seven justices, with the reduction to take place by attrition.

The Executive Branch: On March 6, 1865, President Lincoln nominated Hugh McCulloch to be secretary of the Treasury, and on March 7, 1865, the Senate confirmed McCulloch by voice vote. On March 9, 1865, Lincoln nominated and the Senate confirmed by voice vote, James Harlan to be secretary of the Interior.

After Lincoln's assassination, President Johnson on July 20, 1866, nominated Henry Stanbery to be attorney general, and the Senate confirmed Stanbery by voice vote on July 23, 1866. Johnson nominated, and the Senate confirmed by voice vote, Orville H. Browning to be secretary of the interior. President Johnson did not replace many cabinet-level officials from the previous administration, and no Senate confirmation vote was required for continuing those officials in their positions.

IMPEACHMENTS

None.

CONSTITUTIONAL AMENDMENTS

Congress sent the Fourteenth Amendment to the states for ratification. The amendment consists of five sections, but the most important provisions are those which make it illegal for the states to deny any person the privileges and immunities of citizenship, due process of law, or the equal protection of the laws. The purpose of the Fourteenth Amendment was to establish the supremacy of the federal government over the states, particularly the southern states where states' rights sentiment had helped fuel the Civil War and where the newly freed slaves needed protection from state legislatures. The Fourteenth Amendment was ratified by the required three-fourths of the states effective July 9, 1866. [For the full text of the Fourteenth Amendment, see the copy of the Constitution in Appendix A.]

FURTHER READING

Benedict, Michael. *The Impeachment and Trial of Andrew Johnson*. New York: W.W. Norton & Co., 1972.

Findley, Paul. A. *Lincoln: The Crucible of Congress*. New York: Crown Publishers, Inc., 1979.

Johnson, Andrew. *The Papers of Andrew Johnson*. Knoxville, Tenn.: University of Tennessee Press, 1967-present (seven volumes to date).

Lincoln, Abraham. *The Collected Works of Abraham Lincoln*. New Brunswick, N.J.: Rutgers University Press, 1953 (eight volumes).

Smith, Willard. *Schuyler Colfax: The Changing Fortunes of a Political Idol*. Indianapolis: Indiana Historical Bureau, 1952.

Smock, Raymond. "Searching for the Political Legacy of Thaddeus Stevens." *Pennsylvania History* (April 1993, Volume 60, Number 2): pp. 189-195.

Trefousse, Hans L. *Andrew Johnson*. New York: W.W. Norton & Co., 1989.

The 40th Congress

MARCH 4, 1867 - MARCH 3, 1869

First Session: March 4, 1867-December 1, 1867
Special Senate Session: April 1, 1867-April 20, 1867
Second Session: December 2, 1867-November 10, 1868
Third Session: December 7, 1868-March 3, 1869

The Senate held a special session to vote on the confirmation of presidential appointees to various offices.* [See note 1, p. xxix]

In the 1866 elections for the 40th Congress, the Republicans neither gained nor lost any seats in the Senate, and kept their majority of 42 seats out of the 74. The Democrats gained 1 seat, giving them a total of 11 seats. Of the remaining 21 seats, 20 were vacant due to the secession of Southern states during the Civil War, and 1 seat was held by a senator who was neither a Republican nor a Democrat. In the House, the Republicans lost 6 seats, reducing their majority to 143 of the 243 seats. The Democrats gained 7 seats to give them a total of 49 seats.† All of the remaining 51 seats were vacant due to the secession of southern states during the Civil War. [See notes 2 and 3, p. xxix]

BACKGROUND

Soon after the 40th Congress convened, Secretary of State William H. Seward signed a treaty with the Russian Empire whereby the United States would purchase Alaska for $7.2 million. The Senate approved the treaty on April 9, 1867. The reason behind Russia's decision to sell Alaska was not financial, as evidenced by the small purchase price, but Russia's desire to get the U.S. and Great Britain into a conflict over domination of the northeast Pacific Ocean that would leave the Russians free to pursue their ambitions in China.

In 1868 the House impeached President Andrew Johnson for violating the 1867 Tenure of Office Act passed by the 39th Congress over Johnson's veto. Specifically, Johnson was charged with firing Secretary of War Edwin M. Stanton in violation of the act. The motive for the impeachment was primarily political; the radical Republicans in Congress wanted to remove Johnson, who was from a border state and favored a lenient policy in dealing with the defeated states of the Confederacy. The trial was conducted in the Senate, which failed by one vote to remove Johnson.

SENATE LEADERSHIP

Vice President: None. Andrew Johnson became president on April 15, 1865, after the assassination of President Abraham Lincoln. [See 39th Congress]. (Until the Twenty-fifth Amendment was ratified on February 10, 1967 [See 90th Congress], there was no mechanism for filling vacancies in the office of the vice president. Therefore, there was no president of the Senate during the 40th Congress.)

President Pro Tempore: Benjamin Franklin Wade (Rep., Ohio) was one of the "Radical Republicans," a group which supported harsh

---

* The special Senate session was held while the first session of Congress was in recess.
† During the Civil War, 11 states seceded from the Union: Alabama, Arkansas, Florida, Georgia, Louisiana, Mississippi, North Carolina, South Carolina, Tennessee, Texas and Virginia. Tennessee, under Union military occupation since 1862, was permitted to send senators and representatives beginning in the 39th Congress. During Reconstruction, the same privilege would be restored to the other 10 Southern states.

C H R O N O L O G Y

March 4, 1867:	The 40th Congress and the first session begin. Schuyler Colfax (Rep., Ind.) is reelected Speaker of the House.
April 1, 1867:	A special session of the Senate begins while the first session is in recess.
April 9, 1867:	The Senate ratifies the Alaska Treaty.
April 20, 1867:	The special session of the Senate ends.
July 5, 1867:	Justice James M. Wayne dies, but is not replaced, due to a reduction in the size of the Supreme Court.
August 12, 1867:	President Johnson fires Secretary of War Edwin Stanton.
December 1, 1867:	The first session ends.
December 2, 1867:	The second session begins.
December 7, 1867:	The House votes against impeaching President Johnson.
February 24, 1868:	The House reverses itself, and votes to impeach President Johnson.
March 13, 1868:	The impeachment trial of President Johnson begins in the Senate.
April 23, 1868:	President Johnson nominates John M. Schofield as the new secretary of war.
May 26, 1868:	President Johnson's impeachment trial ends, with the Senate having failed to remove him.
May 27, 1868:	President Johnson nominates Henry Stanbery to serve once again as attorney general.
May 30, 1868:	The Senate confirms Schofield.
June 2, 1868:	The Senate rejects Stanbery's nomination.
June 10, 1868:	Congress readmits most of the former Confederate states to the United States.
June 22, 1868:	President Johnson nominates William M. Evarts to be attorney general.
June 25, 1868:	President Johnson vetoes the readmission of the Confederate states. The veto is overridden by the House and the Senate.
July 15, 1868:	The Senate confirms Evarts.
November 10, 1868:	The second session ends.
December 7, 1868:	The third session begins.
February 20, 1869:	Congress sends the 15th Amendment to the states for ratification.
March 3, 1869:	The third session and the 40th Congress end.

[See note 6, p. xxix]

treatment for the defeated Confederacy in this period of Reconstruction. He stood to become president if the Senate removed Johnson. Wade sought to become the Republican candidate for vice president in the presidential election of 1868, but lost to Speaker of the House Schuyler Colfax. [See note 4, p. xxix]

Majority Leader, Majority Whip, Minority Leader, and Minority Whip: None. These functions did not evolve into formal Senate positions until the 62nd Congress (1911-1913).

Chairmen of Selected Key Committees: [See also Organization and Administration, below]

Committee on Appropriations: Lot Morrill (Rep., Maine)

Committee on Finance: John Sherman (Rep., Ohio)

Committee on Foreign Relations: Charles Sumner (Rep., Mass.)

Committee on the Judiciary: Lyman Trumbull (Rep., Ill.)

Committee on Military Affairs: Henry Wilson (Rep., Mass.)

Committee on Naval Affairs: James Grimes (Rep., Iowa)

HOUSE LEADERSHIP

Speaker of the House: Schuyler Colfax (Rep., Ind.) was reelected Speaker on March 4, 1867. [See biographical note in 38th Congress] Colfax left Congress to become President Grant's vice president after the presidential elections of 1868. Colfax resigned effective March 3, 1869, and Theodore Medad Pomeroy (Rep., N.Y.) was elected the new Speaker that same day.

Majority Leader, Majority Whip, Minority Leader, and Minority Whip: None. These functions did not evolve into formal House positions until the 56th Congress (1899-1901).

Chairmen of Selected Key Committees: [See also Organization and Administration, below]

Committee on Agriculture: Rowland E. Trowbridge (Rep., Mich.)

Committee on Appropriations: Thaddeus Stevens (Rep., Pa.) and Elihu B. Washburne (Rep., Ill.)

Committee on Banking, Finance, and Urban Affairs: Theodore M. Pomeroy (Rep., N.Y.)

Committee on Foreign Affairs: Nathaniel P. Banks (Rep., Mass.)

President Andrew Johnson

Committee on the Judiciary: James F. Wilson (Rep., Iowa)

Committee on Military Affairs: James A. Garfield (Rep., Ohio)

Committee on Naval Affairs: Frederick A. Pike (Rep., Maine)

Committee on Ways and Means: Robert C. Schenck (Rep., Ohio)

ORGANIZATION AND ADMINISTRATION

In this Congress, the Senate established a permanent standing Committee on Appropriations. Also during this Congress, the Senate gave the Judiciary Committee the power to review and investigate all presidential nominees to the federal judiciary. [See note 5, p. xxix]

MAJOR LEGISLATION PASSED

Alaska: In the Alaska Purchase Treaty, the Senate approved a treaty with Russia whereby the U.S. purchased Alaska for $7.2 million.

TABLE OF KEY VOTES

Senate

Subject of Vote	Date of Vote	For	Against
Alaska Treaty Ratification	April 9, 1867	37	2
First Johnson Impeachment Vote (failed: two-thirds needed)	May 16, 1868	35	19
Second Johnson Impeachment Vote (failed: two-thirds needed)	May 26, 1868	35	19
Readmission of Confederate States	June 10, 1868	31	5
15th Amendment	February 17, 1869	35	11

House

Subject of Vote	Date of Vote	For	Against
First Johnson Impeachment Vote	December 7, 1867	57 (failed)	108
Second Johnson Impeachment Vote	February 24, 1868	126 (passed)	47
Readmission of Confederate States	May 14, 1868	110	35
15th Amendment	February 20, 1869	140	37

[See note 7, p. xxix]

Confederate States: In the Omnibus Act, Congress readmitted seven of 11 former Confederate states to the United States: Alabama, Arkansas, Florida, Georgia, Louisiana, North Carolina, and South Carolina.

FAILED LEGISLATION

None of historical significance.

RELATIONS WITH THE PRESIDENT

Relations between President Andrew Johnson and the 40th Congress were extremely bad, leading to Johnson's impeachment. [See Impeachments, p. 174] Johnson vetoed 16 bills during the 40th Congress. One veto concerned the readmission of the Confederate states into the Union. This veto of June 25, 1868, was overridden that same day by the House by a vote of 108 to 32, and by the Senate by a vote of 35 to 8.

NOMINATIONS, APPOINTMENTS, AND CONFIRMATIONS

The Judiciary: The Supreme Court had previously been reduced from ten justices to seven justices, with the reduction to take place by attrition. Thus, when Justice James M. Wayne died on July 5, 1867, the number of justices was reduced from nine to eight, and Wayne was therefore not replaced.

There were, however, two developments in the 40th Congress that would greatly affect the judicial nomination and confirmation process.

Scene in the U.S Senate, May 12th, 1868, previous to the opening of the court of impeachment—
Senator Zachariah Chandler denouncing the Republican senators opposed to conviction.

First, in 1868 the Senate Judiciary Committee became the conduit through which all presidential nominations to the judiciary would have to move. [See Organization and Administration, p. 172] Second, the size of the Supreme Court was increased to nine justices, which has not changed to the present date.

The Executive Branch: While impeachment proceedings, precipitated by the firing of Secretary of War Edwin M. Stanton [See Impeachments, below] were pending, President Johnson on April 23, 1868, nominated John M. Schofield to be the new secretary of war. On May 30, 1868, after the conclusion of the impeachment trial, the Senate confirmed Schofield by a vote of 35 to 2. Also during the impeachment proceedings, Attorney General Henry Stanbery resigned in order to serve as Johnson's defense counsel. On May 27, 1868, the day after the impeachment trial ended in the Senate, Johnson nominated Stanbery to serve

once again as attorney general. The Senate, however, rejected Stanbery's nomination on June 2, 1868, by a vote of 11 in favor of the nomination and 29 against. On June 22, 1868, Johnson nominated William M. Evarts to be attorney general, and on July 15, 1868, the Senate confirmed Evarts by a vote of 27 to 7.

IMPEACHMENTS

President Johnson, a former governor of and senator from Tennessee, favored a lenient approach toward the former rebel states of the South. During his administration, Johnson often used his veto power to thwart civil rights legislation. Johnson became very unpopular in the Republican-dominated Congress. He violated the Tenure of Office Act [See 39th Congress] when on August 12, 1867, he fired his political adversary, the powerful Republican Secretary of War Edwin Stanton without obtaining prior Senate approval. This action gave the congressional Republicans the excuse they needed to try to get rid of Johnson: They impeached him. As required by the Constitution, the process began in the House of Representatives, where a simple majority must vote in favor of impeachment. There were two votes: on December 7, 1867, the House voted 108 to 57 against impeachment; on February 24, 1868, the House voted 126 to 47 in favor of impeachment.

Trial proceedings commenced in the Senate on March 13, 1868, and ended on May 26, 1868. There were two impeachment votes, and although most of the senators voted in favor of removing Johnson from office, both votes were one vote short of the two-thirds majority necessary under the Constitution to remove Johnson. [See Table of Key Votes, p. 173] The impeachment proceedings ended, and Johnson continued as president.

CONSTITUTIONAL AMENDMENTS

Congress sent the Fifteenth Amendment, which protected the right of the newly freed slaves to vote, to the states for ratification. The amendment was ratified by the required three-fourths of the states effective February 3, 1870. [For the text of the Fifteenth Amendment, see the copy of the Constitution in Appendix A]

FURTHER READING

Benedict, Michael. *The Impeachment and Trial of Andrew Johnson*. New York: W.W. Norton & Co., 1972.

Christianson, Stephen G. "President Andrew Johnson Impeachment Trial." In *Great American Trials*, Edited by Edward W. Knappman. Detroit: Gale Research, 1994.

Johnson, Andrew. *The Papers of Andrew Johnson*. Knoxville, Tenn.: University of Tennessee Press, 1967-present (seven volumes to date).

Lanman, Charles. *Dictionary of the United States Congress*. Hartford, Conn.: T. Belknap and H. E. Goodwin, 1868.

Smith, Willard. *Schuyler Colfax: The Changing Fortunes of a Political Idol*. Indianapolis: Indiana Historical Bureau, 1952.

Trefousse, Hans L. *Andrew Johnson*. New York: W.W. Norton & Co., 1989.

The 41st Congress

MARCH 4, 1869-MARCH 3, 1871

First Session: March 4, 1869-April 10, 1869
Special Senate Session: April 12, 1869-April 22, 1869
Second Session: December 6, 1869-July 15, 1870
Third Session: December 5, 1870-March 3, 1871

The Senate held a special session to vote on the confirmation of presidential appointees to various offices. [See note 1, p. xxix]

In the 1868 elections for the 41st Congress, the Republicans gained 14 seats in the Senate to increase their majority to 56 seats out of the 74. The Democrats kept their 11 seats from the 40th Congress. Seven seats were not held by either of the major parties. In the House, the Republicans gained 6 seats to increase their majority to 149 of the 243 seats. The Democrats gained 14 seats, raising their total to 63 seats. Thirty-one seats were not held by either of the major parties. Most of the seats held by neither party were vacancies filled by the end of this Congress as senators and and representatives from southern states readmitted into the Union presented their credentials and were seated. [See notes 2 and 3, p. xxix]

BACKGROUND

According to the census of 1870, the population of the United States as of June 1, 1870, was 39,818,449, resulting in a population density of 13.4 persons for each of the country's 2,969,640 square miles. This was a population increase of 26.6 percent over the 1860 census.

On March 4, 1869, Ulysses S. Grant was inaugurated as the 18th president of the United States. In 1869 two political organizations were formed that would have a major effect on

American history. These organizations were the Prohibition Party, which sought to outlaw all alcoholic beverages, and the National Woman's Suffrage Association, which sought to obtain women's right to vote. On September 24, 1869, an attempt to corner the gold market by Jay Gould, James Fisk Jr., and several associates caused a severe Wall Street panic, called Black Friday. The panic damaged the reputation of the Grant administration, which had been slow to act in the crisis and had close ties to those who had tried to manipulate the market.

In 1870 as southern states were once again permitted representation, the first African Americans took their seats in Congress: Senator Hiram R. Revels (Rep., Miss.) and Representative Joseph H. Rainey (Rep., S.C). In the Senate, the Democrats tried unsuccessfully to block Revels from being seated. [See Organization and Administration, p. 179] Also, Congress established the Department of Justice, and the Fifteenth Amendment protecting the right of former slaves to vote (approved by the 40th Congress) was ratified by the states.

SENATE LEADERSHIP

Vice President: Schuyler Colfax served as Speaker of the House from the 38th Congress through the 40th Congress, after which he left Congress to become President Grant's vice president following the presidential elections of 1868.

C H R O N O L O G Y

March 4, 1869:	The 41st Congress and the first session begin. James Gillespie Blaine (Rep., Maine) is elected Speaker of the House.
March 5, 1869:	President Grant nominates Adolph E. Borie to be secretary of the Navy, Jacob D. Cox to be secretary of the interior, Ebenezer R. Hoar to be attorney general, and Alexander T. Stewart to be secretary of the Treasury. The Senate confirms all of the nominees except Stewart, who declines to serve.
March 11, 1869:	President Grant nominates, and the Senate confirms, George S. Boutwell to be secretary of the Treasury, Hamilton Fish to be secretary of state, and John A. Rawlins to be secretary of war.
March 15, 1869:	Congress passes the Public Credit Act.
April 10, 1869:	The first session ends.
April 12, 1869:	A special session of the Senate begins.
April 22, 1869:	The special session of the Senate ends.
December 6, 1869:	The second session begins. President Grant nominates William W. Belknap to succeed Rawlins as secretary of war and George M. Robeson to succeed Borie as secretary of the Navy.
December 8, 1869:	The Senate confirms both nominees.
January 31, 1870:	Supreme Court Justice Robert Cooper Grier retires.
February 7, 1870:	President Grant nominates William Strong and Joseph P. Bradley to fill two vacant positions on the Court — one created by Grier's retirement and the other by the expansion of the Court to nine seats during the 40th Congress.
February 18, 1870:	The Senate confirms Strong.
February 25, 1870:	A challenge to the credentials of Hiram R. Revels (Rep., Miss.), the first African American senator, fails and Revels is seated.
March 21, 1870:	The Senate confirms Bradley.
June 16, 1870:	Congress establishes the Department of Justice. President Grant nominates Amos T. Akerman to succeed Hoar as attorney general.
June 23, 1870:	The Senate confirms Akerman.
June 30, 1870:	The Senate refuses to ratify the Dominican Republic Treaty.
July 15, 1870:	The second session ends.
December 5, 1870:	The third session begins.
December 6, 1870:	President Grant nominates Columbus Delano to succeed Cox as secretary of the Interior.
December 8, 1870:	The Senate confirms Delano.
March 3, 1871:	The third session and the 41st Congress end.

[See note 6, p. xxix]

The first African American senator and representatives.

President Pro Tempore: Henry Bowen Anthony (Rep., R.I.) was elected on March 23, 1869, April 9, 1869, May 28, 1870, July 1, 1870, and July 14, 1870. [See note 4, p. xxix]

Majority Leader, Majority Whip, Minority Leader, and Minority Whip: None. These functions did not evolve into formal Senate positions until the 62nd Congress (1911-1913).

Chairmen of Selected Key Committees: [See also Organization and Administration, p. 179]

Committee on Appropriations: Lot Morrill (Rep., Maine)

Committee on Finance: John Sherman (Rep., Ohio)

Committee on Foreign Relations: Charles Sumner (Rep., Mass.)

Committee on the Judiciary: Lyman Trumbull (Rep., Ill.)

Committee on Military Affairs: Henry Wilson (Rep., Mass.)

Committee on Naval Affairs: James Grimes (Rep., Iowa) and Aaron Cragin (Rep., N.H.)

HOUSE LEADERSHIP

Speaker of the House: James Gillespie Blaine (Rep., Maine) was elected Speaker on March 4, 1869. He first was elected to Congress in the 38th Congress. Like Schuyler Colfax (Rep., Ind.) before him, who served as Speaker from the 38th Congress through the 40th Congress, Blaine was able to maintain sufficient control over the House to remain as Speaker from the 41st Congress through the 43rd Congress.

Majority Leader, Majority Whip, Minority Leader, and Minority Whip: None. These functions did not evolve into formal House positions until the 56th Congress (1899-1901).

Chairmen of Selected Key Committees: [See also Organization and Administration, p. 179]

Committee on Agriculture: John T. Wilson (Rep., Ohio)

TABLE OF KEY VOTES

Senate

Subject of Vote	Date of Vote	For	Against
Public Credit Act	March 15, 1869	42	13
Seating of First African American Senator	February 25, 1870	48	8
Establishment of Justice Department	June 16, 1870	Passed by voice vote	
Dominican Republic Treaty	June 30, 1870	28	28

House

Subject of Vote	Date of Vote	For	Against
Public Credit Act	March 12, 1869	97	47
Establishment of Justice Department	April 28, 1870	Passed by voice vote	

[See note 7, p. xxix]

Committee on Appropriations: Henry L. Dawes (Rep., Mass.)

Committee on Banking, Finance, and Urban Affairs: James A. Garfield (Rep., Ohio)

Committee on Foreign Affairs: Nathaniel P. Banks (Rep., Mass.)

Committee on the Judiciary: John A. Bingham (Rep., Ohio)

Committee on Military Affairs: John A. Logan (Rep., Ill.)

Committee on Naval Affairs: Glenni W. Scofield (Rep., Pa.)

Committee on Ways and Means: Robert C. Schenck (Rep., Ohio) and Samuel Hooper (Rep., Mass.)

ORGANIZATION AND ADMINISTRATION

Senate Democrats challenged the credentials of Hiram R. Revels (Rep., Miss.), the first African American ever sent to the United States Senate.

The Democrats' arguments were based primarily on simple prejudice: Senators Garrett Davis (Dem., Ky.) and Willard Saulsbury (Dem., Del.) claimed that the Fourteenth Amendment was invalid, and that blacks could never be citizens or be elected to Congress. On February 25, 1870, the Senate voted 48 to 8 that Revels' credentials were valid and that he would be seated. [See note 5, p. xxix]

MAJOR LEGISLATION PASSED

Government Debts: In the Public Credit Act, Congress authorized the federal government to pay its debts in gold.

Justice Department: Congress established the Department of Justice under the authority of the attorney general.

FAILED LEGISLATION

Foreign Policy: The Senate refused to ratify a treaty providing for American annexation of the newly independent Dominican Republic in the Caribbean. The actual vote was 28 to 28, far short of the required two-thirds majority.

RELATIONS WITH
THE PRESIDENT

Like George Washington, Ulysses S. Grant was elected president largely because of his popularity as a successful wartime general. Unlike Washington, however, Grant was a poor leader of the Congress, and his administration was tainted with charges of corruption. During the 41st Congress, Grant vetoed 16 bills, all of which concerned minor matters, such as relief bills for private citizens.

NOMINATIONS, APPOINTMENTS, AND CONFIRMATIONS

The Judiciary: On January 31, 1870, Supreme Court Justice Robert Cooper Grier retired. Grier's retirement reduced the Court from eight to seven members. Since there already was a vacancy on the Court from the previous Congress, President Grant now had two vacancies to fill.

Grant's record so far was not encouraging: He had failed twice to fill the one vacancy on the Court left over from the 40th Congress. Grant had nominated Ebenezer R. Hoar on December 15, 1869, but on February 3, 1870, the Senate voted 33 to 24 against Hoar's confirmation. Then, Grant nominated Edwin M. Stanton on December 20, 1869. The Senate confirmed Stanton that same day by a 46 to 11 vote, but Stanton died on December 24, 1869, before he was even sworn in. On February 7, 1870, after Grier's retirement, Grant nominated William Strong and Joseph P. Bradley to fill the two positions on the Court. The Senate confirmed Strong on February 18, 1870, by voice vote, and confirmed Bradley on March 21, 1870, by a 46 to 9 vote.

The Executive Branch: On March 5, 1869, President Grant nominated Adolph E. Borie to be secretary of the Navy, Jacob D. Cox to be secretary of the Interior, Ebenezer R. Hoar to be attorney general, and Alexander T. Stewart to be secretary of the Treasury. That same day, March 5, the Senate confirmed all of the nominees by voice

vote except Stewart, because Stewart declined to serve. On March 11, 1869, Grant nominated George S. Boutwell to be secretary of the Treasury, Hamilton Fish to be secretary of state, and John A. Rawlins to be secretary of war. All three nominees were confirmed in the Senate by voice vote that same day. On December 6, 1869, Grant nominated William W. Belknap to succeed Rawlins as secretary of war and George M. Robeson to succeed Borie as secretary of the Navy. On December 8, 1869, the Senate confirmed both nominees by voice vote.

On June 16, 1870, Grant nominated Amos T. Akerman to succeed Hoar as attorney general, and on June 23, 1870, the Senate confirmed Akerman by voice vote. On December 6, 1870, Grant nominated Columbus Delano to succeed Cox as secretary of the Interior, and the Senate confirmed Delano by voice vote on December 8, 1870.

IMPEACHMENTS

None.

CONSTITUTIONAL AMENDMENTS

None.

FURTHER READING

McFeely, William S. *Grant: A Biography.* New York: W.W. Norton & Co., 1981.

Muzzey, David S. *James G. Blaine: A Political Idol of Other Days.* Port Washington, N.Y.: Kennikat Press, 1963.

Smith, Willard. *Schuyler Colfax: The Changing Fortunes of a Political Idol.* Indianapolis: Indiana Historical Bureau, 1952.

The 42nd Congress

MARCH 4, 1871-MARCH 3, 1873

First Session: March 4, 1871-April 20, 1871
Special Senate Session: May 10, 1871-May 27, 1871
Second Session: December 4, 1871-June 10, 1872
Third Session: December 2, 1872-March 3, 1873

The Senate held a special session to decide whether to ratify the Treaty of Washington. [See Major Legislation, p. 183] [See note 1, p. xxix]

In the 1870 elections for the 42nd Congress, the Republicans lost 4 seats in the Senate to reduce their majority to 52 seats out of the 74. The Democrats gained 6 seats, giving them a total of 17 seats. Five seats were not held by either of the two major parties. In the House, the Republicans lost 15 seats to reduce their majority to 134 of the 243 seats. The Democrats gained 41 seats raising their a total to 104 seats. Five seats were not held by either major party. In both the House and the Senate, the seats officially held by neither party were in fact predominantly pro-Republican. [See notes 2 and 3, p. xxix]

BACKGROUND

During 1871, railroad lines were expanding rapidly in the West, which had the positive effect of facilitating commerce and the negative effect of encouraging overspeculation by financiers such as Jay Cooke and his Northern Pacific Railroad. The growth of the railroads turned Chicago, an important rail center, into one of America's largest cities. However, the Great Chicago Fire (October 8-11, 1871) destroyed much of the city. In 1872 the Credit Mobilier scandal broke, bring-ing national attention to the corruption surrounding the construction of the Union Pacific Railroad. [See Scandals, p. 184]

SENATE LEADERSHIP

Vice President: Schuyler Colfax served as Speaker of the House from the 38th Congress through the 40th Congress, after which he left Congress to become President Grant's vice president following the presidential elections of 1868. Colfax was unable to run with President Grant in the presidential elections of 1872, because there were allegations of wrongdoing against him in connection with the Credit Mobilier scandal. [See Scandals, p. 184]

President Pro Tempore: Henry Bowen Anthony (Rep., R.I.) was elected on March 10, 1871, April 17, 1871, May 23, 1871, December 21, 1871, February 23, 1872, June 8, 1872, December 4, 1872, December 13, 1872, December 20, 1872, and January 24, 1873. [See note 4, p. xxix]

Majority Leader, Majority Whip, Minority Leader, and Minority Whip: None. These functions did not evolve into formal Senate positions until the 62nd Congress (1911-1913).

Chairmen of Selected Key Committees: [See also Organization and Administration, p. 183]

CHRONOLOGY

March 4, 1871:	The 42nd Congress and the first session begin. James Gillespie Blaine (Rep., Maine) is reelected Speaker of the House.
April 14, 1871:	Congress passes legislation aimed at suppressing the Ku Klux Klan.
April 20, 1871:	The first session ends.
May 10, 1871:	A special session of the Senate begins.
May 24, 1871:	The Senate ratifies the Treaty of Washington, which provides for arbitration of claims with Great Britian arising out of the Civil War.
May 27, 1871:	The special session of the Senate ends.
December 4, 1871:	The second session begins.
December 14, 1871:	President Grant nominates, and the Senate confirms, George H. Williams to be attorney general.
February 27, 1872:	Congress passes the Yellowstone National Park Act.
May 30, 1872:	Congress passes legislation reducing tariffs.
June 10, 1872:	The second session ends.
November 28, 1872:	Supreme Court Justice Samuel Nelson retires.
December 2, 1872:	The third session begins.
December 3, 1872:	President Grant nominates Ward Hunt to replace Nelson.
December 11, 1872:	The Senate confirms Hunt.
January 17, 1873:	Congress passes the Coinage Act of 1873, putting the U.S. on the gold standard.
February 28, 1873:	The House votes to impeach federal Judge Mark H. Delahay, but Delahay resigns before he can be removed by the Senate.
March 3, 1873:	The third session and the 42nd Congress end.

[See note 6, p. xxix]

Committee on Appropriations: Cornelius Cole (Rep., Calif.)

Committee on Finance: John Sherman (Rep., Ohio)

Committee on Foreign Relations: Simon Cameron (Rep., Pa.)

Committee on the Judiciary: Lyman Trumbull (Rep., Ill.) and George Edmunds (Rep., Vt.)

Committee on Military Affairs: Henry Wilson (Rep., Mass.) and John A. Logan (Rep., Ill.)

Committee on Naval Affairs: Aaron Cragin (Rep., N.H.)

HOUSE LEADERSHIP

Speaker of the House: James Gillespie Blaine (Rep., Maine) was reelected Speaker on March 4, 1871. [See biographical note in 41st Congress]

Majority Leader, Majority Whip, Minority Leader, and Minority Whip: None. These functions did not evolve into formal House positions until the 56th Congress (1899-1901).

Chairmen of Selected Key Committees: [See also Organization and Administration, p. 183]

Committee on Agriculture: John T. Wilson (Rep., Ohio)

Committee on Appropriations: James A. Garfield (Rep., Ohio)

Committee on Banking, Finance, and Urban Affairs: Samuel Hooper (Rep., Mass.)

Committee on Foreign Affairs: Nathaniel P. Banks (Rep., Mass.) and Leonard Myers (Rep., Pa.)

Committee on the Judiciary: John A. Bingham (Rep., Ohio)

Committee on Military Affairs: John Coburn (Rep., Ind.)

Committee on Naval Affairs: Glenni W. Scofield (Rep., Pa.)

Committee on Ways and Means: Henry L. Dawes (Rep., Mass.)

ORGANIZATION AND ADMINISTRATION

There have been approximately two thousand committees throughout the history of Congress. However, the modern committee structure and the modern allocation of committee jurisdiction, seniority, and ranking minority member status was not established until after World War II. [See note 5, p. xxix]

MAJOR LEGISLATION PASSED

Currency: In the Coinage Act of 1873, Congress put the United States on the gold standard, and ended the use of silver in currency except for international trade.

Foreign Policy: The Senate approved the Treaty of Washington, in which the United States agreed before an international commission in Geneva, Switzerland, to arbitrate claims against Great Britain for damages done by British-built Confederate raiding ships during the Civil War.

Ku Klux Klan: Congress acted to suppress the KKK and other secret societies that were terrorizing African Americans throughout the old Confederacy where white citizens were resisting the post-Civil War civil rights measures. Congress authorized fines, imprisonment, and even suspending the writ of habeas corpus if necessary.

National Parks: In the Yellowstone National Park Act, Congress designated two million acres of wilderness on the Yellowstone River as a national park dedicated to public enjoyment, and forbade private ownership or commercial development of park lands or resources. This act was the first significant national park legislation in American history.

Tariffs: In the Tariff Act of 1872, Congress cut import tariffs on manufactured goods by ten percent, and reduced tariffs on other imports as well.

FAILED LEGISLATION

None of historical significance.

RELATIONS WITH THE PRESIDENT

Ulysses S. Grant was elected president largely because of his popularity as a successful wartime general. Grant was a poor leader of the Congress, with a limited legislative agenda. Although personally honest, Grant's administration was marred by widespread corruption. During the 42nd Congress Grant vetoed 32 bills, all of which were of minor historical significance and most of which were relief bills for private citizens.

NOMINATIONS, APPOINTMENTS, AND CONFIRMATIONS

The Judiciary: On November 28, 1872, Supreme Court Justice Samuel Nelson retired. President Grant nominated Ward Hunt on December 3, 1872, to replace Nelson, and the Senate confirmed Hunt on December 11, 1872, by voice vote.

The Executive Branch: On December 14, 1871, President Grant nominated, and the Senate confirmed by voice vote, George H. Williams to be attorney general.

IMPEACHMENTS

On February 28, 1873, the House by voice vote voted to impeach federal Judge Mark H. Delahay.

TABLE OF KEY VOTES

Senate

Subject of Vote	Date of Vote	For	Against
Anti-Ku Klux Klan Legislation	April 14, 1871	45	19
Washington Treaty	May 24, 1871	50	12
Yellowstone National Park Act	January 30, 1872	Passed by voice vote	
Tariff Reduction	May 30, 1872	50	3
Gold Standard	January 17, 1873	Passed by voice vote	

House

Subject of Vote	Date of Vote	For	Against
Anti-Ku Klux Klan Legislation	April 6, 1871	118	91
Yellowstone National Park Act	February 27, 1872	115	65
Tariff Reduction	May 20, 1872	149	61
Gold Standard	May 27, 1872	Passed by voice vote	

[See note 7, p. xxix]

Delahay resigned, however, before he could be impeached by the Senate.

CONSTITUTIONAL AMENDMENTS

None.

SCANDALS

In 1872 a scandal that had been simmering for years gained national attention. Representative Oakes Ames (Rep., Mass.), who was a director of the Union Pacific Railroad as well as a member of a House committee that supervised the railroad, had been giving shares of Union Pacific stock to other members of Congress in return for their complicity in the activities of Credit Mobilier of America. Credit Mobilier was supposed to be financing the railroad's construction, but in fact it was more concerned with its own profits from Union Pacific securities, and the railroad was neglected.

FURTHER READING

McFeely, William S. *Grant: A Biography.* New York: W.W. Norton & Co., 1981.

Muzzey, David S. *James G. Blaine: A Political Idol of Other Days.* Port Washington, N.Y.: Kennikat Press, 1963.

Smith, Willard. *Schuyler Colfax: The Changing Fortunes of a Political Idol.* Indianapolis: Indiana Historical Bureau, 1952.

The 43rd Congress

MARCH 4, 1873 - MARCH 3, 1875

Special Senate Session: March 4, 1873-March 26, 1873
First Session: December 1, 1873-June 23, 1874
Second Session: December 7, 1874-March 3, 1875

The Senate held a special session to vote on the confirmation of presidential appointees to various offices.

In the 1872 elections for the 43rd Congress, the Republicans lost 3 seats in the Senate to reduce their majority to 49 seats out of the 74. The Democrats gained 2 seats to raise their total to 19 seats. Six seats were not held by either of the two major parties. Because of the 1870 census [See 41st Congress], the House was reapportioned and increased to 293 members. The Republicans gained 60 seats to increase their majority to 194 of the 293 seats. The Democrats lost 12 seats reducing their total to 92 seats. Seven seats were not held by either of the two major parties. In both the House and the Senate, the seats officially held by neither party were in fact predominantly pro-Republican.

BACKGROUND

Ulysses S. Grant was inaugurated on March 4, 1873, for his second term as the 18th president of the United States. Soon after the 43rd Congress began, America was thrown into an economic crisis, due to the panic of September 18, 1873. The panic was caused by overextension in the financial markets: easy credit, undersecured debt, excessive speculation in railroad securities, and the collapse of the western land boom. One result of the panic was the formation of the Greenback Party, which advocated an inflationary monetary policy using paper currency in order

to alleviate the burden of pre-panic debts on southern and western farmers. In 1875, however, Congress passed the Specie Resumption Act, which aimed to reduce the amount of currency not backed by precious metals in circulation.

SENATE LEADERSHIP

Vice President: Previously a senator from Massachusetts, Henry Wilson originally was born Jeremiah J. Colbath, but had his name legally changed. Wilson started out as a shoemaker but later decided to enter politics, and was elected to the Massachusetts legislature in 1841. Wilson entered the Senate in 1855, and became President Grant's running mate in the presidential elections of 1872 because Grant's vice president in the previous administration (Schuyler Colfax) was implicated in the Credit Mobilier scandal. [See Scandals, p. 184]

President Pro Tempore: Matthew Hale Carpenter (Rep., Wis.) was elected on March 12, 1873, March 26, 1873, December 11, 1873, and December 23, 1874. Henry Bowen Anthony (Rep., R.I.) was elected on January 25, 1875, and February 15, 1875.

Majority Leader, Majority Whip, Minority Leader, and Minority Whip: None. These functions did not evolve into formal Senate positions until the 62nd Congress (1911-1913).

Chairmen of Selected Key Committees: [See also Organization and Administration, p. 187]

C H R O N O L O G Y

March 4, 1873: The 43rd Congress and a special session of the Senate begin.

March 17, 1873: President Grant nominates, and the Senate confirms, William A. Richardson to succeed George S. Boutwell as secretary of the Treasury.

March 26, 1873: The special session of the Senate ends.

May 7, 1873: Supreme Court Chief Justice Salmon P. Chase dies.

December 1, 1873: The first session begins, and James Gillespie Blaine (Rep., Maine) is reelected Speaker of the House.

January 19, 1874: President Grant nominates Morrison R. Waite to replace Chase.

January 21, 1874: The Senate confirms Waite.

June 1, 1874: President Grant nominates Benjamin H. Bristow to succeed Richardson as secretary of the Treasury.

June 2, 1874: The Senate confirms Bristow.

June 18, 1874: Congress reorganizes the government of the District of Columbia.

June 23, 1874: The first session ends.

December 7, 1874: The second session begins.

January 7, 1875: Congress passes the Specie Resumption Act.

February 24, 1875: Congress passes legislation admitting Colorado into the United States.

February 27, 1875: Congress passes the Civil Rights Act of 1875.

March 3, 1875: The second session and the 43rd Congress end.

[See note 6, p. xxix]

Committee on Appropriations: Lot Morrill (Rep., Maine)

Committee on Finance: John Sherman (Rep., Ohio)

Committee on Foreign Relations: Simon Cameron (Rep., Pa.)

Committee on the Judiciary: George Edmunds (Rep., Vt.)

Committee on Military Affairs: John A. Logan (Rep., Ill.)

Committee on Naval Affairs: Aaron Cragin (Rep., N.H.)

Committee on Rules: Thomas Ferry (Rep., Mich.)

HOUSE LEADERSHIP

Speaker of the House: James Gillespie Blaine (Rep., Maine) was reelected Speaker on December 1, 1873. [See biographical note in 42nd Congress]

Majority Leader, Majority Whip, Minority Leader, and Minority Whip: None. These functions did not evolve into formal House positions until the 56th Congress (1899-1901).

Chairmen of Selected Key Committees: [See also Organization and Administration, below]

Committee on Agriculture: Charles Hays (Rep., Ala.)

Committee on Appropriations: James A. Garfield (Rep., Ohio)

TABLE OF KEY VOTES

Senate

Subject of Vote	Date of Vote	For	Against
District of Columbia Reorganization	June 18, 1874	Passed by voice vote	
Reduction in Paper Currency	December 22, 1874	32	14
Admission of Colorado to Union	February 24, 1875	43	13
Civil Rights Act	February 27, 1875	38	26

House

Subject of Vote	Date of Vote	For	Against
Admission of Colorado to Union	June 8, 1874	170	66
District of Columbia Reorganization	June 17, 1874	216	22
Reduction in Paper Currency	January 7, 1875	136	98
Civil Rights Act	February 4, 1875	162	100

[See note 7, p. xxix]

Committee on Banking, Finance, and Urban Affairs: Horace Maynard (Rep., Tenn.)

Committee on Foreign Affairs: Godlove S. Orth (Rep., Ind.)

Committee on the Judiciary: Benjamin F. Butler (Rep., Mass.)

Committee on Military Affairs: John Coburn (Rep., Ind.)

Committee on Naval Affairs: Glenni W. Scofield (Rep., Pa.)

Committee on Ways and Means: Henry L. Dawes (Rep., Mass.)

ORGANIZATION AND ADMINISTRATION

In this Congress, the Senate established a permanent standing Committee on Rules.

There have been approximately two thousand committees throughout the history of Congress. However, the modern committee structure and the modern allocation of committee jurisdiction, seniority, and ranking minority member status was not established until after World War II. [See note 5, p. xxix]

MAJOR LEGISLATION PASSED

Admission of Colorado as a New State: Congress voted to admit Colorado as a state of the Union.

Civil Rights: In the Civil Rights Act of 1875, Congress prohibited discrimination in public accommodations, public conveyances, and jury selection. This legislation was effectively nullified in the courts and by the absence of effective federal enforcement. It would not be until the 1960s that discrimination in these areas would end.

A rare early group photo of the U.S. Senate (1874).

Currency: In the Specie Resumption Act, Congress reduced the amount of paper currency in circulation not backed by precious metals.

District of Columbia: Congress reorganized the government of the District of Columbia by abolishing home rule and installing three commissioners who reported to the president.

FAILED LEGISLATION

None of historical significance.

RELATIONS WITH THE PRESIDENT

Like George Washington, Ulysses S. Grant was elected president largely because of his popularity as a successful wartime general. Unlike Washington, however, Grant had little success with Congress, and his administration was tainted with charges of corruption. During the 43rd Congress, Grant vetoed 16 bills, all of which were of little historic significance and most of which concerned relief bills for private citizens.

NOMINATIONS, APPOINTMENTS, AND CONFIRMATIONS

The Judiciary: On May 7, 1873, Supreme Court Chief Justice Salmon P. Chase died. On January 19, 1874, President Grant nominated Morrison R. Waite to replace Chase, and the Senate confirmed Waite on January 21, 1874, by a 63 to 0 vote.

The Executive Branch: On March 17, 1873, President Grant nominated, and the Senate confirmed by voice vote, William A. Richardson to succeed George S. Boutwell as secretary of the Treasury. On June 1, 1874, Grant nominated Benjamin H. Bristow to succeed Richardson as secretary of the Treasury, and the Senate confirmed Bristow by voice vote the next day. Grant once had nominated Bristow for attorney general, but withdrew the nomination.

IMPEACHMENTS

None.

CONSTITUTIONAL AMENDMENTS

None.

FURTHER READING

Abbott, Richard. *Cobbler in Congress: The Life of Henry Wilson, 1812-1875*. Lexington, Ky.: University Press of Kentucky, 1972.

McFeely, William S. *Grant: A Biography*. New York: W.W. Norton & Co., 1981.

Magrath, C. Peter. *Morrison R. Waite; the Triumph of Character*. New York: Macmillan, 1963.

Muzzey, David S. *James G. Blaine: A Political Idol of Other Days*. Port Washington, N.Y.: Kennikat Press, 1963.

The 44th Congress

MARCH 4, 1875 - MARCH 3, 1877

Special Senate Session: March 5, 1875-March 24, 1875
First Session: December 6, 1875-August 15, 1876
Second Session: December 4, 1876-March 3, 1877

The Senate held a special session to vote on the confirmation of presidential appointees to various offices.

In the 1874 elections for the 44th Congress, the Republicans lost 4 seats in the Senate, reducing their majority to 45 seats out of the 76. The Democrats gained 10 seats for a total of 29 seats. Two seats were not held by either of the major parties. In the House, the Democrats gained 77 seats to give them a new majority of 169 of the 293 seats. The Republicans lost 85 seats, reducing their total to 109 seats. Fifteen seats were not held by either of the two major parties. In the House, the seats officially held by neither party were in fact predominantly pro-Democratic.

BACKGROUND

The 44th Congress began with a major scandal in the administration of President Ulysses S. Grant. In 1875 the Whiskey Ring conspiracy was revealed. The Whiskey Ring, which was composed of major liquor distilling companies, had bribed Treasury Department officers in order to avoid paying federal liquor taxes. Hundreds of people, including many government employees, were involved in the conspiracy and went to trial. The episode severely damaged Grant's standing with the public. Later in 1875 the House of Representatives passed a non-binding resolution directed against Grant, stating that presidents

should not serve more than two terms. Whether because of this resolution or not, Grant did not seek his Republican Party's nomination in the 1876 presidential campaign. The Republicans nominated Rutherford B. Hayes, and the Democrats nominated Samuel J. Tilden. On November 7, 1876, Tilden won a majority of the popular vote, but only 184 of the 185 electoral votes necessary to become president. Twenty electoral votes were in dispute, mostly in the states of the South still under Reconstruction governments. Congress established an electoral commission of eight Republicans and seven Democrats to resolve the issue. The Republicans unanimously voted to give all the disputed electoral votes to Hayes, who had won only 165 electoral votes. With the 20 disputed electoral votes now allotted to him, Hayes thus achieved the 185 electoral votes necessary to win the election, and became president at the beginning of the next Congress.

SENATE LEADERSHIP

Vice President: Henry Wilson was President Grant's vice president until Wilson's death on November 22, 1875. Until the Twenty-fifth Amendment was ratified on February 10, 1967 [See 90th Congress], there was no mechanism for filling vacancies in the office of the vice president. [See note 8, p. xxix]

C H R O N O L O G Y

March 4, 1875: The 44th Congress begins.

March 5, 1875: A special session of the Senate begins.

March 24, 1875: The special session of the Senate ends.

November 22, 1875: Vice President Henry Wilson dies.

December 6, 1875: The first session begins, and Michael Crawford Kerr (Dem., Ind.) is elected Speaker of the House.

December 8, 1875: President Grant nominates Zachariah Chandler to be secretary of the Interior and Edward Pierrepont to be attorney general.

December 9, 1875: The Senate confirms Chandler and Pierrepont.

December 15, 1875: The House passes a resolution against presidents serving more than two terms in office.

March 2, 1876: Secretary of War William Belknap resigns. The House votes to impeach Belknap.

March 7, 1876: President Grant nominates Alphonso Taft to be secretary of war.

March 8, 1876: The Senate confirms Taft.

May 22, 1876: President Grant nominates James D. Cameron to succeed Taft as secretary of war and Taft to succeed Pierrepont as attorney general. The Senate confirms both men.

June 21, 1876: President Grant nominates, and the Senate confirms, Lot M. Morrill to be secretary of the Treasury.

August 1, 1876: The Senate impeachment trial of Belknap ends in an acquittal.

August 15, 1876: The first session ends.

August 19, 1876: Speaker of the House Kerr dies.

November 7, 1876: Democrat Samuel J. Tilden wins a majority of the popular vote for president, but only 184 of the 185 electoral votes necessary to become president.

December 4, 1876: The second session begins, and Samuel Jackson Randall (Dem., Pa.) is elected the new Speaker of the House.

January 26, 1877: Congress establishes an electoral commission to choose the winner of the 1876 presidential election.

March 3, 1877: The second session and the 44th Congress end

[See note 6, p. xxix]

President Pro Tempore: Thomas White Ferry (Rep., Mich.).

Majority Leader, Majority Whip, Minority Leader, and Minority Whip: None. These functions did not evolve into formal Senate positions until the 62nd Congress (1911-1913).

Chairmen of Selected Key Committees: [See also Organization and Administration. p. 193]

Committee on Appropriations: William Windom (Rep., Minn.)

Committee on Finance: John Sherman (Rep., Ohio)

Contemporary depictions from the time of the contested 1876 presidential election.

Committee on Foreign Relations: Simon Cameron (Rep., Pa.)

Committee on the Judiciary: George Edmunds (Rep., Vt.)

Committee on Military Affairs: John A. Logan (Rep., Ill.)

Committee on Naval Affairs: Aaron Cragin (Rep., N.H.)

Committee on Rules: Thomas Ferry (Rep., Mich.)

HOUSE LEADERSHIP

Speaker of the House: Michael Crawford Kerr (Dem., Ind.) was elected Speaker on December 6, 1875. Kerr died on August 19, 1876, and Samuel Jackson Randall (Dem., Pa.) was elected the new Speaker on December 4, 1876. Randall, a former businessman and Civil War veteran, first had been elected to Congress in the 38th Congress, and would serve as Speaker from the 44th Congress through the 46th Congress. He was noted for his involvement in setting forth new internal rules for the House of Representatives.

Majority Leader, Majority Whip, Minority Leader, and Minority Whip: None. These func-tions did not evolve into formal House positions until the 56th Congress (1899-1901).

Chairmen of Selected Key Committees: [See also Organization and Administration, p. 193]

Committee on Agriculture: John H. Caldwell (Dem., Ala.)

Committee on Appropriations: Hiester Clymer (Dem., Pa.), William S. Holman (Dem., Ind.), and Samuel J. Randall (Dem., Pa.)

Committee on Banking, Finance, and Urban Affairs: Samuel S. Cox (Dem., N.Y.)

Committee on Foreign Affairs: Thomas Swann (Dem., Md.)

Committee on the Judiciary: J. Proctor Knott (Dem., Ky.)

Committee on Military Affairs: Henry B. Banning (Dem., Ohio)

Committee on Naval Affairs: Washington C. Whitthorne (Dem., Tenn.)

Committee on Ways and Means: William R. Morrison (Dem., Ill.)

TABLE OF KEY VOTES

Senate

Subject of Vote	Date of Vote	For	Against
Belknap Impeachment Verdict (no two-thirds majority)	August 1, 1876	35	25
		36	25
		36	25
		36	25
		37	25
Electoral Commission Established	January 24, 1877	47	17

House

Subject of Vote	Date of Vote	For	Against
Presidential Terms Resolution	December 15, 1875	234	18
Belknap Impeachment	March 2, 1876	Passed by voice vote	
Electoral Commission Established	January 26, 1877	191	86

[See note 7, p. xxix]

ORGANIZATION AND ADMINISTRATION

There have been approximately two thousand committees throughout the history of Congress. However, the modern committee structure and the modern allocation of committee jurisdiction, seniority, and ranking minority member status was not established until after World War II. [See note 5, p. xxix]

MAJOR LEGISLATION PASSED

Electoral Commission: After the disputed election of 1876 [See Background, p. 190], Congress established an electoral commission to choose the next president of the United States. The commission was composed of 15 members, 8 of whom were Republicans, and the Republicans were thus able to outvote their Democratic opponents 8 to 7 in favor of the Republican presidential candidate.

FAILED LEGISLATION

None of historical significance.

RELATIONS WITH THE PRESIDENT

There was some concern in Congress that President Grant, whose popularity in Congress was very low, might run for a third term as president in the 1876 presidential elections, violating an unwritten rule established by George Washington that no president should serve more than two terms. On December 15, 1875, the House of Representatives passed a non-binding resolution introduced by William M. Springer (Dem., Ill.) opposing presidents serving more than two terms in office. The resolution, passed by a vote of 234 to 18, stated that a third presidential term would "establish a precedent unwise, unpatriotic, and fraught with peril to our free institutions," and was clearly aimed at Grant. The Senate did not take similar action. Presidents would not be legally restricted to two terms until the Twenty-second Amendment was approved by Congress and ratified by the states after the death of Franklin D. Roosevelt, who was elected to four terms in office and has been the only president to serve more than two terms. Grant vetoed 29 bills during the 44th Congress, most of which were of no historic significance and mostly concerned minor legislation such as relief bills for private citizens.

NOMINATIONS, APPOINTMENTS, AND CONFIRMATIONS

The Judiciary: There were no significant nominations, appointments, or confirmations in the federal judiciary during the 44th Congress.

The Executive Branch: On December 8, 1875, President Grant nominated Zachariah Chandler to be secretary of the Interior and Edward Pierrepont to be attorney general. On December 9, 1875, the Senate confirmed Chandler by a vote of 37 to 8 and Pierrepont by voice vote.

On March 7, 1876, Grant nominated Alphonso Taft to be secretary of war, and the Senate confirmed him the next day by voice vote. On May 22, 1876, Grant nominated James D. Cameron to succeed Taft as secretary of war and Taft to succeed Pierrepont as attorney general. Both nominees were confirmed that same day by voice vote. On June 21, 1876, Grant nominated, and the Senate confirmed by voice vote, Lot M. Morrill to be secretary of the Treasury.

IMPEACHMENTS

The House of Representatives impeached Secretary of War William Belknap, for his involvement in the Whiskey Ring and for taking bribes.

Belknap resigned on March 2, 1876, on the same day the House voted to impeach him by voice vote. On August 1, 1876, after five votes, the Senate failed to convict Belknap on the impeachment charges by the necessary two-thirds majority. There was extensive evidence as to Belknap's guilt, but since he was no longer in office, enough senators doubted that the Senate had the necessary jurisdiction to block a removal vote.

CONSTITUTIONAL AMENDMENTS

None.

SCANDALS

The Whiskey Ring scandal [See Background, p. 190] caused the House to impeach Secretary of War William Belknap for his role in the Whiskey Ring and for accepting bribes. [See Impeachment, above, for further details.]

FURTHER READING

Abbott, Richard. *Cobbler in Congress: The Life of Henry Wilson, 1812-1875.* Lexington, Ky.: University Press of Kentucky, 1972.

McFeely, William S. *Grant: A Biography.* New York: W.W. Norton & Co., 1981.

Polakoff, Keith I. *The Politics of Inertia: The Election of 1876 and the End of Reconstruction.* Baton Rouge, La.: Louisiana State University Press, 1973.

The 45th Congress

MARCH 4, 1877 - MARCH 3, 1879

Special Senate Session: March 5, 1877-March 17, 1877
First Session: October 15, 1877-December 3, 1877
Second Session: December 3, 1877-June 20, 1878
Third Session: December 2, 1878-March 3, 1879

The Senate held a special session to vote on the confirmation of presidential appointees to various offices.

In the 1876 elections for the 45th Congress, the Republicans lost 6 seats in the Senate to reduce their majority to 39 seats out of the 76. The Democrats gained 7 seats, giving them a total of 36 seats. One seat was not held by either of the two parties. In the House, the Democrats lost 16 seats, reducing their majority to 153 of the 293 seats. The Republicans gained 31 seats for a total of 140 seats.

BACKGROUND

On March 5, 1877, Rutherford B. Hayes was inaugurated as the 19th president of the United States. During the summer of 1877, the Nez Perce Indians of Idaho rebelled against the U.S. after years of oppression and neglect, but were defeated by October of 1877, despite the talented military leadership of their leader Chief Joseph. There were few events of historical significance during the 45th Congress.

SENATE LEADERSHIP

Vice President: William Almon Wheeler was a former representative from New York who first had been elected to Congress in the 37th Congress. He suffered from health problems, and retired from public life after the Hayes administration.

President Pro Tempore: Thomas White Ferry (Rep., Mich.) was elected on March 5, 1877, February 26, 1878, April 17, 1878, and March 3, 1879.

Majority Leader, Majority Whip, Minority Leader, and Minority Whip: None. These functions did not evolve into formal Senate positions until the 62nd Congress (1911-1913).

Chairmen of Selected Key Committees: [See also Organization and Administration, p. 197]

Committee on Appropriations: William Windom (Rep., Minn.)

Committee on Finance: Justin S. Morrill (Rep., Vt.)

Committee on Foreign Relations: Hannibal Hamlin (Rep., Maine)

Committee on the Judiciary: George Edmunds (Rep., Vt.)

Committee on Military Affairs: George E. Spencer (Rep., Ala.)

Committee on Naval Affairs: Aaron A. Sargent (Rep., Calif.)

Committee on Rules: James Blaine (Rep., Maine)

HOUSE LEADERSHIP

Speaker of the House: Samuel Jackson Randall (Dem., Pa.) was reelected Speaker on October

CHRONOLOGY

March 4, 1877:	The 45th Congress begins. Supreme Court Justice David Davis resigns.
March 5, 1877:	A special session of the Senate begins.
March 7, 1877:	President Hayes nominates Charles Devens to be attorney general, William M. Evarts to be secretary of state, George W. McCrary to be secretary of war, Carl Schurz to be secretary of the Interior, John Sherman to be secretary of the Treasury, and Richard W. Thompson to be secretary of the Navy.
March 8, 1877:	The Senate confirms Sherman.
March 10, 1877:	The Senate confirms the remaining cabinet nominees.
March 17, 1877:	The special session of the Senate ends.
October 15, 1877:	The first session begins, and Samuel Jackson Randall (Dem., Pa.) is reelected Speaker of the House.
October 16, 1877:	President Hayes nominates John M. Harlan to replace Davis.
November 29, 1877:	The Senate confirms Harlan.
December 3, 1877:	The first session ends, and the second session begins.
February 28, 1878:	President Hayes vetoes legislation authorizing the coinage of silver dollars as legal tender. Both the Senate and the House override the veto.
May 27, 1878:	Congress passes legislation reorganizing the District of Columbia's government.
June 8, 1878:	Congress ends the use of Army troops for civilian law enforcement in the former Confederate states.
June 20, 1878:	The second session ends.
December 2, 1878:	The third session begins.
March 1, 1879:	President Hayes vetoes legislation restricting Chinese immigration into the United States. The veto is sustained in the House.
March 3, 1879:	The third session and the 45th Congress end.

[See note 6, p. xxix]

15, 1877. [See biographical note in 44th Congress]

Majority Leader, Majority Whip, Minority Leader, and Minority Whip: None. These functions did not evolve into formal House positions until the 56th Congress (1899-1901).

Chairmen of Selected Key Committees: [See also Organization and Administration, p. 197]

Committee on Agriculture: Augustus W. Cutler (Dem., N.J.)

Committee on Appropriations: John Atkin (Dem., Tenn.)

Committee on Banking, Finance, and Urban Affairs: Aylett H. Buckner (Dem., Mo.)

Committee on Foreign Affairs: Thomas Swann (Dem., Md.)

TABLE OF KEY VOTES

Senate

Subject of Vote	Date of Vote	For	Against
Overriding Legal Tender Veto	February 28, 1878	46	19
District of Columbia Reorganization	May 27, 1878	Passed by voice vote	
Ban on Use of Army Troops for Civilian Law Enforcement	June 8, 1878	Passed by voice vote	

House

Subject of Vote	Date of Vote	For	Against
Overriding Legal Tender Veto	February 28, 1878	196	73
District of Columbia Reorganization	May 7, 1878	Passed by voice vote	
Ban on Use of Army Troops for Civilian Law Enforcement	May 28, 1878	Passed by voice vote	
Overriding Chinese Immigration Veto (not a two-thirds majority)	March 1, 1879	110	96

[See note 7, p. xxix]

Committee on the Judiciary: J. Proctor Knott (Dem., Ky.)

Committee on Military Affairs: Henry B. Banning (Dem., Ohio)

Committee on Naval Affairs: Washington C. Whitthorne (Dem., Tenn.)

Committee on Ways and Means: Fernando Wood (Dem., N.Y.)

ORGANIZATION AND ADMINISTRATION

There have been approximately two thousand committees throughout the history of Congress.

However, the modern committee structure and the modern allocation of committee jurisdiction, seniority, and ranking minority member status was not established until after World War II. [See note 5, p. xxix]

MAJOR LEGISLATION PASSED

Armed Forces: In the Army appropriations legislation of 1878, Congress discontinued the use of Army troops for civilian law enforcement unless expressly authorized by Congress or the Constitution.

District of Columbia: Congress reorganized the District of Columbia's government.

FAILED LEGISLATION

None of historical significance.

RELATIONS WITH THE PRESIDENT

As discussed in the chapter on the 44th Congress, President Rutherford B. Hayes won the 1876 presidential election because he was awarded the 20 disputed electoral votes from the South. Hayes was thus indebted to southerners in Congress, and the Hayes administration ended Reconstruction and the federal military occupation of the South. Hayes vetoed four bills, two of which were of historical significance, during the 45th Congress. One concerned legislation authorizing the coinage of silver dollars as legal tender, which Hayes vetoed on February 28, 1878. However, the veto was overridden that same day in both houses of Congress: in the Senate by a vote of 46 to 19 and in the House by a vote of 196 to 73. Another veto concerned legislation, which Hayes vetoed on March 1, 1879, restricting Chinese immigration into the United States. That same day, the House voted 110 to 96 to overturn the veto, falling short of the required two-thirds majority. With the veto thus sustained in the House, there was no vote in the Senate.

NOMINATIONS, APPOINTMENTS, AND CONFIRMATIONS

The Judiciary: On March 4, 1877, Supreme Court Justice David Davis resigned. On October 16, 1877, President Hayes nominated John M. Harlan to replace Davis, and the Senate confirmed Harlan on November 29, 1877, by voice vote.

The Executive Branch: On March 7, 1877, President Hayes nominated his cabinet: Charles Devens to be attorney general, William M. Evarts to be secretary of state, George W. McCrary to be secretary of war, Carl Schurz to be secretary of the Interior, John Sherman to be secretary of the Treasury, and Richard W. Thompson to be secretary of the Navy. On March 8, 1877, the Senate approved Sherman by a vote of 37 to 11. On March 10, 1877, the Senate approved Evarts by a vote of 44 to 2, Schurz by a vote of 55 to 1, and Devens, McCrary, and Thompson by voice vote.

IMPEACHMENTS

None.

CONSTITUTIONAL AMENDMENTS

None.

FURTHER READING

Clark, Floyd Barzilia. *The Constitutional Doctrines of Justice Harlan.* Baltimore: The Johns Hopkins Press, 1915.

Hoogenboom, Ari. *The Presidency of Rutherford B. Hayes.* Lawrence, Kan.: University Press of Kansas, 1988.

Hoogenboom, Ari. *Rutherford B. Hayes: Warrior and President.* Lawrence, Kan. University Press of Kansas, 1995.

The 46th Congress

MARCH 4, 1879-MARCH 3, 1881

First Session: March 18, 1879-July 1, 1879
Second Session: December 1, 1879-June 16, 1880
Third Session: December 6, 1880-March 3, 1881

In the 1878 elections for the 46th Congress, the Democrats gained 6 seats in the Senate to give them a new majority of 42 seats out of the 76. The Republicans lost 6 seats, reducing their total to 33 seats. One seat was not held by either major party. In the House, the Democrats lost 4 seats to reduce their majority to 149 of the 293 seats. The Republicans lost 10 seats, leaving them with a total of 130. Fourteen seats were not held by either major party; 13 of these seats were held by the Greenback Party, a populist organization that supported paper currency inflation in order to alleviate the debts of southern and western farmers. [See notes 2 and 3, p. xxix]

BACKGROUND

According to the census of 1880, the population of the United States as of June 1, 1880, was 50,155,783, resulting in a population density of 16.9 persons for each of the country's 2,969,640 square miles. This was a population increase of 26 percent over the 1870 census.

When the 46th Congress convened in 1879, anti-immigrant sentiment was rising in the U.S., due to the economic depression of the period and the new influx of non-European immigrants. Prejudice was particularly strong in California, which had a large and growing population of Chinese immigrants. In 1880 a new treaty, called the Chinese Exclusion Treaty, was agreed upon with the Chinese government, which permitted the U.S. to restrict Chinese immigration. The treaty was ratified in the next Congress. Meanwhile, explorers had discovered gold in Alaska, starting a gold rush to that territory and rapidly increasing its population. President Hayes announced that he would keep his campaign promise to not run for a second term, and both parties nominated former generals who were Union veterans of the Civil War. General James A. Garfield was nominated by the Republicans, and General Winfield Scott Hancock by the Democrats.

SENATE LEADERSHIP

Vice President: William Almon Wheeler was a former representative from New York who first had been elected to Congress in the 37th Congress. He suffered from health problems, and after the Hayes administration retired from public life.

President Pro Tempore: Allen Granberry Thurman (Dem., Ohio) first had been elected to Congress in the 29th Congress and was a former chief justice of the Ohio Supreme Court. [See note 4, p. xxix]

Majority Leader, Majority Whip, Minority Leader, and Minority Whip: None. These functions did not evolve into formal Senate positions until the 62nd Congress (1911-1913).

Chairmen of Selected Key Committees: [See also Organization and Administration, below]

C H R O N O L O G Y

March 4, 1879:	The 46th Congress begins.
March 18, 1879:	The first session begins, and Samuel Jackson Randall (Dem., Pa.) is reelected Speaker of the House.
July 1, 1879:	The first session ends.
December 1, 1879:	The second session begins.
December 10, 1879:	President Hayes nominates, and the Senate confirms, Alexander Ramsey to be secretary of war.
June 16, 1880:	The second session ends.
December 6, 1880:	The third session begins.
December 14, 1880:	Supreme Court Justice William Strong retires.
December 15, 1880:	President Hayes nominates William B. Woods to replace Strong.
December 21, 1880:	The Senate confirms Woods.
January 6, 1881:	President Hayes nominates, and the Senate confirms, Nathan Goff Jr. to be secretary of the Navy.
January 24, 1881:	Justice Noah H. Swayne retires, but is not replaced until the 47th Congress.
March 3, 1881:	The third session and the 46th Congress end.

[See note 6, p. xxix]

Committee on Appropriations: Henry G. Davis (Dem., W.Va.)

Committee on Finance: Thomas Bayard (Dem., Del.)

Committee on Foreign Relations: William Eaton (Dem., Conn.)

Committee on the Judiciary: Allen G. Thurman (Dem., Ohio)

Committee on Military Affairs: Theodore Randolph (Dem., N.J.)

Committee on Naval Affairs: John R. McPherson (Dem., N.J.)

Committee on Rules: J.T. Morgan (Dem., Ala.)

HOUSE LEADERSHIP

Speaker of the House: Samuel Jackson Randall (Dem., Pa.) was reelected Speaker on March 18, 1879. [See biographical note in 44th Congress]

Majority Leader, Majority Whip, Minority Leader, and Minority Whip: None. These functions did not evolve into formal House positions until the 56th Congress (1899-1901).

Chairmen of Selected Key Committees: [See also Organization and Administration, below]

Committee on Agriculture: James W. Covert (Dem., N.Y.)

Committee on Appropriations: John Atkins (Dem., Tenn.)

Committee on Banking, Finance, and Urban Affairs: Aylett H. Buckner (Dem., Mo.)

Committee on Foreign Affairs: Samuel S. Cox (Dem., N.Y.)

Committee on the Judiciary: J. Proctor Knott (Dem., Ky.)

Committee on Military Affairs: William A. J. Sparks (Dem., Ill.)

TABLE OF KEY VOTES

Senate

Subject of Vote	Date of Vote	For	Against
Confirmation of Alexander Ramsey to be Secretary of War	December 10, 1879	Passed by voice vote	
Confirmation of William B. Woods to Supreme Court	December 21, 1880	39	8
Confirmation of Nathan Goff Jr. to be Secretary of the Navy	January 6, 1881	Passed by voice vote	

House

(None for this Congress)

[See note 7, p. xxix]

Committee on Naval Affairs: Washington C. Whitthorne (Dem., Tenn.)

Committee on Ways and Means: Fernando Wood (Dem., N.Y.) and John R. Tucker (Dem., Va.)

ORGANIZATION AND ADMINISTRATION

There have been approximately two thousand committees throughout the history of Congress. However, the modern committee structure and the modern allocation of committee jurisdiction, seniority, and ranking minority member status was not established until after World War II. [See note 5, p. xxix]

MAJOR LEGISLATION PASSED

None.

FAILED LEGISLATION

President Hayes wanted to reform the civil service system before the end of his administration, so that government employees would be chosen on the basis of merit rather than political connec-

tions, but failed to gather sufficient support for any legislative initiative in Congress. A reform act eventually was passed in the 47th Congress.

RELATIONS WITH THE PRESIDENT

As discussed under the 44th Congress, President Rutherford B. Hayes won the 1876 presidential election because he was awarded the 20 disputed electoral votes from the South. Thus indebted to southerners in Congress, the Hayes administration ended Reconstruction and the federal military occupation of the South. Hayes vetoed nine bills in the 46th Congress, none of which were historically significant.

NOMINATIONS, APPOINTMENTS, AND CONFIRMATIONS

The Judiciary: On December 14, 1880, Supreme Court Justice William Strong retired. On December 15, 1880, President Hayes nominated William B. Woods to replace Strong, and the Senate confirmed Woods on December 21, 1880, by a 39 to 8 vote. On January 24, 1881, Justice

Noah H. Swayne retired, but would not be replaced until the 47th Congress.

The Executive Branch: On December 10, 1879, President Hayes nominated, and the Senate confirmed by voice vote, Alexander Ramsey to be secretary of war. On January 6, 1881, Hayes nominated, and the Senate confirmed by voice vote, Nathan Goff Jr. to be secretary of the Navy.

IMPEACHMENTS

None.

CONSTITUTIONAL AMENDMENTS

None.

FURTHER READING

Eckenrode, H.J. *Rutherford B. Hayes: Statesman of Reunion.* Norwalk, Conn.: Easton Press, 1988.

Hoogenboom, Ari. *The Presidency of Rutherford B. Hayes.* Lawrence, Kans.: University Press of Kansas, 1988.

Hoogenboom, Ari. *Rutherford B. Hayes: Warrior and President.* Lawrence, Kans.: University Press of Kansas, 1995.

The 47th Congress

MARCH 4, 1881-MARCH 3, 1883

Special Senate Sessions: March 4, 1881-May 20, 1881
and October 10, 1881-October 29, 1881
First Session: December 5, 1881-August 8, 1882
Second Session: December 4, 1882-March 3, 1883

The Senate held two special sessions to vote on the confirmation of presidential appointees to various offices. [See note 1, p. xxix]

In the 1880 elections for the 47th Congress, the Republicans gained 4 seats in the Senate, giving them a total of 37 seats out of the 76. The Democrats also held 37 seats, after losing 5 seats in the elections. Two seats were not held by either of the major parties. In the House, the Republicans gained 17 seats to give them a new and bare majority of 147 of the 293 seats. The Democrats lost 14 seats, leaving them with a total of 135 seats. Eleven seats were not held by either major party. Ten of these seats were held by the Greenback Party. [See notes 2 and 3, p. xxix]

BACKGROUND

On March 4, 1881, James A. Garfield was inaugurated as the 20th president of the United States. Garfield was shot less than four months later, on July 2, by Charles J. Guiteau. Garfield lived for several months afterwards, completely bedridden, and died September 19, 1881. The next day, Vice President Chester A. Arthur was inaugurated as the 21st president.

In 1882 Congress enacted a law forbidding polygamy in U.S. territories that was aimed at the Mormons of Utah. Congress also passed two major immigration laws, the first of which limited Chinese immigration, and the second of which imposed a head tax of fifty cents on immigrants. The immigration legislation was in response to growing pressure on Congress to restrict and regulate the immigrant population, which had previously been largely uncontrolled due to the seemingly endless frontier.

In 1883 Congress passed a civil service reform act concerning the hiring of federal employees, and established a Civil Service Commission.

SENATE LEADERSHIP

Vice President: Chester Alan Arthur was vice president until September 20, 1881, when he became president after the death on September 19, 1881, of President James Abram Garfield. (Until the Twenty-fifth Amendment was ratified on February 10, 1967 [See 90th Congress], there was no mechanism for filling vacancies in the office of the vice president.) [See also, note 8, p. xxix]

President Pro Tempore: Thomas Francis Bayard (Dem., Del.) was elected on October 10, 1881; David Davis (Independent, Ill.) was elected on October 13, 1881, and resigned on March 3, 1883; and George Franklin Edmunds (Rep., Vt.) was elected on March 3, 1883. [See note 4, p. xxix]

Majority Leader, Majority Whip, Minority Leader, and Minority Whip: None. These func-

C H R O N O L O G Y

March 4, 1881:	The 47th Congress and a special session of the Senate begin.
March 5, 1881:	President Garfield nominates his cabinet, and the Senate confirms all of the nominees.
March 14, 1881:	President Garfield nominates Stanley Matthews to fill a position on the Supreme Court left vacant at the end of the 46th Congress.
May 5, 1881:	The Senate ratifies the Chinese Exclusion Treaty.
May 12, 1881:	The Senate confirms Matthews.
May 20, 1881:	The special session of the Senate ends.
July 2, 1881:	Charles J. Guiteau shoots President Garfield who is seriously wounded but survives for more than two months.
July 25, 1881:	Justice Nathan Clifford dies.
September 19, 1881:	President Garfield dies.
September 20, 1881:	Vice President Chester A. Arthur is inaugurated as president.
October 10, 1881:	A special session of the Senate begins.
October 27, 1881:	President Arthur nominates, and the Senate confirms, Charles J. Folger to be secretary of the Treasury.
October 29, 1881:	A special session of the Senate ends.
December 5, 1881:	The first session begins, and Joseph Warren Keifer (Rep., Ohio) is elected Speaker of the House.
December 12, 1881:	President Arthur nominates and the Senate confirms, Frederick T. Frelinghuysen to be secretary of state.
December 16, 1881:	President Arthur nominates Benjamin H. Brewster to be attorney general.
December 19, 1881:	President Arthur nominates Horace Gray to replace Clifford on the Supreme Court. The Senate confirms Brewster to be attorney general.
December 20, 1881:	The Senate confirms Gray.

(continued on p. 205)

tions did not evolve into formal Senate positions until the 62nd Congress (1911-1913).

Chairmen of Selected Key Committees: [See also Organization and Administration, below]

Committee on Appropriations: William Allison (Rep., Iowa)

Committee on Finance: Justin S. Morrill (Rep., Vt.)

Committee on Foreign Relations: William Windom (Rep., Minn.)

Committee on the Judiciary: George Edmunds (Rep., Vt.)

Committee on Military Affairs: John A. Logan (Rep., Ill.)

Committee on Naval Affairs: James Donald Cameron (Rep., Pa.)

Committee on Rules: William Frye (Rep., Maine)

HOUSE LEADERSHIP

Speaker of the House: Joseph Warren Keifer (Rep., Ohio) was elected Speaker on December 5, 1881. Keifer was a Civil War veteran who had risen to the rank of major general in the Union army, and first had been elected to Congress in the 45th Congress. This was Keifer's one and only term as Speaker.

(continued from p. 204)

C H R O N O L O G Y

January 27, 1882: Justice Ward Hunt resigns.

March 13, 1882: Congress passes legislation against polygamy. President Arthur nominates Samuel Blatchford to replace Hunt.

March 27, 1882: The Senate confirms Blatchford.

April 4, 1882: President Arthur vetoes an early version of the Chinese Exclusion Act.

April 5, 1882: The Senate fails to overturn the veto.

April 6, 1882: President Arthur nominates Henry M. Teller to be secretary of the Interior and William E. Chandler to be secretary of the Navy. The Senate confirms Teller.

April 12, 1882: The Senate confirms Chandler.

April 28, 1882: Congress passes a new version of the Chinese Exclusion Act.

July 29, 1882: Congress passes the Immigration Act of 1882.

August 1, 1882: President Arthur vetoes legislation to fund river and harbor improvements.

August 2, 1882: Both the Senate and House override President Arthur's veto of river and harbor improvements.

August 8, 1882: The first session ends.

December 4, 1882: The second session begins.

January 4, 1883: Congress passes the Pendleton Act.

March 3, 1883: The second session and the 47th Congress end.

[See note 6, p. xxix]

Majority Leader, Majority Whip, Minority Leader, and Minority Whip: None. These functions did not evolve into formal House positions until the 56th Congress (1899-1901).

Chairmen of Selected Key Committees: [See also Organization and Administration, below]

Committee on Agriculture: Edward K. Valentine (Rep., Neb.)

Committee on Appropriations: Frank Hiscock (Rep., N.Y.)

Committee on Banking, Finance, and Urban Affairs: William W. Crapo (Rep., Mass.)

Committee on Foreign Affairs: Charles G. Williams (Rep., Wis.)

Committee on the Judiciary: Thomas B. Reed (Rep., Maine)

Committee on Military Affairs: Thomas J. Henderson (Rep., Ill.)

Committee on Naval Affairs: Benjamin W. Harris (Rep., Mass.)

Committee on Rules: J. Warren Keifer (Rep., Ohio)

Committee on Ways and Means: William D. Kelley (Rep., Pa.)

ORGANIZATION AND ADMINISTRATION

At the beginning of this Congress, a standing Committee on Rules became part of the House committee structure. There have been approximately two thousand committees throughout the

TABLE OF KEY VOTES

Senate

Subject of Vote	Date of Vote	For	Against
Chinese Exclusion Treaty	May 5, 1881	48	4
Polygamy Ban	February 16, 1882	Passed by voice vote	
Chinese Exclusion Act	April 28, 1882	32	15
Immigration Act of 1882	July 29, 1882	Passed by voice vote	
Civil Service Reform	December 27, 1882	39	5

House

Subject of Vote	Date of Vote	For	Against
Polygamy Ban	March 13, 1882	199	42
Chinese Exclusion Act	April 17, 1882	202	37
Immigration Act of 1882	June 27, 1882	Passed by voice vote	
Civil Service Reform	January 4, 1883	155	46

[See note 7, p. xxix]

history of Congress. However, the modern committee structure and the modern allocation of committee jurisdiction, seniority, and ranking minority member status was not established until after World War II. [See note 5, p. xxix]

MAJOR LEGISLATION PASSED

Civil Service: In the Pendleton Act, Congress reformed the system for hiring federal employees. Henceforth, there would be a Civil Service Commission, which would administer competitive examinations for federal job applicants. The act also sought to eliminate political party affiliation as a consideration in the hiring process.

Foreign Policy: The Senate approved the Chinese Exclusion Treaty, which was executed between the United States and the Empire of China in the previous Congress and permitted the U.S. to restrict Chinese immigration. Congress then enacted the Chinese Exclusion Act, which placed severe restrictions on Chinese immigration and withheld U.S. citizenship from foreign-born Chinese.

Immigration: In the Immigration Act of 1882, Congress imposed a head tax of fifty cents per immigrant and denied criminals, beggars, and the mentally insane the right to enter the United States.

Polygamy: Congress passed legislation against polygamy that was designed to discourage this particular aspect of the Mormon religion in the territory of Utah, which would soon enter the United States.

FAILED LEGISLATION

None of historical significance.

RELATIONS WITH THE PRESIDENT

President Arthur alienated many of his fellow Republicans in Congress during his administration. Arthur supported the civil service legislation [See Major Legislation Passed, above], which displeased Republican job seekers who wanted to be rewarded for their party loyalty. Arthur vetoed a total of three bills in the 47th Congress; former president, Garfield vetoed none. Arthur vetoed two bills that the Republicans supported. First, on April 4, 1882, Arthur vetoed an early version of the Chinese Exclusion Act. On April 5, 1882, the Senate voted 29 to 21 to overturn the veto, falling short of the required two-thirds majority and thus sustaining the veto without requiring a vote in the House. (Another version of the bill was passed by both Houses later that April and signed into law by the president.) Second, on August 1, 1882, Arthur vetoed legislation to fund river and harbor improvements. This veto was overridden by both houses of Congress on August 2, 1882: the vote was 41 to 16 in the Senate and 122 to 59 in the House.

NOMINATIONS, APPOINTMENTS, AND CONFIRMATIONS

The Judiciary: On January 24, 1881, Justice Noah H. Swayne retired, but was not replaced during the 46th Congress. On March 14, 1881, President Garfield nominated Stanley Matthews to replace Swayne, and the Senate on May 12, 1881, confirmed Matthews by a 24 to 23 vote.

On July 25, 1881, Justice Nathan Clifford died, and President Arthur nominated Horace Gray on December 19, 1881, to replace Clifford. The Senate confirmed Gray on December 20, 1881, by a 51 to 5 vote.

On January 27, 1882, Justice Ward Hunt resigned, and on March 13, 1882, President Arthur nominated Samuel Blatchford to replace Hunt. The Senate confirmed Blatchford on March 27, 1882, by voice vote.

The Executive Branch: On March 5, 1881, President Garfield nominated his cabinet: James G. Blaine to be secretary of state, William H. Hunt to be secretary of the Navy, Samuel J. Kirkwood to be secretary of the Interior, Robert T. Lincoln to be secretary of war, Wayne MacVeagh to be attorney general and William Windom to be secretary of the Treasury. The Senate confirmed all six men by voice vote the same day.

After Garfield's assassination, President Arthur periodically reorganized the cabinet. On October 27, 1881, Arthur nominated, and the Senate confirmed by voice vote, Charles J. Folger to be secretary of the Treasury. On December 12, 1881, Arthur nominated, and the Senate confirmed by voice vote, Frederick T. Frelinghuysen to be secretary of state. Arthur nominated Benjamin H. Brewster to be attorney general on December 16, 1881, and the Senate confirmed Brewster three days later by voice vote. On April 6, 1882, Arthur nominated Henry M. Teller to be secretary of the Interior and William E. Chandler to be secretary of the Navy. The Senate confirmed Teller that same day by voice vote, and Chandler by a vote of 28 to 16 on April 12, 1882.

IMPEACHMENTS

None.

CONSTITUTIONAL AMENDMENTS

None.

FURTHER READING

Clark, James C. *The Murder of James A. Garfield.* Jefferson, N.C.: McFarland, 1993.

Howe, George F. *Chester A. Arthur: A Quarter-Century of Machine Politics.* Norwalk, Conn.: Easton Press, 1987.

Peskin, Allan. *Garfield: A Biography.* Norwalk, Conn.: Easton Press, 1987.

Reeves, Thomas C. *Gentleman Boss: The Life of Chester Alan Arthur.* New York: Knopf, 1975.

The 48th Congress

MARCH 4, 1883 - MARCH 3, 1885

First Session: *December 3, 1883-July 7, 1884*
Second Session: *December 1, 1884-March 3, 1885*

In the 1882 elections for the 48th Congress, the Republicans gained 1 seat in the Senate to give them 38 seats out of the 76. The Democrats lost 1 seat, leaving them with a total of 36 seats, with 2 seats not held by either party. The Republicans held a bare working majority. Because of the 1880 census [See 46th Congress], the House was reapportioned and increased to 332 members. The Democrats gained 62 seats to give them a new majority of 197 of the 332 seats. The Republicans lost 29 seats leaving them with a total of 118 seats. Seventeen seats were not held by either party. Two of these seats were held by the Greenback Party, and the other seats were mostly held by a variety of independent splinter factions from the two main parties. With 180 newcomers to the House of Representatives, the 48th Congress established a record — equaled only by the 54th Congress — for the largest freshman class. [See notes 2 and 3, p. xxix]

BACKGROUND

By the 1880s the labor movement in the United States was finally becoming a significant political force, despite the numerous obstacles placed in its way. Not only did big business oppose organized labor, but the legal system's antiquated view of management-worker relations, namely, as being a system of individual contracts, stymied collective bargaining. Nevertheless, labor had some victories. First, Congress created the Bureau of Labor in 1884. Second, Congress passed a contract labor law in 1885, which attempted to restrict the use of immigrant contract laborers by employers as strike breakers.

SENATE LEADERSHIP

Vice President: None. Vice President Chester Alan Arthur became president after the assassination of President James Abram Garfield on September 19, 1881 [See 47th Congress]. (Until the Twenty-fifth Amendment was ratified on February 10, 1967 [See 90th Congress], there was no mechanism for filling vacancies in the office of the vice president.) [See note 8, p. xxix]

President Pro Tempore: George Franklin Edmunds (Rep., Vt.) first had been elected to the Senate in 1866 to fill a vacancy caused by the death of the previous senator, and was reelected four times thereafter until he resigned in 1891. [See note 4, p. xxix]

Majority Leader, Majority Whip, Minority Leader, and Minority Whip: None. These functions did not evolve into formal Senate positions until the 62nd Congress (1911-1913).

Chairmen of Selected Key Committees: [See also Organization and Administration.]

Committee on Appropriations: William Allison (Rep., Iowa)

Committee on Finance: Justin S. Morrill (Rep., Vt.)

Committee on Foreign Relations: John F. Miller (Rep., Calif.)

C H R O N O L O G Y

March 4, 1883:	The 48th Congress begins.
December 3, 1883:	The first session begins, and John Griffin Carlisle (Dem., Ky.) is elected Speaker of the House.
May 23, 1884:	Congress establishes the Bureau of Labor.
July 7, 1884:	The first session ends.
December 1, 1884:	The second session begins.
December 3, 1884:	President Arthur nominates Hugh McCulloch to be secretary of the Treasury.
December 18, 1884:	The Senate confirms McCulloch.
February 10, 1885:	Congress passes legislation concerning public lands, and also passes legislation concerning contract labor.
March 3, 1885:	The second session and the 48th Congress end.

[See note 6, p. xxix]

Committee on the Judiciary: George Edmunds (Rep., Vt.)

Committee on Military Affairs: John A. Logan (Rep., Ill.)

Committee on Naval Affairs: James Donald Cameron (Rep., Pa.)

Committee on Rules: William Frye (Rep., Maine)

HOUSE LEADERSHIP

Speaker of the House: John Griffin Carlisle (Dem., Ky.) was elected Speaker on December 3, 1883. Carlisle first had been elected to Congress in the 45th Congress, and served as Speaker from the 48th Congress through the 50th Congress.

Majority Leader, Majority Whip, Minority Leader, and Minority Whip: None. These functions did not evolve into formal House positions until the 56th Congress (1899-1901).

Chairmen of Selected Key Committees: [See also Organization and Administration, below]

Committee on Agriculture: William H. Hatch (Dem., Mo.)

Committee on Appropriations: Samuel J. Randall (Dem., Pa.)

Committee on Banking, Finance, and Urban Affairs: Aylett H. Buckner (Dem., Mo.)

Committee on Foreign Affairs: Andrew G. Curtin (Dem., Pa.)

Committee on the Judiciary: John R. Tucker (Dem., Va.)

Committee on Military Affairs: William S. Rosecrans (Dem., Calif.)

Committee on Naval Affairs: Samuel S. Cox (Dem., N.Y.)

Committee on Rules: John G. Carlisle (Dem., Ky.)

Committee on Ways and Means: William R. Morrison (Dem., Ill.)

ORGANIZATION AND ADMINISTRATION

There have been approximately two thousand committees throughout the history of Congress. However, the modern committee structure and the modern allocation of committee jurisdiction,

TABLE OF KEY VOTES

Senate

Subject of Vote	Date of Vote	For	Against
Bureau of Labor Established	May 23, 1884	55	2
Public Lands Protection	February 10, 1885	Passed by voice vote	
Contract Labor Ban	February 18, 1885	50	9

House

Subject of Vote	Date of Vote	For	Against
Bureau of Labor Established	April 19, 1884	182	19
Public Lands Protection	June 3, 1884	Passed by voice vote	
Contract Labor Ban	June 19, 1884	Passed by voice vote	

[See note 7, p. xxix]

seniority, and ranking minority member status was not established until after World War II. [See note 5, p. xxix]

MAJOR LEGISLATION PASSED

Labor: Congress established the Bureau of Labor within the Department of the Interior. In future years, the Bureau would be absorbed into the Department of Labor. Also, Congress made it illegal to bring contract laborers into the United States, except for household servants or certain categories of skilled workers.

Public Lands: Congress acted to protect federal lands in the West by prohibiting illegal fencing and other enclosures on public property by private interests.

FAILED LEGISLATION

None of historical significance.

RELATIONS WITH THE PRESIDENT

President Arthur had alienated many of his fellow Republicans in Congress during the 48th Congress with his support of civil service reform legislation and veto of two bills that the Republicans supported [See Relations with the President, The 47th Congress]. The Republican Party would not renominate Arthur in the presidential election of 1884. Arthur vetoed nine bills during the 48th Congress, none of which were historically significant.

NOMINATIONS, APPOINTMENTS, AND CONFIRMATIONS

The Judiciary: There were no significant nominations, appointments, or confirmations in the federal judiciary during the 48th Congress.

The Executive Branch: On December 3, 1884, President Arthur nominated Hugh McCulloch to be secretary of the Treasury, and on December 18, 1884, the Senate confirmed McCulloch by a vote of 50 to 1.

IMPEACHMENTS

None.

CONSTITUTIONAL AMENDMENTS

None.

FURTHER READING

Reeves, Thomas C. *Gentleman Boss: The Life of Chester Alan Arthur*. New York: Knopf, 1975.

Howe, George F. *Chester A. Arthur: A Quarter-Century of Machine Politics*. Norwalk, Conn.: Easton Press, 1987.

Stealey, Orlando Oscar. *Twenty Years in the Press Gallery: A Concise History of Important Legislation From the 48th to the 58th Congress; the Part Played by the Leading Men of that Period and the Interesting and Impressive Incidents*. New York: Publishers Printing Co., 1906.

The 49th Congress

MARCH 4, 1885 - MARCH 3, 1887

Special Senate Session: March 4, 1885-April 2, 1885
First Session: December 7, 1885-August 5, 1886
Second Session: December 6, 1886-March 3, 1887

The Senate held a special session to vote on the confirmation of presidential appointees to various offices. [See note 1, p. xxix]

In the 1884 elections for the 49th Congress, the Republicans gained 4 seats in the Senate to increase their majority to 42 seats out of the 76. The Democrats lost 2 seats, reducing their total to 34 seats. In the House, the Democrats lost 14 seats to leave them with a majority of 183 of the 332 seats. The Republicans gained 22 seats, for a total of 140 seats. Nine seats were not held by either of the two major parties. One of these seats was held by the Greenback Party. [See notes 2 and 3, p. xxix]

BACKGROUND

On March 4, 1885, Grover Cleveland was inaugurated as the 22nd President of the United States. During this period of history, large American corporations and industrial enterprises were attempting to consolidate their power and eliminate competition by combining into "trusts," controlling all the significant businesses in a particular industry. The law did not yet forbid trusts, and gave big business virtually a free hand in dealing with workers, based on outmoded theories of freedom of contract. The result was conflict between business and the growing organized labor movement. This conflict reached a climax in the Haymarket Riot of 1886, in which a bomb exploded and killed several people during a labor rally in Chicago. Although the action was not a result of the Haymarket Riot, Congress finally took a significant step toward curbing the power of big business in 1887. By passing the Interstate Commerce Act, Congress established the Interstate Commerce Commission to regulate railroad rates and practices.

Also during the 49th Congress, Congress passed a presidential succession act in case the offices of president and vice president both became vacant. Finally, Congress unsuccessfully tried to replace the network of Indian reservations with a system of individual land grants.

SENATE LEADERSHIP

Vice President: Thomas Andrew Hendricks was vice president until his death on November 25, 1885. (Until the Twenty-fifth Amendment was ratified on February 10, 1967 [See 90th Congress], there was no mechanism for filling vacancies in the office of the vice president.) [See note 8, p. xxix]

President Pro Tempore: John Sherman (Rep., Ohio) was elected on December 7, 1885, and resigned on February 26, 1887. John James Ingalls (Rep., Kans.) was elected on February 25, 1887. [See note 4, p. xxix]

C H R O N O L O G Y

March 4, 1885:	The 49th Congress and a special session of the Senate begin.
March 5, 1885:	President Cleveland nominates his cabinet.
March 6, 1885:	The Senate confirms all of the cabinet nominees.
April 2, 1885:	The special session of the Senate ends.
November 25, 1885:	Senate Vice President Thomas Andrew Hendricks dies.
December 7, 1885:	The first session begins, and John Griffin Carlisle (Dem., Ky.) is reelected Speaker of the House.
January 15, 1886:	Congress passes the Presidential Succession Act.
July 30, 1886:	Congress establishes the Interstate Commerce Commission.
August 5, 1886:	The first session ends.
December 6, 1886:	The second session begins.
December 9, 1886:	Congress passes the Electoral Count Act.
December 16, 1886:	Congress passes legislation changing ownership of Native American lands.
March 3, 1887:	Congress repeals the Tenure of Office Act. The second session and the 49th Congress end.

[See note 6, p. xxix]

Majority Leader, Majority Whip, Minority Leader, and Minority Whip: None. These functions did not evolve into formal Senate positions until the 62nd Congress (1911-1913).

Chairmen of Selected Key Committees: [See also Organization and Administration, below]

Committee on Appropriations: William Allison (Rep., Iowa)

Committee on Finance: Justin S. Morrill (Rep., Vt.)

Committee on Foreign Relations: John Sherman (Rep., Ohio)

Committee on the Judiciary: George Edmunds (Rep., Vt.)

Committee on Military Affairs: John A. Logan (Rep., Ill.)

Committee on Naval Affairs: James Donald Cameron (Rep., Pa.)

Committee on Rules: William Frye (Rep., Maine)

HOUSE LEADERSHIP

Speaker of the House: John Griffin Carlisle (Dem., Ky.) was reelected Speaker on December 7, 1885. Carlisle had first been elected to Congress in the 45th Congress, and served as Speaker from the 48th Congress through the 50th Congress.

Majority Leader, Majority Whip, Minority Leader, and Minority Whip: None. These functions did not evolve into formal House positions until the 56th Congress (1899-1901).

Chairmen of Selected Key Committees: [See also Organization and Administration, below]

Committee on Agriculture: William H. Hatch (Dem., Mo.)

Committee on Appropriations: Samuel J. Randall (Dem., Pa.)

TABLE OF KEY VOTES

Senate

Subject of Vote	Date of Vote	For	Against
Presidential Succession	December 17, 1885	Passed by voice vote	
Native American Lands	February 25, 1886	Passed by voice vote	
Presidential Electors	March 17, 1886	Passed by voice vote	
Interstate Commerce Act	May 12, 1886	47	4
Tenure of Office Act	December 17, 1886	30	22

House

Subject of Vote	Date of Vote	For	Against
Presidential Succession	January 15, 1886	186	76
Interstate Commerce Act	July 30, 1886	192	41
Presidential Electors	December 9, 1886	Passed by voice vote	
Native American Lands	December 16, 1886	Passed by voice vote	
Tenure of Office Act	March 3, 1887	171	67

[See note 7, p. xxix]

Committee on Banking, Finance, and Urban Affairs: James F. Miller (Dem., Tex.) and Andrew G. Curtin (Dem., Pa.)

Committee on Foreign Affairs: Perry Belmont (Dem., N.Y.)

Committee on the Judiciary: John R. Tucker (Dem., Va.)

Committee on Military Affairs: Edward S. Bragg (Dem., Wis.)

Committee on Naval Affairs: Hilary A. Herbert (Dem., Ala.)

Committee on Rules: John G. Carlisle (Dem., Ky.)

Committee on Ways and Means: William R. Morrison (Dem., Ill.)

ORGANIZATION AND ADMINISTRATION

There have been approximately two thousand committees throughout the history of Congress. However, the modern committee structure and the modern allocation of committee jurisdiction, seniority, and ranking minority member status was not established until after World War II. [See note 5, p. xxix]

MAJOR LEGISLATION PASSED

Interstate Commerce Commission: In the Interstate Commerce Act, Congress created the Interstate Commerce Commission, which for the first time brought the nation's railroads under federal regulatory supervision.

Native American Lands: In the Severalty Act, Congress authorized a change in the nature of land ownership on Native American reservations. Previously, the land had been held in common by the tribe as a whole. Now, individuals could take a land allotment of up to 160 acres in their own name. Congress believed that the new land ownership system would give Native Americans an incentive to adopt white ways. In reality, the result was that the tribes lost millions of acres of land to whites who purchased land allotments from Native Americans who had fallen into debt.

Presidential Electors: In the Electoral Count Act, Congress fixed a date for presidential electors to meet, and gave the states most of the responsibility for ensuring the accuracy of electoral tallies.

Presidential Succession: In the Presidential Succession Act, Congress provided that if the presidency and the vice presidency were both vacant, the line of succession would consist of the heads of the executive branch departments in the order of the creation of their departments. Thus, the secretary of state would be first in line, because the Department of State was the first executive branch department created by Congress.

Tenure of Office Act: Congress repealed the Tenure of Office Act, which had led to the near removal of President Andrew Johnson [See 39th and 40th Congresses].

FAILED LEGISLATION

None of historical significance.

RELATIONS WITH THE PRESIDENT

Relations between Congress and President Grover Cleveland were usually bad, due in large part to Cleveland's prolific use of the veto power. Cleveland vetoed 202 bills in the 49th Congress, most of which concerned minor legislation of no historical significance. Cleveland vetoed a large number of pension bills and relief bills for private citizens, because he considered such bills to be a misuse of public funds. However, many members of Congress from both parties were irritated by Cleveland's effort to end this traditional form of pork barrel legislation.

NOMINATIONS, APPOINTMENTS, AND CONFIRMATIONS

The Judiciary: There were no significant nominations, appointments, or confirmations in the

federal judiciary during the 49th Congress.

The Executive Branch: On March 5, 1885, President Cleveland nominated his cabinet: Thomas F. Bayard to be secretary of state, William C. Endicott to be secretary of war, Augustus H. Garland to be attorney general, Lucius Q. C. Lamar to be secretary of the Interior, Daniel Manning to be secretary of the Treasury, and William C. Whitney to be secretary of the Navy. The Senate confirmed all six men the next day by voice votes.

IMPEACHMENTS

None.

CONSTITUTIONAL AMENDMENTS

None.

FURTHER READING

Christianson, Stephen G. "Haymarket Trial." In *Great American Trials*, Edited by Edward W. Knappman. Detroit: Gale Research, 1994.

Merrill, Horace S. *Bourbon Leader: Grover Cleveland and the Democratic Party.* Boston: Little, Brown & Co., 1957.

Nevins, Allan. *Grover Cleveland: A Study in Courage.* New York: Dodd, Mead & Co., 1934.

Stealey, Orlando Oscar. *Twenty Years in the Press Gallery: A Concise History of Important Legislation From the 48th to the 58th Congress; the Part Played by the Leading Men of that Period and the Interesting and Impressive Incidents.* New York: Publishers Printing Co., 1906.

The 50th Congress

MARCH 4, 1887-MARCH 3, 1889

First Session: December 5, 1887-October 20, 1888
Second Session: December 3, 1888-March 3, 1889

In the 1886 elections for the 50th Congress, the Republicans lost 3 seats in the Senate to reduce their majority to 39 seats out of the 76. The Democrats gained 3 seats to raise their total to 37 seats. In the House, the Democrats lost 14 seats, cutting their majority to 169 of the 332 seats, and the Republicans gained 12 seats, giving them a total of 152 seats. Eleven seats were not held by either party. Two of these seats were held by the Labor Party and one by the Greenback Party. [See notes 2 and 3, p. xxix]

BACKGROUND

America's industrialization was producing a number of large, powerful, rich corporations, all of which wished to protect their profits and prevent newcomers from disturbing the status quo. Many industries, including oil, distilling, and sugar, were combining into powerful, anti-competitive trusts that monopolized production and pricing. The 50th Congress did nothing, however, to curb the growing abuses by the trusts, while a number of state legislatures passed limited and largely ineffective antitrust laws. In fact, the 50th Congress took very few actions that were of any historical significance.

In the area of science and technology, however, this was a period of enormous progress in America. Nikola Tesla invented several means of utilizing alternating current electricity; Frank Sprague invented the first practical electric trol-

ley for public transportation; George Eastman invented the Kodak camera. The first high-quality steel beams that would make skyscraper construction possible were coming out of the steel forges of Pittsburgh, Pennsylvania. Finally, as the 50th Congress drew to a close during the presidential elections of 1888, the question of whether to reduce tariffs on imports became a significant issue. Incumbent President Grover Cleveland favored tariff reduction, but refused to press the issue in public with Republican candidate Benjamin Harrison, who opposed tariff reduction.

SENATE LEADERSHIP

Vice President: None. Vice President Thomas Andrew Hendricks died on November 25, 1885 [See 49th Congress]. (Until the Twenty-fifth Amendment was ratified on February 10, 1967 [See 90th Congress], there was no mechanism for filling vacancies in the office of the vice president.) [See note 8, p. xxix]

President Pro Tempore: John James Ingalls (Rep., Kans.) first was elected to the Senate in 1872, and would serve until he lost in his bid for reelection in 1890. [See note 4, p. xxix]

Majority Leader, Majority Whip, Minority Leader, and Minority Whip: None. These functions did not evolve into formal Senate positions until the 62nd Congress (1911-1913).

C H R O N O L O G Y

March 4, 1887:	The 50th Congress begins.
May 14, 1887:	Supreme Court Justice William B. Woods dies.
December 5, 1887:	The first session begins, and John Griffin Carlisle (Dem., Ky.) is reelected Speaker of the House.
December 6, 1887:	President Cleveland nominates Lucius Q. C. Lamar to replace Woods, Charles S. Fairchild to be secretary of the Treasury, and William F. Vilas to be secretary of the Interior.
December 15, 1887:	The Senate confirms Fairchild.
January 16, 1888:	The Senate confirms Lamar and Vilas.
March 23, 1888:	Chief Justice Morrison R. Waite dies.
April 30, 1888:	President Cleveland nominates Melville W. Fuller to replace Waite.
May 22, 1888:	Congress creates the Department of Labor.
July 20, 1888:	The Senate confirms Fuller.
September 14, 1888:	Congress passes the Railroad Arbitration Act.
September 21, 1888:	The Department of Agriculture gets cabinet level status.
October 20, 1888:	The first session ends.
December 3, 1888:	The second session begins.
January 18, 1889:	Congress passes legislation admitting North Dakota, South Dakota, Montana, and Washington into the Union.
February 11, 1889:	President Cleveland nominates Norman J. Colman to be secretary of agriculture.
February 13, 1889:	The Senate confirms Colman.
March 3, 1889:	The second session and the 50th Congress end.

[See note 6, p. xxix]

Chairmen of Selected Key Committees: [See also Organization and Administration, below]

Committee on Appropriations: William Allison (Rep., Iowa)

Committee on Finance: Justin S. Morrill (Rep., Vt.)

Committee on Foreign Relations: John Sherman (Rep., Ohio)

Committee on the Judiciary: George Edmunds (Rep., Vt.)

Committee on Military Affairs: Joseph R. Hawley (Rep., Conn.)

Committee on Naval Affairs: James Donald Cameron (Rep., Pa.)

Committee on Rules: Nelson Aldrich (Rep., R.I.)

HOUSE LEADERSHIP

Speaker of the House: John Griffin Carlisle (Dem., Ky.) was reelected Speaker on December 5, 1887. Carlisle first had been elected to Congress in the 45th Congress, and served as Speaker from the 48th Congress through the 50th Congress.

Majority Leader, Majority Whip, Minority Leader, and Minority Whip: None. These func-

TABLE OF KEY VOTES

Senate

Subject of Vote	Date of Vote	For	Against
Admission of North Dakota, South Dakota, Montana, and Washington to the Union	April 19, 1888	26	23
Department of Labor	May 22, 1888	Passed by voice vote	
Railroad Arbitration	September 14, 1888	Passed by voice vote	
Department of Agriculture	September 21, 1888	Passed by voice vote	

House

Subject of Vote	Date of Vote	For	Against
Department of Labor	April 18, 1888	Passed by voice vote	
Railroad Arbitration	April 18, 1888	Passed by voice vote	
Department of Agriculture	May 21, 1888	236	13
Admission of North Dakota, South Dakota, Montana, and Washington to the Union	January 18, 1889	145	98

[See note 7, p. xxix]

tions did not evolve into formal House positions until the 56th Congress (1899-1901).

Chairmen of Selected Key Committees: [See also Organization and Administration, below]

Committee on Agriculture: William H. Hatch (Dem., Mo.)

Committee on Appropriations: Samuel J. Randall (Dem., Pa.)

Committee on Banking, Finance, and Urban Affairs: Beriah Wilkins (Dem., Ohio)

Committee on Foreign Affairs: Perry Belmont (Dem., N.Y.) and James B. McCreary (Dem., Ky.)

Committee on the Judiciary: David B. Culberson (Dem., Tex.)

Committee on Military Affairs: Richard W. Townshend (Dem., Ill.)

Committee on Naval Affairs: Hilary A. Herbert (Dem., Ala.).

Committee on Rules: John G. Carlisle (Dem., Ky.)

Committee on Ways and Means: Roger Q. Mills (Dem., Tex.)

ORGANIZATION AND ADMINISTRATION

There have been approximately two thousand committees throughout the history of Congress. However, the modern committee structure and the modern allocation of committee jurisdiction, seniority, and ranking minority member status was not established until after World War II. [See note 5, p. xxix]

MAJOR LEGISLATION PASSED

Admission of North Dakota, South Dakota, Montana, and Washington as New States: In a combined piece of legislation, Congress voted to admit North Dakota, South Dakota, Montana, and Washington into the United States.

Department of Agriculture: Congress raised the Department of Agriculture to cabinet-level status.

Department of Labor: In the Department of Labor Act, Congress created the Department of Labor, which absorbed the Interior Department's old National Bureau of Labor. The Department of Labor was later renamed the Department of Commerce and Labor.

Railroads: In the Railroad Arbitration Act, Congress established a voluntary arbitration system for railroad labor disputes.

FAILED LEGISLATION

None of historical significance.

RELATIONS WITH THE PRESIDENT

Congress and President Grover Cleveland were often at odds, due in large part to Cleveland's frequent use of his veto power. Cleveland vetoed 212 bills in the 50th Congress, most of which concerned minor legislation of no historical significance. Cleveland vetoed pension bills and relief bills for private citizens, which he considered a misuse of public funds.

NOMINATIONS, APPOINTMENTS, AND CONFIRMATIONS

The Judiciary: On May 14, 1887, Supreme Court Justice William B. Woods died. President Cleveland nominated Lucius Q. C. Lamar on December 6, 1887, and the Senate confirmed Lamar on January 16, 1888, by a 32 to 28 vote.

On March 23, 1888, Chief Justice Morrison R. Waite died, and on April 30, 1888, Cleveland nominated Melville W. Fuller to replace Waite.

The Senate confirmed Fuller on July 20, 1888, by a 41 to 20 vote.

The Executive Branch: On December 6, 1887, President Cleveland nominated Charles S. Fairchild to be secretary of the Treasury and William F. Vilas to be secretary of the Interior. On December 15, 1887, the Senate confirmed Fairchild and on January 16, 1888, Vilas by voice votes. On February 11, 1889, President Cleveland nominated Norman J. Colman to be secretary of agriculture, and on February 13, 1889, the Senate confirmed Colman by voice vote.

IMPEACHMENTS

None.

CONSTITUTIONAL AMENDMENTS

None.

FURTHER READING

King, Willard Leroy. *Melville Weston Fuller, Chief Justice of the United States*. New York: Macmillan, 1950.

Merrill, Horace S. *Bourbon Leader: Grover Cleveland and the Democratic Party*. Boston: Little, Brown & Co., 1957.

Murphy, James B. *L. Q. C. Lamar, Pragmatic Patriot*. Baton Rouge: Louisiana State University Press, 1973.

Nevins, Allan. *Grover Cleveland: A Study in Courage*. New York: Dodd, Mead & Co., 1934.

Stealey, Orlando Oscar. *Twenty Years in the Press Gallery: A Concise History of Important Legislation From the 48th to the 58th Congress; the Part Played by the Leading Men of that Period and the Interesting and Impressive Incidents*. New York: Publishers

The 51st Congress

MARCH 4, 1889-MARCH 3, 1891

Special Senate Session: March 4, 1889-April 2, 1889
First Session: December 2, 1889-October 1, 1890
Second Session: December 1, 1890-March 2, 1891

The Senate held a special session to vote on the confirmation of presidential appointees to various offices. [See note 1, p. xxix]

In the 1888 elections for the 51st Congress, neither party gained nor lost any seats in the Senate, the Republicans keeping their total at 39 of the 76 seats and the Democrats retaining their 37 seats. In the House, the Republicans gained 14 seats, giving them a new majority of 166 of the 332 seats. The Democrats lost 10 seats, reducing their total to 159. Seven seats were not held by either major party. One seat was held by the Labor Party, and most of the remaining seats generally leaned toward the Republicans. [See notes 2 and 3, p. xxix]

BACKGROUND

According to the census of 1890, the population of the United States as of June 1, 1890, was 62,947,714, resulting in a population density of 21.2 persons for each of the country's 2,969,640 square miles. This was a population increase of 25.5 percent over the 1880 census.

On March 4, 1889, Benjamin Harrison was inaugurated as the 23rd president of the United States. Later that year, on April 22, the Oklahoma land rush took place. Those settlers who illegally crossed the territorial boundary in advance to stake out claims were nicknamed "Sooners." On May 31 the Johnstown Flood killed thousands of people in Johnstown, Pennsylvania. The 1890 census, according to historian Frederick Jackson Turner, marked the end of the American frontier, in that it revealed a country settled from coast to coast.

In 1890 Congress finally acted to break up such monopolistic trusts as oil and sugar refining and liquor distilling that were dominating major areas of American industry. The Sherman Antitrust Act of 1890 outlawed trusts, although the government was not aggressive in enforcing the act. That same year, Idaho was admitted to the Union as the 43rd state, and Wyoming was admitted as the 44th. In 1890 Congress also raised tariffs on imports. In 1891, shortly before the end of the 51st Congress, Congress created the U.S. Circuit Courts of Appeals, an intermediate system of appellate courts between federal trial courts and the overworked Supreme Court.

SENATE LEADERSHIP

Vice President: Levi Parsons Morton, President Benjamin Harrison's running mate had served as a representative from New York in the 46th and 47th Congresses and had been the minister to France from 1881 to 1885.

President Pro Tempore: John James Ingalls (Rep., Kans.) was elected on March 7, 1889, April 2, 1889, February 28, 1890, and April 3,

1890. Charles Frederick Manderson (Rep., Neb.) was elected on March 2, 1891. [See note 4, p. xxix]

Majority Leader, Majority Whip, Minority Leader, and Minority Whip: None. These functions did not evolve into formal Senate positions until the 62nd Congress (1911-1913).

Chairmen of Selected Key Committees: [See also Organization and Administration, below]

Committee on Appropriations: William Allison (Rep., Iowa)

Committee on Finance: Justin S. Morrill (Rep., Vt.)

Committee on Foreign Relations: John Sherman (Rep., Ohio)

Committee on the Judiciary: George Edmunds (Rep., Vt.)

Committee on Military Affairs: Joseph R. Hawley (Rep., Conn.)

Committee on Naval Affairs: James Donald Cameron (Rep., Pa.)

Committee on Rules: Nelson Aldrich (Rep., R.I.)

HOUSE LEADERSHIP

Speaker of the House: Thomas Brackett Reed (Rep., Maine) was elected Speaker on December 2, 1889. Reed first had been elected to Congress in the 45th Congress, and served as Speaker in the 51st, 54th, and 55th Congresses. Reed became a powerful Speaker by effectively imposing the Republican majority's will on the Democratic minority. When Democratic members refused to answer quorum calls in order to block votes by making it appear that the necessary majority was not present, Reed would have the House Chamber locked and everyone inside counted as present regardless of whether they answered the roll call or not. Reed also cracked down on the practice of using motions simply for the purpose of delay. Further, as Speaker, Reed also had the Chairmanship of the Rules Committee, which gave him the power to implement changes to streamline the legislative process in the House. Although in the early 20th century Joseph G. Cannon (Rep., Ill.) would abuse the power of the Speakership and the subsequent reaction would end the Speaker's control over the Rules Committee, Reed's actions nevertheless had a lasting effect in making the House a body where legislation does not stall for long if it has the support of the majority.

Majority Leader, Majority Whip, Minority Leader, and Minority Whip: None. These functions did not evolve into formal House positions until the 56th Congress (1899-1901).

Chairmen of Selected Key Committees: [See also Organization and Administration, below]

Committee on Agriculture: Edward H. Funston (Rep., Kans.)

Committee on Appropriations: Joseph G. Cannon (Rep., Ill.)

Committee on Banking, Finance, and Urban Affairs: George W. E. Dorsey (Rep., Neb.)

Committee on Foreign Affairs: Robert R. Hitt (Rep., Ill.)

Committee on the Judiciary: Ezra B. Taylor (Rep., Ohio)

Committee on Military Affairs: Byron M. Cutcheon (Rep., Mich.)

Committee on Naval Affairs: Charles A. Boutelle (Rep., Maine)

Committee on Rules: Thomas B. Reed (Rep., Maine)

Committee on Ways and Means: William McKinley (Rep., Ohio)

ORGANIZATION AND ADMINISTRATION

As has been stated before in this book, from the First Congress until this 51st Congress, the president pro tempore of the Senate was frequently elected for only a specific occasion. On March 12, 1890, the Senate voted that the president pro tempore would hold office "during the pleasure of

CHRONOLOGY

March 4, 1889:	The 51st Congress and a Senate special session begin.
March 5, 1889:	President Harrison nominates his cabinet, and the Senate confirms all of the nominees.
March 22, 1889:	Supreme Court Justice Stanley Matthews dies.
April 2, 1889:	The Senate special session ends.
December 2, 1889:	The first session begins, and Thomas Brackett Reed (Rep., Maine) is elected Speaker.
December 4, 1889:	President Harrison nominates David J. Brewer to replace Matthews.
December 18, 1889:	The Senate confirms Brewer.
March 12, 1890:	The Senate makes the position of president pro tempore a permanent position.
June 17, 1890:	Congress passes the Silver Purchase Act.
June 27, 1890:	Congress passes legislation admitting Wyoming into the United States.
July 1, 1890:	Congress passes legislation admitting Idaho into the United States.
September 10, 1890:	Congress passes legislation raising tariffs.
September 24, 1890:	Congress passes legislation creating the Federal Courts of Appeals.
October 1, 1890:	The first session ends.
October 13, 1890:	Supreme Court Justice Samuel F. Miller dies.
December 1, 1890:	The second session begins.
December 23, 1890:	President Harrison nominates Henry B. Brown to replace Miller.
December 29, 1890:	Congress passes legislation organizing the Oklahoma Territory.
May 1, 1890:	Congress passes the Sherman Antitrust Act.
February 18, 1891:	Congress passes the International Copyright Act.
February 23, 1891:	President Harrison nominates Charles Foster to succeed Windom as secretary of the Treasury.
February 24, 1891:	The Senate confirms Foster.
March 2, 1891:	The second session ends.
March 3, 1891:	The 51st Congress ends.

[See note 6, p. xxix]

the Senate and until another is elected, and shall execute the duties thereof during all future absences of the vice president until the Senate otherwise order." Under article I, section 3, clause 4 of the Constitution the vice president is the president of the Senate, and the president pro tempore was an office to be filled only when the vice president was not present to preside over the Senate. In practice, however, the vice president rarely presides over the Senate except in cases of a tie vote, which is the only time he or she may cast a vote. Since the office of president pro tempore was becoming a practically permanent one anyway, and it rarely possessed anything but ceremonial power, the Senate enacted this measure. [See note 5, p. xxix]

TABLE OF KEY VOTES

Senate

Subject of Vote	Date of Vote	For	Against
Oklahoma Territory Organized	February 13, 1890	Passed by voice vote	
Senate President Pro Tem Made Permanent Position	March 12, 1890	Passed by voice vote	
Sherman Antitrust Bill Passed	April 8, 1890	52	1
Silver Purchase Bill Passed	June 17, 1890	42	25
Admission of Wyoming to Union	June 27, 1890	29	18
Admission of Idaho to Union	July 1, 1890	Passed by voice vote	
Tariffs Raised	September 10, 1890	40	29
Courts of Appeals Bill Passed	September 24, 1890	44	6
Copyright Protection Expanded	February 18, 1891	36	14

House

Subject of Vote	Date of Vote	For	Against
Oklahoma Territory Organized	March 13, 1890	Passed by voice vote	
Admission of Wyoming to Union	March 26, 1890	139	127
Admission of Idaho to Union	April 3, 1890	129	1
Courts of Appeals Bill Passed	April 15, 1890	131	31
Sherman Antitrust Bill Passed	May 1, 1890	Passed by voice vote	
Tariffs Raised	May 21, 1890	164	142
Silver Purchase Bill Passed	June 7, 1890	135	119
Copyright Protection Expanded	December 3, 1890	139	95

[See note 7, p. xxix]

MAJOR LEGISLATION PASSED

Admission of Idaho and Wyoming as New States: Congress voted to admit Idaho and Wyoming into the United States. Although the votes in the House and Senate to admit Wyoming were completed before the votes to admit Idaho, Idaho was formally admitted to the Union (on July 3, 1890) before Wyoming (on July 10, 1890) due to procedural differences concerning the effective date of admission after the state government was organized in each respective legislation.

Antitrust: In the Sherman Antitrust Act, the first federal antitrust act, Congress finally made it a federal offense to monopolize an industry or restrain interstate commerce. At first, the act was not aggressively enforced by the government and faced serious obstacles in the courts. In later years, however, this antitrust act would become important. The act was to be used to crush the railroad strike in 1894, dealing organized labor a major setback.

Copyrights: In the International Copyright Act, Congress gave foreign authors copyright protection under American law if their governments gave similar protection to American authors.

Courts: Congress created the federal Courts of Appeals, which established an intermediate system of appellate courts between federal trial courts and the Supreme Court.

Currency: In the Silver Purchase Act, Congress ordered the Treasury to purchase 4.5 million ounces of silver a month and issue paper money payable in gold or silver at the government's option. This was designed to subsidize western miners and put more silver currency into circulation. The Silver Purchase Act reversed previous acts of Congress that effectively had put the United States on the gold standard.

Oklahoma Territory: Congress created the Oklahoma Territory out of the remaining unorganized territory in the West.

Tariffs: Congress sharply raised tariffs on imports. This increase in tariffs was a Republican concession to American industry, which had made large contributions to Republican political campaigns. The high tariffs were unpopular, however, and the resulting price increases contributed to the Republicans' loss of their majority in the House in the elections for the 52nd Congress.

FAILED LEGISLATION

None of historical significance.

RELATIONS WITH THE PRESIDENT

During the 51st Congress, President Harrison's most significant achievement as president was the passage of the Sherman Antitrust Act. However, Harrison opposed the movement in Congress to raise tariffs, and this unpopular position contributed to his defeat in the 1892 election.

Harrison vetoed 36 bills during the 51st Congress, none of which involved significant legislation.

NOMINATIONS, APPOINTMENTS, AND CONFIRMATIONS

The Judiciary: On March 22, 1889, Supreme Court Justice Stanley Matthews died. President Harrison nominated David J. Brewer on December 4, 1889, to replace Matthews, and the Senate on December 18, 1889, confirmed Brewer by a 53 to 11 vote. On October 13, 1890, Justice Samuel F. Miller died, and on December 23, 1890, President Harrison nominated Henry B. Brown to replace Miller. The Senate confirmed Brown on December 29, 1890, by voice vote.

The Executive Branch: On March 5, 1889, President Harrison nominated, and the Senate confirmed by voice vote, James G. Blaine to be secretary of state, William H.H. Miller to be attorney general, John W. Noble to be secretary of the Interior, Redfield Proctor to be secretary of war, Jeremiah M. Rusk to be secretary of agriculture, Benjamin F. Tracy to be secretary of the Navy, and William Windom to be secretary of the Treasury. On February 23, 1891, President Harrison nominated Charles Foster to succeed Windom as secretary of the Treasury, and the Senate confirmed Foster on February 24 by voice vote.

IMPEACHMENTS

None.

CONSTITUTIONAL AMENDMENTS

None.

FURTHER READING

Robinson, William A. *Thomas B. Reed: Parliamentarian*. New York: Dodd, Mead, 1930.

Sievers, Harry Joseph. *Benjamin Harrison*. New York: University Publishers, 1960.

Stealey, Orlando Oscar. *Twenty Years in the Press Gallery: A Concise History of Important Legislation From the 48th to the 58th Congress; the Part Played by the Leading Men of that Period and the Interesting and Impressive Incidents*. New York: Publishers Printing Co., 1906.

The 52nd Congress

MARCH 4, 1891 - MARCH 3, 1893

First Session: *December 7, 1891-August 5, 1892*
Second Session: *December 5, 1892-March 3, 1893*

In the 1890 elections for the 52nd Congress, the Republicans gained 8 seats in the Senate, raising their majority from 39 to 47 of the 88 seats. The Democrats gained 2 seats for a total of 39. Two seats were held by the People's Party (the Populists). In the House, the Democrats gained 76 seats, giving them a new majority of 235 of the 332 seats. The Republicans lost 78 seats, reducing their total to 88. Nine seats were not held by either major party, eight of which were held by the Populists. [See notes 2 and 3, p. xxix]

BACKGROUND

Economic troubles during the early 1890s created a popular backlash against conventional economic and monetary policies. The Populist Party was formed in the Midwest. Its political platform included the free coinage of silver, in order to help farmers who were hard pressed to repay debts due in gold, and nationalization of the railroads. The Populists nominated James B. Weaver as their candidate in the presidential elections of 1892. Although Weaver ran a distant third in the election, he took a significant eight percent of the popular vote and 22 of the 444 electoral votes.

In 1892, Congress extended the ban on Chinese immigration for another ten years. In 1893 Congress created the diplomatic office of ambassador, which was a promotion for certain U.S. envoys abroad who had the previous title of minister. Meanwhile, on January 17, 1893, a revolution staged by American settlers in the Hawaiian Islands resulted in the overthrow of Queen Liliuokalani and the establishment of a U.S. protectorate over Hawaii.

SENATE LEADERSHIP

Vice President: Levi Parsons Morton, vice president under Benjamin Harrison, had served as a representative from New York in the 46th and 47th Congresses and had been the minister to France from 1881 to 1885.

President Pro Tempore: Charles Frederick Manderson (Rep., Neb.) first was elected to the Senate in 1883 and served until 1895.

Majority Leader, Majority Whip, Minority Leader, and Minority Whip: None. These functions did not evolve into formal Senate positions until the 62nd Congress (1911-1913).

Chairmen of Selected Key Committees: [See note 5, p. xxix]

Committee on Appropriations: William Allison (Rep., Iowa)

Committee on Finance: Justin S. Morrill (Rep., Vt.)

Committee on Foreign Relations: John Sherman (Rep., Ohio)

C H R O N O L O G Y

March 4, 1891:	The 52nd Congress begins.
December 7, 1891:	The first session begins.
December 8, 1891:	Charles Frederick Crisp (Dem., Ga.) is elected Speaker of the House.
December 17, 1891:	President Harrison nominates Stephen B. Elkins to succeed Redfield Proctor as secretary of war.
December 22, 1891:	The Senate confirms Elkins.
January 22, 1892:	Supreme Court Justice Joseph P. Bradley dies.
April 25, 1892:	Congress extends the Chinese Exclusion Act.
June 29, 1892:	President Harrison nominates and the Senate confirms John W. Foster to succeed James G. Blaine as secretary of state.
July 19, 1892:	President Harrison nominates George Shiras to replace Bradley.
July 26, 1892:	The Senate confirms Shiras.
July 28, 1892:	Congress passes a limited eight-hour workday law.
August 5, 1892:	The first session ends.
December 5, 1892:	The second session begins.
January 23, 1893:	Supreme Court Justice Lucius Q.C. Lamar dies.
February 2, 1893:	President Harrison nominates Howell E. Jackson to replace Lamar.
February 11, 1893:	Congress passes the Railway Safety Appliance Act.
February 18, 1893:	The Senate confirms Jackson.
February 23, 1893:	Congress passes legislation authorizing the title of ambassador for U.S. diplomats.
March 3, 1893:	The second session and the 52nd Congress end.

[See note 6, p. xxix]

Committee on the Judiciary: George F. Hoar (Rep., Mass.)

Committee on Military Affairs: Joseph R. Hawley (Rep., Conn.)

Committee on Naval Affairs: James Donald Cameron (Rep., Pa.)

Committee on Rules: Nelson Aldrich (Rep., R.I.)

HOUSE LEADERSHIP

Speaker of the House: Charles Frederick Crisp (Dem., Ga.) was elected on December 8, 1891. Crisp first had been elected to Congress in the 48th Congress and served as Speaker in the 52nd and 53rd Congresses.

Majority Leader, Majority Whip, Minority Leader, and Minority Whip: None. These functions did not evolve into formal House positions until the 56th Congress (1899-1901).

Other House Leaders: William Jennings Bryan (Dem., Neb.) was first elected to the House in the 52nd Congress. He was a leader in the populist and free silver movements and was a controversial but unsuccessful candidate for president in 1896, 1900, and 1908.

Chairmen of Selected Key Committees: [See note 5, p. xxix]

Committee on Agriculture: William H. Hatch (Dem., Mo.)

TABLE OF KEY VOTES

Senate

Subject of Vote	Date of Vote	For	Against
Chinese Exclusion Act Extended	April 25, 1892	Passed by voice vote	
Eight-Hour Workday Law Enacted	July 28, 1892	Passed by voice vote	
Railroads Safety Bill Passed	February 11, 1893	39	10
Diplomatic Title Bill Passed	February 23, 1893	Passed by voice vote	

House

Subject of Vote	Date of Vote	For	Against
Chinese Exclusion Act Extended	April 4, 1892	179	43
Eight-Hour Workday Law Enacted	July 5, 1892	Passed by voice vote	
Railroads Safety Bill Passed	July 8, 1892	Passed by voice vote	
Diplomatic Title Bill Passed	January 31, 1893	Passed by voice vote	

[See note 7, p. xxix]

Committee on Appropriations: William S. Holman (Dem., Ind.)

Committee on Banking, Finance, and Urban Affairs: Henry Bacon (Dem., N.Y.)

Committee on Foreign Affairs: James H. Blount (Dem., Ga.)

Committee on the Judiciary: David B. Culberson (Dem., Tex.)

Committee on Military Affairs: Joseph H. Outhwaite (Dem., Ohio)

Committee on Naval Affairs: Hilary A. Herbert (Dem., Ala.)

Committee on Rules: Charles F. Crisp (Dem., Ga.)

Committee on Ways and Means: William M. Springer (Dem., Ill.)

ORGANIZATION AND ADMINISTRATION

No significant development. [See note 5, p. xxix]

MAJOR LEGISLATION PASSED

Diplomats: Congress authorized the title of ambassador for American envoys abroad, which was a more prestigious title than the previous title of minister. This was in response to the European powers, who were now calling their envoys to the U.S, and to other great powers, ambassadors.

Immigration: Congress extended the Chinese Exclusion Act of 1882 [See 47th Congress], which imposed restrictions on Chinese immigration into the United States.

Labor: Government workers won the eight-hour workday decades before organized labor. Congress instituted the eight-hour workday for laborers and mechanics working for the federal government, the District of Columbia, and public works contractors and subcontractors.

Railroads: The Railway Safety Appliance Act increased railroad safety by requiring the use of certain safety equipment on railroad cars.

FAILED LEGISLATION

None of historical significance.

RELATIONS WITH THE PRESIDENT

Despite the nation's economic problems, President Harrison opposed the movement in Congress to raise tariffs. This unpopular position contributed to his defeat in the 1892 election.

Harrison vetoed eight bills during the 52nd Congress, none of which involved significant legislation.

NOMINATIONS, APPOINTMENTS AND CONFIRMATIONS

The Judiciary: On January 22, 1892, Supreme Court Justice Joseph P. Bradley died. President Harrison nominated George Shiras on July 19, 1892, to replace Bradley, and the Senate confirmed Shiras on July 26, 1892, by voice vote. On January 23, 1893, Justice Lucius Q.C. Lamar died, and President Harrison nominated Howell E. Jackson on February 2, 1893, to replace Lamar. The Senate confirmed Jackson on February 18, 1893, by voice vote.

The Executive Branch: On December 17, 1891, President Harrison nominated Stephen B. Elkins to succeed Redfield Proctor as secretary of war, and on December 22 the Senate confirmed Elkins by voice vote. On June 29, 1892, President Harrison nominated, and the Senate confirmed by voice vote, John W. Foster to succeed James G. Blaine as secretary of state.

IMPEACHMENTS

None.

CONSTITUTIONAL AMENDMENTS

None.

FURTHER READING

Sievers, Harry Joseph. *Benjamin Harrison.* New York: University Publishers, 1960.
Stealey, Orlando Oscar. *Twenty Years in the Press Gallery: A Concise History of Important Legislation From the 48th to the 58th Congress; the Part Played by the Leading Men of that Period and the Interesting and Impressive Incidents.* New York: Publishers Printing Co., 1906.

The 53rd Congress

MARCH 4, 1893 - MARCH 3, 1895

Special Senate Session: March 4, 1893-April 15, 1893
First Session: August 7, 1893-November 3, 1893
Second Session: December 4, 1893-August 28, 1894
Third Session: December 3, 1894-March 3, 1895

The Senate held a special session to vote on the confirmation of presidential appointees to various offices. [See note 1, p. xxix]

In the 1892 elections for the 53rd Congress, the Democrats gained 5 seats in the Senate to hold a new majority of 44 of the 88 seats. The Republicans lost 9 seats, leaving them with 38. Six seats were not held by either major party. Three of these seats were held by the People's Party (the Populists) and 1 seat was held by the Silver Party. Because of the 1890 census [See 51st Congress], the House was reapportioned and increased to 357 members. The Democrats lost 17 seats, reducing their majority from 235 to 218 out of the 357 seats. The Republicans gained 39 seats for a total of 127. Twelve seats were held by neither major party, and 11 of these seats were held by the Populists. [See notes 2 and 3, p. xxix]

BACKGROUND

On March 4, 1893, Grover Cleveland was inaugurated for his second, but non-consecutive, term as president of the United States. Henry Ford built the first practical and efficient gasoline powered engine and began to work on his first automobile designs. The railroad, however, was still the principal means of mechanized transportation, as mass produced automobiles were many years away. In the spring and summer of 1893, there was a major financial crisis due to a stock market collapse, railroad bankruptcies, and a sharp drop in the value of silver. This financial crisis developed into the panic of 1893, in which the financial markets and the economy severely were depressed.

In 1894 Congress enacted the first federal income tax legislation, which was later declared unconstitutional. [See Major Legislation, below] Also during 1894, the Pullman Railroad Car Strike began in Chicago, to be followed by a general railroad strike led by Eugene Debs's American Railway Union. The federal government crushed the strike by sending federal troops into Chicago and using the Sherman Antitrust Act to obtain an injunction against the ARU and Eugene Debs. Organized labor would not fully recover from the defeat until the Great Depression of the 1930s. Finally, the U.S. and Great Britain averted a potential war over a boundary dispute between British Guyana and Venezuela by agreeing to arbitration, and Cuba rebelled against its Spanish colonial government.

SENATE LEADERSHIP

Vice President: Adlai Ewing Stevenson won election on Grover Cleveland's ticket in the election of 1892. Stevenson had served as a representative from Illinois in the 44th and 46th Congresses.

President Pro Tempore: Charles Frederick Manderson (Rep., Neb.) served as president pro tem until he resigned on March 22, 1893. Isham

C H R O N O L O G Y

March 4, 1893:	The 53rd Congress and a special Senate session begin.
March 6, 1893:	President Cleveland nominates his cabinet. The Senate confirms Cleveland's nominees.
April 15, 1893:	The special Senate session ends.
July 7, 1893:	Supreme Court Justice Samuel Blatchford dies.
August 7, 1893:	The first session begins, and Charles Frederick Crisp (Dem., Ga.) is reelected Speaker of the House.
October 17, 1893:	Congress repeals the Silver Purchase Act of 1890.
November 3, 1893:	The first session ends.
December 4, 1893:	The second session begins.
February 19, 1894:	After two unsuccessful nominations, President Cleveland nominates, and the Senate confirms, Edward D. White to succeed Blatchford.
March 29, 1894:	President Cleveland vetoes legislation concerning the coinage of silver bullion.
April 4, 1894:	The House sustains President Cleveland's veto of March 29.
July 2, 1894:	Congress passes the Wilson-Gorman Tariff Act.
July 10, 1894:	Congress passes legislation admitting Utah into the United States.
July 22, 1894:	The House votes in favor of a constitutional amendment providing for the direct election of senators, but the amendment never goes to a vote in the Senate.
August 28, 1894:	The second session ends.
December 3, 1894:	The third session begins.
March 3, 1895:	The third session and the 53rd Congress end.

[See note 6, p. xxix]

Green Harris (Dem., Tenn.) was elected on March 22, 1893. Matt Whitaker Ransom (Dem., N.C.) was elected on January 7, 1895, and resigned on January 10, 1895. Harris was then reelected on January 10, 1895.

Majority Leader, Majority Whip, Minority Leader, and Minority Whip: None. These functions did not evolve into formal Senate positions until the 62nd Congress (1911-1913).

Chairmen of Selected Key Committees: [See note 5, p. xxix]

Committee on Appropriations: Francis Cockrell (Dem., Mo.)

Committee on Finance: Daniel Voorhees (Dem., Ind.)

Committee on Foreign Relations: John T. Morgan (Dem., Ala.)

Committee on the Judiciary: James Pugh (Dem., Ala.)

Committee on Military Affairs: Edward Walthall (Dem., Miss.), who resigned effective January 24,

1894. Joseph R. Hawley (Rep., Conn.) became the next chairman.

Committee on Naval Affairs: John R. McPherson (Dem., N.J.)

Committee on Rules: Joseph C.S. Blackburn (Dem., Ky.)

HOUSE LEADERSHIP

Speaker of the House: Charles Frederick Crisp (Dem., Ga.) was reelected Speaker on August 7, 1893. Crisp first had been elected to Congress in the 48th Congress, and served as Speaker in the 52nd and 53rd Congresses.

Majority Leader, Majority Whip, Minority Leader, and Minority Whip: None. These functions did not evolve into formal House positions until the 56th Congress (1899-1901).

Other House Leaders: William Jennings Bryan (Dem., Neb.), first elected to the House in the 52nd Congress, was a leader in the populist and free silver movements. Bryan was a controversial but unsuccessful candidate for president in 1896, 1900, and 1908. He did not run for reelection to the 54th Congress.

Chairmen of Selected Key Committees: [See note 5, p. xxix]

Committee on Agriculture: William H. Hatch (Dem., Mo.)

Committee on Appropriations: Joseph D. Sayers (Dem., Tex.)

Committee on Banking, Finance, and Urban Affairs: William M. Springer (Dem., Ill.)

Committee on Foreign Affairs: James B. McCreary (Dem., Ky.)

Committee on the Judiciary: David B. Culberson (Dem., Tex.)

Committee on Military Affairs: Joseph H. Outhwaite (Dem., Ohio)

Committee on Naval Affairs: Amos J. Cummings (Dem., N.Y.), who resigned effective November

21, 1894. Jacob Geissenhainer (Dem., N.J.) became the next chairman.

Committee on Rules: Charles F. Crisp (Dem., Ga.)

Committee on Ways and Means: William L. Wilson (Dem., W.Va.)

ORGANIZATION AND ADMINISTRATION

No significant development. [See note 5, p. xxix]

MAJOR LEGISLATION PASSED

Admission of Utah as a New State: Congress voted to admit Utah into the United States after the Utah Mormons agreed to end their practice of polygamy.

Currency: Congress repealed the Silver Purchase Act of 1890, which obligated the U.S. to purchase 4.5 million ounces of silver a month in order to subsidize western miners and put more silver currency into circulation. The act had caused a severe drain on the Treasury's gold reserves because the Treasury had to use gold to purchase silver or use gold to redeem paper money issued for silver.

Revenue: In the Wilson-Gorman Tariff Act, Congress authorized the reduction of duties on imports by an average of 40 percent. The act also authorized a federal income tax on incomes exceeding $4,000 a year. In 1895, however, in the case of *Pollock v. Farmers' Loan and Trust Co.*, the Supreme Court declared that the income tax on revenue derived from property was a "direct tax" requiring apportionment under article I, section 2 of the Constitution. A direct tax in this manner requires the Federal government to determine how much money it wishes to raise, and then that tax is divided or "apportioned" amongst the states according population size. The notion of apportionment inevitably raised tensions between states over which state was paying more or less than they should, particularly if the purpose of the tax was for spending seen as benefitting some states more than others. An income

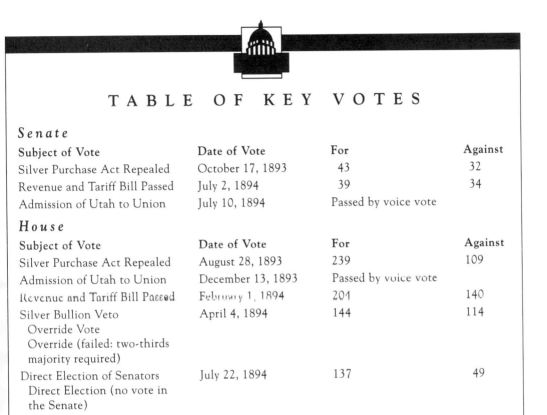

TABLE OF KEY VOTES

Senate

Subject of Vote	Date of Vote	For	Against
Silver Purchase Act Repealed	October 17, 1893	43	32
Revenue and Tariff Bill Passed	July 2, 1894	39	34
Admission of Utah to Union	July 10, 1894	Passed by voice vote	

House

Subject of Vote	Date of Vote	For	Against
Silver Purchase Act Repealed	August 28, 1893	239	109
Admission of Utah to Union	December 13, 1893	Passed by voice vote	
Revenue and Tariff Bill Passed	February 1, 1894	204	140
Silver Bullion Veto Override Vote Override (failed: two-thirds majority required)	April 4, 1894	144	114
Direct Election of Senators Direct Election (no vote in the Senate)	July 22, 1894	137	49

[See note 7, p. xxix]

tax on just earned income or a direct tax apportioned among the states both were politically impossible, and so there was no federal individual income tax until the Sixteenth Amendment was ratified in 1913.

FAILED LEGISLATION

None of historical significance.

RELATIONS WITH THE PRESIDENT

Relations between Congress and President Grover Cleveland were usually poor, due in large part to Cleveland's prolific use of the veto power. Most of Cleveland's vetoes concerned minor legislation of no historic significance, such as pension bills and relief bills for private citizens. He considered such bills to be a misuse of public funds. However, many members of Congress from both parties were irritated by Cleveland's effort to end a long-standing form of patronage for friends, constituents and political supporters.

Cleveland vetoed 81 bills during the 53rd Congress. One bill would have increased the coinage of silver bullion held by the Treasury, but Cleveland had supported the repeal of the Silver Purchase Act. Cleveland vetoed the bill on March 29, 1894. The House sustained the veto on April 4, 1894, when it voted 144 to 114 to override, short of the necessary two-thirds majority, and there was no vote in the Senate.

NOMINATIONS, APPOINTMENTS, AND CONFIRMATIONS

The Judiciary: On July 7, 1893, Supreme Court Justice Samuel Blatchford died. It took President Cleveland three attempts to fill the vacancy. First, Cleveland nominated William B. Hornblower on September 19, 1893, but on January 15, 1894, the Senate voted 30 to 24 against Hornblower's confirmation. Next, Cleveland nominated Wheeler H. Peckham on January 23, 1894, but the Senate on February 16, 1894, voted 41 to 32 against Peckham's confirmation. Finally, on February 19, 1894, Cleveland nominated, and the Senate confirmed by voice vote, Edward D. White to suceed Blatchford.

The Executive Branch: On March 6, 1893, President Cleveland nominated, and the Senate confirmed by voice vote, John G. Carlisle to be secretary of the Treasury, Walter Q. Gresham to be secretary of state, Hilary A. Herbert to be secretary of the Navy, Daniel S. Lamont to be secretary of war, Julius S. Morton to be secretary of agriculture, Richard Olney to be attorney general, and Hoke Smith to be secretary of the Interior.

IMPEACHMENTS

None.

CONSTITUTIONAL AMENDMENTS

On July 22, 1894, the House voted 137 to 49 in favor of a constitutional amendment providing for the direct election of senators. The proposed amendment died in the Senate, where the senators were not yet ready to reform the malfunctioning system whereby state legislatures chose senators. Since the procedure for choosing senators was left to the individual state legislatures, internal disagreements and party politics frequently created deadlocks that lasted for years, leaving a Senate seat simply unfilled in the interim. Many times Senate seats would go to the person who made the most promises of federal jobs and government contracts. By the end of the 19th century, most of the House and in fact most of the state legislatures favored direct election of senators, but since the Constitutional Amendment needed to accomplish this had to get two-thirds of the Senate's approval, those senators who feared facing the electorate directly could block it. There would be no direct election of senators until the Seventeenth Amendment was declared ratified on May 31, 1913. [See 63rd Congress]

FURTHER READING

Merrill, Horace Samuel. *Bourbon Leader: Grover Cleveland and the Democratic Party.* Boston: Little, Brown & Co., 1957.

Nevins, Allan. *Grover Cleveland: A Study in Courage.* New York: Dodd, Mead & Co., 1934.

Stealey, Orlando Oscar. *Twenty Years in the Press Gallery: A Concise History of Important Legislation From the 48th to the 58th Congress; the Part Played by the Leading Men of that Period and the Interesting and Impressive Incidents.* New York: Publishers Printing Co., 1906.

The 54th Congress

MARCH 4, 1895 - MARCH 3, 1897

First Session: December 2, 1895-June 11, 1896
Second Session: December 7, 1896-March 3, 1897

I n the 1894 elections for the 54th Congress, the Republicans gained 6 seats in the Senate to hold a new majority of 44 of the 90 seats. The Democrats lost 4 seats, leaving them with 40. Six seats were not held by either major party. Of the 6 seats, 4 were held by the People's Party (the Populists) and 2 by the Silver Party. In the House, the Republicans gained 117 seats to hold a new majority of 244 of the 357 seats. The Democrats lost 113 seats, reducing their total to 105. Eight seats were held by neither major party. Most of these eight seats were held by the Populists. The number of freshman congressmen in the 54th Congress equaled a record set in the 48th Congress. [See notes 2 and 3, p. xxix]

BACKGROUND

In the 54th Congress, the populist movement for the free coinage of silver grew in popularity and gained more support in Congress, due in large part to the depression caused by the panic of 1893. A group of House Democrats, led by William Jennings Bryan (Dem., Neb.) and Richard P. Bland (Dem., Mo.), unsuccessfully pushed for the free coinage of silver at the ratio of 16 times the level of gold coinage. By 1896 the Democrats were dominated by the populist, free silver faction of the party, while the Republicans supported the traditional and conservative monetary policy based on gold. The Democrats' spokesman, and presidential candidate

in the 1896 elections, was Bryan. Bryan was an eloquent speaker on behalf of the populist and free silver movement, as epitomized by his "cross of gold" speech at the Democratic National Convention in July 1896. Bryan, who was a deeply religious man, equated the conservative gold-based monetary system with the crucifixion of Jesus and humanity. Bryan and the populists lost, however, to Republican William McKinley.

Also in 1896, in the case of *Plessy v. Ferguson*, the Supreme Court legitimized "separate but equal" treatment of blacks and whites, a doctrine which effectively neutralized the Fourteenth and Fifteenth Amendments and Congress's post-Civil War civil rights laws. African Americans were denied the full exercise of their rights as citizens for nearly a century. Another gold strike occurred in Alaska, and the Klondike gold rush caused an influx of settlers into the largely unsettled Alaskan territory.

SENATE LEADERSHIP

Vice President: Adlai Ewing Stevenson had been elected on Grover Cleveland's ticket in 1892. Stevenson previously had served as a representative from Illinois in the 44th and 46th Congresses.

President Pro Tempore: William Pierce Frye (Rep., Maine) was elected on February 7, 1896. Frye first had been elected to Congress in the 42nd Congress, and he served in the House until

C H R O N O L O G Y

March 4, 1895:	The 54th Congress begins.
August 8, 1895:	Supreme Court Justice Howell E. Jackson dies.
December 2, 1895:	The first session begins, and Thomas Brackett Reed (Rep., Maine) is elected Speaker.
December 3, 1895:	President Cleveland nominates Rufus W. Peckham to replace Jackson, Judson Harmon to succeed Richard Olney as attorney general, and Olney to succeed Walter Q. Gresham as secretary of state. The Senate confirms Harmon and Olney.
December 9, 1895:	The Senate confirms Peckham.
February 7, 1896:	William Pierce Frye (Rep., Maine) is elected president pro tem of the Senate.
March 24, 1896:	Congress passes the "Act of Oblivion."
June 11, 1896:	The first session ends.
December 7, 1896:	The second session begins.
December 8, 1896:	President Cleveland nominates David R. Francis to succeed Hoke Smith as secretary of the Interior.
January 18, 1897:	The Senate confirms Francis.
March 3, 1897:	The second session and the 54th Congress end.

[See note 6, p. xxix]

March 17, 1881, when he resigned after being elected senator. Frye served in the Senate until he died on August 8, 1911, and was president pro tem in the 54th through the 62nd Congresses.

Majority Leader, Majority Whip, Minority Leader, and Minority Whip: None. These functions did not evolve into formal Senate positions until the 62nd Congress (1911-1913).

Chairmen of Selected Key Committees: [See note 5, p. xxix]

Committee on Appropriations: William Allison (Rep., Iowa)

Commitee on Finance: Justin S. Morrill (Rep., Vt.)

Committee on Foreign Relations: John Sherman (Rep., Ohio)

Committee on the Judiciary: George F. Hoar (Rep., Mass.)

Committee on Military Affairs: Joseph R. Hawley (Rep., Conn.)

Committee on Naval Affairs: James Donald Cameron (Rep., Pa.)

Committee on Rules: Nelson Aldrich (Rep., R.I.)

HOUSE LEADERSHIP

Speaker of the House: Thomas Brackett Reed (Rep., Maine) was elected Speaker on December 2, 1895. [See biographical note in 51st Congress]

Majority Leader, Majority Whip, Minority Leader, and Minority Whip: These functions did not evolve into formal House positions until the 56th Congress (1899-1901).

Chairmen of Selected Key Committees: [See note 5, p. xxix]

Committee on Agriculture: James W. Wadsworth (Rep., N.Y.)

TABLE OF KEY VOTES

Senate

Subject of Vote	Date of Vote	For	Against
Confirmation of Judson Harmon to be Attorney General and Richard Olney to be Secretary of State	December 3, 1895	Passed by voice votes	
Confirmation of Rufus W. Peckham to Supreme Court	December 9, 1895	Passed by voice vote	
Armed Forces Bill Passed	December 24, 1895	Passed by voice vote	
Confirmation of David R. Francis to be Secretary of the Interior	January 18, 1897	Passed by voice vote	

House

Subject of Vote	Date of Vote	For	Against
Armed Forces Bill Passed	March 24, 1896	Passed by voice vote	

[See note 7, p. xxix]

Committee on Appropriations: Joseph G. Cannon (Rep., Ill.)

Committee on Banking, Finance, and Urban Affairs: Joseph H. Walker (Rep., Mass.)

Committee on Foreign Affairs: Robert R. Hitt (Rep., Ill.)

Committee on the Judiciary: David B. Henderson (Rep., Iowa)

Committee on Military Affairs: John A. T. Hull (Rep., Iowa)

Committee on Naval Affairs: Charles A. Boutelle (Rep., Maine)

Committee on Rules: Thomas B. Reed (Rep., Maine)

Committee on Ways and Means: Nelson Dingley (Rep., Maine)

ORGANIZATION AND ADMINISTRATION

No significant developments. [See note 5, p. xxix]

MAJOR LEGISLATION PASSED

Armed Forces: In legislation nicknamed the "Act of Oblivion," Congress repealed restrictions that formerly had prevented ex-Confederate military officers from serving in the U.S. Army or Navy.

FAILED LEGISLATION

None of historical significance.

RELATIONS WITH THE PRESIDENT

Relations between Congress and President Grover Cleveland were usually poor, due in large part to

Cleveland's prolific use of the veto power. [See 53rd Congress] Cleveland vetoed 89 bills during the 54th Congress, none of which involved significant legislation.

NOMINATIONS, APPOINTMENTS, AND CONFIRMATIONS

The Judiciary: On August 8, 1895, Supreme Court Justice Howell E. Jackson died. President Cleveland nominated Rufus W. Peckham on December 3, 1895, to replace Jackson, and the Senate confirmed Peckham on December 9, 1895, by voice vote.

The Executive Branch: On December 3, 1895, President Cleveland nominated, and the Senate confirmed by voice vote that same day, Judson Harmon to succeed Richard Olney as attorney general and Olney to succeed Walter Q. Gresham as secretary of state. On December 8, 1896, President Cleveland nominated David R. Francis to succeed Hoke Smith as secretary of the Interior. The Senate confirmed Francis by voice vote on January 18, 1897.

IMPEACHMENTS

None.

CONSTITUTIONAL AMENDMENTS

None.

FURTHER READING

Alton, Edmund. *Among the Law-Makers.* New York: Charles Scribner's Sons, 1896.

Merrill, Horace Samuel. *Bourbon Leader: Grover Cleveland and the Democratic Party.* Boston: Little, Brown & Co., 1957.

Nevins, Allan. *Grover Cleveland: A Study in Courage.* New York: Dodd, Mead & Co., 1934.

Robinson, William A. *Thomas B. Reed: Parliamentarian.* New York: Dodd, Mead & Co., 1930.

Stealey, Orlando Oscar. *Twenty Years in the Press Gallery: A Concise History of Important Legislation From the 48th to the 58th Congress; the Part Played by the Leading Men of that Period and the Interesting and Impressive Incidents.* New York: Publishers Printing Co., 1906.

The 55th Congress

MARCH 4, 1897 - MARCH 3, 1899

Special Senate Session: March 4, 1897-March 10, 1897
First Session: March 15, 1897-July 24, 1897
Second Session: December 6, 1897-July 8, 1898
Third Session: December 5, 1898-March 3, 1899

The Senate held a special session to vote on the confirmation of presidential appointees to various offices. [See note 1, p. xxix]

In the 1896 elections for the 55th Congress, the Republicans gained 3 seats in the Senate, raising their majority from 44 to 47 of the 90 seats. The Democrats lost 6 seats, reducing their total to 34. Nine seats were not held by either major party. Five of the seats were held by the People's Party (the Populists) and 2 by the Silver Party. In the House, the Republicans lost 40 seats reducing their majority from 244 to 204 of the 357 seats. The Democrats gained 8 seats to hold a total of 113. Forty seats were held by neither major party. Of these seats, 22 were held by the Populists, 1 by the Silver Party, and the remaining 17 seats generally leaned toward the Democrats. [See notes 2 and 3, p. xxix]

BACKGROUND

On March 4, 1897, William McKinley was inaugurated as the 25th president of the United States. During 1897 the issue of tariffs on imported goods was politically important, and Congress passed tariff legislation that raised import duties to the highest rates in U.S. history. The tariff law was a victory for the Republicans, who supported high tariffs in order to protect domestic industry, even though American industrial enterprises were now some of the largest and most competitive in the world and did not need protectionist tariffs.

In 1898 the nation's attention turned to the Spanish American War. On February 25, 1898, the U.S. battleship *Maine* exploded in the harbor of Havana, Cuba, for reasons that were never positively determined. In the U.S., however, public opinion already was heavily in favor of the Cuban rebels, who were fighting the Spanish colonial government, as being responsible. Further, America had expansionist ambitions in the Caribbean and Central America. The *Maine* incident led to a U.S. declaration of war against Spain, and American naval, marine, and volunteer army forces were victorious in actions against the Spanish from Manila Bay in the Philippines to Guantanamo, Cuba, and Puerto Rico. Spain conceded defeat in August 1898, and the Treaty of Paris ended the war. Cuba became independent, although in reality it was now a semicolonial possession of the U.S., and the U.S. took Guam, the Philippines, and Puerto Rico from Spain. As a side effect of the war, interest grew in the possibility of a canal across the narrow lands of Central America, which would reduce the travel time of American warships and merchant vessels between the Atlantic and Pacific Oceans. Also in 1898, America acquired yet more territory when Congress in a joint resolution approved the annexation of Hawaii.

CHRONOLOGY

March 4, 1897:	The 55th Congress and a special Senate session begin.
March 5, 1897:	President McKinley nominates his cabinet, and the Senate confirms his nominees.
March 10, 1897:	The special Senate session ends.
March 15, 1897:	The first session begins and Thomas Brackett Reed (Rep., Maine) is reelected Speaker of the House.
July 7, 1897:	Congress passes the Dingley Tariff Act.
July 24, 1897:	The first session ends.
December 1, 1897:	Supreme Court Justice Stephen J. Field retires.
December 6, 1897:	The second session begins.
December 16, 1897:	President McKinley nominates Joseph McKenna to replace Field.
January 21, 1898:	The Senate confirms McKenna.
April 25, 1898:	Congress passes a declaration of war against Spain.
July 6, 1898:	Congress passes legislation annexing the Hawaiian Islands.
July 8, 1898:	The second session ends.
December 5, 1898:	The third session begins.
February 6, 1899:	The Senate approves the Treaty of Paris.
March 3, 1899:	The third session and the 55th Congress end.

[See note 6, p. xxix]

SENATE LEADERSHIP

Vice President: Garret Augustus Hobart was elected on William McKinley's ticket in the 1896 elections. Hobart had never served in Congress, but he had been prominent in the Republican Party, having served as a member of the Republican National Committee from 1884 to 1896.

President Pro Tempore: William Pierce Frye (Rep., Maine). [See biographical note in 54th Congress]

Majority Leader, Majority Whip, Minority Leader, and Minority Whip: None. These functions did not evolve into formal Senate positions until the 62nd Congress (1911-1913).

Chairmen of Selected Key Committees: [See note 5, p. xxix]

Committee on Appropriations: William Allison (Rep., Iowa)

Committee on Finance: Justin S. Morrill (Rep., Vt.), who died on December 28, 1898. Nelson Aldrich (Rep., R.I.) became the next chairman.

Committee on Foreign Relations: William P. Frye (Rep., Maine) and Cushman Davis (Rep., Minn.)

Committee on the Judiciary: George F. Hoar (Rep., Mass.)

Committee on Military Affairs: Joseph R. Hawley (Rep., Conn.)

Committee on Naval Affairs: Eugene Hale (Rep., Maine)

Committee on Rules: Nelson Aldrich (Rep., R.I.)

TABLE OF KEY VOTES

Senate

Subject of Vote	Date of Vote	For	Against
Tariffs Raised	July 7, 1897	38	28
Declaration of War With Spain	April 25, 1898	Passed by voice vote	
Hawaii Annexation Passed	July 6, 1898	42	21
Treaty of Paris Approved	February 6, 1899	57	27

House

Subject of Vote	Date of Vote	For	Against
Tariffs Raised	March 31, 1897	205	122
Declaration of War With Spain	April 25, 1898	Passed by voice vote	
Hawaii Annexation Passed	June 15, 1898	209	91

[See note 7, p. xxix]

HOUSE LEADERSHIP

Speaker of the House: Thomas Brackett Reed (Rep., Maine) was reelected Speaker on March 15, 1897. [See biographical note in 51st Congress]

Majority Leader, Majority Whip, Minority Leader, and Minority Whip: None: These functions did not evolve into formal House positions until the 56th Congress (1899-1901).

Chairmen of Selected Key Committees: [See note 5, p. xxix]

Committee on Agriculture: James W. Wadsworth (Rep., N.Y.)

Committee on Appropriations: Joseph G. Cannon (Rep., Ill.)

Committee on Banking, Finance, and Urban Affairs: Joseph H. Walker (Rep., Mass.)

Committee on Foreign Affairs: Robert R. Hitt (Rep., Ill.)

Committee on the Judiciary: David B. Henderson (Rep., Iowa)

Committee on Military Affairs: John A. T. Hull (Rep., Iowa)

Committee on Naval Affairs: Charles A. Boutelle (Rep., Maine)

Committee on Rules: Thomas B. Reed (Rep., Maine)

Committee on Ways and Means: Nelson Dingley (Rep., Maine), who died on January 13, 1899. Sereno E. Payne (Rep., N.Y.) became the next chairman.

ORGANIZATION AND ADMINISTRATION

No developments of significance. [See note 5, p. xxix]

MAJOR LEGISLATION PASSED

Hawaii: Congress voted to annex the Hawaiian Islands, which were a U.S protectorate, as part of the United States. As a result, the Hawaiian Islands could eventually qualify for statehood.

Spanish American War: Congress declared war

on Spain after the *Maine* incident in Cuba. [See Background, above] The war ended during this Congress when Spain conceded defeat, and the Senate approved the Treaty of Paris.

Tariffs: In the Dingley Tariff Act, Congress raised duties on imports to an average of 57 percent on their value, the highest tariff rate in U.S. history.

FAILED LEGISLATION

None of historical significance.

RELATIONS WITH THE PRESIDENT

President McKinley's relations with Congress were generally smoother than President Cleveland's. McKinley strongly supported high tariffs in order to protect American industry, and successfully pushed higher tariff legislation through Congress. McKinley vetoed seven bills during the 55th Congress, none of which involved significant legislation.

NOMINATIONS, APPOINTMENTS, AND CONFIRMATIONS

The Judiciary: On December 1, 1897, Supreme Court Justice Stephen J. Field retired. President McKinley nominated Joseph McKenna on December 16, 1897, to replace Field, and the Senate confirmed McKenna on January 21, 1898, by voice vote.

The Executive Branch: President McKinley frequently reorganized his cabinet during the 55th Congress. All nominees were confirmed by the Senate by voice vote. On March 5, 1897, President McKinley nominated, and the Senate confirmed, Russel A. Alger to be secretary of war, Cornelius N. Bliss to be secretary of the Interior, Lyman J. Gage to be secretary of the Treasury, John D. Long to be secretary of the Navy, Joseph McKenna to be attorney general, John Sherman to be secretary of state, and James Wilson to be secretary of agriculture. John W. Griggs was nominated to be attorney general on January 22, 1898, and confirmed on January 25, 1898; William R.

Day was both nominated and confirmed to be secretary of state on April 26, 1898. On December 6, 1898, John Hay was nominated to be secretary of state, and Ethan A. Hitchcock was nominated to be secretary of the Interior. Both Hay and Hitchcock were confirmed on December 7, 1898.

IMPEACHMENTS

None.

CONSTITUTIONAL AMENDMENTS

None.

FURTHER READING

Gould, Lewis L. *William McKinley: A Bibliography.* Westport, Conn.: Meckler, 1988.

McDevitt, Brother Matthew. *Joseph McKenna: Associate Justice of the United States.* New York: Da Capo Press, 1974 (reprint of 1946 edition).

Merrill, Horace Samuel & Merrill, Marion Galbraith. *The Republican Command, 1897-1913.* Lexington: University Press of Kentucky, 1971.

Rhodes, James Ford. *The McKinley and Roosevelt Administrations, 1897-1909.* Port Washington, N.Y.: Kennikat Press, 1965 (reprint of 1922 edition).

Robinson, William A. *Thomas B. Reed: Parliamentarian.* New York: Dodd, Mead, & Co., 1930.

Stealey, Orlando Oscar. *Twenty Years in the Press Gallery: A Concise History of Important Legislation From the 48th to the 58th Congress; the Part Played by the Leading Men of that Period and the Interesting and Impressive Incidents.* New York: Publishers Printing Co., 1906.

The 56th Congress

MARCH 4, 1899 - MARCH 3, 1901

First Session: December 4, 1899-June 7, 1900
Second Session: December 3, 1900-March 3, 1901

In the 1898 elections for the 56th Congress, the Republicans gained 6 seats in the Senate, raising their majority from 47 to 53 of the 90 seats. The Democrats lost 8 seats, reducing their total to 26. Eleven seats were held by neither major party. Of these 11 seats, 5 were held by the People's Party (the Populists), 2 by the Silver Party, and 3 by a splinter group called the Silver Republicans. In the House, the Republicans lost 19 seats, reducing their majority from 204 to 185 of the 357 seats. The Democrats gained 50 seats, raising their total to 163. Nine seats were held by neither party. Of these 9 seats, 5 were held by the Populists, 1 seat was held by an "Independent Populist," 1 seat was held by the Silver Party, and 2 seats were held by the Silver Republicans. [See notes 2 and 3, p. xxix]

BACKGROUND.

According to the Census of 1900, the population of the United States as of June 1, 1900, was 75,994,575, resulting in a population density of 25.6 persons for each of the country's 2,969,834 square miles. This was a population increase of 20.7 percent over the 1890 census.

In 1899 the first serious international convention on disarmament was organized by Czar Nicholas II of Russia, and envoys from 26 nations including the U.S. met at The Hague, Netherlands, from May 18 to July 29. The assembled nations agreed to establish the Permanent Court of International Arbitration to mediate international disputes. However, the arbitration was purely voluntary, with the U.S. reserving the right to invoke the Monroe Doctrine, and nothing of significance was accomplished concerning disarmament. Also during 1899, there was a continuing guerrilla war in the Philippines between Filipino rebels and the American forces that had occupied the country after the Spanish American War.

In 1900 the Boxer Rebellion broke out in China. The Boxers were ultranationalist rebels who wanted to expel all the foreigners from China and keep the country free from western culture and influences. The Boxers took the capital, Beijing, on June 20 and took the resident diplomatic community hostage. Six nations, including the U.S., assembled an expeditionary force that went to China and took Beijing on August 14. By September 7, the Chinese Imperial government was back in power and was forced to pay $333 million in reparations, of which the U.S. received $24.5 million.

Domestically, in 1900 Congress passed legislation that put the U.S. back on the gold standard, which was a severe defeat for the free silver and populist movement led by William Jennings Bryan. Congress established the territory of Hawaii, and on June 14, 1900, President McKinley appointed Sanford B. Dole as the first territorial governor. Also in 1900, Minneapolis, Minnesota, experimented with the first direct primary election in U.S. history. As a result, many states became inter-

CHRONOLOGY

March 4, 1899:	The 56th Congress begins.
December 4, 1899:	The first session begins and David Bremner Henderson (Rep., Iowa) is elected Speaker.
December 6, 1899:	President McKinley nominates, and the Senate confirms, Elihu Root to succeed Russell A. Alger as secretary of war.
February 15, 1900:	Congress passes the Currency Act of 1900.
February 28, 1900:	Congress passes legislation reorganizing the government of Puerto Rico.
April 6, 1900:	Congress passes legislation concerning Hawaii's territorial status.
June 7, 1900:	The first session ends.
December 3, 1900:	The second session begins.
February 27, 1901:	Congress passes the Platt Amendment.
March 3, 1901:	The second session and the 56th Congress end.

[See note 6, p. xxix]

ested in the primary system, and Wisconsin became the first to implement the direct primary on a state-wide basis in 1903. Finally, by the end of 1900, the Olds Company had built in Detroit, Michigan, the first mass production automobile factory in the United States.

In 1901 Congress approved the Platt Amendment to the Army Appropriation Act of 1901, which effectively required Cuba to become a U.S. protectorate as the condition for the withdrawal of American troops. By the end of the 56th Congress, the United States Steel Corporation was formed and in time would become the first billion dollar corporation in American history. At the same time, a surge of oil exploration and development occurred in Texas due to the vast oil reservoirs discovered near Beaumont, Texas. Texas would become the center of the petroleum industry in the future.

SENATE LEADERSHIP

Vice President: Garret Augustus Hobart won election on McKinley's ticket in 1896. He had never served in Congress, but he was prominent in the Republican Party, having been a member of the Republican National Committee from 1884 to 1896. Hobart died on November 21, 1899 and the vice presidency remained vacant for the balance of McKinley's first term. (Until the Twenty-fifth Amendment was ratified on February 10, 1967 [See 90th Congress], there was no mechanism for filling vacancies in the office of the vice president.)

President Pro Tempore: William Pierce Frye (Rep., Maine). [See biographical note in 54th Congress]

Majority Leader, Majority Whip, Minority Leader, and Minority Whip: None. These functions did not evolve into formal Senate positions until the 62nd Congress (1911-1913).

Chairmen of Selected Key Committees: [See also Organization and Administration, below]

Committee on Appropriations: William Allison (Rep., Iowa)

Committee on Finance: Nelson Aldrich (Rep., R.I.)

TABLE OF KEY VOTES

Senate

Subject of Vote	Date of Vote	For	Against
Silver Purchase Bill Passed	February 15, 1900	46	29
Hawaii Territory Bill Passed	March 1, 1900	Passed by voice vote	
Puerto Rico Territory Bill Passed	April 3, 1900	40	31
Platt Amendment Passed	February 27, 1901	43	18

House

Subject of Vote	Date of Vote	For	Against
Silver Purchase Bill Passed	December 18, 1899	190	150
Puerto Rico Territory Bill Passed	February 28, 1900	172	160
Hawaii Territory Bill Passed	April 6, 1900	Passed by voice vote	
Platt Amendment Passed	February 12, 1901	Passed by voice vote	

[See note 7, p. xxix]

Committee on Foreign Relations: Cushman Davis (Rep., Minn.)

Committee on the Judiciary: George F. Hoar (Rep., Mass.)

Committee on Military Affairs: Joseph R. Hawley (Rep., Conn.)

Committee on Naval Affairs: Eugene Hale (Rep., Maine)

Committee on Rules: John C. Spooner (Rep., Wis.)

HOUSE LEADERSHIP

Speaker of the House: David Bremner Henderson (Rep., Iowa) was elected Speaker on December 4, 1899. Henderson first had been elected to Congress in the 48th Congress, and served as Speaker in the 56th and 57th Congresses.

Majority Leader: Sereno E. Payne (Rep., N.Y.)

Majority Whip: James A. Tawney (Rep., Minn.)

Minority Leader: James D. Richardson (Dem., Tenn.)

Minority Whip: Oscar W. Underwood (Dem., Ala.)

Chairmen of Selected Key Committees: [See also Organization and Administration, below]

Committee on Agriculture: James W. Wadsworth (Rep., N.Y.)

Committee on Appropriations: Joseph G. Cannon (Rep., Ill.)

Committee on Banking, Finance and Urban Affairs: Marriott Brosius (Rep., Pa.)

Committee on Foreign Affairs: Robert R. Hitt (Rep., Ill.)

Committee on the Judiciary: George W. Ray (Rep., N.Y.)

Committee on Military Affairs: John A. T. Hull (Rep., Iowa)

Committee on Naval Affairs: Charles A. Boutelle

(Rep., Maine), who resigned effective March 3, 1901, on the last day of the 56th Congress. George E. Foss (Rep., Ill.) became the next Chairman.

Committee on Rules: David B. Henderson (Rep., Iowa)

Committee on Ways and Means: Sereno E. Payne (Rep., N.Y.)

ORGANIZATION AND ADMINISTRATION

In the House, the offices of majority leader, majority whip, minority leader, and minority whip became formal positions during this Congress. The majority leader is the Speaker of the House's second in command and is supposed to lead the majority party in the House. The majority whip is the Speaker's third in command and is supposed to keep majority party members informed of party objectives and ensure their loyalty to the party's agenda. These offices may be viewed as a line of succession as well: If a Speaker leaves office, the majority leader usually becomes the next Speaker if his or her party stays in the majority. The majority whip then rises to become the majority leader, and a new person is chosen to become the majority whip. The minority leader and minority whip serve similar functions. The minority leader represents the minority party, and the minority whip keeps the members of that party in line with the party's agenda. Of course, these positions can reverse themselves. For example, if the majority party loses control of the House in an election, the former minority leader then becomes the number one figure in the new majority party, and is usually elected Speaker of the House. Conversely, the former Speaker may find himself or herself the new minority leader. [See note 5, p. xxix]

MAJOR LEGISLATION PASSED

Cuba: In the Platt Amendment to the Army Appropriations Act of 1901, Congress gave the U.S. the right to intervene in Cuban political affairs, disapprove treaties made by Cuba, and acquire land from Cuba for naval bases.

Currency: In the Currency Act of 1900, Congress officially put the United States back on the gold standard, based on the gold dollar with a standard weight of 25.8 grains of gold.

Hawaii: Congress established the Hawaiian Islands as an "incorporated territory," with the residents being protected by the Constitution and eligible for U.S. citizenship.

Puerto Rico: Congress established Puerto Rico as an "unorganized territory," and gave it a new form of government. The governor and upper house of the legislature would be appointed by the U.S. president, and the lower house of the legislature would be elected by the people. The residents were made citizens of Puerto Rico but not yet given U.S. citizenship.

FAILED LEGISLATION

None of historical significance.

RELATIONS WITH THE PRESIDENT

President McKinley's relations with Congress, which continued under Republican control, remained good. [See 55th Congress] McKinley vetoed 35 bills during the 56th Congress, none of which involved significant legislation.

NOMINATIONS, APPOINTMENTS, AND CONFIRMATIONS

The Judiciary: There were no significant nominations, appointments, or confirmations in the federal judiciary during the 56th Congress.

The Executive Branch: On December 6, 1899, President McKinley nominated, and the Senate confirmed, Elihu Root to succeed Russell A. Alger as secretary of war.

IMPEACHMENTS
None.

CONSTITUTIONAL AMENDMENTS
None.

FURTHER READING

Gould, Lewis L. _William McKinley: A Bibliography_. Westport, Conn.: Meckler, 1988.

Merrill, Horace Samuel & Merrill, Marion Galbraith. _The Republican Command, 1897-1913_. Lexington: University Press of Kentucky, 1971.

Rhodes, James Ford. _The McKinley and Roosevelt Administrations, 1897-1909_. Port Washington, N.Y.: Kennikat Press, 1965 (reprint of 1922 edition).

Stealey, Orlando Oscar. _Twenty Years in the Press Gallery: A Concise History of Important Legislation From the 48th to the 58th Congress; the Part Played by the Leading Men of that Period and the Interesting and Impressive Incidents_. New York: Publishers Printing Co., 1906.

The 57th Congress

MARCH 4, 1901-MARCH 3, 1903

Special Senate Session: *March 4, 1901-March 9, 1901*
First Session: *December 2, 1901-July 1, 1902*
Second Session: *December 1, 1902-March 3, 1903*

The Senate held a special session to vote on the confirmation of presidential appointees to various offices. [See note 1, p. xxix]

In the 1900 elections for the 57th Congress, the Republicans gained 2 seats in the Senate, raising their majority from 53 to 55 of the 90 seats. The Democrats gained 5 seats for a total of 31. Four seats were held by neither major party. Two of these seats were held by the People's Party (the Populists). In the House, the Republicans gained 12 seats, raising their majority from 185 to 197 of the 357 seats. The Democrats lost 12 seats, reducing their total to 151. Nine seats were not held by either major party. Five of these seats were held by the Populists. [See notes 2 and 3, p. xxix]

BACKGROUND.

On March 4, 1901, William McKinley was inaugurated for his second term as the 25th president of the United States. An anarchist named Leon Czolgosz shot McKinley on September 6, 1901, and the president died eight days later, early on the morning of September 14. Vice President Theodore Roosevelt was sworn in as the 26th president that same day. Roosevelt was 42 years old, the youngest person to become president.

During 1901 American troops in the Philippines captured Emilio Aguinaldo, the most important leader of the Filipino guerrilla resistance to the U.S. occupation, and the rebel move-ment was effectively crushed. In the *Insular Cases*, the Supreme Court held that the Philippines and other territories acquired from Spain due to the Spanish American War were not entitled to the same constitutional protections as other territories, such as Alaska and Hawaii, that would eventually become states. Finally, the U.S. and Great Britain signed the Hay-Pauncefote Treaty, according to which Britain consented to the American construction and control of a canal across Panama in order to link the Atlantic and Pacific Oceans. In 1902 Congress passed legislation authorizing the construction of the Panama Canal.

President Roosevelt started the first major antitrust prosecution under the Sherman Act against the Northern Securities Company in 1902. Congress also enacted legislation reorganizing the government of the Philippines, and passed the Newlands Reclamation Act, which established the Interior Department's Bureau of Reclamation as part of a series of land conservation measures. In 1903 Congress passed the Elkins Act, designed to strengthen existing legislation against the widespread and illegal railroad practice of giving rebates to certain favored shippers.

SENATE LEADERSHIP

Vice President: Theodore Roosevelt had been elected vice president on William McKinley's ticket in 1900 and became president on September 14, 1901, after the assassination of

C H R O N O L O G Y

March 4, 1901:	The 57th Congress and a special Senate session begin.
March 5, 1901:	President McKinley renominates, and the Senate reconfirms, his cabinet.
March 7, 1901:	William Pierce Frye (Rep., Maine) is reelected president pro tem of the Senate.
March 9, 1901:	The special Senate session ends.
December 2, 1901:	The first session begins and David Bremner Henderson (Rep., Iowa) is elected Speaker of the House.
December 16, 1901:	The Senate approves the Hay-Pauncefote Treaty.
February 17, 1902:	Congress passes legislation making the Census Bureau a permanent agency.
June 13, 1902:	Congress passes the Newlands Reclamation Act.
June 19, 1902:	Congress passes legislation furthering the construction of the Panama Canal.
June 26, 1902:	Congress passes the Philippine Government Act.
July 1, 1902:	The first session ends.
September 15, 1902:	Supreme Court Justice Horace Gray dies.
December 1, 1902:	The second session begins.
December 2, 1902:	President Roosevelt nominates, and the Senate confirms, Oliver Wendell Holmes to replace Gray.
January 17, 1903:	Congress passes legislation making the Department of Commerce and Labor a cabinet-level agency.
February 5, 1903:	Congress passes new antitrust legislation.
February 13, 1903:	Congress passes the Elkins Act.
February 23, 1903:	Supreme Court Justice George Shiras retires.
March 2, 1903:	President Roosevelt nominates, and the Senate confirms, William R. Day to replace Shiras.
March 3, 1903:	The second session and the 57th Congress end.

[See note 6, p. xxix]

McKinley. Since until the Twenty-fifth Amendment was ratified on February 10, 1967 [See 90th Congress], there was no mechanism for filling vacancies in the office of the vice president, the vice presidency remained vacant for the balance of Roosevelt's first term.

President Pro Tempore: William Pierce Frye (Rep., Maine) was reelected on March 7, 1901. [See biographical note in 54th Congress]

Majority Leader, Majority Whip, Minority Leader, and Minority Whip: None. These functions did not evolve into formal Senate positions until the 62nd Congress (1911-1913).

Chairmen of Selected Key Committees: [See note 5, p. xxix]

Committee on Appropriations: William Allison (Rep., Iowa)

TABLE OF KEY VOTES

Senate

Subject of Vote	Date of Vote	For	Against
Hay-Pauncefote Treaty	December 16, 1901	72	6
Department of Commerce and Labor Elevated	January 28, 1902	Passed by voice vote	
Census Bureau Established	February 17, 1902	Passed by voice vote	
Land Reclamation Bill Passed	March 1, 1902	Passed by voice vote	
Philippines Territorial Government Established	June 3, 1902	48	30
Panama Canal Authorized	June 19, 1902	67	6
Anti-Rebate Bill Passed	February 3, 1903	Passed by voice vote	
Antitrust Enforcement Strengthened	February 4, 1903	Passed by voice vote	

House

Subject of Vote	Date of Vote	For	Against
Panama Canal Authorized	January 9, 1902	308	2
Census Bureau Established	January 13, 1902	Passed by voice vote	
Land Reclamation Bill Passed	June 13, 1902	146	55
Philippines Territorial Government Established	June 26, 1902	140	97
Department of Commerce and Labor Elevated	January 17, 1903	135	42
Antitrust Enforcement Strengthened	February 5, 1903	Passed by voice vote	
Anti-Rebate Bill Passed	February 13, 1903	250	6

[See note 7, p. xxix]

Committee on Finance: Nelson Aldrich (Rep., R.I.)

Committee on Foreign Relations: Shelby Cullom (Rep., Ill.)

Committee on the Judiciary: George F. Hoar (Rep., Mass.)

Committee on Military Affairs: Joseph R. Hawley (Rep., Conn.)

Committee on Naval Affairs: Eugene Hale (Rep., Maine)

Committee on Rules: John C. Spooner (Rep., Wis.)

HOUSE LEADERSHIP

Speaker of the House: David Bremner Henderson (Rep., Iowa) was elected Speaker on December 2, 1901. Henderson first had been elected to Congress in the 48th Congress and served as Speaker in the 56th and 57th Congresses.

Majority Leader: Sereno E. Payne (Rep., N.Y.)

Majority Whip: James A. Tawney (Rep., Minn.)

Minority Leader: James D. Richardson (Dem., Tenn.)

Minority Whip: James T. Lloyd (Dem., Mo.)

Chairmen of Selected Key Committees: [See note 5, p. xxix]

Committee on Agriculture: James W. Wadsworth (Rep., N.Y.)

Committee on Appropriations: Joseph G. Cannon (Rep., Ill.)

Committee on Banking, Finance, and Urban Affairs: Charles N. Fowler (Rep., N.J.)

Committee on Foreign Affairs: Robert R. Hitt (Rep., Ill.)

Committee on the Judiciary: George W. Ray (Rep., N.Y.)

Committee on Military Affairs: John A. T. Hull (Rep., Iowa)

Committee on Naval Affairs: George E. Foss (Rep., Ill.)

Committee on Rules: David B. Henderson (Rep., Iowa)

Committee on Ways and Means: Sereno E. Payne (Rep., N.Y.)

ORGANIZATION AND ADMINISTRATION

No developments of significance. [See note 5, p. xxix]

MAJOR LEGISLATION PASSED

Antitrust: Congress passed legislation to expedite federal antitrust prosecutions by giving such litigation priority in federal courts.

Census: Congress made the Census Bureau, which supervises the national census that takes place every ten years, a permanent government agency.

Department of Commerce and Labor: Congress promoted the Department of Commerce and Labor to a cabinet-level agency.

Land Reclamation: In the Newlands Reclamation Act, Congress established the Interior Department's Bureau of Reclamation and authorized a series of land conservation and irrigation projects, which were financed by the sale of public lands and contributions from local settlers.

Panama Canal: The Senate approved the Hay-Pauncefote Treaty, in which Britain agreed to let the U.S. build and operate a Panama Canal under exclusive U.S. control. This treaty terminated the Clayton-Bulwer Treaty of 1850 [See 31st Congress], which had contemplated a Panama Canal under joint U.S.-British control. Congress then passed legislation authorizing the government to buy the necessary rights from the New Panama Canal Company of France, which had unsuccessfully attempted to build a canal, and the Republic of Colombia, to which Panama belonged.

Philippines: In the Philippine Government Act, Congress made the Philippines an "unorganized territory," and established a new form of government. The Philippines would remain under U.S. protection and control, but there would be a popularly elected Philippine Assembly. Philippine residents were not given U.S. citizenship.

Shipping: In the Elkins Act, Congress strengthened existing legislation against illegal railroad shipping rebates.

FAILED LEGISLATION

None of historical significance.

RELATIONS WITH THE PRESIDENT

Roosevelt successfully pursued a progressive legislative agenda in Congress. He supported legislation that increased the federal government's ability to regulate business and successfully backed new environmental and labor legislation. Roosevelt vetoed 21 bills during the 57th Congress, none of which involved major legislation. McKinley vetoed none in his brief tenure as president during this congress.

NOMINATIONS, APPOINTMENTS, AND CONFIRMATIONS

The Judiciary: On September 15, 1902, Supreme Court Justice Horace Gray died. President Theodore Roosevelt nominated, and the Senate confirmed by voice vote, Oliver Wendell Holmes on December 2, 1902, to replace Gray. On February 23, 1903, Justice George Shiras retired. President Roosevelt nominated William R. Day on March 2, 1903, to replace Shiras, and the Senate confirmed him that same day by voice vote.

The Executive Branch: Although not required by law to do so, on March 5, 1901, President McKinley renominated his cabinet [See 55th and 56th Congresses] as he entered his second term. On that same day the Senate reconfirmed the cabinet by voice vote. After McKinley's assassination, President Roosevelt kept most of McKinley's cabinet, and made only four major changes during the 57th Congress. First, on December 4, 1901, Roosevelt nominated Philander C. Knox to succeed John W. Griggs as attorney general, and on December 16, 1901, the senator confirmed Knox by a voice vote. Second, on January 7, 1902, Roosevelt nominated Leslie M. Shaw to succeed Lyman J. Gage as secretary of the Treasury, and on January 9, 1902, the Senate confirmed Shaw by voice vote. Third, on April 29, 1902, Roosevelt nominated, and the Senate confirmed by voice vote, William H. Moody to succeed John D. Long as secretary of the Navy. Finally, on February 16, 1903, Roosevelt nominated, and the Senate confirmed by voice vote, George B. Cortelyou to be secretary of commerce and labor, a position which first achieved cabinet status in this Congress. [See Major Legislation, p. 251]

IMPEACHMENTS

None.

CONSTITUTIONAL AMENDMENTS

None.

FURTHER READING

Harbaugh, William Henry. *The Life and Times of Theodore Roosevelt.* New York: Collier Books, 1963.

Gould, Lewis L. *William McKinley: A Bibliography.* Westport, Conn: Meckler, 1988.

Merrill, Horace Samuel & Merrill, Marion Galbraith. *The Republican Command, 1897-1913.* Lexington: University Press of Kentucky, 1971.

Novick, Sheldon M.. *Honorable Justice: The Life of Oliver Wendell Holmes.* Boston: Little, Brown & Co., 1989.

Rhodes, James Ford. *The McKinley and Roosevelt Administrations, 1897-1909.* Port Washington, N.Y.: Kennikat Press, 1965 (reprint of 1922 edition).

Stealey, Orlando Oscar. *Twenty Years in the Press Gallery: A Concise History of Important Legislation From the 48th to the 58th Congress; the Part Played by the Leading Men of that Period and the Interesting and Impressive Incidents.* New York: Publishers Printing Co., 1906.

The 58th Congress

MARCH 4, 1903-MARCH 3, 1905

Special Senate Session: March 5, 1903-March 19, 1903
First Session: November 9, 1903-December 7, 1903
Second Session: December 7, 1903-May 7, 1904
Third Session: December 5, 1904-March 3, 1905

The Senate held a special session to vote on the confirmation of presidential appointees to various offices. [See note 1, p. xxix]

In the 1902 elections for the 58th Congress, the Republicans gained 2 seats in the Senate, raising their majority from 55 to 57 of the 90 seats. The Democrats gained 2 seats to hold a total of 33. Because of the 1900 census [See 56th Congress], the House was reapportioned and increased to 391 members. The Republicans gained 11 seats for a majority of 208 of the 391 seats, and the Democrats gained 27 seats to hold a total of 178. Five seats were not held by either major party. Three of these seats were held by a splinter faction calling themselves Independent Republicans. [See notes 2 and 3, p. xxix]

BACKGROUND

In 1903 Orville and Wilbur Wright made the first recorded heavier-than-air powered flight at Kitty Hawk, North Carolina. The Wright brothers' aircraft flew for only 12 seconds and went just over 100 feet, but their aircraft had proven itself to be a feasible means of mechanized flight. Also during 1903, several events occurred concerning Panama, where the U.S. wanted to build and control a canal linking the Atlantic and Pacific Oceans. First, President Roosevelt sent the Navy to Panama on November 2. Then, a Panamanian revolt planned and supported by the U.S. overthrew the local Colombian authorities on November 3, and the U.S. officially recognized the new Republic of Panama on November 6. On November 18 the U.S. and Panama signed the Hay-Bunau-Varilla Treaty, which gave the Canal Zone to the U.S.

In 1904 the government won its antitrust prosecution against the Northern Securities Company when the Supreme Court ordered the dissolution of the corporation, which was controlled by the powerful financier J.P. Morgan. For the first time, the Sherman Antitrust Act of 1890 had been used successfully to break up a powerful and monopolistic business enterprise.

In foreign affairs, in February 1904 the empires of Russia and Japan went to war over which nation would dominate Korea and other regions of the Pacific far east. Europe and the U.S. assumed that Russia, which had millions of troops and vast resources, would defeat Japan. The Japanese surprised everyone by winning some important naval and land engagements, and the defeats led to civil unrest within Russia. In the next Congress, Roosevelt would make a peace initiative to both sides that would end the war and establish Roosevelt as an international leader.

SENATE LEADERSHIP

Vice President: None. [See 57th Congress]

President Pro Tempore: William Pierce Frye (Rep., Maine). [See biographical note in 54th Congress]

CHRONOLOGY

March 4, 1903:	The 58th Congress begins.
March 5, 1903:	The Senate special session begins.
March 19, 1903:	The Senate special session ends.
November 9, 1903:	The first session begins, and Joseph Gurney Cannon (Rep., Ill.) is elected Speaker of the House.
December 7, 1903:	The first session ends, and the second session begins.
January 4, 1904:	President Roosevelt nominates William H. Taft to succeed Elihu Root as secretary of war.
January 11, 1904:	The Senate confirms Taft.
February 23, 1904:	The Senate approves the Hay-Bunau-Varilla Treaty.
May 7, 1904:	The second session ends.
December 5, 1904:	The third session begins.
December 6, 1904:	President Roosevelt nominates Paul Morton to succeed William H. Moody as secretary of the Navy, Moody to succeed Philander C. Knox as attorney general, and Victor H. Metcalf to succeed George B. Cortelyou as secretary of commerce and labor.
December 7, 1904:	The Senate confirms Morton, Moody, and Metcalf.
January 17, 1905:	Congress passes the Transfer Act of 1905.
March 3, 1905:	The third session and the 58th Congress end.

[See note 6, p. xxix]

Majority Leader, Majority Whip, Minority Leader, and Minority Whip: None. These functions did not evolve into formal Senate positions until the 62nd Congress (1911-1913).

Chairmen of Selected Key Committees: [See note 5, p. xxix]

Committee on Appropriations: William Allison (Rep., Iowa)

Committee on Finance: Nelson Aldrich (Rep., R.I.)

Committee on Foreign Relations: Shelby Cullom (Rep., Ill.)

Committee on the Judiciary: George F. Hoar (Rep., Mass.), who died on September 30, 1904. Orville Platt (Rep., Conn.) became the next chairman.

Committee on Military Affairs: Joseph R. Hawley (Rep., Conn.)

Committee on Naval Affairs: Eugene Hale (Rep., Maine)

Committee on Rules: John C. Spooner (Rep., Wis.)

HOUSE LEADERSHIP

Speaker of the House: Joseph Gurney Cannon (Rep., Ill.) was elected Speaker on November 9, 1903. Cannon first had been elected to Congress in the 43rd Congress and served as Speaker from the 58th through the 61st Congresses. Cannon exploited the Speaker's traditional chairmanship of the Rules Committee to give himself more control over the House than any other Speaker had ever held, causing a revolt against his dictatorial rule in 1910 during the 61st Congress.

Four powerful senators in the early 1900s. From left to right: Orville H. Platt (Rep., Conn.; Chairman of Judiciary Committee), John C. Spooner (Rep., Wis.; Chairman of Rules Committee), William B. Allison (Rep., Iowa; Chairman of Appropriations Committee) and Nelson W. Aldrich (Rep., R.I.; Chairman of Finance Committee.

Majority Leader: Sereno E. Payne (Rep., N.Y.)

Majority Whip: James A. Tawney (Rep., Minn.)

Minority Leader: John Sharp Williams (Dem., Miss.)

Minority Whip: James T. Lloyd (Dem., Mo.)

Chairmen of Selected Key Committees: [See note 5, p. xxix]

Committee on Agriculture: James W. Wadsworth (Rep., N.Y.)

Committee on Appropriations: James A. Hemenway (Rep., Ind.)

Committee on Banking, Finance and Urban Affairs: Charles N. Fowler (Rep., N.J.)

Committee on Foreign Affairs: Robert R. Hitt (Rep., Ill.)

Committee on the Judiciary: John J. Jenkins (Rep., Wis.)

Committee on Military Affairs: John A.T. Hull (Rep., Iowa)

Committee on Naval Affairs: George E. Foss (Rep., Ill.)

Committee on Rules: Joseph G. Cannon (Rep., Ill.)

Committee on Ways and Means: Sereno E. Payne (Rep., N.Y.)

ORGANIZATION AND ADMINISTRATION

No significant developments. [See note 5, p. xxix]

MAJOR LEGISLATION PASSED

Forests: In the Transfer Act of 1905, Congress transferred supervision of the national forests from the Department of the Interior to the Department of Agriculture.

Panama Canal: The Senate approved the Hay-Bunau-Varilla Treaty between the United States and the newly independent nation of Panama, which gave the Canal Zone to the U.S.

TABLE OF KEY VOTES

Senate

Subject of Vote	Date of Vote	For	Against
Confirmation of William H. Taft to be Secretary of War	January 11, 1904	Passed by voice vote	
Hay-Bunau-Varilla Treaty Approved	February 23, 1904	66	14
Confirmation of Paul Morton to be Secretary of the Navy, William H. Moody to be Attorney General, and Victor H. Metcalf to be Secretary of Commerce and Labor	December 7, 1904	Passed by voice votes	
National Forests Transferred to Department of Agriculture	January 17, 1905	Passed by voice vote	

House

Subject of Vote	Date of Vote	For	Against
National Forests Transferred to Department of Agriculture	December 12, 1904	Passed by voice vote	

FAILED LEGISLATION

None of historical significance.

RELATIONS WITH THE PRESIDENT

Roosevelt was so successful in engineering the acquisition of the Panama Canal and winning public support for his actions that, when the Hay-Bunau-Varilla Treaty went to the Senate, there actually was some opposition to treaty provisions providing for a less than complete U.S. takeover of the Canal Zone. Specifically, the treaty provided for $250,000 annual rent payment to Panama, and Panama would retain titular, but effectively meaningless, sovereignty over the Canal Zone. The opposition relented after Secretary of

War Taft explained that these provisions were simply to mollify the sentimental "Spanish Mind," and the Senate approved the treaty.

Roosevelt vetoed two bills during the 58th Congress, neither of which involved significant legislation.

NOMINATIONS, APPOINTMENTS, AND CONFIRMATIONS

The Judiciary: There were no significant nominations, appointments, or confirmations in the federal judiciary during the 58th Congress.

The Executive Branch: On January 4, 1904, President Roosevelt nominated William H. Taft to succeed Elihu Root as secretary of war, and on January 11 the Senate confirmed Taft by voice vote.

Roosevelt nominated Paul Morton to succeed William H. Moody as secretary of the Navy on December 6, 1904, and the Senate confirmed Morton by voice vote the next day. Also on December 6, 1904, Roosevelt nominated Moody to succeed Philander C. Knox as attorney general, and Victor H. Metcalf to succeed George B. Cortelyou as secretary of commerce and labor. The Senate confirmed both men by voice votes the next day.

IMPEACHMENTS

Charles Swayne, a federal judge for the northern district of Florida, was accused of abusing his power to hold people in contempt of court, cheating on his expense accounts, and making personal use of property held under judicial receivership. Swayne was impeached, but on February 27, 1905, the Senate found him not guilty after 12 separate votes on the various charges against him.

CONSTITUTIONAL AMENDMENTS

None.

FURTHER READING

Bolles, Blair. *Tyrant From Illinois: Uncle Joe Cannon's Experiment With Personal Power.* New York: W.W. Norton & Co., 1951.

Harbaugh, William Henry. *The Life and Times of Theodore Roosevelt.* New York: Collier Books, 1963.

Rhodes, James Ford. *The McKinley and Roosevelt Administrations, 1897-1909.* Port Washington, N.Y.: Kennikat Press, 1965 (reprint of 1922 edition).

Stealey, Orlando Oscar. *Twenty Years in the Press Gallery: A Concise History of Important Legislation From the 48th to the 58th Congress; the Part Played by the Leading Men of that Period and the Interesting and Impressive Incidents.* New York: Publishers Printing Co., 1906.

The 59th Congress

MARCH 4, 1905 - MARCH 3, 1907

Special Senate Session: March 4, 1905-March 18, 1905
First Session: December 4, 1905-June 30, 1906
Second Session: December 3, 1906-March 3, 1907

The Senate held a special session to vote on the confirmation of presidential appointees to various offices. [See note 1, p. xxix]

In the 1904 elections for the 59th Congress, neither party gained nor lost any seats in the Senate, the Republicans keeping their total at 57 of the 90 seats and the Democrats retaining their 33 seats. In the House, the Republicans gained 42 seats, giving them a majority of 250 of the 391, and the Democrats lost 42 seats, reducing their total to 136. Five seats were not held by either of the major parties. [See notes 2 and 3, p. xxix]

BACKGROUND

On March 4, 1905, Theodore Roosevelt was inaugurated for his first full term as the 26th president of the United States. The empires of Russia and Japan had been fighting the Russo-Japanese War since 1904. [See 58th Congress] Roosevelt sent a diplomatic note to both nations on June 8, 1905, inviting them to send representatives to the U.S. to meet and negotiate a peace under Roosevelt's mediation. Both sides agreed. They met at Portsmouth, New Hampshire, from August 9, 1905, until September 5, 1905, and with encouragement from the president, the parties concluded the Treaty of Portsmouth. The treaty effectively recognized Japan as the winner of the war, and Japan

received Korea as part of its sphere of influence, as well as other territorial concessions on the mainland of Asia. Roosevelt was able to preserve the Open Door policy for U.S. interests in China, and to some extent, the regional balance of power. Roosevelt won the 1906 Nobel Peace Prize for arranging the end of the war. He was the first American ever to win a Nobel Prize.

Also in 1905, the International Workers of the World, a radical labor organization known as the Wobblies, was formed.

On April 18, 1906, an earthquake struck San Francisco, California, starting fires that swept through most of the city. It took three days to bring the fires under control, and nearly a quarter of a million people were left homeless. Also in 1906, Congress realized that the legislation passed in 1902 [See 57th Congress] to end illegal railroad rebates to favored shippers was ineffective. After months of debate, Congress passed the Hepburn Act. The act gave more power to the Interstate Commerce Commission to regulate and enforce rates. Congress also passed the Pure Food and Drug Act, which would lead to the establishment of the U.S. Food and Drug Administration.

SENATE LEADERSHIP

Vice President: Charles Warren Fairbanks was elected as Roosevelt's running mate in 1904. Fairbanks had served in the Senate (Rep., Ind.)

C H R O N O L O G Y

March 4, 1905:	The 59th Congress and a special Senate session begin.
March 18, 1905:	The special Senate session ends.
December 4, 1905:	The first session begins, and Joseph Gurney Cannon (Rep., Ill.) is reelected Speaker of the House.
December 5, 1905:	President Roosevelt nominates Charles J. Bonaparte to be secretary of the Navy and Elihu Root to be secretary of state.
December 6, 1905:	The Senate confirms Root.
December 7, 1905:	The Senate confirms Bonaparte.
March 9, 1906:	Congress passes legislation admitting Oklahoma into the United States.
May 18, 1906:	Congress passes the Hepburn Act.
May 28, 1906:	Supreme Court Justice Henry B. Brown retires.
June 23, 1906:	Congress passes the Pure Food and Drug Act.
June 27, 1906:	Congress passes immigration legislation.
June 30, 1906:	The first session ends.
December 3, 1906:	The second session begins, and President Theodore Roosevelt nominates William H. Moody to replace Brown, Charles J. Bonaparte to be attorney general, George B. Cortelyou to be secretary of the Treasury, James R. Garfield to be secretary of the Interior, Victor H. Metcalf to succeed Bonaparte as secretary of the Navy, and Oscar S. Straus to be secretary of commerce and labor.
December 12, 1906:	The Senate confirms Moody, Bonaparte, Metcalf, and Straus.
January 15, 1907:	The Senate confirms Cortelyou and Garfield.
February 27, 1907:	Congress passes the Citizenship and Expatriation Act.
March 3, 1907:	The second session and the 59th Congress end.

[See note 6, p. xxix]

from 1896 until March 3, 1905, when he resigned in order to become vice president.

President Pro Tempore: William Pierce Frye (Rep., Maine). [See biographical note in 54th Congress]

Majority Leader, Majority Whip, Minority Leader, and Minority Whip: None. These functions did not evolve into formal Senate positions until the 62nd Congress (1911-1913).

Chairmen of Selected Key Committees: [See note 5, p. xxix]

Committee on Appropriations: William Allison (Rep., Iowa)

Committee on Finance: Nelson Aldrich (Rep., R.I.)

Committee on Foreign Relations: Shelby Cullom (Rep., Ill.)

TABLE OF KEY VOTES

Senate

Subject of Vote	Date of Vote	For	Against
Pure Food and Drug Act Passed	February 21, 1906	63	4
Oklahoma Admitted to Union	March 9, 1906	Passed by voice vote	
Railroads Regulation Strengthened	May 18, 1906	71	3
Immigration Bureau Established	June 27, 1906	Passed by voice vote	
Citizenship and Expatriation Bill Passed	February 27, 1907	Passed by voice vote	

House

Subject of Vote	Date of Vote	For	Against
Oklahoma Admitted to Union	January 25, 1906	195	150
Railroads Regulation Strengthened	February 8, 1906	346	7
Immigration Bureau Established	June 5, 1906	Passed by voice vote	
Pure Food and Drug Act Passed	June 23, 1906	241	17
Citizenship and Expatriation Bill Passed	January 21, 1907	Passed by voice vote	

[See note 7, p. xxix]

Committee on the Judiciary: Orville Platt (Rep., Conn.), who died on April 21, 1905. Clarence D. Clark (Rep., Wyo.) became the next chairman.

Committee on Military Affairs: Francis E. Warren (Rep., Wyo.)

Committee on Naval Affairs: Eugene Hale (Rep., Maine)

Committee on Rules: John C. Spooner (Rep., Wis.)

HOUSE LEADERSHIP

Speaker of the House: Joseph Gurney Cannon (Rep., Ill.) was reelected Speaker on December 4, 1905. [See biographical note in 58th Congress]

Majority Leader: Sereno E. Payne (Rep., N.Y.)

Majority Whip: James E. Watson (Rep., Ind.)

Minority Leader: John Sharp Williams (Dem., Miss.)

Minority Whip: James T. Lloyd (Dem., Mo.)

Chairmen of Selected Key Committees: [See note 5, p. xxix]

Committee on Agriculture: James W. Wadsworth (Rep., N.Y.)

Committee on Appropriations: James A. Tawney (Rep., Minn.)

Committee on Banking, Finance, and Urban Affairs: Charles N. Fowler (Rep., N.J.)

Committee on Foreign Affairs: Robert R. Hitt (Rep., Ill.)

Committee on the Judiciary: John J. Jenkins (Rep., Wis.)

Committee on Military Affairs: John A.T. Hull (Rep., Iowa)

Committee on Naval Affairs: George E. Foss (Rep., Ill.)

Committee on Rules: Joseph G. Cannon (Rep., Ill.)

Committee on Ways and Means: Sereno E. Payne (Rep., N.Y.)

ORGANIZATION AND ADMINISTRATION

No developments of significance. [See note 5, p. xxix]

MAJOR LEGISLATION PASSED

Admission of Oklahoma as a New State: Congress voted to admit Oklahoma into the United States.

Citizenship and Expatriation: In the Citizenship and Expatriation Act, Congress established procedures for the expatriation of U.S. citizens and for giving U.S. citizenship to aliens married to U.S. citizens.

Immigration: Congress established the Bureau of Immigration and Naturalization and set forth uniform regulations for the naturalization of aliens in the U.S.

Pure Food and Drug Act: In response to publicity, such as Upton Sinclair's book *The Jungle* about unsanitary conditions in the food processing industry, Congress enacted the Pure Food and Drug Act. The act was the first serious federal effort to regulate and improve the production and sale of food, drugs, and other substances to the public.

Railroads: Congress passed the Hepburn Act, which expanded and strengthened the Interstate Commerce Commission's authority over railroads and railroad rates.

FAILED LEGISLATION

None of historical significance.

RELATIONS WITH THE PRESIDENT

President Roosevelt successfully pursued a progressive legislative agenda in Congress. He supported legislation that increased the federal government's ability to regulate business and successfully backed new environmental and labor legislation. In particular, Roosevelt won a significant victory when Congress passed the Pure Food and Drug Act. This legislation was opposed by virtually every sector of the food processing industry from meat packers to candy manufacturers.

Roosevelt vetoed 33 bills during the 59th Congress, none of which involved significant legislation.

NOMINATIONS, APPOINTMENTS, AND CONFIRMATIONS

The Judiciary: Supreme Court Justice Henry B. Brown retired on May 28, 1906. President Theodore Roosevelt nominated William H. Moody on December 3, 1906, to replace Brown, and the Senate confirmed Moody by voice vote on December 12, 1906.

The Executive Branch: Upon entering his new term, President Roosevelt did not significantly reorganize his cabinet, but during the course of the 59th Congress he did make several changes. On

December 5, 1905, Roosevelt nominated Charles J. Bonaparte to be secretary of the Navy and Elihu Root to be secretary of state. The Senate confirmed Root on December 6, 1905, by voice vote and Bonaparte the next day by voice vote. On December 3, 1906, Roosevelt nominated Charles J. Bonaparte to be attorney general, George B. Cortelyou to be secretary of the Treasury, James R. Garfield to be secretary of the Interior, Victor H. Metcalf to succeed Bonaparte as secretary of the Navy, and Oscar S. Straus to be secretary of commerce and labor. On December 12, 1906, the Senate confirmed Bonaparte, Metcalf, and Straus by voice votes and on January 15, 1907, Cortelyou and Garfield by voice votes.

IMPEACHMENTS

None.

CONSTITUTIONAL AMENDMENTS

None.

FURTHER READING

Bolles, Blair. *Tyrant From Illinois: Uncle Joe Cannon's Experiment With Personal Power.* New York: W.W. Norton & Co., 1951.

Harbaugh, William Henry. *The Life and Times of Theodore Roosevelt.* New York: Collier Books, 1963.

Merrill, Horace Samuel & Merrill, Marion Galbraith. *The Republican Command, 1897-1913.* Lexington: University Press of Kentucky, 1971.

Rhodes, James Ford. *The McKinley and Roosevelt Administrations, 1897-1909.* Port Washington, N.Y.: Kennikat Press, 1965 (reprint of 1922 edition).

The 60th Congress

MARCH 4, 1907-MARCH 3, 1909

First Session: December 2, 1907-May 30, 1908
Second Session: December 7, 1908-March 3, 1909

In the 1906 elections for the 60th Congress, the Republicans gained 4 seats in the Senate, raising their majority from 57 to 61 of the 92 seats, and the Democrats lost 2 seats, reducing their total to 31. In the House, the Republicans lost 28 seats, reducing their majority from 250 to 222 of the 391 seats. The Democrats gained 28 seats, giving them a total of 164 seats. Five seats were not held by either major party. One seat was held by an Independent Republican. [See notes 2 and 3, p. xxix]

BACKGROUND

On March 13, 1907, nine days after the 60th Congress met, the stock market dropped sharply. The primary cause was overextended and unregulated bank credit, which supported excessive speculation in the financial markets. The government took no actions to address these problems, however, and on October 21, 1907, the collapse of the Knickerbocker Trust Company caused the panic of 1907. The panic was a severe depression in the financial markets and the economy. The Russian czar, Nicholas II, convened the second International Peace Conference in The Hague, Netherlands, in 1907. The conference's most significant action was to approve an Argentinian proposal that Western nations should not use force to collect debts from Latin American nations.

Another important event in 1907 was Roosevelt's decision to display the new power of the U.S. Navy, which had built a fleet of battleships in order to project American power into the open ocean. Historically, possessing a prestigious "white water" navy with the ability to conduct major naval operations beyond national shores and coastal waters, had been limited to the European powers. On December 16, 1907, a squadron of battleships left the U.S. for a two-year voyage, stopping at important ports throughout the world in order to show off the fleet. The ships returned in 1909, having succeeded in impressing the Europeans with America's growing naval power.

In 1908 Congress enacted a child labor law for the District of Columbia. Congress wanted the law to become a piece of model legislation for the states, but the states were slow to follow Congress's lead. Also in 1908, Roosevelt decided that he would not seek another term as president, even though he had not held two full terms (he became president only after President William McKinley was assassinated in 1901). Roosevelt used his influence to see that William Howard Taft, rather than Vice President Fairbanks, would be the next Republican Party candidate for president.

During 1908 Henry Ford introduced the Model T, an inexpensive and reliable automobile, which became extremely popular and made Ford Motor Company the industry leader. In 1909, before the 60th Congress ended, the U.S. ended its military occupation of Cuba.

SENATE LEADERSHIP

Vice President: Charles Warren Fairbanks had served in the Senate (Rep., Ind.) from 1896 until

C H R O N O L O G Y

March 4, 1907: The 60th Congress begins.

December 2, 1907: The first session begins, and Joseph Gurney Cannon (Rep., Ill.) is reelected Speaker of the House.

December 5, 1907: William Frye (Rep., Maine) is reelected president pro tem of the Senate.

May 6, 1908: Congress passes a child labor law for the District of Columbia.

May 15, 1908: Congress passes the Aldrich-Vreeland Emergency Currency Act in response to the panic of 1907.

May 30, 1908: The first session ends.

December 7, 1908: The second session begins.

December 8, 1908: President Roosevelt nominates Truman H. Newberry to succeed Victor H. Metcalf as secretary of the Navy and Luke E. Wright to succeed William H. Taft as secretary of war.

December 9, 1908: The Senate confirms Newberry and Wright.

January 25, 1909: President Roosevelt nominates Robert Bacon to succeed Elihu Root as secretary of state.

January 27, 1909: The Senate confirms Bacon.

March 3, 1909: The second session and the 60th Congress end.

[See note 6, p. xxix]

March 3, 1905, when he resigned in order to become Roosevelt's vice president after having been elected to that office in the 1904 elections.

President Pro Tempore: William Frye (Rep., Maine) was reelected on December 5, 1907. [See biographical note in 54th Congress]

Majority Leader, Majority Whip, Minority Leader, and Minority Whip: None. These functions did not evolve into formal Senate positions until the 62nd Congress (1911-1913).

Chairmen of Selected Key Committees: [See note 5, p. xxix]

Committee on Appropriations: William Allison (Rep., Iowa), who died on August 4, 1908. Eugene Hale (Rep., Maine) became the next chairman.

Committee on Finance: Nelson Aldrich (Rep., R.I.)

Committee on Foreign Relations: Shelby Cullom

(Rep., Ill.)

Committee on the Judiciary: Clarence D. Clark (Rep., Wyo.)

Committee on Military Affairs: Francis E. Warren (Rep., Wyo.)

Committee on Naval Affairs: Eugene Hale (Rep., Maine)

Committee on Rules: Philander C. Knox (Rep., Pa.)

HOUSE LEADERSHIP

Speaker of the House: Joseph Gurney Cannon (Rep., Ill.) was reelected Speaker on December 2, 1907. [See biographical note in 58th Congress]

Majority Leader: Sereno E. Payne (Rep., N.Y.)

Majority Whip: James E. Watson (Rep., Ind.)

TABLE OF KEY VOTES

Senate

Subject of Vote	Date of Vote	For	Against
D.C. Child Labor Law Passed	May 6, 1908	Passed by voice vote	
Panic of 1907 Investigation Bill Passed	May 15, 1908	47	20
Confirmation of Truman H. Newberry to be Secretary of the Navy and Luke E. Wright to be Secretary of War	December 9, 1908	Passed by voice votes	
Confirmation of Robert Bacon to be Secretary of State	January 27, 1909	Passed by voice vote	

House

Subject of Vote	Date of Vote	For	Against
D.C. Child Labor Law Passed	May 4, 1908	200	0
Panic of 1907 Investigation Bill Passed	May 12, 1908	185	145

[See note 7, p. xxix]

Minority Leader: Champ Clark (Dem., Mo.)

Minority Whip: James T. Lloyd (Dem., Mo.)

Chairmen of Selected Key Committees: [See note 5, p. xxix]

Committee on Agriculture: Charles F. Scott (Rep., Kans.)

Committee on Appropriations: James A. Tawney (Rep., Minn.)

Committee on Banking, Finance and Urban Affairs: Charles N. Fowler (Rep., N.J.)

Committee on Foreign Affairs: Robert G. Cousins (Rep., Iowa)

Committee on the Judiciary: John J. Jenkins (Rep., Wis.)

Committee on Military Affairs: John A. T. Hull (Rep., Iowa)

Committee on Naval Affairs: George E. Foss (Rep., Ill.)

Committee on Rules: Joseph G. Cannon (Rep., Ill.)

Committee on Ways and Means: Sereno E. Payne (Rep., N.Y.)

ORGANIZATION AND ADMINISTRATION

No developments of significance. [See note 5, p. xxix]

MAJOR LEGISLATION PASSED

Child Labor: Congress passed a child labor law for the District of Columbia.

Panic of 1907: In the Aldrich-Vreeland Emergency Currency Act, Congress established a

National Monetary Commission to investigate the American banking, credit and currency system. The act was a response to the panic of 1907.

FAILED LEGISLATION

None of historical significance.

RELATIONS WITH THE PRESIDENT

President Roosevelt continued to pursue a progressive legislative agenda in Congress, athough at a slower pace than during the previous few years. He supported legislation that increased the government's power to regulate business, such as the model child labor law Congress passed for the District of Columbia, and supported a more active Federal role in protecting the environment and what was left of the frontier from rapacious mining interests and other big businesses.

Roosevelt vetoed 26 bills during the 60th Congress, none of which involved significant legislation.

NOMINATIONS, APPOINTMENTS, AND CONFIRMATIONS

The Judiciary: There were no significant nominations, appointments, or confirmations in the federal judiciary during the 60th Congress.

The Executive Branch: On December 8, 1908, President Roosevelt nominated Truman H. Newberry to succeed Victor H. Metcalf as secretary of the Navy and Luke E. Wright to succeed William H. Taft as secretary of war. On December 9, 1908, the Senate confirmed both men by voice votes. On January 25, 1909, Roosevelt nominated Robert Bacon to succeed Elihu Root as secretary

of state, and on January 27, 1909, the Senate confirmed Bacon by voice vote.

IMPEACHMENTS

None.

CONSTITUTIONAL AMENDMENTS

None.

FURTHER READING

Bolles, Blair. *Tyrant From Illinois: Uncle Joe Cannon's Experiment With Personal Power.* New York: W.W. Norton & Co., 1951.

Harbaugh, William Henry. *The Life and Times of Theodore Roosevelt.* New York: Collier Books, 1963.

Merrill, Horace Samuel & Merrill, Marion Galbraith. *The Republican Command, 1897-1913.* Lexington: University Press of Kentucky, 1971.

Rhodes, James Ford. *The McKinley and Roosevelt Administrations, 1897-1909.* Port Washington, N.Y.: Kennikat Press, 1965 (reprint of 1922 edition).

Woodrow, Wilson (the future president). *Congressional Government.* Boston and New York: Houghton Mifflin Co., 1885.

The 61st Congress

MARCH 4, 1909 - MARCH 3, 1911

Special Senate Session: March 4, 1909-March 6, 1909
First Session: March 15, 1909-August 5, 1909
Second Session: December 6, 1909-June 25, 1910
Third Session: December 5, 1910-March 3, 1911

The Senate held a special session to vote on the confirmation of presidential appointees to various offices. [See note 1, p. xxix]

In the 1908 elections for the 61st Congress, the Republicans lost 1 seat in the Senate, reducing their majority from 61 to 60 of the 92 seats. The Democrats gained 1 seat to hold a total of 32. In the House, the Republicans lost 3 seats reducing their majority from 222 to 219 of the 391 seats, and the Democrats gained 8 seats to hold a total of 172. [See notes 2 and 3, p. xxix]

BACKGROUND

According to the census of 1910, the population of the United States as of April 15, 1910, was 91,972,266, resulting in a population density of 31 persons for each of the country's 2,969,565 square miles. This was a population increase of 21 percent over the 1900 census.

William Howard Taft was inaugurated as the 27th president of the United States on March 4, 1909. Tariffs on imports were a politically sensitive topic, and Taft supported lower tariffs. He was unable to obtain significant tariff reductions, however, in the 1909 Payne-Aldrich Tariff Act. Congress in 1909 sent the proposed Sixteenth Amendment to the Constitution, which permitted a federal income tax without the necessity of apportioning it among the states for ratification. In the same year, an American expedition under

Robert E. Peary became the first in history to reach the North Pole. Also in 1909, the Navy dispatched two ships to Nicaragua in order to protect Americans there from the growing civil unrest caused by dictator Jose Santos Zelaya's effort to suppress a popular rebellion. The American presence and tacit support for the rebels caused Zelaya to resign on December 16, 1909.

In 1910 the House of Representatives restructured the Rules Committee, removing the Speaker's power to appoint committee members. Congress enacted legislation that expanded the Interstate Commerce Commission's jurisdiction to include telephone and telegraph companies. Congress also enacted the Mann Act, which made it illegal to transport women across state lines for "immoral purposes," in order to end the use of immigrant girls from Europe in brothels, a practice popularly called "white slavery."

The U.S. and Great Britain in 1910 resolved a dispute over fishing rights off the coast of Newfoundland, Canada, before the International Court of Arbitration in The Hague, Netherlands.

SENATE LEADERSHIP

Vice President: James Schoolcraft Sherman was elected vice president on Taft's ticket in the 1908 elections. Sherman first had been elected to Congress in the 50th Congress as a representative from New York and had served in the House until he was elected vice president.

CHRONOLOGY

March 4, 1909:	The 61st Congress and a special Senate session begin.
March 5, 1909:	President Taft nominates his cabinet, and the Senate confirms all of the nominees.
March 6, 1909:	The special Senate session ends.
March 15, 1909:	The first session begins, and Joseph Gurney Cannon (Rep., Ill.) is reelected Speaker of the House.
July 8, 1909:	Congress passes the Payne-Aldrich Tariff Act.
July 12, 1909:	Congress sends the 16th Amendment (permitting income taxes) to the states for ratification.
August 5, 1909:	The first session ends.
October 24, 1909:	Supreme Court Justice Rufus W. Peckham dies.
December 6, 1909:	The second session begins.
December 13, 1909:	President William Howard Taft nominates Horace H. Lurton to replace Peckham.
December 20, 1909:	The Senate confirms Lurton.
March 19, 1910:	The House acts to limit the power of Speaker Joe Cannon.
March 28, 1910:	Supreme Court Justice David J. Brewer dies.
April 25, 1910:	President Taft nominates Charles Evans Hughes to replace Brewer.
May 2, 1910:	The Senate confirms Hughes.
June 3, 1910:	Congress passes legislation increasing the authority of the Interstate Commerce Commission.
June 22, 1910:	Congress passes legislation concerning campaign contributions.
June 25, 1910:	Congress passes the Mann Act and the second session ends.
July 4, 1910:	Supreme Court Justice Melville W. Fuller dies.
November 20. 1910:	Supreme Court Justice William H. Moody resigns.
December 5, 1910:	The third session begins.
December 12, 1910:	President Taft nominates Willis Van Devanter and Joseph R. Lamar to the Supreme Court.
December 15, 1910:	The Senate confirms Van Devanter and Lamar.
February 15, 1911:	Congress passes the Weeks Act.
March 3, 1911:	The third session and the 61st Congress end.

[See note 6, p. xxix]

President Pro Tempore: William Pierce Frye (Rep., Maine). [See biographical note in 54th Congress]

Majority Leader, Majority Whip, Minority Leader, and Minority Whip: None. These functions did not evolve into formal Senate positions until the 62nd Congress (1911-1913).

Chairmen of Selected Key Committees: [See also Organization and Administration, below]

Committee on Appropriations: Eugene Hale (Rep., Maine)

Committee on Finance: Nelson Aldrich (Rep., R.I.)

Committee on Foreign Relations: Shelby Cullom (Rep., Ill.)

Committee on the Judiciary: Clarence D. Clark (Rep., Wyo.)

Committee on Military Affairs: Francis E. Warren (Rep., Wyo.)

Committee on Naval Affairs: George C. Perkins (Rep., Calif.)

Committee on Rules: W. Murray Crane (Rep., Mass.)

HOUSE LEADERSHIP

Speaker of the House: Joseph Gurney Cannon (Rep., Ill.) was reelected Speaker on March 15, 1909. [See biographical note in 58th Congress] Cannon exploited the Speaker's traditional chairmanship of the Rules Committee to give himself more control over the House than any other Speaker ever had held, causing a revolt against his dictatorial rule in this Congress. On March 19, 1910, the House removed the Speaker's power to appoint the members of the Rules Committee and replaced Cannon as committee chairman. However, Cannon stayed on as Speaker through the end of this Congress.

Majority Leader: Sereno E. Payne (Rep., N.Y.)

Majority Whip: John W. Dwight (Rep., N.Y.)

Minority Leader: Champ Clark (Dem., Mo.)

Minority Whip: None.

Chairmen of Selected Key Committees: [See also Organization and Administration, below]

Committee on Agriculture: Charles F. Scott (Rep., Kans.)

Committee on Appropriations: James A. Tawney (Rep., Minn.)

Committee on Banking, Finance, and Urban Affairs: Edward B. Vreeland (Rep., N.Y.)

Committee on Foreign Affairs: David J. Foster (Rep., Vt.) and James B. Perkins (Rep., N.Y.)

Committee on the Judiciary: Richard W. Parker (Rep., N.J.)

Committee on Military Affairs: John A.T. Hull (Rep., Iowa)

Committee on Naval Affairs: George E. Foss (Rep., Ill.)

Committee on Rules: Joseph G. Cannon (Rep., Ill.), until he was replaced by John Dalzell (Rep., Pa.) on March 19, 1910

Committee on Ways and Means: Sereno E. Payne (Rep., N.Y.)

ORGANIZATION AND ADMINISTRATION

In an episode sometimes referred to as the "Cannon revolt," members of the House placed limits on the power of Speaker Joe Cannon. [See House Leadership, above] [See note 5, p. xxix]

MAJOR LEGISLATION PASSED

Campaign Contributions: Congress required that candidates in elections for the House of Representatives report campaign contributions of $10 or more and made these contributions a matter of public record.

Interstate Commerce Commission: Congress expanded the jurisdiction of the Interstate Commerce Commission to include telephone and telegraph companies.

Natural Resources: In the Weeks Act, Congress authorized several measures to help conserve national forests and waterways.

Tariffs: In the Payne-Aldrich Tariff Act, Congress lowered duties on imports to an average level of 38 percent and established the Tariff Commission.

White Slavery: In the Mann Act, Congress made it illegal to transport women across state lines for immoral purposes, in order to end the use of immigrant women from Europe in brothels.

TABLE OF KEY VOTES

Senate

Subject of Vote	Date of Vote	For	Against
16th Amendment Passed	July 5, 1909	77	0
Tariffs Reduced	July 8, 1909	45	34
Interstate Commerce Commission Granted Wider Jurisdiction	June 3, 1910	50	12
Campaign Contribution Bill Passed	June 22, 1910	Passed by voice vote	
Mann Act Passed	June 25, 1910	Passed by voice vote	
Natural Resources Bill Passed	February 15, 1911	57	9

House

Subject of Vote	Date of Vote	For	Against
Tariffs Reduced	April 9, 1909	217	161
16th Amendment Passed	July 12, 1909	318	14
Mann Act Passed	January 26, 1910	Passed by voice vote	
Campaign Contribution Bill Passed	April 18, 1910	Passed by voice vote	
Interstate Commerce Commission Granted Wider Jurisdiction	May 10, 1910	201	126
Natural Resources Bill Passed	June 23, 1910	130	111

[See note 7, p. xxix]

FAILED LEGISLATION

None of historical significance.

RELATIONS WITH THE PRESIDENT

Unlike his predecessor, President Roosevelt, President Taft was not forceful and lacked charisma. His real ambition was to become chief justice of the Supreme Court. His lack of energy or a vigorous legislative agenda alienated the progressives in Congress.

Taft vetoed 13 bills during the 61st Congress, none of which involved significant legislation.

NOMINATIONS, APPOINTMENTS, AND CONFIRMATIONS

The Judiciary: On October 24, 1909, Supreme Court Justice Rufus W. Peckham died. President William Howard Taft nominated Horace H. Lurton on December 13, 1909, to replace Peckham, and the Senate confirmed Lurton on December 20, 1909, by voice vote. During 1910 three more vacancies opened on the Court: Justice David J. Brewer died on March 28, 1910; Justice Melville W. Fuller died on July 4, 1910; and Justice William H. Moody resigned on November 20, 1910. President Taft filled all three vacancies by the end of the 61st Congress. First, Taft nominated Charles Evans Hughes on April 25, 1910, and the Senate confirmed Hughes on May 2, 1910, by voice vote. Second, Taft nominated Willis Van Devanter and Joseph R. Lamar on December 12, 1910, and the Senate confirmed both nominees by voice votes on December 15, 1910.

The Executive Branch: President Taft nominated his cabinet on March 5, 1909, and the Senate confirmed all of the nominees the same day by voice votes. The nominees were Richard A. Ballinger to be secretary of the Interior, Jacob M. Dickinson to be secretary of war, Philander C. Knox to be secretary of state, Franklin MacVeagh to be secretary of the Treasury, George von L. Meyer to be secretary of the Navy, Charles Nagel to be secretary of commerce and labor, George W. Wickersham to be attorney general, and James Wilson to be secretary of agriculture.

IMPEACHMENTS

None.

CONSTITUTIONAL AMENDMENTS

Congress sent the Sixteenth Amendment, which permitted a federal income tax without the necessity of apportionment, to the states for ratification. The Sixteenth Amendment was ratified by the required three-fourths of the states effective February 3, 1913. [For the actual text of the Sixteenth Amendment, see the copy of the Constitution at Appendix A.]

FURTHER READING

Bolles, Blair. *Tyrant From Illinois: Uncle Joe Cannon's Experiment With Personal Power.* New York: W.W. Norton & Co., 1951.

Coletta, Paolo Enrico. *William Howard Taft: A Bibliography.* Westport, Conn.: Meckler, 1989.

Lamar, Clarinda Huntington. *The Life of Joseph Rucker Lamar, 1857-1916.* New York: G. P. Putnam's Sons, 1926.

Merrill, Horace Samuel & Merrill, Marion Galbraith. *The Republican Command, 1897-1913.* Lexington: University Press of Kentucky, 1971.

Pringle, Henry F. *The Life and Times of William Howard Taft: A Biography.* Norwalk, Conn.: Easton Press, 1986 (reprint of the 1939 edition).

Pusey, Merlo John. *Charles Evans Hughes.* New York: Macmillan, 1951.

The 62nd Congress

MARCH 4, 1911 - MARCH 3, 1913

First Session: April 4, 1911-August 22, 1911
Second Session: December 4, 1911-August 26, 1912
Third Session: December 2, 1912-March 3, 1913

In the 1910 elections for the 62nd Congress, the Republicans lost 9 seats in the Senate, reducing their majority from 60 to 51 of the 92 seats. The Democrats gained 9 seats to hold a total of 41. In the House, the Democrats gained 56 seats to hold a new majority of 228 of the 391 seats. The Republicans lost 58 seats, reducing their total to 161. Two seats were held by neither major party. One seat was held by the Socialist Party, and 1 seat was held by a Progressive Republican. [See notes 2 and 3, p. xxix]

BACKGROUND

By 1911 American industry had grown rapidly. In many ways, the U.S. was the most advanced industrial nation in the world, but its labor and safety regulations had not kept up with its industrial advances. This problem received national attention when on March 25, 1911, a fire in the Triangle Shirtwaist Company's New York City sweatshop killed over one hundred employees. The workers were unable to escape the burning building because the exits were blocked, and no serious fire safety precautions were in effect.

Also in 1911 there was the problem with trusts, which were amalgamations of the leading companies in certain industry sectors. These trusts were formed in the 19th century for the purpose of supressing competition and protecting profits. Despite the Sherman Antitrust Act of 1890, the only significant trust to be dissolved was the Northern Securities Company, which was dissolved during the Roosevelt administration. On May 15, 1911, however, an antitrust prosecution against the Standard Oil Company, which dominated the petroleum industry, resulted in a Supreme Court order dissolving the company. Standard Oil was fragmented into a number of new companies, many of which have survived to the present: Standard Oil of New Jersey (Exxon), Standard Oil of Indiana (Amoco), and Standard Oil of Ohio (Sohio). In 1911 Arizona was ready for statehood, but President Taft vetoed Congress's approval because he disapproved of the judicial recall provision in the Arizona constitution. Arizona removed the judicial recall provision and was ultimately admitted into the United States.

In 1912 the radical International Workers of the World, or *Wobblies*, achieved recognition as an important part of the labor movement after leading a well-publicized textile strike in Lawrence, Massachusetts. Congress passed a law that guaranteed an eight-hour workday to federal contract employees. On its first voyage, the British passenger ship *Titanic* struck an iceberg off the Newfoundland coast and sank in one of the greatest maritime disasters in history. Former President Theodore Roosevelt, who had declined to run in the presidential election of 1908, decided to enter the 1912 election. He ran as a third party candidate, nominated by the Progressive or Bull Moose Party, and came closer to winning the presidency than any other third party candidate in the 20th century. In 1913, before the 62nd Congress ended, the Sixteenth Amendment to the Constitution was passed (approved by the 61st Congress), which, once ratified by the required three-quarters of the states, permitted a federal income tax without requiring apportionment amongst the states.

SENATE LEADERSHIP

Vice President: James Schoolcraft Sherman, who had been elected on Taft's ticket in 1908, was vice president until he died on October 30, 1912, leaving the post of president of the Senate open until March 4, 1913. (Until the Twenty-Fifth Amendment was ratified on February 10, 1967 [See 90th Congress], there was no mechanism for filling vacancies in the office of the vice president.) Sherman first had been elected to Congress in the 50th Congress as a representative from New York and had served in the House until he was elected vice president in the 1908 elections.

President Pro Tempore: William Pierce Frye (Rep., Maine) served until he resigned on April 27, 1911. Frye's resignation and the later death of the vice president resulted in considerable turnover in the office of president pro tempore. The following senators held the office during the remainder of the 62nd Congress: Augustus Octavius Bacon (Dem., Ga.), January 15-17, 1912; March 11-12, 1912; April 8, 1912; May 10, 1912; May 30-June 3, 1912; June 13-July 5, 1912; August 1-August 10, 1912; August 27-December 15, 1912; January 5-18, 1913; and February 2-15, 1913. Frank Bosworth Brandegee (Rep., Conn.), May 25, 1912. Charles Curtis (Rep., Kans.), December 4-12, 1911. Jacob Harold Gallinger (Rep., N.H.), February 12-14, 1912; April 26-27, 1912; May 7, 1912; July 6-31, 1912; August 12-26, 1912; December 16, 1912-January 4, 1913; January 19-February 1, 1913; and February 16-March 3, 1913. Henry Cabot Lodge (Rep., Mass.), March 25-26, 1912.

Majority Leader: Shelby M. Cullom (Rep., Ill.)

Majority Whip: None. This function did not evolve into a formal position until the 63rd Congress (1913-1915).

Minority Leader: Thomas S. Martin (Dem., Va.)

Minority Whip: None. This function did not evolve into a formal position until the 64th Congress (1915-1917).

Chairmen of Selected Key Committees: [See also Organization and Administration, below]

Committee on Appropriations: Francis E. Warren (Rep., Wyo.)

Committee on Finance: Boies Penrose (Rep., Pa.)

Committee on Foreign Relations: Shelby Cullom (Rep., Ill.)

Committee on the Judiciary: Clarence D. Clark (Rep., Wyo.) and Charles A. Culberson (Dem., Tex.)

Committee on Military Affairs: Henry A. du Pont (Rep., Del.)

Committee on Naval Affairs: George C. Perkins (Rep., Calif.)

Committee on Rules: W. Murray Crane (Rep., Mass.)

HOUSE LEADERSHIP

Speaker of the House: Champ Clark (Dem., Mo.) was elected Speaker on April 4, 1911. His full name was James Beauchamp Clark. Clark first had been elected to Congress in the 53rd Congress, and had served as minority leader in the 60th and 61st Congresses. He was Speaker from the 62nd through the 65th Congresses.

Majority Leader: Oscar W. Underwood (Dem., Ala.)

Majority Whip: None.

Minority Leader: James R. Mann (Rep., Ill.)

Minority Whip: John W. Dwight (Rep., N.Y.)

Chairmen of Selected Key Committees: [See also Organization and Administration, below]

Committee on Agriculture: John Lamb (Dem., Va.)

Committee on Appropriations: John J. Fitzgerald (Dem., N.Y.)

Committee on Banking, Finance, and Urban Affairs: Arsene P. Pujo (Dem., La.)

Committee on Foreign Affairs: There were three chairmen during this Congress. The first chairman was William Sulzer (Dem., N.Y.), who resigned effective December 31, 1912, because he had been elected governor of New York. During the final months of the 62nd Congress both Charles B. Smith (Dem., N.Y.) and Henry D. Flood (Dem., Va.) served as chairman.

Committee on the Judiciary: Henry D. Clayton (Dem., Ala.)

Committee on Military Affairs: James Hay (Dem., Va.)

Committee on Naval Affairs: Lemuel P. Padgett (Dem., Tenn.)

Committee on Rules: Robert L. Henry (Dem., Tex.)

Committee on Ways and Means: Oscar W. Underwood (Dem., Ala.)

ORGANIZATION AND ADMINISTRATION

In the Senate, the offices of majority leader and minority leader became formal positions during this Congress. The majority leader is the leader of the majority party in the Senate, and the minority leader represents the minority party. These positions can reverse themselves. For example, if the majority party loses control of the Senate in an election, the former minority leader now becomes the majority leader and the former majority leader then becomes the minority leader. [See note 5, p. xxix]

MAJOR LEGISLATION PASSED

Admission of New Mexico and Arizona as New States: In a combined piece of legislation, Congress voted to admit both New Mexico and Arizona into the United States.

Alaska: Congress created the territory of Alaska and gave the residents both U.S. citizenship and the right to elect a territorial legislative assembly.

Department of Commerce, Department of Labor: The full title of the Department of Commerce had been the Department of Commerce and Labor. Congress split the department into the Department of Commerce and the Department of Labor and gave both departments cabinet-level status.

Labor: Congress gave all workers under federal contract the right to an eight-hour workday.

FAILED LEGISLATION

None of historical significance.

RELATIONS WITH THE PRESIDENT

Taft's uninspired presidency and legislative agenda had finally so alienated the Progressives in Congress that Progressive Senator Robert M. LaFollette (Rep., Wis.) formed a National Progressive Republican League and challenged Taft for the upcoming 1912 Republican presidential nomination. Former President Theodore Roosevelt also challenged Taft for the nomination, and went on to run as a third party candidate after Taft successfully overcame the Progressive challenge for the nomination. Democrat Woodrow Wilson benefitted from this conflict and won the 1912 election. In later years, Taft would realize his dream of becoming Chief Justice of the Supreme Court, which he really desired more than he ever had desired the presidency.

Taft vetoed 26 bills during the 62nd Congress. One veto was reasonably significant. On August 15, 1911, Taft vetoed legislation admitting Arizona and New Mexico into the United States because he disapproved of the judicial recall provision in the Arizona constitution. Neither the House nor the Senate tried to override the veto. Arizona removed the judicial recall provision and Congress passed new legislation to admit

C H R O N O L O G Y

March 4, 1911: The 62nd Congress begins.

April 4, 1911: The first session begins, and Champ Clark (Dem., Mo.) is elected Speaker of the House.

April 10, 1911: President Taft nominates Walter L. Fisher to succeed Richard A. Ballinger as secretary of the Interior.

April 17, 1911: The Senate confirms Fisher.

April 27, 1911: Senate president pro tem William P. Frye (Rep., Maine) resigns.

May 15, 1911: President Taft nominates Henry L. Stimson to succeed Jacob M. Dickinson as secretary of war.

May 16, 1911: The Senate confirms Stimson.

June 12, 1911: Congress sends the 17th Amendment to the states for ratification.

August 15, 1911: President Taft vetoes legislation concerning the admission of Arizona and New Mexico into the United States. The veto is not challenged.

August 19, 1911: Congress passes new legislation, which is not vetoed, admitting New Mexico and Arizona into the United States.

August 22, 1911: The first session ends.

October 14, 1911: Supreme Court Justice John Marshall Harlan dies.

December 4, 1911: The second session begins.

February 19, 1912: President Taft nominates Mahlon Pitney to replace Harlan.

March 13, 1912: The Senate confirms Pitney.

May 31, 1912: Congress passes labor legislation granting federal workers an eight-hour workday.

July 24, 1912: Congress passes legislation creating the territory of Alaska.

August 26, 1912: The second session ends.

December 2, 1912: The third session begins.

February 26, 1913: Congress passes legislation separating the Departments of Commerce and Labor.

March 3, 1913: The third session and the 62nd Congress end.

[See note 6, p. xxix]

---

both states into the Union. Taft also vetoed a tariff bill, a budget bill and an immigration bill, all of which Congress failed to override.

NOMINATIONS, APPOINTMENTS, AND CONFIRMATIONS

The Judiciary: On October 14, 1911, Supreme Court Justice John Marshall Harlan died. President William Howard Taft nominated Mahlon Pitney on February 19, 1912, to replace Harlan, and the Senate confirmed Pitney on March 13, 1912, by a 50 to 26 vote.

The Executive Branch: On April 10, 1911, President Taft nominated Walter L. Fisher to succeed Richard A. Ballinger as secretary of the Interior, and on April 17, 1911, the Senate confirmed Fisher by voice vote. On May 15, 1911, Taft nominated Henry L. Stimson to succeed

TABLE OF KEY VOTES

Senate

Subject of Vote	Date of Vote	For	Against
17th Amendment Passed	June 12, 1911	64	24
Admission of New Mexico and Arizona to Union	August 18, 1911	53	9
Eight-Hour Day Law Passed	May 31, 1912	45	11
Alaska Territory Legislation Passed	July 24, 1912	Passed by voice vote	
Departments of Commerce and Labor Separated	February 26, 1913	Passed by voice vote	

House

Subject of Vote	Date of Vote	For	Against
17th Amendment Passed	April 13, 1911	296	16
Admission of New Mexico and Arizona to Union	August 19, 1911	Passed by voice vote	
Eight-Hour Day Law Passed	December 14, 1911	Passed by voice vote	
Alaska Territory Legislation Passed	April 24, 1912	Passed by voice vote	
Departments of Commerce and Labor Separated	July 17, 1912	Passed by voice vote	

[See note 7, p. xxix]

Jacob M. Dickinson as secretary of war, and on May 16, 1911, the Senate confirmed Stimson by voice vote. The Department of Commerce and Labor was split into two cabinet-level agencies towards the end of this Congress. [See Major Legislation, above]. President Woodrow Wilson would appoint their secretaries in the 63rd Congress.

IMPEACHMENTS

Robert W. Archbald, an associate judge of the U.S. Commerce Court, was accused of accepting improper gifts while in office, such as free trips to Europe. The House voted to impeach Archbald on July 11, 1912, and on January 13, 1913 the Senate removed him from office.

CONSTITUTIONAL AMENDMENTS

Congress sent to the states for ratification, the Seventeenth Amendment, which replaced the system whereby senators were chosen by their state legislatures, with the modern system whereby senators are directly elected by the people. Also, vacancies can be filled by the state's chief executive pending the next election. Previously, attempts to pass a Constitutional Amendment providing for direct election of Senators had been supported by the states and the House, but blocked in the Senate where there were enough Senators who feared popular elections to block the necessary two-thirds majority vote. See, for example, the 53rd Congress [Constitutional Amendments]. Starting with Oregon in 1901, the reform movement began to gain ground by getting the states to pass legislation providing for a system of electing state legislators in which the legislators would commit themselves to voting for the Senate candidate chosen by popular ballot. The states could not just provide for the direct popular election of their Senators, since article I, section 3 of the Constitution says that Senators from each state must be chosen "by the Legislature thereof." Nevertheless, by the 62nd Congress nearly half of the states had followed the Oregon model, and in those states the role of the legislature was often just a formality. In other states there were calls for a second Constitutional Convention, which would not need Senate approval to pass a direct election amendment. The Senate finally gave in to these pressures in this Congress.

The Seventeenth Amendment was ratified by the required three-fourths of the states effective April 8, 1913, and became binding on the Senate when the amendment was officially declared ratified on May 31, 1913. [For the actual text of the Seventeenth Amendment, see the copy of the Constitution at Appendix A]

FURTHER READING

Christianson, Stephen G. "Triangle Shirtwaist Fire Trial." In *Great American Trials*, Edited by Edward W. Knappman. Detroit: Gale Research, 1994.

Clark, Champ. *My Quarter Century of American Politics*. 2 vols. New York: Harper, 1920.

Coletta, Paolo Enrico. *William Howard Taft: a Bibliography*. Westport, Conn.: Meckler, 1989.

Merrill, Horace Samuel & Merrill, Marion Galbraith. *The Republican Command, 1897-1913*. Lexington: University Press of Kentucky, 1971.

Pringle, Henry F. *The Life and Times of William Howard Taft: A Biography*. Norwalk, Conn.: Easton Press, 1986 (reprint of the 1939 edition).

The 63rd Congress

MARCH 4, 1913 - MARCH 3, 1915

Special Senate Session: March 4, 1913-March 17, 1913
First Session: April 7, 1913-December 1, 1913
Second Session: December 1, 1913-October 24, 1914
Third Session: December 7, 1914-March 3, 1915

The Senate held a special session to vote on the confirmation of presidential appointees to various offices. [See note 1, p. xxix]

In the 1912 elections for the 63rd Congress, the Democrats gained 10 seats in the Senate to hold a new majority of 51 of the 96 seats. The Republicans lost 7 seats, leaving them with 44. One seat was held by a Progressive. Because of the 1910 census [See 61st Congress], the House was reapportioned and increased to 435 members. (Except for a brief period from 1959 to 1963 [See 86th and 87th Congresses], the House has stayed at 435 members throughout subsequent decennial reapportionments.) The Democrats gained 63 seats, raising their majority from 228 to 291 of the 435 House seats. The Republicans lost 34 seats, reducing their total to 127. Seventeen seats were held by neither of the two major parties. Nine of these seats were held by the Progressive Party, 1 was held by an independent, and the other 7 seats generally leaned toward the Republicans. [See notes 2 and 3, p. xxix]

BACKGROUND

Woodrow Wilson was inaugurated as the 28th president of the United States on March 4, 1913. Ever since the panic of 1907, the government had been aware of the need to institute some sort of supervision over the nation's banks and financial

system. The unregulated system led to recurring periods of overexpansion and then economically damaging collapses. The 63rd Congress finally took action and established the Federal Reserve System in 1913. The Federal Reserve System consists of a Federal Reserve Board and 12 subordinate regional Federal Reserve Banks throughout the United States. All national banks, which means virtually all large banks, are required to join the system. By controlling interest rates and credit among banks, the Federal Reserve influences economic growth and inflation. Because the Federal Reserve is an independent body and allegedly free from political pressure, it can adopt expansive or restrictive monetary policies depending principally on what it thinks is best for the economy.

Also during 1913, the states ratified the Seventeenth Amendment (approved by the 62nd Congress)to the Constitution, which provided for the direct election of senators by the voters of each state.

The Panama Canal was finished and officially opened on August 15, 1914. Meanwhile, Archduke Ferdinand of Austria-Hungary had been assassinated on June 28, 1914, in the Bosnian city of Sarajevo. After Austria-Hungary declared war on Serbia, the network of military alliances across Europe brought most of the nations of Europe into the war. Great Britain, France, Italy, Serbia, and Russia were allied against Germany, Austria-Hungary, and the

C H R O N O L O G Y

March 4, 1913:	The 63rd Congress and a special Senate session begin.
March 5, 1913:	President Wilson nominates his cabinet, and the Senate confirms all of the nominees.
March 13, 1913:	James Paul Clarke (Dem., Ark.) is elected Senate president pro tem.
March 17, 1913:	The special Senate session ends.
April 7, 1913:	The first session begins and Champ Clark (Dem., Mo.) is reelected Speaker of the House.
April 7, 1913:	Woodrow Wilson became the first president since John Adams to address a joint session of Congress. Intervening presidents simply had sent their messages for a clerk to read.
May 22, 1913:	The Senate creates a Committee on Banking and Currency.
September 10, 1913:	Congress passes the Underwood-Simmons Tariff Act.
December 1, 1913:	The first session ends and the second session begins.
December 19, 1913:	Congress passes legislation creating the Federal Reserve System.
July 12, 1914:	Supreme Court Justice Horace H. Lurton dies.
August 5, 1914:	Congress passes the Federal Trade Commission Act.
August 19, 1914:	President Woodrow Wilson nominates Attorney General James C. McReynolds to replace Lurton and Thomas W. Gregory to succeed McReynolds as attorney general.
August 25, 1914:	Congress passes the Clayton Antitrust Act of 1914.
August 29, 1914:	The Senate confirms McReynolds and Gregory.
October 24, 1914:	The second session ends.
December 7, 1914:	The third session begins.
January 20, 1915:	Congress passes legislation creating the Coast Guard.
March 3, 1915:	The third session and the 63rd Congress end.

[See note 6, p. xxix]

Ottoman Empire. On August 4 the U.S. declared that it wished to remain neutral from the conflict, which in the future would be called the Great War or World War I.

SENATE LEADERSHIP

Vice President: Thomas Riley Marshall was elected on Woodrow Wilson's ticket in the election of 1912. Marshall never had served in Congress, but he had been governor of Indiana from 1909 to 1913, when he resigned to assume his position as vice president.

President Pro Tempore: James Paul Clarke (Dem., Ark.) was elected on March 13, 1913. Clarke had been the governor of Arkansas from 1895 to 1896 and had been elected to the Senate in 1903. He served in the Senate until his death on October 1, 1916, and was president pro tem in the 63rd and 64th Congresses.

Majority Leader: John W. Kern (Dem., Ind.)

Majority Whip: J. Hamilton Lewis (Dem., Ill.)

Minority Leader: Jacob H. Gallinger (Rep., N.H.)

Minority Whip: None. This function did not evolve into a formal position until the 64th Congress (1915-1917).

Chairmen of Selected Key Committees: [See also Organization and Administration, below]

Committee on Appropriations: Thomas S. Martin (Dem., Va.)

Committee on Banking and Currency: Robert L. Owen (Dem., Okla.)

Committee on Finance: Furnifold M. Simmons (Dem., N.C.)

Committee on Foreign Relations: Augustus O. Bacon (Dem., Ga.), who died on February 14, 1914. William J. Stone (Dem., Mo.) became the next chairman.

Committee on the Judiciary: Charles A. Culberson (Dem., Tex.)

Committee on Military Affairs: Joseph F. Johnston (Dem., Ala.), who died on August 8, 1913. George E. Chamberlain (Dem., Ore.) became the next chairman.

Committee on Naval Affairs: Benjamin Tillman (Dem., S.C.)

Committee on Rules: Lee S. Overman (Dem., N.C.)

HOUSE LEADERSHIP

Speaker of the House: Champ Clark (Dem., Mo.) was reelected Speaker on April 7, 1913. [See biographical note in 62nd Congress]

Majority Leader: Oscar W. Underwood (Dem., Ala.)

Majority Whip: Thomas M. Bell (Dem., Ga.)

Minority Leader: James R. Mann (Rep., Ill.)

Minority Whip: Charles H. Burke (Rep., S.D.)

Chairmen of Selected Key Committees: [See also Organization and Administration, below]

Committee on Agriculture: Asbury F. Lever (Dem., S.C.)

Committee on Appropriations: John J. Fitzgerald (Dem., N.Y.)

Committee on Banking, Finance, and Urban Affairs: Carter Glass (Dem., Va.)

Committee on Foreign Affairs: Henry D. Flood (Dem., Va.)

Committee on the Judiciary: Henry D. Clayton (Dem., Ala.), who resigned from Congress effective May 25, 1914, in order to accept a position as a federal judge. Edwin Y. Webb (Dem., N.C.) became the next chairman.

Committee on Military Affairs: James Hay (Dem., Va.)

Committee on Naval Affairs: Lemuel P. Padgett (Dem., Tenn.)

Committee on Rules: Robert L. Henry (Dem., Tex.)

Committee on Ways and Means: Oscar W. Underwood (Dem., Ala.)

ORGANIZATION AND ADMINISTRATION

In the Senate, the office of majority whip became a formal position during this Congress. The majority whip is the Senate majority leader's second in command and is supposed to keep majority party members informed of party objectives and ensure their loyalty to the party's agenda. If a majority leader leaves office, the majority whip usually rises to become the new majority leader, and a new person is chosen to become the majority whip.

On May 22, 1913, the Senate created a Committee on Banking and Currency. The House already had a Committee on Banking, Finance, and Urban Affairs. [See note 5, p. xxix]

MAJOR LEGISLATION PASSED

Antitrust: Congress passed the Clayton Antitrust Act of 1914, one of the most important antitrust acts in American history. The Clayton Act expanded the scope of antitrust law, prohibited anticompetitive price discrimination and "tying

TABLE OF KEY VOTES

Senate

Subject of Vote	Date of Vote	For	Against
Tariffs Lowered	September 10, 1913	44	37
Federal Reserve System Created	December 19, 1913	54	34
Coast Guard Established	March 12, 1914	Passed by voice vote	
Federal Trade Commission Established	August 5, 1914	53	16
Antitrust Laws Strengthened	August 25, 1914	46	16

House

Subject of Vote	Date of Vote	For	Against
Tariffs Lowered	May 8, 1913	281	139
Federal Reserve System Established	September 18, 1913	286	85
Federal Trade Commission Established	June 5, 1914	Passed by voice vote	
Antitrust Laws Strengthened	June 5, 1914	277	54
Coast Guard Established	January 20, 1915	210	79

[See note 7, p. xxix]

contracts" that prevented purchasers from handling goods from the seller's competitors. The act also limited the use of antitrust law as a weapon against organized labor.

Coast Guard: Congress created the United States Coast Guard, which absorbed the Life Saving Service and the Revenue Cutter Service.

Federal Reserve System: Congress established the Federal Reserve System. [See Background, above]

Federal Trade Commission: In the Federal Trade Commission Act, Congress established the Federal Trade Commission and gave the FTC a mandate to prevent unfair business practices.

Tariffs: In the Underwood-Simmons Tariff Act, Congress lowered duties on imports from an average of 38 percent to under 30 percent and imposed a graduated income tax of 1 to 6 percent on incomes over $2,000 a year.

FAILED LEGISLATION

None of historical significance.

RELATIONS WITH THE PRESIDENT

President Wilson generally was successful in pursuing domestic reform legislation through Congress, but was less successful in foreign policy. The Wilson administration, which broke its promise to keep America neutral during World

War I, is remembered for its eventual failure to get the Treaty of Versailles through the Senate. [See 66th Congress]

Wilson vetoed four bills during the 63rd Congress, none of which involved significant legislation.

NOMINATIONS, APPOINTMENTS, AND CONFIRMATIONS

The Judiciary: Supreme Court Justice Horace H. Lurton died on July 12, 1914. President Woodrow Wilson nominated Attorney General James C. McReynolds on August 19 to replace Lurton, and the Senate confirmed him on August 29 by a 44 to 6 vote.

The Executive Branch: On March 5, 1913, President Wilson nominated his cabinet, and the Senate confirmed all of the nominees by voice vote the same day. The nominees were William Jennings Bryan to be secretary of state, Josephus Daniels to be secretary of the Navy, Lindley M. Garrison to be secretary of war, David F. Houston to be secretary of agriculture, Franklin K. Lane to be secretary of the Interior, William G. McAdoo to be secretary of the Treasury, James C. McReynolds to be attorney general, William C. Redfield to be secretary of commerce, and William B. Wilson to be secretary of labor. On August 19, 1914, Wilson nominated Thomas W. Gregory to succeed McReynolds as attorney general, and the Senate confirmed him by voice vote on August 29.

IMPEACHMENTS

None.

CONSTITUTIONAL AMENDMENTS

The Seventeenth Amendment, which provided for the direct election of senators by the voters of each state, was ratified by the required three-fourths of the states effective April 8, 1913. The amendment became binding when it was officially declared ratified on May 31, 1913. [The Seventeenth Amendment was approved in the 62nd Congress: see 62nd Congress, Constitutional Amendments, for further details. For the actual text of the Seventeenth Amendment, see the copy of the Constitution at Appendix A.]

FURTHER READING

Clark, Champ. *My Quarter Century of American Politics.* 2 vols. New York: Harper, 1920.

Levin, Norman Gordon. *Woodrow Wilson and World Politics; America's Response to War and Revolution.* New York: Oxford University Press, 1968.

Stimson, Henry Lewis. *Initiative and Responsibility of the Executive; a Remedy for Inefficient Legislation.* Philadelphia: G. Dukes, Printer, 1913.

Walworth, Arthur Clarence. *Woodrow Wilson.* Boston: Houghton Mifflin Co., 1965.

The 64th Congress

MARCH 4, 1915 - MARCH 3, 1917

First Session: December 6, 1915-September 8, 1916
Second Session: December 4, 1916-March 3, 1917

In the 1914 elections for the 64th Congress, the Democrats gained 5 seats in the Senate raising their majority from 51 to 56 of the 96 seats. The Republicans lost 4 seats to hold a total of 40. In the House, the Democrats lost 61 seats, lowering their majority from 291 to 230 of the 435. House Republicans gained 69 seats to hold a total of 196. Nine seats were not held by either of the two major parties. Of these 9 seats, 6 were held by the Progressive Party, 1 seat by the Socialist Party, 1 seat by the Prohibitionist Party, and 1 seat by an independent. When the Seventeenth Amendment was declared ratified on May 31, 1913 [See 63rd Congress], United States senators were directly elected by the voters of their respective states for the first time in American history. [See note 3, p. xxix]

BACKGROUND

In 1915 the major European powers all were engaged in World War I, but the United States was still neutral. America had never before become involved in a European war, and most Americans wanted to stay out of the conflict. The causes of the war and the objectives of the combatants were unclear. Millions of Americans had ancestral ties to Great Britain, but millions of others had immigrated from Germany, Britain's enemy. Britain was the original mother country prior to the American Revolution and English was America's language, but many Americans remembered that historically Britain had twice fought wars with America — the Revolution and the War of 1812 — while Germany had never been an enemy of the United States. American public opinion, however, began to turn against Germany in 1915. On May 7 a German submarine torpedoed and sank the British passenger ship *Lusitania*, and 114 American passengers aboard drowned. For months, the Germans had been issuing public warnings to American travelers that Germany considered all British flag ships to be enemy vessels subject to attack. President Wilson sent diplomatic notes to Germany protesting the action. Germany defended the sinking of the *Lusitania* as a legitimate act of self-defense, but promised that it would not attack clearly marked ships of neutral nations. Wilson, however, continued to criticize Germany and public opinion turned against the Germans.

In 1916 Wilson was preparing for the November presidential election. He ran using the campaign theme "he kept us out of war." In reality, Wilson got the U.S. involved in two conflicts. First, after a minor border raid by the Mexican bandit Pancho Villa, Wilson sent American troops into Mexico to capture Villa and gain control over the U.S.-Mexico border area. The resulting loss in American and Mexican lives far exceeded the damage done in Villa's raid, and after a year of failure in searching for Villa, Wilson withdrew the U.S. forces.

Second, Wilson demanded that Germany

cease its submarine operations, or else the U.S. would sever diplomatic relations. Meanwhile, under the National Defense Act passed by Congress in 1916, the size of the combined U.S. Army and National Guard was increased to 625,000. In 1917, citing the difficulty in distinguishing between neutral and enemy ships, Germany announced that it would recommence unrestricted submarine attacks on shipping. Also in 1917, the British forwarded to the U.S. the decoded text of the "Zimmermann Telegram," a secret message from the German foreign minister to his ambassador in Mexico proposing an alliance between the two countries should the U.S. declare war on Germany.

During the 64th Congress, the pro-neutrality faction in Congress saw its power and influence slip away as the country drifted toward war. Pacifist leaders Senator Robert M. LaFollette (Rep., Wis.) and Senator George W. Norris (Rep., Neb.) unsuccessfully opposed the National Defense Act. Secretary of State William Jennings Bryan, an ally of LaFollette, had resigned when Wilson's diplomacy with Germany hardened after the sinking of the *Lusitania*. The "pro-military preparedness" faction within Congress was led by Wilson himself and two influential members of his cabinet: Secretary of the Navy Josephus Daniels and Secretary of War Newton Baker. Even though LaFollette and Norris were prepared to back a measure authorizing the president to arm U.S. merchant ships. Wilson armed the ships on his own authority and prepared to ask the incoming 65th Congress for a declaration of war against Germany.

SENATE LEADERSHIP

Vice President: Thomas Riley Marshall, Wilson's vice president, had never served in Congress, but had been governor of Indiana from 1909 to 1913, when he resigned in order to become vice president.

President Pro Tempore: James Paul Clarke (Dem., Ark.) was reelected on December 6, 1915. Clarke had been governor of Arkansas from 1895 to 1896 and had been elected to the Senate in

1903. He served in the Senate until his death on October 1, 1916, and was president pro tem in the 63rd and 64th Congresses. After Clarke died, Willard Saulsbury (Dem., Del.) was elected on December 14, 1916. Saulsbury served in the Senate from 1913 until 1919, and was president pro tem in the 64th and 65th Congresses.

Majority Leader: John W. Kern (Dem., Ind.)

Majority Whip: J. Hamilton Lewis (Dem., Ill.)

Minority Leader: Jacob H. Gallinger (Rep., N.H.)

Minority Whip: Charles Curtis (Rep., Kans.), except for the week of December 6-December 13, 1915, when James W. Wadsworth Jr. (Rep., N.Y.) served as minority whip.

Chairmen of Selected Key Committees: [See also Organization and Administration, below]

Committee on Appropriations: Thomas S. Martin (Dem., Va.)

Committee on Banking and Currency: Robert L. Owen (Dem., Okla.)

Committee on Finance: Furnifold M. Simmons (Dem., N.C.)

Committee on Foreign Relations: William J. Stone (Dem., Mo.)

Committee on the Judiciary: Charles A. Culberson (Dem., Tex.)

Committee on Military Affairs: George E. Chamberlain (Dem., Ore.)

Committee on Naval Affairs: Benjamin Tillman (Dem., S.C.)

Committee on Rules: Lee S. Overman (Dem., N.C.)

HOUSE LEADERSHIP

Speaker of the House: Champ Clark (Dem., Mo.) was reelected Speaker on December 15, 1915. [See biographical note in 62nd Congress]

Majority Leader: Claude Kitchin (Dem., N.C.)

Majority Whip: None.

C H R O N O L O G Y

March 4, 1915:	The 64th Congress begins.
December 6, 1915:	The first session begins, and James Paul Clarke (Dem., Ark.) is reelected Senate president pro tem.
December 7, 1915:	President Wilson nominates Robert Lansing to succeed William Jennings Bryan as secretary of state.
December 13, 1915:	The Senate confirms Lansing.
December 15, 1915:	Champ Clark (Dem., Mo.) is reelected Speaker of the House.
January 2, 1916:	Supreme Court Justice Joseph R. Lamar dies.
January 28, 1916:	President Wilson nominates Louis D. Brandeis to replace Lamar.
March 7, 1916:	President Wilson nominates, and the Senate confirms, Newton D. Baker to succeed Lindley M. Garrison as secretary of war.
April 17, 1916:	Congress passes the National Defense Act.
May 1, 1916:	Congress passes legislation concerning the Philippines.
May 15, 1916:	Congress passes the Federal Farm Loan Bank Act.
June 1, 1916:	The Senate confirms Brandeis.
June 10, 1916:	Supreme Court Justice Charles Evans Hughes resigns.
July 14, 1916:	President Wilson nominates John H. Clarke to replace Hughes.
July 24, 1916:	The Senate confirms Clarke.
August 5, 1916:	Congress passes child labor legislation.
September 7, 1916:	The Senate approves a treaty to purchase the Virgin Islands.
September 8, 1916:	The first session ends.
December 4, 1916:	The second session begins.
December 13, 1916:	Congress passes immigration legislation.
January 29, 1917:	President Wilson vetoes the immigration legislation.
February 1, 1917:	The House overrides Wilson's immigration veto.
February 5, 1917:	The Senate overrides Wilson's immigration veto.
March 3, 1917:	The second session and the 64th Congress end.

[See note 6, p. xxix]

Minority Leader: James R. Mann (Rep., Ill.)

Minority Whip: Charles M. Hamilton (Rep., N.Y.)

Chairmen of Selected Key Committees: [See also Organization and Administration, below]

Committee on Agriculture: Asbury F. Lever (Dem., S.C.)

Committee on Appropriations: John J. Fitzgerald (Dem., N.Y.)

Committee on Banking, Finance, and Urban Affairs: Carter Glass (Dem., Va.)

Committee on Foreign Affairs: Henry D. Flood (Dem., Va.)

Committee on the Judiciary: Edwin Y. Webb (Dem., N.C.)

Committee on Military Affairs: James Hay (Dem., Va.)

TABLE OF KEY VOTES

Senate

Subject of Vote	Date of Vote	For	Against
Philippines Given More Autonomy	February 3, 1916	52	24
Armed Forces Reorganized	April 17, 1916	Passed by voice vote	
Farm Loan Board Established	May 3, 1916	58	5
Child Labor Restricted	August 5, 1916	52	12
Virgin Islands Treaty Approved	September 7, 1916	Unanimous voice vote	
Immigration Law Passed	December 13, 1916	64	7

House

Subject of Vote	Date of Vote	For	Against
Child Labor Restricted	February 2, 1916	337	46
Armed Forces Reorganized	March 23, 1916	403	2
Immigration Law Passed	March 30, 1916	307	87
Philippines Given More Autonomy	May 1, 1916	Passed by voice vote	
Farm Loan Board Established	May 15, 1916	295	10

[See note 7, p. xxix]

Committee on Naval Affairs: Lemuel P. Padgett (Dem., Tenn.)

Committee on Rules: Robert L. Henry (Dem., Tex.)

Committee on Ways and Means: Claude Kitchin (Dem., N.C.)

ORGANIZATION AND ADMINISTRATION

In the Senate, the office of minority whip became a formal position. The minority whip is the minority leader's second in command, and is supposed to keep members of the minority party informed of party objectives and ensure their loyalty to the party's agenda. [See note 5, p. xxix]

MAJOR LEGISLATION PASSED

Armed Forces: In the National Defense Act,

Congress reorganized American land forces into the regular Army, the Reserves, and the National Guard. The Army was increased to 175,000 troops and the National Guard to 450,000, for a total of 625,000 troops. Further, the act established the Reserve Officer Training Corps at institutions of higher learning.

Child Labor: Congress attempted to regulate and restrict child labor, making it illegal for factories to hire children under the age of 14 or mining companies to hire children under the age of 16. The Supreme Court nullified much of this legislation in the 1918 case of *Hammer v. Dagenhart*.

Farm Loans: In the Federal Farm Loan Bank Act, Congress established 12 regional Federal Land Banks with a Federal Farm Loan Board to supervise the system.

Immigration: Congress imposed a literacy test requirement on immigrants, with an exemption for refugees from religious persecution. President Wilson vetoed the bill, but his veto was overridden [See Relations with the President, below].

Philippines: Congress gave more autonomy to the local government of the U.S. occupied Philippine Islands.

Virgin Islands: The Senate approved a treaty between the United States and Denmark whereby the U.S. purchased the Danish West Indies islands, now known as the Virgin Islands, for $22 million.

FAILED LEGISLATION

None of historical significance.

RELATIONS WITH THE PRESIDENT

President Wilson was generally successful in pursuing domestic reform legislation through Congress, but was less successful in foreign policy. The Wilson administration, which broke its promise to keep America neutral during World War I, is remembered for its eventual failure [See 66th Congress] to get the Treaty of Versailles through the Senate.

Wilson vetoed six bills during the 64th Congress. One veto, involving immigration legislation [See Major Legislation, above], resulted in a defeat for Wilson. Wilson vetoed the bill on January 29, 1917. The House overrode the veto on February 1, 1917, by a vote of 287 to 106, and the Senate overrode the veto on February 5, 1917, by a vote of 62 to 19.

NOMINATIONS, APPOINTMENTS, AND CONFIRMATIONS

The Judiciary: On January 2, 1916, Supreme Court Justice Joseph R. Lamar died. President Woodrow Wilson nominated Louis D. Brandeis on January 28, 1916, to replace Lamar, and on June 1, 1916, the Senate confirmed Brandeis by a 47

to 22 vote. Justice Charles Evans Hughes resigned on June 10, 1916. President Wilson nominated John H. Clarke on July 14, 1916, to replace Hughes, and the Senate confirmed Clarke by voice vote on July 24, 1916.

The Executive Branch: On December 7, 1915, President Wilson nominated Robert Lansing to succeed William Jennings Bryan as secretary of state, and on December 13, 1915, the Senate confirmed Lansing by voice vote. On March 7, 1916, Wilson nominated, and the Senate confirmed by voice vote, Newton D. Baker to succeed Lindley M. Garrison as secretary of war.

IMPEACHMENTS

None.

CONSTITUTIONAL AMENDMENTS

None.

FURTHER READING

Clark, Champ. *My Quarter Century of American Politics.* 2 vols. New York: Harper, 1920.

Levin, Norman Gordon. *Woodrow Wilson and World Politics; America's Response to War and Revolution.* New York: Oxford University Press, 1968.

Strum, Philippa. *Louis D. Brandeis: Justice for the People.* New York: Schocken Books, 1989.

Walworth, Arthur Clarence. *Woodrow Wilson.* Boston: Houghton Mifflin Co., 1965.

The 65th Congress

MARCH 4, 1917 - MARCH 3, 1919

Special Senate Session: March 5, 1917-March 16, 1917
First Session: April 2, 1917-October 6, 1917
Second Session: December 3, 1917-November 21, 1918
Third Session: December 2, 1918-March 3, 1919

The Senate held a special session to vote on the confirmation of presidential appointees to various offices. [See note 1, p. xxix]

In the 1916 elections for the 65th Congress, the Democrats lost 3 seats in the Senate, reducing their majority from 56 to 53 of the 96 seats. The Republicans gained 2 seats to hold a total of 42. One seat was held by neither major party. In the House, the Democrats lost 14 seats, reducing their majority from 230 to 216 of the 435 seats. The Republicans gained 14 seats to hold a total of 210. Nine seats were not held by either major party. Three of these seats were held by the Progressive Party, 1 seat by the Socialist Party, 1 seat by the Prohibitionist Party, and 1 seat by an Independent Republican. [See note 3, p. xxix]

BACKGROUND

Woodrow Wilson was inaugurated for his second term as the 28th president of the United States on March 5, 1917. By the start of the 65th Congress, the United States was getting ready to enter World War I on the side of Great Britain, France, and Russia (plus other minor powers) against Germany, Austria-Hungary, and the Ottoman Empire. On April 2, 1917, the first day of the first session of this Congress, Wilson asked Congress to declare war. Within a few days, both houses of Congress approved Wilson's war resolution, and the U.S. went to war. By June, the first American troops had arrived in France, where the two sides were engaged in large-scale trench warfare that had largely resulted in a stalemate since 1914.

Nineteen seventeen was a busy year in the 65th Congress, due mostly to war-related legislation. Congress passed the Liberty Loan Act, authorizing $5 billion in war bonds; the Selective Service Act, which required all men between the ages of 21 and 30 to register for the draft; and the Espionage Act, which set severe penalties for treasonous activities. Congress also approved the Eighteenth Amendment, which would establish Prohibition, and sent the amendment to the states for ratification. Finally, the House seated its first female member, Jeannette Rankin (Rep., Mont.), who would cast one of fifty votes against Wilson's proposed declaration of war.

In 1918 Wilson issued his Fourteen Points, proposing the basis for an end to the war and a fair and permanent peace. Congress passed the Sedition Act, which curbed freedom of expression by making it illegal to speak against or criticize the U.S. or the war. By the summer and fall of 1918, millions of American troops were fighting in Europe, putting the Germans and their allies on the defensive. The development of the tank also meant that the German trenches finally were vulnerable to Allied attacks. On October 6 the German chancellor, Prince Max of Baden, approached Wilson about a truce along the lines of the Fourteen Points. The German initiative led to the Armistice on November 11.

In 1919 the Paris Peace Conference convened in order to formulate the terms for ending the war. On February 14, 1919, Wilson asked the conference to endorse his idea for a League of Nations. The league would be a worldwide representative body, in which nations could express their grievances and act to avoid conflicts such as World War I.

SENATE LEADERSHIP

Vice President: Thomas Riley Marshall had never served in Congress, but he had been governor of Indiana from 1909 to 1913, when he resigned in order to become vice president after having been elected to that office on Wilson's ticket in the 1912 elections.

President Pro Tempore: Willard Saulsbury (Dem., Del.) had served in the Senate from 1913 until 1919 and was president pro tem in the 64th and 65th Congresses.

Majority Leader: Thomas S. Martin (Dem., Va.)

Majority Whip: J. Hamilton Lewis (Dem., Ill.)

Minority Leader: Jacob H. Gallinger (Rep., N.H.), until August 17, 1918, when he died. Henry Cabot Lodge (Rep., Mass.) became the new minority leader on August 24, 1918.

Minority Whip: Charles Curtis (Rep., Kans.)

Chairmen of Selected Key Committees: [See also Organization and Administration, below]

Committee on Appropriations: Thomas S. Martin (Dem., Va.)

Committee on Banking and Currency: Robert L. Owen (Dem., Okla.)

Committee on Finance: Furnifold M. Simmons (Dem., N.C.)

Committee on Foreign Relations: William J. Stone (Dem., Mo.), who died on April 14, 1918. Gilbert M. Hitchcock (Dem., Neb.) became the next chairman.

Committee on the Judiciary: Charles A. Culberson (Dem., Tex.)

Committee on Military Affairs: George E. Chamberlain (Dem., Ore.)

Committee on Naval Affairs: Benjamin Tillman (Dem., S.C.), who died on July 3, 1918. Claude A. Swanson (Dem., Va.) became the next chairman.

Committee on Rules: Lee S. Overman (Dem., N.C.)

HOUSE LEADERSHIP

Speaker of the House: Champ Clark (Dem., Mo.) was reelected Speaker on April 2, 1917. [See biographical note in 62nd Congress]

Majority Leader: Claude Kitchin (Dem., N.C.)

Majority Whip: None

Minority Leader: James R. Mann (Rep., Ill.)

Minority Whip: Charles M. Hamilton (Rep., N.Y.)

Chairmen of Selected Key Committees: [See also Organization and Administration, below]

Committee on Agriculture: Asbury F. Lever (Dem., S.C.)

Committee on Appropriations: John J. Fitzgerald (Dem., N.Y.), who resigned effective December 31, 1917. J. Swagar Sherley (Dem., Ky.) became the next chairman.

Committee on Banking, Finance, and Urban Affairs: Carter Glass (Dem., Va.), who resigned effective December 16, 1918, to become secretary of the Treasury. Michael F. Phelan (Dem., Mass.) became the next chairman.

Committee on Foreign Affairs: Henry D. Flood (Dem., Va.)

C H R O N O L O G Y

March 4, 1917:	The 65th Congress begins.
March 5, 1917:	A special Senate session begins.
March 8, 1917:	The Senate adopts its first cloture rule.
March 16, 1917:	The special Senate session ends.
April 2, 1917:	The first session begins, and Champ Clark (Dem., Mo.) is reelected Speaker of the House.
April 5, 1917:	Congress passes a declaration of war against Germany.
April 17, 1917:	Congress passes liberty loan legislation.
April 30, 1917:	Congress passes selective service legislation.
May 11, 1917:	Congress passes espionage legislation.
August 15, 1917:	Congress passes legislation raising taxes for the war effort.
September 12, 1917:	Congress passes the Trading With The Enemy Act.
October 6, 1917:	The first session ends.
December 3, 1917:	The second session begins.
December 7, 1917:	Congress passes a declaration of war against Austria-Hungary.
December 17, 1917:	Congress sends the 18th Amendment, establishing prohibition of alcoholic beverages, to the states for ratification.
March 6, 1918:	Congress passes the Sabotage Act.
March 15, 1918:	Congress passes legislation establishing Daylight Saving Time.
April 6, 1918:	Congress passes the Sedition Act.
November 21, 1918:	The second session ends.
December 2, 1918:	The third session begins.
December 3, 1918:	President Wilson nominates Carter Glass to succeed William G. McAdoo as secretary of the Treasury.
December 6, 1918:	The Senate confirms Glass.

[See note 6, p. xxix]

Committee on the Judiciary: Edwin Y. Webb (Dem., N.C.)

Committee on Military Affairs: Stanley Hubert Dent Jr. (Dem., Ala.)

Committee on Naval Affairs: Lemuel P. Padgett (Dem., Tenn.)

Committee on Rules: Edward W. Pou (Dem., N.C.)

Committee on Ways and Means: Claude Kitchin (Dem., N.C.)

ORGANIZATION AND ADMINISTRATION

The Senate has always found it much more difficult than the House to limit the right of members to speak for as long as they want, generally because the Senate is a smaller and more collegial body. Effective March 8, 1917, the Senate adopted its first *cloture* rule. Cloture means to shut off debate. Under this first cloture rule, two-thirds of the senators present and voting could stop members from speaking. The cloture rule and the majority necessary to invoke cloture have been revised periodically, but still exist. [See note 5, p. xxix]

MAJOR LEGISLATION PASSED

Daylight Saving Time: In the Daylight Saving Time Act, Congress ordered clocks to be set ahead by one hour between March and October in order to conserve electricity.

Espionage: In the Espionage Act, Congress set severe penalties for treasonous activities and gave the Post Office the power to censor the mail.

Liberty Loans: In the Liberty Loan Act, Congress authorized the sale of $5 billion in war bonds.

Revenue: In order to finance the war effort, Congress increased income taxes on individuals and corporations and imposed luxury, excise, and excess-profits taxes.

Sabotage: In the Sabotage Act, Congress established punishments for people who illegally obstructed the war effort.

Sedition: In the Sedition Act, Congress made it illegal to speak against or criticize the U.S. or the war.

Selective Service: In the Selective Service Act, Congress required all men between the ages of 21 and 30 to register for the draft, with actual draftees to be chosen by lot.

Trade: In the Trading With the Enemy Act, Congress outlawed trade with nations at war with the United States.

World War I: Congress declared war against Germany and Austria-Hungary, bringing the United States into World War I.

FAILED LEGISLATION

None of historical significance.

RELATIONS WITH THE PRESIDENT

President Wilson successfully pursued his wartime legislative agenda with Congress, and secured the passage of legislation such as the Sedition Act that arguably violated constitutional liberties. When the war ended, however, Wilson found that the American tradition of isolationism still was very strong. His idea for a League of Nations would not be well received by the 66th Congress.

Wilson vetoed six bills during the 65th Congress, none of which involved significant legislation.

NOMINATIONS, APPOINTMENTS, AND CONFIRMATIONS

The Judiciary: There were no significant nominations, appointments, or confirmations in the federal judiciary during the 65th Congress.

The Executive Branch: On December 3, 1918, President Wilson nominated Carter Glass to succeed William G. McAdoo as secretary of the Treasury, and the Senate confirmed Glass by voice vote on December 6, 1918.

IMPEACHMENTS

None.

CONSTITUTIONAL AMENDMENTS

Congress sent the Eighteenth Amendment, which established Prohibition, to the states for ratification. The Eighteenth Amendment was ratified by the required three-fourths of the states effective January 16, 1919. [For the actual text of the Eighteenth Amendment, see the copy of the Constitution at Appendix A.]

Prohibition was the final victory of the Temperance Movement, which started in the late 19th century as an off-shoot of the movement for social reform known generally as Progressivism. The Temperance Movement, led by Wayne B. Wheeler's Anti-Saloon League and Frances Willard's Women's Christian Temperance Union, believed that alcohol largely was responsible for social evils such as poverty and crime. Religious Fundamentalists supported temperance and so did the Women's Suffrage Movement, which sought to associate a woman's right to vote with other high moral ideals. By 1917, 27 states had gone "dry" by enacting legislation against alco-

TABLE OF KEY VOTES

Senate

Subject of Vote	Date of Vote	For	Against
Declaration of War Against Germany	April 4, 1917	82	6
Sabotage Act Passed	April 9, 1917	Passed by voice vote	
Liberty Bond Sale Authorized	April 17, 1917	84	0
Selective Service Established	April 30, 1917	Passed by voice vote	
Espionage Act Passed	May 11, 1917	77	6
Daylight Saving Time Established	June 27, 1917	Passed by voice vote	
18th Amendment Sent to States	July 31, 1917	65	20
Income Tax Raised	August 15, 1917	69	4
Trading with Enemy Barred	September 12, 1917	Passed by voice vote	
Declaration of War Against Austria-Hungary	December 7, 1917	74	0
Sedition Act Passed	April 6, 1918	Passed by voice vote	

House

Subject of Vote	Date of Vote	For	Against
Declaration of War Against Germany	April 5, 1917	373	50
Liberty Bond Sale Authorized	April 14, 1917	390	0
Selective Service Established	April 28, 1917	397	24
Espionage Act Passed	May 4, 1917	260	107
Income Tax Raised	May 23, 1917	329	76
Trading with Enemy Barred	July 11, 1917	Passed by voice vote	
Declaration of War Against Austria-Hungary	December 7, 1917	365	1
18th Amendment Sent to States	December 17, 1917	282	128
Sedition Act Passed	March 4, 1918	Passed by voice vote	
Sabotage Act Passed	March 6, 1918	321	0
Daylight Saving Time Established	March 15, 1918	252	40

[See note 7, p. xxix]

holic beverages, but their efforts were hampered by the availability of alcohol in neighboring "wet" states. This factor, and the so-called "spirit of sacrifice" created by World War I, caused Congress to endorse the Temperance and Suffrage Movements' push for national Prohibition and send the Eighteenth Amendment to the states. The Republicans generally supported Prohibition, but the Democrats were divided between southern Democrats who supported Prohibition and northern Democrats who had strong labor union constituencies in the cities that did not want to lose jobs in the brewing and distilling industries and wanted to preserve what was considered the working man's traditional form of after-hours relaxation. President Wilson took no firm position on the issue, although he would veto the Volstead Act in the 66th Congress, probably because his fellow Democrats were divided.

FURTHER READING

Clark, Champ. *My Quarter Century of American Politics.* 2 vols. New York: Harper, 1920.

Levin, Norman Gordon. *Woodrow Wilson and World Politics; America's Response to War and Revolution.* New York: Oxford University Press, 1968.

Walworth, Arthur Clarence. *Woodrow Wilson.* Boston: Houghton Mifflin Co., 1965.

The 66th Congress

MARCH 4, 1919 - MARCH 3, 1921

First Session: *May 19, 1919-November 19, 1919*
Second Session: *December 1, 1919-June 5, 1920*
Third Session: *December 6, 1920-March 3, 1921*

In the 1918 elections for the 66th Congress, the Republicans gained 7 seats in the Senate, creating a new majority of 49 of the 96 seats. The Democrats lost 6 seats, reducing their total to 47. In the House, the Republicans gained 30 seats, creating a new majority of 240 of the 435 seats. The Democrats lost 26 seats, reducing their total to 190. Five seats were not held by either major party. One seat was held by the Prohibitionist Party and 1 seat by the Union Labor Party. [See note 3, p. xxix]

BACKGROUND

According to the census of 1920, the population of the United States as of January 1, 1920, was 105,710,620, resulting in a population density of 35.6 persons for each of the country's 2,969,451 square miles. This was a population increase of 14.9 percent over the 1910 census.

By the summer of 1919, the Paris Peace Conference had agreed on the terms of the Treaty of Versailles to end World War I and to establish the League of Nations. Wilson sent the treaty, which would bring the U.S. into the league, to the Senate for approval on July 10, 1919. Despite Wilson's nationwide speaking tour on behalf of the proposed league, the American public was ready to forget the war and international politics. The Senate voted on the Versailles Treaty twice during the 66th Congress, and on both occasions the treaty failed to get the two-thirds majority necessary for approval. Thus, the U.S. did not join the League of Nations. [See Relations with the President, p. 297]

Also in 1919, Congress acted on the Eighteenth Amendment establishing Prohibition and passed the Volstead Act in order to implement it. [See 65th Congress, Constitutional Amendments, for more background on the Eighteenth Amendment] Wilson vetoed the act, but Congress overrode his veto. The Volstead Act, or National Prohibition Act, made it a federal offense to produce, sell, or consume any beverage that contained more than one-half of one percent of alcohol. Under the Act, the states also had the right to enact or enforce existing prohibition legislation of their own. Wilson had taken no firm position for or against Prohibition during his administration, due to internal divisions within his Democratic Party over the issue and his desire not to alienate the Suffrage Movement, which favored Prohibition, or to distract attention from the League of Nations and the Treaty of Versailles. In the end Wilson vetoed the Volstead Act because it opened the way for an enormous increase in federal enforcement in an area that he thought should be left to the states. Congress overrode the veto.

In 1920 the Democratic Party's candidate for president was James M. Cox. Cox wanted America to enter the League of Nations, but his Republican opponent Warren G. Harding was indifferent to the issue. When Cox lost the election in

November, any chance for U.S. entry into the league also was lost. Nevertheless, Wilson won the Nobel Peace Prize on November 20 for having launched the league and for his efforts to achieve world peace. Also in 1920, Congress passed a Merchant Marine Act in order to stimulate the American shipping industry. The act provided for the sale of government surplus ships to U.S. shipping companies and made loans available through a new Merchant Fleet Corporation. Finally, the Nineteenth Amendment, granting women the right to vote, was ratified.

Before the 66th Congress ended, the Census Bureau not only had completed the 1920 census, but also had released a study on American urban development. For the first time in U.S. history, the majority of the population was not rural. 51 percent lived in cities or towns of more than 2,500 people. The reason for this change was industrialization and mechanized agriculture, which made it possible for a nation to have large urban populations that could support themselves without the necessity of growing their own food. America would henceforth become a nation of cities, making the Jeffersonian ideal of a republic of small farmers obsolete, but the implications of American urbanization would not be realized for many years.

SENATE LEADERSHIP

Vice President: Thomas Riley Marshall [See biographical note in 65th Congress]

President Pro Tempore: Albert Baird Cummins (Rep., Iowa) was elected president pro tempore on May 19, 1919. Cummins had been governor of Iowa from 1902 to 1908, served in the Senate from 1908 until he died on July 30, 1926, and was president pro tem from the 66th through the 69th Congresses.

Majority Leader: Henry Cabot Lodge (Rep., Mass.) Lodge first was elected to the Senate in 1893 and served until he died on November 9, 1924. Lodge was also Chairman of the Foreign Relations Committee, which put him in a very powerful position when Democratic President

Woodrow Wilson sought to have the Treaty of Versailles approved by the Senate. [See Relations with the President, below]

Majority Whip: Charles Curtis (Rep., Kans.)

Minority Leader: Thomas S. Martin (Dem., Va.), until he died on November 12, 1919. Gilbert M. Hitchcock (Dem., Neb.) served as acting minority leader until April 27, 1920, when Oscar W. Underwood (Dem., Ala.) became the new minority leader.

Minority Whip: Peter G. Gerry (Dem., R.I.)

Chairmen of Selected Key Committees: [See also Organization and Administration, below]

Committee on Appropriations: Francis E. Warren (Rep., Wyo.)

Committee on Banking and Currency: George P. McLean (Rep., Conn.)

Committee on Finance: Boies Penrose (Rep., Pa.)

Committee on Foreign Relations: Henry Cabot Lodge (Rep., Mass.)

Committee on the Judiciary: Knute Nelson (Rep., Minn.)

Committee on Military Affairs: James W. Wadsworth Jr. (Rep., N.Y.)

Committee on Naval Affairs: Carroll S. Page (Rep., Vt.)

Committee on Rules: Philander C. Knox (Rep., Pa.)

HOUSE LEADERSHIP

Speaker of the House: Frederick Huntington Gillett (Rep., Mass.) was elected Speaker on May 19, 1919. Gillett first had been elected to Congress in the 53rd Congress and served as Speaker in the 66th through the 68th Congresses.

Majority Leader: Franklin W. Mondell (Rep., Wyo.)

Majority Whip: Harold Knutson (Rep., Minn.)

C H R O N O L O G Y

March 4, 1919:	The 66th Congress begins.
May 19, 1919:	The first session begins. Frederick Huntington Gillett (Rep., Mass.) is elected Speaker of the House, and Albert Baird Cummins (Rep., Iowa) is elected Senate president pro tem.
May 23, 1919:	President Wilson nominates A. Mitchell Palmer to succeed Thomas W. Gregory as attorney general.
June 3, 1919:	Congress passes the 19th Amendment, granting women the right to vote, and sends it to the states for ratification.
August 29, 1919:	The Senate confirms Palmer.
September 5, 1919:	Congress passes the Volstead Act establishing Prohibition.
October 27, 1919:	President Wilson vetoes the Volstead Act. The House overrides the veto.
October 28, 1919:	The Senate also votes to override Wilson's veto.
November 19, 1919:	The Senate fails to approve the Treaty of Versailles, and the first session ends.
December 1, 1919:	The second session begins.
December 4, 1919:	President Wilson nominates Joshua W. Alexander to succeed William C. Redfield as secretary of commerce.
December 11, 1919:	The Senate confirms Alexander.
December 16, 1919:	Congress passes the Esch-Cummins Transportation Act concerning railroads.
January 15, 1920:	Congress passes the Water Power Act.
January 27, 1920:	President Wilson nominates David F. Houston to succeed Carter Glass as secretary of the Treasury and Edwin T. Meredith to take over Houston's former position as secretary of agriculture.
January 31, 1920:	The Senate confirms Houston and Meredith.
February 13, 1920:	President Wilson nominates John B. Payne to succeed Franklin K. Lane as secretary of the Interior.
February 25, 1920:	President Wilson nominates Bainbridge Colby to succeed Robert Lansing as secretary of state.
February 28, 1920:	The Senate confirms Payne.
March 19, 1920:	The Senate again fails to approve the Treaty of Versailles.
March 22, 1920:	The Senate confirms Colby.
May 21, 1920:	Congress passes the Jones Merchant Marine Act.
May 27, 1920:	The Senate eliminates 42 obsolete committees.
June 5, 1920:	The second session ends.
December 6, 1920:	The third session begins.
March 3, 1921:	The third session and the 66th Congress end.

[See note 6, p. xxix]

Minority Leader: Champ Clark (Dem., Mo.)

Minority Whip: None.

Chairmen of Selected Key Committees: [See also Organization and Administration, below]

Committee on Agriculture: Gilbert N. Haugen (Rep., Iowa.)

Committee on Appropriations: James W. Good (Rep., Iowa)

Committee on Banking, Finance and Urban Affairs: Edmund Platt (Rep., N.Y.), who resigned effective June 7, 1920. Louis T. McFadden (Rep., Pa.) became the next chairman.

Committee on Foreign Affairs: Stephen G. Porter (Rep., Pa.)

Committee on the Judiciary: Andrew J. Volstead (Rep., Minn.)

Committee on Military Affairs: Julius Kahn (Rep., Calif.)

Committee on Naval Affairs: Thomas S. Butler (Rep., Pa.)

Committee on Rules: Philip P. Campbell (Rep., Kans.)

Committee on Ways and Means: Joseph W. Fordney (Rep., Mich.)

ORGANIZATION AND ADMINISTRATION

On May 27, 1920, the Senate eliminated 42 obsolete committees. Most of these committees, such as the Committee on Revolutionary War Claims, existed only to justify office space and support staff for majority party senators. [See note 5, p. xxix]

MAJOR LEGISLATION PASSED

Prohibition: In the Volstead Act, Congress implemented the Eighteenth Amendment and established national Prohibition. [See Background, above]

Public Waterways: In the Water Power Act, Congress established the Federal Power Commission and gave the commission the power to license dams and hydroelectric facilities.

Railroads: In the Esch-Cummins Transportation Act, Congress ended the wartime controls that had been imposed on the railroads, established a Railroad Labor Board to handle labor disputes, and exempted the railroads from the antitrust laws, while simultaneously increasing the power of the Interstate Commerce Commission.

Shipping: In the Jones Merchant Marine Act, Congress attempted to stimulate the American shipping industry by providing for the sale of government surplus ships to U.S. flag shipping companies and in making loans available through a new Merchant Fleet Corporation.

FAILED LEGISLATION

World War I: The Senate twice refused to ratify the Treaty of Versailles, which would have brought the United States into the League of Nations. [See Relations with the President, below]

RELATIONS WITH THE PRESIDENT

The greatest defeat of the Wilson Administration was its failure to get the Treaty of Versailles approved by the Senate. The treaty was the product of the Paris Peace Conference, where the Allied victors of World War I endorsed President Wilson's idea of a League of Nations to prevent future wars, punished the defeated Germans, and redrew the map of Eastern and Central Europe.

The Senate was divided into three factions. First, there were those Republicans who had seen their party retake the Senate after the November 1918 elections and were determined to renew the traditional American policy of isolationism. Senators William E. Borah (Rep., Idaho), Hiram W. Johnson (Rep. Calif.), Philander C. Knox (Rep., Pa.), Robert M. LaFollette (Rep, Wis.), Joseph M. McCormick (Rep., Ill.), and George H. Moses (Rep., N.H.) were particularly determined to reassert Republican strength and defeat the treaty. Second, there were the loyal Wilson Democrats, led by Senator Gilbert M. Hitchcock (Dem., Neb.), who would support the treaty.

TABLE OF KEY VOTES

Senate

Subject of Vote	Date of Vote	For	Against
19th Amendment Sent to States	June 3, 1919	56	25
Prohibition Implemented	September 5, 1919	Passed by voice vote	
First Versailles Treaty Vote	November 19, 1919	38	53
Railroad Control Lifted	December 16, 1919	46	30
Federal Power Commission Established	January 15, 1920	52	18
Second Versailles Treaty Vote (failed to reach two-thirds)	March 19, 1920	49	35

House

Subject of Vote	Date of Vote	For	Against
19th Amendment Sent to States	May 21, 1919	304	89
Federal Power Commission Established	July 1, 1919	Passed by voice vote	
Prohibition Implemented	July 22, 1919	289	100
Shipping Act Passed	November 8, 1919	240	8
Railroad Control Lifted	November 17, 1919	204	161

[See note 7, p. xxix]

Third, in the middle were both Democrats and Republicans who, as the expression went, had "mild reservations" about the treaty. For example, there was support in this group for a declaration that the United States would not commit itself to sending military forces to defend the various new nations and national borders that had emerged in post-war Europe under the treaty. The leader of this middle group was Henry Cabot Lodge (Rep., Mass.), the Chairman of the Senate Foreign Relations Committee and Majority Leader.

After Wilson sent the treaty to the Senate on July 10, 1919, it soon became apparent that passage would be impossible without some concessions to Lodge's faction, since the loyal Democrats did not have the necessary two-thirds majority to approve the treaty. Wilson did not wish to compromise, however, and beginning on September 4, 1919, began a cross-county speaking tour to rally public support behind the treaty. Three weeks later, on September 25, Wilson suffered a heart attack that left him incapacitated until early November. Senator Hitchcock was left to speak for a President who was unable to effectively support him and who still refused to make concessions to Lodge and the Centrists. On November 19, 1919, the Treaty of Versailles was rejected by the Senate, and again on March 19, 1920. [See Table of Key Votes, above]

Wilson vetoed 28 bills during the 66th Congress, including the Volstead Act, which established Prohibition [See Major Legislation, above]. On October 27, 1919, the House voted 175 to 55 to override Wilson's veto, and on October 28, 1919, the Senate voted 65 to 20 to override.

NOMINATIONS, APPOINTMENTS, AND CONFIRMATIONS

The Judiciary: There were no significant nominations, appointments, or confirmations in the federal judiciary during the 66th Congress.

The Executive Branch: On May 23, 1919, President Wilson nominated A. Mitchell Palmer to succeed Thomas W. Gregory as attorney general, and on August 29, 1919, the Senate confirmed Palmer by voice vote. Wilson nominated Joshua W. Alexander on December 4, 1919, to succeed William C. Redfield as secretary of commerce, and the Senate confirmed Alexander by voice vote on December 11, 1919. On January 27, 1920, Wilson nominated David F. Houston to succeed Carter Glass as secretary of the Treasury, and Edwin T. Meredith to take over Houston's former position as secretary of agriculture. The Senate confirmed both men by voice vote on January 31, 1920. On February 13, 1920, Wilson nominated John B. Payne to succeed Franklin K. Lane as secretary of the Interior, and on February 25, 1920, Wilson nominated Bainbridge Colby to succeed Robert Lansing as secretary of state. The Senate confirmed Payne by voice vote on February 28, 1920, and Colby by voice vote on March 22, 1920.

IMPEACHMENTS

None.

CONSTITUTIONAL AMENDMENTS

Congress sent the Nineteenth Amendment, which gave women the right to vote, to the states for ratification. The Nineteenth Amendment was ratified by the required three-fourths of the states effective August 26, 1920. [For the actual text of the Nineteenth Amendment, see the copy of the Constitution at Appendix A]

FURTHER READING

Hamm, Richard F. *Shaping the Eighteenth Amendment: Temperance Reform, Legal Culture, and the Polity, 1889-1920.* Chapel Hill, N.C.. University of North Carolina Press, 1995.

Levin, Norman Gordon. *Woodrow Wilson and World Politics; America's Response to War and Revolution.* New York: Oxford University Press, 1968.

Margulies, Herbert F. *The Mild Reservationists and the League of Nations Controversy in the Senate.* Columbia, Mo.: University of Missouri Press, 1989.

Walworth, Arthur Clarence. *Woodrow Wilson.* Boston: Houghton Mifflin Co., 1965.

The 67th Congress

MARCH 4, 1921 - MARCH 3, 1923

Special Senate Session: March 4, 1921-March 15, 1921
First Session: April 11, 1921-November 23, 1921
Second Session: December 5, 1921-September 22, 1922
Third Session: November 20, 1922-December 4, 1922
Fourth Session: December 4, 1922-March 3, 1923

The Senate held a special session to vote on the confirmation of presidential appointees to various offices. [See note 1, p. xxix]

In the 1920 elections for the 67th Congress, the Republicans gained 10 seats in the Senate, raising their majority from 49 to 59 of the 96 seats. The Democrats lost 10 seats, reducing their total to 37. In the House, the Republicans gained 61 seats, giving them a majority of 301 of the 435 seats. The Democrats lost 59 seats, leaving them with a total of 131. Three seats were not held by either major party. One seat was held by the Socialist Party and one seat was held by an Independent Republican. [See note 3, p. xxix]

BACKGROUND

Warren G. Harding was inaugurated as the 29th president of the United States on March 4, 1921. Harding was the first incumbent senator to be elected president.

One of the 67th Congress's first actions was to pass legislation broadly restricting immigration into the U.S. Unlike prior measures, which had been directed at certain groups, like the Chinese, there was now a quota system applicable to all foreigners seeking to enter the U.S. The number of annual immigrants from each nation could not exceed three percent of the number of people from that nation already present in the U.S. as calcu-

lated by the 1910 census. The combined number of annual immigrants was capped at 357,803.

Also in 1921, on November 12, the Washington (D.C.) Conference for Limitation of Armaments began. The U.S. sponsored the conference and invited representatives of the world's major maritime powers to attend in order to discuss limiting the growth of their navies. The conference resulted in three treaties [See Major Legislation, below], all of which were passed by the Senate but none of which made a lasting contribution to naval disarmament or world peace.

In 1922 Congress created the Foreign Debt Commission to work out a schedule for the repayment of U.S. loans to France, Great Britain, Italy, and other countries during World War I. The final terms of repayment were fairly generous: repayment was stretched out over 62 years at just over two percent interest. The European economy, however, was weak, and the debtor countries depended on unrealistic German reparation obligations. Thus, most of the war debt to the U.S. was never repaid. On October 3, 1922, 87-year-old Rebecca L. Felton (Dem., Ga.) became the first female senator in U.S. history. Georgia Governor Thomas W. Hardwick appointed her after the death of former Senator Thomas E. Watson (Dem., Ga.). When the Senate convened in November, Felton served a single day and then stepped aside for her elected successor.

C H R O N O L O G Y

March 4, 1921:	The 67th Congress and a special Senate session begin.
March 7, 1921:	Albert Baird Cummins (Rep., Iowa) is reelected Senate president pro tem.
March 15, 1921:	The special Senate session ends.
April 11, 1921:	The first session begins, and Frederick Huntington Gillett (Rep., Mass.) is reelected Speaker of the House.
May 2, 1921:	Congress passes immigration quota legislation.
May 5, 1921:	Congress passes the National Budget and Accounting Act.
July 20, 1921:	Congress establishes the Veterans Bureau.
November 23, 1921:	The first session ends.
December 5, 1921:	The second session begins.
January 25, 1922:	Congress establishes the Foreign Debt Commission.
March 24, 1922:	The Senate approves the Four-Power Treaty.
March 29, 1922:	The Senate approves the Five-Power Treaty.
March 30, 1922:	The Senate approves the Nine-Power Treaty.
April 15, 1922:	Senator John B. Kendrick (Dem., Wyo.) introduces a resolution concerning Interior Secretary Albert B. Fall that begins the Teapot Dome scandal. [See Scandals, below]
August 3, 1922:	Congress passes the Fordney-McCumber Tariff Act.
September 9, 1922:	Congress passes citizenship legislation concerning married women.
September 19, 1922:	President Harding vetoes veterans legislation.
September 20, 1922:	The House overrides Harding's veto, but the Senate does not.
September 22, 1922:	The second session ends.
October 3, 1922:	Rebecca L. Felton (Dem., Ga.) becomes the first female senator.
November 20, 1922:	The third session begins.
December 4, 1922:	The third session ends.
December 4, 1922:	The fourth session begins.
March 1, 1923:	Congress passes farm loan legislation.
March 3, 1923:	The fourth session and the 67th Congress end.

[See note 6, p. xxix]

SENATE LEADERSHIP

Vice President: Calvin Coolidge had never served in Congress, but he had been governor of Massachusetts from 1919 to 1920 before being elected vice president on Warren Harding's ticket in the election of 1920.

President Pro Tempore: Albert Baird Cummins (Rep., Iowa) was reelected on March 7, 1921. [See biographical note in 66th Congress]

Majority Leader: Henry Cabot Lodge (Rep., Mass.)

Majority Whip: Charles Curtis (Rep., Kans.)

Minority Leader: Oscar W. Underwood (Dem., Ala.)

Minority Whip: Peter G. Gerry (Dem., R.I.)

Chairmen of Selected Key Committees: [See note 5, p. xxix]

Committee on Appropriations: Francis E. Warren (Rep., Wyo.)

Committee on Banking and Currency: George P. McLean (Rep., Conn.)

Committee on Finance: Boies Penrose (Rep., Pa.), who died on December 31, 1921. Porter J. McCumber (Rep., N.D.) became the next chairman.

Committee on Foreign Relations: Henry Cabot Lodge (Rep., Mass.)

Committee on the Judiciary: Knute Nelson (Rep., Minn.)

Committee on Military Affairs: James W. Wadsworth Jr. (Rep., N.Y.)

Committee on Naval Affairs: Carroll S. Page (Rep., Vt.)

Committee on Rules: Charles Curtis (Rep., Kans.)

HOUSE LEADERSHIP

Speaker of the House: Frederick Huntington Gillett (Rep., Mass.) was reelected Speaker on April 11, 1921. Gillett first had been elected to Congress in the 53rd Congress and served as Speaker in the 66th through the 68th Congresses.

Majority Leader: Franklin W. Mondell (Rep., Wyo.)

Majority Whip: Harold Knutson (Rep., Minn.)

Minority Leader: Claude Kitchin (Dem., N.C.)

Minority Whip: William A. Oldfield (Dem., Ark.)

Chairmen of Selected Key Committees: [See note 5, p. xxix]

Committee on Agriculture: Gilbert N. Haugen (Rep., Iowa)

Committee on Appropriations: James W. Good (Rep., Iowa), who resigned effective June 15, 1921. Charles R. Davis (Rep., Minn.) became the next chairman.

Committee on Banking, Finance, and Urban Affairs: Louis T. McFadden (Rep., Pa.)

Committee on Foreign Affairs: Stephen G. Porter (Rep., Pa.)

Committee on the Judiciary: Andrew J. Volstead (Rep., Minn.)

Committee on Military Affairs: Julius Kahn (Rep., Calif.)

Committee on Naval Affairs: Thomas S. Butler (Rep., Pa.)

Committee on Rules: Philip P. Campbell (Rep., Kans.)

Committee on Ways and Means: Joseph W. Fordney (Rep., Mich.)

ORGANIZATION AND ADMINISTRATION

No significant developments. [See note 5, p. xxix]

MAJOR LEGISLATION PASSED

Budget and Accounting: In the National Budget and Accounting Act, Congress created the General Accounting Office under the supervision of the comptroller general of the United States to keep an independent accounting of the government's income and disbursements. The act also created a Budget Bureau as part of the Treasury Department.

Citizenship: Congress made the U.S. citizenship of married women independent of their husbands' citizenship. Thus, a woman could no longer lose her U.S. citizenship if she married an alien.

Farm Loans: Congress established 12 Intermediate Credit Banks, located in the Federal Reserve System districts, and funded each bank with $5 million for farm loans.

Foreign Debts: Congress established a Foreign Debt Commission. [See Background, above]

TABLE OF KEY VOTES

Senate

Subject of Vote	Date of Vote	For	Against
GAO Created	April 25, 1921	Passed by voice vote	
Immigration Quotas Established	May 2, 1921	78	1
Veterans Bureau Created	July 20, 1921	Passed by voice vote	
Foreign Debt Commission Created	January 25, 1922	39	26
Four-Power Treaty Approved	March 24, 1922	67	27
Five-Power Treaty Approved	March 29, 1922	74	1
Nine-Power Treaty Approved	March 30, 1922	66	0
Agricultural Tariffs Raised	August 3, 1922	48	25
Women's Citizenship Legislation Passed	September 9, 1922	Passed by voice vote	
Farm Loan Program Established	January 16, 1923	Passed by voice vote	

House

Subject of Vote	Date of Vote	For	Against
Immigration Quotas Established	April 22, 1921	Passed by voice vote	
GAO Created	May 5, 1921	344	9
Veterans Bureau Created	June 10, 1921	335	0
Agricultural Tariffs Raised	June 21, 1921	288	127
Foreign Debt Commission Created	October 24, 1921	200	117
Women's Citizenship Legislation Passed	June 20, 1922	206	9
Farm Loan Program Established	March 1, 1923	306	36

[See note 7, p. xxix]

Foreign Policy: The Senate approved the three major treaties that came out of the Washington (D.C.) Conference for Limitation of Armaments. [See Background, above] First, there was the Four-Power Pacific Treaty, in which Britain, France, Japan, and the U.S. agreed to respect each other's territories in the Pacific Ocean and terminated the Anglo-Japanese Alliance of 1902. Second, there was the Five-Power Naval Limitation Treaty, which established a warship ratio for the major naval powers: five each for the U.S. and Great Britain, three for Japan, and 1.6 each for France and Italy. Third, in the Nine-Power Treaty, Belgium, Britain, France, Holland, Italy, Japan, Portugal, and the U.S. agreed with China to respect China's sovereign independence and to endorse the Open Door policy, of maintaining its territorial integrity.

Immigration: Congress passed immigration quota legislation. [See Background, above]

Tariffs: In the Fordney-McCumber Tariff Act, Congress responded to pressure from the sugar and textile industries as well as agricultural interests, and raised by 10-30 percent the tariffs on a variety of agricultural commodies and raw materials.

Veterans Bureau: Congress established the Veterans Bureau to oversee veterans' programs.

FAILED LEGISLATION

None of historical significance.

RELATIONS WITH
THE PRESIDENT

Harding was largely a passive president who let Congress take the initiative on legislative matters. His administration also was tainted by the Teapot Dome scandal.

Harding vetoed six bills during the 67th Congress. One veto was significant. On September 19, 1922, Harding vetoed veterans legislation adjusting benefits for veterans of World War I. The House voted to override the veto on September 20, 1922, by a vote of 258 to 54, but on the same day the Senate voted 44 to 28 to override, falling short of the required two-thirds majority, and thus the veto stood.

NOMINATIONS, APPOINTMENTS, AND CONFIRMATIONS

The Judiciary: On May 19, 1921, Supreme Court Chief Justice Edward D. White died. President Warren G. Harding nominated, and the Senate confirmed by voice vote, former President William H. Taft on June 30, 1921, to replace White. During 1922, three more vacancies opened on the Court. Justice John H. Clarke resigned on September 18, 1922; Justice William R. Day retired on November 13, 1922; and Justice Mahlon Pitney resigned on December 31, 1922.

President Harding filled all three vacancies by the end of the 67th Congress. First, Harding nominated, and the Senate confirmed by voice vote, George Sutherland on September 5, 1922. Second, Harding nominated Pierce Butler on December 5, 1922, and the Senate confirmed Butler on December 21, 1922, by a 61 to 8 vote. Finally, Harding nominated Edward T. Sanford on January 24, 1923, and the Senate confirmed Sanford on January 29, 1923, without a vote.

The Executive Branch: On March 4, 1921, President Harding nominated his cabinet, and the Senate confirmed all of the nominees by voice vote the same day. The nominees were Harry M. Daugherty to be attorney general, James J. Davis to be secretary of labor, Edwin Denby to be secretary of the Navy, Albert B. Fall to be secretary of the Interior, Herbert C. Hoover to be secretary of commerce, Charles Evans Hughes to be secretary of state, Andrew W. Mellon to be secretary of the Treasury, Henry A. Wallace to be secretary of agriculture, and John W. Weeks to be secretary of war. On February 27, 1923, Harding nominated Hubert Work to replace Fall as secretary of the Interior, due to Fall's involvement in the growing Teapot Dome scandal, and the Senate confirmed Work by voice vote the same day. [See Scandals, below]

IMPEACHMENTS

None.

CONSTITUTIONAL AMENDMENTS

None.

SCANDALS

The Teapot Dome scandal is discussed in the 68th Congress, but it began in the 66th Congress when Senator John B. Kendrick (Dem., Wyo.) introduced a resolution requesting Interior Secretary Albert B. Fall to explain the illegal drilling on public lands in Wyoming. Kendrick's resolution was Senate Resolution 277, which was "considered by unanimous consent and agreed to."

FURTHER READING

Frederick, Richard G. *Warren G. Harding: A Bibliography.* Westport, Conn.: Greenwood Press, 1992.

Murray, Robert K. *The Politics of Normalcy: Governmental Theory and Practice in the Harding-Coolidge Era.* New York: W.W. Norton,& Co. 1973.

Talmadge, John E. *Rebecca Latimer Felton: Nine Stormy Decades.* Athens, Ga.: University of Georgia Press, 1960.

The 68th Congress

MARCH 4, 1923 - MARCH 3, 1925

First Session: *December 3, 1923-June 7, 1924*
Second Session: *December 1, 1924-March 3, 1925*

In the 1922 elections for the 68th Congress, the Republicans lost 8 seats in the Senate, reducing their majority from 59 to 51 of the 96 seats. The Democrats gained 6 seats to hold a total of 43. Two seats were not held by either major party. One seat was held by the Farmer-Labor Party. In the House, the Republicans lost 76 seats, reducing their majority from 301 to 225 of the 435 seats. The Democrats gained 74 seats, to hold a total of 205. Five seats were held by neither major party. Two seats were held by the Farmer-Labor Party and 1 seat by the Socialist Party. [See note 3, p. xxix]

BACKGROUND

With his administration mired in the Teapot Dome scandal, President Warren G. Harding left Washington in the summer of 1923 to visit the West and recover his health. During the trip, Harding caught pneumonia, suffered from food poisoning, and died from an embolism on August 2, 1923, in San Francisco, California. The next day, Vice President Calvin Coolidge was sworn in as the 30th president of the United States.

After the collapse of the German economy in 1923 and the resulting hyperinflation that threatened to destabilize Europe, Coolidge appointed banker (and future vice president) Charles G. Dawes as the head of a commission formed to investigate the situation. On April 9, 1924, the commission proposed the Dawes Plan for restructuring and reducing Germany's debts. The Dawes Plan ultimately was adopted, and succeeded in stabilizing the German mark.

In 1924 Congress sent to the states for ratification a proposed constitutional amendment giving Congress the power to regulate child labor, but the necessary three-fourths of the states have never ratified it. Nellie Taylor Ross was elected the governor of Wyoming to complete the balance of her deceased husband's term. She was the first female governor in American history. Finally, Senator Robert M. LaFollette (Rep., Wis.) ran as the Progressive candidate in the 1924 presidential election. Approximately 16 percent of the American electorate voted for LaFollette, a percentage that would not be exceeded by an independent candidate until H. Ross Perot ran for president in 1992.

SENATE LEADERSHIP

Vice President: Calvin Coolidge served as vice president until he became president after the death of former President Warren G. Harding on August 2, 1923, leaving the Senate without a president until March 4, 1925. (Until the Twenty-fifth Amendment was ratified on February 10, 1967 [See 90th Congress], there was no mechanism for filling vacancies in the office of the vice president.) Coolidge had never served in Congress, but he had been governor of Massachusetts from 1919 to 1920 before being elected vice president.

President Pro Tempore: Albert Baird Cummins (Rep., Iowa). Cummins had been governor of Iowa from 1902 to 1908 and served in the Senate from 1908 until he died on July 30, 1926. He was president pro tem from the 66th through the 69th Congresses.

Majority Leader: Henry Cabot Lodge (Rep., Mass.), until he died on November 9, 1924. Charles Curtis (Rep., Kans.) became the new majority leader on November 28, 1924.

Majority Whip: Charles Curtis (Rep., Kans.), until he became the majority leader on November 28, 1924. Wesley L. Jones (Rep., Wash.) became the new majority whip the same day.

Minority Leader: Joseph T. Robinson (Dem., Ark.)

Minority Whip: Peter G. Gerry (Dem., R.I.)

Chairmen of Selected Key Committees: [See note 5, p. xxix]

Committee on Appropriations: Francis E. Warren (Rep., Wyo.)

Committee on Banking and Currency: George P. McLean (Rep., Conn.)

Committee on Finance: Reed Smoot (Rep., Utah)

Committee on Foreign Relations: Henry Cabot Lodge (Rep., Mass.), who died on November 9, 1924. William E. Borah (Rep., Idaho) became the next chairman.

Committee on the Judiciary: Frank B. Brandegee (Rep., Conn.), who died on October 14, 1924. Albert B. Cummins (Rep., Iowa) became the next chairman.

Committee on Military Affairs: James W. Wadsworth Jr. (Rep., N.Y.)

Committee on Rules: Charles Curtis (Rep., Kans.)

HOUSE LEADERSHIP

Speaker of the House: Frederick Huntington Gillett (Rep., Mass.) was reelected Speaker on December 3, 1923. Gillett first had been elected to Congress in the 53rd Congress and served as Speaker in the 66th through the 68th Congresses.

Majority Leader: Nicholas Longworth (Rep., Ohio)

Majority Whip: Albert H. Vestal (Rep., Ind.)

Minority Leader: Finis J. Garrett (Dem., Tenn.)

Minority Whip: William A. Oldfield (Dem., Ark.)

Chairmen of Selected Key Committees: [See note 5, p. xxix]

Committee on Agriculture: Gilbert N. Haugen (Rep., Iowa.)

Committee on Appropriations: Martin B. Madden (Rep., Ill.)

Committee on Banking, Finance and Urban Affairs: Louis T. McFadden (Rep., Pa.)

Committee on Foreign Affairs: Stephen G. Porter (Rep., Pa.)

Committee on the Judiciary: George S. Graham (Rep., Pa.)

Committee on Military Affairs: Julius Kahn (Rep., Calif.), who died on December 18, 1924. John C. McKenzie (Rep., Ill.) became the next chairman.

Committee on Naval Affairs: Thomas S. Butler (Rep., Pa.)

Committee on Rules: Bertrand H. Snell (Rep., N.Y.)

Committee on Ways and Means: William R. Green (Rep., Iowa)

ORGANIZATION AND ADMINISTRATION

No developments of significance. [See note 5, p. xxix]

MAJOR LEGISLATION PASSED

Foreign Service: Congress created the modern foreign service by consolidating the administration of American diplomats and consuls and providing for a system of hiring by examination and merit-based promotions.

C H R O N O L O G Y

March 4, 1923:	The 68th Congress begins.
October 1923:	Senate Public Lands Committee begins investigation of Teapot Dome affair.
December 3, 1923:	The first session begins, and Frederick Huntington Gillett (Rep., Mass.) is reelected Speaker of the House.
March 14, 1924:	President Coolidge nominates Curtis D. Wilbur to succeed Edwin Denby as secretary of the Navy.
March 18, 1924:	The Senate confirms Wilbur.
April 2, 1924:	Coolidge nominates Harlan F. Stone to succeed Harry M. Daugherty as attorney general.
April 7, 1924:	The Senate confirms Stone.
April 12, 1924:	Congress passes immigration legislation.
April 21, 1924:	Congress passes the Soldiers Bonus Bill.
May 14, 1924:	Congress passes legislation to reorganize the Foreign Service.
May 14, 1924:	Congress passes legislation making Native Americans U.S. citizens.
May 31, 1924:	Congress sends a Child Labor Amendment to the states for ratification, but it is never ratified.
June 7, 1924:	The first session ends.
December 1, 1924:	The second session begins.
December 2, 1924:	President Coolidge nominates Howard M. Gore to succeed Henry A. Wallace as secretary of agriculture.
December 4, 1924:	The Senate confirms Gore.
January 5, 1925:	Supreme Court Justice Joseph McKenna retires, and President Coolidge nominates Harlan F. Stone to replace McKenna.
February 5, 1925:	The Senate confirms Stone.
February 14, 1925:	President Coolidge nominates Frank B. Kellogg to succeed Charles Evans Hughes as secretary of state and William M. Jardine to succeed Howard M. Gore as secretary of agriculture.
February 16, 1925:	The Senate confirms Kellogg.
February 17, 1925:	The Senate confirms Jardine.
March 3, 1925:	The second session and the 68th Congress end.

[See note 6, p. xxix]

Immigration: Congress tightened the immigration quota system. The number of annual immigrants from each nation could not exceed 2 percent of the number of people from that nation already present in the U.S. as calculated by the 1890 census. The total number of immigrants was limited to 150,000, and Japanese immigration was completely prohibited.

Native Americans: Congress gave U.S. citizenship to all Native Americans.

Veterans: In the Soldiers Bonus Bill, Congress

TABLE OF KEY VOTES

Senate

Subject of Vote	Date of Vote	For	Against
Immigration Quotas Tightened	April 10, 1924	62	6
Veterans Bonus Authorized	April 21, 1924	67	17
Foreign Service Reorganized	May 14, 1924	Passed by voice vote	
Native Americans Given Citizenship	May 14, 1924	Passed by voice vote	
Child Labor Amendment Passed	May 31, 1924	62	23

House

Subject of Vote	Date of Vote	For	Against
Veterans Bonus Authorized	March 18, 1924	355	54
Native Americans Given Citizenship	March 18, 1924	Passed by voice vote	
Immigration Quotas Tightened	April 12, 1924	323	71
Child Labor Amendment Passed	April 26, 1924	297	69
Foreign Service Reorganized	May 1, 1924	134	27

[See note 7, p. xxix]

authorized a bonus for World War I veterans based on length of service. The bonus was in the form of a twenty-year annuity policy.

FAILED LEGISLATION

None of historical significance.

RELATIONS WITH THE PRESIDENT

Harding was largely a passive president who let Congress take the initiative on legislative matters. His administration also was tainted by the Teapot Dome scandal. President Coolidge also was a passive president, but he was very careful to avoid any taint from the Teapot Dome scandal, making no effort to protect the members of the Harding administration who were involved.

Coolidge vetoed seven bills during the 68th Congress, none of which involved significant legislation. Harding vetoed none.

NOMINATIONS, APPOINTMENTS, AND CONFIRMATIONS

The Judiciary: On January 5, 1925, Supreme Court Justice Joseph McKenna retired. President Calvin Coolidge nominated Harlan F. Stone to replace McKenna on the same day, and on February 5, 1925, the Senate confirmed Stone by a 71 to 6 vote.

The Executive Branch: After President Harding's death, President Calvin Coolidge kept a significant portion of Harding's cabinet [See 67th Congress], and no Senate confirmation vote was required for continuing those officials. On March 14, 1924, Coolidge nominated Curtis D. Wilbur to succeed Edwin Denby as secretary of the Navy, and on March 18, 1924, the Senate confirmed Wilbur by voice vote. On April 2, 1924, Coolidge nominated Harlan F. Stone to succeed Harry M. Daugherty as attorney general, and the Senate confirmed Stone by voice vote on April 7, 1924. On December 2, 1924, Coolidge nominated Howard M. Gore to succeed Henry A. Wallace as secretary of agriculture, and two days later the Senate confirmed Gore by voice vote. On February 14, 1925, Coolidge nominated Frank B. Kellogg to succeed Charles Evans Hughes as secretary of state and William M. Jardine to succeed Howard M. Gore as secretary of agriculture. The Senate confirmed Kellogg by voice vote on February 16, 1925, and confirmed Jardine on February 17, 1925, by voice vote.

IMPEACHMENTS

None.

CONSTITUTIONAL AMENDMENTS

Congress approved a Child Labor Amendment to the Constitution, which would have given Congress the power to regulate child labor throughout the nation, and sent it to the states for ratification. The necessary three-fourths of the states did not ratify it, however. The amendment was a response to restrictive Supreme Court decisions limiting Congress's power to legislate on matters traditionally reserved for the states. In the mid-1930s, however, the Supreme Court began to adopt a more liberal position, letting Congress use constitutional provisions, such as the federal power to regulate interstate commerce, in order to legislate with respect to such "state" matters as child labor. The Child Labor Amendment thus became largely irrelevant.

SCANDALS

By the 68th Congress, the Teapot Dome scandal had received national publicity. The scandal started when Senator John B. Kendrick (Dem., Wyo.) introduced a resolution on April 15, 1922, in the 67th Congress, asking Interior Secretary Albert B. Fall to explain the secret lease of federal lands in Wyoming to a private enterprise. The lands in question were an oil rich area known as the Teapot Dome, which was supposed to be held as a petroleum reserve for the U.S. Navy. Instead, Harry F. Sinclair's Mammoth Oil Company was drilling in the area. Congressional hearings led to the replacement of Fall as secretary of the Interior shortly before the end of the 67th Congress [See Executive Branch nominations]. Other members of the Harding administration were implicated in the scandal, which may have been the cause of Harding's subsequent health problems. The Teapot Dome scandal resulted in federal grand jury indictments of former Interior Secretary Fall and other persons involved in the affair. Fall was eventually convicted for accepting bribes and sent to prison.

FURTHER READING

Frederick, Richard G. *Warren G. Harding: A Bibliography.* Westport, Conn.: Greenwood Press, 1992.

Mason, Alpheus Thomas. *Harlan Fiske Stone: Pillar of the Law.* New York: Viking Press, 1956.

Murray, Robert K. *The Politics of Normalcy: Governmental Theory and Practice in the Harding-Coolidge Era.* New York: W.W. Norton & Co., 1973.

The 69th Congress

MARCH 4, 1925 - MARCH 3, 1927

Special Senate Session: March 4, 1925-March 18, 1925
First Session: December 7, 1925-July 3, 1926
Second Session: December 6, 1926-March 3, 1927

The Senate held a special session to vote on the confirmation of presidential appointees to various offices. [See note 1, p. xxix]

In the 1924 elections for the 69th Congress, the Republicans gained 5 seats in the Senate, raising their majority from 51 to 56 of the 96 seats. The Democrats lost 4 seats, reducing their total to 39. One seat was held by the Farmer Labor Party. In the House, the Republicans gained 22 seats, giving them a majority of 247 of the 435 seats. The Democrats lost 22 seats, leaving them with a total of 183. Five seats were not held by either major party. Three of these seats were held by the Farmer-Labor Party, 1 seat by the American Labor Party, and 1 seat by the Socialist Party. [See note 3, p. xxix]

BACKGROUND

On March 4, 1925, Calvin Coolidge was inaugurated for his first full term as the 30th president of the United States. During the summer of 1925, the famous Scopes "monkey trial" took place in Tennessee. Former presidential candidate William Jennings Bryan assisted the prosecution in its effort to enforce a state law against teaching evolution. Although John T. Scopes was convicted and fined $100 for teaching evolution, the case made fundamentalist religious principles appear foolish in the face of modern science.

If science was making progress, race relations were not. The Ku Klux Klan had become a pow-

erful political organization, claiming to have millions of members nationwide. Tens of thousands of KKK members marched in Washington, D.C., on August 8, 1925 in a show of strength.

The Senate on January 27, 1926, approved an agreement whereby the U.S. could join the Permanent Court of International Justice, which was then part of the League of Nations and is now known as the World Court. The Senate attached five conditions to U.S. membership, however, and one condition concerning advisory opinions was not acceptable to the court. Therefore, the U.S. did not become a member of the court. Also in 1926, Congress passed the Revenue Act of 1926, which reduced federal taxes. American Marines landed in Nicaragua on May 10 in order to stabilize the government after a local rebellion. Congress created the Army Air Corps, in recognition of the growing military value of aircraft, although the most progressive advocates of air power such as General "Billy" Mitchell, still were ignored and their views ridiculed. In 1926 Henry Ford adopted the 40-hour work week for workers at the Ford Motor Company, setting a progressive precedent for American industry and organized labor.

Before the 69th Congress ended in 1927, Coolidge called for another international convention on naval disarmament. Only three great powers including the U.S. attended the conference, which ended in failure. Finally, Congress established a Federal Radio Commission with the

C H R O N O L O G Y

March 4, 1925:	The 69th Congress and a special Senate session begin.
March 5, 1925:	President Coolidge nominates Charles B. Warren to succeed Harlan F. Stone as attorney general.
March 6, 1925:	The Senate elects Albert Baird Cummins (Rep., Iowa) and George Higgins Moses (Rep., N.H.) presidents pro tem.
March 10, 1925:	The Senate votes not to confirm Warren.
March 12, 1925:	President Coolidge nominates Warren again.
March 16, 1925:	The Senate again votes not to confirm Warren.
March 17, 1925:	President Coolidge nominates, and the Senate confirms, John G. Sargent to be attorney general.
March 18, 1925:	The special Senate session ends.
December 7, 1925:	The first session begins, and Nicholas Longworth (Rep., Ohio) is elected Speaker of the House.
December 8, 1925:	President Coolidge nominates Dwight F. Davis to succeed John W. Weeks as secretary of war.
December 15, 1925:	The Senate confirms Davis.
January 27, 1926:	The Senate approves U.S. membership in the Permanent Court of International Justice (the World Court), but attaches five conditions that ultimately derail U.S. membership.
February 1, 1926:	Congress passes the Revenue Act of 1926.
April 12, 1926:	Congress passes the Air Commerce Act.
May 10, 1926:	Congress passes legislation concerning railroad labor disputes.
June 2, 1926:	Congress passes legislation creating the Army Air Corps.
July 1, 1926:	Congress passes the Radio Control Act.
July 3, 1926:	The first session ends.
December 6, 1926:	The second session begins.
March 3, 1927:	The second session and the 69th Congress end.

[See note 6, p. xxix]

authority to regulate broadcasters and issue rules on such matters as transmission frequencies. The Federal Radio Commission was the predecessor of today's Federal Communications Commission.

SENATE LEADERSHIP

Vice President: Charles Gates Dawes was elected vice president on the Coolidge ticket in November 1924. Dawes had never served in Congress, but he had a distinguished career in government before becoming vice president. He had been director of the Bureau of the Budget, served on the Allied Reparations Commission, and shared the 1925 Nobel Peace Prize for drafting the "Dawes Plan," which helped to stabilize Germany's economy and currency.

Presidents Pro Tempore: In an unusual procedural move, the Senate elected Albert Baird Cummins (Rep., Iowa) and George Higgins Moses (Rep., N.H.) presidents pro tempore on March

Robert M. LaFollette (Rep., Wis.) was first elected to the 69th Congress after his unsuccessful campaign for the presidency as a Progressive in 1924.

6, 1925. Cummins had been governor of Iowa from 1902 to 1908 and served in the Senate from 1908 until he died on July 30, 1926. He was president pro tem from the 66th through the 69th Congresses. Moses first had been elected to the Senate in 1918 and was president pro tem from the 69th through the 72nd Congresses.

Majority Leader: Charles Curtis (Rep., Kans.)

Majority Whip: Wesley L. Jones (Rep., Wash.)

Minority Leader: Joseph T. Robinson (Dem., Ark.)

Minority Whip: Peter G. Gerry (Dem., R.I.)

Chairmen of Selected Key Committees: [See note 5, p. xxix]

Committee on Appropriations: Francis E. Warren (Rep., Wyo.)

Committee on Banking and Currency: George P. McLean (Rep., Conn.)

Committee on Finance: Reed Smoot (Rep., Utah)

Committee on Foreign Relations: William E. Borah (Rep., Idaho)

Committee on the Judiciary: Albert B. Cummins (Rep., Iowa), who died on July 30, 1926. George W. Norris (Rep., Neb.) became the next chairman.

Committee on Military Affairs: James W. Wadsworth Jr. (Rep., N.Y.)

Committee on Naval Affairs: Frederick Hale (Rep., Maine)

Committee on Rules: Charles Curtis (Rep., Kans.)

HOUSE LEADERSHIP

Speaker of the House: Nicholas Longworth (Rep., Ohio) was elected Speaker on December 7, 1925. Longworth first had been elected to Congress in the 58th Congress and served as Speaker from the 69th through the 71st Congresses. Longworth reestablished some of the power of the speakership that had been lost under Speaker Joseph G. Cannon (Rep., Ill.; Speaker 1903-1911). Longworth used his power to determine committee seniority, to take seniority from fellow Republicans who opposed him, and like Cannon, he used a small group of trusted loyalists to enforce his will on the House. However, Longworth never went as far as Cannon did in arbitrarily changing House rules at his whim, and was much more willing to use compromise and negotiation.

Majority Leader: Nicholas Longworth, until he became Speaker of the House on December 7, 1925. John Q. Tilson (Rep., Conn.) became the new majority leader that same day.

Majority Whip: Albert H. Vestal (Rep., Ind.)

Minority Leader: Finis J. Garrett (Dem., Tenn.)

Minority Whip: William A. Oldfield (Dem., Ark.)

Chairmen of Selected Key Committees: [See note 5, p. xxix]

Committee on Agriculture: Gilbert N. Haugen

TABLE OF KEY VOTES

Senate

Subject of Vote	Date of Vote	For	Against
Aviation Bureau Established	December 16, 1925	Passed by voice vote	
World Court Membership Approved	January 27, 1926	76	17
Taxes Reduced	February 1, 1926	58	9
Railroad Mediation Board Established	May 10, 1926	69	13
Army Air Corps Established	June 2, 1926	Passed by voice vote	
Radio Commission Established	July 1, 1926	Passed by voice vote	

House

Subject of Vote	Date of Vote	For	Against
Taxes Reduced	December 18, 1925	390	25
Railroad Mediation Board Established	March 1, 1926	381	13
Radio Commission Established	March 15, 1926	218	123
Aviation Bureau Established	April 12, 1926	229	80
Army Air Corps Established	May 5, 1926	Passed by voice vote	

[See note 7, p. xxix]

(Rep., Iowa)

Committee on Appropriations: Martin B. Madden (Rep., Ill.)

Committee on Banking, Finance, and Urban Affairs: Louis T. McFadden (Rep., Pa.)

Committee on Foreign Affairs: Stephen G. Porter (Rep., Pa.)

Committee on the Judiciary: George S. Graham (Rep., Pa.)

Committee on Military Affairs: John M. Morin (Rep., Pa.)

Committee on Naval Affairs: Thomas S. Butle (Rep., Pa.)

Committee on Rules: Bertrand H. Snell (Rep. N.Y.)

Committee on Ways and Means: William R Green (Rep., Iowa)

ORGANIZATION AND ADMINISTRATION

No developments of significance [See note 5, p xxix]

MAJOR LEGISLATION PASSED

Army Air Corps: Congress established the Army Air Corps.

Aviation: In the Air Commerce Act, Congress established an Air Commerce Bureau within the Department of Commerce to supervise civil aviation, license pilots and their aircraft, and issue safety regulations.

Permanent Court of International Justice: The Senate approved an international agreement whereby the U.S. would join the Permanent Court of International Justice (now the World Court), but the Senate attached conditions to its acceptance, which resulted in the U.S. not becoming a member of the Court. [See Background, above]

Radio: In the Radio Control Act, Congress established the Federal Radio Commission and gave it the authority to regulate radio broadcasters and issue rules on such matters as transmission frequencies. The Federal Radio Commission was the predecessor to the modern Federal Communications Commission.

Railroads: Congress reorganized the system for resolving railroad labor disputes and replaced the Railroad Labor Board with a Board of Mediation.

Taxes: In the Revenue Act of 1926, Congress reduced the federal income tax for individuals, and also reduced inheritance taxes and excise taxes. For corporations, however, Congress raised taxes.

FAILED LEGISLATION

None of historical significance.

RELATIONS WITH THE PRESIDENT

Like his predecessor, Warren G. Harding, President Coolidge was largely a passive president with no major agenda in Congress. Coolidge was probusiness and made no effort to stem the growing speculation on Wall Street that was propelling the stock market to record levels and also encouraging risky investment schemes that had little or no financial underpinnings.

Coolidge vetoed 11 bills during the 69th Congress, none of which involved significant legislation.

NOMINATIONS, APPOINTMENTS, AND CONFIRMATIONS

The Judiciary: There were no significant nominations, appointments, or confirmations in the federal judiciary during the 69th Congress.

The Executive Branch: Twice, President Coolidge tried to get Charles B. Warren confirmed to succeed Harlan F. Stone as attorney general. Coolidge first nominated Warren on March 5, 1925, and the Senate vote on March 10, 1925, was 39 in favor and 41 against. Warren, a prominent attorney, was attacked for his close ties with the monopolistic sugar industry, and his critics felt that as attorney general he could not be trusted to enforce the anti-trust laws. On March 12, 1925, Coolidge nominated Warren again, and on March 16, 1925, the Senate vote was 39 in favor and 46 against. Finally, on March 17, 1925, Coolidge nominated John G. Sargent to be attorney general, and on the same day the Senate confirmed Sargent by voice vote. On December 8, 1925, Coolidge nominated Dwight F. Davis to succeed John W. Weeks as secretary of war, and on December 15, 1925, the Senate confirmed Davis by voice vote.

IMPEACHMENTS

The House voted to impeach federal Judge George W. English, but he resigned and thus avoided trial in the Senate. English, a judge in the eastern district of Illinois, was accused of abusing the power of his office by making overly harsh and oppressive rulings against parties he disfavored. His case was dismissed on December 13, 1926.

CONSTITUTIONAL AMENDMENTS

None.

Further Reading

Fuess, Claude Moore. *Calvin Coolidge, The Man From Vermont*. Hamden, Conn.: Archon Books, 1965.

Murray, Robert K. *The Politics of Normalcy: Governmental Theory and Practice in the Harding-Coolidge Era*. New York: W.W. Norton & Co., 1973.

Timmons, Bascom N. *Charles G. Dawes: Portrait of an American*. New York: Garland Publishers, 1979 (reprint of 1953 edition).

The 70th Congress

MARCH 4, 1927-MARCH 3, 1929

First Session: December 5, 1927-May 29, 1928
Second Session: December 3, 1928-March 3, 1929

In the 1926 elections for the 70th Congress, the Republicans lost 7 seats in the Senate, reducing their majority from 56 to 49 of the 96 seats. The Democrats gained 7 seats to hold a total of 46. One seat was held by the Farmer-Labor Party. In the House, the Republicans lost 10 seats, reducing their majority from 247 to 237 of the 435 seats. The Democrats gained 12 seats to hold a total of 195. Three seats were not held by either major party. Two of these seats were held by the Farmer-Labor Party and 1 seat by the Socialist Party. [See note 3, p. xxix]

BACKGROUND

In the 70th Congress, the decade known as the Roaring Twenties was coming to a close. Most Americans believed that their country was entering a new era of prosperity, and the financial markets were experiencing unprecedented growth. Behind the appearance of prosperity, however, there were deep-seated economic problems.

First, Europe really had never recovered from World War I, and its stability depended on America's ability and willingness to support the western world's economy and credit markets. Second, rural poverty at home was on the rise. Improvements in transportation and mechanized agriculture meant that farmers faced both increased competition and lower prices for their products. In the South, rural poverty was particularly acute. African American farmers, who usually did not own their own land but were share-croppers, were reduced to a condition of servitude not much better than pre-Civil War slavery. This was due to the system in the South known as peonage, where white-dominated legislatures passed laws that made offenses such as breach of contract and vagrancy a crime. The effect of these legal measures was to discourage African Americans from breaking out of their share-cropper status and migrating to the cities in search of greater economic opportunities. Third, much of the boom in the financial markets of Wall Street was due to overspeculation and high risk borrowing. For example, Samuel Insull created a holding company empire in the electric utility industry, and shares of his companies were popular with investors. In reality however, his companies, burdened by large debts, were greatly over-valued and eventually collapsed in 1932 with huge losses for investors.

President Coolidge did nothing during the 70th Congress to restrain the over-heated economy. Coolidge may have feared that the end was near, because on August 2, 1927, he announced that he would not run for reelection in the 1928 elections.

The major legislative achievements of the 70th Congress included a Merchant Marine Act, which attempted to stimulate the depressed American shipping industry by providing subsidies and generous government contracts, and ratification of the Kellogg-Briand Peace Pact on January 15, 1929. The peace pact, initiated by the French foreign minister, was an agreement by the major powers, including the United States,

CHRONOLOGY

March 4, 1927:	The 70th Congress begins.
December 5, 1927:	The first session begins, and Nicholas Longworth (Rep., Ohio) is reelected Speaker.
December 15, 1927:	George Higgins Moses (Rep., N.H.) is reelected Senate president pro tem.
April 24, 1928:	Congress passes flood control legislation.
May 5, 1928:	Congress passes the Jones-White Merchant Marine Act.
May 29, 1928:	The first session ends.
December 3, 1928:	The second session begins.
December 6, 1928:	President Coolidge nominates William F. Whiting to succeed Herbert C. Hoover as secretary of commerce and Roy O. West to succeed Hubert Work as secretary of the Interior.
December 11, 1928:	The Senate confirms Whiting.
January 15, 1929:	The Senate approves the Kellogg-Briand Treaty.
January 21, 1929:	The Senate confirms West.
February 13, 1929:	Congress passes legislation concerning American Samoa.
March 3, 1929:	The second session and the 70th Congress end.

[See note 6, p. xxix]

to outlaw war and use arbitration as a means of resolving international disputes.

SENATE LEADERSHIP

Vice President: Charles Gates Dawes. [See biographical note in 69th Congress]

President Pro Tempore: George Higgins Moses (Rep., N.H.) was reelected on December 15, 1927. Moses first had been elected to the Senate in 1918 and was president pro tem from the 69th through the 72nd Congresses.

Majority Leader: Charles Curtis (Rep., Kans.)

Majority Whip: Wesley L. Jones (Rep., Wash.)

Minority Leader: Joseph T. Robinson (Dem., Ark.)

Minority Whip: Peter G. Gerry (Dem., R.I.)

Chairmen of Selected Key Committees: [See note 5, p. xxix]

Committee on Appropriations: Francis E. Warren (Rep., Wyo.)

Committee on Banking and Currency: Peter Norbeck (Rep., S.D.)

Committee on Finance: Reed Smoot (Rep., Utah)

Committee on Foreign Relations: William E. Borah (Rep., Idaho)

Committee on the Judiciary: George W. Norris (Rep., Neb.)

Committee on Military Affairs: David Reed

TABLE OF KEY VOTES

Senate

Subject of Vote	Date of Vote	For	Against
Shipping Industry Aid Passed	January 31, 1928	53	31
Flood Control Bill Passed	March 27, 1928	70	0
American Samoa Administration Established	May 3, 1928	Passed by voice vote	
Kellogg-Briand Treaty Approved	January 15, 1929	85	1

House

Subject of Vote	Date of Vote	For	Against
Flood Control Bill Passed	April 24, 1928	254	91
Shipping Industry Aid Passed	May 5, 1928	Passed by voice vote	
American Samoa Administration Established	February 13, 1929	Passed by voice vote	

[See note 7, p. xxix]

(Rep., Pa.)

Committee on Naval Affairs: Frederick Hale (Rep., Maine)

Committee on Rules: Charles Curtis (Rep., Kans.)

HOUSE LEADERSHIP

Speaker of the House: Nicholas Longworth (Rep., Ohio) was reelected Speaker on December 5, 1927. [See biographical note in 69th Congress]

Majority Leader: John Q. Tilson (Rep., Conn.)

Majority Whip: Albert H. Vestal (Rep., Ind.)

Minority Leader: Finis J. Garrett (Dem., Tenn.)

Minority Whip: William A. Oldfield (Dem., Ark.) until he died on November 19, 1928. John McDuffie (Dem., Ala.) became the new minority whip on December 3, 1928.

Chairmen of Selected Key Committees: [See note 5, p. xxix]

Committee on Agriculture: Gilbert N. Haugen (Rep., Iowa)

Committee on Appropriations: Martin B. Madden (Rep., Ill.), who died on April 27, 1928. Daniel R. Anthony Jr. (Rep., Kans.) became the next chairman.

Committee on Banking, Finance and Urban Affairs: Louis T. McFadden (Rep., Pa.)

Committee on Foreign Affairs: Stephen G. Porter (Rep., Pa.)

Committee on the Judiciary: George S. Graham (Rep., Pa.)

Committee on Military Affairs: John M. Morin (Rep., Pa.)

Committee on Naval Affairs: Thomas S. Butler (Rep., Pa.), who died on May 26, 1928. Frederick A. Britten (Rep., Ill.) became the next chairman.

Committee on Rules: Bertrand H. Snell (Rep., N.Y.)

Committee on Ways and Means: William R. Green (Rep., Iowa), who resigned effective March 31, 1928. Willis C. Hawley (Rep., Ore.) became the next chairman.

ORGANIZATION AND ADMINISTRATION

No developments of significance. [See note 5, p. xxix]

MAJOR LEGISLATION PASSED

American Samoa: Congress provided for the administration of the islands that comprise American Samoa.

Flood Control: Congress authorized $325 million for a ten-year program to improve flood control in the Mississippi Valley.

Foreign Policy: The Senate approved the Kellogg-Briand Peace Pact, in which the major powers renounced war in favor of international arbitration. [See Background, above]

Shipping: In the Jones-White Merchant Marine Act, Congress attempted to stimulate the depressed American shipping industry by providing subsidies and generous government contracts. The act's measures included a ship-construction loan fund, long-term mail carriage contracts, and the sale of government ships at bargain prices to private concerns.

FAILED LEGISLATION

None of historical significance.

RELATIONS WITH THE PRESIDENT

President Coolidge closed out his administration with an unambitious legislative agenda, and no effort to stem the speculative tide on Wall Street that would lead to disaster for the economy in the 71st Congress.

Coolidge vetoed 32 bills during the 70th Congress, none of which involved significant legislation.

NOMINATIONS, APPOINTMENTS, AND CONFIRMATIONS

The Judiciary: There were no significant nominations, appointments, or confirmations in the federal judiciary during the 70th Congress.

The Executive Branch: On December 6, 1928, President Coolidge nominated William F. Whiting to succeed Herbert C. Hoover as secretary of commerce and Roy O. West to succeed Hubert Work as secretary of the Interior. The Senate confirmed Whiting on December 11, 1928, by voice vote, and confirmed West on January 21, 1929, by a vote of 53 to 27.

IMPEACHMENTS

None.

CONSTITUTIONAL AMENDMENTS

None.

FURTHER READING

Fuess, Claude Moore. *Calvin Coolidge, The Man From Vermont.* Hamden, Conn.: Archon Books, 1965.

Murray, Robert K. *The Politics of Normalcy: Governmental Theory and Practice in the Harding-Coolidge Era.* New York: W.W. Norton & Co., 1973.

Timmons, Bascom N. *Charles G. Dawes: Portrait of an American.* New York: Garland Publishers, 1979 (reprint of 1953 edition).

The 71st Congress

MARCH 4, 1929-MARCH 3, 1931

Special Senate Session: March 4, 1929-March 5, 1929
First Session: April 15, 1929-November 22, 1929
Second Session: December 2, 1929-July 3, 1930
Special Senate Session: July 7, 1930-July 21, 1930
Third Session: December 1, 1930-March 3, 1931

The Senate held a special session in March of 1929 to vote on the confirmation of presidential appointees to various offices. [See note 1, p. xxix] The Senate held a second special session in July 1930 to decide whether to ratify a naval arms treaty.

In the 1928 elections for the 71st Congress, the Republicans gained 7 seats in the Senate, raising their majority from 49 to 56 of the 96 seats. The Democrats lost 7 seats, reducing their total to 39. One seat was held by the Farmer-Labor Party. In the House, the Republicans gained 30 seats, giving them a majority of 267 of the 435 seats. The Democrats lost 28 seats, leaving them with a total of 167 seats. One seat was held by the Farmer-Labor Party. [See note 3, p. xxix]

BACKGROUND

According to the census of 1930, the population of the United States as of April 1, 1930, was 122,775,046, resulting in a population density of 41.2 persons for each of the country's 2,977,128 square miles. This was a population increase of 16.1 percent over the 1920 census.

Herbert Hoover was inaugurated on March 4, 1929, as the 31st president of the United States. In 1929 the financial markets were booming, as represented by the Dow Jones Industrial Average of 30 leading New York Stock Exchange companies, which was setting historic highs. This apparent prosperity, however, masked deep-rooted economic problems. In September 1929 the government released statistics showing that over 50 percent of American families had annual incomes of less than $2,000, which was considered the basic income necessary to sustain a household. Congress did take some action to help the nation's farmers by passing the Agricultural Marketing Act, which created a Federal Farm Board to establish cooperatives and other entities for marketing farm products. The act also provided for low interest loans, government purchases of excess crops, and subsidized export sales to other nations.

On October 29, 1929, the Wall Street collapse known as Black Tuesday occurred. A record 16 million shares of stock were traded on the New York Stock Exchange, the largest stock market in the United States, and prices dropped more than 12 percent that day. During the remainder of 1929 and throughout 1930, stock prices continued to decline. From a high of 381.2 during 1929, the Dow Jones Industrial Average went as low as 160 during 1930, a loss of over 50 percent of its value. The stock market crash was the beginning of the Great Depression, which would not end until World War II. The Great Depression was not limited to the United States, and the western world's entire economic system went into a slump.

In 1930 Congress tried to protect American industry from world economic troubles by enacting the Hawley-Smoot Tariff Act. The act raised tariffs on imported goods in order to protect

CHRONOLOGY

March 4, 1929:	The 71st Congress and a special Senate session begin.
March 5, 1929:	President Hoover nominates his cabinet, and the Senate confirms all of the nominees. The special Senate session ends.
April 15, 1929:	The first session begins, and Nicholas Longworth (Rep., Ohio) is reelected Speaker of the House.
May 7, 1929:	Congress passes the Agricultural Marketing Act.
May 21, 1929:	The Senate ends the practice of routinely holding executive sessions (on treaties and nominations) behind closed doors.
November 22, 1929:	The first session ends.
December 2, 1929:	The second session begins.
December 9, 1929:	Hoover nominates, and the Senate confirms, Patrick J. Hurley to succeed James W. Good as secretary of war.
February 3, 1930:	Supreme Court Chief Justice William H. Taft retires, and President Hoover nominates Charles Evans Hughes to replace Taft.
February 13, 1930:	The Senate confirms Hughes.
March 8, 1930:	Supreme Court Justice Edward T. Sanford dies.
March 21, 1930:	President Hoover nominates John J. Parker to replace Sanford.
March 24, 1930:	Congress passes the Hawley-Smoot Tariff Act.
May 7, 1930:	The Senate votes not to confirm Parker.
May 9, 1930:	President Hoover nominates Owen J. Roberts to replace Justice Sanford.
May 20, 1930:	The Senate confirms Roberts.
June 30, 1930:	Congress creates the Veterans Administration.
July 3, 1930:	The second session ends.
July 7, 1930:	A second special Senate session begins.
July 21, 1930:	The second special Senate session ends.
December 1, 1930:	The third session begins.
December 3, 1930:	President Hoover nominates William N. Doak to succeed James J. Davis as secretary of labor.
December 8, 1930:	The Senate confirms Doak.
December 11, 1930:	Congress passes public works legislation.
February 17, 1931:	Congress passes legislation adopting the national anthem.
March 3, 1931:	The third session and the 71st Congress end.

[See note 6, p. xxix]

domestic markets. Instead of helping American industry, the act hurt international trade and made economic conditions worse, because most major nations retaliated by raising their tariffs on American goods. Also during 1930, Congress created the Veterans Administration and enacted public works legislation in order to create jobs for the unemployed.

In 1931, before the end of the 71st Congress, the Wickersham Commission issued a report or

January 19 stating that Prohibition was ineffective and that the Eighteenth Amendment should be revised. The government had found that Prohibition practically was impossible to enforce, since a large section of the public opposed it and continued to drink alcoholic beverages, creating a large illegal market serviced by organized crime.

SENATE LEADERSHIP

Vice President: Charles Curtis first had been elected to Congress as a representative from Kansas in the 53rd Congress and had been elected to the Senate in 1907. Curtis left the Senate when he was elected vice president on Herbert Hoover's ticket in the 1928 elections.

President Pro Tempore: George Higgins Moses (Rep., N.H.). Moses first had been elected to the Senate in 1918 and was president pro tem from the 69th through the 72nd Congresses.

Majority Leader: James E. Watson (Rep., Ind.)

Majority Whip: Simeon D. Fess (Rep., Ohio)

Minority Leader: Joseph T. Robinson (Dem., Ark.)

Minority Whip: Morris Sheppard (Dem., Tex.)

Chairmen of Selected Key Committees: [See also Organization and Administration, below]

Committee on Appropriations: Francis E. Warren (Rep., Wyo.), who died on November 24, 1929. Wesley L. Jones (Rep., Wash.) became the next chairman.

Committee on Banking and Currency: Peter Norbeck (Rep., S.D.)

Committee on Finance: Reed Smoot (Rep., Utah)

Committee on Foreign Relations: William E. Borah (Rep., Idaho)

Committee on the Judiciary: George W. Norris (Rep., Neb.)

Committee on Military Affairs: David Reed (Rep., Pa.)

Committee on Naval Affairs: Frederick Hale (Rep., Maine)

Committee on Rules: George H. Moses (Rep., N.H.)

HOUSE LEADERSHIP

Speaker of the House: Nicholas Longworth (Rep., Ohio) was reelected Speaker on April 15, 1929. [See biographical note in 69th Congress]

Majority Leader: John Q. Tilson (Rep., Conn.)

Majority Whip: Albert H. Vestal (Rep., Ind.)

Minority Leader: John N. Garner (Dem., Tex.)

Minority Whip: John McDuffie (Dem., Ala.)

Chairmen of Selected Key Committees: [See also Organization and Administration, below]

Committee on Agriculture: Gilbert N. Haugen (Rep., Iowa).

Committee on Appropriations: William R. Wood (Rep., Ind.).

Committee on Banking, Finance, and Urban Affairs: Louis T. McFadden (Rep., Pa.)

Committee on Foreign Affairs: Stephen G. Porter (Rep., Pa.)

Committee on the Judiciary: George S. Graham (Rep., Pa.)

Committee on Military Affairs: W. Francis James (Rep., Mich.)

Committee on Naval Affairs: Frederick A. Britten (Rep., Ill.)

Committee on Rules: Bertrand H. Snell (Rep., N.Y.)

Committee on Ways and Means: Willis C. Hawley (Rep., Ore.)

ORGANIZATION AND ADMINISTRATION

The Senate has the exclusive responsibility for confirming presidential nominees and for approv-

TABLE OF KEY VOTES

Senate

Subject of Vote	Date of Vote	For	Against
Aid to Farmers Approved	May 7, 1929	54	39
Tariffs Raised	March 24, 1930	53	31
Veterans Administration Created	June 30, 1930	Passed by voice vote	
Public Works Bill Passed	December 11, 1930	Passed by voice vote	
National Anthem Adopted	February 17, 1931	Passed by voice vote	

House

Subject of Vote	Date of Vote	For	Against
Aid to Farmers Approved	April 25, 1929	366	35
Tariffs Raised	May 28, 1929	264	147
National Anthem Adopted	April 21, 1930	Passed by voice vote	
Veterans Administration Created	April 29, 1930	190	61
Public Works Bill Passed	December 9, 1930	Passed by voice vote	

[See note 7, p. xxix]

ing treaties. During this Congress, the Senate largely abandoned its historic practice of conducting "executive sessions" in secrecy. There were so many leaks to the press that the executive sessions in reality had not been secret for many years. [See note 5, p. xxix]

MAJOR LEGISLATION PASSED

Agriculture: In the Agricultural Marketing Act, Congress created the Federal Farm Board and approved several measures to help the nation's farmers. [See Background, above]

National Anthem: Congress adopted "The Star Spangled Banner" by Francis Scott Key as the national anthem.

Public Works: Congress approved some limited public works spending in order to create jobs for the unemployed during the growing Great Depression.

Tariffs: In the Hawley-Smoot Tariff Act, Congress raised duties on imports in an unsuccessful effort to protect American industry from the worldwide economic depression. [See Background, above] This legislation was initially intended by President Hoover to raise tariffs primarily on agricultural imports. Congress, however, added so many additional tariff hikes on industrial goods that in its final form the bill raised tariffs on nearly 900 items. Hoover refused to block this expansion of tariff protectionism by Congress, even though 1,028 economists signed a joint letter urging him to do so. The economists' warning to Hoover proved to be correct, as over two dozen countries retaliated by raising their tariffs on U.S. goods.

Veterans: Congress created the Veterans Administration, with jurisdiction over all veteran programs.

FAILED LEGISLATION

None of historical significance.

RELATIONS WITH THE PRESIDENT

President Hoover had a distinguished career in public service, but had the misfortune to be president during the onset of the Great Depression. Hoover believed that the economy would correct itself, and opposed anti-Depression measures in Congress.

Hoover vetoed 19 bills during the 71st Congress, none of which involved significant legislation.

NOMINATIONS, APPOINTMENTS, AND CONFIRMATIONS

The Judiciary: On February 3, 1930, Supreme Court Chief Justice William H. Taft retired and President Hoover nominated Charles Evans Hughes, a former justice of the Court who had resigned during the 64th Congress, to replace him. The Senate confirmed Hughes by a 52 to 26 vote on February 13, 1930. Justice Edward T. Sanford died on March 8, 1930, and President Hoover nominated John J. Parker to replace him on March 21, 1930. The Senate rejected Parker's nomination by a 41 to 39 vote on May 7, 1930. On May 9, 1930, President Hoover nominated Owen J. Roberts, and the Senate confirmed Roberts on May 20, 1930, by voice vote.

The Executive Branch: On March 5, 1929, President Hoover nominated Charles F. Adams to be secretary of the Navy, James W. Good to be secretary of war, Arthur M. Hyde to be secretary of agriculture, Robert P. Lamont to be secretary of commerce, William DeWitt Mitchell to be attorney general, Henry L. Stimson to be secretary of state, and Ray L. Wilbur to be secretary of the Interior. The Senate confirmed all of the nominees the same day. Hoover kept two Coolidge administration officials, namely, Secretary of Labor James J. Davis and Secretary

of the Treasury Andrew W. Mellon, for whom no Senate confirmation vote was required. On December 9, 1929, Hoover nominated, and the Senate confirmed by voice vote, Patrick J. Hurley to succeed Good as secretary of war. On December 3, 1930, Hoover nominated William N. Doak to succeed Davis as secretary of labor, and the Senate confirmed Doak by voice vote on December 8, 1930.

IMPEACHMENTS

None.

CONSTITUTIONAL AMENDMENTS

None.

FURTHER READING

Burner, David. *Herbert Hoover, A Public Life.* New York: Alfred A. Knopf, 1979.

Clavin, Patricia. *The Failure of Economic Diplomacy: Britain, Germany, France, and the United States 1931-1936.* New York: St. Martin's Press, 1995.

Liebovich, Louis. *Bylines in Despair: Herbert Hoover, the Great Depression, and the U.S. News Media.* Westport, Conn.: Praeger, 1994.

Lyons, Eugene. *Herbert Hoover: A Biography.* Norwalk, Conn.: Easton Press, 1989 (reprint of 1964 edition).

McElvaine, Robert S. *The Great Depression: America, 1929-1941.* New York: Times Books, 1993.

The 72nd Congress

MARCH 4, 1931 - MARCH 3, 1933

First Session: *December 7, 1931-July 16, 1932*
Second Session: *December 5, 1932-March 3, 1933*

In the 1930 elections for the 72nd Congress, the Republicans lost 8 seats in the Senate, reducing their majority from 56 to 48 of the 96 seats. The Democrats gained 8 seats to give them a total of 47. One seat was held by the Farmer-Labor Party. In the House, the Democrats gained 53 seats, giving them a new majority of 220 of the 435 seats. The Republicans lost 53 seats, reducing their total to 214. One seat was held by the Farmer-Labor Party. [See note 3, p. xxix]

BACKGROUND

During the 72nd Congress, President Hoover tried unsuccessfully to reverse America's economic decline and end the Great Depression. On June 20, 1931, Hoover proposed an international moratorium on debts and reparations due between nations as a result of World War I. Although the financial markets were initially optimistic about Hoover's proposal, nothing substantive resulted, and the financial markets resumed their slow and steady decline. During the 72nd Congress, the Dow Jones Industrial Average would reach a Great Depression low of 41.2, a decline of nearly 90 percent from the 1929 high of 381.2. Since stocks and bonds had lost virtually all of their value, many banks became insolvent and went out of business. Because there was no government protection for depositors, millions of Americans lost their savings as well as their jobs.

The economy continued to decline in 1932 and millions more people lost their jobs, but organized labor did achieve a significant leg-

islative victory. Congress enacted the Norris-LaGuardia Act, also known as the Federal Anti-Injunction Law. The act abolished the use of court injunctions to break strikes and suppress such union activities as marches, boycotts, and protests. President Hoover also endorsed the concept of a five-day work week by adopting it for the majority of federal government workers. This Norris-LaGuardia Act was important for the labor movement, which had lost approximately one-third of its membership from 1920 to 1931 and was suffering from the competition presented by millions of unemployed workers. Nevertheless, the employment situation in the U.S. remained grim. Even workers who were able to keep their jobs suffered, as wages declined by an average of 60 percent from 1929 to 1932, although price deflation offset some of the impact of falling wages.

Beginning on May 29, 1932, veterans groups started gathering in Washington, D.C., to petition the government for early payments on their service benefits under the Soldier Bonus Bill. [see p. 308-309] Many of the veterans were unemployed, and wanted their benefits immediately, rather than live in poverty. The veterans' gathering, nicknamed the Bonus Army, camped out near Capitol Hill and increased to nearly 20,000 during the summer of 1932. The House of Representatives passed legislation permitting bonus payments, but the law did not pass the Senate. [See Failed Legislation, below] On July 28, the government used troops under the com-

Hattie Caraway (Dem., Ark.), one of the first women to serve in the Senate, was first elected in the 72nd Congress.

mand of General Douglas MacArthur to force the Bonus Army out of Washington.

SENATE LEADERSHIP

Vice President: Charles Curtis. [See biographical note in 71st Congress]

President Pro Tempore: George Higgins Moses (Rep., N.H.) first had been elected to the Senate in 1918 and was president pro tem from the 69th through the 72nd Congresses.

Majority Leader: James E. Watson (Rep., Ind.)

Majority Whip: Simeon D. Fess (Rep., Ohio)

Minority Leader: Joseph T. Robinson (Dem., Ark.)

Minority Whip: Morris Sheppard (Dem., Tex.)

Chairmen of Selected Key Committees: [See note 5, p. xxix]

Committee on Appropriations: Wesley L. Jones (Rep., Wash.), who died on November 19, 1932.

Carter Glass (Dem., Va.) became the next chairman.

Committee on Banking and Currency: Peter Norbeck (Rep., S.D.)

Committee on Finance: Reed Smoot (Rep., Utah)

Committee on Foreign Relations: William E. Borah (Rep., Idaho)

Committee on the Judiciary: George W. Norris (Rep., Neb.)

Committee on Military Affairs: David Reed (Rep., Pa.)

Committee on Naval Affairs: Frederick Hale (Rep., Maine)

Committee on Rules: George H. Moses (Rep., N.H.)

HOUSE LEADERSHIP

Speaker of the House: John Nance Garner (Dem., Tex.) was elected Speaker on December 7, 1931. Garner first had been elected to Congress in the 58th Congress and served as Speaker in the 72nd Congress before he was elected vice president on Franklin D. Roosevelt's ticket in the 1932 elections. Garner was vice president from 1933 to 1941.

Majority Leader: Henry T. Rainey (Dem., Ill.)

Majority Whip: John McDuffie (Dem., Ala.)

Minority Leader: Bertrand H. Snell (Rep., N.Y.)

Minority Whip: Carl G. Bachmann (Rep., W.Va.)

Chairmen of Selected Key Committees: [See note 5, p. xxix]

Committee on Agriculture: J. Marvin Jones (Dem., Tex.)

Committee on Appropriations: Joseph W. Byrns (Dem., Tenn.)

Committee on Banking, Finance, and Urban Affairs: Henry B. Steagall (Dem., Ala.)

Committee on Foreign Affairs: J. Charles Linthicum (Dem., Md.), who died on October 5,

C H R O N O L O G Y

March 4, 1931:	The 72nd Congress begins.
December 7, 1931:	The first session begins, and John Nance Garner (Dem., Tex.) is elected Speaker of the House.
January 12, 1932:	Supreme Court Justice Oliver Wendell Holmes retires.
January 18, 1932:	Congress creates the Reconstruction Finance Corporation.
February 15, 1932:	President Hoover nominates Benjamin N. Cardozo to replace Holmes.
February 16, 1932:	Congress sends the 20th Amendment, changing the dates when new Congresses and presidental terms begin, to the states for ratification.
February 24, 1932:	The Senate confirms Cardozo.
March 9, 1932:	Congress passes the Norris-LaGuardia Anti-Injunction Act.
June 17, 1932:	Congress fails to pass the Bonus Bill.
July 11, 1932:	Congress passes legislation creating the Federal Home Loan Bank Board. President Hoover vetoes a bill to expand the powers of the Reconstruction Finance Corporation. Neither the House nor the Senate attempted to override the veto.
July 16, 1932:	The first session ends.
December 5, 1932:	The second session begins.
January 13, 1933:	President Hoover vetoes a Philippine independence bill, and the House votes to override the veto.
January 17, 1933:	The Senate votes to override Hoover's Philippine independence bill veto.
February 20, 1933:	Congress sends the 21st Amendment, repealing Prohibition, to the states for ratification.
March 3, 1933:	The second session and the 72nd Congress end.

[See note 6, p. xxix]

1932. Samuel D. McReynolds (Dem., Tenn.) became the next chairman.

Committee on the Judiciary: Hatton W. Sumners (Dem., Tex.)

Committee on Military Affairs: Percy E. Quin (Dem., Miss.), who died on February 4, 1932. John J. McSwain (Dem., S.C.) became the next chairman.

Committee on Naval Affairs: Carl Vinson (Dem., Ga.)

Committee on Rules: Edward W. Pou (Dem., N.C.)

Committee on Ways and Means: James W. Collier (Dem., Miss.)

ORGANIZATION AND ADMINISTRATION

No developments of significance. [See note 5, p. xxix]

Huey P. Long, the prominent Populist governor of Louisiana, went to the Senate beginning in the 72nd Congress and served until he was assassinated in 1935.

MAJOR LEGISLATION PASSED

Financial: Congress created the Reconstruction Finance Corporation, and gave it the power to raise money by selling tax exempt bonds and then lend the proceeds to banks, other financial institutions, railroads, and other businesses as emergency financing.

Housing: Congress established the Federal Home Loan Bank Board and a banking network in order to provide capital for home mortgages.

Labor: In the Norris-LaGuardia Anti-Injunction Act, Congress abolished the use of court injunctions to break strikes and suppress such union activities as marches, boycotts, and protests.

FAILED LEGISLATION

Bonus Bill: Largely in response to veterans groups marching in Washington, D.C. [See Background, above], the House approved legislation that would have given veterans certain service benefits in advance. [See Veterans: Soldiers Bonus Bill under Major Legislation in the 68th Congress] The Senate, however, refused to pass the Soldier's Bonus Bill.

RELATIONS WITH THE PRESIDENT

President Hoover finally endorsed some anti-Depression measures [See Background, above], but it was a classic example of too little, too late. The Democrats had retaken the House, were gaining in the Senate, and after Roosevelt won the 1932 presidential election Hoover was a weak lame duck president for the whole second session of this Congress.

Hoover vetoed 18 bills during the 72nd Congress. Two vetos were significant. First, on July 11, 1932, Hoover vetoed a bill that would have expanded the powers of the Reconstruction Finance Corporation to combat the depression. Neither the House nor the Senate attempted to override his veto. Second, on January 13, 1933, Hoover vetoed a Philippine independence bill. The same day, the House voted 274 to 94 to override the veto, and on January 17, 1933, the Senate by a vote of 66 to 26 also voted to override.

TABLE OF KEY VOTES

Senate

Subject of Vote	Date of Vote	For	Against
20th Amendment Approved	January 6, 1932	63	7
Reconstruction Finance Corporation Created	January 18, 1932	Passed by voice vote	
Labor Reform Passed	March 9, 1932	Passed by voice vote	
Bonus Bill Approved	June 17, 1932	18	62
Housing Mortgage Aid Approved	July 11, 1932	Passed by voice vote	
21st Amendment Approved	February 10, 1933	63	23

House

Subject of Vote	Date of Vote	For	Against
Reconstruction Finance Corporation Created	January 15, 1932	335	56
20th Amendment Approved	February 16, 1932	336	56
Labor Reform Passed	March 8, 1932	362	14
Bonus Bill Approved	June 15, 1932	211	176
Housing Mortgage Aid Approved	June 15, 1932	Passed by voice vote	
21st Amendment Approved	February 20, 1933	289	121

[See note 7, p. xxix]

NOMINATIONS, APPOINTMENTS, AND CONFIRMATIONS

The Judiciary: On January 12, 1932, Supreme Court Justice Oliver Wendell Holmes retired. President Herbert Hoover nominated Benjamin N. Cardozo on February 15, 1932, to replace Holmes, and the Senate confirmed Cardoza on February 24, 1932, by voice vote.

The Executive Branch: In early February of 1932 President Hoover nominated Ogden L. Mills to succeed Andrew W. Mellon as secretary of the Treasury, since Mellon had been appointed an ambassador. The Senate confirmed Mills on February 10, 1932, by voice vote. Later in 1932, Hoover nominated Roy D. Chapin to succeed Robert P. Lamont as secretary of commerce. The Senate confirmed Chapin in December of 1932.

Unfortunately, more accurate information is not available, due to missing information from Senate records. These records are in the process of being reconstructed, but as of this writing the project was not yet complete.

IMPEACHMENTS

None.

CONSTITUTIONAL AMENDMENTS

Congress sent two amendments to the states for ratification. First, the Twentieth Amendment provided that Congress begin and end on January

3 and that the terms of the president and vice president end at noon on January 20. By moving up the date of presidential inaugurations from March 4, the Twentieth Amendment eliminated the need for special lame-duck sessions of the Senate to vote on such matters as the new president's appointees to high offices. The Twentieth Amendment was ratified by the required three-fourths of the states effective January 23, 1933, and in accordance with section five of the amendment took effect on October 15, 1933, during the 73rd Congress. Second, Congress sent the Twenty-first Amendment, which repealed the Eighteenth Amendment and thus ended Prohibition, to the states. The Twenty-first Amendment was ratified by the required three-fourths of the states effective December 5, 1933. [For the actual text of the Twentieth and Twenty-first Amendments, see the copy of the Constitution at Appendix A]

FURTHER READING

Burner, David. *Herbert Hoover, A Public Life*. New York: Alfred A. Knopf, 1979.

Liebovich, Louis. *Bylines in Despair: Herbert Hoover, the Great Depression, and the U.S. News Media*. Westport, Conn.: Praeger, 1994.

Lisio, Donald J. *The President and Protest: Hoover, MacArthur, and the Bonus Riot*. New York: Fordham University Press, 1994.

Lyons, Eugene. *Herbert Hoover: A Biography*. Norwalk, Conn.: Easton Press, 1989 (reprint of 1964 edition).

The 73rd Congress

MARCH 4, 1933 - JANUARY 3, 1935

Special Senate Session: March 4, 1933-March 6, 1933
First Session: March 9, 1933-June 15, 1933
Second Session: January 3, 1934-June 18, 1934

The Senate held a special session to vote on the confirmation of presidential appointees to various offices. [See note 1, p. xxix] This was the last Senate special session in congressional history, because the Twentieth Amendment to the Constitution enabled the Senate to deal with confirmations during regular sessions. [See Background below]

In the 1932 elections for the 73rd Congress, the Democrats gained 13 seats in the Senate to hold a new majority of 60 of the 96 seats. The Republicans lost 13 seats, reducing their total to 35. One seat was held by the Farmer-Labor Party. In the House, the Democrats gained 90 seats, raising their majority from 220 to 310 of the 435 seats. The Republicans lost 97 seats, lowering their total to 117. Eight seats were not held by either major party. Five of the seats were held by the Farmer-Labor Party. [See note 3, p. xxix]

BACKGROUND

The Twentieth Amendment to the Constitution, which became effective on October 15, 1933, during this Congress, [See 72nd Congress] provides that Congress begins and ends on January 3, and also provides that the terms of the president and vice president end at noon on January 20. Therefore, the 73rd Congress was two months shorter than usual, since it began on March 4, 1933, before the Twentieth Amendment became effective, but ended on the new date of January 3, 1935.

On March 4, 1933, Franklin D. Roosevelt was inaugurated as the 32nd president of the United States. The Democrats now controlled the presidency and had large majorities in both houses of Congress. This put Roosevelt in a strong position to implement his New Deal package of economic stimulus and reform programs. Therefore, the 73rd Congress was one of the most active and significant Congresses in history, passing a blitz of legislation during its first 100 days. By focusing on domestic legislation, however, Roosevelt and Congress ignored ominous developments abroad. Dictator Joseph Stalin was consolidating his power in the Soviet Union, and Adolf Hitler's Nazis ended democracy in Germany.

In 1933 Congress, with its Democratic majorities, passed the first series of New Deal laws. The Reforestation Unemployment Act created the Civilian Conservation Corps, designed to create jobs and replenish the nation's forests. The Agricultural Adjustment Act placed quotas on certain crops in order to support prices and subsidized farmers left with unused land. The Federal Emergency Relief Act provided $500 million in funding for the Federal Emergency Relief Administration. The Tennessee Valley Act created the Tennessee Valley Authority which, in addition to building dams and controlling the waters of the Tennessee River valley area, was designed to create jobs in one of the poorest regions of the country and provide inexpensive rural electricity. The Securities Act of 1933 gave the federal government extensive powers over the registration and regulation of new stock and bond issues, which was a response to the specu-

Everett Dirksen (Rep., Ill.) (featured here on the right; Gerald Ford is on the left) was first elected to the 73rd Congress.

lative excesses of the 1920s. The National Industrial Recovery Act created the National Recovery Administration and the Public Works Administration. The Banking Act of 1933 created the Federal Deposit Insurance Corporation, which guaranteed that the federal government would insure bank deposits up to a certain amount, thereby helping to restore the middle class's faith in the banking system.

By 1934 the worst of the Great Depression appeared to be over. Although the economy still was weak, employment and wages were rising. Meanwhile, Congress continued to pass New Deal legislation. The Farm Mortgage Refinancing Act created the Federal Farm Mortgage Corporation in order to provide low cost loans to the nation's farmers and help them avoid foreclosure. The Securities Exchange Act gave the Securities and Exchange Commission the power to regulate transactions in the stock and bond markets. Although the Roosevelt administration had many successes during the 73rd Congress, there were significant defeats as well. Corporate America resisted many New Deal laws, particularly those in the area of labor-management relations. This resistance took place in the federal courts, and the Supreme Court struck down several New Deal laws as unconstitutional, notably the National Industrial Recovery Act.

SENATE LEADERSHIP

Vice President: John Nance Garner first had been elected to Congress in the 58th Congress and had served as Speaker of the House in the 72nd Congress before he was elected vice president on Roosevelt's ticket in the 1932 elections. Garner was vice president from 1933 to 1941.

President Pro Tempore: Key Pittman (Dem., Nev.) was elected on March 9, 1933. Pittman first had been elected to the Senate in 1913, where he served until he died on November 10, 1940. He was president pro tem in the 73rd through the 76th Congresses.

Majority Leader: Joseph T. Robinson (Dem., Ark.)

Majority Whip: J. Hamilton Lewis (Dem., Ill.)

Minority Leader: Charles L. McNary (Rep., Ore.)

Minority Whip: Felix Hebert (Rep., R.I.)

Chairmen of Selected Key Committees: [See note 5, p. xxix]

Committee on Appropriations: Carter Glass (Dem., Va.)

Committee on Banking and Currency: Duncan U. Fletcher (Dem., Fla.)

Committee on Finance: Pat Harrison (Dem., Miss.)

Committee on Foreign Relations: Key Pittman (Dem., Nev.)

Committee on the Judiciary: Henry F. Ashurst (Dem., Ariz.)

Committee on Military Affairs: Morris Sheppard (Dem., Tex.)

Committee on Naval Affairs: Park Trammell (Dem., Fla.)

Committee on Rules: Royal S. Copeland (Dem., N.Y.)

HOUSE LEADERSHIP

Speaker of the House: Henry Thomas Rainey (Dem., Ill.) was elected Speaker on March 9, 1933. Rainey first was elected to Congress in the 58th Congress and served as Speaker in the 58th Congress only. He died on August 19, 1934, after the second and last session had adjourned; therefore, no new Speaker was elected during this Congress.

Majority Leader: Joseph W. Byrns (Dem., Tenn.)

Majority Whip: Arthur H. Greenwood (Dem., Ind.)

Minority Leader: Bertrand H. Snell (Rep., N.Y.)

Minority Whip: Harry L. Englebright (Rep., Calif.)

Chairmen of Selected Key Committees: [See note 5, p. xxix]

Committee on Agriculture: J. Marvin Jones (Dem., Tex.)

Committee on Appropriations: James P. Buchanan (Dem., Tex.)

Committee on Banking, Finance, and Urban Affairs: Henry B. Steagall (Dem., Ala.)

Committee on Foreign Affairs: Samuel D. McReynolds (Dem., Tenn.)

Committee on the Judiciary: Hatton W. Sumners (Dem., Tex.)

Committee on Military Affairs: John J. McSwain (Dem., S.C.)

Committee on Naval Affairs: Carl Vinson (Dem., Ga.)

Committee on Rules: Edward W. Pou (Dem., N.C.), who died on April 1, 1934. William B. Bankhead (Dem., Ala.) became the next chairman.

Committee on Ways and Means: Robert L. Doughton (Dem., N.C.)

ORGANIZATION AND ADMINISTRATION

No developments of significance. [See note 5, p. xxix]

MAJOR LEGISLATION PASSED

Agriculture: In the Agricultural Adjustment Act, Congress tried to help the nation's farmers by inflating the severely depressed prices of farm products. In order to raise prices, Congress placed quotas on crop production, aimed at reducing the surpluses that were keeping prices down, and subsidized those farmers left with unused farm land.

Banking: In the Emergency Banking Relief Act, Congress confirmed the Roosevelt administration's emergency actions with respect to the national banking system. Further, the act made it illegal for Americans to own gold and ordered all citizens to turn their gold over to the Treasury in exchange for currency.

Civilian Conservation Corps: In the Reforestation Unemployment Act, Congress established the Civilian Conservation Corps in order to create jobs and replenish the nation's forests.

Communications: In the Communications Act of 1934, Congress established the Federal Communications Commission and gave it jurisdiction over radio, telegraph, and other forms of communication. The FCC absorbed the old Federal Radio Commission.

Emergency Relief: The Federal Emergency Relief Act provided half a billion dollars in funding for the Federal Emergency Relief Administration, which was to work with state and local authorities to help the poor.

FDIC: In the Banking Act of 1933, Congress created the Federal Deposit Insurance Corporation, which guarantees individual bank deposits up to a certain limit.

Farm Mortgages: In the Farm Mortgage Refinancing Act, Congress established the Federal Farm Mortgage Corporation to help farmers refinance their debts.

C H R O N O L O G Y

March 4, 1933:	The 73rd Congress and a special Senate session begin. President Roosevelt nominates his cabinet, and the Senate confirms all of the nominees.
March 6, 1933:	The special Senate session ends.
March 9, 1933:	The first session begins, and Congress passes the Emergency Banking Relief Act. Henry Thomas Rainey (Dem., Ill.) is elected Speaker of the House, and Key Pittman (Dem., Nev.) is elected Senate president pro tem.
March 29, 1933:	Congress passes legislation creating the Civilian Conservation Corps.
April 27, 1933:	Congress passes the Agricultural Adjustment Act.
May 1, 1933:	Congress passes the Federal Emergency Relief Act and legislation creating the Tennessee Valley Authority.
May 8, 1933:	Congress passes the Securities Act of 1933.
May 25, 1933:	Congress passes legislation creating the Federal Deposit Insurance Corporation.
June 3, 1933:	Congress passes legislation taking the U.S. off the gold standard.
June 5, 1933:	Congress passes the Home Owners Loan Act of 1933.
June 8, 1933:	Congress passes the National Industrial Recovery Act.
June 15, 1933:	The first session ends.
January 3, 1934:	The second session begins.
January 4, 1934:	President Roosevelt nominates Henry Morgenthau Jr. to succeed William H. Woodin as secretary of the Treasury.
January 8, 1934:	The Senate confirms Morgenthau.
January 22, 1934:	Congress passes legislation establishing the Federal Farm Mortgage Corporation.
January 26, 1934:	Congress passes the Gold Reserve Act of 1934.
March 5, 1934:	Congress passes the Naval Parity Act.
April 5, 1934:	Congress passes the Home Owners Loan Act of 1934.
May 12, 1934:	Congress passes the Securities Exchange Act.
June 2, 1934:	Congress passes legislation creating the Federal Communications Commission.
June 4, 1934:	Congress passes the Reciprocal Trade Agreements Act.
June 16, 1934:	Congress passes the National Housing Act.
June 18, 1934:	The second session ends.
January 3, 1935:	The 73rd Congress ends.

[See note 6, p. xxix]

Gold: In 1933 Congress officially took the United States off the gold standard. In 1934 in the Gold Reserve Act of 1934, Congress gave the federal government further controls over the nation's gold supply and established an Exchange Stabilization Fund to help stabilize the dollar

TABLE OF KEY VOTES

Senate

Subject of Vote	Date of Vote	For	Against
Emergency Banking Actions Approved	March 9, 1933	73	7
Civilian Conservation Corps Established	March 28, 1933	Passed by voice vote	
Agricultural Adjustment Act Passed	April 27, 1933	64	20
Emergency Relief Bill Passed	May 1, 1933	Passed by voice vote	
Tennessee Valley Authority Established	May 1, 1933	63	20
Securities Regulation Passed	May 8, 1933	Passed by voice vote	
FDIC Established	May 25, 1933	Passed by voice vote	
Gold Standard Ended	June 3, 1933	48	20
Home Owners Refinancing Passed	June 5, 1933	Passed by voice vote	
National Recovery Administration Established	June 8, 1933	58	24
Farm Mortgage Refinancing Passed	January 22, 1934	Passed by voice vote	
Gold Reserve Act Passed	January 26, 1934	66	23
Navy Shipbuilding Program Passed	March 5, 1934	65	18
Home Refinancing Expanded	March 19, 1934	Passed by voice vote	
Securities Exchange Commission Established	May 12, 1934	62	13
FCC Established	May 14, 1934	Passed by voice vote	
Trade Negotiations Approved	June 4, 1934	57	33
FHA Established	June 16, 1934	71	12

(continued on p. 337)

against other currencies.

Housing: In the Home Owners Loan Act of 1933, Congress created a Home Owners Loan Corporation to help homeowners refinance their home mortgages. In the Home Owners Loan Act of 1934, Congress increased the funds available to the Home Owners Loan Corporation. Finally, in the National Housing Act, Congress created the Federal Housing Administration (FHA) in order to stimulate the housing industry by providing federal loan insurance.

National Recovery Administration: In the National Industrial Recovery Act, Congress established the National Recovery Administration and

TABLE OF KEY VOTES

House

Subject of Vote	Date of Vote	For	Against
Emergency Banking Actions Approved	March 9, 1933	Passed by voice vote	
Agriculture Adjustment Act Passed	March 22, 1933	315	98
Civilian Conservation Corps Established	March 29, 1933	Passed by voice vote	
Emergency Relief Bill Passed	April 21, 1933	331	42
Tennessee Valley Authority Established	April 25, 1933	306	92
Home Owners Refinancing Passed	April 28, 1933	383	4
Securities Regulation Passed	May 5, 1933	Passed by voice vote	
FDIC Established	May 23, 1933	262	19
National Recovery Administration Established	May 26, 1933	325	76
Gold Standard Ended	May 29, 1933	283	57
Farm Mortgage Refinancing Passed	January 16, 1934	Passed by voice vote	
Gold Reserve Act Passed	January 20, 1934	360	40
Navy Shipbuilding Program Passed	January 30, 1934	Passed by voice vote	
Trade Negotiations Approved	March 29, 1934	274	111
Home Owners Refinancing Expanded	April 5, 1934	339	1
Securities Exchange Commission Established	May 4, 1934	281	84
FCC Established	June 2, 1934	Passed by voice vote	
FHA Established	June 13, 1934	176	19

[See note 7, p. xxix]

the Public Works Administration. The act established extensive industrial and trade regulations over the economy and authorized massive new public works projects, all intended to help America out of the Great Depression. The act was initially very popular and successful, but administrative problems caused the initial enthusiasm to wane and the whole program to decline.

The final blow came on May 27, 1935, shortly before the expiration of the act, when the Supreme Court declared the act unconstitutional in the case of *Schechter Poultry Corp. v. U.S.*

Navy: In the Naval Parity Act, Congress authorized additional ship building to bring the U.S. Navy up to full strength.

Securities: Congress passed two major pieces of securities legislation. First, the Securities Act of 1933 gave the federal government extensive powers over the registration and regulation of new securities. Second, the Securities Exchange Act created the Securities and Exchange Commission, which was to enforce the new regulations overseeing securities transactions that were designed to prevent excessive speculation and fraudulent activities.

Tennessee Valley Authority: In the Tennessee Valley Act, Congress created the Tennessee Valley Authority in order to build dams and hydroelectric facilities in the waterways of the Tennessee River valley area. Congress intended to bring jobs, cheap electricity, and industrial development into one of the poorest regions of the United States.

Trade: In the Reciprocal Trade Agreements Act, Congress authorized the president to enter into agreements with other nations for the mutual and equal reduction of trade tariffs.

FAILED LEGISLATION

None of historical significance.

RELATIONS WITH THE PRESIDENT

President Roosevelt's fellow Democrats held large majorities in both houses of Congress, and thus Roosevelt generally was able to get his New Deal legislation through Congress without great difficulty. The first session of this Congress is known as the "100 days" for the large amount of legislation passed at Roosevelt's initiative.

Roosevelt vetoed 73 bills during the 73rd Congress, most of which concerned minor legislation such as private relief bills.

NOMINATIONS, APPOINTMENTS, AND CONFIRMATIONS

The Judiciary: There were no significant nominations, appointments, or confirmations in the federal judiciary during the 73rd Congress.

The Executive Branch: On March 4, 1933,

President Franklin D. Roosevelt nominated, and the Senate confirmed by voice vote, all of his cabinet nominees. The nominees were Homer S. Cummings to be attorney general, George H. Dern to be secretary of war, Cordell Hull to be secretary of state, Harold L. Ickes to be secretary of the Interior, Frances Perkins to be secretary of labor, Daniel C. Roper to be secretary of commerce, Claude A. Swanson to be secretary of the Navy, Henry A. Wallace to be secretary of agriculture, and William H. Woodin to be secretary of the Treasury. On January 4, 1934, Roosevelt nominated Henry Morgenthau Jr. to succeed William H. Woodin as secretary of the Treasury, and on January 8, 1934, the Senate confirmed Morgenthau by voice vote.

IMPEACHMENTS

Federal Judge Harold Louderback was impeached for appointing incompetent bankruptcy officials and letting them take excessive fees from receivership cases. The Senate found him not guilty on May 24, 1933.

CONSTITUTIONAL AMENDMENTS

None.

Further Reading

Conklin, Paul Keith. *The New Deal.* Arlington Heights, Ill.: Harlan Davidson, 1992.

Maney, Patrick J. *The Roosevelt Presence: A Biography of Franklin Roosevelt.* New York: Twayne Publishers and Macmillan International, 1992.

Waller, Robert A. *Rainey of Illinois: A Political Biography, 1903-1934.* Urbana, Ill.: University of Illinois Press, 1977.

The 74th Congress

JANUARY 3, 1935 - JANUARY 3, 1937

First Session: *January 3, 1935-August 26, 1935*
Second Session: *January 3, 1936-June 20, 1936*

In the 1934 elections for the 74th Congress, the Democrats gained 9 seats in the Senate, raising their majority from 60 to 69 of the 96 seats. The Republicans lost 10 seats, reducing their total to 25. Two seats were not held by either major party. One seat was held by the Farmer-Labor Party and 1 seat by the Progressive Party. In the House, the Democrats gained 9 seats, raising their majority from 310 to 319 of the 435 seats. The Republicans lost 14 seats, leaving them with a total of 103. Thirteen seats were not held by either major party. Seven of these seats were held by the Progressives and 3 by the Farmer-Labor Party. [See note 3, p. xxix]

BACKGROUND

The Roosevelt administration continued to press forward with New Deal legislation in the 74th Congress. The preoccupation with domestic matters, however, caused the nation to take a largely isolationist view toward foreign affairs. For example, one of the first actions of the Senate in the 74th Congress was to refuse to ratify U.S. membership in the World Court. Adolf Hitler was rearming Germany, while the U.S. and other powers did nothing to enforce the disarmament provisions of the Treaty of Versailles.

In 1935 the Supreme Court dealt the New Deal a serious blow. On May 27 the Court unanimously held in the case of *Schechter Poultry Corp. v. U.S.* that the National Industrial Recovery Act of 1933 was unconstitutional because it exceeded the government's authority to set prices, wages and working conditions. In particular, the Supreme Court's decision threatened the progress that organized labor was making. Since President Roosevelt and the Democrats, who controlled both houses of Congress, depended on the votes of organized labor, Congress quickly enacted the National Labor Relations Act [or Wagner-Connery Act], which reestablished the National Labor Relations Board's power to regulate labor-management disputes and prevent unfair practices against organized labor. Also during 1935, Congress enacted the Social Security Act, which for the first time in American history provided for a government regulated system of pension and retirement benefits for senior citizens based upon their lifetime earnings.

In 1936 the 74th Congress was not very active, largely because President Roosevelt was focusing on his reelection campaign. The U.S. continued to ignore growing threats to international peace. After killing millions of people in order to collectivize Soviet agriculture, Joseph Stalin began instituting purges throughout the Soviet Communist Party and Red Army in order to eliminate any opposition to his totalitarian rule. Adolf Hitler's Germany reoccupied the Rhineland in violation of the Treaty of Versailles, while Benito Mussolini's Italy conquered Ethiopia, an empire thousands of years old and one of the last remaining independent African states. By not taking

C H R O N O L O G Y

January 3, 1935:	The 74th Congress and the first session begin. Joseph Wellington Byrns (Dem., Tenn.) is elected Speaker of the House.
January 7, 1935:	Key Pittman (Dem., Nev.) is reelected Senate president pro tem.
January 29, 1935:	The Senate rejects a World Court Treaty.
March 23, 1935:	Congress passes the Emergency Relief Appropriations Act.
May 27, 1935:	The Supreme Court holds that the National Industrial Recovery Act is unconstitutional.
June 19, 1935:	Congress passes legislation creating the Social Security system and the National Labor Relations Board.
July 1, 1935:	The Senate creates the position of Senate parliamentarian.
July 2, 1935:	Congress passes the Public Utility Holding Company Act.
August 1, 1935:	Congress passes legislation expanding the power of the Interstate Commerce Commission.
August 23, 1935:	Congress passes the Neutrality Act of 1935.
August 26, 1935:	The first session ends.
January 3, 1936:	The second session begins.
April 9, 1936:	Congress passes the Rural Electrification Act.
June 1, 1936:	Congress passes legislation against predatory pricing.
June 4, 1936:	Speaker of the House Byrns dies, and William Brockman Bankhead (Dem., Ala.) is elected the new Speaker.
June 18, 1936:	Congress passes shipping legislation.
June 20, 1936:	The second session ends.
January 3, 1937:	The 74th Congress ends.

[See note 6, p. xxix]

serious measures in response to these actions, the U.S. and other Western powers effectively encouraged further aggressions in the years leading up to World War II.

SENATE LEADERSHIP

Vice President: John Nance Garner. [See biographical note in 73rd Congress]

President Pro Tempore: Key Pittman (Dem., Nev.) was reelected on January 7, 1935. [See biographical note in 73rd Congress]

Majority Leader: Joseph T. Robinson (Dem., Ark.)

Majority Whip: J. Hamilton Lewis (Dem., Ill.)

Minority Leader: Charles L. McNary (Rep., Ore.)

Minority Whip: None.

Chairmen of Selected Key Committees: [See also Organization and Administration, below]

Committee on Appropriations: Carter Glass (Dem., Va.)

Committee on Banking and Currency: Duncan U. Fletcher (Dem., Fla.), who died on June 17, 1936. Robert F. Wagner (Dem., N.Y.) became the next chairman.

Committee on Finance: Pat Harrison (Dem., Miss.)

Committee on Foreign Relations: Key Pittman (Dem., Nev.)

Committee on the Judiciary: Henry F. Ashurst (Dem., Ariz.)

Committee on Military Affairs: Morris Sheppard (Dem., Tex.)

Committee on Naval Affairs: Park Trammell (Dem., Fla.)

Committee on Rules: Royal S. Copeland (Dem., N.Y.) and Matthew M. Neely (Dem., W.Va.)

HOUSE LEADERSHIP

Speaker of the House: Joseph Wellington Byrns (Dem., Tenn.) was elected Speaker on January 3, 1935. Byrns died on June 4, 1936, and William Brockman Bankhead (Dem., Ala.) was elected the new Speaker on June 4, 1936. Bankhead first had been elected to Congress in the 65th Congress and served as Speaker from the 74th through the 76th Congresses.

Majority Leader: William B. Bankhead (Dem., Ala.), until he became the Speaker of the House on June 4, 1936. The vacancy was not filled during the 74th Congress.

Majority Whip: Patrick J. Boland (Dem., Pa.)

Minority Leader: Bertrand H. Snell (Rep., N.Y.)

Minority Whip: Harry L. Englebright (Rep., Calif.)

Chairmen of Selected Key Committees: [See also Organization and Administration, below]

Committee on Agriculture: J. Marvin Jones (Dem., Tex.)

Committee on Appropriations: James P. Buchanan (Dem., Tex.)

Committee on Banking, Finance, and Urban Affairs: Henry B. Steagall (Dem., Ala.)

Committee on Foreign Affairs: Samuel D. McReynolds (Dem., Tenn.)

Committee on the Judiciary: Hatton W. Sumners (Dem., Tex.)

Committee on Military Affairs: John J. McSwain (Dem., S.C.)

Committee on Naval Affairs: Carl Vinson (Dem., Ga.)

Committee on Rules: John J. O'Connor (Dem., N.Y.)

Committee on Ways and Means: Robert L. Doughton (Dem., N.C.)

ORGANIZATION AND ADMINISTRATION

On July 1, 1935, the Senate created the position of Senate Parliamentarian. The parliamentarian advises senators on Senate rules and procedure. [See note 5, p. xxix]

MAJOR LEGISLATION PASSED

Emergency Relief: In the Emergency Relief Appropriations Act, Congress funded large state and local work relief programs for the unemployed. The act also established the Works Progress Administration.

Foreign Policy: In the Neutrality Act of 1935, Congress made it illegal to export military supplies to countries at war or for American-flag ships to carry military supplies to countries at war.

Interstate Commerce Commission: Congress expanded the ICC's jurisdiction to include interstate bus transportation.

Labor Relations: In the National Labor Relations Act, also known as the Wagner-Connery Act, Congress empowered the National Labor Relations Board to certify trade unions as lawful collective bargaining units, to supervise union elections, and to take legal actions against unfair labor practices.

Predatory Pricing: In the Anti-Price Discrimina-

TABLE OF KEY VOTES

Senate

Subject of Vote	Date of Vote	For	Against
World Court Treaty Rejected (failed: two-thirds majority required)	January 29, 1935	52	36
Emergency Relief Funds Appropriated	March 23, 1935	68	16
Interstate Commerce Commission Powers Expanded	April 16, 1935	Passed by voice vote	
National Labor Relations Board Established	May 16, 1935	63	12
Public Utilities Regulations	June 11, 1935	56	32
Social Security Bill Passed	June 19, 1935	77	6
Neutrality Act Passed	August 20, 1935	Passed by voice vote	
Rural Electrification Program Established	March 2, 1936	Passed by voice vote	
Predatory Pricing Outlawed	June 1, 1936	Passed by voice vote	
Shipping Regulations Revised	June 18, 1936	Passed by voice vote	

House

Subject of Vote	Date of Vote	For	Against
Emergency Relief Funds Appropriated	January 24, 1935	329	78
Social Security Bill Passed	April 19, 1935	372	33
National Labor Relations Board Established	June 19, 1935	Passed by voice vote	
Shipping Regulations Revised	June 27, 1935	194	186
Public Utilities Regulations	July 2, 1935	323	81
Interstate Commerce Commission Powers Expanded	August 1, 1935	193	18
Neutrality Act Passed	August 23, 1935	Passed by voice vote	
Rural Electrification Program Established	April 9, 1936	Passed by voice vote	
Predatory Pricing Outlawed	May 28, 1936	290	16

[See note 7, p. xxix]

tion Act, Congress outlawed a tactic known as *predatory pricing*. (Predatory pricing is when a large company seeking to preserve its dominant or monopolistic share of a market cuts prices so low that smaller competitors, who can't bear temporary losses for as long a period, are driven out of business and the large company can then raise prices.) Congress gave the Federal Trade Commission the power to enforce the act. The act was primarily the result of concerns that large chain stores were driving their mom-and-pop competitors out of business.

Public Utilities: In the Public Utility Holding Company Act, Congress gave the Securities and Exchange Commission the power to regulate the financial operations of public utility holding companies. This was a reaction to excessive speculation in utility company stocks and the financial manipulations by such holding company kingpins as Samuel Insull during the 1920s.

Rural Electrification: In the Rural Electrification Act, Congress created the Rural Electrification Administration with the power to finance rural electric cooperatives and other initiatives for bringing electricity to rural areas.

Shipping: Congress established the United States Maritime Commission and revised the system for the regulation and support of the American merchant marine industry.

Social Security: In the Social Security Act, Congress established a system of pension and retirement benefits funded by payroll taxes on employers and employees. Individual entitlements depended upon individual lifetime earnings. Congress also established the Social Security Board to administer the system.

World Court: The Senate rejected a treaty that would have brought the United States into the World Court. [See also the 69th Congress and information concerning the Permanent Court of International Justice]

FAILED LEGISLATION

None of historical significance.

RELATIONS WITH THE PRESIDENT

President Roosevelt's fellow Democrats continued to hold, and even increased, their large majorities in both Houses of Congress. Although the volume of New Deal legislation passed was not quite as large as in the 73rd Congress with its famous "100

days" of new bills, Roosevelt and the Democrats' agenda was nevertheless successful and impressive. [See Major Legislation]

Roosevelt vetoed 148 bills during the 74th Congress. None involved major legislation and largely rejected private relief bills.

NOMINATIONS, APPOINTMENTS, AND CONFIRMATIONS

There were no significant nominations, appointments, or confirmations in the federal judiciary or the executive branch during the 74th Congress.

IMPEACHMENTS

Federal Judge Halsted Ritter was impeached for taking kickbacks, running a private practice while on the Bench, and filing false tax returns. The Senate voted to remove him from office on April 17, 1936.

CONSTITUTIONAL AMENDMENTS

None.

FURTHER READING

Altmeyer, Arthur J. *The Formative Years of Social Security.* Madison, Wis.: University of Wisconsin Press, 1966.

Conklin, Paul Keith. *The New Deal.* Arlington Heights, Ill.: Harlan Davidson, 1992.

Maney, Patrick J. *The Roosevelt Presence: A Biography of Franklin Roosevelt.* New York: Twayne Publishers and Macmillan International, 1992.

Roos, Charles Frederick. *NRA Economic Planning.* New York: Da Capo Press, 1971 (Reprint of 1937 ed.).

The 75th Congress

JANUARY 3, 1937-JANUARY 3, 1939

First Session: January 5, 1937-August 21, 1937
Second Session: November 15, 1937-December 21, 1937
Third Session: January 3, 1938-June 16, 1938

In the 1936 elections for the 75th Congress, the Democrats gained 7 seats in the Senate, raising their majority from 69 to 76 of the 96 seats. The Republicans lost 9 seats, reducing their total to 16 seats. Four seats were not held by either major party. Two seats were held by the Farmer-Labor Party, 1 seat by the Progressive Party, and 1 seat by an independent. In the House, the Democrats gained 12 seats, raising their majority from 319 to 331 of the 435 seats. The Republicans lost 14 seats, reducing their total to 89. Fifteen seats were not held by either major party. Eight of these seats were held by the Progressive Party and 5 were held by the Farmer-Labor Party. [See note 3, p. xxix]

BACKGROUND

Franklin D. Roosevelt was inaugurated on January 20, 1937, for his second term as the 32nd president of the United States. One of Roosevelt's first moves was to meet with congressional leaders on February 5, 1937, to discuss revisions to the federal courts, particularly the Supreme Court. After the Supreme Court had declared the National Industrial Recovery Act to be unconstitutional in 1936 Roosevelt's primary aim was to increase the number of Supreme Court justices, so he would then be able to nominate new justices and thus be able to "pack" the Court with New Deal supporters. If the "court-packing" plan succeeded, the Supreme Court would not be able to block key New Deal legislation, as the Court

had during the previous Congress when it held the National Industrial Recovery Act to be unconstitutional. The court-packing proposal was unpopular, however, and went nowhere in Congress.

During 1937 the national economy initially showed many signs of improvement, but the recovery collapsed in the summer and fall. By the end of the year, both the economy and the financial markets once again were declining.

In 1938 Congress enacted the Revenue Act of 1938, which reduced business taxes in order to stimulate economic activity. Congress hoped that the tax cut would reinvigorate the recovery that had begun in 1937, but failed to sustain itself. In the same year, Congress also enacted the Naval Expansion Act, which authorized more than a billion dollars for the construction of new warships, established a minimum hourly wage for most workers, instituted the 40-hour work week, and passed a Civil Aeronautics Act establishing a new and more comprehensive system of federal supervision over the airline industry.

Toward the end of its final session, Congress and the Roosevelt administration were paying more attention to developments in Europe that were leading toward World War II. On September 26, 1938, Roosevelt sent a diplomatic note to Czechoslovakia, France, Great Britain, and Nazi Germany concerning Hitler's demand that Czechoslovakia cede to Germany that portion of Czech territory known as the Sudetenland. The Sudetenland was a strip of territory adjacent to

Lyndon Baines Johnson (Dem., Tex.) was first elected to the 75th Congress.

Germany that contained a substantial German ethnic population. Roosevelt asked the four countries to submit the crisis to international arbitration. France and Great Britain, however, gave in to Hitler's demands in the Munich Pact of September 29, 1938, which authorized Germany to take the Sudetenland without Czechoslovakia's consent and encouraged Hitler to continue his plans for Gernamy's expansion.

SENATE LEADERSHIP

Vice President: John Nance Garner. [See biographical note in 73rd Congress]

President Pro Tempore: Key Pittman (Dem., Nev.) [See biographical note in 73rd Congress]

Majority Leader: Joseph T. Robinson (Dem., Ark.), until he died on July 14, 1937. Alben W. Barkley (Dem., Ky.) became the new majority leader on July 22, 1937.

Majority Whip: J. Hamilton Lewis (Dem., Ill.)

Minority Leader: Charles L. McNary (Rep., Ore.)

Minority Whip: None.

Chairmen of Selected Key Committees: [See note 5, p. xxix]

Committee on Appropriations: Carter Glass (Dem., Va.)

Committee on Banking and Currency: Robert F. Wagner (Dem., N.Y.)

Committee on Finance: Pat Harrison (Dem., Miss.)

Committee on Foreign Relations: Key Pittman (Dem., Nev.)

Committee on the Judiciary: Henry F. Ashurst (Dem., Ariz.)

Committee on Military Affairs: Morris Sheppard (Dem., Tex.)

Committee on Naval Affairs: David I. Walsh (Dem., Mass.)

Committee on Rules: Matthew M. Neely (Dem., W.Va.)

HOUSE LEADERSHIP

Speaker of the House: William Brockman Bankhead (Dem., Ala.) was reelected Speaker on January 5, 1937. [See biographical note in 73rd Congress]

Majority Leader: Sam Rayburn (Dem., Tex.)

Majority Whip: Patrick J. Boland (Dem., Pa.)

Minority Leader: Bertrand H. Snell (Rep., N.Y.)

Minority Whip: Harry L. Englebright (Rep., Calif.)

Chairmen of Selected Key Committees: [See note 5, p. xxix]

Committee on Agriculture: J. Marvin Jones (Dem., Tex.)

Committee on Appropriations: James P. Buchanan (Dem., Tex.), who died on February 22, 1937. Edward T. Taylor (Dem., Colo.) became the next chairman.

CHRONOLOGY

January 3, 1937:	The 75th Congress begins.
January 5, 1937:	The first session begins, and William Brockman Bankhead (Dem., Ala.) is reelected Speaker of the House.
February 5, 1937:	President Roosevelt submits his court packing plan, which dies in committee.
April 27, 1937:	President Roosevelt nominates Harry H. Woodring to be secretary of war.
May 6, 1937:	The Senate confirms Woodring.
June 2, 1937:	Supreme Court Justice Willis Van Devanter retires.
August 12, 1937:	President Roosevelt nominates Hugo L. Black to replace Van Devanter.
August 17, 1937:	The Senate confirms Black.
August 19, 1937:	Congress passes the Revenue Act of 1937.
August 21, 1937:	The first session ends.
November 15, 1937:	The second session begins.
December 17, 1937:	Congress passes the Agricultural Adjustment Act of 1938.
December 21, 1937:	The second session ends.
January 3, 1938:	The third session begins.
January 17, 1938:	Supreme Court Justice George Sutherland retires. (President Roosevelt already had nominated Stanley F. Reed to replace Sutherland.)
January 25, 1938:	The Senate confirms Reed.
April 9, 1938:	Congress passes the Revenue Act of 1938.
May 3, 1938:	Congress passes legislation to expand the Navy.
May 18, 1938:	Congress passes the Civil Aeronautics Act.
May 24, 1938:	Congress passes the Fair Labor Standards Act.
June 1, 1938:	Congress passes legislation increasing federal supervision over the sale of food, drugs, and cosmetics.
June 16, 1938:	The third session ends.
July 9, 1938:	Supreme Court Justice Benjamin N. Cardozo dies, but is not replaced until the 76th Congress.
January 3, 1939:	The 75th Congress ends.

[See note 6, p. xxix]

Committee on Banking, Finance, and Urban Affairs: Henry B. Steagall (Dem., Ala.)

Committee on Foreign Affairs: Samuel D. McReynolds (Dem., Tenn.)

Committee on the Judiciary: Hatton W. Sumners (Dem., Tex.)

Committee on Military Affairs: J. Lister Hill (Dem., Ala.)

Committee on Naval Affairs: Carl Vinson (Dem., Ga.)

Committee on Rules: John J. O'Connor (Dem., N.Y.)

TABLE OF KEY VOTES

Senate

Subject of Vote	Date of Vote	For	Against
FDA Powers Increased	March 9, 1937	Passed by voice vote	
Fair Labor Bill Passed	July 3, 1937	56	28
Tax Loopholes Closed	August 19, 1937	Passed by voice vote	
Agricultural Price Supports Revised	December 17, 1937	59	29
Business Taxes Cut	April 9, 1938	Passed by voice vote	
Navy Program Passed	May 3, 1938	56	28
Civil Aviation Bill Passed	May 16, 1938	Passed by voice vote	

House

Subject of Vote	Date of Vote	For	Against
Tax Loopholes Closed	August 16, 1937	173	0
Agriculture Price Supports Revised	December 10, 1937	267	130
Business Taxes Cut	March 11, 1938	293	97
Navy Program Passed	March 21, 1938	294	100
Civil Aviation Bill Passed	May 18, 1938	Passed by voice vote	
Fair Labor Standards Bill Passed	May 24, 1938	314	97
FDA Powers Increased	June 1, 1938	Passed by voice vote	

[See note 7, p. xxix]

Committee on Ways and Means: Robert L. Doughton (Dem., N.C.)

ORGANIZATION AND ADMINISTRATION

No developments of significance. [See note 5, p. xxix]

MAJOR LEGISLATION PASSED

Agriculture: In the Agricultural Adjustment Act of 1938, Congress revised the system of price supports and surplus crop quotas.

Aviation: In the Civil Aeronautics Act, Congress established the Civil Aeronautics Authority and implemented a new and more comprehensive system of federal supervision over the airline industry.

Food, Drugs, and Cosmetics: In the Food, Drug, and Cosmetics Act, Congress increased the powers of the Food and Drug Administration and required manufacturers to list ingredients on product containers. Congress also increased the power of the Federal Trade Commission to prevent false and misleading advertising.

Labor: In the Fair Labor Standards Act, Congress for the first time established a minimum hourly wage, which initially was set at 25 cents. Congress also put the principle of the 40-hour work week into effect for all workers.

Navy: In the Naval Expansion Act of 1938, Congress authorized over a billion dollars in new ship construction for the United States Navy. The act was a reaction to growing war tension in Europe.

Revenue: The 75th Congress passed two important revenue bills. First, in the Revenue Act of 1937, Congress attempted to cut down on tax evasion by ending certain loopholes. Second, in the Revenue Act of 1938, Congress reduced the corporate tax rate and the capital gains tax in order to stimulate business activity.

FAILED LEGISLATION

Federal Courts: On February 5, 1937, President Roosevelt submitted his court-packing plan to Congress. [See Background, p. 344] The proposal was very controversial, and many of Roosevelt's fellow Democrats criticized it. The court-packing plan died in the Senate Judiciary Committee.

RELATIONS WITH THE PRESIDENT

President Roosevelt's fellow Democrats held huge majorities in both houses of Congress, and thus Roosevelt was generally able to get his New Deal legislation through Congress with little difficulty. However, even Democrats criticized Roosevelt's Supreme Court-packing plan. Finally, as the 1938 elections approached, conservatives in Congress formed a "Conservative Coalition" to oppose Roosevelt's liberal agenda.

Roosevelt vetoed 117 bills during the 75th Congress, most of which concerned such minor legislation as private relief bills.

NOMINATIONS, APPOINTMENTS, AND CONFIRMATIONS

The Judiciary: Supreme Court Justice Willis Van Devanter retired on June 2, 1937. On August 12, 1937, President Franklin D. Roosevelt nominated Hugo L. Black to replace Van Devanter, and on August 17, 1937, the Senate confirmed Black by a 63 to 16 vote. Justice George Sutherland retired on January 17, 1938. President Roosevelt already had nominated Stanley F. Reed on January 15,

1938, to replace Sutherland. The Senate confirmed Reed on January 25, 1938, by voice vote. On July 9, 1938, Justice Benjamin N. Cardozo died, but he was not replaced until the 76th Congress.

The Executive Branch: On April 27, 1937, President Roosevelt nominated Harry H. Woodring to be secretary of war, and on May 6, 1937, the Senate confirmed Woodring by voice vote.

IMPEACHMENTS

None.

CONSTITUTIONAL AMENDMENTS

None.

FURTHER READING

Conklin, Paul Keith. *The New Deal.* Arlington Heights, Ill.: Harlan Davidson, 1992.

Davis, Kenneth Sydney. *FDR: Into the Storm, 1937-1940: A History.* New York: Random House, 1993.

Maney, Patrick J. *The Roosevelt Presence: A Biography of Franklin Roosevelt.* New York: Twayne Publishers and Macmillan International, 1992.

Patterson, James T. *Congressional Conservatism and the New Deal: The Growth of the Conservative Coalition in Congress, 1933-1939.* Westport, CT: Greenwood Press, 1981 (Reprint of 1967 edition).

Ponsford, Pearl Olive. *Evil Results of Mid-Term Congressional Elections and a Suggested Remedy.* Los Angeles: The University of Southern California Press, 1937.

Yarbrough, Tinsley E. *Mr. Justice Black and His Critics.* Durham, N.C.: Duke University Press, 1988.

The 76th Congress

JANUARY 3, 1939-JANUARY 3, 1941

First Session: January 3, 1939-August 5, 1939
Second Session: September 21, 1939-November 3, 1939
Third Session: January 3, 1940-January 3, 1941

In the 1938 elections for the 76th Congress, the Democrats lost 7 seats in the Senate, reducing their majority from 76 to 69 of the 96 seats. The Republicans gained 7 seats to hold a total of 23. Four seats were not held by either major party. Two of these seats were held by the Farmer-Labor Party, 1 seat by the Progressive Party, and 1 seat by an independent. In the House, the Democrats lost 70 seats, reducing their majority from 331 to 261 of the 435 seats. The Republicans gained 75 seats to hold a total of 164. Ten seats were not held by either major party. Two of these seats were held by the Farmer-Labor Party and 1 seat by the American Labor Party. [See note 3, p. xxix]

BACKGROUND

According to the census of 1940, the population of the United States as of April 1, 1940, was 131,669,275, resulting in a population density of 44.2 persons for each of the country's 2,977,128 square miles. This was a population increase of 7.2 percent over the 1930 census.

In 1939 the American economy began to recover significantly from the Great Depression, largely because of industrial exports to nations that were preparing for World War II. The Munich Pact of 1938 had sought to appease Hitler's territorial ambitions in Europe by giving Nazi Germany the Sudetenland of Czechoslovakia. When Hitler did not stop with the Sudetenland, but took all of Czechoslovakia, the Western powers were finally convinced that Hitler's ambitions could not be stopped by peaceful means. Hitler began to make aggressive moves against Poland. France and Great Britain declared that they would go to war against Germany if it attacked Poland. On August 23, 1939, Germany and the Soviet Union signed a non-aggression treaty and agreed to divide Poland between them. Hitler invaded Poland on September 1, and on September 3, France and Great Britain followed through with their pledge to declare war on Germany.

On September 21, Roosevelt convened the second session of the 76th Congress, and requested that it repeal legislation that prevented the United States from exporting military supplies to nations at war. Roosevelt wanted the United States to be able to ship supplies to the British and French in their war against Nazi Germany. Congress complied, enacting the Neutrality Act of 1939. Also during 1939, physicists in America were achieving significant breakthroughs in developing atomic power through the controlled fission of radioactive atoms. Their discoveries would lead to the development of nuclear weapons by the end of World War II and change forever the nature of warfare.

In 1940 Europe was at war, and President Roosevelt was preparing to campaign for his third term as president. George Washington had declined to serve more than two terms, and

C H R O N O L O G Y

January 3, 1939:	The 76th Congress and the first session begin. William Brockman Bankhead (Dem., Ala.) is reelected Speaker of the House.
January 5, 1939:	President Roosevelt nominates Frank Murphy to succeed Homer S. Cummings as attorney general and Harry L. Hopkins to succeed Daniel C. Roper as secretary of commerce. Roosevelt also nominates Felix Frankfurter to replace Supreme Court Justice Benjamin N. Cardozo, who died during the 75th Congress.
January 17, 1939:	The Senate confirms Murphy and Frankfurter.
January 23, 1939:	The Senate confirms Hopkins.
February 13, 1939:	Supreme Court Justice Louis D. Brandeis retires.
March 20, 1939:	President Roosevelt nominates William O. Douglas to replace Brandeis.
March 22, 1939:	Congress passes the Administrative Reorganization Act of 1939.
April 4, 1939:	The Senate confirms Douglas.
July 13, 1939:	Congress passes Social Security revisions.
July 20, 1939:	Congress passes the Hatch Act.
July 29, 1939:	Congress passes the Alien Registration Act.
August 5, 1939:	The first session ends.
September 21, 1939:	The second session begins.
October 27, 1939:	Congress passes the Neutrality Act of 1939.
November 3, 1939:	The second session ends.
November 16, 1939:	Supreme Court Justice Pierce Butler dies.
January 3, 1940:	The third session begins.
January 4, 1940:	President Roosevelt nominates Frank Murphy to replace Butler, Charles Edison to succeed Claude A. Swanson as secretary of the Navy, and Robert H. Jackson to succeed Frank Murphy as attorney general.

(Continued on p. 351)

although there was not yet any constitutional prohibition against holding more than two terms as president, until 1940 no president had dared to violate this precedent. Like so many leaders throughout history, Roosevelt thought that he was indispensable in a time of national crisis. Finally during 1940, Congress enacted the Alien Registration Act, which provided for the federal registration of over five million aliens on American territory, and passed a selective service act requiring all men between the ages of 21 and 35 to register for the military draft.

SENATE LEADERSHIP

Vice President: John Nance Garner first was elected to Congress in the 58th Congress and served as Speaker of the House in the 72nd Congress before he was elected vice president in the 1932 elections. Garner was vice president from 1933 to 1941.

President Pro Tempore: Key Pittman (Dem, Nev.), until he died on November 10, 1940. William Henry King (Dem, Utah) was elected on November 19, 1940. Pittman first was elected to Congress when he was elected to the Senate in

C H R O N O L O G Y

January 11, 1940:   The Senate confirms Edison.

January 16, 1940:   The Senate confirms Murphy and Jackson.

June 20, 1940:   President Roosevelt nominates Henry L. Stimson to succeed Harry H. Woodring as secretary of war and Frank Knox to succeed Charles Edison as secretary of the Navy.

July 9, 1940:   The Senate confirms Stimson.

July 10, 1940:   The Senate confirms Knox.

August 14, 1940:   President Roosevelt nominates Claude R. Wickard to succeed Henry A. Wallace as secretary of agriculture.

August 23, 1940:   The Senate confirms Wickard.

September 7, 1940:   Congress passes selective service legislation.

September 13, 1940:   President Roosevelt nominates Jesse H. Jones to succeed Harry L. Hopkins as secretary of commerce.

September 14, 1940:   The Senate confirms Jones.

September 15, 1940:   Speaker of the House Bankhead dies.

September 16, 1940:   Samuel Taliaferro Rayburn (Dem., Tex.) is elected the new Speaker of the House.

November 10, 1940:   Senate President Pro Tem Key Pittman (Dem., Nev.) dies.

November 19, 1940:   William Henry King (Dem., Utah) is elected the new Senate president pro tem.

January 3, 1941:   The third session and the 76th Congress end.

[See note 6, p. xxix]

1913, where he served until he died in this congress. He was president pro tem in the 73rd through the 76th Congresses. King first was elected to Congress as a representative in the 55th Congress, and was elected to the Senate in 1916. The 76th Congress was King's only Congress as president pro tem. [See biographical note in 73rd Congress]

Majority Leader: Alben W. Barkley (Dem., Ky.)

Majority Whip: Sherman Minton (Dem., Ind.)

Minority Leader: Charles L. McNary (Rep., Ore.)

Minority Whip: None.

Chairmen of Selected Key Committees: [See note 5, p. xxix]

Committee on Appropriations: Carter Glass (Dem., Va.)

Committee on Banking and Currency: Robert F. Wagner (Dem., N.Y.)

Committee on Finance: Pat Harrison (Dem., Miss.)

Committee on Foreign Relations: Key Pittman (Dem., Nev.)

Committee on the Judiciary: Henry F. Ashurst (Dem., Ariz.)

TABLE OF KEY VOTES

Senate

Subject of Vote	Date of Vote	For	Against
Government Reorganization Authorized	March 22, 1939	63	23
Hatch Act Passed	April 13, 1939	Passed by voice vote	
Social Security Revised	July 13, 1939	57	8
Neutrality Act Revised	October 27, 1939	63	30
Alien Registration Required	June 15, 1940	Passed by voice vote	
Selective Service Bill Passed	August 28, 1940	58	31

House

Subject of Vote	Date of Vote	For	Against
Government Reorganization Authorized	March 8, 1939	246	153
Social Security Revised	June 10, 1939	364	2
Neutrality Act Revised	June 30, 1939	201	187
Hatch Act Passed	July 20, 1939	241	134
Alien Registration Required	July 29, 1939	Passed by voice vote	
Selective Service Bill Passed	September 7, 1940	Passed by voice vote	

[See note 7, p. xxix]

Committee on Military Affairs: Morris Sheppard (Dem., Tex.)

Committee on Naval Affairs: David I. Walsh (Dem., Mass.)

Committee on Rules: Matthew M. Neely (Dem., W.Va.)

HOUSE LEADERSHIP

Speaker of the House: William Brockman Bankhead (Dem., Ala.) was reelected Speaker on January 3, 1939. Bankhead died on September 15, 1940, and Samuel Taliaferro Rayburn (Dem., Tex.) was elected the new Speaker on September 16, 1940. Bankhead first had been elected to Congress in the 65th Congress and served as Speaker from the 74th through the 76th Congresses. Rayburn first had been elected to Congress in the 63rd Congress and served as Speaker in the 77th through 79th, 81st, and 82nd, and 84th through 87th Congresses. Rayburn was a persuasive leader and a master of Democratic party politics, qualities which made him one of the most powerful Speakers in history.

Majority Leader: Sam Rayburn (Dem., Tex.), until he was elected the new Speaker of the House on September 16, 1940. John W. McCormack (Dem., Mass.) became the new majority leader on September 26, 1940.

Majority Whip: Patrick J. Boland (Dem., Pa.).

Minority Leader: Joseph W. Martin Jr. (Rep., Mass.) first had been elected to Congress in the 69th Congress and became the leader of the

House Republicans in the 76th Congress, taking the post of minority leader. Martin was the leader of the House Republicans for the next 20 years and served as minority leader through the 85th Congress except for the 80th and the 83rd Congresses, when the Republicans had a majority in the House and elected Martin the Speaker.

Minority Whip: Harry L. Englebright (Rep., Calif.).

Chairmen of Selected Key Committees: [See note 5, p. xxix]

Committee on Agriculture: J. Marvin Jones (Dem., Tex.), who resigned effective November 20, 1940, to accept an appointment to the U.S. Court of Claims. Hampton P. Fulmer (Dem., S.C.) became the next chairman.

Committee on Appropriations: Edward T. Taylor (Dem., Colo.)

Committee on Banking, Finance, and Urban Affairs: Henry B. Steagall (Dem., Ala.)

Committee on Foreign Affairs: Samuel D. McReynolds (Dem., Tenn.), who died on July 11, 1939. Sol Bloom (Dem., N.Y.) became the next chairman.

Committee on the Judiciary: Hatton W. Sumners (Dem., Tex.)

Committee on Military Affairs: Andrew J. May (Dem., Ky.)

Committee on Naval Affairs: Carl Vinson (Dem., Ga.)

Committee on Rules: Adolph J. Sabath (Dem., Ill.)

Committee on Ways and Means: Robert L. Doughton (Dem., N.C.)

ORGANIZATION AND ADMINISTRATION

No developments of significance. [See note 5, p. xxix]

MAJOR LEGISLATION PASSED

Aliens: In the Alien Registration Act, Congress required over five million aliens to register with federal authorities.

Foreign Policy: In the Neutrality Act of 1939, Congress repealed many of the restrictions on selling military supplies to nations at war.

Government: In the Administrative Reorganization Act of 1939, Congress gave the president the authority to reorganize executive agencies.

Government Employees: In the Hatch Act, Congress placed restrictions on how involved federal employees could be in political campaigns and elections.

Selective Service: In the Selective Training and Service Act, Congress required all men between the ages of 21 and 35 to register for the draft.

Social Security: Congress implemented various revisions and amendments to the Social Security system established by the 74th Congress.

FAILED LEGISLATION

None of historical significance.

RELATIONS WITH THE PRESIDENT

President Roosevelt's fellow Democrats held comfortable majorities in both houses of Congress, despite the loss of 70 seats in the House, and thus Roosevelt was still able to get legislation, most of which dealt with foreign policy and defense, through Congress without great difficulty.

Roosevelt vetoed 167 bills during the 76th Congress, most of which concerned such minor legislation as private relief bills.

NOMINATIONS, APPOINTMENTS, AND CONFIRMATIONS

The Judiciary: Supreme Court Justice Benjamin N. Cardozo had died on July 9, 1938, and had not been replaced during the 75th Congress. President Franklin D. Roosevelt nominated Felix

Frankfurter on January 5, 1939, to replace Cardozo, and the Senate confirmed Frankfurter on January 17, 1939, by voice vote. On February 13, 1939, Justice Louis D. Brandeis retired, and President Roosevelt nominated William O. Douglas on March 20, 1939, to replace Brandeis. The Senate confirmed Douglas on April 4, 1939, by a 62 to 4 vote. Justice Pierce Butler died on November 16, 1939, and President Roosevelt nominated Frank Murphy on January 4, 1940, to replace Butler. The Senate confirmed Murphy on January 16, 1940, by voice vote.

The Executive Branch: On January 5, 1939, President Roosevelt nominated Frank Murphy to succeed Homer S. Cummings as attorney general and Harry L. Hopkins to succeed Daniel C. Roper as secretary of commerce. The Senate confirmed Murphy by a vote of 78 to 7 on January 17, 1939, and Hopkins by a vote of 58 to 27 on January 23, 1939. On January 4, 1940, Roosevelt nominated Charles Edison to succeed Claude A. Swanson as secretary of the Navy and Robert H. Jackson to succeed Frank Murphy as attorney general. The Senate confirmed Edison by voice vote on January 11, 1940, and Jackson by voice vote on January 16, 1940. On June 20, 1940, Roosevelt nominated Henry L. Stimson to succeed Harry H. Woodring as secretary of war and Frank Knox to succeed Charles Edison as secretary of the Navy. The Senate confirmed Stimson by a vote of 56 to 28 on July 9, 1940, and Knox by a vote of 66 to 16 on July 10, 1940. Roosevelt nominated Claude R. Wickard to succeed Henry A. Wallace as secretary of agriculture on August 14, 1940, and on August 23, 1940, the Senate confirmed Wickard by voice vote. On September 13, 1940, Roosevelt nominated Jesse H. Jones to succeed Harry L. Hopkins as secretary of commerce, and on September 14, 1940, the Senate confirmed Jones by voice vote.

IMPEACHMENTS

None.

CONSTITUTIONAL AMENDMENTS

None.

FURTHER READING

Conklin, Paul Keith. *The New Deal.* Arlington Heights, Ill.: Harlan Davidson, 1992.

Davis, Kenneth Sydney. *FDRep., Into the Storm, 1937-1940: A History.* New York: Random House, 1993.

Douglas, William O. *The Court Years, 1939-1975.* New York: Random House, 1980.

Hardeman, D.B., and Donald C. Bacon. *Rayburn: A Biography.* Austin: Texas Monthly Press, 1987.

Herzstein, Robert Edwin. *Roosevelt & Hitler: Prelude to War.* New York: J. Wiley, 1994.

Maney, Patrick J. *The Roosevelt Presence: A Biography of Franklin Roosevelt.* New York: Twayne Publishers and Macmillan International, 1992.

Patterson, James T. *Congressional Conservatism and the New Deal: The Growth of the Conservative Coalition in Congress, 1933-1939.* Westport, CT: Greenwood Press, 1981 (Reprint of 1967 edition).

Parrish, Michael E. *Felix Frankfurter and His Times.* New York: Free Press, 1982.

The 77th Congress

JANUARY 3, 1941-JANUARY 3, 1943

First Session: January 3, 1941-January 2, 1942
Second Session: January 5, 1942-December 16, 1942

In the 1940 elections for the 77th Congress, the Democrats lost 3 seats in the Senate, reducing their majority from 69 to 66 of the 96 seats. The Republicans gained 5 seats to hold a total of 28. Two seats were not held by either major party. One seat was held by the Progressive Party and 1 seat by an independent. In the House, the Democrats gained 7 seats, increasing their majority from 261 to 268 of the 435 seats. The Republicans lost 2 seats, reducing their total to 162. Five seats were not held by either major party. Three seats were held by the Progressive Party, 1 seat by the Farmer-Labor Party and 1 seat by the American Labor Party. [See note 3, p. xxix]

BACKGROUND

Franklin D. Roosevelt was inaugurated for his third term as the 32nd president of the United States on January 20, 1941. Roosevelt was the only president to break the tradition of serving only two terms that was set by George Washington. During 1941 most of the 77th Congress's legislation was related to World War II. Although the United States still officially was neutral, it was providing assistance to the Allies against Nazi Germany. For example, Congress passed the Lend-Lease Act, which provided for "loans" of military supplies to the Allies. On May 27, after the Nazis took Yugoslavia and Greece, Roosevelt declared a state of national emergency. On June 14 Roosevelt froze German and Italian assets in the United States and on June 16 closed all the German consulates in the U.S. On July 25 Roosevelt also took actions

against the empire of Japan, which was allied with Germany and Italy. Roosevelt froze all Japanese assets in the U.S. and halted exports of gasoline and scrap iron from the U.S. to Japan. On August 12 Roosevelt and Winston Churchill, the prime minister of Great Britain, secretly agreed on the terms of the Atlantic Charter. The Atlantic Charter was to be a wartime alliance between the U.S. and Great Britain and was the forerunner of the North Atlantic Treaty Organization (NATO).

Meanwhile, the Allies were suffering military defeats in 1941. Hitler had conquered all of continental Western Europe, except for the neutral nations of Portugal, Spain, Sweden, and Switzerland. The Allies consisted of Great Britain and the governments-in-exile of France, Poland, and other conquered nations. On June 22 the Germans invaded the Soviet Union and were closing in on Moscow by the end of the year. By the end of 1941, however, the U.S. had joined the Allies. On December 7 the Japanese attacked Pearl Harbor, and on December 8 Congress declared war on Japan. Several days later, Germany and Italy declared war on the U.S., and Congress in turn declared war against those nations as well.

In 1942 the nation was mobilizing for war, and Congress delegated extensive powers to President Roosevelt as the commander in chief. For example, the Emergency Price Control Act created the Office of Price Administration, which effectively gave the executive branch control over the entire economy. During the first half of 1942, American involvement in World War II was focused on the

Pacific, where U.S. forces were defeated in the Battle of the Java Sea, lost the Philippines, and lost the Battle of the Coral Sea. In the summer, the situation began to turn in America's favor. The U.S. won the Battle of Midway, which lasted from June 4 until June 6. On August 7 the U.S. went on the offensive against the Japanese when the Marines landed on the island of Guadalcanal. American forces also went on the offensive against Nazi Germany, when on November 7 U.S. troops invaded Nazi-occupied North Africa. Although the war effort was achieving some successes by the end of the 77th Congress, it also was very expensive, and the budget bills passed by Congress included some of the largest budget deficits in American history.

SENATE LEADERSHIP

Vice President: John Nance Garner was vice president until Henry Agard Wallace became the new vice president at noon on January 20, 1941. [See note 8, p. xxix] When President Roosevelt was elected to a third term in the elections of November 1940, his running mate was Wallace, not Garner. Wallace had been Roosevelt's secretary of agriculture from 1933 to 1940 and had never served in Congress.

President Pro Tempore: Pat Harrison (Dem., Miss.) was elected on January 6, 1941. Harrison first had been elected to Congress as a representative to the 62nd Congress and had been elected to the Senate in 1918, where he served as president pro tem in only the 77th Congress. Harrison died on June 22, 1941, and Carter Glass (Dem., Va.) was elected on July 10, 1941. Glass first had been elected to Congress as a representative to the 57th Congress, had served as President Wilson's secretary of the Treasury from 1918 to 1920, and had left the cabinet for the Senate in 1920. Glass served as president pro tem in the 77th and 78th Congresses.

Majority Leader: Alben W. Barkley (Dem., Ky.)

Majority Whip: Lister Hill (Dem., Ala.)

Minority Leader: Charles L. McNary (Rep., Ore.)

Minority Whip: None.

Chairmen of Selected Key Committees: [See note 5, p. xxix]

Committee on Appropriations: Carter Glass (Dem., Va.)

Committee on Banking and Currency: Robert F. Wagner (Dem., N.Y.)

Committee on Finance: Pat Harrison (Dem., Miss.), who died on June 22, 1941. Walter F. George (Dem., Ga.) became the next chairman.

Committee on Foreign Relations: Walter F. George (Dem., Ga.), until he became chairman of the Finance Committee. Tom Connally (Dem., Tex.) became the next chairman.

Committee on the Judiciary: Frederick Van Nuys (Dem., Ind.)

Committee on Military Affairs: Morris Sheppard (Dem., Tex.), who died on April 9, 1941. Robert R. Reynolds (Dem., N.C.) became the next chairman.

Committee on Naval Affairs: David I. Walsh (Dem., Mass.)

Committee on Rules: Harry Flood Byrd (Dem., Va.)

HOUSE LEADERSHIP

Speaker of the House: Samuel Taliaferro Rayburn (Dem., Tex.) was reelected Speaker on January 3, 1941. [See biographical note in 76th Congress]

Majority Leader: John W. McCormack (Dem., Mass.)

Majority Whip: Patrick J. Boland (Dem., Pa.), until he died on May 18, 1942. Robert Ramspeck (Dem., Ga.) became the new majority whip on June 8, 1942.

Minority Leader: Joseph W. Martin Jr. (Rep., Mass.). [See biographical note in 76th Congress]

Minority Whip: Harry L. Englebright (Rep., Calif.)

Chairmen of Selected Key Committees: [See note 5, p. xxix]

C H R O N O L O G Y

January 3, 1941:	The 77th Congress and the first session begin. Samuel Taliaferro Rayburn (Dem., Tex.) is reelected Speaker of the House.
January 6, 1941:	Pat Harrison (Dem., Miss.) is elected Senate president pro tem.
February 1, 1941:	Supreme Court Justice James C. McReynolds retires.
March 8, 1941:	Congress passes the Lend-Lease Act.
June 12, 1941:	President Roosevelt nominates James F. Byrnes and Robert H. Jackson to replace McReynolds and retiring Chief Justice Charles Evans Hughes. The Senate confirms Byrnes.
June 22, 1941:	Senate President Pro Tem Harrison dies.
July 7, 1941:	The Senate confirms Jackson.
July 10, 1941:	Carter Glass (Dem., Va.) is elected the new Senate president pro tem.
August 12, 1941:	Congress passes prewar selective service legislation.
August 25, 1941:	President Roosevelt nominates Francis Biddle to succeed Robert H. Jackson as attorney general.
September 5, 1941:	The Senate confirms Biddle.
December 8, 1941:	Congress passes a declaration of war against Japan.
December 11, 1941:	Congress passes declarations of war against Germany and Italy.
December 17, 1941:	Congress passes the War Powers Act of 1941.
December 18, 1941:	Congress passes another wartime selective service act.
January 2, 1942:	The first session ends.
January 5, 1942:	The second session begins.
January 10, 1942:	Congress passes legislation creating the Office of Price Administration.
February 28, 1942:	Congress passes the War Powers Act of 1942.
October 3, 1942:	Supreme Court Justice Byrnes resigns and is not replaced until the 78th Congress.
October 24, 1942:	Congress passes the Teenage Draft Act of 1942.
December 16, 1942:	The second session ends.
January 3, 1943:	The 77th Congress ends.

[See note 6, p. xxix]

Committee on Agriculture: Hampton P. Fulmer (Dem., S.C.)

Committee on Appropriations: Edward T. Taylor (Dem., Colo.), who died on September 3, 1941. Clarence A. Cannon (Dem., Mo.) became the next chairman.

Committee on Banking, Finance, and Urban Affairs: Henry B. Steagall (Dem., Ala.)

Committee on Foreign Affairs: Sol Bloom (Dem., N.Y.)

Committee on the Judiciary: Hatton W. Sumners (Dem., Tex.)

Committee on Military Affairs: Andrew J. May (Dem., Ky.)

Committee on Naval Affairs: Carl Vinson (Dem., Ga.)

TABLE OF KEY VOTES

Senate

Subject of Vote	Date of Vote	For	Against
Lend-Lease Bill Passed	March 8, 1941	60	31
First 1941 Selective Service Act Passed	August 7, 1941	45	30
Declaration of War Against Japan Adopted	December 8, 1941	82	0
Declaration of War Against Germany Adopted	December 11, 1941	88	0
Declaration of War Against Italy Adopted	December 11, 1941	90	0
War Powers Act of 1941 Passed	December 17, 1941	Passed by voice vote	
Second 1941 Selective Service Act Passed	December 18, 1941	79	2
Office of Price Administration Established	January 10, 1942	84	1
War Powers Act of 1942 Passed	January 28, 1942	Passed by voice vote	
Teenage Draft Act Passed	October 24, 1942	58	5

House

Subject of Vote	Date of Vote	For	Against
Lend-Lease Bill Passed	February 8, 1941	260	165
First 1941 Selective Service Act Passed	August 12, 1941	203	202
Office of Price Administration Established	November 28, 1941	224	161
Declaration of War Against Japan Adopted	December 8, 1941	Passed by voice vote	
Declaration of War Against Germany Adopted	December 11, 1941	Passed by voice vote	
Declaration of War Against Italy Adopted	December 11, 1941	399	0*
War Powers Act of 1941 Passed	December 17, 1941	Passed by voice vote	
Second 1941 Selective Service Act Passed	December 17, 1941	Passed by voice vote	
War Powers Act of 1942 Passed	February 28, 1942	Passed by voice vote	
Teenage Draft Act Passed	October 17, 1942	345	16

[See note 7, p. xxix]

* Jeannette Rankin (Rep., Mont.) voted "not present," which was not recorded as a vote against the declaration of war, but simply as the only member not present. Rankin was the only member of Congress to express such reluctance to entering the war. After her vote, she had to be escorted to her office by Capital Building security men in order to protect her.

Committee on Rules: Adolph J. Sabath (Dem., Ill.)

Committee on Ways and Means: Robert L. Doughton (Dem., N.C.)

ORGANIZATION AND ADMINISTRATION

No developments of significance. [See note 5, p. xxix]

MAJOR LEGISLATION PASSED

Declarations of War: After Pearl Harbor, Congress passed three declarations of war within a few days. Congress declared war on Japan, Germany, and Italy.

Lend-Lease: In the Lend-Lease Act, Congress authorized the president to provide military supplies to nations deemed vital to American national security.

Office of Price Administration: In the Emergency Price Control Act, Congress created the Office of Price Administration and gave it extensive powers over the economy, including implementation of rent and price controls.

Selective Service: In anticipation of World War II in the Summer of 1941, Congress increased draftees' term of service from one year to 30 months. In the House, antiwar sentiment was very strong, and the Selective Service legislation passed by only one vote. After Congress declared war against the Axis powers, it passed another selective service act, which required all men between the ages of 18 and 65 to register for the draft and made all men between the ages of 20 and 45 subject to immediate induction. (In the Table of Key Votes below, these acts are referred to as the First 1941 Selective Service Act and the Second 1941 Selective Service Act.) Finally, in the Teenage Draft Act of 1942, Congress expanded the scope of immediate induction to include 18-year-old and 19-year-old men.

War Powers: In the War Powers Act of 1941, Congress gave the president virtually unlimited power to mobilize and reorganize the government for war. In the War Powers Act of 1942, Congress gave the president the power to order the transfer of economic resources into war production.

FAILED LEGISLATION

None of historical significance.

RELATIONS WITH THE PRESIDENT

With fellow Democrats holding comfortable majorities in both houses of Congress, President Roosevelt generally was able to get his wartime legislation through Congress without great difficulty.

Roosevelt vetoed 82 bills during the 77th Congress, which concerned such minor legislation as private relief bills.

NOMINATIONS, APPOINTMENTS, AND CONFIRMATIONS

The Judiciary: Two justices of the Supreme Court retired in 1941: James C. McReynolds on February 1, 1941, and Chief Justice Charles Evans Hughes on July 1, 1941. President Franklin D. Roosevelt filled both vacancies by the end of 1941: He nominated James F. Byrnes and Robert H. Jackson on June 12, 1941. The Senate confirmed Byrnes on June 12, 1941, by voice vote and Jackson on July 7, 1941, without a vote. On October 3, 1942, Justice Byrnes resigned and was not replaced until the 78th Congress. Also on June 12, 1941, Roosevelt nominated Associate Justice Harlan F. Stone to be the next chief justice, and on June 27, 1941, the Senate confirmed Stone by a voice vote.

The Executive Branch: President Roosevelt nominated Francis Biddle on August 25, 1941, to succeed Robert H. Jackson as attorney general, and the Senate confirmed Biddle by voice vote on September 5, 1941.

IMPEACHMENTS

None.

CONSTITUTIONAL AMENDMENTS

None.

FURTHER READING

Brinkley, David. *Washington Goes to War*. New York: Alfred A. Knopf, 1988.

Gerhart, Eugene C. *America's Advocate: Robert H. Jackson*. Indianapolis, Ind.: Bobbs-Merrill, 1958.

Goodwin, Doris Kearns. *No Ordinary Time: Franklin and Eleanor Roosevelt: The Home Front in World War Two*. New York: Simon & Schuster, 1994.

Hardeman, D.B., and Donald C. Bacon. *Rayburn: A Biography*. Austin: Texas Monthly Press, 1987.

Maney, Patrick J. *The Roosevelt Presence: A Biography of Franklin Roosevelt*. New York: Twayne Publishers and Macmillan International, 1992.

Robertson, David. *Sly and Able: A Political Biography of James F. Byrnes*. New York: Norton, 1994.

The 78th Congress

JANUARY 3, 1943-JANUARY 3, 1945

First Session: January 6, 1943-December 21, 1943
Second Session: January 10, 1944-December 19, 1944

In the 1942 elections for the 78th Congress, the Democrats lost 8 seats in the Senate, reducing their majority from 66 to 58 of the 96 seats. The Republicans gained 9 seats to hold a total of 37. One seat was held by the Progressive Party. In the House, the Democrats lost 50 seats, reducing their majority from 268 to 218 of the 435 seats. The Republicans gained 46 seats to hold a total of 208. Nine seats were not held by either major party. Two of these seats were held by the Progressive Party, 1 seat by the Farmer-Labor Party, and 1 seat by the American Labor Party. [See note 3, p. xxix]

BACKGROUND

By 1943 the United States and the other Allies were beginning to win World War II. The Allies had stopped the German and Japanese offensives in Europe and the Pacific and were beginning to push the enemy back. The Allies took North Africa, invaded Sicily and Italy, and U.S. forces defeated the Japanese throughout the Pacific. From November 21, 1943, until December 1, 1943, Roosevelt met with Great Britain's Prime Minister Winston Churchill and Soviet dictator Joseph Stalin to make plans for the impending invasion of Nazi-occupied Europe.

Also during 1943, Congress passed some significant nonwar legislation, namely, the Current Tax Payment Act. The act fundamentally changed the nature of the federal income tax system. Prior to the act, taxpayers made quarterly estimated tax payments and thus had to pay money to the government every three months. The act introduced the modern system of withholding taxes from individual paychecks. By withholding small amounts from weekly or biweekly paychecks, the government could collect more taxes than under the previous system, where people were forced to make large lump sum payments every three months. The new "pay as you go" system drew upon the experience of the American retail sales industry, which had known for many decades that it was easier to get Americans to spend their money in a series of small payments made very frequently (such as the monthly installment plan), rather than a few large payments. By drawing upon private industry's experience with consumer psychology, Congress was able to set up a federal income tax system that made massive tax increases possible.

On June 6, 1944, the Allies invaded Normandy and began the liberation of Western Europe. The U.S. also was advancing against the Japanese in the Pacific. Elsewhere, the Soviets were forcing the Germans to retreat all along the Eastern Front. On August 21, 1945, representatives of the United States, China, Great Britain, and the Soviet Union met at the Dumbarton Oaks Conference in Washington,

D.C. At the conference, the Allies agreed in principle to establish the United Nations after the war. By the end of 1944 the Nazis were nearly defeated, despite a short-lived German counteroffensive in the Battle of the Bulge during December. Finally, the 78th Congress passed the Servicemen's Readjustment Act, which gave extensive benefits to World War II veterans, such as financial assistance for higher education. These benefits were known as the G.I. Bill.

SENATE LEADERSHIP

Vice President: Henry Agard Wallace had been elected vice president on Roosevelt's ticket in 1940 after serving as secretary of agriculture from 1933 to 1940. He had never served in Congress.

President Pro Tempore: Carter Glass (Dem., Va.). [See biographical note in 77th Congress]

Majority Leader: Alben W. Barkley (Dem., Ky.)

Majority Whip: Lister Hill (Dem., Ala.)

Minority Leader: Charles L. McNary (Rep., Ore.)

Minority Whip: Kenneth Wherry (Rep., Neb.)

Chairmen of Selected Key Committees: [See note 5, p. xxix]

Committee on Appropriations: Carter Glass (Dem., Va.)

Committee on Banking and Currency: Robert F. Wagner (Dem., N.Y.)

Committee on Finance: Walter F. George (Dem., Ga.)

Committee on Foreign Relations: Tom Connally (Dem., Tex.)

Committee on the Judiciary: Frederick Van Nuys (Dem., Ind.)

Committee on Military Affairs: Robert R. Reynolds (Dem., N.C.)

Committee on Naval Affairs: David I. Walsh (Dem., Mass.)

Committee on Rules: Harry Flood Byrd (Dem., Va.)

HOUSE LEADERSHIP

Speaker of the House: Samuel Taliaferro Rayburn (Dem., Tex.) was reelected Speaker on January 6, 1943. [See biographical note in 76th Congress]

Majority Leader: John W. McCormack (Dem., Mass.)

Majority Whip: Robert Ramspeck (Dem., Ga.)

Minority Leader: Joseph W. Martin Jr. (Rep., Mass.) [See biographical note in 76th Congress]

Minority Whip: Leslie C. Arends (Rep., Ill.)

Chairmen of Selected Key Committees: [See note 5, p. xxix]

Committee on Agriculture: Hampton P. Fulmer (Dem., S.C.), who died on October 19, 1944. John W. Flannagan Jr. (Dem., Va.) became the next chairman.

Committee on Appropriations: Clarence A. Cannon (Dem., Mo.)

Committee on Banking, Finance, and Urban Affairs: Henry B. Steagall (Dem., Ala.), who died on November 22, 1943. Brent Spence (Dem., Ky.) became the next chairman.

Committee on Foreign Affairs: Sol Bloom (Dem., N.Y.)

Committee on the Judiciary: Hatton W. Sumners (Dem., Tex.)

Committee on Military Affairs: Andrew J. May (Dem., Ky.)

Committee on Naval Affairs: Carl Vinson (Dem., Ga.)

Committee on Rules: Adolph J. Sabath (Dem., Ill.)

Committee on Ways and Means: Robert L. Doughton (Dem., N.C.)

ORGANIZATION AND ADMINISTRATION

No developments of significance. [See note 5, p. xxix]

C H R O N O L O G Y

January 3, 1943:	The 78th Congress begins.
January 6, 1943:	The first session begins, and Samuel Taliaferro Rayburn (Dem., Tex.) is reelected Speaker of the House.
January 11, 1943:	President Franklin D. Roosevelt nominates Wiley B. Rutledge to replace Supreme Court Justice James F. Byrnes, who resigned during the 77th Congress.
February 8, 1943:	The Senate confirms Rutledge.
May 14, 1943:	Congress passes the Current Tax Payment Act.
June 4, 1943:	Congress passes the Smith-Connally Anti-Strike Act.
June 25, 1943:	President Roosevelt vetoes a wartime industry bill restricting strikes and other labor activities. The Senate and the House vote to override the veto.
December 21, 1943:	The first session ends.
January 10, 1944:	The second session begins.
February 22, 1944:	President Roosevelt vetoes a revenue act.
February 24, 1944:	The House votes to override the veto.
February 25, 1944:	The Senate also votes to override the veto.
May 10, 1944:	President Roosevelt nominates James V. Forrestal to succeed Frank Knox as secretary of the Navy.
May 17, 1944:	The Senate confirms Forrestal.
May 18, 1944:	Congress passes the G.I. Bill.
August 25, 1944:	Congress passes legislation concerning surplus government property.
August 31, 1944:	Congress passes legislation to implement the transition from a wartime ecomomy back to a civilian economy.
November 27, 1944:	President Roosevelt nominates Edward R. Stettinius to succeed Cordell Hull as secretary of state.
November 30, 1944:	The Senate confirms Stettinius.
December 19, 1944:	The second session ends.
January 3, 1945:	The 78th Congress ends.

[See note 6, p. xxix]

MAJOR LEGISLATION PASSED

G.I. Bill: In the Servicemen's Readjustment Act of 1944, Congress passed the G.I. Bill, which gave veterans extensive benefits. These benefits included educational assistance, which would help millions of Americans get a higher education that they otherwise could not have afforded, and government insured home mortgages for veterans. Roosevelt was wary of the bill, which was sponsored by the American Legion and passed with the support of a coalition of southern Democrats and moderate Republicans.

Labor: In the Smith-Connally Anti-Strike Act, Congress placed severe restrictions on the ability

TABLE OF KEY VOTES

Senate

Subject of Vote	Date of Vote	For	Against
Income Taxes Made Pay-As-You-Go	May 14, 1943	49	30
Anti-Strike Bill Passed	May 15, 1943	63	16
G.I. Bill Passed	March 24, 1944	50	0
Reconversion Plan Authorized	August 11, 1944	55	19
Surplus Property Bill Passed	August 25, 1944	Passed by voice vote	

House

Subject of Vote	Date of Vote	For	Against
Income Taxes Made Pay-As-You-Go	May 4, 1943	313	95
Anti-Strike Bill Passed	June 4, 1943	233	141
G.I. Bill Passed	May 18, 1944	388	0
Surplus Property Bill Passed	August 22, 1944	Passed by voice vote	
Reconversion Plan Authorized	August 31, 1944	Passed by voice vote	

[See note 7, p. xxix]

---

of unions to go on strike during wartime and made strikes illegal in "war industries."

Reconversion: In the War Mobilization and Reconversion Act, Congress gave the Office of War Mobilization and Reconversion the power and responsibility for reconverting the wartime economy back to a civilian economy.

Surplus Property: In the Surplus Property Act of 1944, Congress provided for auctions and other means to dispose of surplus government property, primarily excess war material.

Taxes: In the Current Tax Payment Act, Congess created the modern "pay-as-you-go" system of withholding taxes. [See Background, above]

FAILED LEGISLATION

None of historical significance.

RELATIONS WITH THE PRESIDENT

President Roosevelt did not dominate this Congress as he had previous Congresses. After the 1942 elections, the Democratic majorities in both houses were significantly narrowed. Furthermore Roosevelt's health was failing, and he was no longer the dynamic leader of former years.

Roosevelt vetoed 46 bills during the 78th Congress. Two important vetoes were overridden by Congress. First, on June 25, 1943, Roosevelt vetoed a bill concerning the wartime control of industrial facilities by the government, which also restricted strikes and other labor activities. On that same day, the Senate voted 56 to 25 to override the veto, and the House also voted to override by a vote of 244 to 108. Second, on February 22, 1944, Roosevelt vetoed a revenue act. On February 24, 1944, the House voted 299 to 95 to override the veto, and on February 25, 1944, the Senate also voted to override by a vote of 72 to 14.

NOMINATIONS, APPOINTMENTS, AND CONFIRMATIONS

The Judiciary: On October 3, 1942, during the 77th Congress, Supreme Court Justice James F. Byrnes resigned. President Franklin D. Roosevelt nominated Wiley B. Rutledge on January 11, 1943, to replace Byrnes, and the Senate on February 8, 1943, confirmed Rutledge without a vote.

The Executive Branch: On May 10, 1944, President Roosevelt nominated James V. Forrestal to succeed Frank Knox as secretary of the Navy, and on May 17, 1944, the Senate confirmed Forrestal by voice vote. Roosevelt nominated Edward R. Stettinius to succeed Cordell Hull as secretary of state on November 27, 1944, and the Senate confirmed Stettinius by a 68 to 1 vote on November 30, 1944.

IMPEACHMENTS

None.

CONSTITUTIONAL AMENDMENTS

None.

FURTHER READING

Brinkley, David. *Washington Goes to War.* New York: Alfred A. Knopf, 1988.

Goodwin, Doris Kearns. *No Ordinary Time: Franklin and Eleanor Roosevelt: The Home Front in World War Two.* New York: Simon & Schuster, 1994.

Hardeman, D.B., and Donald C. Bacon. *Rayburn: A Biography.* Austin: Texas Monthly Press, 1987.

Maney, Patrick J. *The Roosevelt Presence: A Biography of Franklin Roosevelt.* New York: Twayne Publishers and Macmillan International, 1992.

The 79th Congress

JANUARY 3, 1945 - JANUARY 3, 1947

First Session: *January 3, 1945-December 21, 1945*
Second Session: *January 14, 1946-August 2, 1946*

In the 1944 elections for the 79th Congress, the Democrats lost 2 seats in the Senate, reducing their majority from 58 to 56 of the 96 seats. The Republicans gained 1 seat to hold a total of 38. Two seats were not held by either major party. One of these seats was held by the Progressive Party. In the House, the Democrats gained 24 seats, increasing their majority from 218 to 242 of the 435 seats. The Republicans lost 18 seats, reducing their total to 190. Three seats were not held by either major party. One seat was held by the Progressive Party and 1 seat by the American Labor Party. [See note 3, p. xxix]

BACKGROUND

Franklin D. Roosevelt was inaugurated for his fourth term as the 32nd president of the United States on January 20, 1945. Roosevelt was the only president to serve more than two terms. In 1945 the U.S. and the other Allies were nearing final victory in World War II as they entered German territory and closed in on the home islands of Japan. Roosevelt met with the other Allied leaders on several occasions in order to prepare for the postwar situation in Europe and the world. From February 4 until February 11, 1945, Roosevelt met with Great Britain's Prime Minister Winston Churchill and Soviet dictator Joseph Stalin in the Yalta Conference, which was held in the Soviet Union. On February 12 the Allied leaders issued a resolution calling for a

United Nations Conference, which met on April 24 in San Francisco, California. Roosevelt died on April 12 before the conference began, and Harry S. Truman was sworn in as the 33rd president of the United States. Germany surrendered to the Allies on May 7, and the United Nations Conference ended on June 26 when 50 countries signed the new Charter of the United Nations. The U.S. Senate approved the United Nations Charter on July 28. Meanwhile, in the Pacific the U.S. decided to use a new weapon in the war against Japan, rather than risk the heavy casualties that were predicted from a conventional invasion of the Japanese home islands. That weapon was the atomic bomb, developed in the Manhattan Project, which was kept so secret that although over $2 billion in defense funds were spent, the Congress and Vice President Truman were kept in the dark about the bomb's existence. When he became president after Roosevelt's death and learned about the bomb, Truman formed an "Interim Committee" to decide whether the bomb should be used on the Japanese. The committee had no members of Congress on it, but was composed solely of seven senior members of Truman's administration. On June 1, 1945 the committee advised Truman that the bomb should be used on Japan. That same day, Truman sent Congress a message, promising to pursue the policy of unconditional surrender with the Japanese "using ships, aircraft, armor, artillery, and all other material in massive concentration. We have the men, the material, the skill, the leadership, the fortitude to achieve total victory." Other than this elliptical reference to the use of massive force, Congress received no formal notification or consultation concerning Truman's decision to use the bomb. The United States dropped an atomic bomb on Hiroshima on August 6, and a second atomic bomb on Nagasaki on August 9. The Japanese surrendered on August 14, 1945.

World War II was over. The United States was victorious, and it was unquestionably the most powerful country in the world. Unlike the other Allies, the U.S. had experienced very little conflict on its own territory, and thus its population and economic base were undamaged. In fact, the war had helped the American economy and brought it out of the Great Depression. Furthermore, the U.S. was the only country in the world with nuclear weapons. In order to control this new technology, Congress passed the Atomic Energy Act, which created the Atomic Energy Commission. Congress gave the commission the authority to regulate various matters relating to atomic energy. Finally, by the end of the 79th Congress, Congress was beginning to remove the wartime controls over the civilian economy. For example, most of the World War II wage and price controls, with the exception of rent control, were lifted by the end of 1946.

SENATE LEADERSHIP

Vice President: Henry Agard Wallace, who had been elected on FDR's ticket in 1940, was vice president until January 20, 1945, when Harry S. Truman, elected with Roosevelt in November 1944, became the new vice president. [See note 8, p. xxix] Prior to becoming vice president, Truman had served as a senator from Missouri since 1935. He became president upon the death of President Franklin Delano Roosevelt on April 12, 1945, leaving the Senate without a president until January 20, 1949. (Until the Twenty-fifth Amendment was ratified on February 10, 1967 [See 90th Congress], there was no mechanism for filling vacancies in the office of the vice president.)

President Pro Tempore: Kenneth McKellar (Dem., Tenn.) was elected on January 6, 1945. McKellar first had been elected as a representative to the 62nd Congress and had been elected to the Senate in 1916. McKellar served as president pro tem in the 79th, 81st, and 82nd Congresses.

Majority Leader: Alben W. Barkley (Dem., Ky.)

Majority Whip: Lister Hill (Dem., Ala.)

Minority Leader: Wallace H. White Jr. (Rep., Maine)

Minority Whip: Kenneth Wherry (Rep., Neb.)

Chairmen of Selected Key Committees: [See also Organization and Administration, below]

Committee on Appropriations: Carter Glass (Dem., Va.)

Committee on Banking and Currency: Robert F. Wagner (Dem., N.Y.)

Committee on Finance: Walter F. George (Dem., Ga.)

Committee on Foreign Relations: Tom Connally (Dem., Tex.)

Committee on the Judiciary: Pat McCarran (Dem., Nev.)

Committee on Military Affairs: Elbert Thomas (Dem., Utah)

Committee on Naval Affairs: David I. Walsh (Dem., Mass.)

Committee on Rules: Harry Flood Byrd (Dem., Va.)

HOUSE LEADERSHIP

Speaker of the House: Samuel Taliaferro Rayburn (Dem., Tex.) was reelected Speaker on January 3, 1945. [See biographical note in 76th Congress]

Majority Leader: John W. McCormack (Dem., Mass.)

Majority Whip: Robert Ramspeck (Dem., Ga.), until he resigned on December 31, 1945. John J.

C H R O N O L O G Y

January 3, 1945:	The 79th Congress and the first session begin. Samuel Taliaferro Rayburn (Dem., Tex.) is reelected Speaker of the House. The House makes its Committee on Un-American Activities a permanent committee.
January 6, 1945:	Kenneth McKellar (Dem., Tenn.) is elected Senate president pro tem.
July 19, 1945:	Congress passes legislation implementing the Bretton Woods agreements.
July 28, 1945:	The Senate approves the U.N. Charter.
July 31, 1945:	Supreme Court Justice Owen J. Roberts resigns.
September 18, 1945:	President Truman nominates Harold H. Burton to replace Roberts.
September 19, 1945:	The Senate confirms Burton.
December 14, 1945:	Congress passes the Employment Act of 1946.
December 21, 1945:	The first session ends.
January 14, 1946:	The second session begins.
April 22, 1946:	Chief Justice Harlan F. Stone dies.
June 6, 1946:	President Truman nominates Fred M. Vinson to replace Stone.
June 20, 1946:	The Senate confirms Vinson.
July 13, 1946:	Congress approves a loan to Great Britain.
July 20, 1946:	Congress passes the Atomic Energy Act.
July 25, 1946:	Congress passes sweeping internal reorganization legislation.
July 27, 1946:	Congress passes legislation creating the Fulbright Scholars program.
August 2, 1946:	The second session ends.
January 3, 1947:	The 79th Congress ends.

[See note 6, p. xxix]

Sparkman (Dem., Ala.) became the new majority whip on January 14, 1946.

Minority Leader: Joseph W. Martin Jr. (Rep., Mass.) [See biographical note in 76th Congress]

Minority Whip: Leslie C. Arends (Rep., Ill.)

Chairmen of Selected Key Committees: [See also Organization and Administration, below]

Committee on Agriculture: John W. Flannagan Jr. (Dem., Va.)

Committee on Appropriations: Clarence A. Cannon (Dem., Mo.)

Committee on Banking, Finance, and Urban Affairs: Brent Spence (Dem., Ky.)

Committee on Foreign Affairs: Sol Bloom (Dem., N.Y.)

Committee on the Judiciary: Hatton W. Sumners (Dem., Tex.)

Committee on Military Affairs: Andrew J. May (Dem., Ky.)

Committee on Naval Affairs: Carl Vinson (Dem., Ga.)

Committee on Rules: Adolph J. Sabath (Dem., Ill.)

Committee on Ways and Means: Robert L. Doughton (Dem., N.C.)

ORGANIZATION AND ADMINISTRATION

In the Legislative Reorganization Act of 1946, Congress completely revamped its internal organization. The act provided for professional staff for the first time, and the committee structure was consolidated, with an emphasis on powerful standing committees that specifically had defined jurisdiction over particular legislative matters. Further, a clearly defined seniority system was established for members of both parties on the committee, and both the chairman (the senior member of the majority party) and the ranking minority member (the senior member of the minority party) would receive office space, staff, and an administrative budget for their committee duties. These committees and their members grew in influence and power as the federal government grew after World War II. Thus, beginning in the next Congress when the act took effect, there are expanded committee listings for both the Senate and the House under the heading chairman and ranking minority members of Key Committees.

Also during this Congress, the House voted to upgrade its Committee on Un-American Activities from a special committee to a permanent committee. [See Table of Key Votes, below] [See note 5, p. xxix] The committee originally was formed as part of the war effort to investigate potentially subversive activities, and after the end of the war turned its attention to the perceived threat from Communism and the Soviet Union. This committee and its counterpart in the Senate would achieve notoriety in the 1950s when alleged Communist infiltration of American society would become a national obsession.

MAJOR LEGISLATION PASSED

Bretton Woods Agreements: In an elite New Hampshire enclave known as Bretton Woods, representatives from the United States and other Western powers reached several agreements concerning the post-World War II international financial structure. The agreements included U.S. involvement in the International Monetary Fund and the International Bank for Reconstruction and Development.

British Loan: Congress appropriated $3.75 billion for a postwar economic recovery loan to Great Britain.

Congressional Reorganization: Congress passed the Legislative Reorganization Act of 1946. [See Organization and Administration, above]

Fulbright Scholars: In an amendment to the Surplus Property Act of 1944, Congress diverted funds to establish the Fulbright Scholars program to assist American students abroad and foreign students in the U.S.

Labor: In the Employment Act of 1946, Congress created the Council of Economic Advisers and made it the government's objective to achieve maximum national employment and industrial output.

Nuclear Power: In the Atomic Energy Act, Congress established a civilian Atomic Energy Commission to control nuclear power research and development, ending the wartime control by the military.

United Nations: The United States and the other victorious nations of World War II agreed on a charter establishing a framework for the United Nations. The international agreement setting forth the charter was approved by the Senate.

FAILED LEGISLATION

None of historical significance.

RELATIONS WITH THE PRESIDENT

The new president, Harry S. Truman, did not get along well with Congress. For example, after World War II ended Truman unsuccessfully lobbied Congress to continue his wartime control over the economy. Although Truman's blunt mannerisms and penchant for controversy would make him a popular president in retrospect, during his

TABLE OF KEY VOTES

Senate

Subject of Vote	Date of Vote	For				Against			
		D	R	I	Total	D	R	I	Total
Bretton Woods Agreement Approved	July 19, 1945	41	19	1	61	2	14	0	16
UN Charter Approved	July 28, 1945	53	35	1	89	0	2	0	2
Employment Act Passed	September 10, 1945	43	27	1	71	4	6	0	10
British Loan Approved	May 10, 1946	29	17	0	46	15	18	1	34
Atomic Energy Commission Established	June 1, 1946	passed by voice vote							
Legislative Reorganization Passed	June 10, 1946	26	22	1	49	13	3	0	16
Fulbright Scholars Program Established	July 27, 1946	passed by voice vote							

House

Subject of Vote	Date of Vote	For				Against			
		D	R	I	Total	D	R	I	Total
Un-American Activities Committee Made Permanent	January 3, 1945	70	138	0	208	150	34	2	186
Bretton Woods Agreement Approved	June 7, 1945	205	138	2	345	0	18	0	18
Employment Act Passed	December 14, 1945	195	58	2	255	21	105	0	126
British Loan Approved	July 13, 1946	157	61	1	219	32	122	1	155
Atomic Energy Commission Established	July 20, 1946	158	105	2	265	12	67	0	79
Legislative Reorganization Passed	July 25, 1946	standing vote* 229				standing vote* 61			
Fulbright Scholars Program Established	July 26, 1946	passed by voice vote							

[See note 7, p. xxix]

*A standing vote is essentially a head count, not broken down by party. The for and against votes are tallied by having all the persons voting "yes" stand and be counted, and then all the persons voting "no" stand and be counted.

administration his popularity often was very low.

Roosevelt had vetoed two bills during the 79th Congress before he died. Truman vetoed 74 bills during the remainder of the 79th Congress. None of the vetoes was of major political or historic significance.

NOMINATIONS, APPOINTMENTS, AND CONFIRMATIONS

The Judiciary: On July 31, 1945, Supreme Court Justice Owen J. Roberts resigned. President Harry S. Truman nominated Harold H. Burton on

September 18, 1945, to replace Roberts, and the Senate confirmed Burton by voice vote the next day. Chief Justice Harlan F. Stone died on April 22, 1946. President Truman nominated Fred M. Vinson on June 6, 1946, to replace Stone, and the Senate on June 20, 1946, confirmed Vinson by voice vote.

The Executive Branch: Before President Roosevelt died, he nominated Henry A. Wallace on January 20, 1945, to succeed Jesse H. Jones as secretary of commerce. On March 1, 1945, the Senate confirmed Wallace by a vote of 56 to 32. After Roosevelt died, President Truman initially kept all of Roosevelt's cabinet, and Senate confirmation votes were not required for continuing those officials. On May 23, 1945, Truman nominated Lewis B. Schwellenbach to succeed Frances Perkins as secretary of labor, Clinton B. Anderson to succeed Claude R. Wickard as secretary of agriculture, and Tom C. Clark to succeed Francis Biddle as attorney general. The Senate confirmed all three nominees by voice vote: Schwellenbach on May 31, 1945, Anderson on June 1, 1945, and Clark on June 14, 1945. On July 2, 1945, Truman nominated, and the Senate confirmed, James F. Byrnes to succeed Edward R. Stettinius as secretary of state. On July 16, 1945, Truman nominated Fred M. Vinson to succeed Henry Morgenthau Jr. as secretary of the Treasury, and on July 17, 1945, the Senate confirmed Vinson by voice vote. On September 18, 1945, Truman nominated Robert P. Patterson to succeed Henry L. Stimson as secretary of war, and on September 20, 1945, the Senate confirmed Patterson by voice vote. On February 26, 1946, Truman nominated Julius A. Krug to succeed Harold L. Ickes as secretary of the Interior, and the Senate confirmed Krug on March 5, 1946, by voice vote. Finally, on June 6, 1946, Truman nominated John W. Snyder to succeed Vinson as secretary of the Treasury, and on June 11, 1946, the Senate confirmed Snyder by voice vote.

IMPEACHMENTS

None.

CONSTITUTIONAL AMENDMENTS

None.

FURTHER READING

Ferrell, Robert H. *Harry S. Truman: A Life.* Columbia, Mo.: University of Missouri Press, 1994.

Hamby, Alonzo L. *American Democrat: Harry S. Truman.* New York: Oxford University Press, 1995.

Hardeman, D.B., and Donald C. Bacon. *Rayburn: A Biography.* Austin: Texas Monthly Press, 1987.

Maney, Patrick J. *The Roosevelt Presence: A Biography of Franklin Roosevelt.* New York: Twayne Publishers and Macmillan International, 1992.

McCullough, David. *Truman.* New York: Simon & Schuster, 1992.

Pritchett, Charles Herman. *Civil Liberties and the Vinson Court.* Chicago: University of Chicago Press, 1954.

The 80th Congress

JANUARY 3, 1947-JANUARY 3, 1949

First Session: January 3, 1947-December 19, 1947
Second Session: January 6, 1948-December 31, 1948

In the 1946 elections for the 80th Congress, the Republicans gained 13 seats in the Senate to hold a new majority of 51 of the 96 seats. The Democrats lost 11 seats, lowering their total from 56 to 45 seats. In the House, the Republicans gained 55 seats to give them a new majority of 245 of the 435 seats, and the Democrats lost 54 seats, leaving them with a total of 188. Two seats were not held by either major party. One seat was held by the American Labor Party. [See note 3, p. xxix]

BACKGROUND

With the end of World War II in 1945 during the 79th Congress, the American economy was shifting from wartime production back to civilian consumer goods. There was some concern that the Great Depression might resume, now that the economy no longer had the stimulus of war production and government spending. The Great Depression did not resume, however, as the end of wartime rationing caused an upsurge in consumer spending. In fact, the combination of the release of pent up consumer demand and the return home of millions of American soldiers caused a period of high inflation during the late 1940s.

In 1947 the cold war between the U.S. and its former ally, the Soviet Union, began as it became clear that the Soviets intended to challenge U.S. domination in Europe and in the world. The Truman administration was concerned about European vulnerability to Communism, since the European economy virtually had been destroyed by the war. During 1947 Congress passed the first major piece of postwar aid legislation, authorizing $400 million in aid to Turkey and Greece. This aid was primarily intended to prevent Turkey and Greece from falling within the sphere of Soviet influence that now had encompassed most of Eastern Europe, and which threatened to give the Soviets control over the Black Sea passage into the Mediterranean. On June 5, 1947, Secretary of State George C. Marshall proposed the Marshall Plan, which would be a comprehensive economic aid package for Western Europe.

In domestic matters, Congress enacted the National Security Act of 1947, which created the Air Force and brought the American armed forces under the control of a single secretary of defense with cabinet-level status. The act also created the Central Intelligence Agency and the National Security Council. The act was designed to centralize the American military and intelligence services and thus increase their efficiency. There was also a growing fear of Communism and Communist infiltration in American society. In the House, J. Parnell Thomas (Rep., N.J.), Chairman of the House Un-American Activities Committee, aggressively pursued allegations of Communist influence in Hollywood and the movie industry. Future President Ronald Reagan

ation of the United Nations, serving as one of the eight U.S. delegates to the San Francisco conference that defeated the U.N. Charter, and was determined to prevent the U.S. from slipping back into isolationism. Unlike a parallel figure after World War I, namely Senator Henry Cabot Lodge (Rep., Mass.), Vandenberg used his influence to support American involvement in the affairs of post-war Europe and helped push the Marshall Plan through the Senate in order to counter the growing Soviet menace. Vandenberg is especially noteworthy for his effort to bring both Democrats and Republicans into the decision-making process, so that measures such as the Marshall Plan would not be characterized as a victory or loss for a particular party, but as the result of bi-partisan cooperation.

Majority Leader: Wallace H. White Jr. (Rep., Maine)

Majority Whip: Kenneth Wherry (Rep., Neb.)

Minority Leader: Alben W. Barkley (Dem., Ky.)

Minority Whip: Scott Lucas (Dem., Ill.)

Chairman and Ranking Minority Members of Key Committees: [See also Organization and Administration, below]

Committee on Agriculture and Forestry: Chairman: Arthur Capper (Rep., Kans.); Ranking Minority Member: Elmer Thomas (Dem., Okla.)

Committee on Appropriations: Chairman: H. Styles Bridges (Rep., N.H.); Ranking Minority Member: Kenneth D. McKellar (Dem., Tenn.)

Committee on Armed Services: Chairman: J. Chandler Gurney (Rep., S.D.); Ranking Minority Member: Millard E. Tydings (Dem., Md.)

Committee on Banking and Currency: Chairman: Charles W. Tobey (Rep., N.H.); Ranking Minority Member: Robert F. Wagner (Dem., N.Y.)

Committee on Finance: Chairman: Eugene D. Millikin (Rep., Colo.); Ranking Minority Member: Walter F. George (Dem., Ga.)

Joseph R. McCarthy (Rep., Wis.) was first elected to the 80th Congress.

was a witness in an investigation of the Screen Actors Guild. However, anti-Communist legislation passed by the House died in the Senate. [See Failed Legislation, below]

SENATE LEADERSHIP

Vice President: None. Truman became President after the death of former President Franklin Delano Roosevelt on April 12, 1945. [See 79th Congress] Until the Twenty-fifth Amendment was ratified on February 10, 1967 [See 90th Congress], there was no mechanism for filling vacancies in the office of the vice president.

President Pro Tempore: Arthur Hendrick Vandenberg (Rep., Mich.) was elected on January 4, 1947. Vandenberg first was elected to the Senate in 1928 and served as president pro tem in only the 80th Congress. Vanderberg, who was also the Chairman of the Senate Foreign Relations Committee, played an important role in getting the Marshall Plan passed. [See Major Legislation, below] He had supported the cre-

Committee on Foreign Relations: Chairman: Arthur H. Vandenberg (Rep., Mich.); Ranking Minority Member: Thomas T. Connally (Dem., Tex.)

Committee on Interstate and Foreign Commerce: Chairman: Wallace H. White Jr. (Rep., Maine); Ranking Minority Member: Edwin C. Johnson (Dem., Colo.)

Committee on the Judiciary: Chairman: Alexander Wiley (Rep., Wis.); Ranking Minority Member: Patrick A. McCarran (Dem., Nev.)

Committee on Labor and Public Welfare: Chairman: Robert A. Taft (Rep., Ohio); Ranking Minority Member: Elbert D. Thomas (Dem., Utah)

Committee on Public Lands: Chairman: Hugh A. Butler (Rep., Neb.); Ranking Minority Member: Carl A. Hatch (Dem., N.M.)

Committee on Public Works: Chairman: W. Chapman Revercomb (Rep., W.Va.); Ranking Minority Member: John H. Overton (Dem., La.), who died on May 14, 1948. Dennis Chavez (Dem., N.M.) became the next ranking minority member.

Committee on Rules and Administration: Chairman: C. Wayland Brooks (Rep., Ill.); Ranking Minority Member: Carl Hayden (Dem., Ariz.)

HOUSE LEADERSHIP

Speaker of the House: Joseph William Martin Jr. (Rep., Mass.) was elected Speaker on January 3, 1947. [See biographical note in 76th Congress]

Majority Leader: Charles A. Halleck (Rep., Ind.)

Majority Whip: Leslie C. Arends (Rep., Ill.)

Minority Leader: Samuel T. Rayburn (Dem., Tex.), formerly the Speaker of the House, became the minority leader since the Republicans were now the majority party. [See biographical note in 76th Congress]

Minority Whip: John W. McCormack (Dem., Mass.)

Other House Leaders:

Richard M. Nixon (Rep., Calif.): Nixon, a future vice president and president of the U.S., first was elected to the 80th Congress. He quickly became a prominent figure, although he occasionally was involved in controversial matters, such as when he cosponsored an anti-Communist bill in the House. [See Failed Legislation, below]

Chairman and Ranking Minority Members of Key Committees: [See also Organization and Administration, below]

Committee on Agriculture: Chairman: Clifford R. Hope (Rep., Kans.); Ranking Minority Member: John W. Flannagan Jr. (Dem., Va.)

Committee on Appropriations: Chairman: John Taber (Rep., N.Y.); Ranking Minority Member: Clarence Cannon (Dem., Mo.)

Committee on Armed Services: Chairman: Walter G. Andrews (Rep., N.Y.); Ranking Minority Member: Carl Vinson (Dem., Ga.)

Committee on Banking and Currency: Chairman: Jesse P. Wolcott (Rep., Mich.); Ranking Minority Member: Brent Spence (Dem., Ky.)

Committee on Education and Labor: Chairman: Fred A. Hartley Jr. (Rep., N.J.); Ranking Minority Member: John Lesinski (Dem., Mich.)

Committee on Foreign Affairs: Chairman: Charles A. Eaton (Rep., N.J.); Ranking Minority Member: Sol Bloom (Dem., N.Y.)

Committee on Interstate and Foreign Commerce: Chairman: Charles A. Wolverton (Rep., N.J.); Ranking Minority Member: Clarence F. Lea (Dem., Calif.)

Committee on the Judiciary: Chairman: Earl C. Michener (Rep., Mich.); Ranking Minority Member: Emanuel Celler (Dem., N.Y.)

Committee on Public Lands: Chairman: Richard J. Welch (Rep., Calif.); Ranking Minority Member: Andrew L. Somers (Dem., N.Y.)

Committee on Public Works: Chairman: George A. Dondero (Rep., Mich.); Ranking Minority

C H R O N O L O G Y

January 3, 1947:	The 80th Congress and the first session begin. Joseph William Martin Jr. (Rep., Mass.) is elected Speaker of the House.
January 4, 1947:	Arthur Hendrick Vandenberg (Rep., Mich.) is elected Senate president pro tem.
January 8, 1947:	President Truman nominates George C. Marshall to succeed James F. Byrnes as secretary of state and W. Averell Harriman to succeed Henry A. Wallace as secretary of commerce. The Senate confirms Marshall.
January 27, 1947:	The Senate confirms Harriman.
March 12, 1947:	Congress sends the 22nd Amendment, limiting presidents to two terms, to the states for ratification.
May 9, 1947:	Congress authorizes aid to Greece and Turkey.
June 20, 1947:	President Truman vetoes the Taft-Hartley Labor-Management Relations Act. The House votes to override the veto.
June 23, 1947:	The Senate votes to override Truman's veto.
July 18, 1947:	Congress passes the Presidential Succession Act. President Truman nominates Kenneth C. Royall to succeed Robert P. Patterson as secretary of war.
July 19, 1947:	The Senate confirms Royall, and Congress passes the National Security Act.
July 26, 1947:	President Truman nominates, and the Senate confirms, James V. Forrestal to be secretary of defense.
December 8, 1947:	The Senate approves the Rio Treaty.
December 19, 1947:	The first session ends.
January 6, 1948:	The second session begins.
March 31, 1948:	Congress authorizes the Marshall Plan.
April 22, 1948:	President Truman nominates Charles Sawyer to succeed Harriman as secretary of commerce.
May 5, 1948:	The Senate confirms Sawyer.
May 19, 1948:	The House passes anti-Communist legislation, but the Senate takes no action and the legislation dies.
May 24, 1948:	President Truman nominates Charles F. Brannan to succeed Clinton B. Anderson as secretary of agriculture.
May 28, 1948:	The Senate confirms Brannan.
August 7, 1948:	The Senate rejects a proposal to give the president more economic controls.
December 31, 1948:	The second session ends.
January 3, 1949:	The 80th Congress ends.

[See note 6, p. xxix]

Member: Joseph J. Mansfield (Dem., Tex.), who died on July 12, 1947. William M. Whittington (Dem., Miss.) became the next ranking minority member.

Committee on Rules: Chairman: Leo E. Allen (Rep., Ill.); Ranking Minority Member: Adolph J. Sabath (Dem., Ill.)

Committee on Ways and Means: Chairman: Harold Knutson (Rep., Minn.); Ranking Minority Member: Robert L. Doughton (Dem., N.C.)

ORGANIZATION AND ADMINISTRATION

The Legislative Reorganization Act of 1946 took effect in this Congress. [See 79th Congress] In the Senate, the Committee on Public Lands was renamed the Committee on Interior and Insular Affairs on January 28, 1948. [See note 5, p. xxix]

MAJOR LEGISLATION PASSED

Foreign Aid: Congress authorized $400 million in military and economic aid to Greece and Turkey to prevent them from falling under Soviet control.

Labor: In the Taft-Hartley Labor-Management Relations Act, Congress overrode President Truman's veto and imposed a series of new restrictions on organized labor. These included presidential authority to impose 60-day cooling-off periods in strikes affecting interstate commerce and prohibition on unions from making political campaign contributions.

Marshall Plan: In the Economic Cooperation Act of 1948, Congress funded the Marshall Plan with over $5 billion in economic assistance for Western Europe in just the first year. Additional assistance was authorized for China, Greece, Turkey, and a United Nations children's fund.

National Security: In the National Security Act, Congress abolished the War department and the Navy Department, made the Air Force an independent service, and put the new departments of the Army, Navy, and Air under the control of a single secretary of defense with cabinet-level status. The actual Department of Defense was not created until the 81st Congress, however. The act also created the Central Intelligence Agency and the National Security Council.

Presidential Succession: In the Presidential Succession Act, Congress changed the order of presidential succession as follows: first, the vice president, then the Speaker of the House, and then the president pro tempore of the Senate.

Rio Treaty: The Senate approved the Inter-American Treaty of Reciprocal Assistance, commonly known as the Rio Treaty, which bound the United States and 18 Latin American countries into a pact of mutual assistance if any one of them were attacked.

FAILED LEGISLATION

Communism: The House passed legislation against "un-American" activities that would impose registration requirements and other restrictions on Communist organizations. President Truman never took a formal position on the bill, but did express opposition to making a political party illegal. The bill died in the Senate, which took no action. [See also Other House Leaders, above]

Economic Controls: Despite fears about postwar inflation, the Senate rejected a proposed amendment to a Senate Joint Resolution (Joint Resolution Number 157) that would give the president standby rationing and wage-and-price control powers.

RELATIONS WITH THE PRESIDENT

President Truman, a Democrat, got along poorly with Congress, where both houses now were controlled by the Republicans. During the 1948 presidential campaign, Truman derided the 80th Congress, calling it anti-labor, anti-farmer, and "do-nothing." However, the Republican leadership generally supported Truman's efforts to contain Communism and rebuild wartorn Europe.

TABLE OF KEY VOTES

Senate

Subject of Vote	Date of Vote	For D	R	I	Total	Against D	R	I	Total
22nd Amendment Approved	March 12, 1947	13	46	0	59	23	0	0	23
Greece/Turkey Aid Bill Passed	April 27, 1947	32	35	0	67	7	16	0	23
Taft-Hartley Veto Overridden	June 23, 1947	20	48	0	68	22	3	0	25
Presidential Succession Bill Passed	June 27, 1947	3	47	0	50	35	0	0	35
National Security Act Passed	July 9, 1947	Passed by voice vote							
Rio Treaty Approved	December 8, 1947	32	40	0	72	0	1	0	1
Marshall Plan Funded	March 13, 1948	38	31	0	69	4	13	0	17
Economic Controls Rejected	August 7, 1948	32	1	0	33	6	47	0	53

House

Subject of Vote	Date of Vote	For D	R	I	Total	Against D	R	I	Total
22nd Amendment Approved	February 6, 1947	47	238	0	285	120	0	1	121
Greece/Turkey Aid Bill Passed	May 9, 1947	160	127	0	287	13	94	1	108
Taft-Hartley Veto Overridden	June 20, 1947	106	225	0	331	71	11	1	73
Presidential Succession Bill Passed	July 18, 1947	142	222	1	365	10	1	0	11
National Security Act Passed	July 19, 1947	Passed by voice vote							
Marshall Plan Funded	March 31, 1948	158	171	0	329	11	61	2	74
Anti-Communist Measures Passed (No Senate Action)	May 19, 1948	104	215	0	319	18	8	2	58

[See note 7, p. xxix]

Truman vetoed 75 bills during the 80th Congress. On June 20, 1947, he vetoed the Taft-Hartley Labor-Management Relations Act [See Major Legislation, above], and his veto was overriden. [See Table of Key Votes, above]

NOMINATIONS, APPOINTMENTS, AND CONFIRMATIONS

The Judiciary: There were no significant nominations, appointments, or confirmations in the federal judiciary during the 80th Congress.

The Executive Branch: On January 8, 1947, President Truman nominated George C. Marshall to succeed James F. Byrnes as secretary of state and W. Averell Harriman to succeed Henry A. Wallace as secretary of commerce. The Senate confirmed both men by voice vote: Marshall was confirmed the same day he was nominated, and Harriman was confirmed on January 27, 1947. Truman nominated Kenneth C. Royall on July 18, 1947, to succeed Robert P. Patterson and serve as the last secretary of war before that department was absorbed into the new Department of Defense. On July 19, 1947, the Senate confirmed Royall by voice vote. On July 26, 1947, Truman nominated, and the Senate confirmed by voice vote, James V. Forrestal to be the first secretary of defense. On April 22, 1948, Truman nominated Charles Sawyer to replace Harriman as secretary of commerce, and on May 5, 1948, the Senate confirmed Sawyer by voice vote. Finally, on May 24, 1948, Truman nominated Charles F. Brannan to succeed Clinton B. Anderson as secretary of agriculture, and on May 28, 1948, the Senate confirmed Brannan by voice vote.

IMPEACHMENTS

None.

CONSTITUTIONAL AMENDMENTS

Congress sent the Twenty-second Amendment to the states for ratification. Sometimes nicknamed the Roosevelt Amendment, it prevents any person from holding more than two full terms as the president of the United States. Before Franklin D. Roosevelt was elected to four terms as president (in 1932, 1936, 1940, and 1944), no president tried to serve more than two terms. The Twenty-second Amendment made this custom, established by George Washington, a binding provision of the Constitution when it was ratified by the required three-fourths of the states effective February 27, 1951. [For the actual text of the Twenty-second Amendment, see the copy of the Constitution at Appendix A]

FURTHER READING

Ferrell, Robert H. *Harry S. Truman: A Life.* Columbia, Mo.: University of Missouri Press, 1994.

Hamby, Alonzo L. *American Democrat: Harry S. Truman.* New York: Oxford University Press, 1995.

McCullough, David. *Truman.* New York: Simon & Schuster, 1992.

Tompkins, C. David. *Senator Arthur H. Vandenberg: The Evolution of a Modern Republican, 1884-1945.* Lansing: Michigan State University Press, 1970.

The 81st Congress

JANUARY 3, 1949 - JANUARY 3, 1951

First Session: *January 3, 1949-October 19, 1949*
Second Session: *January 3, 1950-January 2, 1951*

In the 1948 elections for the 81st Congress, the Democrats gained 9 seats in the Senate to hold a new majority of 54 of the 96 seats. The Republicans lost 9 seats to hold a total of 42. In the House, the Democrats gained 75 seats to give them a new majority of 263 of the 435 seats. The Republicans lost 74 seats, leaving them with a total of 171. One seat was held by the American Labor Party. [See note 3, p. xxix]

BACKGROUND

According to the census of 1950, the population of the United States as of April 1, 1950, was 151,325,798, resulting in a population density of 42.6 persons for each of the country's 3,552,206 square miles (this figure includes Alaska and Hawaii for the first time). This was a population increase of 14.5 percent over the 1940 census.

Harry S. Truman was inaugurated on January 20, 1949 for his second term as the 33rd president of the United States. World War II now had been over for nearly four years, but world peace once again was threatened, this time by the rivalry between the United States and the Soviet Union, known as the cold war. Unlike the United States, the Soviets had not withdrawn their forces from Europe after the defeat of Nazi Germany, instead installing submissive Communist governments throughout Soviet-occupied Eastern Europe. In response to the Soviet military presence, the United States organized the North Atlantic Treaty Organization (NATO). NATO was formed on April 4, 1949, when the U.S., Belgium, Canada, Denmark, France, Great Britain, Italy, Iceland, Luxembourg, the Netherlands, Norway, and Portugal executed the North Atlantic Treaty in Washington, D.C. The Senate approved the North Atlantic Treaty on July 21, 1949.

In 1950 the cold war escalated into a regional conflict in the Korean Peninsula. Korea was divided into two nations, North Korea and South Korea. North Korea had a Communist government and was allied with the Soviet Union and the People's Republic of China. South Korea was largely a dictatorship, but it was friendly toward the U.S. and the West and was trying to develop its economy along western lines. The North Koreans, however, had been concentrating their resources on military development and on June 25, 1950, invaded South Korea. The American government viewed North Korea's attack as part of a larger plan by Soviet dictator Joseph Stalin to expand world Communism. Although Stalin and his Chinese allies could not directly invade neighboring non-Communist countries without risking nuclear war with the U.S., they could expand Communism by encouraging and supporting their Third World Communist allies, such as North Korea, in regional wars of expansion.

Truman quickly responded by sending American military assistance to South Korea. By July 1 American troops were in South Korea, and a naval blockade was in progress against North Korea. Truman was able to get United Nations support for the defense of South Korea, when the U.N. Security Council authorized military assistance to South Korea and cleared the way for U.N. contingents to join the American forces. The Soviet delegate to the Security Council, whose vote could have vetoed the entire U.S. proposal, was not present.

Now that the cold war had broken out into a "hot" action, there was a mood of national concern about Communist infiltration within the United States. Although the American Communist Party never had been more than a minor fringe organization, Congress overrode Truman's veto and passed the McCarran Internal Security Act of 1950 to restrain Communist activity. A former State Department official named Alger Hiss was tried for passing classified documents to a Soviet agent, and Representative Richard M. Nixon (Rep., Calif.) was the leading figure in the Hiss investigation conducted by the House Un-American Committee. Senator Joseph McCarthy (Rep., Wis.) was getting national attention with his allegations that the State Department had been penetrated by Communists, a claim that appeared to be valid when FBI Director J. Edgar Hoover stated that there were half a million Communist sympathizers in the United States. Senator William E. Jenner (Rep., Ind.) also achieved notoriety with his accusations that senior members of the government and the military were responsible for having "lost China" to the Communists, even when Jenner called General George C. Marshall "a front man for traitors."

By the end of the 81st Congress, American forces defeated the North Koreans and launched a counteroffensive into North Korea that reached the Yalu River on the Chinese border. On November 29, 1950, hundreds of thousands of Chinese Red Army troops launched a new offensive in order to rescue North Korea, and the American forces retreated. The Chinese troops were supposedly volunteers, and there were no declarations of war between the People's Republic of China and the United States.

SENATE LEADERSHIP

Vice President: Alben William Barkley was elected vice president on Truman's ticket in 1948. Barkley first had been elected to Congress as a representative from Kentucky to the 63rd Congress and had been elected to the Senate in 1926. He was the leader of the Senate Democrats from 1937 until his election as vice president.

President Pro Tempore: Kenneth Douglas McKellar (Dem., Tenn.) was elected on January 3, 1949. McKellar first had been elected to Congress as a representative to the 62nd Congress and was elected to the Senate in 1916. McKellar served as president pro tem in the 79th, 81st, and 82nd Congresses.

Majority Leader: Scott W. Lucas (Dem., Ill.)

Majority Whip: Francis Myers (Dem., Pa.)

Minority Leader: Kenneth S. Wherry (Rep., Neb.)

Minority Whip: Leverett Saltonstall (Rep., Mass.)

Chairman and Ranking Minority Members of Key Committees:

Committee on Agriculture and Forestry: Chairman: Elmer Thomas (Dem., Okla.); Ranking Minority Member: George D. Aiken (Rep., Vt.)

Committee on Appropriations: Chairman: Kenneth D. McKellar (Dem., Tenn.); Ranking Minority Member: H. Styles Bridges (Rep., N.H.)

Committee on Armed Services: Chairman: Millard E. Tydings (Dem., Md.); Ranking Minority Member: H. Styles Bridges (Rep., N.H.)

Committee on Banking and Currency: Chairman: Burnet R. Maybank (Dem., S.C.); Ranking Minority Member: Charles W. Tobey (Rep., N.H.)

Committee on Finance: Chairman: Walter F. George (Dem., Ga.); Ranking Minority Member: Eugene D. Millikin (Rep., Colo.)

C H R O N O L O G Y

January 3, 1949: The 81st Congress and the first session begin. Samuel Taliaferro Rayburn (Dem., Tex.) is elected Speaker of the House, and Kenneth Douglas McKellar (Dem., Tenn.) is elected Senate president pro tem. The House amends its procedures concerning the Rules Committee.

May 16, 1949: Congress passes the Executive Reorganization Act of 1949.

June 29, 1949: Congress passes housing legislation.

July 18, 1949: Congress passes legislation establishing the Department of Defense.

July 19, 1949: Supreme Court Justice Frank Murphy dies.

July 21, 1949: The Senate approves the North Atlantic Treaty.

August 2, 1949: President Truman nominates Thomas C. Clark to replace Murphy.

August 18, 1949: The Senate confirms Clark.

September 10, 1949: Supreme Court Justice Wiley B. Rutledge dies.

September 15, 1949: President Truman nominates Sherman Minton to replace Rutledge.

September 22, 1949: Congress passes mutual defense legislation.

October 4, 1949: The Senate confirms Minton.

October 19, 1949: The first session ends.

January 3, 1950: The second session begins.

May 5, 1950: Congress passes the Foreign Economic Assistance Act of 1950.

June 20, 1950: Congress passes legislation expanding Social Security.

July 17, 1950: Congress fails to approve a constitutional amendment concerning the allocation of electoral votes.

August 21, 1950: Congress passes the Defense Production Act of 1950.

September 22, 1950: President Truman vetoes the McCarran Internal Security Act of 1950. Both chambers of Congress vote to override Truman's veto.

January 2, 1951: The second session ends.

January 3, 1951: The 81st Congress ends.

[See note 6, p. xxix]

Committee on Foreign Relations: Chairman. Thomas T. Connally (Dem., Tex.); Ranking Minority Member: Arthur H. Vandenberg (Rep., Mich.)

Committee on Interior and Insular Affairs: Chairman: Joseph C. O'Mahoney (Dem., Wyo.); Ranking Minority Member: Hugh A. Butler (Rep., Neb.)

Committee on Interstate and Foreign Commerce: Chairman: Edwin C. Johnson (Dem., Colo.);

Ranking Minority Member. Charles W. Tobey (Rep., N.H.)

Committee on the Judiciary: Chairman: Patrick A. McCarran (Dem., Nev.); Ranking Minority Member: Alexander Wiley (Rep., Wis.)

Committee on Labor and Public Welfare: Chairman: Elbert D. Thomas (Dem., Utah); Ranking Minority Member: Robert A. Taft (Rep., Ohio)

Committee on Public Works: Chairman: Dennis Chavez (Dem., N.M.); Ranking Minority Member: Harry P. Cain (Rep., Wash.)

Committee on Rules and Administration: Chairman: Carl Hayden (Dem., Ariz.); Ranking Minority Member: Kenneth S. Wherry (Rep., Neb.)

HOUSE LEADERSHIP

Speaker of the House: Samuel Taliaferro Rayburn (Dem., Tex.) was elected Speaker on January 3, 1949. [See biographical note in 76th Congress]

Majority Leader: John W. McCormack (Dem., Mass.)

Majority Whip: J. Percy Priest (Dem., Tenn.)

Minority Leader: Joseph W. Martin Jr. (Rep., Mass.). [See biographical note in 76th Congress]

Minority Whip: Leslie C. Arends (Rep., Ill.)

Chairman and Ranking Minority Members of Key Committees: [See also Organization and Administration, below]

Committee on Agriculture: Chairman: Harold D. Cooley (Dem., N.C.); Ranking Minority Member: Clifford R. Hope (Rep., Kans.)

Committee on Appropriations: Chairman: Clarence Cannon (Dem., Mo.); Ranking Minority Member: John Taber (Rep., N.Y.)

Committee on Armed Services: Chairman: Carl Vinson (Dem., Ga.); Ranking Minority Member: Dewey Short (Rep., Mo.)

Committee on Banking and Currency: Chairman: Brent Spence (Dem., Ky.); Ranking Minority Member: Jesse P. Wolcott (Rep., Mich.)

Committee on Education and Labor: Chairman: John Lesinski (Dem., Mich.), who died on May 27, 1950. Graham A. Barden (Dem., N.C.) became the next chairman effective June 6, 1950. Ranking Minority Member: Samuel K. McConnell Jr. (Rep., Pa.)

Committee on Foreign Affairs: Chairman: Sol Bloom (Dem., N.Y.), who died on March 7, 1949.

John Kee (Dem., W.Va.) became the next chairman effective March 11, 1949. Ranking Minority Member: Charles A. Eaton (Rep., N.J.)

Committee on Interstate and Foreign Commerce: Chairman: Robert Crosser (Dem., Ohio); Ranking Minority Member: Charles A. Wolverton (Rep., N.J.)

Committee on the Judiciary: Chairman: Emanuel Celler (Dem., N.Y.); Ranking Minority Member: Earl C. Michener (Rep., Mich.)

Committee on Public Lands: Chairman: Andrew L. Somers (Dem., N.Y.), who died on April 6, 1949. J. Hardin Peterson (Dem., Fla.) became the new chairman effective April 13, 1949. Ranking Minority Member: Richard J. Welch (Rep., Calif.), who died on September 10, 1949. Fred L. Crawford (Rep., Mich.) became the next ranking minority member effective that same day.

Committee on Public Works: Chairman: William M. Whittington (Dem., Miss.); Ranking Minority Member: George A. Dondero (Rep., Mich.)

Committee on Rules: Chairman: Adolph J. Sabath (Dem., Ill.); Ranking Minority Member: Leo E. Allen (Rep., Ill.)

Committee on Ways and Means: Chairman: Robert L. Doughton (Dem., N.C.); Ranking Minority Member: Daniel A. Reed (Rep., N.Y.)

ORGANIZATION AND ADMINISTRATION

The House amended its rules in order to permit committee chairmen to bypass the Rules Committee [See Table of Key Votes, below] by asking the House membership to consider legislation approved by the chairman's committee within 21 days of its introduction. [See note 5, p. xxix]

MAJOR LEGISLATION PASSED

Executive Branch: In the Executive Reorganization Act of 1949, Congress gave the president extensive powers to reorganize the agencies of the executive branch until April 1, 1953. Presidential actions were subject to a vote of disapproval by either the House or the Senate.

Foreign Aid: In the Foreign Economic Assistance Act of 1950, Congress appropriated $3 billion for five foreign aid programs aimed primarily at the Third World and China.

Housing: In the Housing Act of 1949, Congress established the first large-scale program of federal assistance for subsidized public housing and urban renewal.

Mutual Defense: Congress authorized funding for the American participation in NATO. Congress also extended the Marshall Plan and authorized over $3 billion in additional assistance.

NATO: The Senate approved the North Atlantic Treaty, which established the North Atlantic Treaty Organization (NATO), the principal mutual defense alliance in the post-World War II period between the U.S. and Western Europe against the Soviet Union and its allies.

National Security: Congress amended the National Security Act [See 80th Congress], which created the position of secretary of defense, by consolidating the armed services (the Departments of the Army, Navy, and Air Force) into a single Department of Defense. In the Defense Production Act of 1950, Congress provided for emergency controls over industrial facilities, resources, wages, and prices. Finally, Congress overrode President Truman's veto and passed the McCarran Internal Security Act of 1950, which established a Subversive Activities Control Board and imposed several restrictions on Communist activity in the U.S. In the 1960s, there were several Supreme Court decisions holding provisions of the McCarran Act unconstitutional.

Social Security: Congress expanded the Social Security system's public assistance, child welfare, and insurance benefits.

FAILED LEGISLATION

There was an effort, which failed, to amend the Constitution with respect to the allocation of electoral votes. [See Constitutional Amendments, below]

RELATIONS WITH THE PRESIDENT

Even though his fellow Democrats had regained the majority in both houses, President Truman got along poorly with Congress. The Republicans remembered that Truman had run his 1948 campaign in large part against the "do-nothing" 80th Congress that they controlled. Even though both chambers now were controlled by the Democrats, enough of their conservatives sided with the Republicans to block Truman's "Fair Deal" initiatives to expand the New Deal.

Truman vetoed 79 bills during the 81st Congress. On September 22, 1950, Truman vetoed the McCarran Internal Security Act of 1950 [See Major Legislation, above], but Congress overrode his veto the same day. [See Table of Key Votes, below]

NOMINATIONS, APPOINTMENTS, AND CONFIRMATIONS

The Judiciary: On July 19, 1949, Supreme Court Justice Frank Murphy died. President Truman nominated Thomas C. Clark on August 2, 1949, to replace Murphy, and the Senate confirmed Clark on August 18, 1949, by a 73 to 8 vote. Justice Wiley B. Rutledge died on September 10, 1949. President Truman nominated Sherman Minton to replace Rutledge on September 15, 1949, and the Senate confirmed Minton on October 4, 1949, by a 48 to 16 vote.

The Executive Branch: On January 10, 1949, President Truman nominated Dean G. Acheson to succeed George C. Marshall as secretary of state, and on January 18, 1949, the Senate voted 83 to 6 to confirm Acheson. Truman nominated Maurice J. Tobin on January 17, 1949, to succeed Lewis B. Schwellenbach as secretary of labor, and on January 31, 1949, the Senate confirmed Tobin by voice vote. On March 4, 1949, Truman nominated Louis A. Johnson to succeed James V. Forrestal as secretary of defense, and on March 23, 1949, the Senate confirmed Johnson by voice

TABLE OF KEY VOTES

Senate

Subject of Vote	Date of Vote	For				Against			
		D	R	I	Total	D	R	I	Total
Housing Program Passed	April 21, 1949	33	24	0	57	2	11	0	13
Executive Reorganization Authorized	May 16, 1949	Passed by voice vote							
Department of Defense Established	May 26, 1949	Passed by voice vote							
NATO Treaty Approved	July 21, 1949	50	32	0	82	2	11	0	13
Mutual Defense Legislation Passed	September 22, 1949	36	19	0	55	10	14	0	24
Amendment on Electoral College Approved	February 1, 1950	46	18	0	64	4	23	0	27
Foreign Aid Bill Passed	May 5, 1950	36	24	0	60	1	7	0	8
Social Security Expanded	June 20, 1950	46	35	0	81	0	2	0	2
Defense Production Bill Passed	August 21, 1950	49	36	0	85	0	3	0	3
Internal Security Veto Overridden	September 22, 1950	26	31	0	57	10	0	0	10

House

Subject of Vote	Date of Vote	For				Against			
		D	R	I	Total	D	R	I	Total
House Rules Amended	January 3, 1949	225	49	1	275	31	112	0	143
Executive Reorganization Authorized	February 7, 1949	228	129	1	358	1	8	0	9
Housing Program Passed	June 29, 1949	192	34	1	227	55	131	0	186
Department of Defense Established	July 18, 1949	Passed by voice vote							
Mutual Defense Legislation Passed	August 18, 1949	187	51	0	238	27	94	1	122
Social Security Expanded	October 5, 1949	202	130	1	333	1	12	0	14
Foreign Aid Bill Passed	March 31, 1950	209	78	0	287	16	69	1	86
Amendment on Electoral College Defeated	July 17, 1950	86	48	0	134	116	93	1	210
Defense Production Bill Passed	August 10, 1950	242	141	0	383	0	11	1	12
Internal Security Veto Overridden	September 22, 1950	160	126	0	286	45	2	1	48

[See note 7, p. xxix]

vote. Truman nominated J. Howard McGrath on August 2, 1949, to succeed Tom C. Clark as attorney general, and the Senate confirmed McGrath by voice vote on August 18, 1949. On December 1, 1949, Truman nominated Oscar L. Chapman to succeed Julius A. Krug as secretary of the Interior, and on January 18, 1950, the Senate confirmed Chapman by voice vote. Also on September 13, 1950, Truman nominated George C. Marshall to succeed Louis A. Johnson as secretary of defense, and on September 19 the Senate confirmed Marshall by a 57 to 11 vote.

IMPEACHMENTS

None.

CONSTITUTIONAL AMENDMENTS

The Senate passed a resolution to amend the Constitution so that in a presidential election the electoral votes of each state would be proportional to the number of votes actually cast in each state. The House rejected the resolution.

FURTHER READING

Davis, Polly. *Alben Barkley: Senate Majority Leader and Vice President*. New York: Garland Publishing, 1979.

Ferrell, Robert H. *Harry S. Truman: A Life*. Columbia, Mo.: University of Missouri Press, 1994.

Hamby, Alonzo L. *American Democrat: Harry S. Truman*. New York: Oxford University Press, 1995.

Hardeman, D.B., and Donald C. Bacon. *Rayburn: A Biography*. Austin: Texas Monthly Press, 1987.

McCullough, David. *Truman*. New York: Simon & Schuster, 1992.

The 82nd Congress

JANUARY 3, 1951 - JANUARY 3, 1953

First Session: January 3, 1951-October 20, 1951
Second Session: January 8, 1952-July 7, 1952

In the 1950 elections for the 82nd Congress, the Democrats lost 5 seats in the Senate, reducing their majority from 54 to 49 of the 96 seats. The Republicans gained 5 seats to hold a total of 47. In the House, the Democrats lost 29 seats, reducing their majority from 263 to 234 of the 435 seats. The Republicans gained 28 seats for a total of 199. Two seats were not held by either major party. One seat was held by an independent. [See note 3, p. xxix]

BACKGROUND

In 1951 the U.S. was at war for the second time in a decade. During the previous Congress, North Korea had invaded South Korea, but the U.N. counteroffensive led by the U.S. had been so successful that it took American troops right to the border of Communist China. At that point, hundreds of thousands of Chinese troops, under the guise of "volunteer" units, went to rescue Communist North Korea and forced the U.S. to retreat. By January 4, 1951, the Chinese had taken Seoul, the capital of South Korea. In training and equipment, the Chinese military was inferior to the U.S. military, but its greater numbers and contiguous border with North Korea made it possible for the Chinese to overwhelm the American forces. For a time, conservative senior military officers, notably General Douglas MacArthur, urged using atomic weapons against the Chinese,

since the Chinese did not yet have any nuclear capability. President Truman did not want to risk war with China and possibly the Soviet Union, however, and so the Korean War was fought to the end with conventional weapons.

By the spring of 1951, American forces were able to regroup and slowly force the Chinese to retreat to approximately the 38th parallel, which was roughly the border between North and South Korea before the war. Meanwhile, Truman became increasingly irritated with General MacArthur's behavior. MacArthur made several public statements to the press criticizing Truman's decision not to expand war operations into Chinese territory, snubbed the president during a meeting in the Pacific, and even sent House Minority Leader Joseph W. Martin Jr. (Rep., Mass.) a letter calling for military victory in Korea in order to decide the global contest for supremacy with the Communists. On April 11, 1951, Truman relieved MacArthur of all his commanding positions, to be replaced by Lieutenant General Matthew Ridgway. MacArthur returned to the U.S., where he still was very popular, and on April 19 addressed a joint session of Congress to give his farewell statement. Invoking the army song "Old Soldiers Never Die, They Just Fade Away," MacArthur said, "I now close my military career and just fade away, an old soldier who tried to do his duty as God gave him the light to see that duty."

In 1952 the Korean War had become a stale-

C H R O N O L O G Y

January 3, 1951:	The 82nd Congress and the first session begin. Samuel Taliaferro Rayburn (Dem., Tex.) is reelected Speaker of the House, and Kenneth Douglas McKellar (Dem., Tenn.) is reelected Senate president pro tem.
February 2, 1951:	The House Committee on Public Lands is renamed.
May 24, 1951:	Congress authorizes aid to India.
August 28, 1951:	Congress passes the Mutual Defense Assistance Control Act.
August 31, 1951:	Congress passes the Mutual Security Act of 1951.
September 12, 1951:	President Truman nominates Robert A. Lovett to succeed George C. Marshall as secretary of defense.
September 14, 1951:	The Senate confirms Lovett.
October 20, 1951:	The first session ends.
January 8, 1952:	The second session begins.
March 20, 1952:	The Senate approves a formal peace treaty with Japan.
April 4, 1952:	President Truman nominates James P. McGranery to succeed J. Howard McGrath as attorney general. The House creates a select committee concerning tax exempt organizations.
May 20, 1952:	The Senate votes to confirm McGranery.
May 28, 1952:	Congress passes the Mutual Security Act of 1952.
June 25, 1952:	President Truman vetoes the McCarran-Walter Immigration and Nationality Act.
June 26, 1952:	The House votes to override Truman's veto.
June 27, 1952:	The Senate votes to override Truman's veto.
June 28, 1952:	Congress passes legislation expanding the G.I. Bill.
July 1, 1952:	Congress gives Puerto Rico a new constitution.
July 7, 1952:	The second session ends.
January 3, 1953:	The 82nd Congress ends.

[See note 6, p. xxix]

mate, both at the battle front along the 38th parallel and at the truce talks. Meanwhile, the Senate approved a peace treaty that finally put a formal end to World War II between the U.S. and Japan. Congress also overrode Truman's veto of an immigration reform bill and enacted a G.I. Bill of Rights for Korean veterans.

SENATE LEADERSHIP

Vice President: Alben William Barkley. [See biographical note in 81st Congress]

President Pro Tempore: Kenneth Douglas McKellar (Dem., Tenn.) was elected on January 3, 1951. [See biographical note in 79th Congress]

McKellar served as president pro tem in the 79th, 81st, and 82nd Congresses.

Majority Leader: Ernest W. McFarland (Dem., Ariz.)

Majority Whip: Lyndon B. Johnson (Dem., Tex.)

Minority Leader: Kenneth S. Wherry (Rep., Neb.), until he died on November 29, 1951. H. Styles Bridges (Rep., N.H.) became the new minority leader on January 8, 1952.

Minority Whip: Leverett Saltonstall (Rep., Mass.)

Chairman and Ranking Minority Members of Key Committees:

Committee on Agriculture and Forestry: Chairman: Allen J. Ellender, (Dem., La.); Ranking Minority Member: George D. Aiken (Rep., Vt.)

Committee on Appropriations: Chairman: Kenneth D. McKellar (Dem., Tenn.); Ranking Minority Member: H. Styles Bridges (Rep., N.H.)

Committee on Armed Services: Chairman: Richard B. Russell (Dem., Ga.); Ranking Minority Member: H. Styles Bridges (Rep., N.H.)

Committee on Banking and Currency: Chairman: Burnet R. Maybank (Dem., S.C.); Ranking Minority Member: Homer E. Capehart (Rep., Ind.)

Committee on Finance: Chairman: Walter F. George (Dem., Ga.); Ranking Minority Member: Eugene D. Millikin (Rep., Colo.)

Committee on Foreign Relations: Chairman: Thomas T. Connally (Dem., Tex.); Ranking Minority Member: Arthur H. Vandenberg (Rep., Mich.), who died on April 18, 1951. Alexander Wiley (Rep., Wis.) became the next ranking minority member effective the same day.

Committee on Interior and Insular Affairs: Chairman: Joseph C. O'Mahoney (Dem., Wyo.); Ranking Minority Member: Hugh A. Butler (Rep., Neb.)

Committee on Interstate and Foreign Commerce: Chairman: Edwin C. Johnson (Dem., Colo.); Ranking Minority Member: Charles W. Tobey (Rep., N.H.)

Committee on the Judiciary: Chairman: Patrick A. McCarran (Dem., Nev.); Ranking Minority Member: Alexander Wiley (Rep., Wis.)

Committee on Labor and Public Welfare: Chairman: James E. Murray (Dem., Mont.); Ranking Minority Member: Robert A. Taft (Rep., Ohio)

Committee on Public Works: Chairman: Dennis Chavez (Dem., N.M.); Ranking Minority Member: Harry P. Cain (Rep., Wash.)

Committee on Rules and Administration: Chairman: Carl Hayden (Dem., Ariz.); Ranking Minority Member: Kenneth S. Wherry (Rep., Neb.), who died on November 29, 1951. Henry Cabot Lodge Jr. (Rep., Mass.) became the next ranking minority member effective the same day.

HOUSE LEADERSHIP

Speaker of the House: Samuel Taliaferro Rayburn (Dem., Tex.) was reelected Speaker on January 3, 1951. [See biographical note in 76th Cobgress]

Majority Leader: John W. McCormack (Dem., Mass.)

Majority Whip: J. Percy Priest (Dem., Tenn.)

Minority Leader: Joseph W. Martin Jr. (Rep., Mass.) [See biographical note in 76th Congress]

Minority Whip: Leslie C. Arends (Rep., Ill.)

Chairmen and Ranking Minority Members of Key Committees: [See also Organization and Administration, below]

Committee on Agriculture: Chairman: Harold D. Cooley (Dem., N.C.); Ranking Minority Member: Clifford R. Hope (Rep., Kans.)

Committee on Appropriations: Chairman: Clarence Cannon (Dem., Mo.); Ranking Minority Member: John Taber (Rep., N.Y.)

Committee on Armed Services: Chairman: Carl Vinson (Dem., Ga.); Ranking Minority Member: Dewey Short (Rep., Mo.)

TABLE OF KEY VOTES

Senate

Subject of Vote	Date of Vote	For D	For R	For Total	Against D	Against R	Against Total
India Food Act Approved	May 16, 1951	15	37	52	30	2	32
Mutual Defense Assistance Act Passed	August 28, 1951	37	18	55	0	16	16
Mutual Security Act of 1951 Passed	August 31, 1951	39	22	61	0	5	5
Japan Peace Treaty Approved	March 20, 1952	38	28	66	1	9	10
Mutual Security Act of 1952 Passed	May 28, 1952	39	25	64	1	9	10
Immigration Veto Overridden	June 27, 1952	25	32	57	18	8	26
G.I. Bill of Rights Passed	June 28, 1952	Passed by voice vote					
Puerto Rican Constitution Approved	July 1, 1952	Passed by voice vote					

House

Subject of Vote	Date of Vote	For D	For R	For I	For Total	Against D	Against R	Against I	Against Total
India Food Act Approved	May 24, 1951	171	121	1	293	36	58	0	94
Mutual Defense Assistance Act Passed	August 2, 1951	Passed by voice vote							
Mutual Security Act of 1951 Passed	August 17, 1951	179	80	1	260	20	81	0	101
Mutual Security Act of 1952 Passed	May 23, 1952	168	78	0	246	20	89	0	109
G.I. Bill of Rights Passed	June 5, 1952	Not Available			361	0	1	0	1
Immigration Veto Overridden	June 26, 1952	107	170	1	278	90	23	0	113
Puerto Rican Constitution Approved	June 30, 1952	Passed by voice vote							

[See note 7, p. xxix]

Committee on Banking and Currency: Chairman: Brent Spence (Dem., Ky.); Ranking Minority Member: Jesse P. Wolcott (Rep., Mich.)

Committee on Education and Labor: Chairman: Graham A. Barden (Dem., N.C.); Ranking

Minority Member: Samuel K. McConnell Jr. (Rep., Pa.)

Committee on Foreign Affairs: Chairman: John Kee (Dem., W.Va.), who died on May 8, 1951. James P. Richards (Dem., S.C.) became the next chairman effective May 15, 1951. Ranking Minority Member: Charles A. Eaton (Rep., N.J.)

Committee on Interior and Insular Affairs: Chairman: John R. Murdock (Dem., Ariz.); Ranking Minority Member: Fred L. Crawford (Rep., Mich.)

Committee on Interstate and Foreign Commerce: Chairman: Robert Crosser (Dem., Ohio); Ranking Minority Member: Charles A. Wolverton (Rep., N.J.)

Committee on the Judiciary: Chairman: Emanuel Celler (Dem., N.Y.); Ranking Minority Member: Chauncey W. Reed (Rep., Ill.)

Committee on Public Works: Chairman: Charles A. Buckley (Dem., N.Y.); Ranking Minority Member: George A. Dondero (Rep., Mich.)

Committee on Rules: Chairman: Adolph J. Sabath (Dem., Ill.); Ranking Minority Member: Leo E. Allen (Rep., Ill.)

Committee on Ways and Means: Chairman: Robert L. Doughton (Dem., N.C.); Ranking Minority Member: Daniel A. Reed (Rep., N.Y.)

ORGANIZATION AND ADMINISTRATION

The House Committee on Public Lands was renamed the Committee on Interior and Insular Affairs effective February 2, 1951. Also, on April 4, 1952, the House voted 194 to 158 to establish a select committee to investigate tax exempt organizations allegedly involved in "subversive" activities. [See note 5, p. xxix]

MAJOR LEGISLATION PASSED

G.I. Bill of Rights: In the Veterans Readjustment Assistance Act of 1952, Congress added the so-called G.I. Bill of Rights to the original G.I. Bill [See 78th Congress] and included Korean War veterans among those entitled to benefits.

Immigration: Congress overrode President Truman's veto and passed the McCarran-Walter Immigration and Nationality Act, which elimi-

nated the ban on Asian immigration, and provided for the exclusion and deportation of aliens considered to be a threat to the nation. In the 1960s the Supreme Court held that certain provisions were unconstitutional.

India: Congress sent nearly $200 million in food aid to India, which was experiencing a severe famine.

Mutual Security: In the Mutual Security Act of 1951, Congress appropriated approximately $7.5 billion for foreign aid in technical, military, and economic areas. The act also created the Mutual Security Agency. Congress also passed the Mutual Defense Assistance Control Act, which automatically ended aid to any country providing military supplies to Soviet dominated countries. Finally, Congress passed the Mutual Security Act of 1952, which authorized assistance for non-Communist countries in the Third World.

Peace With Japan: The Senate approved the Peace Treaty with Japan, thus formally ending World War II in the Pacific.

Puerto Rico: Congress approved a new constitution for the Commonwealth of Puerto Rico.

FAILED LEGISLATION

None of historical significance.

RELATIONS WITH THE PRESIDENT

Even though his fellow Democrats were in control of both Chambers, Truman's Congressional relations were poor. General MacArthur, who was relieved of duty by Truman, was enthusiastically received when he gave his farewell address before Congress. Further, Conservative Democrats sided with the Republicans to block Turman's "Fair Deal" initiatives to expand the New Deal.

Truman vetoed 22 bills during the 82nd Congress. On June 25, 1952, Truman vetoed the McCarran-Walter Immigration and Nationality Act [See Major Legislation, above], but Congress overrode the veto. [See Table of Key Votes, above]

NOMINATIONS, APPOINTMENTS, AND CONFIRMATIONS

The Judiciary: There were no significant nominations, appointments, or confirmations in the federal judiciary during the 82nd Congress.

The Executive Branch: On September 12, 1951, President Truman nominated Robert A. Lovett to succeed George C. Marshall as secretary of defense, and on September 14, 1951, the Senate confirmed Lovett by voice vote. On April 4, 1952, Truman nominated James P. McGranery to succeed J. Howard McGrath as attorney general, and the Senate voted 52 to 18 to confirm McGranery on May 20, 1952.

IMPEACHMENTS

None.

CONSTITUTIONAL AMENDMENTS

None.

FURTHER READING

Davis, Polly. *Alben Barkley: Senate Majority Leader and Vice President.* New York: Garland Publishing, 1979.

Ferrell, Robert H. *Harry S. Truman: A Life.* Columbia, Mo.: University of Missouri Press, 1994.

Hamby, Alonzo L. *American Democrat: Harry S. Truman.* New York: Oxford University Press, 1995.

Hardeman, D.B., and Donald C. Bacon. *Rayburn: A Biography.* Austin,: Texas Monthly Press, 1987.

McCullough, David. *Truman.* New York: Simon & Schuster, 1992.

The 83rd Congress

JANUARY 3, 1953-JANUARY 3, 1955

First Session: *January 3, 1953-August 3, 1953*
Second Session: *January 6, 1954-December 2, 1954*

In the 1952 elections for the 83rd Congress, the Republicans gained 1 seat in the Senate to create a new, if bare, majority of 48 of the 96 seats. The Democrats lost 2 seats for a total of 47. One seat was held by an independent. In the House, the Republicans gained 22 seats to give them a new majority of 221 of the 435 seats. The Democrats lost 23 seats, leaving them with a total of 211. Three seats were not held by either major party. [See note 3, p. xxix]

BACKGROUND

Dwight D. Eisenhower was inaugurated as the 34th president of the United States on January 20, 1953. Early in the Eisenhower administration, on February 22, 1953, the Presidential Commission on the Health Needs of the Nation made one of the first comprehensive proposals for a system of national health insurance. The proposal did not result in a national health insurance plan, but Congress did create the Department of Health, Education, and Welfare soon thereafter. Also during 1953, Senator Joseph McCarthy (Rep., Wis.) had become a national figure with his public accusations of Communist infiltration within the American government. McCarthy was becoming an influential figure in the Senate, a development which many members of Congress considered dangerous. Meanwhile, the Korean War ended in an armistice at the Panmunjon Truce Talks between the two sides. The border between North Korea and South Korea after the war was very close to the prewar border.

In 1954 one of the most serious incidents of terrorism in Congress occurred. On March 1 a few militant supporters of Puerto Rican independence were able to bring firearms into the House of Representatives and shoot five congressmen on the House floor. None of the congressmen was killed.

Also during 1954, Senator McCarthy's power in Congress came to an end. From April 23, 1954, until June 17, 1954, McCarthy's Senate Permanent Subcommittee on Investigations held televised hearings on the alleged Communist penetration of the American military. McCarthy's attacks on the military backfired when his allegations resulted in negative publicity and the collapse of his public support. McCarthy's fellow Republican, Senator Ralph E. Flanders (Rep., Vt.), introduced a resolution to censure McCarthy for conduct unbecoming a United States senator. The Senate passed the Flanders resolution on December 2.

There were two other significant developments during the 83rd Congress. First, in the case of *Brown v. Board of Education*, the Supreme Court held that racially segregated public schools were unconstitutional and overturned a 19th-

Robert Carlyle Byrd (Dem., W. Va.) was first elected to the 83rd Congress.

century decision permitting "separate but equal" treatment of African Americans. Despite the Supreme Court's clear signal that segregation was no longer constitutionally permissible, most southern states resisted desegregation for nearly two more decades. Second, the French military was defeated at the Battle of Dien Bien Phu in Vietnam on May 7, 1954. The French would withdraw from Vietnam a year later, leaving behind a strong Vietnamese Communist movement, a threat that would result in American concern for the region and ultimately the Vietnam War.

SENATE LEADERSHIP

Vice President: Alben William Barkley was vice president, until January 20, 1953, when Richard Milhous Nixon became the new vice president. [See note 8, p. xxix] Nixon first had been elected to Congress in the 80th Congress as a representative from California and had been elected to the Senate in 1950, where he served until he was elected vice president in the 1952 elections. Nixon was reelected vice president in 1956 and unsuccessfully ran for president in 1960. He successfully ran for president in 1968 and 1972.

President Pro Tempore: H. Styles Bridges (Rep., N.H.) was elected on January 3, 1953. Bridges had been governor of New Hampshire from 1934 to 1936, when he had been elected to the Senate. He served as president pro tem only in the 83rd Congress.

Majority Leader: Robert A. Taft (Rep., Ohio) was majority leader until he died on July 31, 1953. William F. Knowland (Rep., Calif.) became the new majority leader on August 4, 1953, and remained the majority leader throughout the 83rd Congress, even though Taft's empty seat was filled by Democrat Thomas Burke on November 10, 1953, giving the Democrats a 48 to 47 (one independent) majority.

Majority Whip: Leverett Saltonstall (Rep., Mass.)

Minority Leader: Lyndon B. Johnson (Dem., Tex.) first had been elected to Congress as a representative to the 75th Congress and had been elected to the Senate in 1948. He became the leader of the Senate Democrats in the 83rd Congress. When the Democrats regained the majority in the 84th Congress, Johnson became majority leader, a position he retained until he was elected vice president in 1960. He would become president after John F. Kennedy was assassinated in 1963. Johnson was a deft politician, who successfully combined strong-arm tactics with an ability to make strategic compromises. These skills made him a powerful leader with one of the most successful legislative records in history.

Minority Whip: Earle Clements (Dem., Ky.)

Chairman and Ranking Minority Members of Key Committees:

Committee on Agriculture and Forestry: Chairman: George D. Aiken (Rep., Vt.); Ranking Minority Member: Allen J. Ellender (Dem., La.)

Committee on Appropriations: Chairman: H.

Styles Bridges (Rep., N.H.); Ranking Minority Member: Carl Hayden (Dem., Ariz.)

Committee on Armed Services: Chairman: Leverett Saltonstall (Rep., Mass.); Ranking Minority Member: Richard B. Russell (Dem., Ga.)

Committee on Banking and Currency: Chairman: Homer E. Capehart (Rep., Ind.); Ranking Minority Member: Burnet R. Maybank (Dem., S.C.), who died on September 1, 1954. J. William Fulbright (Dem., Ark.) became the next ranking minority member effective the same day.

Committee on Finance: Chairman: Eugene D. Millikin (Rep., Colo.); Ranking Minority Member: Walter F. George (Dem., Ga.)

Committee on Foreign Relations: Chairman: Alexander Wiley (Rep., Wis.); Ranking Minority Member: Walter F. George (Dem., Ga.)

Committee on Interior and Insular Affairs: Chairman: Hugh A. Butler (Rep., Neb.), who died on July 1, 1954. Guy Cordon (Rep., Ore.) became the next chairman effective July 9, 1954. Ranking Minority Member: James E. Murray (Dem., Mont.)

Committee on Interstate and Foreign Commerce: Chairman: Charles W. Tobey (Rep., N.H.), who died on July 24, 1953. John W. Bricker (Rep., Ohio) became the next chairman effective July 29, 1953. Ranking Minority Member: Edwin C. Johnson (Dem., Colo.)

Committee on the Judiciary: Chairman: William Langer (Rep., N.D.); Ranking Minority Member: Patrick A. McCarran (Dem., Nev.), who died on September 28, 1954. Harley M. Kilgore (Dem., W.Va.) became the next ranking minority member effective the same day.

Committee on Labor and Public Welfare: Chairman: H. Alexander Smith (Rep., N.J.); Ranking Minority Member: James E. Murray (Dem., Mont.)

Committee on Public Works: Chairman: Edward Martin (Rep., Pa.); Ranking Minority Member: Dennis Chavez (Dem., N.M.)

Committee on Rules and Administration: Chairman: William E. Jenner (Rep., Ind.); Ranking Minority Member: Carl Hayden (Dem., Ariz.)

HOUSE LEADERSHIP

Speaker of the House: Joseph William Martin (Rep., Mass.) was elected Speaker on January 3, 1953. [See biographical note in 76th Congress]

Majority Leader: Charles A. Halleck (Rep., Ind.)

Majority Whip: Leslie C. Arends (Rep., Ill.)

Minority Leader: Samuel T. Rayburn (Dem., Tex.) Rayburn, formerly the Speaker of the House, became the minority leader because the Republicans were now the majority party. [See biographical note in 76th Congress]

Minority Whip: John W. McCormack (Dem., Mass.)

Chairman and Ranking Minority Members of Key Committees:

Committee on Agriculture: Chairman: Clifford R. Hope (Rep., Kans.); Ranking Minority Member: Harold D. Cooley (Dem., N.C.)

Committee on Appropriations: Chairman: John Taber (Rep., N.Y.); Ranking Minority Member: Clarence Cannon (Dem., Mo.)

Committee on Armed Services: Chairman: Dewey Short (Rep., Mo.); Ranking Minority Member: Carl Vinson (Dem., Ga.)

Committee on Banking and Currency: Chairman: Jesse P. Wolcott (Rep., Mich.); Ranking Minority Member: Brent Spence (Dem., Ky.)

Committee on Education and Labor: Chairman: Samuel K. McConnell Jr. (Rep., Pa.); Ranking Minority Member: Graham A. Barden (Dem., N.C.)

Committee on Foreign Affairs: Chairman: Robert B. Chiperfield (Rep., Ill.); Ranking Minority Member: James P. Richards (Dem., S.C.)

Committee on Interior and Insular Affairs: Chairman: Arthur L. Miller (Rep., Neb.); Ranking Minority Member: Clair Engle (Dem., Calif.)

C H R O N O L O G Y

January 3, 1953:	The 83rd Congress and the first session begin. Joseph William Martin (Rep., Mass.) is elected Speaker of the House, and H. Styles Bridges (Rep., N.H.) is elected Senate president pro tem.
January 20, 1953:	President Eisenhower nominates most of his cabinet.
January 21, 1953:	The Senate confirms Eisenhower's nominees.
January 22, 1953:	President Eisenhower nominates Charles E. Wilson to be secretary of defense.
January 26, 1953:	The Senate confirms Wilson.
March 30, 1953:	Congress passes legislation creating the Department of Health, Education, and Welfare.
April 2, 1953:	President Eisenhower nominates Oveta C. Hobby to be secretary of health, education, and welfare.
April 10, 1953:	The Senate confirms Hobby.
July 20, 1953:	Congress passes legislation creating the Small Business Administration.
July 29, 1953:	Congress passes the Refugee Relief Act of 1953.
August 3, 1953:	The first session ends.
September 8, 1953:	Supreme Court Chief Justice Fred M. Vinson dies.
January 6, 1954:	The second session begins.
January 11, 1954:	President Eisenhower nominates Earl Warren to replace Vinson and James P. Mitchell to succeed Martin P. Durkin as secretary of labor.
January 19, 1954:	The Senate confirms Mitchell.
February 26, 1954:	The Senate rejects a proposed constitutional amendment concerning treaties.
March 1, 1954:	The Senate confirms Warren as Chief Justice.
May 6, 1954:	Congress passes the St. Lawrence Seaway Act of 1954.
July 27, 1954:	Congress passes nuclear power legislation.
July 28, 1954:	Congress passes a comprehensive overhaul of the federal tax system and passes the Housing Act of 1954.
August 12, 1954:	Congress passes legislation reforming the system of customs tariffs.
October 9, 1954:	Supreme Court Justice Robert H. Jackson dies. (He will not be replaced until the 84th Congress.)
December 2, 1954:	The Senate censures Senator Joseph McCarthy (Rep., Wis.), and the second session ends.
January 3, 1955:	The 83rd Congress ends.

[See note 6, p. xxix]

TABLE OF KEY VOTES

Senate

Subject of Vote	Date of Vote	For D	R	I	Total	Against D	R	I	Total
HEW Established	March 30, 1953	Passed by voice vote							
Small Business Administration Established	July 20, 1953	Passed by voice vote							
Refugee Relief Legislation Passed	July 29, 1953	24	38	1	63	22	8	0	30
St. Lawrence Seaway Approved	January 20, 1954	25	25	1	51	18	15	0	33
Bricker Amendment Rejected	February 26, 1954	28	32	0	60	16	14	1	31
Internal Revenue Code Revised	June 29, 1954	19	42	0	61	22	3	1	26
Private Nuclear Power Approved	July 27, 1954	13	44	0	57	25	2	1	28
Housing Act Passed	July 28, 1954	21	38	0	59	17	4	0	21
Customs Simplified	August 12, 1954	Passed by voice vote							
McCarthy Censured	December 2, 1954	44	22	1	67	0	22	0	22

House

Subject of Vote	Date of Vote	For D	R	I	Total	Against D	R	I	Total
HEW Established	March 18, 1953	96	194	1	291	73	13	0	86
Small Business Administration Established	June 5, 1953	Passed by voice vote							
Refugee Relief Legislation Passed	July 28, 1953	88	132	1	221	111	74	0	185
St. Lawrence Seaway Approved	May 6, 1954	96	144	1	241	94	64	0	158
Housing Act Passed	July 20, 1954	161	196	1	358	23	7	0	30
Private Nuclear Power Approved	July 26, 1954	36	195	0	231	146	7	1	154
Customs Simplified	July 26, 1954	Passed by voice vote							
Internal Revenue Code Revised	July 28, 1954	114	201	0	315	73	3	1	77

[See note 7, p. xxix]

Barry Goldwater (Rep., Ariz.; left) was first elected to the 83rd Congress. Seen here with Carl Hayden (Dem., Ariz.; center) and Paul Fannin (Rep., Ariz.).

Committee on Interstate and Foreign Commerce: Chairman: Charles A. Wolverton (Rep., N.J.); Ranking Minority Member: Robert Crosser (Dem., Ohio)

Committee on the Judiciary: Chairman: Chauncey W. Reed (Rep., Ill.); Ranking Minority Member: Emanuel Celler (Dem., N.Y.)

Committee on Public Works: Chairman: George A. Dondero (Rep., Mich.); Ranking Minority Member: Charles A. Buckley (Dem., N.Y.)

Committee on Rules: Chairman: Leo E. Allen (Rep., Ill.); Ranking Minority Member: Howard W. Smith (Dem., Va.)

Committee on Ways and Means: Chairman: Daniel A. Reed (Rep., N.Y.); Ranking Minority Member: Jere Cooper (Dem., Tenn.)

ORGANIZATION AND ADMINISTRATION

No developments of historical significance. [See note 5, p. xxix]

MAJOR LEGISLATION PASSED

Customs: Congress passed the Customs Simplification Act of 1954, which sought to review and simplify the system of tariff classifications and schedules.

HEW: Congress established the Department of Health, Education, and Welfare (HEW), which absorbed several federal agencies, such as the Food and Drug Administration and the Social Security Administration.

Housing: In the Housing Act of 1954, Congress allocated funds for 35,000 new public housing units in order to accommodate people displaced by urban renewal programs. There were significant differences between the legislation passed by the House and that passed by the Senate, but the two chambers finally passed a conference committee version of the bill.

Internal Revenue Code: Congress passed the Internal Revenue Code of 1954, which overhauled the entire system of Federal tax laws and regulations and provided the basic structure of the federal tax system until, 1986, when there was another major revision. The 1954 code called for relatively high tax rates, subject to a wide variety of deductions and exempt income.

Nuclear Power: In the Atomic Energy Act of 1954, Congress ended the federal monopoly on nuclear science and research and authorized private sector involvement and investment.

Refugees: In the Refugee Relief Act of 1953, Congress permitted an additional 209,000 refugees to enter the U.S. beyond the regular immigration quotas.

St. Lawrence Seaway: In the St. Lawrence Seaway Act of 1954, Congress created the St. Lawrence Seaway Development Corporation to participate with the government of Canada in the construction of the Seaway.

Small Business Administration: In the Small Business Administration Act, Congress terminated the old Reconstruction Finance Corporation and created the Small Business Administration. Congress also authorized funds for small business loans.

FAILED LEGISLATION

The Senate rejected a proposed constitutional amendment to limit the effect of treaties. [See Constitutional Amendments, below]

RELATIONS WITH THE PRESIDENT

Eisenhower's agenda rarely put him in serious conflict with Congress. He was a fiscal conservative, and kept budget deficits to a minimum during his administration. Once the commander in chief of Allied forces during World War II, Eisenhower was suspicious of what he termed the "military-industrial complex" and opposed those in Congress who wanted to large increases in military spending in response to the cold war.

Eisenhower vetoed 52 bills during the 83rd Congress.

NOMINATIONS, APPOINTMENTS, AND CONFIRMATIONS

The Judiciary: On September 8, 1953, Supreme Court Chief Justice Fred M. Vinson died. President Dwight D. Eisenhower nominated Earl Warren on January 11, 1954, to replace Vinson, and the Senate on March 1, 1954, confirmed Warren by voice vote. On October 9, 1954, Justice Robert H. Jackson died, but was not replaced until the 84th Congress.

The Executive Branch: President Eisenhower replaced all of former President Truman's cabinet. On January 20, 1953, Ezra Taft Benson was nominated to be secretary of agriculture; Herbert Brownell Jr. to be attorney general; John Foster Dulles to be secretary of state; Martin P. Durkin to be secretary of labor; George M. Humphrey to be secretary of the Treasury; Douglas McKay to be secretary of the Interior; and Sinclair Weeks to be secretary of commerce. All of these men were confirmed on January 21, 1953. Charles E Wilson was nominated on January 22, 1953, to be secretary of defense and was confirmed on January 26, 1953. On April 2, 1953, Oveta C. Hobby was nominated to be secretary of health, education, and welfare. Hobby was confirmed on April 10, 1953. The Senate confirmed all of the nominees by voice vote, except for Wilson, who was approved by a vote of 77 to 6.

On January 11, 1954, Eisenhower nominated James P. Mitchell to succeed Durkin as secretary of labor, and on January 19, 1954, the Senate confirmed Mitchell by voice vote.

IMPEACHMENTS

None.

CONSTITUTIONAL AMENDMENTS

The Senate rejected a constitutional amendment proposed by John W. Bricker (Rep., Ohio) to limit the effect of treaties. The proposed amendment stated that treaties in conflict with the Constitution were invalid and that international agreements had to be implemented by Congress before they could take effect within the U.S.

SCANDALS

The Senate passed a resolution proposed by Senator Ralph E. Flanders (Rep., Vt.) to censure Senator Joseph McCarthy (Rep., Wis.) for conduct unbecoming a member of the Senate. [See Background, above]

FURTHER READING

Ambrose, Stephen E. *Eisenhower*. New York: Simon & Schuster, 1983-1984.

Lee, R. Alton. *Dwight D. Eisenhower: A Bibliography of His Times and Presidency*. Wilmington, Del.: Scholarly Resources Inc., 1991.

Oshinsky, David. *A Conspiracy So Immense: The World of Joseph McCarthy*. New York: The Free Press, 1983.

Reichard, Gary W. *The Reaffirmation of Republicanism: Eisenhower and the Eighty-third Congress*. Knoxville: University of Tennessee Press, 1975.

Schwartz, Bernard. *Super Chief, Earl Warren and His Supreme Court, a Judicial Biography*. New York: New York University Press, 1983.

The 84th Congress

JANUARY 3, 1955-JANUARY 3, 1957

First Session: *January 5, 1955-August 2, 1955*
Second Session: *January 3, 1956-July 27, 1956*

In the 1954 elections for the 84th Congress, the Democrats gained 1 seat in the Senate to create a new majority of 48 of the 96 seats. The Republicans lost 1 seat, reducing their total to 47. One seat was held by an independent. In the House, the Democrats gained 21 seats to create a new majority of 232 of the 435 seats. The Republicans lost 18 seats, reducing their total to 203 seats. [See note 3, p. xxix]

BACKGROUND

Government spending during the Korean War had continued to stimulate the economy, which had been growing steadily since the end of World War II. The unemployment rate remained low even after the Korean War ended. Although the cold war with the Soviet Union continued, there was some hope that tensions would subside when Eisenhower met in 1955 with Soviet leader Nikita Khruschev at the Geneva Conference. This combination of domestic prosperity and international tranquility may explain why the 84th Congress was not a particularly active one.

During 1955 the Senate approved the continuing investigation of possible Communist influence in the U.S., despite the end of McCarthyism in the 83rd Congress. Congress also approved American military support for Formosa (now Taiwan) and the Pescadores, islands off the coast of Communist China that had governments independent of the Communist regime. During the 84th Congress, American foreign aid continued to grow and now exceeded $3 billion a year. From the post-World War II Marshall Plan to rebuild Europe, foreign aid had evolved into a permanent part of the federal budget, largely because America was using economic and military aid to prevent the spread of Soviet influence. Congress also authorized an increase in the reserve units of the American armed forces from 800,000 to approximately 2.9 million. In response to growing unrest in Southeast Asia, the Senate approved the Southeast Asia Treaty Organization (SEATO), a military alliance between the U.S., France, and Great Britain with Australia, New Zealand, Pakistan, the Philippines, and Thailand.

Before the end of the 84th Congress, there was an important reorganization in the American labor movement. The two largest labor organizations, the American Federation of Labor and the Congress of Industrial Organizations, merged to form the AFL-CIO. Dr. Jonas E. Salk discovered a vaccine for polio, and within a few years polio virtually was eliminated as a medical problem in the U.S. Finally, the Atomic Energy Commission authorized the first privately owned and operated nuclear power facilities on May 4, 1956.

SENATE LEADERSHIP

Vice President: Richard Milhous Nixon had been elected on the Eisenhower ticket in November 1952. [See biographical note in 83rd Congress]

C H R O N O L O G Y

January 3, 1955:	The 84th Congress begins.
January 5, 1955:	The first session begins. Samuel Taliaferro Rayburn (Dem., Tex.) is elected Speaker of the House, and Walter Franklin George (Dem., Ga.) is elected Senate president pro tem.
January 10, 1955:	President Eisenhower nominates John M. Harlan II to replace Supreme Court Justice Robert H. Jackson, who died during the 83rd Congress.
January 28, 1955:	Congress authorizes the use of force in the Formosa region.
February 1, 1955:	The Senate approves the SEATO Treaty.
March 16, 1955:	The Senate confirms Harlan.
April 1, 1955:	The Senate approves a German occupation treaty and a treaty concerning Germany and NATO.
June 17, 1955:	The Senate approves a treaty concerning the postwar status of Austria.
June 29, 1955:	The Senate passes a bill on D.C. home rule, which dies in the House.
July 13, 1955:	President Eisenhower nominates Marion B. Folsom to succeed Oveta C. Hobby as secretary of health, education, and welfare.
July 14, 1955:	Congress passes the Reserve Forces Act of 1955.
July 20, 1955:	The Senate confirms Folsom.
August 2, 1955:	The first session ends.
January 3, 1956:	The second session begins.
March 1, 1956:	Congress passes dam and irrigation project legislation.
May 28, 1956:	President Eisenhower nominates Frederick A. Seaton to succeed Douglas McKay as secretary of the Interior.
May 29, 1956:	Congress passes interstate highway development legislation.
June 6, 1956:	The Senate confirms Seaton.
July 27, 1956:	The second session ends.
October 15, 1956:	Supreme Court Justice Sherman Minton retires. He was not replaced until the 85th Congress.
January 3, 1957:	The 84th Congress ends.

[See note 6, p. xxix]

President Pro Tempore: Walter Franklin George (Dem., Ga.) was elected on January 5, 1955. George first had been elected to the Senate in 1922 and served as president pro tem in only the 84th Congress.

Majority Leader: Lyndon B. Johnson (Dem.,

Tex.) [See biographical note in 83rd Congress]

Majority Whip: Earle Clements (Dem., Ky.)

Minority Leader: William F. Knowland (Rep., Calif.)

Minority Whip: Leverett Saltonstall (Rep., Mass.)

Chairman and Ranking Minority Members of Key Committees:

Committee on Agriculture and Forestry: Chairman: Allen J. Ellender (Dem., La.); Ranking Minority Member: George D. Aiken (Rep., Vt.)

Committee on Appropriations: Chairman: Carl Hayden (Dem., Ariz.); ranking minority member: H. Styles Bridges (Rep., N.H.)

Committee on Armed Services: Chairman: Richard B. Russell (Dem., Ga.); Ranking Minority Member: H. Styles Bridges (Rep., N.H.), until February 23, 1955, when he switched with Leverett Saltonstall (Rep., Mass.) to become Ranking Minority Member on the Appropriations Committee for the remainder of the Congress.

Committee on Banking and Currency: Chairman: William J. Fulbright (Dem., Ark.); Ranking Minority Member: Homer E. Capehart (Rep., Ind.)

Committee on Finance: Chairman: Harry Flood Byrd (Dem., Va.); Ranking Minority Member: Eugene D. Millikin (Rep., Colo.)

Committee on Foreign Relations: Chairman: Walter F. George (Dem., Ga.); Ranking Minority Member: Alexander Wiley (Rep., Wis.)

Committee on Interior and Insular Affairs: Chairman: James E. Murray (Dem., Mont.); Ranking Minority Member: Eugene D. Millikin (Rep., Colo.)

Committee on Interstate and Foreign Commerce: Chairman: Warren G. Magnuson (Dem., Wash.); Ranking Minority Member: John W. Bricker (Rep., Ohio)

Committee on the Judiciary: Chairman: Harley M. Kilgore (Dem., W.Va.), who died on February 28, 1956. James O. Eastland (Dem., Miss.) became the next chairman effective March 2, 1956. Ranking Minority Member: Alexander Wiley (Rep., Wis.)

Committee on Labor and Public Welfare: Chairman: J. Lister Hill (Dem., Ala.); Ranking Minority Member: H. Alexander Smith (Rep., N.J.)

Committee on Public Works: Chairman: Dennis Chavez (Dem., N.M.); Ranking Minority Member: Edward Martin (Rep., Pa.)

Committee on Rules and Administration: Chairman: Theodore F. Green (Dem., R.I.); Ranking Minority Member: William E. Jenner (Rep., Ind.)

HOUSE LEADERSHIP

Speaker of the House: Samuel Taliaferro Rayburn (Dem., Tex.) was elected Speaker on January 5, 1955. [See biographical note in 76th Congress]

Majority Leader: John W. McCormack (Dem., Mass.)

Majority Whip: Carl Albert (Dem., Okla.)

Minority Leader: Joseph W. Martin Jr. (Rep., Mass.) [See biographical note in 76th Congress]

Minority Whip: Leslie C. Arends (Rep., Ill.)

Chairman and Ranking Minority Members of Key Committees:

Committee on Agriculture: Chairman: Harold D. Cooley (Dem., N.C.); Ranking Minority Member: Clifford R. Hope (Rep., Kans.)

Committee on Appropriations: Chairman: Clarence Cannon (Dem., Mo.); Ranking Minority Member: John Taber (Rep., N.Y.)

Committee on Armed Services: Chairman: Carl Vinson (Dem., Ga.); Ranking Minority Member: Dewey Short (Rep., Mo.)

Committee on Banking and Currency: Chairman: Brent Spence (Dem., Ky.); Ranking Minority Member: Jesse P. Wolcott (Rep., Mich.)

Committee on Education and Labor: Chairman: Graham A. Barden (Dem., N.C.); Ranking Minority Member: Samuel K. McConnell Jr. (Rep., Pa.)

Committee on Foreign Affairs: Chairman: James P. Richards (Dem., S.C.); Ranking Minority Member: Robert B. Chiperfield (Rep., Ill.)

TABLE OF KEY VOTES

Senate

Subject of Vote	Date of Vote	For D	For R	For Total	Against D	Against R	Against Total
Protection of Formosa Approved	January 28, 1955	42	43	85	2	1	3
SEATO Treaty Approved	February 1, 1955	42	40	2	0	1	1
German Occupation Treaty Approved	April 1, 1955	43	33	76	0	2	2
Germany/NATO Treaty Approved	April 1, 1955	43	33	76	0	2	2
Colorado Dams Project Passed	April 20, 1955	31	27	58	15	8	23
Austria Treaty Approved	June 17, 1955	35	28	63	0	3	3
D.C. Home Rule Bill Passed	June 29, 1955	28	31	59	12	3	15
		(no vote in House: bill never passed into law)					
Military Reserves Expanded	July 14, 1955	39	41	80	0	1	1
Highways Bill Passed	May 29, 1956	Passed by voice vote					

House

Subject of Vote	Date of Vote	For D	For R	For Total	Against D	Against R	Against Total
Protection of Formosa Approved	January 25, 1955	225	185	410	1	2	3
Military Reserves Expanded	July 1, 1955	Passed by voice vote					
Colorado Dams Project Passed	March 1, 1956	136	120	256	63	73	136
Highways Bill Passed	April 27, 1956	200	188	388	15	4	19

[See note 7, p. xxix]

ommittee on Interior and Insular Affairs: hairman: Clair Engle (Dem., Calif.); Ranking **l**inority Member: Arthur L. Miller (Rep., Neb.)

ommittee on Interstate and Foreign Commerce: hairman: J. Percy Priest (Dem., Tenn.); Ranking Minority Member: Charles A. Wolverton (Rep., N.J.)

Committee on the Judiciary: Chairman: Emanuel Celler (Dem., N.Y.); Ranking Minority Member: Chauncey W. Reed (Rep., Ill.), who died on

February 9, 1956. Kenneth B. Keating (Rep., N.Y.) became the next ranking minority member effective that same day.

Committee on Public Works: Chairman: Charles A. Buckley (Dem., N.Y.); Ranking Minority Member: George A. Dondero (Rep., Mich.)

Committee on Rules: Chairman: Howard W. Smith (Dem., Va.); Ranking Minority Member: Leo E. Allen (Rep., Ill.)

Committee on Ways and Means: Chairman: Jere Cooper (Dem., Tenn.); Ranking Minority Member: Daniel A. Reed (Rep., N.Y.)

ORGANIZATION AND ADMINISTRATION

A Senate initiative to give the District of Columbia home rule legislation died in the House. [See Failed Legislation, below and note 5, p. xxix]

MAJOR LEGISLATION PASSED

Dams: Congress appropriated funds for a series of dams and related irrigation projects known collectively as the Upper Colorado River Project.

Formosa (Taiwan): After the Communist Chinese moved to occupy some islands near Formosa (known as Nationalist China or more commonly Taiwan), Congress authorized the president to use American forces to protect Formosa and nearby Pescadores islands from invasion.

Germany and Austria: The Senate approved three treaties concerning Germany and Austria. The first treaty ended the postwar occupation of West Germany, except for certain Allied military bases. The second permitted West Germany to join the North Atlantic Treaty Organization (NATO). The third was a peace treaty with Austria, which recognized it as a sovereign state, forbade it from entering into another anschluss, or union, with Germany, and effectively required Austria to become a neutral state.

Highways: In the Highway Act of 1956, Congress authorized over $30 billion for the development of an interstate highway network and established a Highway Trust Fund supported by certain taxes to finance further interstate highway development.

Military Reserves: In the Reserve Forces Act of 1955, Congress permitted 250,000 men a year to enter the Ready Reserves for eight years of reserve status in exchange for exemption from the draft.

SEATO: The Senate approved the Southeast Asia Treaty Organization (SEATO) treaty, in which the U.S., Britain, and France committed themselves to the defense of South East Asia (including Australia and New Zealand, but excluding Formosa/Taiwan).

FAILED LEGISLATION

D.C. Home Rule: The Senate passed a bill providing for home rule in the District of Columbia which as the enclave of the federal government was then under federal control and management. The Senate bill provided for a D.C. mayor and city council. Once the bill went to the House however, the House District Committee failed to act on it, and the bill was never voted on by the full House.

RELATIONS WITH THE PRESIDENT

The Democrats had regained control of both Chambers of Congress, but with the end of McCarthyism and Eisenhower's mild legislative agenda, there was little serious conflict between the president and Congress.

Eisenhower vetoed 34 bills during the 84th Congress. None was of historical importance.

NOMINATIONS, APPOINTMENTS, AND CONFIRMATIONS

The Judiciary: On October 9, 1954, Supreme Court Justice Robert H. Jackson died and was not replaced during the 83rd Congress. President Dwight D. Eisenhower nominated John M. Harlan II on January 10, 1955, to replace Jackson, and the Senate confirmed Harlan on March 16, 1955, by a 71 to 11 vote. On October 15, 1956, Justice

Sherman Minton retired and was not replaced until the 85th Congress.

The Executive Branch: On July 13, 1955, President Eisenhower nominated Marion B. Folsom to succeed Oveta C. Hobby as secretary of health, education, and welfare. The Senate confirmed Folsom by voice vote on July 20, 1955. On May 28, 1956, Eisenhower nominated Frederick A. Seaton to succeed Douglas McKay as secretary of the Interior, and on June 6, 1956, the Senate confirmed Seaton by voice vote.

IMPEACHMENTS

None.

CONSTITUTIONAL AMENDMENTS

None.

FURTHER READING

Ambrose, Stephen E. *Eisenhower.* New York: Simon & Schuster, 1983-1984.

Hardeman, D.B., and Donald C. Bacon. *Rayburn: A Biography.* Austin: Texas Monthly Press, 1987.

Lee, R. Alton. *Dwight D. Eisenhower: A Bibliography of His Times and Presidency.* Wilmington, Del.: Scholarly Resources, 1991.

Yarbrough, Tinsley E. *John Marshall Harlan: Great Dissenter of the Warren Court.* New York: Oxford University Press, 1992.

The 85th Congress

JANUARY 3, 1957-JANUARY 3, 1959

First Session: January 3, 1957-August 30, 1957
Second Session: January 7, 1958-August 24, 1958

In the 1956 elections for the 85th Congress, the Democrats gained 1 seat in the Senate, raising their majority from 48 to 49 of the 96 seats. The Republicans retained their 47 seats. In the House, the Democrats gained 1 seat, raising their majority from 232 to 233 of the 435 seats. The Republicans lost 3 seats, reducing their total to 200 seats. Two seats were not held by either major party. [See note 3, p. xxix]

BACKGROUND

Dwight D. Eisenhower was inaugurated for his second term as the 34th president of the United States on January 20, 1957. Shortly thereafter, Eisenhower spoke to a joint session of Congress. In his speech, Eisenhower made a proposal known as the Eisenhower Doctrine, which would extend American military protection against Communism to friendly Middle Eastern countries. Eisenhower was unable, however, to create any kind of cohesive Middle Eastern military alliance under U.S. control. Middle Eastern nations were concerned more with their own regional political, ethnic, and religious rivalries than they were with the cold war between the U.S. and the Soviet Union. Furthermore, America's support for the Jewish state of Israel was unpopular with the predominantly Moslem nations of the Middle East. Finally, many countries developed a pattern of playing the U.S. and the Soviet Union against each other, taking economic aid from the U.S. and military hardware from the Soviets.

Until 1957 the American government and the public had been deeply concerned about the cold war, but there never really had been any serious doubt that America was superior to the Soviet Union militarily, economically, and of course technologically. America was the first country in the world to develop the atomic bomb, and American industry was the largest and most productive in the world. The U.S. considered the Soviet Union to be technologically backward, even though the Soviets had developed their own nuclear capability years ahead of U.S. predictions. On October 4, 1957, the Soviets stunned the U.S. and the world when they launched the first artificial satellite into an orbit around the earth. The launch of the satellite, called *Sputnik*, was a significant publicity victory for the Soviet Union and destroyed American complacency about Soviet technological capabilities.

On January 31, 1958, the United States launched its first orbital satellite, named *Explorer I*. Eisenhower was concerned about American overreaction to the Soviet launch of *Sputnik*, but he could not prevent the rush to match the Soviets in what would become nicknamed the "Space Race." Also during 1958, Congress approved the admission of Alaska to the Union as the 49th state.

Finally, Congress passed legislation establishing the National Aeronautics and Space Administration (NASA) and passed the National Defense Education Act of 1958, which sought to further mathematics, science, and foreign language education. Both measures were a reaction to the perceived Soviet advantages in outer space and the need for Americans to "catch up" in certain areas important to defense.

SENATE LEADERSHIP

Vice President: Richard Milhous Nixon was reelected with Eisenhower in the November 1956 elections. [See biographical note in 83rd Congress]

President Pro Tempore: Carl Hayden (Dem., Ariz.) was elected on January 3, 1957. Hayden first had been elected to Congress as a representative to the 62nd Congress and had been elected to the Senate in 1926. He served as president pro tem in the 85th through the 90th Congresses.

Majority Leader: Lyndon B. Johnson (Dem., Tex.) [See biographical note in 83rd Congress]

Majority Whip: Michael J. Mansfield (Dem., Mont.)

Minority Leader: William F. Knowland (Rep., Calif.)

Minority Whip: Everett McKinley Dirksen (Rep., Ill.)

Chairman and Ranking Minority Members of Key Committees:

Committee on Agriculture and Forestry: Chairman: Allen J. Ellender, (Dem., La.); Ranking Minority Member: George D. Aiken (Rep., Vt.)

Committee on Appropriations: Chairman: Carl Hayden (Dem., Ariz.); Ranking Minority Member: H. Styles Bridges (Rep., N.H.)

Committee on Armed Services: Chairman: Richard B. Russell (Dem., Ga.); Ranking Minority Member: H. Styles Bridges (Rep., N.H.), until January 22, 1957, when he became the ranking minority member of the Appropriations Committee. Leverett Saltonstall (Rep., Mass.) became the next ranking minority member.

Committee on Banking and Currency: Chairman: William J. Fulbright (Dem., Ark.); Ranking Minority Member: Homer E. Capehart (Rep., Ind.)

Committee on Finance: Chairman: Harry Flood Byrd (Dem., Va.); Ranking Minority Member: Edward Martin (Rep., Pa.)

Committee on Foreign Relations: Chairman: Theodore F. Green (Dem., R.I.); Ranking Minority Member: Alexander Wiley (Rep., Wis.)

Committee on Interior and Insular Affairs: Chairman: James E. Murray (Dem., Mont.); Ranking Minority Member: George W. Malone (Rep., Nev.)

Committee on Interstate and Foreign Commerce: Chairman: Warren G. Magnuson (Dem., Wash.); Ranking Minority Member: John W. Bricker (Rep., Ohio)

Committee on the Judiciary: Chairman: James O. Eastland (Dem., Miss.); Ranking Minority Member: Alexander Wiley (Rep., Wis.)

Committee on Labor and Public Welfare: Chairman: J. Lister Hill (Dem., Ala.); Ranking Minority Member: H. Alexander Smith (Rep., N.J.)

Committee on Public Works: Chairman: Dennis Chavez (Dem., N.M.); Ranking Minority Member: Edward Martin (Rep., Pa.)

Committee on Rules and Administration: Chairman: Thomas C. Hennings Jr. (Dem., Mo.); Ranking Minority Member: Carl T. Curtis (Rep., Neb.)

HOUSE LEADERSHIP

Speaker of the House: Samuel Taliaferro Rayburn (Dem., Tex.) was reelected Speaker on January 3, 1957. [See biographical note in 76th Congress]

Majority Leader: John W. McCormack (Dem., Mass.)

Majority Whip: Carl Albert (Dem., Okla.)

C H R O N O L O G Y

January 3, 1957:	The 85th Congress and the first session begin. Samuel Taliaferro Rayburn (Dem., Tex.) is reelected Speaker of the House, and Carl Hayden (Dem., Ariz.) is elected Senate president pro tem.
January 14, 1957:	President Eisenhower nominates William J. Brennan to replace Supreme Court Justice Sherman Minton, who had retired during the 84th Congress and had not been replaced.
February 25, 1957:	Supreme Court Justice Stanley F. Reed retires.
March 2, 1957:	President Eisenhower nominates Charles E. Whittaker to replace Reed.
March 5, 1957:	Congress authorizes assistance to Mideast countries.
March 19, 1957:	The Senate confirms Brennan and Whittaker.
May 29, 1957:	President Eisenhower nominates Robert B. Anderson to succeed George M. Humphrey as secretary of the Treasury.
June 18, 1957:	The Senate approves the International Atomic Energy Treaty.
July 2, 1957:	The Senate confirms Anderson.
August 7, 1957:	Congress passes the Civil Rights Act of 1957. President Eisenhower nominates Neil H. McElroy to succeed Charles E. Wilson as secretary of defense.
August 9, 1957:	Congress passes legislation implementing the International Atomic Energy Treaty.
August 19, 1957:	The Senate confirms McElroy.
August 30, 1957:	The first session ends.
January 7, 1958:	The second session begins.
January 13, 1958:	President Eisenhower nominates William P. Rogers to succeed Herbert Brownell Jr. as attorney general.
January 27, 1958:	The Senate confirms Rogers.
May 7, 1958:	President Eisenhower nominates Arthur S. Flemming to succeed Marion B. Folsom as secretary of health, education, and welfare.
June 16, 1958:	Congress passes legislation creating NASA.
June 30, 1958:	Congress passes legislation admitting Alaska into the United States.
July 9, 1958:	The Senate confirms Flemming.
July 18, 1958:	Congress passes the Defense Department Reorganization Act of 1958.
August 13, 1958:	Congress passes the National Defense Education Act of 1958.
August 24, 1958:	The second session ends.
October 13, 1958:	Supreme Court Justice Harold H. Burton retires and will not be replaced until the 86th Congress.
January 3, 1959:	The 85th Congress ends.

[See note 6, p. xxix]

Minority Leader: Joseph W. Martin Jr. (Rep., Mass.) [See biographical note in 76th Congress]

Minority Whip: Leslie C. Arends (Rep., Ill.)

Chairman and Ranking Minority Members of Key Committees:

Committee on Agriculture: Chairman: Harold D. Cooley (Dem., N.C.); Ranking Minority Member: August H. Andresen (Rep., Minn.), who died on January 14, 1958. William S. Hill (Rep., Colo.) became the next ranking minority member effective that same day.

Committee on Appropriations: Chairman: Clarence Cannon (Dem., Mo.); Ranking Minority Member: John Taber (Rep., N.Y.)

Committee on Armed Services: Chairman: Carl Vinson (Dem., Ga.); Ranking Minority Member: Leslie C. Arends (Rep., Ill.)

Committee on Banking and Currency: Chairman: Brent Spence (Dem., Ky.); Ranking Minority Member: Henry O. Talle (Rep., Iowa)

Committee on Education and Labor: Chairman: Graham A. Barden (Dem., N.C.); Ranking Minority Member: Samuel K. McConnell Jr. (Rep., Pa.), who retired effective September 1, 1957. Ralph W. Gwinn (Rep., N.Y.) became the next ranking minority member effective the same day.

Committee on Foreign Affairs: Chairman: Thomas S. Gordon (Dem., Ill.); Ranking Minority Member: Robert B. Chiperfield (Rep., Ill.)

Committee on Interior and Insular Affairs: Chairman: Clair Engle (Dem., Calif.), Ranking Minority Member: Arthur L. Miller (Rep., Neb.)

Committee on Interstate and Foreign Commerce: Chairman: Oren Harris (Dem., Ark.); Ranking Minority Member: Charles A. Wolverton (Rep., N.J.)

Committee on the Judiciary: Chairman: Emanuel Celler (Dem., N.Y.); Ranking Minority Member: Kenneth B. Keating (Rep., N.Y.)

Committee on Public Works: Chairman: Charles A. Buckley (Dem., N.Y.); Ranking Minority Member: J. Harry McGregor (Rep., Ohio)

Committee on Rules: Chairman: Howard W. Smith (Dem., Va.); Ranking Minority Member: Leo E. Allen (Rep., Ill.)

Committee on Ways and Means: Chairman: Jere Cooper (Dem., Tenn.), who died on December 18, 1957. Wilbur D. Mills (Dem., Ark.) became the next chairman effective January 7, 1958. Ranking Minority Member: Daniel A. Reed (Rep., N.Y.)

ORGANIZATION AND ADMINISTRATION

The Senate considered but ultimately rejected a move to ease rules on limiting debate. The initiative was an attempt to prepare the way for more civil rights legislation by making cloture easier to invoke but it was blocked by Majority Leader Lyndon B. Johnson (Dem., Tex.). [See note 5, p. xxix]

MAJOR LEGISLATION PASSED

Admission of Alaska as a New State: Congress passed legislation providing for the admission of Alaska to the Union as the 49th state. Alaska was officially admitted to the Union on January 3, 1959.

Civil Defense Reorganization: Through inaction, Congress permitted President Eisenhower to combine the Federal Civil Defense Administration with the Office of Defense Mobilization into a new Office of Civil Defense Mobilization. Eisenhower had the authority to reorganize executive branch agencies unless Congress exercised its power to prevent such a reorganization. Congress did not exercise that power because civil defense was a low priority concern (thus, there are no votes included in the Table of Key Votes, below).

Civil Rights: In the Civil Rights Act of 1957, Congress created the Civil Rights Division of the Department of Justice and gave the attorney general the power to seek injunctions against the denial of voting rights.

TABLE OF KEY VOTES

Senate

Subject of Vote	Date of Vote	For			Against		
		D	R	Total	D	R	Total
Middle East Resolution Passed	March 5, 1957	30	42	72	16	3	19
IAEA Treaty Approved	June 18, 1957	35	32	67	9	10	19
Civil Rights Act Passed	August 7, 1957	29	43	72	18	0	18
IAEA Act Passed	August 9, 1957	Passed by voice vote					
NASA Established	June 16, 1958	Passed by voice vote					
Alaska Statehood Bill Passed	June 30, 1958	31	33	64	13	7	20
Defense Department Reorganization Approved	July 18, 1958	40	40	80	0	0	0
Defense and Education Bill Passed	August 13, 1958	35	27	62	10	16	26

House

Subject of Vote	Date of Vote	For			Against		
		D	R	Total	D	R	Total
Middle East Resolution Passed	January 30, 1957	188	167	355	35	26	61
Civil Rights Act Passed	June 18, 1957	118	168	286	107	19	126
IAEA Act Passed	August 8, 1957	Passed by voice vote					
Alaska Statehood Bill Passed	May 28, 1958	118	92	210	81	85	166
NASA Established	June 2, 1958	Passed by voice vote					
Defense Department Reorganization Approved	June 12, 1958	216	186	402	0	1	1
Defense and Education Bill Passed	August 8, 1958	Passed by voice vote					

[See note 7, p. xxix]

Defense and Education: In the National Defense Education Act of 1958, Congress appropriated $1 billion to improve mathematics, science, and foreign language education. The act was primarily a reaction to the public perception after the *Sputnik* launching that the U.S. was lagging behind the Soviets. [See Background, above]

Defense Department: In the Defense Department Reorganization Act of 1958, Congress authorize the secretary of defense to consolidate the suppo and supply services for the armed forces and th eliminate unnecesary duplication between th Army, Navy, and Air Force.

International Atomic Energy Agency: The Sena approved the International Atomic Energy Treat which established the International Atomic Energ gency (IAEA). The IAEA promotes the safe and peaceful development of nuclear power through-out the world. Further, Congress passed the International Atomic Energy Participation Act of 1957, which permitted the U.S. to participate in IAEA-related organizations.

Middle East: Congress passed a resolution autho-zing the president to work with Middle East countries that desired military and economic assis-ance against potential Communist aggression.

NASA: Congress established the National Aeronautics and Space Administration (NASA) to lead the American exploration of outer space.

FAILED LEGISLATION

None of historical significance.

RELATIONS WITH THE PRESIDENT

Eisenhower's support of civil rights legislation and use of federal troops on September 24, 1957, to enforce the desegregation of Central High School in Little Rock, Arkansas, alienated many southern Democrats. Although Eisenhower had some doubts about the wisdom of desegregation, he enforced the Supreme Court's mandate of desegregation in the Little Rock situation despite the southern opposition in Congress.

Eisenhower vetoed 51 bills during the 85th Congress, none of historical significance.

NOMINATIONS, APPOINTMENTS, AND CONFIRMATIONS

The Judiciary: On October 15, 1956, Supreme Court Justice Sherman Minton retired and had not been replaced during the 84th Congress. Then, on February 25, 1957, Justice Stanley F. Reed retired, leaving President Dwight D. Eisenhower with two vacancies on the Court to fill: On January 14, 1957, Eisenhower nominated William J. Brennan Jr., and the Senate confirmed Brennan on March 19, 1957, without a vote. On March 2, 1957, Eisenhower nominated Charles E. Whittaker, and the Senate confirmed Whittaker

by voice vote, on March 19, 1957. On October 13, 1958, Justice Harold H. Burton retired and would not be replaced until the 86th Congress.

The Executive Branch: On May 29, 1957, Eisenhower nominated Robert B. Anderson to succeed George M. Humphrey as secretary of the Treasury, and on July 2, 1957, the Senate con-firmed Anderson by voice vote. On August 7, 1957, Eisenhower nominated Neil H. McElroy to succeed Charles E. Wilson as secretary of defense, and on August 19, 1957, the Senate con-firmed McElroy by voice vote. On January 13, 1958, Eisenhower nominated William P. Rogers to succeed Herbert Brownell Jr. as attorney gen-eral, and on January 27, 1958, the Senate con-firmed Rogers by voice vote. On May 7, 1958, Eisenhower nominated Arthur S. Flemming to succeed Marion B. Folsom as secretary of health, education, and welfare, and on July 9, 1958, the Senate confirmed Flemming by voice vote.

IMPEACHMENTS

None.

CONSTITUTIONAL AMENDMENTS

None.

FURTHER READING

Ambrose, Stephen E. _Eisenhower_. New York: Simon & Schuster, 1983-1984.

Divine, Robert A. _The Sputnik Challenge_. New York: Oxford University Press, 1993.

Hardeman, D.B., and Donald C. Bacon. _Rayburn: A Biography_. Austin: Texas Monthly Press, 1987.

Lee, R. Alton. _Dwight D. Eisenhower: A Bibliography of His Times and Presidency_. Wilmington, Del.: Scholarly Resources, 1991.

The 86th Congress

JANUARY 3, 1959-JANUARY 3, 1961

First Session: *January 7, 1959-September 15, 1959*
Second Session: *January 6, 1960-September 1, 1960*

In the 1958 elections for the 86th Congress, the Democrats gained 15 seats in the Senate, raising their majority from 49 to 64 of the 98 seats. The Republicans lost 13 seats, reducing their total to 34. In the House, the Democrats gained 50 seats, increasing their majority from 233 to 283 of the 436 seats. The Republicans lost 47 seats, reducing their total to 153 seats. Congress had provided for the newly admitted state of Alaska to have 1 representative pending the next census and reapportionment. [See note 3, p. xxix]

BACKGROUND

According to the census of 1960, the population of the United States as of April 1, 1960, was 179,323,175, resulting in a population density of 50.6 persons for each of the country's 3,540,911 square miles. This was a population increase of 18.5 percent over the 1950 census.

During 1959 Hawaii became the 50th state of the United States, the last state to be admitted to the Union to date. On July 4, 1960, a new American flag containing 50 stars officially was introduced. The American space program continued to expand, due to the Soviet challenge presented by the launching of *Sputnik* in 1957, which was the first artificial satellite to orbit the earth. The U.S. launched a series of satellites for military and weather reconnaissance purposes. Vice President Richard Nixon visited the Soviet Union during December 1959, positioning himself for the Republican nomination in the 1960 presidential elections. Several months after Nixon completed his visit to the Soviet Union, Soviet leader Nikita Khruschev visited the United States.

In 1960 the competition between the United States and the Soviet Union in outer space was compounded by fears of a "missile gap," based on the premise that the U.S. was lagging behind the Soviet Union in rocket technology. After several well-publicized failures, the U. S. space program finally began manned space launches in the Project Mercury program. The U.S. continued to underestimate Soviet technological ability, however, and was taken by surprise on May 1, 1960, when the Soviets used new surface-to-air missiles to shoot down a high-altitude Air Force U2 reconnaissance plane over the Soviet Union. The American government had assumed that the U2 spy missions were being flown above the range of Soviet air defenses. I was forced to admit that the U.S. had been conducting illegal spy missions over Soviet territory. The U2 episode was a serious embarrassment for President Eisenhower.

Philip A. Hart (Dem., Mich.) was first elected to the 86th Congress.

Also during 1960, for the first time, television became a decisive factor in American politics. Vice President Richard Nixon won the Republican nomination for president in the 1960 elections, and Senator John F. Kennedy (Dem., Mass.) was the Democratic candidate. Nixon was older and more experienced than Kennedy. Kennedy, however, had the political backing of organized labor and the financial backing of his wealthy father, former Ambassador Joseph P. Kennedy. In the first nationally televised debates between presidential candidates, Kennedy defeated Nixon, largely because Kennedy looked better on television than Nixon did. Significantly, a majority of people who listened to the debate on radio rather than watching it on television believed that Nixon, not Kennedy, had won the debate. Henceforth, a politician's ability to conduct himself or herself before the television camera would become just as important as the substance of the message being conveyed.

SENATE LEADERSHIP

Vice President: Richard Milhous Nixon, had been reelected with Eisenhower in 1956. [See biographical note in 83rd Congress]

President Pro Tempore: Carl Hayden (Dem., Ariz.) was elected on January 7, 1959. [See biographical note in 85th Congress]

Majority Leader: Lyndon B. Johnson (Dem., Tex.) [See biographical note in 83rd Congress]

Majority Whip: Michael J. Mansfield (Dem., Mont.)

Minority Leader: Everett McKinley Dirksen (Rep., Ill.) first had been elected to Congress as a representative to the 73rd Congress and had been elected to the Senate in 1950. Dirksen became the leader of the Senate Republicans in the 86th Congress and served in that position until the 91st Congress. Even though his party was in the minority, Dirksen was an important figure due to his ability to negotiate and to compromise. He worked well with Republicans and Democrats alike.

Minority Whip: Thomas H. Kuchel (Rep., Calif.)

Chairman and Ranking Minority Members of Key Committees:

Committee on Agriculture and Forestry: Chairman: Allen J. Ellender, (Dem., La.); Ranking Minority Member: George D. Aiken (Rep., Vt.)

Committee on Appropriations: Chairman: Carl Hayden (Dem., Ariz.); Ranking Minority Member: H. Styles Bridges (Rep., N.H.)

Committee on Armed Services: Chairman: Richard B. Russell (Dem., Ga.); Ranking Minority Member: H. Styles Bridges (Rep., N.H.), until January 23, 1959, when he became the ranking minority member of the Appropriations Committee. Leverett Saltonstall (Rep., Mass.) became the next ranking minority member.

Committee on Banking and Currency: Chairman: William J. Fulbright (Dem., Ark.), until he left to become chairman of the Senate Foreign Relations Committee on February 6, 1959. A. Willis

C H R O N O L O G Y

January 3, 1959:	The 86th Congress begins.
January 7, 1959:	The first session begins. Samuel Taliaferro Rayburn (Dem., Tex.) is reelected Speaker of the House, and Carl Hayden (Dem., Ariz.) is reelected Senate president pro tem.
January 17, 1959:	President Eisenhower nominates Potter Stewart to replace Supreme Court Justice Harold H. Burton, who had retired in the 85th Congress. Eisenhower also nominates Lewis L. Strauss to succeed Sinclair Weeks as secretary of commerce.
March 12, 1959:	Congress passes legislation admitting Hawaii into the United States.
April 20, 1959:	President Eisenhower nominates Christian A. Herter to succeed John Foster Dulles as secretary of state.
April 21, 1959:	The Senate confirms Herter.
May 5, 1959:	The Senate confirms Stewart.
June 18, 1959:	The Senate votes against confirming Strauss.
July 21, 1959:	President Eisenhower nominates Frederick H. Mueller to be secretary of commerce.
August 6, 1959:	The Senate confirms Mueller.
August 14, 1959:	Congress passes the Labor-Management Reporting and Disclosure Act of 1959.
September 1, 1959:	Congress passes health insurance for federal employees legislation.
September 15, 1959:	The first session ends.
January 6, 1960:	The second session begins.
January 11, 1960:	President Eisenhower nominates Thomas S. Gates Jr. to succeed Neil H. McElroy as secretary of defense.
January 26, 1960:	The Senate confirms Gates.
April 8, 1960:	Congress passes the Civil Rights Act of 1960.
June 16, 1960:	Congress sends the 23rd Amendment, giving D.C. residents the vote in presidential elections, to the states for ratification.
June 22, 1960:	The Senate approves a military treaty with Japan.
August 23, 1960:	Congress passes legislation increasing Social Security benefits, although a proposal to grant medical benefits for retirees over the age of 68 fails.
September 1, 1960:	The second session ends.
January 3, 1961:	The 86th Congress ends.

[See note 6, p. xxix]

Robertson (Dem., Va.) became the next chairman effective the same day. Ranking Minority Member: Homer E. Capehart (Rep., Ind.)

Committee on Finance: Chairman: Harry Flood Byrd (Dem., Va.); Ranking Minority Member: John J. Williams (Rep., Del.)

Committee on Foreign Relations: Chairman: Theodore F. Green (Dem., R.I.) until February 6, 1959, when he resigned as chairman. J. William Fulbright (Dem., Ark.) became the next chairman effective the same day. Ranking Minority Member: Alexander Wiley (Rep., Wis.)

Committee on Interior and Insular Affairs: Chairman: James E. Murray (Dem., Mont.); Ranking Minority Member: Henry C. Dworshak (Rep., Idaho)

Committee on Interstate and Foreign Commerce: Chairman: Warren G. Magnuson (Dem., Wash.); Ranking Minority Member: Andrew F. Schoeppel (Rep., Kans.)

Committee on the Judiciary: Chairman: James O. Eastland (Dem., Miss.); Ranking Minority Member: Alexander Wiley (Rep., Wis.)

Committee on Labor and Public Welfare: Chairman: J. Lister Hill (Dem., Ala.); Ranking Minority Member: Barry M. Goldwater (Rep., Ariz.)

Committee on Public Works: Chairman: Dennis Chavez (Dem., N.M.); Ranking Minority Member: Francis H. Case (Rep., S.D.)

Committee on Rules and Administration: Chairman: Thomas C. Hennings Jr. (Dem., Mo.); Ranking Minority Member: Carl T. Curtis (Rep., Neb.)

HOUSE LEADERSHIP

Speaker of the House: Samuel Taliaferro Rayburn (Dem., Tex.) was reelected Speaker on January 7, 1959. [See biographical note in 76th Congress]

Majority Leader: John W. McCormack (Dem., Mass.)

Majority Whip: Carl Albert (Dem., Okla.)

Minority Leader: Charles A. Halleck (Rep., Ind.)

Minority Whip: Leslie C. Arends (Rep., Ill.)

Chairman and Ranking Minority Members of Key Committees:

Committee on Agriculture: Chairman: Harold D. Cooley (Dem., N.C.); Ranking Minority Member: Charles B. Hoeven (Rep., Iowa)

Committee on Appropriations: Chairman: Clarence Cannon (Dem., Mo.); Ranking Minority Member: John Taber (Rep., N.Y.)

Committee on Armed Services: Chairman: Carl Vinson (Dem., Ga.); Ranking Minority Member: Leslie C. Arends (Rep., Ill.)

Committee on Banking and Currency: Chairman: Brent Spence (Dem., Ky.); Ranking Minority Member: Clarence E. Kilburn (Rep., N.Y.)

Committee on Education and Labor: Chairman: Graham A. Barden (Dem., N.C.); Ranking Minority Member: Carroll D. Kearns (Rep., Pa.)

Committee on Foreign Affairs: Chairman: Thomas E. Morgan (Dem., Pa.); Ranking Minority Member: Robert B. Chiperfield (Rep., Ill.)

Committee on Interior and Insular Affairs: Chairman: Wayne N. Aspinall (Dem., Colo.); Ranking Minority Member: John P. Saylor (Rep., Pa.)

Committee on Interstate and Foreign Commerce: Chairman: Oren Harris (Dem., Ark.); Ranking Minority Member: John B. Bennett (Rep., Mich.)

Committee on the Judiciary: Chairman: Emanuel Celler (Dem., N.Y.); Ranking Minority Member: William M. McCulloch (Rep., Ohio)

Committee on Public Works: Chairman: Charles A. Buckley (Dem., N.Y.); Ranking Minority Member: James C. Auchincloss (Rep., N.J.)

Committee on Rules: Chairman: Howard W. Smith (Dem., Va.); Ranking Minority Member: Leo E. Allen (Rep., Ill.)

Committee on Ways and Means: Chairman: Wilbur D. Mills (Dem., Ark.); Ranking Minority

Member: There were three ranking minority members during this Congress. The first was Daniel A. Reed (Rep., N.Y.), who died on February 19, 1959. Richard M. Simpson (Rep., Pa.) succeeded Reed effective the same day, but died on January 7, 1960. Noah M. Mason (Rep., Ill.) became the third and final ranking minority member effective the same day.

ORGANIZATION AND ADMINISTRATION

No developments of historical significance. [See note 5, p. xxix]

MAJOR LEGISLATION PASSED

Admission of Hawaii as a New State: Congress passed legislation providing for the admission of Hawaii into the Union as the 50th state. Hawaii was officially admitted August 21, 1959.

Civil Rights: In the Civil Rights Act of 1960, Congress gave further protection to people exercising their right to vote and increased the penalties for bombings, mob violence, and other obstructionist tactics.

Federal Employees: In the Federal Employees Health Benefits Act of 1959, Congress created a new health insurance plan covering over two million federal employees and dependents.

Labor Relations: In the Labor-Management Reporting and Disclosure Act of 1959 (popularly known as the Landrum-Griffin Act), Congress guaranteed union members a "bill of rights" and imposed various registration and reporting requirements on unions. The act also increased the level of federal supervision over union elections.

Social Security: In the 1960 amendments to the Social Security Act, Congress established the Medical Assistance to the Aged program and increased federal assistance to the states for the medical care of financially needy senior citizens. An amendment to give medical benefits to all retirees over the age of 68 failed, however. [See Failed Legislation, below]

Treaty With Japan: The Senate approved a Treaty of Mutual Cooperation and Security with Japan. In the treaty, Japan agreed to the continuing American military presence on its territory, and the U.S. agreed to consult the Japanese government before undertaking any combat actions from Japanese bases.

FAILED LEGISLATION

Although Congress passed a series of amendments to the Social Security Act [See Major Legislation, above], the Senate rejected Senator Clinton B. Anderson's (Dem., N.M.) amendment to increase the payroll tax and use the proceeds to provide medical benefits to all retirees over the age of 68. When Anderson's amendment was brought to a vote on August 23, 1960, the vote was 44 in favor and 51 against.

RELATIONS WITH THE PRESIDENT

However, Eisenhower's relations with Congress soured to a degree in this Congress as the Democrats expected victory in the 1960 presidential election. The Senate defeat of Lewis Strauss for secretary of commerce [See Nominations, below] was a major embarassment to Eisenhower, and was the first cabinet rejection since Charles Warren in the 1920s.

Eisenhower vetoed 44 bills during the 86th Congress. None was of historical importance.

NOMINATIONS, APPOINTMENTS, AND CONFIRMATIONS

The Judiciary: On October 13, 1958, Supreme Court Justice Harold H. Burton had retired and had not been replaced during the 85th Congress. President Dwight D. Eisenhower nominated Potter Stewart on January 17, 1959, to replace Burton, and on May 5, 1959, the Senate confirmed Stewart by a 70 to 17 vote.

The Executive Branch: On January 17, 1959, President Eisenhower nominated Lewis L. Strauss to succeed Sinclair Weeks as secretary of commerce, but on June 18, 1959, the Senate vote was

TABLE OF KEY VOTES

Senate

Subject of Vote	Date of Vote	For			Against		
		D	R	Total	D	R	Total
Hawaii Admitted to the Union	March 11, 1959	46	30	76	14	1	15
Labor Relations Bill Passed	April 25, 1959	60	30	90	0	1	1
Strauss confirmation as Commerce Secretary rejected	June 18, 1959	15	31	46	47	2	49
Federal Employees Given Health Benefits	July 16, 1959	55	26	81	0	4	4
Civil Rights Bill Passed	April 8, 1960	42	29	71	18	0	18
23rd Amendment Sent to States	June 16, 1960	Passed by voice vote					
Treaty With Japan Approved	June 22, 1960	57	33	90	2	0	2
Social Security Revised	August 23, 1960	60	31	91	1	1	2

House

Subject of Vote	Date of Vote	For			Against		
		D	R	Total	D	R	Total
Hawaii Admitted to the Union	March 12, 1959	203	120	323	65	24	89
Labor Relations Bill Passed	August 14, 1959	156	147	303	122	3	125
Federal Employees Given Health Benefits	September 1, 1959	253	130	383	1	3	4
Civil Rights Bill Passed	March 24, 1960	179	132	311	94	15	109
23rd Amendment Sent to States	June 16, 1960	Passed by voice vote					
Social Security Revised	June 23, 1960	244	137	381	16	7	23

[See note 7, p. xxix]

46 in favor and 49 against Strauss. Strauss was very conservative, had participated in the attacks on atomic scientist J. Robert Oppenheimer in the early 1950s, and allegedly had withheld information from Congress while chairman of the Atomic Energy Commission from 1953 to 1958.

Meanwhile, on April 20, 1959, Eisenhower nominated Christian A. Herter to succeed John Foster Dulles as secretary of state, and on April 21, 1959, the Senate voted 93 to 0 to confirm Herter. On July 21, 1959, Eisenhower nominated Frederick H. Mueller instead of Strauss to be secretary of commerce, and on August 6, 1959, the Senate confirmed Mueller by voice vote. On January 11, 1960, Eisenhower nominated Thomas S. Gates Jr. to succeed Neil H. McElroy as secretary of defense, and on January 26, 1960, the Senate confirmed Gates by voice vote.

IMPEACHMENTS

None.

CONSTITUTIONAL AMENDMENTS

Congress sent the Twenty-third Amendment to the states for ratification. The Twenty-third Amendment gives District of Columbia citizens the right to vote in presidential elections and gives the District three votes in the electoral college. The amendment was ratified by the required three-fourths of the states effective March 29, 1961. [For the actual text of the Twenty-third Amendment, see the copy of the Constitution at Appendix A]

FURTHER READING

Ambrose, Stephen E. *Eisenhower.* New York: Simon & Schuster, 1983-1984.

Hardeman, D.B., and Donald C. Bacon. *Rayburn: A Biography.* Austin: Texas Monthly Press, 1987.

Lee, R. Alton. *Dwight D. Eisenhower: A Bibliography of His Times and Presidency.* Wilmington, Del.: Scholarly Resources, 1991.

Schapsmeier, Edward, and Frederick Schapsmeier. *Dirksen of Illinois: Senatorial Statesman.* Urbana, Ill.: University of Illinois Press, 1985.

The 87th Congress

JANUARY 3, 1961 - JANUARY 3, 1963

First Session: January 3, 1961-September 27, 1961
Second Session: January 10, 1962-October 13, 1962

In the 1960 elections for the 87th Congress, the Democrats gained 1 seat in the Senate, increasing their majority from 64 to 65 of the 98 seats. The Republicans also gained 1 seat, giving them a total of 35 seats. In the House, the Democrats lost 20 seats, lowering their majority from 283 to 263 of the 437 seats. The Republicans gained 21 seats, raising their total to 174 seats. Congress had provided for the newly admitted states of Alaska and Hawaii to each have 1 representative pending the next census and reapportionment. [See note 3, p. xxix]

BACKGROUND

John F. Kennedy was inaugurated as the 35th president of the United States on January 20, 1961. Shortly before, on January 3, 1961 (the first day of the 87th Congress), the United States had cut off diplomatic relations with the Carribean nation of Cuba. There had been a revolution in Cuba, and the country's leader was now Fidel Castro. The break in diplomatic relations followed two years of increasing hostility between the U.S. and the leftist Castro government. The revolution in Cuba and Castro's adoption of socialist measures, such as the nationalization of private property, had caused tens of thousands of Cubans to leave for the United States. Many of these exiles had been prosperous middle class businessmen and professionals in

Cuba, who lost everything they owned in the revolution. Therefore, the Cuban exile community in America was strongly anti-Communist and anti-Castro. From this community, the Kennedy administration secretly recruited and trained 1,500 men to land in Cuba, overthrow Castro, and install a pro-American government.

The CIA trained and armed the Cuban force, which landed in Cuba on April 17, 1961, at the Bay of Pigs. The exile force was not able to gain the support of the local population, and troops loyal to Castro surrounded and defeated the invaders. Kennedy refused to use air strikes in order to support the exiles, who were taken prisoner and placed in Cuban jails. The Bay of Pigs disaster was a serious embarrassment for the Kennedy administration, and on April 24, 1961, Kennedy admitted that the U.S. had been involved and accepted the responsibility. The episode only succeeded in prompting Castro to forge closer ties with the Soviet Union.

In 1962 the first American astronaut orbited the earth, and Drs. James D. Watson and Francis H. Crick were awarded the Nobel Prize for their discovery of the structure of DNA. During the spring of 1962 and into the summer, the U.S., Soviet Union, and Great Britain continued disarmament negotiations in Geneva, Switzerland, concentrating on achieving an international nuclear test ban. The most important event of

Edward M. Kennedy (Dem., Mass.) was first elected to the 87th Congress.

the year began on October 22, when on national television President Kennedy announced that the Soviet Union was constructing nuclear missile facilities in Cuba. Kennedy imposed a naval blockade of Cuba and declared that any nuclear missile launched from Cuba against the United States or another country of the Western Hemisphere would be considered an act of war on the part of the Soviet Union against the U.S. After six days of tense negotiations, on October 28 the Soviets agreed to withdraw their missiles. In return, the U.S. agreed to lift its naval blockade, and promised that it would not invade Cuba or sponsor any more "Bay of Pigs" style operations.

SENATE LEADERSHIP

Vice President: Richard Milhous Nixon had been vice president until January 20, 1961, when Lyndon Baines Johnson became the new vice president. [See biographical note in 83rd Congress] [See note 8, p. xxix]

President Pro Tempore: Carl Hayden (Dem., Ariz.) [See biographical note in 85th Congress]

Majority Leader: Michael J. Mansfield (Dem., Mont.) first had been elected to Congress as a representative to the 78th Congress and had been elected to the Senate in 1952. When Lyndon B. Johnson was elected vice president in 1960, Mansfield rose from majority whip to majority leader, a position he would retain for 16 years.

Majority Whip: Hubert H. Humphrey (Dem., Minn.)

Minority Leader: Everett McKinley Dirksen (Rep., Ill.) [See biographical note in 86th Congress]

Minority Whip: Thomas H. Kuchel (Rep., Calif.)

Chairman and Ranking Minority Members of Key Committees: [See also Organization and Administration, below]

Committee on Agriculture and Forestry: Chairman: Allen J. Ellender, (Dem., La.); Ranking Minority Member: George D. Aiken (Rep., Vt.)

Committee on Appropriations: Chairman: Carl Hayden (Dem., Ariz.); Ranking Minority Member: H. Styles Bridges (Rep., N.H.), who died on November 26, 1961. Leverett Saltonstall (Rep., Mass.) became the next ranking minority member effective the same day.

Committee on Armed Services: Chairman: Richard B. Russell (Dem., Ga.); Ranking Minority Member: H. Styles Bridges (Rep., N.H.), until January 26, 1961, when he became the ranking minority member of the Appropriations Committee. Leverett Saltonstall (Rep., Mass.) became the next ranking minority member effective the same day.

Committee on Banking and Currency: Chairman: A. Willis Robertson (Dem., Va.); Ranking Minority Member: Homer E. Capehart (Rep., Ind.)

Committee on Commerce: Chairman: Warren G. Magnuson (Dem., Wash.); Ranking Minority Member: Andrew F. Schoeppel (Rep., Kans.), who died on January 21, 1962. John Marshall Butler (Rep., Md.) became the next ranking minority member effective the same day.

C H R O N O L O G Y

January 3, 1961:	The 87th Congress and the first session begin.
January 20, 1961:	President Kennedy nominates his cabinet.
January 21, 1961:	The Senate confirms Kennedy's cabinet.
January 31, 1961:	The House increases the size of its Rules Committee.
March 16, 1961:	The Senate approves the Convention on the Organization for Economic Cooperation and Development.
March 29, 1961:	Congress passes the Area Redevelopment Act.
April 13, 1961:	The Senate renames its Committee on Interstate and Foreign Commerce the Committee on Commerce.
August 30, 1961:	The House rejects an Emergency Educational Aid Act.
September 14, 1961:	Congress passes legislation to create the Peace Corps.
September 19, 1961:	Congress passes the Arms Control and Disarmament Act.
September 27, 1961:	The first session ends.
November 16, 1961:	Speaker of the House Sam Rayburn (Dem., Tex.) dies.
January 10, 1962:	The second session begins, and John William McCormack (Dem., Mass.) is elected the new Speaker of the House.
February 28, 1962:	Congress passes labor legislation for unemployed workers.
April 1, 1962:	Supreme Court Justice Charles E. Whittaker retires.
April 3, 1962:	President Kennedy nominates Byron R. White to replace Whittaker.
April 11, 1962:	The Senate confirms White.
July 12, 1962:	Congress passes the Foreign Assistance Act of 1962.
July 16, 1962:	President Kennedy nominates Anthony J. Celebrezze to succeed Abraham A. Ribicoff as secretary of health, education, and welfare.
July 17, 1962:	Congress passes legislation increasing federal involvement in welfare.
July 20, 1962:	The Senate confirms Celebrezze.
August 17, 1962:	Congress authorizes the creation of COMSAT.
August 27, 1962:	Congress sends the 24th Amendment, outlawing poll taxes, to the states for ratification.
August 28, 1962:	Justice Felix Frankfurter retires.
August 31, 1962:	President Kennedy nominates Arthur J. Goldberg to replace Frankfurter and W. Willard Wirtz to succeed Goldberg as secretary of labor.
September 20, 1962:	The Senate confirms Wirtz.
September 25, 1962:	The Senate confirms Goldberg.
October 13, 1962:	The second session ends.
January 3, 1963:	The 87th Congress ends.

[See note 6, p. xxix]

Committee on Finance: Chairman: Harry Flood Byrd (Dem., Va.); Ranking Minority Member: John J. Williams (Rep., Del.)

Committee on Foreign Relations: Chairman: J. William Fulbright (Dem., Ark.); Ranking Minority Member: Alexander Wiley (Rep., Wis.)

Committee on Interior and Insular Affairs: Chairman: Clinton B. Anderson (Dem., N.M.); Ranking Minority Member: Henry C. Dworshak (Rep., Idaho), who died on July 23, 1962. Thomas H. Kuchel (Rep., Calif.) became the next ranking minority member effective the same day.

Committee on the Judiciary: Chairman: James O. Eastland (Dem., Miss.); Ranking Minority Member: Alexander Wiley (Rep., Wis.)

Committee on Labor and Public Welfare: Chairman: J. Lister Hill (Dem., Ala.); Ranking Minority Member: Barry M. Goldwater (Rep., Ariz.)

Committee on Public Works: Chairman: Dennis Chavez (Dem., N.M.); Ranking Minority Member: Francis H. Case (Rep., S.D.), who died on June 22, 1962. John Sherman Cooper (Rep., Ky.) became the next ranking minority member effective the same day.

Committee on Rules and Administration: Chairman: Michael J. Mansfield (Dem., Mont.); Ranking Minority Member: Carl T. Curtis (Rep., Neb.)

HOUSE LEADERSHIP

Speaker of the House: Samuel Taliaferro Rayburn (Dem., Tex.) was Speaker until he died on November 16, 1961. [See biographical note in 76th Congress] John William McCormack (Dem., Mass.) was elected the new Speaker on January 10, 1962. McCormack first had been elected to Congress in the 70th Congress and served as Speaker in the 87th through the 91st Congresses. McCormack had a distinguished career in Congress, but was not as powerful a Speaker as Rayburn.

Majority Leader: John W. McCormack (Dem., Mass.), until he was elected the new Speaker on January 10, 1962. Carl Albert (Dem., Okla.) became the new majority leader the same day.

Majority Whip: Carl Albert (Dem., Okla.), until he became the majority leader on January 10, 1962. Hale Boggs (Dem., La.) became the new majority whip the same day.

Minority Leader: Charles A. Halleck (Rep., Ind.)

Minority Whip: Leslie C. Arends (Rep., Ill.)

Chairman and Ranking Minority Members of Key Committees: [See also Organization and Administration, below]

Committee on Agriculture: Chairman: Harold D. Cooley (Dem., N.C.); Ranking Minority Member: Charles B. Hoeven (Rep., Iowa)

Committee on Appropriations: Chairman: Clarence Cannon (Dem., Mo.); Ranking Minority Member: John Taber (Rep., N.Y.)

Committee on Armed Services: Chairman: Carl Vinson (Dem., Ga.); Ranking Minority Member: Leslie C. Arends (Rep., Ill.)

Committee on Banking and Currency: Chairman: Brent Spence (Dem., Ky.); Ranking Minority Member: Clarence E. Kilburn (Rep., N.Y.)

Committee on Education and Labor: Chairman: Adam Clayton Powell Jr. (Dem., N.Y.); Ranking Minority Member: Carroll D. Kearns (Rep., Pa.)

Committee on Foreign Affairs: Chairman: Thomas E. Morgan (Dem., Pa.); Ranking Minority Member: Robert B. Chiperfield (Rep., Ill.)

Committee on Interior and Insular Affairs: Chairman: Wayne N. Aspinall (Dem., Colo.); Ranking Minority Member: John P. Saylor (Rep., Pa.)

Committee on Interstate and Foreign Commerce: Chairman: Oren Harris (Dem., Ark.); Ranking Minority Member: John B. Bennett (Rep., Mich.)

Committee on the Judiciary: Chairman: Emanuel Celler (Dem., N.Y.); Ranking Minority Member: William M. McCulloch (Rep., Ohio)

Committee on Public Works: Chairman: Charles A. Buckley (Dem., N.Y.); Ranking Minority Member: James C. Auchincloss (Rep., N.J.)

Committee on Rules: Chairman: Howard W. Smith (Dem., Va.); Ranking Minority Member: Clarence J. Brown (Rep., Ohio)

TABLE OF KEY VOTES

Senate

Subject of Vote	Date of Vote	For			Against		
		D	R	Total	D	R	Total
Area Redevelopment Act Passed	March 15, 1961	48	15	63	11	16	27
OECD Membership Approved	March 16, 1961	48	24	72	11	7	18
Labor Training Bill Passed	August 23, 1961	44	16	60	14	17	31
Peace Corps Established	August 25, 1961	Passed by voice vote					
Arms Control Agency Established	September 8, 1961	48	25	73	8	6	14
24th Amendment Sent to States	March 27, 1962	Passed by voice vote					
Foreign Aid Restricted	June 7, 1962	38	23	61	13	10	23
Welfare Bill Passed	July 17, 1962	Passed by voice vote					
COMSAT Established	August 17, 1962	37	29	66	11	0	1

House

Subject of Vote	Date of Vote	For			Against		
		D	R	Total	D	R	Total
Rules Committee Increase Passed	January 31, 1961	195	22	217	64	148	212
Area Redevelopment Act Passed	March 29, 1961	208	43	251	42	125	167
Emergency Educational Aid Defeated	August 30, 1961	164	6	170	82	160	242
Peace Corps Established	September 14, 1961	206	82	288	29	68	97
Arms Control Agency Established	September 19, 1961	194	96	290	16	38	54
Labor Training Bill Passed	February 28, 1962	209	145	354	40	22	62
Welfare Bill Passed	March 15, 1962	224	96	320	3	66	69
COMSAT Established	May 3, 1962	201	153	354	9	0	9
Foreign Aid Restricted	July 12, 1962	178	72	50	68	96	164
24th Amendment Sent to States	August 27, 1962	163	132	295	71	15	86

[See note 7, p. xxix]

Robert Dole (Rep., Kans.) was first elected to the 87th Congress.

Committee on Ways and Means: Chairman: Wilbur D. Mills (Dem., Ark.); Ranking Minority Member: Noah M. Mason (Rep., Ill.)

ORGANIZATION AND ADMINISTRATION

On April 13, 1961, the Senate Committee on Interstate and Foreign Commerce was officially renamed the Committee on Commerce.

The House increased the size of the House Rules Committee from 12 to 15 members. Of the three new members, two were to be Democrats and one would be a Republican. The move was engineered by northern Democrats and moderate Republicans, with White House support, to diminish the ability of committee chairman Howard W. Smith (Dem., Va.) to block civil rights legislation from reaching the floor of the House for a vote. [See note 5, p. xxix]

MAJOR LEGISLATION PASSED

Arms Control: In the Arms Control and Disarmament Act, Congress created the U.S. Arms Control and Disarmament Agency to supervise international disarmament negotiations.

COMSAT: In the Communications Satellite Act of 1962, Congress authorized the creation of the Communications Satellite Corporation (COMSAT) in order to promote the development of communications satellite technology. COMSAT would begin as a government corporation and thereafter rapidly be privatized.

Economic Recovery: In the Area Redevelopment Act, Congress appropriated funds for industrial redevelopment and training assistance programs.

Foreign Aid: In the Foreign Assistance Act of 1962, Congress specifically denied any assistance to a list of Communist nations and to any nation aiding Cuba.

Labor: In the Manpower Training and Development Act of 1962, Congress appropriated funds for training programs for unemployed workers.

OECD: The Senate approved the Convention on the Organization for Economic Cooperation and Development (OECD), in which the U.S., Canada, and most of Western Europe joined the newly established OECD.

Peace Corps: In the Peace Corps Act of 1961, Congress established a Peace Corps of volunteers to work on development programs in the Third World.

Welfare: In the Public Welfare Amendments of 1962, Congress increased federal assistance for the poor and transferred the financial burden of certain programs from the states to the federal government.

FAILED LEGISLATION

The House rejected an Emergency Educational Aid Act, which would have increased federal funding of school construction programs and continued defense-related student loan programs. There was no Senate vote.

RELATIONS WITH THE PRESIDENT

Although some of his objectives were controversial, particularly in the area of civil rights,

Kennedy generally enjoyed good relations with Congress. Part of this success was due to his vice president, Lyndon Johnson, who formerly had been the Senate majority leader and had considerable experience in dealing with Congress.

Kennedy vetoed 20 bills during the 87th Congress. None was of historical significance.

NOMINATIONS, APPOINTMENTS, AND CONFIRMATIONS

The Judiciary: On April 1, 1962, Supreme Court Justice Charles E. Whittaker retired. President John F. Kennedy nominated Byron R. White on April 3, 1962, to replace Whittaker, and the Senate on April 11, 1962, confirmed White by voice vote. On August 28, 1962, Justice Felix Frankfurter retired. President Kennedy nominated Arthur J. Goldberg on August 31, 1962, to replace Frankfurter, and the Senate on September 25, 1962, confirmed Goldberg by voice vote.

The Executive Branch: On January 20, 1961, President Kennedy nominated Douglas Dillon to be secretary of the Treasury, Orville L. Freeman to be secretary of agriculture, Arthur J. Goldberg to be secretary of labor, Luther H. Hodges to be secretary of commerce, Robert F. Kennedy (the president's brother) to be attorney general, Robert S. McNamara to be secretary of defense, Abraham A. Ribicoff to be secretary of health, education, and welfare, Dean Rusk to be secretary of state, and Stewart L. Udall to be secretary of the Interior. On January 21, 1961, the Senate confirmed all of the nominees by voice vote. On July 16, 1962, Kennedy nominated Anthony J. Celebrezze to succeed Ribicoff as secretary of health, education, and welfare, and on July 20, 1962, the Senate confirmed Celebrezze by voice vote. On August 31, 1962, Kennedy nominated W. Willard Wirtz to succeed Goldberg as secretary of labor, and on September 20, 1962, the Senate confirmed Wirtz by voice vote.

IMPEACHMENTS

None.

CONSTITUTIONAL AMENDMENTS

Congress sent the Twenty-fourth Amendment to the states for ratification. The Twenty-fourth Amendment states that no one can be denied the right to vote in a federal election for failing to pay any tax, including a poll tax. The amendment was ratified by the required three-fourths of the states effective January 23, 1964. [For the actual text of the Twenty-fourth Amendment, see the copy of the Constitution at Appendix A]

FURTHER READING

Baldwin, Louis. *Honorable Politician: Mike Mansfield of Montana*. Missoula, Mont.: Mountain Press, 1979.

Goldman, Martin S. *John F. Kennedy, Portrait of a President*. New York: Facts on File, 1995.

Hardeman, D.B., and Donald C. Bacon. *Rayburn: A Biography*. Austin: Texas Monthly Press, 1987.

Kennedy, John F. *Profiles in Courage*. New York: Harper, 1961.

Reeves, Richard. *President Kennedy: Profile of Power*. New York: Simon & Schuster, 1993.

Schapsmeier, Edward, and Schapsmeier, Frederick. *Dirksen of Illinois: Senatorial Statesman*. Urbana, Ill.: University of Illinois Press, 1985.

The 88th Congress

JANUARY 3, 1963-JANUARY 3, 1965

First Session: *January 9, 1963-December 30, 1963*
Second Session: *January 7, 1964-October 3, 1964*

In the 1962 elections for the 88th Congress, the Democrats gained 2 seats in the Senate, increasing their majority from 65 to 67 of the 100 seats. The Republicans lost 2 seats, leaving them with a total of 33. After the 1960 census [See 86th Congress], the House was reapportioned and fixed at 435 members, a reduction from the temporary level of 437 members during the 86th and 87th Congresses. The Democrats lost 5 seats, lowering their majority from 263 to 258 of the 435 seats. The Republicans gained 3 seats, raising their total to 177. [See note 3, p. xxix]

BACKGROUND

In 1963 tensions between the U.S. and the Soviet Union increased and arms control negotiations collapsed. During the summer of 1963, President Kennedy made a 10-day speaking tour of Western Europe. The purpose of the tour was to reassure American allies about the U.S. commitment to European security after the collapse of the disarmament talks. It was during this tour that Kennedy went to West Berlin and made the famous statement "I am a Berliner." Also during the summer of 1963, the Civil Rights movement was gaining momentum, and a group of the movement's leaders organized a Freedom March on Washington, D.C. On August 28 Reverend Martin Luther King Jr. spoke to nearly a quarter of a million people about the problems of injus-

tice and racial inequality in America. It was during this speech that King made another famous statement, namely, "I have a dream," forseeing an America free from segregation and prejudice.

In the fall of 1963 the U.S., the Soviet Union, and Great Britain finally agreed upon the terms of a limited nuclear test ban treaty. The treaty banned nuclear testing in the atmosphere, outer space, and under water, but not underground. The Kennedy administration came to a sudden and violent end on November 22, 1963, when the president was shot and killed while riding in his limousine through downtown Dallas, Texas. Lyndon B. Johnson was sworn in the same day as the 36th president of the United States. One of Johnson's first actions was to establish the Warren Commission on November 29 in order to investigate the Kennedy assassination. The Warren Commission, named after Supreme Court Chief Justice Earl Warren who was the chairman, eventually released a lengthy report concluding that assassin Lee Harvey Oswald had acted alone. Despite several popular conspiracy theories that have lasted until the present day, there has never been any concrete evidence that there was a conspiracy to kill President Kennedy.

In 1964 President Johnson proposed civil rights legislation to Congress that would result in the historic Civil Rights Act of 1964. The act forbade most aspects of segregation throughout the country and would have a particularly significant impact on the South. For this reason, southern senators organized a 75-day-long filibuster, in an unsuccessful attempt to block passage of the act. On January 23, 1964, the Twenty-fourth Amendment to the Constitution was ratified by the states. The amendment banned the poll tax, which was a tax on voter registration. Many states, especially in the South, used the poll tax not to raise revenue, but to discourage poor blacks from voting. Finally, by the end of the 88th Congress, the United States was on its way toward full-scale military involvement in Vietnam. In the Gulf of Tonkin off Vietnam, three North Vietnamese naval vessels attacked the American destroyer *Maddox* in international waters. The U.S. retaliated with air strikes on North Vietnamese military installations, and on August 7 Congress passed a joint resolution authorizing American military action in Vietnam.

SENATE LEADERSHIP

Vice President: Lyndon Baines Johnson had been vice president until he became president after the assassination of President John Fitzgerald Kennedy on November 22, 1963. [See biographical note in 83rd Congress] Until the Twenty-fifth Amendment was ratified on February 10, 1967 [See 90th Congress], there was no mechanism for filling vacancies in the office of the vice president.

President Pro Tempore: Carl Hayden (Dem., Ariz.) [See biographical note in 85th Congress]

Majority Leader: Michael J. Mansfield (Dem., Mont.) [See biographical note in 87th Congress]

Majority Whip: Hubert H. Humphrey (Dem., Minn.)

Minority Leader: Everett McKinley Dirksen (Rep., Ill.) [See biographical note in 86th Congress]

Minority Whip: Thomas H. Kuchel (Rep., Calif.)

Chairman and Ranking Minority Members of Key Committees: [See also Organization and Administration, below]

Committee on Agriculture and Forestry: Chairman: Allen J. Ellender, (Dem., La.); Ranking Minority Member: George D. Aiken (Rep., Vt.)

Committee on Appropriations: Chairman: Carl Hayden (Dem., Ariz.); Ranking Minority Member: Leverett Saltonstall (Rep., Mass.)

Committee on Armed Services: Chairman: Richard B. Russell (Dem., Ga.); Ranking Minority Member: Leverett Saltonstall (Rep., Mass.)

Committee on Banking and Currency: Chairman: A. Willis Robertson (Dem., Va.); Ranking Minority Member: Wallace F. Bennett (Rep., Utah)

Committee on Commerce: Chairman: Warren G. Magnuson (Dem., Wash.); Ranking Minority Member: Norris Cotton (Rep., N.H.)

Committee on Finance: Chairman: Harry Flood Byrd (Dem., Va.); Ranking Minority Member: John J. Williams (Rep., Del.)

Committee on Foreign Relations: Chairman: J. William Fulbright (Dem., Ark.); Ranking Minority Member: Bourke B. Hickenlooper (Rep., Iowa)

Committee on Interior and Insular Affairs: Chairman: Henry M. Jackson (Dem., Wash.); Ranking Minority Member: Thomas H. Kuchel (Rep., Calif.)

Committee on the Judiciary: Chairman: James O. Eastland (Dem., Miss.); Ranking Minority Member: Everett M. Dirksen (Rep., Ill.)

Committee on Labor and Public Welfare: Chairman: J. Lister Hill (Dem., Ala.); Ranking Minority Member: Barry M. Goldwater (Rep., Ariz.)

Committee on Public Works: Chairman: Patrick V. McNamara (Dem., Mich.); Ranking Minority Member: John Sherman Cooper (Rep., Ky.)

Committee on Rules and Administration: Chairman: B. Everett Jordan (Dem., N.C.); Ranking Minority Member: Carl T. Curtis (Rep., Neb.)

CHRONOLOGY

January 3, 1963:	The 88th Congress begins.
January 9, 1963:	The first session begins.
May 23, 1963:	Congress passes the Equal Pay Act of 1963.
September 24, 1963:	The Senate approves the Nuclear Test Ban Treaty.
November 22, 1963:	President Kennedy is assassinated.
December 30, 1963:	The first session ends.
January 7, 1964:	The second session begins.
February 7, 1964:	Congress passes the Revenue Act of 1964.
June 10, 1964:	Senate cloture vote on civil rights legislation.
June 19, 1964:	Congress passes the Civil Rights Act of 1964.
August 7, 1964:	Congress passes the Gulf of Tonkin Resolution.
August 8, 1964:	Congress passes War on Poverty legislation.
October 3, 1964:	The second session ends.
January 3, 1965:	The 88th Congress ends.

[See note 6, p. xxix]

HOUSE LEADERSHIP

Speaker of the House: John William McCormack (Dem., Mass.) [See biographical note in 87th Congress]

Majority Leader: Carl Albert (Dem., Okla.)

Majority Whip: Hale Boggs (Dem., La.)

Minority Leader: Charles A. Halleck (Rep., Ind.)

Minority Whip: Leslie C. Arends (Rep., Ill.)

Chairman and Ranking Minority Members of Key Committees: [See also Organization and Administration, below]

Committee on Agriculture: Chairman: Harold D. Cooley (Dem., N.C.); Ranking Minority Member: Charles B. Hoeven (Rep., Iowa)

Committee on Appropriations: Chairman: Clarence Cannon (Dem., Mo.), who died on May 12, 1964. George H. Mahon (Dem., Tex.) became the next chairman effective the same day. Ranking Minority Member: Ben F. Jensen (Rep., Iowa)

Committee on Armed Services: Chairman: Carl Vinson (Dem., Ga.); Ranking Minority Member: Leslie C. Arends (Rep., Ill.)

Committee on Banking and Currency: Chairman: J.W. Wright Patman (Dem., Tex.); Ranking Minority Member: Clarence E. Kilburn (Rep., N.Y.)

Committee on Education and Labor: Chairman: Adam Clayton Powell Jr. (Dem., N.Y.); Ranking Minority Member: Peter H.B. Frelinghuysen (Rep., N.J.)

Committee on Foreign Affairs: Chairman: Thomas E. Morgan (Dem., Pa.); Ranking Minority Member: Frances P. Bolton (Rep., Ohio)

Committee on Interior and Insular Affairs: Chairman: Wayne N. Aspinall (Dem., Colo.); Ranking Minority Member: John P. Saylor (Rep., Pa.)

Committee on Interstate and Foreign Commerce: Chairman: Oren Harris (Dem., Ark.); Ranking Minority Member: John B. Bennett (Rep., Mich.), who died on August 9, 1964. William L. Springer

(Rep., Ill.) became the next ranking minority member effective the same day.

Committee on the Judiciary: Chairman: Emanuel Celler (Dem., N.Y.); Ranking Minority Member: William M. McCulloch (Rep., Ohio)

Committee on Public Works: Chairman: Charles A. Buckley (Dem., N.Y.); Ranking Minority Member: James C. Auchincloss (Rep., N.J.)

Committee on Rules: Chairman: Howard W. Smith (Dem., Va.); Ranking Minority Member: Clarence J. Brown (Rep., Ohio)

Committee on Ways and Means: Chairman: Wilbur D. Mills (Dem., Ark.); Ranking Minority Member: John W. Byrnes (Rep., Wis.)

ORGANIZATION AND ADMINISTRATION

In the 87th Congress, the House had increased the size of the House Rules Committee from 12 members to 15 members. This increase was made permanent during this Congress. [See Table of Key Votes, below] [See note 5, p. xxix]

MAJOR LEGISLATION PASSED

Civil Rights: In the Civil Rights Act of 1964, Congress strengthened the federal government's power to prevent voting obstruction and to force states and localities to end segregation. In addition to the passage of the act itself, a key vote occurred when the Senate voted to invoke cloture (meaning to stop debate) on the lengthy southern filibuster against the act. Unlike the House rules, the Senate rules required a vote to close off debate.

Equal Rights: In the Equal Pay Act of 1963, Congress made it illegal for an employer to pay female employees less than male employees in jobs of equal skill, effort, and responsibility.

Food Stamps: Congress passed the Food Stamp Act of 1964, which created a federally subsidized food stamp program to help poor people purchase food and also help farmers by reducing agricultural surpluses.

Gulf of Tonkin: Congress gave the president the authority to pursue the Vietnam War, even though there was no formal declaration of war between the U.S. and North Vietnam.

Nuclear Weapons: The Senate approved the Nuclear Test Ban Treaty, in which the U.S., the Soviet Union, and most of the international community agreed not to test nuclear weapons in the atmosphere, outer space, or in the seas.

Taxation: In the Revenue Act of 1964, Congress lowered individual income taxes, corporate taxes, and withholding taxes. The act also created a minimum standard deduction and a lower capital gains rate for people over the age of 65.

War on Poverty: In response to President Johnson's initiative for a War on Poverty, Congress passed the Economic Opportunity Act of 1964, which appropriated funds for nearly a dozen programs against poverty.

FAILED LEGISLATION

None of historical significance.

RELATIONS WITH THE PRESIDENT

Although Kennedy supported the growing civil rights movement, he needed the support of southern Democrats, who were influential in Congress and had helped him get elected in 1960. Martin Luther King Jr.'s Freedom March in the Summer of 1963 strained these conflicting loyalties, and Kennedy privately expressed political reservations about the march. After Kennedy was assassinated in November of 1963, however, President Lyndon Johnson (a southern Democrat from Texas) firmly endorsed Kennedy's civil rights agenda and pushed measures such as the 1964 Civil Rights Act through Congress despite resistance from fellow southern Democrats.

Kennedy vetoed one bill during the 88th Congress before he was assassinated. Johnson vetoed eight bills during the remainder of the 88th Congress. None of the vetoes was particularly significant.

TABLE OF KEY VOTES

Senate

Subject of Vote	Date of Vote	For			Against		
		D	R	Total	D	R	Total
Equal Pay Act Passed	May 17, 1963	Passed by voice vote					
Nuclear Test Ban Treaty Approved	September 24, 1963	55	25	80	11	8	19
Taxes Lowered	February 7, 1964	56	21	77	11	10	21
Civil Rights: Cloture Voted	June 10, 1964	44	27	71	23	6	29
1964 Civil Rights Act Passed	June 19, 1964	46	27	73	21	6	27
Economic Opportunity Act Passed	July 23, 1964	51	10	61	12	22	34
Tonkin Gulf Resolution Passed	August 7, 1964	56	32	88	2	0	2

House

Subject of Vote	Date of Vote	For			Against		
		D	R	Total	D	R	Total
Rules Committee Size Established	January 9, 1963	207	28	235	48	148	196
Equal Pay Act Passed	May 23, 1963	Passed by voice vote					
Taxes Lowered	September 25, 1963	223	48	271	29	126	155
1964 Civil Rights Act Passed	February 10, 1964	152	138	290	96	34	130
Tonkin Gulf Resolution Passed	August 7, 1964	241	175	416	0	0	0
Economic Opportunity Act Passed	August 8, 1964	204	22	226	40	145	185

[See note 7, p. xxix]

NOMINATIONS, APPOINTMENTS, AND CONFIRMATIONS

The Judiciary: There were no significant nominations, appointments, or confirmations in the federal judiciary during the 88th Congress.

The Executive Branch: There were no significant nominations, appointments, or confirmations in the executive branch during the 88th Congress. President Johnson did not replace Kennedy's cabinet, and Senate confirmation votes were not required for continuing those officials.

IMPEACHMENTS

None.

CONSTITUTIONAL AMENDMENTS

None.

FURTHER READING

Baldwin, Louis. *Honorable Politician: Mike Mansfield of Montana*. Missoula, Mont.: Mountain Press, 1979.

Bernstein, Irving. *The Presidency of Lyndon Johnson*. New York: Oxford University Press, 1995.

Califano, Joseph A. *The Triumph & Tragedy of Lyndon Johnson: The White House Years*. New York: Simon & Schuster, 1991.

Goldman, Martin S. *John F. Kennedy, Portrait of a President*. New York: Facts on File, 1995.

Kennedy, John F. *Profiles in Courage*. New York: Harper, 1961.

Reeves, Richard. *President Kennedy: Profile of Power*. New York: Simon & Schuster, 1993.

Schapsmeier, Edward, and Frederick Schapsmeier. *Dirksen of Illinois: Senatorial Statesman*. Urbana, Ill.: University of Illinois Press, 1985.

United States Warren Commission. *The Warren Commission Report: The Official Report of the President's Commission on the Assassination of President John F. Kennedy*. Stamford, Conn.: Longmeadow Press, 1993.

The 89th Congress

JANUARY 3, 1965-JANUARY 3, 1967

First Session: January 4, 1965-October 23, 1965
Second Session: January 10, 1966-October 22, 1966

In the 1964 elections for the 89th Congress, the Democrats gained 1 seat in the Senate, increasing their majority from 67 to 68 of the 100 seats. The Republicans lost 1 seat, leaving them with 32 seats. In the House, the Democrats gained 37 seats, increasing their majority from 258 to 295 of the 435 seats. The Republicans lost 37 seats, reducing their total to 140. [See note 3, p. xxix]

BACKGROUND

Lyndon B. Johnson was inaugurated for his first full term as the 36th president of the United States on January 20, 1965. One of Johnson's first actions was to propose a Twenty-fifth Amendment to the Constitution to Congress, which would provide for filling a vacancy in the office of the vice president and also permit a vice president to serve as acting president should the president become disabled. The Kennedy assassination during the previous Congress, which had made former Vice President Johnson the president, brought attention to the Constitution's failure to provide for filling vice presidential vacancies. From the first Congress until the 90th Congress, when the Twenty-fifth Amendment was ratified by the required three-fourths of the states, there were many occasions in which there was no serving vice president.

During 1965 Johnson made some new civil rights proposals to Congress, capitalizing on his victory in getting the Civil Rights Act of 1964

passed by the previous Congress and the new Twenty-fourth Amendment to the Constitution banning the poll tax. On March 15 Johnson made a nationally televised speech to a joint session of Congress, and proposed comprehensive voting rights legislation. Soon thereafter, Congress enacted the Voting Rights Act of 1965, which authorized the federal government to ensure that minorities were not denied their right to vote by discriminatory state voter registration practices. The act, together with a series of Supreme Court decisions enforcing constitutional guarantees against discrimination, helped end such practices as using a literacy test requirement to deny African Americans the right to vote. That year also brought Reverend Martin Luther King Jr.'s famous civil rights march from Selma to Montgomery, Alabama.

Less positive developments during 1965 include the riots in the Los Angeles ghetto of Watts, an increase in the number of troops deployed in South Vietnam to 125,000, and the assassination of Nation of Islam leader Malcolm X.

In 1966 the Vietnam War was escalating, and so was popular opposition to it. The U.S. was now conducting bombing missions over North Vietnam, and the total number of American troops present in South Vietnam increased to nearly 300,000. Antiwar protestors organized mass protest demonstrations across the country.

In the area of civil rights, the Senate confirmed Robert C. Weaver as the first secretary of

Robert F. Kennedy (Dem., N.Y.) was elected senator to the 89th Congress. He was assassinated on June 6, 1968, during the 90th Congress.

the new Department of Housing and Urban Development; Weaver thus became the first African American confirmed to a cabinet-level position. The courts in 1966 upheld the constitutionality of the Voting Rights Act of 1965, and a White House Conference on Civil Rights composed of over 2,000 leaders of the Civil Rights movement asked Congress to pass additional civil rights legislation.

SENATE LEADERSHIP

Vice President: Hubert Horatio Humphrey had been elected vice president on Lyndon B. Johnson's ticket in the November 1964 elections. He became vice president effective January 20, 1965. [See note 8, p. xxix] Humphrey first had been elected to Congress in 1948 as a senator from Minnesota. During the 1950s, he was a major spokesman for the liberal wing of the Democratic Party in Congress and was an especially forceful advocate of civil rights for African Americans. After President Johnson decided not to run for reelection in 1968, Humphrey became the Democratic nominee that year for president, but lost the election.

President Pro Tempore: Carl Hayden (Dem., Ariz.) [See biographical note in 85th Congress]

Majority Leader: Michael J. Mansfield (Dem., Mont.) [See biographical note in 87th Congress]

Majority Whip: Russell Long (Dem., La.)

Minority Leader: Everett McKinley Dirksen (Rep., Ill.) [See biographical note in 86th Congress]

Minority Whip: Thomas H. Kuchel (Rep., Calif.)

Chairman and Ranking Minority Members of Key Committees:

Committee on Agriculture and Forestry: Chairman: Allen J. Ellender, (Dem., La.); Ranking Minority Member: George D. Aiken (Rep., Vt.)

Committee on Appropriations: Chairman: Carl Hayden (Dem., Ariz.); Ranking Minority Member: Leverett Saltonstall (Rep., Mass.)

Committee on Armed Services: Chairman: Richard B. Russell (Dem., Ga.); Ranking Minority Member: Leverett Saltonstall (Rep., Mass.)

Committee on Banking and Currency: Chairman: A. Willis Robertson (Dem., Va.); Ranking Minority Member: Wallace F. Bennett (Rep., Utah)

Committee on Commerce: Chairman: Warren G. Magnuson (Dem., Wash.); Ranking Minority Member: Norris Cotton (Rep., N.H.)

Committee on Finance: Chairman: Harry Flood Byrd (Dem., Va.), who resigned effective November 10, 1965. Russell B. Long (Dem., La.) became the next chairman effective January 14, 1966. Ranking Minority Member: John J. Williams (Rep., Del.)

Committee on Foreign Relations: Chairman: J. William Fulbright (Dem., Ark.); Ranking Minority Member: Bourke B. Hickenlooper (Rep., Iowa)

Committee on Interior and Insular Affairs: Chairman: Henry M. Jackson (Dem., Wash.); Ranking Minority Member: Thomas H. Kuchel (Rep., Calif.)

C H R O N O L O G Y

January 3, 1965:	The 89th Congress begins.
January 4, 1965:	The first session begins.
January 6, 1965:	President Johnson nominates John T. Connor to succeed Luther H. Hodges as secretary of commerce.
January 15, 1965:	The Senate confirms Connor.
January 28, 1965:	President Johnson nominates Nicholas Katzenbach to succeed Robert F. Kennedy as attorney general.
February 10, 1965:	The Senate confirms Katzenbach.
March 18, 1965:	President Johnson nominates Henry H. Fowler to succeed Douglas Dillon as secretary of the Treasury.
March 25, 1965:	The Senate confirms Fowler.
April 13, 1965:	Congress sends the 25th Amendment, providing a mechanism for filling vacancies in the office of the vice presidency, to the states for ratification.
May 11, 1965:	The Senate rejects a ban on state and local poll taxes.
May 25, 1965:	The Senate invokes cloture on a southern filibuster against civil rights legislation.
July 9, 1965:	Congress passes the Voting Rights Act of 1965 and also passes Medicare and Medicaid legislation.
July 15, 1965:	Congress passes the Housing and Urban Development Act of 1965.
July 25, 1965:	Supreme Court Justice Arthur J. Goldberg resigns.
July 27, 1965:	President Johnson nominates John W. Gardner to succeed Anthony J. Celebrezze as secretary of health, education, and welfare.
July 28, 1965:	President Johnson nominates Abe Fortas to replace Goldberg.
August 11, 1965:	Congress passes legislation creating the Department of Housing and Urban Development. The Senate confirms Gardner and Fortas.
October 23, 1965:	The first session ends.
January 10, 1966:	The second session begins.
January 14, 1966:	President Johnson nominates Robert C. Weaver to be secretary of housing and urban development.
January 17, 1966:	The Senate confirms Weaver.
September 29, 1966:	Congress passes legislation creating the Department of Transportation.
October 22, 1966:	The second session ends.
January 3, 1967:	The 89th Congress ends.

[See note 6, p. xxix]

Committee on the Judiciary: Chairman: James O. Eastland (Dem., Miss.); Ranking Minority Member: Everett M. Dirksen (Rep., Ill.)

Committee on Labor and Public Welfare: Chairman: J. Lister Hill (Dem., Ala.); Ranking Minority Member: Jacob K. Javits (Rep., N.Y.)

Committee on Public Works: Chairman: Patrick V. McNamara (Dem., Mich.), who died on April 30, 1966. Jennings Randolph (Dem., W.Va.) became the new chairman effective May 5, 1966. Ranking Minority Member: John Sherman Cooper (Rep., Ky.)

Committee on Rules and Administration: Chairman: B. Everett Jordan (Dem., N.C.); Ranking Minority Member: Carl T. Curtis (Rep., Neb.)

HOUSE LEADERSHIP

Speaker of the House: John William McCormack (Dem., Mass.) [See biographical note in 87th Congress]

Majority Leader: Carl Albert (Dem., Okla.)

Majority Whip: Hale Boggs (Dem., La.)

Minority Leader: Gerald R. Ford (Rep., Mich.)

Minority Whip: Leslie C. Arends (Rep., Ill.)

Chairman and Ranking Minority Members of Key Committees:

Committee on Agriculture: Chairman: Harold D. Cooley (Dem., N.C.); Ranking Minority Member: Paul B. Dague (Rep., Pa.)

Committee on Appropriations: Chairman: George H. Mahon (Dem., Tex.); Ranking Minority Member: Frank T. Bow (Rep., Ohio)

Committee on Armed Services: Chairman: L. Mendel Rivers (Dem., S.C.); Ranking Minority Member: William H. Bates (Rep., Mass.)

Committee on Banking and Currency: Chairman: J.W. Wright Patman (Dem., Tex.); Ranking Minority Member: William B. Widnall (Rep., N.J.)

Committee on Education and Labor: Chairman: Adam Clayton Powell Jr. (Dem., N.Y.); Ranking Minority Member: William H. Ayres (Rep., Ohio)

Committee on Foreign Affairs: Chairman: Thomas E. Morgan (Dem., Pa.); Ranking Minority Member: Frances P. Bolton (Rep., Ohio)

Committee on Interior and Insular Affairs: Chairman: Wayne N. Aspinall (Dem., Colo.); Ranking Minority Member: John P. Saylor (Rep., Pa.)

Committee on Interstate and Foreign Commerce: Chairman: Oren Harris (Dem., Ark.), who resigned effective January 13, 1966, in order to become a federal judge. Harley O. Staggers (Dem., W.Va.) became the next ranking minority member effective the same day. Ranking Minority Member: William L. Springer (Rep., Ill.)

Committee on the Judiciary: Chairman: Emanuel Celler (Dem., N.Y.); Ranking Minority Member: William M. McCulloch (Rep., Ohio)

Committee on Public Works: Chairman: George H. Fallon (Dem., Md.); Ranking Minority Member: William C. Cramer (Rep., Fla.)

Committee on Rules: Chairman: Howard W. Smith (Dem., Va.); Ranking Minority Member: Clarence J. Brown (Rep., Ohio), who died on August 23, 1965. H. Allen Smith (Rep., Calif.) became the next ranking minority member effective the same day.

Committee on Ways and Means: Chairman: Wilbur D. Mills (Dem., Ark.); Ranking Minority Member: John W. Byrnes (Rep., Wis.)

ORGANIZATION AND ADMINISTRATION

No developments of historical significance. [See note 5, p. xxix]

MAJOR LEGISLATION PASSED

Civil Rights: Congress recognized that despite the civil rights legislation passed by previous Congresses, African Americans were still effectively barred from voting in many state localities, particularly in the South. In the Voting Rights Act of 1965, Congress authorized federal authorities to take over voter registration in areas where African American voter participation was under a certain percentage and ended the use of voter qualification obstacles such as literacy tests.

TABLE OF KEY VOTES

Senate

Subject of Vote	Date of Vote	For			Against		
		D	R	Total	D	R	Total
25th Amendment Sent to States	February 19, 1965	48	24	72	0	0	0
Ending State & Local Poll Taxes Defeated	May 11, 1965	39	6	45	24	25	49
Civil Rights: Cloture Voted	May 25, 1965	47	23	70	21	9	30
Voting Rights Act of 1965 Passed	May 26, 1965	47	30	77	17	2	19
Medicare and Medicaid Bill Passed	July 9, 1965	55	13	68	7	14	21
Housing Programs Approved	July 15, 1965	47	7	54	11	19	30
HUD Established	August 11, 1965	47	10	57	14	19	33
Department of Transportation Established	September 29, 1966	48	16	64	1	1	2

House

Subject of Vote	Date of Vote	For			Against		
		D	R	Total	D	R	Total
25th Amendment Sent to States	April 13, 1965	246	122	368	21	8	29
Medicare and Medicaid Bill Passed	April 18, 1965	248	65	313	42	73	115
HUD Established	June 16, 1965	208	9	217	118	66	184
Housing Programs Approved	June 30, 1965	219	26	245	60	109	169
Voting Rights Act of 1965 Passed	July 9, 1965	221	112	333	61	24	85
Department of Transportation Established	August 30, 1966	235	101	336	23	19	42

[See note 7, p. xxix]

As with the 1964 Civil Rights Act in the 88th Congress, in addition to the passage of the act itself, a key Senate vote invoked cloture (meaning to stop debate) on a southern filibuster against the act. Unlike the House rules, the Senate rules required a vote to close off debate.

Culture: In the National Foundation on the Arts and Humanities Act of 1965, Congress established that foundation and two national endowments, one for the arts and one for the humanities.

Department of Transportation: In the Department of Transportation Act, Congress consolidated nearly three dozen federal agencies into the Department of Transportation (DOT) and gave DOT cabinet-level status.

Environment: In the Water Quality Act of 1965, Congress made the states take steps to set and enforce water quality standards.

Freedom of Information: In the Freedom of Information Act, Congress enabled private citizens to obtain information and copies of records from federal agencies, subject to several important exceptions.

Housing and Urban Development: Congress appropriated funds for a variety of new programs in the Housing and Urban Development Act of 1965. Further, in the Department of Housing and Urban Development Act, Congress combined a number of existing agencies into that department (HUD) and gave HUD cabinet-level status.

Medicare and Medicaid: Congress passed a series of Social Security amendments, creating (1) a program of medical assistance for the senior citzens called Medicare, and (2) a program of medical assistance for the poor called Medicaid.

FAILED LEGISLATION

State and Local Poll Taxes: Since the Twenty-fourth Amendment [See 87th Congress] does not explicitly ban the poll tax in state and local elections but only in federal elections, Senator Edward M. Kennedy (Dem., Mass.) tried to get Congress to pass legislation banning state and local poll taxes. The Senate rejected Kennedy's initiative, preferring to let the attorney general challenge such state and local poll taxes in the courts as discriminatory. [See Table of Key Votes, below]

RELATIONS WITH THE PRESIDENT

President Lyndon Johnson, who formerly had been vice president in the Kennedy administration and was once the Senate majority leader, had considerable experience in dealing with Congress. Johnson capitalized on this experience to push through his civil rights and war on poverty legislation.

Johnson vetoed 14 bills during the 89th Congress. None was particularly significant.

NOMINATIONS, APPOINTMENTS, AND CONFIRMATIONS

The Judiciary: On July 25, 1965, Supreme Court Justice Arthur J. Goldberg resigned. President Lyndon B. Johnson nominated Abe Fortas on July 28, 1965, to replace Goldberg, and on August 11, 1965, the Senate confirmed Fortas by voice vote.

The Executive Branch: On January 6, 1965, President Johnson nominated John T. Connor to succeed Luther H. Hodges as secretary of commerce, and on January 15, 1965, the Senate confirmed Connor by voice vote. Johnson nominated Nicholas Katzenbach to succeed Robert F. Kennedy as attorney general on January 28, 1965, and on February 10, 1965, the Senate confirmed Katzenbach by voice vote. On March 18, 1965, Johnson nominated Henry H. Fowler to succeed Douglas Dillon as secretary of the Treasury, and on March 25, 1965, the Senate confirmed Fowler by voice vote. On July 27, 1965, Johnson nominated John W. Gardner to succeed Anthony J. Celebrezze as secretary of health, education, and welfare, and on August 11, 1965, the Senate confirmed Gardner by voice vote. Finally, on January 14, 1966, Johnson nominated Robert C. Weaver to be secretary of housing and urban development, now a cabinet-level position, and on January 17, 1966, the Senate confirmed Weaver by voice vote.

IMPEACHMENTS

None.

CONSTITUTIONAL AMENDMENTS

Congress sent the Twenty-fifth Amendment to the states for ratification. The Twenty-fifth Amendment permits the vice president to become acting president if the president is unable to perform his or her duties or there is a finding that he or she is incapacitated. The Twenty-fifth Amendment further provides a mechanism for filling vacancies in the office of the vice president. Previously, if a president died and the vice president became president, or a vice president died, there was no new vice president until the next presidential election. The amendment was ratified by the required three-fourths of the states effective February 10, 1967. [For the actual text of the Twenty-fifth Amendment, see the copy of the Constitution at Appendix A.]

Also during this Congress, Senator Everett Dirksen (Rep., Ill.) proposed two Constitutional amendments. One amendment would have permited a state to apportion one house of its legislature on a basis other than one-man, one-vote; the other amendment would have reversed the Supreme Court decision to permit voluntary school prayer. Both of Dirksen's proposals died in the Senate.

FURTHER READING

Baldwin, Louis. *Honorable Politician: Mike Mansfield of Montana*. Missoula, Mont.: Mountain Press, 1979.

Bernstein, Irving. *The Presidency of Lyndon Johnson*. New York: Oxford University Press, 1995.

Califano, Joseph A. *The Triumph & Tragedy of Lyndon Johnson: The White House Years*. New York: Simon & Schuster, 1991.

Goodwin, Doris Kearns. *Lyndon Johnson and the American Dream*. New York: St. Martin's Press, 1991.

Kalman, Laura. *Abe Fortas: a Biography*. New Haven, Conn.: Yale University Press, 1990.

Schapsmeier, Edward, and Frederick Schapsmeier. *Dirksen of Illinois: Senatorial Statesman*. Urbana, Ill.: University of Illinois Press, 1985.

VanDeMark, Brian. *Into the Quagmire: Lyndon Johnson and the Escalation of the Vietnam War*. New York: Oxford University Press, 1991.

The 90th Congress

JANUARY 3, 1967-JANUARY 3, 1969

First Session: January 10, 1967-December 15, 1967
Second Session: January 15, 1968-October 14, 1968

In the 1966 elections for the 90th Congress, the Democrats lost 4 seats in the Senate, lowering their majority from 68 to 64 of the 100 seats. The Republicans gained 4 seats, raising their total to 36. In the House, the Democrats lost 48 seats, reducing their majority from 295 to 247 of the 435 seats. The Republicans gained 47 seats to give them a total of 187. One seat was held by neither major party. [See note 3, p. xxix]

BACKGROUND

In 1967 President Lyndon B. Johnson continued to press forward with his Great Society programs in Congress, but because of the increasing cost of the Vietnam War Congress also was forced to authorize record defense budgets. The number of Americans killed in Vietnam approached 20,000, and the U.S. had to support an increasingly expensive and unpopular war in Vietnam while maintaining its military commitments around the world. By the end of 1967 there were nearly 500,000 American troops in Vietnam. The American forces were militarily and technologically superior to the North Vietnamese army and the Communist guerrillas. The Vietnamese population, however, resented the American presence, seeing it as the continuation of decades of Western colonialism that had begun with the French in the 19th century. The North Vietnamese also were receiving support from the Soviet Union and Communist China, two nations that were now enemies in

many respects but had a common desire to see the United States humiliated in the Third World. Despite the enormous resources that the American government had committed to Vietnam, the war showed no signs of ending, and antiwar protests were becoming larger and more frequent.

On February 10, 1967, the Twenty-fifth Amendment to the Constitution was ratified. The Twenty-fifth Amendment provides for a mechanism to fill vacancies in the office of the vice president, and to make the vice president the acting president should the president become disabled. The Twenty-fifth Amendment originally had been proposed by President Johnson after he had been elevated from vice president to president upon the assassination of John F. Kennedy. The amendment remedied the Constitution's failure to provide for vice presidential vacancies.

Also during 1967, the space program was close to achieving its goal of landing a man on the moon by the end of the decade. Several unmanned spacecraft already had orbited the moon, and preparations were underway for a manned mission. Problems in the space program including a fire in an *Apollo* launch vehicle that killed three astronauts, delayed the manned moon launch until 1969, however. Finally, during 1967 Thurgood Marshall became the first African American justice on the Supreme Court.

In 1968 the Vietnam War continued to escalate, and so did the domestic violence surrounding the antiwar and Civil Rights movements. On

C H R O N O L O G Y

January 3, 1967:	The 90th Congress begins.
January 10, 1967:	The first session begins. President Johnson nominates Alan S. Boyd to be secretary of transportation.
January 12, 1967:	The Senate confirms Boyd.
February 28, 1967:	President Johnson nominates Ramsey Clark to succeed Nicholas Katzenbach as attorney general.
March 2, 1967:	The Senate confirms Clark.
March 16, 1967:	The Senate approves a consular convention with the Soviet Union.
April 25, 1967:	The Senate approves a treaty on the use of outer space.
May 23, 1967:	President Johnson nominates Alexander B. Trowbridge to succeed John T. Connor as secretary of commerce.
June 8, 1967:	The Senate confirms Trowbridge.
June 12, 1967:	Supreme Court Justice Thomas C. Clark retires.
June 13, 1967:	President Johnson nominates Thurgood Marshall to replace Clark.
August 30, 1967:	The Senate confirms Marshall.
September 21, 1967:	Congress passes the Public Broadcasting Act of 1967.
November 2, 1967:	Congress passes the Air Quality Control Act of 1967.
December 15, 1967:	The first session ends.
January 15, 1968:	The second session begins.
January 22, 1968:	President Johnson nominates Clark M. Clifford to succeed Robert S. McNamara as secretary of defense.
January 30, 1968:	The Senate confirms Clifford.

(Continued on p. 441)

the Vietnamese New Year, called Tet, North Vietnam launched a massive offensive involving both regular troops and guerrilla forces. The American Embassy grounds in Saigon briefly were penetrated, and the Marine Corps base at Khe Sanh was cut off and besieged. American forces counterattacked and eventually drove the enemy back, but television coverage of the fighting and the casualties served to increase popular dissatisfaction with the war and with the Johnson administration. Shortly after the end of the Tet offensive, on March 31, 1968, President Johnson announced that he would not seek or accept the nomination of his Democratic Party as the candidate for president in the upcoming 1968 elections. Contributing to Johnson's decision was the surprising strength of anti-war challenger Senator

Eugene McCarthy (Dem., Minn.) who won 42 percent of the vote in the March 12, 1968, Democratic primary in New Hampshire, a surprisingly strong showing even though Johnson narrowly won with 48 percent of the vote.

On April 4, 1968, civil rights leader Reverend Martin Luther King Jr. was assassinated in Memphis, Tennessee. Afterward, there were days of violent riots in African American communities across the United States, particularly in Washington, D.C. Two months later, another prominent individual was assassinated. Senator Robert F. Kennedy (Dem., N.Y.), the brother of late President John F. Kennedy and a former U.S. attorney general, had been campaigning in the Democratic primaries for the upcoming 1968 presidential elections. On June 5 after Kennedy gave

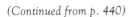

(Continued from p. 440)

C H R O N O L O G Y

February 1, 1968:	Congress passes truth-in-lending legislation.
February 19, 1968:	President Johnson nominates Cyrus R. Smith to succeed Alexander B. Trowbridge as secretary of commerce.
March 1, 1968:	The Senate confirms Smith.
March 11, 1968:	Congress passes the Civil Rights Act of 1968.
March 25, 1968:	President Johnson nominates Wilbur J. Cohen to succeed John W. Gardner as secretary of health, education, and welfare.
May 9, 1968:	The Senate confirms Cohen.
May 16, 1968:	Congress passes dams and irrigation legislation.
June 20, 1968:	Congress passes legislation imposing a tax surcharge to finance the Vietnam War.
June 26, 1968:	President Johnson nominates Associate Justice Abe Fortas to succeed Chief Justice Earl Warren, who wished to resign. Johnson also nominated Homer Thornberry to succeed Fortas.
September 18, 1968:	Congress passes gun control legislation.
October 4, 1968:	President Johnson withdraws the Fortas and Thornberry nominations before any vote was taken.
October 14, 1968:	The second session ends.
January 3, 1969:	The 90th Congress ends.

[See note 6, p. xxix]

a victory speech in the California primary, a Jordanian named Sirhan Sirhan shot and killed the candidate. Despite the turmoil in the Civil Rights movement and his own decision to not seek reelection, President Johnson was nevertheless successful in getting Congress to enact the 1968 Civil Rights Act, which outlawed racial discrimination in housing.

SENATE LEADERSHIP

Vice President: Hubert Horatio Humphrey first had been elected to Congress in 1948 as a senator from Minnesota and was elected vice president on Lyndon B. Johnson's ticket in November 1967. After President Johnson decided not to run for reelection in 1968, Humphrey became the Democratic nominee that year for president, but lost the election.

President Pro Tempore: Carl Hayden (Dem., Ariz.) [See biographical note in 85th Congress]

Majority Leader: Michael J. Mansfield (Dem., Mont.) [See biographical note in 87th Congress]

Majority Whip: Russell Long (Dem., La.)

Minority Leader: Everett McKinley Dirksen (Rep., Ill.) [See biographical note in 86th Congress]

Minority Whip: Thomas H. Kuchel (Rep., Calif.)

Chairman and Ranking Minority Members of Key Committees:

Committee on Agriculture and Forestry: Chairman:

TABLE OF KEY VOTES

Senate

Subject of Vote	Date of Vote	For D	For R	For Total	Against D	Against R	Against Total
U.S.-Soviet Consul Agreement Approved	March 16, 1967	44	22	66	15	13	28
Outer Space Treaty Approved	April 25, 1967	58	30	88	0	0	0
Public Broadcasting Bill Passed	May 17, 1967	Passed by voice vote					
Truth in Lending Bill Passed	July 11, 1967	56	36	92	0	0	0
Air Pollution Bill Passed	July 18, 1967	55	33	88	0	Ø	0
Dams and Irrigation Program Passed	August 7, 1967	Passed by voice vote					
Civil Rights Act of 1968 Passed	March 11, 1968	42	29	71	17	3	20
Tax Surcharge Imposed	April 2, 1968	22	31	53	32	3	35
Gun Control Bill Passed	September 18, 1968	39	31	70	13	4	17

House

Subject of Vote	Date of Vote	For D	For R	For Total	Against D	Against R	Against Total
Civil Rights Act of 1968 Passed	August 16, 1967	166	161	327	68	25	93
Public Broadcasting Bill Passed	September 21, 1967	166	99	265	36	55	91
Air Pollution Bill Passed	November 2, 1967	201	161	362	0	0	0
Truth in Lending Bill Passed	February 1, 1968	218	165	383	3	1	4
Dams and Irrigation Program Passed	May 16, 1968	Passed by voice vote					
Tax Surcharge Imposed	June 20, 1968	154	114	268	77	73	150
Gun Control Bill Passed	July 24, 1968	158	147	305	79	39	118

[See note 7, p. xxix]

Allen J. Ellender (Dem., La.); Ranking Minority Member: George D. Aiken (Rep., Vt.)

Committee on Appropriations: Chairman: Carl Hayden (Dem., Ariz.); Ranking Minority Member: Milton R. Young (Rep., N.D.)

Committee on Armed Services: Chairman: Richard B. Russell (Dem., Ga.); Ranking Minority

Member: Margaret Chase Smith (Rep., Maine)

Committee on Banking and Currency: Chairman: John J. Sparkman (Dem., Ala.); Ranking Minority Member: Wallace F. Bennett (Rep., Utah)

Committee on Commerce: Chairman: Warren G. Magnuson (Dem., Wash.); Ranking Minority

Member: Norris Cotton (Rep., N.H.)

Committee on Finance: Chairman: Russell B. Long (Dem., La.); Ranking Minority Member: John J. Williams (Rep., Del.)

Committee on Foreign Relations: Chairman: J. William Fulbright (Dem., Ark.); Ranking Minority Member: Bourke B. Hickenlooper (Rep., Iowa)

Committee on Interior and Insular Affairs: Chairman: Henry M. Jackson (Dem., Wash.); Ranking Minority Member: Thomas H. Kuchel (Rep., Calif.)

Committee on the Judiciary: Chairman: James O. Eastland (Dem., Miss.); Ranking Minority Member: Everett M. Dirksen (Rep., Ill.)

Committee on Labor and Public Welfare: Chairman: J. Lister Hill (Dem., Ala.); Ranking Minority Member: Jacob K. Javits (Rep., N.Y.)

Committee on Public Works: Chairman: Jennings Randolph (Dem., W.Va.); Ranking Minority Member: John Sherman Cooper (Rep., Ky.)

Committee on Rules and Administration: Chairman: B. Everett Jordan (Dem., N.C.); Ranking Minority Member: Carl T. Curtis (Rep., Neb.)

HOUSE LEADERSHIP

Speaker of the House: John William McCormack (Dem., Mass.). [See biographical note in 87th Congress]

Majority Leader: Carl Albert (Dem., Okla.)

Majority Whip: Hale Boggs (Dem., La.)

Minority Leader: Gerald R. Ford (Rep., Mich.)

Minority Whip: Leslie C. Arends (Rep., Ill.)

Chairman and Ranking Minority Members of Key Committees:

Committee on Agriculture: Chairman: William R. Poage (Dem., Tex.); Ranking Minority Member: Page H. Belcher (Rep., Okla.)

Committee on Appropriations: Chairman: George H. Mahon (Dem., Tex.); Ranking Minority Member: Frank T. Bow (Rep., Ohio)

Committee on Armed Services: Chairman: L. Mendel Rivers (Dem., S.C.); Ranking Minority Member: William H. Bates (Rep., Mass.)

Committee on Banking and Currency: Chairman: J.W. Wright Patman (Dem., Tex.); Ranking Minority Member: William B. Widnall (Rep., N.J.)

Committee on Education and Labor: Chairman: Carl D. Perkins (Dem., Ky.); Ranking Minority Member: William H. Ayres (Rep., Ohio)

Committee on Foreign Affairs: Chairman: Thomas E. Morgan (Dem., Pa.); Ranking Minority Member: Frances P. Bolton (Rep., Ohio)

Committee on Interior and Insular Affairs: Chairman: Wayne N. Aspinall (Dem., Colo.); Ranking Minority Member: John P. Saylor (Rep., Pa.)

Committee on Interstate and Foreign Commerce: Chairman: Harley O. Staggers (Dem., W.Va.); Ranking Minority Member: William L. Springer (Rep., Ill.)

Committee on the Judiciary: Chairman: Emanuel Celler (Dem., N.Y.); Ranking Minority Member: William M. McCulloch (Rep., Ohio)

Committee on Public Works: Chairman: George H. Fallon (Dem., Md.); Ranking Minority Member: William C. Cramer (Rep., Fla.)

Committee on Rules: Chairman: William M. Colmer (Dem., Miss.); Ranking Minority Member: H. Allen Smith (Rep., Calif.)

Committee on Ways and Means: Chairman: Wilbur D. Mills (Dem., Ark.); Ranking Minority Member: John W. Byrnes (Rep., Wis.)

ORGANIZATION AND ADMINISTRATION

No developments of historical significance. [See note 5, p. xxix]

MAJOR LEGISLATION PASSED

Civil Rights: Congress passed the Civil Rights Act of 1968, which among other measures, outlawed racial discrimination in selling or renting houses.

Dams and Irrigation: In the Colorado River Basin Project Act, Congress appropriated funds for several large water development projects in the Southwest, particularly the Central Arizona Project.

Environment: Congress passed the Air Quality Control Act of 1967, which increased the level of federal involvement in the effort to control and reduce air pollution.

Gun Control: In the Gun Control Act of 1968, Congress took some tentative steps to limit the availability of firearms, such as limiting sales to minors and the importation of foreign military surplus weapons.

Outer Space: The Senate approved the Multilateral Treaty on Principles Governing the Activities of States in the Exploration and Use of Outer Space Bodies. Under the treaty, the U.S., the Soviet Union, and most of the international community agreed to the peaceful development of outer space. This agreement includes a prohibition against nuclear weapons in space and prohibits any nation from asserting a claim to the Moon or any other territory in space.

Public Broadcasting: In the Public Broadcasting Act of 1967, Congress created the Corporation for Public Broadcasting in order to promote noncommercial educational programming.

Tax Surcharge: Because of the increasing expense of the Vietnam War, Congress imposed a 10 percent surcharge on individual and corporate income taxes. The surcharge was added by the Senate as an amendment to a tax bill that the House had already passed, and the House voted to accept the Senate's amended version of the bill.

Truth In Lending: In the Consumer Credit Protection Act, popularly known as the Truth In Lending Act, Congress required lenders and cred-itors to make certain disclosures concerning the cost of loans, installment plans, and other forms of consumer credit. The act also limited the amount of take-home pay subject to garnishment.

U.S.-Soviet Consuls: The Senate approved a Consular Convention and Protocol with the Soviet Union, which enabled each country to open consulates on the other's territory.

FAILED LEGISLATION

None of historical significance.

RELATIONS WITH THE PRESIDENT

The final Congress of the Johnson administration is noted for many landmark legislative achievements in civil rights, the environment, and consumer protection. However, the Vietnam War was increasingly unpopular in Congress and with the public, and the Tax Surcharge [See Major Legislation, above] furthered this dissatisfaction. Several members of Congress, such as Senator Eugene McCarthy (Dem., Minn.) [See Background, above], openly criticized the war and Johnson's leadership.

Johnson vetoed eight bills during the 90th Congress.

NOMINATIONS, APPOINTMENTS, AND CONFIRMATIONS

The Judiciary: When Supreme Court Justice Thomas C. Clark retired on June 12, 1967, President Lyndon B. Johnson nominated Thurgood Marshall, the first African American to be nominated to the Court, on June 13, 1967, to replace him. On August 30, 1967, the Senate confirmed Marshall by a 69 to 11 vote. During 1968 Chief Justice Earl Warren announced that he wished to resign in the near future. On June 26, 1968, President Johnson nominated Associate Justice Abe Fortas to succeed Warren as chief justice, and simultaneously nominated Homer Thornberry to succeed Fortas as an associate justice. The Fortas nomination drew criticism in the Senate, however, due to questions about his conduct on the bench. Fortas allegedly had helped President Johnson draft legislation and had advised Johnson on Vietnam policy. Further, Fortas was criticized for taking a $15,000 fee to teach a summer seminar at American University. On October 4, 1968, Johnson withdrew the nominations before any vote was taken. Warren did not resign and no successor was named until the next Congress.

The Executive Branch: On January 10, 1967, President Johnson nominated Alan S. Boyd to be secretary of transportation, now a cabinet-level position. On January 12, 1967, the Senate confirmed Boyd by voice vote. On February 28, 1967, Johnson nominated Ramsey Clark to succeed Nicholas Katzenbach as attorney general, and on March 2, 1967, the Senate confirmed Clark by voice vote. On May 23, 1967, Johnson nominated Alexander B. Trowbridge to succeed John T. Connor as secretary of commerce, and on June 8, 1967, the Senate confirmed Trowbridge by voice vote. On January 22, 1968, Johnson nominated Clark M. Clifford to succeed Robert S. McNamara as secretary of defense, and on January 30, 1968, the Senate confirmed Clifford by voice vote. On February 19, 1968, Johnson nominated Cyrus R. Smith to succeed Trowbridge as secretary of commerce, and on March 1, 1968, the Senate confirmed Smith by voice vote. Finally, on March 25, 1968, Johnson nominated Wilbur J. Cohen to succeed John W. Gardner as secretary of health, education, and welfare, and on May 9, 1968, the Senate confirmed Cohen by voice vote.

IMPEACHMENTS

None.

CONSTITUTIONAL AMENDMENTS

None.

SCANDALS

Both chambers of Congress acted to discipline a member. The House excluded Representative Adam Clayton Powell (Dem., N.Y.) from the House for misuse of committee funds. The Senate censured Senator Thomas J. Dodd (Dem., Conn.) for using political funds for personal expenses. In the next Congress, the Supreme Court in the case of *Powell v. McCormack, et al.* (McCormack was the Speaker of the House) held that Powell's exclusion was illegal since the Constitution does not specifically make "improprieties" a basis for exclusion. The Court's decision was moot, however, since Powell had been reelected to the 91st Congress despite his exclusion during the prior Congress.

FURTHER READING

Baldwin, Louis. *Honorable Politician: Mike Mansfield of Montana*. Missoula Mont.: Mountain Press, 1979.

Bernstein, Irving. *The Presidency of Lyndon Johnson*. New York: Oxford University Press, 1995.

Califano, Joseph A. *The Triumph & Tragedy of Lyndon Johnson: The White House Years*. New York: Simon & Schuster, 1991.

Goodwin, Doris Kearns. *Lyndon Johnson and the American Dream*. New York: St. Martin's Press, 1991.

Kluger, Richard. *Simple Justice: The History of Brown v. Board of Education and Black America's Struggle for Equality*. New York: Vintage Books, 1977.

Schapsmeier, Edward, and Frederick Schapsmeier. *Dirksen of Illinois: Senatorial Statesman*. Urbana: University of Illinois Press, 1985.

VanDeMark, Brian. *Into the Quagmire: Lyndon Johnson and the Escalation of the Vietnam War*. New York: Oxford University Press, 1991.

The 91st Congress

JANUARY 3, 1969-JANUARY 3, 1971

First Session: *January 3, 1969-December 23, 1969*
Second Session: *January 19, 1970-January 2, 1971*

In the 1968 elections for the 91st Congress, the Democrats lost 7 seats in the Senate, reducing their majority from 64 to 57 of the 100 seats. The Republicans gained 7 seats, giving them a total of 43. In the House, the Democrats lost 4 seats, reducing their majority from 247 to 243 of the 435 seats. The Republicans gained 5 seats, giving them a total of 192. [See note 3, p. xxix]

BACKGROUND

According to the census of 1970, the population of the United States as of April 1, 1970, was 203,302,031, resulting in a population density of 57.4 persons for each of the country's 3,540,023 square miles. This was a population increase of 13.4 percent over the 1960 census.

Richard M. Nixon was inaugurated as the 37th president of the United States on January 20, 1969. Nixon had been the vice president during the Eisenhower administration and had lost to John F. Kennedy in the presidential election of 1960. Nixon inherited the Vietnam War from former Presidents Kennedy and Johnson. Peace talks in Paris, France, between the U.S. and North Vietnam were progressing slowly, and by the spring of 1969 the number of Americans killed in Vietnam had exceeded the number killed in the Korean War. By the fall of 1969, millions of Americans were participating in antiwar demonstrations and other protest activities.

On October 15, 1969, the first Vietnam Moratorium Day was held, and on November 14 there was a second Vietnam Moratorium Day, which included a march on Washington, D.C., by over 250,000 people. In Congress, there were allegations that Nixon was conducting combat activities in Laos, a country bordering Vietnam that was supposed to be outside the sphere of military operations. In addition to the antiwar movement, a movement to assist American prisoners of war (POWs) held by the North Vietnamese was gaining supporters. After years of combat, North Vietnam was holding many captured American servicemen. The movement to rescue the POWs gained national publicity when Texas businessman H. Ross Perot chartered a plane and filled it with Christmas gifts for delivery to the POWs in North Vietnam.

Also during 1969, the American space program landed a manned spacecraft on the surface of the moon. The lunar landing was not only an achievement for the space program that had been started by President Kennedy, but was a milestone in human history. On July 20, *Apollo 11* astronauts Edwin E. Aldrin and Neil Armstrong landed on that portion of the moon known as the Sea of Tranquillity aboard the LEM (Lunar Excursion Module) *Eagle*. Upon landing and emerging from the LEM to step forth on the moon, Armstrong made the famous statement, "That's one small step for man, one giant leap for mankind." Although the space program had succeeded in landing a man on the moon, the original objective of proving American superiority over the Soviets by defeating them in the conquest of outer space largely had disappeared given the preoccupation with the Vietnam War.

In 1970 the Nixon administration was successful in reducing the American presence in Vietnam to fewer than 350,000 troops. Under the Johnson administration, there had been more than 500,000 soldiers in Vietnam. Nevertheless, the troop reductions did not defuse the antiwar movement, both because the number of American dead climbed to over 44,000 and because Nixon started a very unpopular offensive against North Vietnamese bases in Cambodia. On May 4, U.S. National Guard troops opened fire on antiwar demonstrators at Ohio's Kent State University and killed four students. The Kent State incident served to increase the number of antiwar demonstrations on college campuses throughout the nation.

SENATE LEADERSHIP

Vice President: Hubert Horatio Humphrey had served as vice president until January 20, 1969, when Spiro Theodore Agnew became the new vice president. Agnew had never served in Congress, but he had been elected governor of Maryland in 1966, and had resigned after he was elected vice president in the 1968 elections. [See note 8, p. xxix]

President Pro Tempore: Richard Brevard Russell (Dem., Ga.) had been governor of Georgia from 1931 until 1933, when he was elected to the Senate. Russell served as president pro tem in the 91st and 92nd Congresses.

Majority Leader: Michael J. Mansfield (Dem., Mont.) [See biographical note in 87th Congress]

Majority Whip: Edward M. Kennedy (Dem., Mass.)

Minority Leader: Everett McKinley Dirksen (Rep., Ill.), until he died on September 7, 1969. [See biographical note in 86th Congress] Hugh Scott (Rep., Pa.) became the new minority leader on September 24, 1969.

Minority Whip: Hugh Scott (Rep., Pa.), until he became the new minority leader on September 24, 1969. Robert P. Griffin (Rep., Mich.) became the new minority whip on that same day.

Chairman and Ranking Minority Members of Key Committees: [See also Organization and Administration, below]

Committee on Agriculture and Forestry: Chairman: Allen J. Ellender, (Dem., La.); Ranking Minority Member: George D. Aiken (Rep., Vt.)

Committee on Appropriations: Chairman: Richard B. Russell (Dem., Ga.); Ranking Minority Member: Milton R. Young (Rep., N.D.)

Committee on Armed Services: Chairman: John C. Stennis (Dem., Miss.); Ranking Minority Member: Margaret Chase Smith (Rep., Maine)

Committee on Banking, Housing, and Urban Affairs: Chairman: John J. Sparkman (Dem., Ala.); Ranking Minority Member: Wallace F. Bennett (Rep., Utah)

Committee on Commerce: Chairman: Warren G. Magnuson (Dem., Wash.); Ranking Minority Member: Norris Cotton (Rep., N.H.)

Committee on Finance: Chairman: Russell B. Long (Dem., La.); Ranking Minority Member: John J. Williams (Rep., Del.), who retired effective December 31, 1970. Wallace F. Bennett (Rep., Utah) became the next ranking minority member effective the same day.

Committee on Foreign Relations: Chairman: J. William Fulbright (Dem., Ark.); Ranking Minority Member: George D. Aiken (Rep., Vt.)

Committee on Interior and Insular Affairs: Chairman: Henry M. Jackson (Dem., Wash.); Ranking Minority Member: Gordon L. Allott (Rep., Colo.)

Committee on the Judiciary: Chairman: James O. Eastland (Dem., Miss.); Ranking Minority Member: Everett M. Dirksen (Rep., Ill.), who died on September 7, 1969. Roman L. Hruska (Rep., Neb.) became the next ranking minority member effective the same day.

C H R O N O L O G Y

January 3, 1969:	The 91st Congress and the first session begin.
January 20, 1969:	President Nixon nominates his cabinet, and the Senate confirms all of the nominees except for Walter J. Hickel, Nixon's nominee for secretary of the Interior.
January 23, 1969:	The Senate confirms Hickel.
March 13, 1969:	The Senate approves a nuclear non-proliferation treaty.
May 14, 1969:	Supreme Court Justice Abe Fortas resigns.
May 21, 1969:	President Nixon nominates Warren E. Burger to be the new chief justice, to replace Chief Justice Earl Warren who plans to resign.
June 9, 1969:	The Senate confirms Burger. President Nixon nominates Elliot L. Richardson to succeed Robert H. Finch as secretary of health, education, and welfare.
June 23, 1969:	Chief Justice Earl Warren resigns.
September 4, 1969:	Congress passes child safety legislation.
September 23, 1969:	Congress passes the National Environmental Policy Act of 1969.
October 8, 1969:	Congress passes water quality legislation.
December 23, 1969:	The first session ends.
January 19, 1970:	The second session begins.
March 13, 1970:	Congress passes voting rights legislation.
April 15, 1970:	After two unsuccessful nominations, President Nixon nominates Harry A. Blackmun to replace Fortas.
May 12, 1970:	The Senate confirms Blackmun.
June 12, 1970:	Nixon nominates James D. Hodgson to succeed George P. Shultz as secretary of labor.
June 15, 1970:	The Senate confirms Richardson.
June 17, 1970:	The Senate confirms Hodgson.
August 25, 1970:	The Senate rejects a volunteer army bill.
September 17, 1970:	Congress fails to approve a constitutional amendment concerning the electoral college.
October 7, 1970:	Congress passes the Organized Crime Control Act.
October 14, 1970:	Congress passes legislation creating the National Railroad Passenger Corporation.
December 10, 1970:	Congress passes the Securities Investor Protection Act of 1970.
January 2, 1971:	The second session ends.
January 3, 1971:	The 91st Congress ends.

[See note 6, p. xxix]

Committee on Labor and Public Welfare: Chairman: Ralph W. Yarborough (Dem., Tex.); Ranking Minority Member: Jacob K. Javits (Rep., N.Y.)

Committee on Public Works: Chairman: Jennings Randolph (Dem., W.Va.); Ranking Minority Member: John Sherman Cooper (Rep., Ky.)

Committee on Rules and Administration: Chairman: B. Everett Jordan (Dem., N.C.); Ranking Minority Member: Carl T. Curtis (Rep., Neb.)

HOUSE LEADERSHIP

Speaker of the House: John William McCormack (Dem., Mass.) [See biographical note in 87th Congress]

Majority Leader: Carl Albert (Dem., Okla.)

Majority Whip: Hale Boggs (Dem., La.)

Minority Leader: Gerald R. Ford (Rep., Mich.)

Minority Whip: Leslie C. Arends (Rep., Ill.)

Chairman and Ranking Minority Members of Key Committees: [See also Organization and Administration, below]

Committee on Agriculture: Chairman: William R. Poage (Dem., Tex.); Ranking Minority Member: Page H. Belcher (Rep., Okla.)

Committee on Appropriations: Chairman: George H. Mahon (Dem., Tex.); Ranking Minority Member: Frank T. Bow (Rep., Ohio)

Committee on Armed Services: Chairman: L Mendel Rivers (Dem., S.C.), who died on December 28, 1970. On December 30, 1970, Philip J. Philbin (Dem., Mass.) became the next chairman effective the same day. Ranking Minority Member: William H. Bates (Rep., Mass.), who died on June 22, 1969. Leslie C. Arends (Rep., Ill.) became the next ranking minority member effective the same day.

Committee on Banking and Currency: Chairman: J.W. Wright Patman (Dem., Tex.); Ranking

Minority Member: William B. Widnall (Rep., N.J.)

Committee on Education and Labor: Chairman: Carl D. Perkins (Dem., Ky.); Ranking Minority Member: William H. Ayres (Rep., Ohio)

Committee on Foreign Affairs: Chairman: Thomas E. Morgan (Dem., Pa.); Ranking Minority Member: E. Ross Adair (Rep., Ind.)

Committee on Interior and Insular Affairs: Chairman: Wayne N. Aspinall (Dem., Colo.); Ranking Minority Member: John P. Saylor (Rep., Pa.)

Committee on Interstate and Foreign Commerce: Chairman: Harley O. Staggers (Dem., W.Va.); Ranking Minority Member: William L. Springer (Rep., Ill.)

Committee on the Judiciary: Chairman: Emanuel Celler (Dem., N.Y.); Ranking Minority Member: William M. McCulloch (Rep., Ohio)

Committee on Public Works: Chairman: George H. Fallon (Dem., Md.), Ranking Minority Member: William C. Cramer (Rep., Fla.)

Committee on Rules: Chairman: William M. Colmer (Dem., Miss.); Ranking Minority Member: H. Allen Smith (Rep., Calif.)

Committee on Ways and Means: Chairman: Wilbur D. Mills (Dem., Ark.); Ranking Minority Member: John W. Byrnes (Rep., Wis.)

ORGANIZATION AND ADMINISTRATION

On October 26, 1970, the Senate Committee on Banking and Currency was renamed the Committee on Banking, Housing, and Urban Affairs. [See note 5, p. xxix]

MAJOR LEGISLATION PASSED

Child Safety: In the Child Protection and Toy Safety Act of 1969, Congress outlawed the sale of hazardous toys.

Crime: In the Organized Crime Control Act, Congress increased the power of federal authorities to obtain evidence regarding organized crime, and sought to prevent money derived from organized crime from being laundered through legitimate businesses.

Environment: In the National Environmental Policy Act of 1969, Congress made it a national priority to address environmental problems, and established the Council on Environmental Quality. In addition, Congress passed the Federal Water Quality Improvement Act of 1970, which placed stricter controls over sewage, pesticide, petroleum, and thermal pollution in the nation's waters. Finally, by not exercising its veto power over executive branch reorganizations, Congress permitted President Nixon to consolidate the federal government's environmental initiatives in a new Environmental Protection Agency (thus, there is no vote in the Table of Key Votes below).

Nuclear Non-Proliferation: The Senate approved the Nuclear Non-Proliferation Treaty between the U.S., the Soviet Union, and 60 other countries. The treaty sought to prevent the spread of nuclear weapons technology.

Railways: In the Rail Passenger Service Act of 1970, Congress created the National Railroad Passenger Corporation to take over railway operations from bankrupt private railroads.

Securities: In the Securities Investor Protection Act of 1970, Congress acted to protect investors in their dealings with securities dealers and brokers. The act also created an insurance fund to protect investors from insolvent brokers.

Voting: Congress amended the Voting Rights Act of 1965 to extend its effect until 1975, and lowered the voting age in all elections to 18. The Supreme Court, however, held that Congress could lower only the voting age to 18 in federal elections, and this decision would be the motivation for the passage of the Twenty-sixth Amendment in the next Congress.

FAILED LEGISLATION

Electoral College: A proposed constitutional amendment to abolish the electoral college passed the House but died in the Senate. [See Constitutional Amendments, below]

Volunteer Army: There was an initiative in the Senate to speed up the planned transition from the draft to a volunteer army. This initiative, in the form of an amendment to the fiscal 1971 defense bill, failed on August 25, 1970. [See Table of Key Votes, below] There was no vote in the House.

RELATIONS WITH THE PRESIDENT

During his first term, President Richard Nixon generally was successful in his dealings with Congress, despite substantial Democratic majorities in both Houses, but experienced growing discontent over the Vietnam War.

Nixon vetoed 11 bills during the 91st Congress.

NOMINATIONS, APPOINTMENTS, AND CONFIRMATIONS

The Judiciary: On May 14, 1969, Supreme Court Justice Abe Fortas resigned, and on June 23, 1969, Chief Justice Earl Warren resigned. President Richard M. Nixon nominated Warren E. Burger on May 21, 1969, to be the new chief justice, and the Senate confirmed Burger on June 9, 1969, by a 74 to 3 vote. It took Nixon three attempts, however, before he could replace Fortas. First, Nixon nominated Clement Haynsworth Jr. on August 18, 1969, but the Senate voted against Haynsworth's confirmation on November 21, 1969, by a 55 to 45 vote. Labor and civil rights groups criticized Haynsworth's conservative background, and there were allegations that he had participated in cases involving corporations in which he had a financial interest. Second, Nixon nominated G. Harrold Carswell on January 19, 1970, and the Senate voted against Carswell's confirmation on April 8, 1970, by a 51 to 45 vote. Carswell was attacked for various racist comments he made and for his poor record while serving as a Federal District Court Judge for the northern district of Florida. Finally, Nixon nominated Harry A. Blackmun on April 15, 1970, and the

TABLE OF KEY VOTES

Senate

Subject of Vote	Date of Vote	For D	R	Total	Against D	R	Total
Nuclear Non-Proliferation Treaty Approved	March 13, 1969	49	34	83	7	8	15
Child Safety Bill Passed	June 30, 1969	Passed by voice vote					
Environmental Policy Law Passed	July 10, 1969	Passed by voice vote					
Water Quality Bill Passed	October 8, 1969	46	40	86	0	0	0
Organized Crime Bill Passed	January 23, 1970	45	28	73	1	0	1
Voting Act Amendments Passed	March 13, 1970	31	33	64	11	1	12
Volunteer Army Bill Defeated	August 25, 1970	15	20	35	34	18	52
Electoral College Defeated	September 17, 1970	33	21	54	18	18	36
Railway Corporation Established	October 14, 1970	Passed by voice vote					
Securities Reform Passed	December 10, 1970	46	31	77	0	0	0

House

Subject of Vote	Date of Vote	For D	R	Total	Against D	R	Total
Water Quality Bill Passed	April 16, 1969	218	174	392	0	1	1
Child Safety Bill Passed	September 4, 1969	182	145	327	0	0	0
Electoral College Approved	September 18, 1969	184	154	338	44	26	70
Environmental Policy Law Passed	September 23, 1969	208	164	372	8	7	15
Voting Act Amendments Passed	December 11, 1969	82	152	234	153	26	179
Organized Crime Bill Passed	October 7, 1970	181	160	341	26	0	26
Railway Corporation Established	October 14, 1970	Passed by voice vote					
Securities Reform Passed	December 1, 1970	202	157	359	2	1	3

[See note 7, p. xxix]

enate confirmed Blackmun on May 12, 1970, y a 94 to 0 vote.

he Executive Branch: On January 20, 1969, resident Nixon nominated his cabinet: Robert I. Finch to be secretary of health, education, and welfare; Clifford M. Hardin to be secretary of agriculture; Walter J. Hickel to be secretary of the Interior; David M. Kennedy to be secretary of the Treasury; Melvin R. Laird to be secretary of defense; John N. Mitchell to be attorney general; William P. Rogers to be secretary of state; George Romney to be secretary of housing and urban development; George P. Shultz to be secretary of labor; Maurice H. Stans to be secretary of commerce; and John A. Volpe to be secretary of transportation. On that same day, the Senate confirmed all of the nominees except Hickel by voice vote. On January 23, 1969, the Senate confirmed Hickel by a vote of 73 to 16. On June 9, 1970, Nixon nominated Elliot L. Richardson to succeed Finch as secretary of health, education, and welfare, and on June 15, 1970, the Senate confirmed Richardson by voice vote. Finally, on June 12, 1970, Nixon nominated James D. Hodgson to succeed Shultz as secretary of labor, and on June 17, 1970, the Senate confirmed him by voice vote.

IMPEACHMENTS

None.

CONSTITUTIONAL AMENDMENTS

During the 1968 presidential election, the strong showing made by third-party candidate George Wallace raised concerns that no candidate would receive the required number of electoral votes and that under the Constitution the House would have to select the next president. This did not happen, but the possibility of it occurring drew some criticism of the electoral college as being outdated. In 1969 the House passed a resolution in favor of a constitutional amendment abolishing the electoral college, but in 1970 a similar resolution simply died in the Senate when the leadership couldn't raise the necessary 60 votes to invoke cloture (meaning to end debate).

FURTHER READING

Baldwin, Louis. *Honorable Politician: Mike Mansfield of Montana.* Missoula Mont.: Mountain Press, 1979.

Nixon, Richard Milhous. *RN: The Memoirs of Richard Nixon.* New York: Simon & Schuster, 1990 (reprint of the 1975 edition).

Schapsmeier, Edward, and Frederick Schapsmeier. *Dirksen of Illinois: Senatorial Statesman.* Urbana: University of Illinois Press, 1985.

Schwartz, Bernard. *The Ascent of Pragmatism: The Burger Court in Action.* Reading, Mass.: Addison-Wesley Pub. Co., 1990.

The 92nd Congress

JANUARY 3, 1971-JANUARY 3, 1973

First Session: January 21, 1971-December 17, 1971
Second Session: January 18, 1972-October 18, 1972

In the 1970 elections for the 92nd Congress, the Democrats lost 3 seats in the Senate, reducing their majority from 57 to 54 of the 100 seats. The Republicans gained 1 seat, raising their total to 44. Two seats were held by independents. In the House, the Democrats gained 11 seats, increasing their majority from 243 to 254 of the 435 seats. The Republicans lost 12 seats, reducing their total to 180. One seat was not held by either major party. [See note 3, p. xxix]

BACKGROUND

Under the Nixon administration, the U.S. continued to disengage itself from the Vietnam War. By the end of 1971, the total number of U.S. troops in Vietnam was less than half of the peak figure it had reached during the previous Johnson administration. Nevertheless, antiwar demonstrations continued, including a May Day (a socialist holiday) protest in Washington, D.C., and a veterans' protest where servicemen from Vietnam threw away their military medals and ribbons. One consequence of the anti-Vietnam movement was a change in popular opinion on what the proper age requirement for voting should be. The draft age began at age 18, and a large percentage of the American forces in Vietnam were young men. Nevertheless, the voting age in many states was 21. Therefore, especially with President Nixon's policy of withdrawing troops from Vietnam, there were thousands of veterans

returning to the United States who had survived combat tours of duty, only to be told that they were not mature enough to vote. This inequity resulted in the ratification of the Twenty-sixth Amendment to the Constitution on June 30, 1971, which provides that the voting age in all federal and state elections must be 18.

Another positive result from Nixon's policy of disengagement from Vietnam was the first step toward normalization in U.S.-Chinese relations. During December 1971, the U.S. announced that it would not oppose Communist China's admission into the United Nations, and that President Nixon would visit China during 1972. Nixon also planned to visit the Soviet Union and was pursuing the Strategic Arms Limitation Talks (SALT), aimed at reducing the superpowers' stockpiles of nuclear weapons. Finally, during 1971 Nixon instituted wage and price controls in order to reduce inflation.

President Nixon left for Communist China on February 21, 1972, where he met with Chinese leaders for a week. On February 27 the U.S. and China issued a joint statement called the Shanghai Communique, which pledged a mutual commitment to reduce cold war tensions and normalize relations. In the communique, Nixon distanced himself from America's ally Taiwan and stated that the U.S. recognized that there was but one Chinese nation. This statement was a concession to the Communist Chinese, who claimed that Taiwan was part of Chinese territory, and a rejection of the

Taiwanese position that they were an independent nation. Nixon was unable, however, to reach an accord with the North Vietnamese in the Paris Peace Talks, and on March 30 the North Vietnamese launched a new offensive against South Vietnam. American air power helped the South Vietnamese defeat the Communist offensive, and Nixon continued his policy of withdrawing American combat troops. By August 1972 American front line combat troops in Vietnam had been withdrawn except for prisoners held by the Communists and those missing in action. The American front line troops were replaced by South Vietnamese ARVN units (Army of the Republic of Viet-Nam).

Also during 1972, Nixon became the first American president to visit Moscow, the capital of the Soviet Union. Nixon also made progress in the arms talks with the Soviets, which resulted in the SALT I agreement.

SENATE LEADERSHIP

Vice President: Spiro Theodore Agnew had never served in Congress, but he had been elected governor of Maryland in 1966, a post he left after he was elected vice president in the 1968 elections on the Nixon ticket.

President Pro Tempore: Richard Brevard Russell Jr. (Dem., Ga.) served until he died on January 21, 1971. Allen Joseph Ellender (Dem., La.) was elected the new president pro tempore on January 22, 1971. Ellender died on July 27, 1972, and James Oliver Eastland (Dem., Miss.) was elected the new president pro tempore on July 28, 1972.

Majority Leader: Michael J. Mansfield (Dem., Mont.) [See biographical note in 85th Congress]

Majority Whip: Robert C. Byrd (Dem., W.Va.)

Minority Leader: Hugh Scott (Rep., Pa.)

Minority Whip: Robert P. Griffin (Rep., Mich.)

Chairman and Ranking Minority Members of Key Committees:

Committee on Agriculture and Forestry: Chairman: Herman E. Talmadge (Dem., Ga.); Ranking

Minority Member: Jack R. Miller (Rep., Iowa)

Committee on Appropriations: Chairman: Allen J. Ellender (Dem., La.), who died on July 27, 1972. John L. McClellan (Dem., Ark.) became the new chairman effective August 2, 1972. Ranking Minority Member: Milton R. Young (Rep., N.D.)

Committee on Armed Services: Chairman: John C. Stennis (Dem., Miss.); Ranking Minority Member: Margaret Chase Smith (Rep., Maine)

Committee on Banking, Housing, and Urban Affairs: Chairman: John J. Sparkman (Dem., Ala.); Ranking Minority Member: John G. Tower (Rep., Tex.)

Committee on Commerce: Chairman: Warren G. Magnuson (Dem., Wash.); Ranking Minority Member: Norris Cotton (Rep., N.H.)

Committee on Finance: Chairman: Russell B. Long (Dem., La.); Ranking Minority Member: Wallace F. Bennett (Rep., Utah)

Committee on Foreign Relations: Chairman: J. William Fulbright (Dem., Ark.); Ranking Minority Member: George D. Aiken (Rep., Vt.)

Committee on Interior and Insular Affairs: Chairman: Henry M. Jackson (Dem., Wash.); Ranking Minority Member: Gordon L. Allott (Rep., Colo.)

Committee on the Judiciary: Chairman: James O. Eastland (Dem., Miss.); Ranking Minority Member: Roman L. Hruska (Rep., Neb.)

Committee on Labor and Public Welfare: Chairman: Harrison A. Williams Jr. (Dem., N.J.); Ranking Minority Member: Jacob K. Javits (Rep., N.Y.)

Committee on Public Works: Chairman: Jenning Randolph (Dem., W.Va.); Ranking Minority Member: John Sherman Cooper (Rep., Ky.)

Committee on Rules and Administration Chairman: B. Everett Jordan (Dem., N.C.) Ranking Minority Member: Winston L. Prouty (Rep., Vt.)

HOUSE LEADERSHIP

Speaker of the House: Carl Bert Albert (Dem., Okla.) first had been elected to Congress in the 80th Congress and served as Speaker in the 92nd through the 94th Congresses.

Majority Leader: Hale Boggs (Dem., La.)

Majority Whip: Thomas P. O'Neill Jr. (Dem., Mass.)

Minority Leader: Gerald R. Ford (Rep., Mich.)

Minority Whip: Leslie C. Arends (Rep., Ill.)

Chairman and Ranking Minority Members of Key Committees:

Committee on Agriculture: Chairman: William R. Poage (Dem., Tex.); Ranking Minority Member: Page H. Belcher (Rep., Okla.)

Committee on Appropriations: Chairman: George H. Mahon (Dem., Tex.); Ranking Minority Member: Frank T. Bow (Rep., Ohio)

Committee on Armed Services: Chairman: F. Edward Hebert (Dem., La.); Ranking Minority Member: Leslie C. Arends (Rep., Ill.)

Committee on Banking and Currency: Chairman: J.W. Wright Patman (Dem., Tex.); Ranking Minority Member: William B. Widnall (Rep., N.J.)

Committee on Education and Labor: Chairman: Carl D. Perkins (Dem., Ky.); Ranking Minority Member: Albert H. Quie (Rep., Minn.)

Committee on Foreign Affairs: Chairman: Thomas E. Morgan (Dem., Pa.); Ranking Minority Member: William S. Maillard (Rep., Calif.)

Committee on Interior and Insular Affairs: Chairman: Wayne N. Aspinall (Dem., Colo.); Ranking Minority Member: John P. Saylor (Rep., Pa.)

Committee on Interstate and Foreign Commerce: Chairman: Harley O. Staggers (Dem., W.Va.); Ranking Minority Member: William L. Springer (Rep., Ill.)

Committee on the Judiciary: Chairman: Emanuel Celler (Dem., N.Y.); Ranking Minority Member: William M. McCulloch (Rep., Ohio)

Committee on Public Works: Chairman: John A. Blatnik (Dem., Minn.); Ranking Minority Member: William H. Harsha Jr. (Rep., Ohio)

Committee on Rules: Chairman: William M. Colmer (Dem., Miss.); Ranking Minority Member: H. Allen Smith (Rep., Calif.)

Committee on Ways and Means: Chairman: Wilbur D. Mills (Dem., Ark.); Ranking Minority Member: John W. Byrnes (Rep., Wis.)

ORGANIZATION AND ADMINISTRATION

No developments of historical significance. [See note 5, p. xxix]

MAJOR LEGISLATION PASSED

Consumer Protection: In the Consumer Product Safety Act, Congress established the Consumer Product Safety Commission with the power to set safety regulations concerning consumer products.

Economy: In the Economic Stabilization Act Amendments of 1971, Congress gave the president the power to limit wages, prices, interest rates, dividends, and other matters in an effort to control inflation.

Elections: In the Federal Election Campaign Act of 1971, Congress placed limits on campaign spending in federal elections. (The Supreme Court later held that parts of the act were unconstitutional).

Environment: In the Federal Water Pollution Control Act Amendments of 1972, Congress issued new and much stricter regulations concerning water quality and appropriated funds for a number of programs that greatly expanded the federal government's effort to combat water pollution. The legislation was passed over President Nixon's veto.

Lockheed: In the Emergency Loan Guarantee

C H R O N O L O G Y

January 3, 1971: The 92nd Congress begins.

January 21, 1971: The first session begins. Senate President Pro Tem Richard Brevard Russell Jr. (Dem., Ga.) dies.

January 22, 1971: Allen Joseph Ellender (Dem., La.) is elected the new Senate president pro tem.

January 25, 1971: President Nixon nominates John B. Connally to succeed David M. Kennedy as secretary of the Treasury and Rogers C.B. Morton to succeed Walter J. Hickel as secretary of the Interior.

January 28, 1971: The Senate confirms Morton.

February 8, 1971: The Senate confirms Connally.

March 23, 1971: Congress sends the 26th Amendment, lowering the voting age to 18, to the states for ratification.

August 2, 1971: Congress approves a financial bailout of Lockheed, a large defense contractor.

September 17, 1971: Supreme Court Justice Hugo L. Black retires.

September 23, 1971: Supreme Court Justice John M. Harlan II retires.

October 22, 1971: President Nixon nominates Lewis F. Powell Jr. to replace Black and William H. Rehnquist to replace Harlan.

November 11, 1971: President Nixon nominates Earl L. Butz to succeed Clifford M. Hardin as secretary of agriculture.

November 30, 1971: Congress passes the Federal Election Campaign Act of 1971.

December 2, 1971: The Senate confirms Butz.

December 6, 1971: The Senate confirms Powell.

December 10, 1971: Congress passes economic stabilization legislation. The Senate confirms Rehnquist.

December 17, 1971: The first session ends.

(Continued on p. 457)

Act, Congress gave banks lending money to the Lockheed Corporation a federal guarantee of repayment. Lockheed, a major defense contractor, was in serious financial difficulty.

U.S.-Soviet Relations: There were two major developments during this Congress. First, the Senate approved the Anti-Ballistic Missile Treaty, which limited the U.S. and the Soviet Union to two ABM sites. Second, Congress passed the Strategic Arms Limitation Act, which approved the agreements reached in the Strategic Arms Limitation Talks.

FAILED LEGISLATION

Desegregating Schools: Congress rejected a proposal to mandate the nationwide integration of schools. The proposal would have required northern school systems where housing patterns, rather than legally mandated segregation, generally determined the ethnic mix, to forcibly integrate. On the other hand, Congress rejected a bill that would have ended busing.

Supersonic Transport (SST): Congress refused to continue funding for the SST airplane project despite the ongoing SST programs in Europe and the Soviet Union.

(Continued from p. 456)

C H R O N O L O G Y

January 18, 1972:   The second session begins.

January 27, 1972:   President Nixon nominates Peter G. Peterson to succeed Maurice H. Stans as secretary of commerce.

February 15, 1972:   President Nixon nominates Richard G. Kleindienst to succeed John N. Mitchell as attorney general.

February 21, 1972:   The Senate confirms Peterson.

March 22, 1972:   Congress sends the Equal Rights Amendment to the states for ratification, but the states eventually fail to ratify it.

May 17, 1972:   President Nixon nominates George P. Shultz to succeed John B. Connally as secretary of the Treasury.

June 8, 1972:   The Senate confirms Kleindienst and Shultz.

June 17, 1972:   The Watergate affair begins.

July 27, 1972:   Senate President Pro Tem Allen Joseph Ellender (Dem., La.) dies.

July 28, 1972:   James Oliver Eastland (Dem., Miss.) is elected as the new Senate president pro tem.

August 3, 1972:   The Senate approves the Anti-Ballistic Missile Treaty.

September 20, 1972:   Congress passes the Consumer Product Safety Act.

September 25, 1972:   Congress passes legislation implementing SALT.

October 17, 1972:   President Nixon vetoes the Federal Water Pollution Control Act Amendments of 1972.

October 18, 1972:   Both chambers of Congress vote to override Nixon's veto. The second session ends.

January 3, 1973:   The 92nd Congress ends.

[See note 6, p. xxix]

---

ietnam: The Senate came close to voting that efense appropriations for Vietnam could only e used for the withdrawal of U.S. troops, but ie administration successfully prevented this om occurring.

ELATIONS WITH
HE PRESIDENT

espite Democratic majorities in both Houses of ongress, President Richard Nixon generally was iccessful in his dealings with Congress. However, ie administration came under increasing pressure om Congress to accelerate its disengagement

from the Vietnam War.

Nixon vetoed 20 bills during the 92nd Congress. Four were particularly significant. First, on June 29, 1971, Nixon vetoed a public works bill that included $2 billion for public works jobs that Nixon thought were wasteful. The Senate on July 14, 1971, voted 57 to 36 to override the veto, but was short of the two-thirds majority necessary to override a veto, and thus there was no vote in the House. Second, on December 9, 1971, Nixon vetoed funding for a comprehensive child care program. On December 10, 1971, the Senate voted 51 to 36 to override the veto, short of the required two-thirds majority, and thus there

TABLE OF KEY VOTES

Senate

Subject of Vote	Date of Vote	For D	For R	For Total	Against D	Against R	Against Total
26th Amendment Approved	March 10, 1971	51	43	94	0	0	0
Lockheed Bailout Passed	August 2, 1971	22	27	49	31	17	48
Campaign Spending Limits Passed	August 5, 1971	51	37	88	0	2	2
Economic Stabilization Bill Passed	December 1, 1971	45	41	86	3	1	4
Equal Rights Amendment Approved	March 22, 1972	47	37	84	2	6	8
Consumer Protection Voted	June 21, 1972	38	31	69	3	7	10
ABM Treaty Approved	August 3, 1972	48	40	88	1	1	2
SALT Act Passed	September 14, 1972	50	38	88	2	0	2
Environment Veto Overridden	October 18, 1972	34	18	52	4	8	12

House

Subject of Vote	Date of Vote	For D	For R	For Total	Against D	Against R	Against Total
26th Amendment Approved	March 23, 1971	Passed by voice vote					
Lockheed Bailout Passed	July 30, 1971	102	90	192	129	60	189
Equal Rights Amendment Approved	October 12, 1971	217	137	354	12	12	24
Campaign Spending Limits Passed	November 30, 1971	219	153	372	11	12	23
Economic Stabilization Bill Passed	December 10, 1971	184	142	326	22	11	33
Consumer Protection Voted	September 20, 1972	193	126	319	27	23	50
SALT Act Passed	September 25, 1972	182	126	308	3	1	4
Environment Veto Overridden	October 18, 1972	152	95	247	10	13	23

[See note 7, p. xxix]

was no vote in the House. Third, on August 16, 1972, Nixon vetoed an appropriations bill for the Department of Health, Education, and Welfare and the Department of Labor that Nixon thought should be cut by $1.8 billion. That same day, the House voted 203 to 171 to override the veto, short of the required two-thirds majority and thus there was no vote in the Senate. Finally, o[n] October 17, 1972, Nixon vetoed the Feder[al] Water Pollution Control Act Amendments [of] 1972 [See Major Legislation, above] as being to[o] costly, but Congress overrode his veto the ne[xt] day. [See Table of Key Votes, above]

NOMINATIONS, APPOINTMENTS, AND CONFIRMATIONS

The Judiciary: On September 17, 1971, Supreme Court Justice Hugo L. Black retired, and on September 23, 1971, Justice John M. Harlan II retired. To fill the two vacancies on the Court, President Richard M. Nixon nominated Lewis F. Powell Jr. and William H. Rehnquist on October 22, 1971. The Senate confirmed Powell on December 6, 1971, by an 89 to 1 vote and Rehnquist on December 10, 1971, by a 68 to 26 vote.

The Executive Branch: On January 25, 1971, Nixon nominated John B. Connally to succeed David M. Kennedy as secretary of the Treasury and Rogers C.B. Morton to succeed Walter J. Hickel as secretary of the Interior. On January 28, 1971, the Senate confirmed Morton by voice vote, and on February 8, 1971, the Senate confirmed Connally by voice vote. On November 11, 1971, Nixon nominated Earl L. Butz to succeed Clifford M. Hardin as secretary of agriculture, and on December 2, 1971, the Senate confirmed him by a vote of 51 to 44. On January 27, 1972, Nixon nominated Peter G. Peterson to succeed Maurice H. Stans as secretary of commerce, and on February 21, 1972, the Senate confirmed Peterson by voice vote. On February 15, 1972, Nixon nominated Richard G. Kleindienst to succeed John N. Mitchell as attorney general, and on May 17, 1972, Nixon nominated George P. Shultz to succeed John B. Connally as secretary of the Treasury. On June 8, 1972, the Senate confirmed Kleindienst by a vote of 64 to 19 and Shultz by a vote of 83 to 0.

IMPEACHMENTS

None.

CONSTITUTIONAL AMENDMENTS

Congress sent the Twenty-sixth Amendment to the states for ratification. The Twenty-sixth Amendment states that anyone who is 18 years of age or older cannot be denied the right to vote on account of age in any federal, state, or local election. The amendment was ratified by the required three-fourths of the states effective June 30, 1971. Congress also sent the Equal Rights Amendment (ERA), which would require equal rights regardless of gender, to the states for ratification. The necessary three-fourths of the states did not ratify the ERA, however. [For the actual text of the Twenty-sixth Amendment, see the copy of the Constitution in Appendix A]

SCANDALS

On June 17, 1972, the Watergate affair began when District of Columbia police arrested five men for breaking into the Democratic National Committee headquarters in the Watergate building. The attempted cover-up of the burglary by the Nixon administration eventually would lead to President Nixon's resignation in 1974.

FURTHER READING

Baldwin, Louis. *Honorable Politician: Mike Mansfield of Montana.* Missoula, Mont.: Mountain Press, 1979.

Davis, Sue. *Justice Rehnquist and the Constitution.* Princeton, N.J.: Princeton University Press, 1989.

Emery, Fred. *Watergate: The Corruption of American Politics and the Fall of Richard Nixon.* New York: Times Books, 1994.

Nixon, Richard Milhous. *RN: The Memoirs of Richard Nixon.* New York: Simon & Schuster, 1990 (reprint of the 1975 edition).

The 93rd Congress

JANUARY 3, 1973-JANUARY 3, 1975

First Session: *January 3, 1973-December 22, 1973*
Second Session: *January 21, 1974-December 20, 1974*

In the 1972 elections for the 93rd Congress, the Democrats gained 2 seats in the Senate, increasing their majority from 54 to 56 of the 100 seats. The Republicans lost 2 seats, reducing their total to 42. Two seats were held by independents. In the House, the Democrats lost 15 seats, reducing their majority from 254 to 239 of the 435 seats. The Republicans gained 12 seats, giving them a total of 192. Two seats were vacant because House Majority Leader Hale Briggs (Dem., La.) and Representative Nick Begich (Dem., Alaska) were missing on an airplane flight over Alaska. They were declared dead, and their seats were filled in a special election in March 1973. Two seats were not held by either major party. One of these seats was held by an Independent Democrat. [See note 3, p. xxix]

BACKGROUND

Richard M. Nixon was inaugurated for his second term as the 37th president of the United States on January 20, 1973. Two days later, the long-standing Paris Peace Talks finally resulted in a peace accord between the United States and North Vietnam. The terms of the agreement provided for an independent South Vietnam, a mutual cease-fire, and withdrawal of the remaining American military presence in South Vietnam. Both sides were to release their prisoners of war (POWs), and North Vietnam and South Vietnam were to pursue reunification

through peaceful negotiations. Although it wa highly doubtful that North Vietnam would obe the agreement's terms once the United State had withdrawn militarily, the American govern ment was anxious to put the unpopular wa behind it. In later years, many veterans group would accuse the government of abandonin American soldiers who were missing in actio (MIAs) or held as POWs by not insisting tha North Vietnam thoroughly account for and tur over all MIAs and POWs in its possession befor the U.S. made a complete military withdrawal

Although the political problem of the Vietnar War was now diminishing for President Nixor the new problem of the Watergate scandal wa increasing. Government investigators and new. paper journalists were uncovering evidence c high-level White House involvement in th break-in at the Democratic Party offices in th Watergate hotel and apartment complex i Washington, D.C. By the end of April 1973, fi senior Nixon Administration officials ha resigned because of their involvement in th Watergate affair: White House Counsel Joh Dean, Domestic Policy Assistant Joh Ehrlichman, FBI Director L. Patrick Gray, Whi House Chief of Staff H. R. Haldeman, and U.. Attorney General Richard G. Kleindienst. I May, the Senate Select Committee o Presidential Campaign Activities began an inve tigation into Watergate, chaired by Senator Sa J. Ervin (Dem., N.C.). In addition, Archiba

chose Representative Gerald R. Ford (Rep., Mich.) to be the new vice president. By the end of 1973, the House of Representatives was considering eight different impeachment resolutions against President Nixon.

Also during 1973, the Organization of Petroleum Exporting Countries (OPEC), which consisted mostly of Arab nations in the Middle East, imposed an oil embargo on the U.S. in retaliation for its support of the Jewish state of Israel. The Arab oil embargo caused a gasoline shortage in the U.S., and served to put the economy into a recession and heightened the inflation problem.

In 1974 Congress was moving toward the second impeachment of a president in United States history, the first having been that of Andrew Johnson after the Civil War. [See 40th Congress] In response to Senate subpoenas, Nixon turned over various documents and tapes of White House conversations concerning Watergate, but did not make a full disclosure of all the materials in his possession. Nixon claimed that "executive privilege" entitled him to withhold sensitive documents from the Senate's and special prosecuter's inquiries into Watergate. Ultimately, it was the Supreme Court's decision in *U.S. v. Nixon* that caused Nixon to resign from the presidency. In a unanimous decision, the justices of the Supreme Court held that Nixon had to release the requested materials. On August 9, 1974, Nixon resigned, and Vice President Gerald R. Ford was sworn in as the 38th president of the United States. Shortly thereafter, President Ford exercised his constitutional power to pardon Nixon for any crimes committed while in office, and thus ended the Watergate affair with respect to Nixon. The Nixon pardon, however, would remain as a political liability to Ford throughout his presidency.

SENATE LEADERSHIP

Vice President: Spiro T. Agnew served as vice president until he resigned on October 10, 1973. On October 12, 1973 President Nixon nominated Representative Gerald R. Ford (Rep., Mich.) to

Senator Howard Baker (Rep., Tenn.) during the Watergate hearings.

Cox was named the special federal prosecutor for the Watergate affair by the new attorney general.

During the summer of 1973, Leonid Brezhnev, the leader of the Soviet Union, visited the U.S. to reciprocate for Nixon's visit to the Soviet Union during the previous Congress. Nixon and Brezhnev executed several agreements designed to continue the lessening of cold war tensions, but Brezhnev's visit was overshadowed by the Senate's continuing Watergate hearings. Former White House Counsel John Dean gave extensive testimony, which was televised nationally, that implicated Nixon in the Watergate affair. In what was becoming a power struggle between Congress and the presidency, Nixon refused to relinquish control over tape recordings of conversations that he had made in the White House concerning the Watergate affair. Senator Ervin's committee subpoenaed Nixon's tapes. Nixon refused to honor the subpoena and left the matter to the federal courts to resolve.

On October 10, 1973, Nixon's vice president, Spiro Agnew, resigned because of an unrelated scandal concerning income tax evasion. Nixon

C H R O N O L O G Y

January 3, 1973:	The 93rd Congress and the first session begin. President Nixon made numerous changes to his cabinet before he resigned from office. [See Nominations, Appointments, and Confirmations: The Executive Branch, below.]
April 19, 1973:	Congress passes the Highway Act of 1973.
July 19, 1973:	Congress passes the Agriculture and Consumer Protection Act of 1973.
August 2, 1973:	Congress approves the Alaskan pipeline.
September 18, 1973:	Congress passes endangered species legislation.
October 10, 1973:	Vice President Spiro T. Agnew resigns.
October 12, 1973:	President Nixon nominates Gerald Ford to be the new vice president.
October 24, 1973:	President Nixon vetoes the War Powers Resolution.
November 7, 1973:	Both chambers of Congress vote to override Nixon's veto.
December 6, 1973:	Congress approves Gerald Ford as the new vice president.
December 11, 1973:	Congress passes the Regional Rail Reorganization Act of 1973.
December 22, 1973:	The first session ends.
January 21, 1974:	The second session begins.
February 28, 1974:	Congress passes ERISA.
July 12, 1974:	Both the House and the Senate establish standing budget committees.
August 9, 1974:	President Nixon resigns.
August 20, 1974:	President Ford nominates Nelson Rockefeller to be the new vice president.
November 21, 1974:	Congress passes legislation to expand the Freedom of Information Act.
December 13, 1974:	Congress passes the Trade Act of 1974.
December 19, 1974:	Congress approves Nelson Rockefeller as the new vice president.
December 20, 1974:	The second session ends.
January 3, 1975:	The 93rd Congress ends.

[See note 6, p. xxix]

be the new vice president, and Ford thus became the first vice president to be nominated by the president and approved by Congress pursuant to the Twenty-fifth Amendment. [See Table of Key Votes, below] Ford became president on August 9, 1974, when President Nixon resigned. On August 20, 1974, Ford nominated Nelson A. Rockefeller, former governor of New York, to be vice president and Congress approved Rockefelle as well. [See Table of Key Votes, below]

President Pro Tempore: James Oliver Eastlan

(Dem., Miss.) had been elected to the Senate in 1942 and served as president pro tem in the 92nd through the 95th Congresses.

Majority Leader: Michael J. Mansfield (Dem., Mont.) [See biographical note in 85th Congress]

Majority Whip: Robert C. Byrd (Dem., W.Va.)

Minority Leader: Hugh Scott (Rep., Pa.)

Minority Whip: Robert P. Griffin (Rep., Mich.)

Chairman and Ranking Minority Members of Key Committees: [See also Organization and Administration, below]

Committee on Agriculture and Forestry: Chairman: Herman E. Talmadge (Dem., Ga.); Ranking Minority Member: Carl T. Curtis (Rep., Neb.)

Committee on Appropriations: Chairman: John L. McClellan, (Dem., Ark.); Ranking Minority Member: Milton R. Young (Rep., N.D.)

Committee on Armed Services: Chairman: John C. Stennis (Dem., Miss.); Ranking Minority Member: J. Strom Thurmond (Rep., S.C.)

Committee on Banking, Housing, and Urban Affairs: Chairman: John J. Sparkman (Dem., Ala.); Ranking Minority Member: John G. Tower (Rep., Tex.)

Committee on the Budget: Chairman: Edmund S. Muskie (Dem., Maine); Ranking Minority Member: Peter H. Dominick (Rep., Colo.)

Committee on Commerce: Chairman: Warren G. Magnuson (Dem., Wash.); Ranking Minority Member: Norris Cotton (Rep., N.H.)

Committee on Finance: Chairman: Russell B. Long (Dem., La.); Ranking Minority Member: Wallace F. Bennett (Rep., Utah)

Committee on Foreign Relations: Chairman: J. William Fulbright (Dem., Ark.); Ranking Minority Member: George D. Aiken (Rep., Vt.)

Committee on Interior and Insular Affairs: Chairman: Henry M. Jackson (Dem., Wash.); Ranking Minority Member: Paul J. Fannin (Rep., Ariz.)

Committee on the Judiciary: Chairman: James O. Eastland (Dem., Miss.); Ranking Minority Member: Roman L. Hruska (Rep., Neb.)

Committee on Labor and Public Welfare: Chairman: Harrison A. Williams Jr. (Dem., N.J.); Ranking Minority Member: Jacob K. Javits (Rep., N.Y.)

Committee on Public Works: Chairman: Jennings Randolph (Dem., W.Va.); Ranking Minority Member: Howard H. Baker Jr. (Rep., Tenn.)

Committee on Rules and Administration: Chairman: Howard W. Cannon (Dem., Nev.); Ranking Minority Member: Marlow W. Cook (Rep., Ky.)

HOUSE LEADERSHIP

Speaker of the House: Carl Bert Albert (Dem., Okla.) first had been elected to Congress in the 80th Congress and served as Speaker in the 92nd through the 94th Congresses.

Majority Leader: Thomas P. O'Neill Jr. (Dem., Mass.)

Majority Whip: John J. McFall (Dem., Calif.)

Minority Leader: Gerald R. Ford (Rep., Mich.), until he resigned on December 6, 1973 to become vice president. John J. Rhodes (Rep., Ariz.) became the new minority leader on December 7, 1973.

Minority Whip: Leslie C. Arends (Rep., Ill.)

Chairman and Ranking Minority Members of Key Committees: [See also Organization and Administration, below]

Committee on Agriculture: Chairman: William R. Poage (Dem., Tex.); Ranking Minority Member: Charles M. Teague (Rep., Calif.), who died on January 1, 1974. William C. Wampler (Rep., Va.) became the next ranking minority member effective the same day.

Committee on Appropriations: Chairman: George H. Mahon (Dem., Tex.); Ranking Minority Member: Elford A. Cederberg (Rep., Mich.)

TABLE OF KEY VOTES

Senate

Subject of Vote	Date of Vote	For			Against		
		D	R	Total	D	R	Total
1973 Highway Act Passed	March 15, 1973	47	30	77	1	4	5
Agriculture Aid Expanded	June 8, 1973	48	30	78	2	7	9
Alaskan Pipeline Authorized	July 17, 1973	38	39	77	17	3	20
Endangered Species Bill Passed	July 24, 1973	54	38	92	0	0	0
ERISA Passed	September 19, 1973	55	38	93	0	0	0
War Powers Resolution Veto Overridden	November 7, 1973	50	25	75	3	15	18
Vice President Ford Approved	November 27, 1973	52	40	92	3	0	3
Railroads Reorganized	December 11, 1973	47	22	69	5	17	22
Freedom of Information Bill Passed	November 21, 1974	47	18	65	7	20	27
Vice President Rockefeller Approved	December 10, 1974	53	37	90	4	3	7
1974 Trade Act Passed	December 13, 1974	45	32	77	3	1	4

House

Subject of Vote	Date of Vote	For			Against		
		D	R	Total	D	R	Total
1973 Highway Act Passed	April 19, 1973	Passed by voice vote					
Agriculture Aid Expanded	July 19, 1973	139	87	226	88	94	182
Alaskan Pipeline Authorized	August 2, 1973	177	179	356	52	8	60
Endangered Species Bill Passed	September 18, 1973	221	169	390	3	9	12
War Powers Resolution Veto Overridden	November 7, 1973	198	86	284	32	103	135
Railroads Reorganized	November 8, 1973	196	110	306	20	62	82
Vice President Ford Approved	December 6, 1973	201	186	387	35	0	35
1974 Trade Act Passed	December 11, 1973	112	160	272	121	19	140
ERISA Passed	February 28, 1974	210	166	376	1	3	4
Freedom of Information Bill Passed	November 20, 1974	225	146	371	6	25	31
Vice President Rockefeller Approved	December 19, 1974	134	153	287	99	29	128

[See note 7, p. xxix]

Committee on Armed Services: Chairman: F. Edward Hebert (Dem., La.); Ranking Minority Member: William G. Bray (Rep., Ind.)

Committee on Banking and Currency: Chairman: J.W. Wright Patman (Dem., Tex.); Ranking Minority Member: William B. Widnall (Rep., N.J.)

Committee on the Budget: Chairman: Albert C. Ullman (Dem., Ore.); Ranking Minority Member: John J. Rhodes (Rep., Ariz.)

Committee on Education and Labor: Chairman: Carl D. Perkins (Dem., Ky.); Ranking Minority Member: Albert H. Quie (Rep., Minn.)

Committee on Foreign Affairs: Chairman: Thomas E. Morgan (Dem., Pa.), Ranking Minority Member: William S. Maillard (Rep., Calif.), who resigned effective March 5, 1974, in order to accept an ambassadorship. Peter H.B. Frelinghuysen (Rep., N.J.) became the next ranking minority member effective the same day.

Committee on Interior and Insular Affairs: Chairman: James A. Haley (Dem., Fla.); Ranking Minority Member: John P. Saylor (Rep., Pa.), who died on October 28, 1973. Craig Hosmer (Rep., Calif.) became the next ranking minority member effective the same day.

Committee on Interstate and Foreign Commerce: Chairman: Harley O. Staggers (Dem., W.Va.); Ranking Minority Member: Samuel L. Devine (Rep., Ohio)

Committee on the Judiciary: Chairman: Peter W. Rodino Jr. (Dem., N.J.); Ranking Minority Member: J. Edward Hutchinson (Rep., Mich.)

Committee on Public Works: Chairman: John A. Blatnik (Dem., Minn.); Ranking Minority Member: William H. Harsha Jr. (Rep., Ohio)

Committee on Rules: Chairman: Ray J. Madden (Dem., Ind.); Ranking Minority Member: David T. Martin (Rep., Neb.)

Committee on Ways and Means: Chairman: Wilbur D. Mills (Dem., Ark.); Ranking Minority Member: Herman T. Schneebeli (Rep., Pa.)

ORGANIZATION AND ADMINISTRATION

Effective July 12, 1974, both the House and the Senate established standing committees on the budget. From this Congress forward, the chairmen and ranking minority members of these committees are listed above. [See note 5, p. xxix]

The House Democratic caucus also forced Chairman Wilbur Mills (Dem., Ark.) to divide the Ways and Means Committee into four subcommittees, each headed by an independent chairman. The caucus also voted to enlarge the committee from 12 to 35 members in a further move to weaken the power of Mills. [See Scandals, below]

The tradition of selecting committee chairmen purely on the basis of seniority was repudiated in theory but continued in practice in the 93rd Congress. Both the Republicans and Democrats in the Senate and House voted in January 1973 to have committee chairman and ranking members determined by votes of the party members serving on the committee and ratified by votes of the party caucuses. In the votes for chairman and ranking minority members every House and Senate committee followed the seniority principle.

A new electronic voting system was inaugurated in the House on January 23, 1973. In another modest reform, both the House and Senate voted in December 1973 to restrict the franking privilege (postage-free mailing for members) to official business. The bill was signed into law by President Nixon on December 18, 1974.

MAJOR LEGISLATION PASSED

Agriculture: In the Agriculture and Consumer Protection Act of 1973, Congress authorized a number of agricultural assistance measures, such as increased price supports, export promotion, and an extension of the food stamp program.

Alaskan Pipeline: In the Trans-Alaska Pipeline Authorization Act, Congress ordered the expedited bureaucratic approval of pipeline construction from the new oil fields in northern Alaska to the south Alaska port of Valdez.

Environment: In the Endangered Species Act of 1973, Congress expanded federal protection for species threatened with extinction and increased the federal penalties for violating the law.

ERISA: Congress passed the Employee Retirement Income Security Act of 1974 (ERISA), which imposed federal regulations on private pension plans.

Freedom of Information: In the Freedom of Information Act (FOIA) Amendments of 1974, Congress gave federal courts the power to review federal agency FOIA denials and set deadlines for responding to FOIA information requests.

Highways: In the Highway Act of 1973, Congress not only appropriated funds for interstate highway projects, but for the first time included spending for mass transit programs.

Railroads: In the Regional Rail Reorganization Act of 1973, Congress created the U.S. Railway Association, which took over the operations of several bankrupt railroads including the massive Penn Central network.

Trade: In the Trade Act of 1974, Congress increased the president's authority to enter into international trade agreements, but made more liberal emigration a precondition to greater trade with the Soviet Union.

War Powers Resolution: Congress passed a resolution over President Nixon's veto that limited the president's power to use military forces abroad. The War Powers Resolution, which has been criticized by many presidents as an intrusion into executive power, gives the president 60 days to use forces abroad before having to obtain Congress's permission.

FAILED LEGISLATION

Energy Crisis: Congress considered, but rejected, proposals to institute mandatory gasoline rationing and to place limits on petroleum prices and oil company profits.

NATO: For the first time, the Senate voted to reduce the number of American troops committed to the NATO alliance abroad, but quickly reversed its decision.

Trident Submarine: The Senate rejected a move by Senator Thomas J. McIntyre (Dem., N.H.) to cut the defense budget appropriation for the expensive Trident nuclear missile submarine program.

RELATIONS WITH THE PRESIDENT

President Nixon's relations with Congress were particularly tense, due to the Watergate affair and the investigation by Sam Ervin's subcommittee. [See Background, above] When Senator Sam Ervin's (Dem., N.C.) committee first began its investigation and opened its nationally televised hearings, the tendency of the Republicans was to unite behind their president, taking the position that the Democrats simply were using their power as the Majority party in both Chambers of Congress to go after a Republican president. As the evidence of Nixon's involvement became increasingly clear, and Nixon fought the committee's attempt to obtain his tapes of White House conversations concerning Watergate, the Republicans began to distance themselves from Nixon. The ranking Republican on Ervin's committee, Howard H. Baker Jr. (Rep., Tenn.) joined in the interrogation of witnesses, repeatedly asking: "How much did the president know, and when did he know it?" By the summer of 1974, many Republicans were openly joining the Democrats in calling for Nixon's resignation or impeachment. When the House Judiciary Committee, under its chairman Peter W. Rodino Jr. (Dem., N.J.), from July 27 – July 30, 1974, approved three articles of impeachment against Nixon, seven of the 17 Republicans on the 38-member committee voted in favor of at least one of these three articles. After Nixon released the tapes on August 5, 1974, with their incontrovertible evidence of his involvement in Watergate, the 10 Republicans on the House Judiciary Committee who had voted against impeachment reversed themselves and joined the call for impeachment or resignation. If Nixon had not resigned on August 9, 1974, there is little doubt that both Democrats and Republicans in the House would have supported impeachment

After Nixon resigned, shortly before the end of this Congress, his successor Gerald R. Ford was widely criticized in Congress for pardoning Nixon.

Nixon vetoed 12 bills during the 93rd Congress before he resigned. Ford vetoed 27 bills during the remainder of the 93rd Congress. Two of Nixon's vetoes were particularly significant. First, on September 6, 1973, Nixon vetoed a bill to increase the minimum wage, in part because there was no lesser minimum wage for teenagers. On September 19, 1973, the House voted 259 to 164 to override the veto, short of the required two-thirds majority, and thus the veto was sustained and there was no vote in the Senate. Second, on October 24, 1973, Nixon vetoed the War Powers Resolution, and Congress overrode his veto. [See Major Legislation, above and Table of Key Votes, below]

NOMINATIONS, APPOINTMENTS, AND CONFIRMATIONS

The Judiciary: There were no significant nominations, appointments, or confirmations in the federal judiciary during the 93rd Congress.

The Executive Branch: On January 3, 1973, Nixon significantly reorganized his cabinet. Nixon nominated Peter J. Brennan to succeed James D. Hodgson as secretary of labor, Claude S. Brinegar to succeed John A. Volpe as secretary of transportation, Frederick B. Dent to succeed Peter G. Peterson as secretary of commerce, James T. Lynn to succeed George Romney as secretary of housing and urban development, Elliot L. Richardson to succeed Melvin R. Laird as secretary of defense, and Caspar W. Weinberger to succeed Richardson as secretary of health, education, and welfare. On January 18, 1973, the Senate confirmed Brinegar and Dent by voice vote; on January 29, 1973, the Senate confirmed Richardson by a vote of 81 to 1; on January 31, 1973, the Senate confirmed Brennan by a vote of 81 to 3 and Lynn by voice vote; and on February 8, 1973, the Senate confirmed Weinberger by a vote of 61 to 10.

On May 1, 1973, Nixon nominated Richardson to succeed Richard G. Kleindienst as attorney general, and on May 23, 1973, the Senate con-

firmed Richardson by a vote of 82 to 3. On May 24, 1973, Nixon nominated James R. Schlesinger to succeed Richardson as the secretary of defense, and on June 28, 1973, the Senate confirmed Schlesinger by a vote of 91 to 0. On September 5, 1973, Nixon nominated Henry A. Kissinger to succeed William P. Rogers as secretary of state, and on September 20, 1973, the Senate confirmed Kissinger by a vote of 78 to 7. Nixon nominated William B. Saxbe to succeed Richardson as attorney general on December 10, 1973, and the Senate confirmed Saxbe by a vote of 75 to 10 on December 17, 1973. Finally, on April 22, 1974, Nixon nominated William E. Simon to succeed George P. Shultz as secretary of the Treasury, and on April 30, 1974, the Senate confirmed Simon by voice vote.

After Nixon resigned, President Ford kept Nixon's cabinet, and no Senate confirmation vote was required for continuing these officials in office.

IMPEACHMENTS

None.

CONSTITUTIONAL AMENDMENTS

None.

SCANDALS

The Watergate affair, which caused President Nixon's resignation, is discussed in Background, and Relations with the President above.

In October 1974, Wilbur Mills (Dem., Ark.), the powerful chairman of the House Ways and Means Committee, embarrassed the Democratic leadership when a striptease dancer working under the name of Fanne Fox leaped from Mills's car into the waters of Washington's Tidal Basin when the car was stopped by police. When Mills appeared on stage with the stripper two months later, House Speaker Carl Albert said Mills would not be permitted to continue his chairmanship during the next Congress. Mills soon afterwards checked himself into a hospital to undergo treatment for alcoholism.

FURTHER READING

Baldwin, Louis. *Honorable Politician: Mike Mansfield of Montana*. Missoula, Mont.: Mountain Press, 1979.

Cannon, James M. *Time and Chance: Gerald Ford's Appointment With History*. New York: HarperCollins, 1994.

Emery, Fred. *Watergate: The Corruption of American Politics and the Fall of Richard Nixon*. New York: Times Books, 1994.

Gerald R. Ford and the Politics of Post-Watergate America. Westport, Conn.: Greenwood Press, 1993.

Nixon, Richard Milhous. *RN: The Memoirs of Richard Nixon*. New York: Simon & Schuster, 1990 (reprint of the 1975 edition).

The 94th Congress

JANUARY 3, 1975 - JANUARY 3, 1977

First Session: *January 14, 1975-December 19, 1975*
Second Session: *January 19, 1976-October 1, 1976*

In the 1974 elections for the 94th Congress, the Democrats gained 4 seats in the Senate, increasing their majority from 56 to 60 of the 100 seats. The Republicans lost 5 seats, reducing their total to 37. One seat was vacant and two seats were held by independents. The vacant seat would ultimately be taken by a Republican. In the House, the Democrats gained 52 seats, increasing their majority from 239 to 291 of the 435 seats. The Republicans lost 48 seats, leaving them with a total of 144. [See note 3, p. xxix]

BACKGROUND

During the 94th Congress, North Vietnam broke the Paris peace accord that it had executed with the United States and South Vietnam on January 22, 1973. [See 93rd Congress] Pursuant to the accord, the U.S. had withdrawn its forces from Vietnam, and the North promised to pursue reunification with the South by peaceful means. The leaders of the North were aware of how unpopular the Vietnam War was with the American public by the time of the Paris accord, and successfully gambled that President Ford and Congress would not send troops back to Vietnam to protect the South. When the North attacked South Vietnam in January 1975 and the South's military collapsed, the U.S. did nothing. On April 30, 1975, the U.S. evacuated the last of its citizens from Saigon, the South's capital. The South surrendered the same day. In Cambodia, the

Communist Khmer Rouge also had seized power by the end of April.

Former President Nixon had wanted to get the U.S. out of Vietnam but end the war on terms of "peace with honor." The Paris agreement gave the U.S. a way to exit Vietnam without admitting defeat. Now, the Communist victory in Vietnam and Cambodia made it clear that the U.S. had lost a war for the first time. The Vietnam experience made the American public and Congress reluctant to get the American military involved in other regional conflicts, such as in Angola in southwest Africa.

Also during 1975, Cambodia on May 12 seized the *Mayaguez*, a civilian U.S. vessel, and on May 14 American forces staged a successful operation to rescue the crew. During the summer, the U.S. and the Soviet Union conducted the joint *Apollo-Soyuz* space mission, and 35 nations including the U.S. executed an agreement in Helsinki, Finland, pledging to respect the post-World War II national borders in Europe. In November, New York City came close to bankruptcy due to years of mismanaged finances and excessive spending and borrowing, and the federal government was forced to rescue the city by providing over $2 billion in loans.

In 1976 *Viking I* and *Viking II* became the first spacecraft to land on Mars. The Viking probes detected no signs of life. Finally, in the 1976 presidential campaign for the upcoming November election, the first televised debates between an incumbent president and another candidate took place (the Kennedy-Nixon debates in 1960 had not involved incumbent President Eisenhower, who already had served two terms). President Ford, a Republican, debated Democratic candidate Jimmy Carter three times. In addition, Ford's vice presidental running mate, Senator Robert Dole (Rep., Kans.), debated Carter's running mate Senator Walter Mondale (Dem., Minn.) in the first television debate to ever take place between candidates for vice president.

SENATE LEADERSHIP

Vice President: Nelson A. Rockefeller had been governor of New York from 1959 to 1973 and became vice president in the 93rd Congress when he was nominated to that position by President Ford and confirmed by Congress.

President Pro Tempore: James Oliver Eastland (Dem., Miss.) first had been elected to the Senate in 1942 and served as president pro tem in the 92nd through the 95th Congresses.

Majority Leader: Michael J. Mansfield (Dem., Mont.) [See biographical note in 85th Congress]

Majority Whip: Robert C. Byrd (Dem., W.Va.)

Minority Leader: Hugh Scott (Rep., Pa.)

Minority Whip: Robert P. Griffin (Rep., Mich.)

Chairman and Ranking Minority Members of Key Committees:

Committee on Agriculture and Forestry: Chairman: Herman E. Talmadge, (Dem., Ga.); Ranking Minority Member: Robert J. Dole (Rep., Kans.)

Committee on Appropriations: Chairman: John L. McClellan (Dem., Ark.); Ranking Minority Member: Milton R. Young (Rep., N.D.)

Committee on Armed Services: Chairman: John C. Stennis (Dem., Miss.); Ranking Minority Member: J. Strom Thurmond (Rep., S.C.)

Committee on Banking, Housing, and Urban Affairs: Chairman: William Proxmire (Dem., Wis.); Ranking Minority Member: John G. Tower (Rep., Tex.)

Committee on the Budget: Chairman: Edmund S. Muskie (Dem., Maine); Ranking Minority Member: Henry Bellmon (Rep., Okla.)

Committee on Commerce: Chairman: Warren G. Magnuson (Dem., Wash.); Ranking Minority Member: James B. Pearson (Rep., Kans.)

Committee on Finance: Chairman: Russell B. Long (Dem., La.); Ranking Minority Member: Carl T. Curtis (Rep., Neb.)

Committee on Foreign Relations: Chairman: John J. Sparkman (Dem., Ala.); Ranking Minority Member: Clifford P. Case (Rep., N.J.)

Committee on Interior and Insular Affairs: Chairman: Henry M. Jackson (Dem., Wash.); Ranking Minority Member: Paul J. Fannin (Rep., Ariz.)

Committee on the Judiciary: Chairman: James O. Eastland (Dem., Miss.); Ranking Minority Member: Roman L. Hruska (Rep., Neb.)

Committee on Labor and Public Welfare: Chairman: Harrison A. Williams Jr. (Dem., N.J.); Ranking Minority Member: Jacob K. Javits (Rep., N.Y.)

Committee on Public Works: Chairman: Jennings Randolph (Dem., W.Va.); Ranking Minority Member: Howard H. Baker Jr. (Rep., Tenn.)

Committee on Rules and Administration: Chairman: Howard W. Cannon (Dem., Nev.); Ranking Minority Member: Mark O. Hatfield (Rep., Ore.)

HOUSE LEADERSHIP

Speaker of the House: Carl Bert Albert (Dem., Okla.) first had been elected to Congress in the 80th Congress and served as Speaker in the 92nd through the 94th Congresses.

Majority Leader: Thomas P. O'Neill Jr. (Dem., Mass.)

Majority Whip: John J. McFall (Dem., Calif.)

C H R O N O L O G Y

January 3, 1975:	The 94th Congress begins. During this Congress, President Ford made numerous changes to his cabinet. [See Nominations, Appointments, and Confirmations: The Executive Branch, below.]
January 14, 1975:	The first session begins.
March 7, 1975:	The Senate revises its filibuster rule.
May 1, 1975:	The House rejects legislation authorizing the president to use the military during the final evacuation of South Vietnam.
November 12, 1975:	Supreme Court Justice William O. Douglas retires.
November 28, 1975:	President Gerald Ford nominates John Paul Stevens to replace Douglas.
December 6, 1975:	Congress approves a financial bailout for New York City.
December 17, 1975:	Congress passes the Energy Policy and Conservation Act. The Senate confirms Stevens.
December 19, 1975:	The first session ends.
January 19, 1976:	The second session begins.
January 28, 1976:	Congress passes fisheries legislation.
June 14, 1976:	Congress passes the International Security Assistance and Arms Export Control Act of 1976.
July 28, 1976:	Congress passes the Government in the Sunshine Act.
August 6, 1976:	Congress passes the Tax Reform Act of 1976.
September 1, 1976:	A scandal forces House Administration Committee Chairman Wayne Hays (Dem., Ohio) to resign.
September 22, 1976:	Congress passes copyright reform legislation.
October 1, 1976:	The second session ends.
January 3, 1977:	The 94th Congress ends.

[See note 6, p. xxix]

Minority Leader: John J. Rhodes (Rep., Ariz.)

Minority Whip: Robert H. Michel (Rep., Ill.)

Chairman and Ranking Minority Members of Key Committees: [See also Organization and Administration, below]

Committee on Agriculture: Chairman: Thomas S. Foley (Dem., Wash.); Ranking Minority Member: William C. Wampler (Rep., Va.)

Committee on Appropriations: Chairman: George H. Mahon (Dem., Tex.); Ranking Minority

Member: Elford A. Cederberg (Rep., Mich.)

Committee on Armed Services: Chairman: C. Melvin Price (Dem., Ill.); Ranking Minority Member: Robert C. Wilson (Rep., Calif.)

Committee on Banking, Currency, and Housing: Chairman: Henry S. Reuss (Dem., Wis.); Ranking Minority Member: Albert W. Johnson (Rep., Pa.)

Committee on the Budget: Chairman: Brock Adams (Dem., Wash.); Ranking Minority Member: Delbert L. Latta (Rep., Ohio)

Committee on Education and Labor: Chairman: Carl D. Perkins (Dem., Ky.); Ranking Minority Member: Albert H. Quie (Rep., Minn.)

Committee on Interior and Insular Affairs: Chairman: James A. Haley (Dem., Fla.); Ranking Minority Member: Joe Skubitz (Rep., Kans.)

Committee on International Relations: Chairman: Thomas E. Morgan (Dem., Pa.); Ranking Minority Member: William S. Broomfield (Rep., Mich.)

Committee on Interstate and Foreign Commerce: Chairman: Harley O. Staggers (Dem., W.Va.); Ranking Minority Member: Samuel L. Devine (Rep., Ohio)

Committee on the Judiciary: Chairman: Peter W. Rodino, Jr. (Dem., N.J.); Ranking Minority Member: J. Edward Hutchinson (Rep., Mich.)

Committee on Public Works and Transportation: Chairman: Robert E. Jones Jr. (Dem., Ala.); Ranking Minority Member: William H. Harsha Jr. (Rep., Ohio)

Committee on Rules: Chairman: Ray J. Madden (Dem., Ind.); Ranking Minority Member: James H. Quillen (Rep., Tenn.)

Committee on Ways and Means: Chairman: Albert C. Ullman (Dem., Ore.); Ranking Minority Member: Herman T. Schneebeli (Rep., Pa.)

ORGANIZATION AND ADMINISTRATION

The Senate on March 7, 1975, voted 56 to 27 to revise its filibuster rule. The majority necessary to "invoke cloture," or end debate and get to a vote, was changed from two-thirds of the senators present and voting to three-fifths of all the Senate membership (in other words, 60 of the 100 senators, regardless of whether all the senators were present). With respect to future changes in the Senate rules themselves, however, the old two-thirds rule still applied.

House Administration Committee Chairman Wayne Hays (Dem., Ohio) was involved in a sex

scandal that also concerned the abuse of his office. [See Scandals, below] The Republicans launched an initiative, which ultimately failed, to strip future Administration Committee chairmen of some of their powers.

Also in the House, the name of the Committee on Banking and Currency was changed to the Committee on Banking, Currency, and Housing effective January 3, 1975. The name of the Committee on Public Works was changed to the Committee on Public Works and Transportation effective January 5, 1975, and the name of the Committee on Foreign Affairs was changed to the Committee on International Relations effective March 19, 1975. [See note 5, p. xxix]

MAJOR LEGISLATION PASSED

Arms Exports: In the International Security Assistance and Arms Export Control Act of 1976, Congress expanded federal controls over exports of military equipment.

Copyrights: In the Copyright Law Revision of 1976, Congress revised the outdated copyright statutes and made American copyright law conform more closely to international copyright law. Further, the new copyright laws contained provisions concerning modern technology such as copying machines and cable television.

Energy: In the Energy Policy and Conservation Act, Congress enacted measures designed to encourage domestic energy production and conservation and established a strategic petroleum reserve. The act actually was composed of five bills, and it took several months for the House and Senate to agree on the final form of legislation.

Fisheries: In the Fishery Conservation and Management Act of 1976, Congress expanded the coastal fishing zone where only U.S. ships could fish from 12 miles to 200 miles.

Government: In the Sunshine Act, Congress established a policy of holding high-level government meetings open to the public. This law was part of the reaction against government

TABLE OF KEY VOTES

Senate

Subject of Vote	Date of Vote	For			Against		
		D	R	Total	D	R	Total
Sunshine Legislation Passed	November 6, 1975	59	35	94	0	0	0
New York City Loans Approved	December 6, 1975	41	16	57	14	16	30
Energy Conservation Bill Passed	December 17, 1975	50	8	58	10	30	40
Fisheries Zone Extended	January 28, 1976	49	28	77	11	8	19
Copyright Laws Revised	February 19, 1976	61	36	97	0	0	0
Arms Export Control Tightened	June 14, 1976	38	24	62	11	7	18
Tax Reforms Passed	August 6, 1976	27	22	49	17	5	22

House

Subject of Vote	Date of Vote	For			Against		
		D	R	Total	D	R	Total
Fisheries Zone Extended	October 9, 1975	131	77	208	77	24	101
New York City Loans Approved	December 2, 1975	175	38	213	103	100	203
Tax Reforms Passed	December 4, 1975	225	32	257	57	111	168
Energy Conservation Bill Passed	December 15, 1975	202	34	236	59	101	160
Arms Export Control Tightened	June 2, 1976	185	70	255	78	62	140
Sunshine Legislation Passed	July 28, 1976	256	134	390	3	2	5
Copyright Laws Revised	September 22, 1976	209	107	316	4	3	7

[See note 7, p. xxix]

secrecy after Watergate. When the Heads of government agencies met, and "where such deliberations determine or result in the joint conduct or disposition of official agency business," the meetings were supposed to be open to the public. There were a variety of exceptions, however, so that Cabinet meetings, informal discussions, or meetings concerning classified matters didn't have to be held in public.

New York City: In the New York City Seasonal Financing Act of 1975, Congress gave the Treasury permission to loan New York City $2.3 billion a year until 1978 to tide the city over during seasonal cash shortages.

Taxation: In the Tax Reform Act of 1976, Congress revised many provisions of the Internal Revenue Code, including various deductions, exlusions, credits, and shelters.

FAILED LEGISLATION

Vietnam: As the North Vietnamese forces approached Saigon, Congress procrastinated on whether to allow the president to use the military in the evacuation of Americans and loyal South Vietnamese. The fear was that such an authorization would involve the U.S. in Vietnam again, or be used as a precedent for future intervention. On May 1, 1975, the final phase of authorizing legislation, namely, the conference committee's compromise version of legislation passed by the House and Senate, was rejected by the House 246 to 162 as moot. The day before, April 30, the North Vietnamese already had occupied Saigon.

RELATIONS WITH
THE PRESIDENT

President Gerald R. Ford, who went from vice president to president when former President Richard M. Nixon resigned, inherited the Watergate stigma when he pardoned Nixon. Ford had no major legislative agenda with Congress, and his relations with Congress can best be described as unremarkable.

Ford vetoed 39 bills during the 94th Congress. None of these vetoes was particularly significant.

NOMINATIONS, APPOINTMENTS, AND CONFIRMATIONS

The Judiciary: On November 12, 1975, Supreme Court Justice William O. Douglas retired. President Gerald R. Ford nominated John Paul Stevens on November 28, 1975, to replace Douglas, and the Senate on December 17, 1975, confirmed Stevens by a 98 to 0 vote.

The Executive Branch: After President Nixon resigned during the 93rd Congress, President Ford kept Nixon's cabinet, and no Senate confirmation vote was required for continuing these officials. On January 16, 1975, Ford nominated William

T. Coleman Jr. to succeed Claude S. Brinegar as secretary of transportation and Edward H. Levi to succeed William B. Saxbe as attorney general. On February 5, 1975, the Senate confirmed Levi by voice vote, and on March 3, 1975, the Senate confirmed Coleman by voice vote. On February 18, 1975, Ford nominated John T. Dunlop to succeed Peter J. Brennan as secretary of labor, and on March 6, 1975, the Senate confirmed Dunlop by voice vote. On February 20, 1975, Ford nominated Carla A. Hills to succeed James T. Lynn as secretary of housing and urban development, and on March 5, 1975, the Senate confirmed Hills by a vote of 85 to 5. On April 7, 1975, Ford nominated Rogers C.B. Morton to succeed Frederick B. Dent as secretary of commerce and Stanley K. Hathaway to succeed Morton as secretary of the Interior. On April 25, 1975, the Senate confirmed Morton by voice vote, and on June 11, 1975, the Senate confirmed Hathaway by a vote of 60 to 36. On June 26, 1975, Ford nominated F. David Mathews to succeed Caspar W. Weinberger as secretary of health, education, and welfare, and on July 22, 1975, the Senate confirmed Mathews by voice vote. On September 9, 1975, Ford nominated Thomas S. Kleppe to succeed Hathaway as secretary of the Interior, and on October 9, 1975, the Senate confirmed Kleppe by voice vote. On November 4, 1975, Ford nominated Donald H. Rumsfeld to succeed James R. Schlesinger as secretary of defense, and on November 18, 1975, the Senate confirmed Rumsfeld by a vote of 95 to 2. On November 20, 1975, Ford nominated Elliot L. Richardson to succeed Morton as secretary of commerce, and on December 11, 1975, the Senate confirmed Richardson by voice vote. Finally, on January 22, 1976, Ford nominated Willie J. Usery Jr. to succeed Dunlop as secretary of labor, and on February 4, 1976, the Senate confirmed Usery by a vote of 79 to 7.

IMPEACHMENTS

None.

CONSTITUTIONAL AMENDMENTS

None.

SCANDALS

In 1976 a major scandal hit Congress. The Justice Department conducted an investigation that revealed that several members of Congress had accepted large sums of money from South Korean lobbyists. The lobbyists were attempting to buy influence for the pro-U.S., but authoritarian South Korean government of Park Chung Hee. The scandal was nicknamed "Koreagate," a pun on the recent Watergate affair.

Also during this Congress, House Administration Committee Chairman Wayne Hays (Dem., Ohio) resigned on September 1, 1976. There were allegations that he had abused his office by putting his mistress, Elizabeth Ray, on the payroll. Further, many representatives had grudges against Hays's committee, which controlled internal administrative matters, such as office space assignments. Hays resigned after the House Ethics Committee decided to investigate the allegations against him.

FURTHER READING

Baldwin, Louis. *Honorable Politician: Mike Mansfield of Montana*. Missoula, Mont.: Mountain Press, 1979.

Cannon, James M. *Time and Chance: Gerald Ford's Appointment With History*. New York: HarperCollins, 1994.

Gerald R. Ford and the Politics of Post-Watergate America. Westport, Conn.: Greenwood Press, 1993.

Greene, John Robert. *The Presidency of Gerald R. Ford*. Lawrence, Kans.: University Press of Kansas, 1995.

Persico, Joseph. *The Imperial Rockefeller*. New York: Simon & Schuster, 1982.

The 95th Congress

JANUARY 3, 1977-JANUARY 3, 1979

First Session: January 4, 1977-December 15, 1977
Second Session: January 19, 1978-October 15, 1978

In the 1976 elections for the 95th Congress, the Democrats gained 1 seat in the Senate, increasing their majority from 60 to 61 of the 100 seats. The Republicans gained 1 seat to give them a total of 38. One seat was held by an independent. In the House, the Democrats gained 1 seat, raising their majority from 291 to 292 of the 435 seats. The Republicans lost 1 seat, leaving them with a total of 143. [See note 3, p. xxix]

BACKGROUND

Jimmy Carter was inaugurated as the 39th president of the United States on January 20, 1977. Carter was the only Democrat to win the presidency from 1968 to 1992, and the principal reason for his victory was the popular backlash against the Republicans after the Watergate affair, which had forced President Nixon to resign in disgrace in 1974. Furthermore, when Nixon's Vice President Gerald Ford became president after Nixon resigned, he made a politically unpopular decision to pardon Nixon for any crimes Nixon may have committed. This decision also served to discredit the Republicans. Carter took his first action as president on January 21, 1977, when he pardoned most of the people who had evaded the draft during the Vietnam War.

On August 12, 1977, NASA launched the first space shuttle, called the *Enterprise*. Unlike previous spacecraft, the space shuttle was a reusable vehicle, capable of attaining an orbit around the Earth and returning again. The United States and Panama agreed upon the terms of two Panama Canal treaties, pursuant to which the United States would return the Canal to Panama by the end of the century.

By 1978 the American economy had become mired in the phenomenon known as *stagflation*. The federal budget deficit was at record levels, inflation and interest rates were increasing, the national trade deficit was growing, and economic growth was low. Although there was no economic crisis like that of the Great Depression or the oil embargo of 1973-1974, the lack of economic progress increased a popular sense of disappointment in America following Vietnam and Watergate. Carter was not an inspirational president who could erase the impression of national unease or rally Congress to pass reform legislation. Carter did succeed, however, in preventing a sale of U.S. fighter jets to Middle Eastern nations from being blocked by the Senate. He also persuaded the Senate to approve the two Panama Canal treaties.

Also during 1978, on June 6, California voters approved Proposition 13, a state constitutional amendment that cut property taxes by over 50 percent. The Supreme Court in *Bakke v. The University of California* ruled that racial quotas, that constituted reverse discrimination were unconstitutional. Finally, by the end of the 95th Congress, Carter achieved a major victory in foreign policy. Ever since the late 1940s, the newly created Jewish state of Israel in the Middle East had faced a hostile alliance of Islamic nations in the region. Within this alliance, Egypt was the most populous and militarily powerful state and received considerable economic and military assistance from the Soviet Union. Israel and Egypt had fought several wars, and due to American military aid and superior troops the Israelis always had won. Nevertheless, Israel politically and militarily was isolated in the Middle East. Carter arranged a peace conference between Israeli leader Menachem Begin and Egyptian leader Anwar Sadat, which took place at the Camp David presidential retreat in Maryland from September 6 until September 17, 1978. The result was a peace treaty between the two countries, and Egypt's defection from the Arab anti-Israel alliance.

SENATE LEADERSHIP

Vice President: Nelson A. Rockefeller had served as vice president until January 20, 1977, when Walter F. Mondale became the new vice president. Mondale had been elected to Congress as a senator from Minnesota in 1966 and had served in the Senate until he was elected vice president in 1976. After President Carter lost his bid for reelection in 1980, Mondale unsuccessfully ran for president on the Democratic ticket in 1984. [See note 8, p. xxix]

President Pro Tempore: James Oliver Eastland (Dem., Miss.) first had been elected to the Senate in 1942 and served as president pro tem in the 92nd through the 95th Congresses.

Majority Leader: Robert C. Byrd (Dem., W.Va.) first had been elected to Congress as a representative to the 83rd Congress and had been elected to the Senate in 1958. Byrd became the leader of the Senate Democrats in the 95th Congress and remained in that position through the 100th Congress. Byrd's extensive knowledge of Senate procedure made him a consummate parliamentarian, but he often was criticized for his

unabashed use of governmental funds (pork barrel politics) to benefit his home state.

Majority Whip: Alan Cranston (Dem., Calif.)

Minority Leader: Howard H. Baker Jr. (Rep., Tenn.) was the son-in-law of former Senate Republican leader Everett Dirksen and first had been elected to the Senate in 1966. He was the leader of the Senate Republicans in the 95th through the 98th Congresses.

Minority Whip: Theodore F. Stevens (Rep., Alaska)

Chairman and Ranking Minority Members of Key Committees: [See also Organization and Administration, below]

Committee on Agriculture, Nutrition, and Forestry: Chairman: Herman E. Talmadge, (Dem., Ga.); Ranking Minority Member: Robert J. Dole (Rep., Kans.)

Committee on Appropriations: Chairman: John L. McClellan (Dem., Ark.), who died on November 28, 1977. Warren G. Magnuson (Dem., Wash.) became the new chairman effective January 27, 1978. Ranking Minority Member: Milton R. Young (Rep., N.D.)

Committee on Armed Services: Chairman: John C. Stennis (Dem., Miss.); Ranking Minority Member: J. Strom Thurmond (Rep., S.C.), until January 22, 1977, when he became the ranking minority member of the Judiciary Committee. John G. Tower (Rep., Tex.) became the next ranking minority member effective the same day.

Committee on Banking, Housing, and Urban Affairs: Chairman: William Proxmire (Dem., Wis.); Ranking Minority Member: John G. Tower (Rep., Tex.), until January 22, 1977, when he became the ranking minority member on the Armed Services Committee. Edward W. Brooke (Rep., Mass.) became the next ranking minority member effective the same day.

Committee on the Budget: Chairman: Edmund S. Muskie (Dem., Maine); Ranking Minority Member: Henry Bellmon (Rep., Okla.)

Committee on Commerce, Science, and Transportation: Chairman: Warren G. Magnuson (Dem., Wash.), until January 27, 1978, when he became chairman of the Appropriations Committee. Howard W. Cannon (Dem., Nev.) became the next chairman effective the same day. Ranking Minority Member: James B. Pearson (Rep., Kans.)

Committee on Finance: Chairman: Russell B. Long (Dem., La.); Ranking Minority Member: Carl T. Curtis (Rep., Neb.)

Committee on Foreign Relations: Chairman: John J. Sparkman (Dem., Ala.); Ranking Minority Member: Clifford P. Case (Rep., N.J.)

Committee on Interior and Insular Affairs: Chairman: Henry M. Jackson (Dem., Wash.); Ranking Minority Member: Clifford P. Hansen (Rep., Wyo.)

Committee on the Judiciary: Chairman: James O. Eastland (Dem., Miss.); Ranking Minority Member: J. Strom Thurmond (Rep., S.C.)

Committee on Labor and Public Welfare: Chairman: Harrison A. Williams Jr. (Dem., N.J.); Ranking Minority Member: Jacob K. Javits (Rep., N.Y.)

Committee on Public Works: Chairman: Jennings Randolph (Dem., W.Va.); Ranking Minority Member: Robert T. Stafford (Rep., Vt.)

Committee on Rules and Administration: Chairman: Howard W. Cannon (Dem., Nev.) until January 27, 1978, when he became chairman of the Committee on Commerce, Science, and Transportation. Claiborne D. Pell (Dem., R.I.) became the next chairman effective the same day. Ranking Minority Member: Mark O. Hatfield (Rep., Ore.)

HOUSE LEADERSHIP

Speaker of the House: Thomas Phillip "Tip" O'Neill Jr. (Dem., Mass.) first had been elected to Congress in the 83rd Congress and served as Speaker in the 95th through the 99th Congresses. O'Neill first achieved recognition in the late 1960s when he criticized Democratic President Lyndon Johnson's policy in Vietnam, and he gained enough support amongst liberal Democrats to become Majority Whip in the early 1970s. From that position he rose, through the attrition of his seniors, to the Speakership even though he was not a particularly dynamic leader. As Speaker, his efforts to impose discipline on liberals and conservatives alike usually failed. For example, when Democrat Phil Gramm refused to follow the party line and O'Neill removed Gramm from the House Budget Committee, Gramm became a Republican and returned to the Budget Committee as a member of the minority. When the Republicans took the White House in the 1980 elections, however, O'Neill became more important for his role as a national spokesman for the Democrats. Other than Senator Ted Kennedy (Dem., Mass.), there were few senior Democrats with such established liberal views and loyal party ties as O'Neill, and during the 1980s it was frequently O'Neill who spoke out against Republican initiatives to increase defense spending and cut social programs.

Majority Leader: James C. Wright (Dem., Tex.)

Majority Whip: John Brademas (Dem., Ind.)

Minority Leader: John J. Rhodes (Rep., Ariz.)

Minority Whip: Robert H. Michel (Rep., Ill.)

Chairman and Ranking Minority Members of Key Committees: [See also Organization and Administration, below]

Committee on Agriculture: Chairman: Thomas S. Foley (Dem., Wash.); Ranking Minority Member: William C. Wampler (Rep., Va.)

Committee on Appropriations: Chairman: George H. Mahon (Dem., Tex.); Ranking Minority Member: Elford A. Cederberg (Rep., Mich.)

Committee on Armed Services: Chairman: C. Melvin Price (Dem., Ill.); Ranking Minority Member: Robert C. Wilson (Rep., Calif.)

Committee on Banking, Finance, and Urban Affairs: Chairman: Henry S. Reuss (Dem., Wis.);

C H R O N O L O G Y

January 3, 1977:	The 95th Congress begins.
January 4, 1977:	The first session begins.
January 20, 1977:	President Carter nominates his cabinet, and the Senate confirms most of the nominees.
June 3, 1977:	Congress passes legislation creating the Department of Energy.
June 10, 1977:	Congress passes the Clean Air Act Amendments of 1977.
August 4, 1977:	President Carter nominates, and the Senate confirms, James R. Schlesinger to be secretary of energy.
December 15, 1977:	The first session ends.
January 19, 1978:	The second session begins.
March 16, 1978:	The Senate approves the Panama Canal Treaty.
April 18, 1978:	The Senate approves a Panama Canal neutrality treaty.
May 15, 1978:	The Senate fails to vote against Mideast arms exports.
August 22, 1978:	Congress sends a constitutional amendment concerning the District of Columbia to the states for ratification, but the states never ratify it.
September 21, 1978:	Congress passes airline deregulation legislation.
September 27, 1978:	Congress passes the Ethics in Government Act of 1978.
October 10, 1978:	Congress passes the Revenue Act of 1978.
October 13, 1978:	Congress passes full employment legislation and the Presidential Records Act of 1978.
October 15, 1978:	The second session ends.
January 3, 1979:	The 95th Congress ends.

[See note 6, p. xxix]

Ranking Minority Member: J. William Stanton (Rep., Ohio)

Committee on the Budget: Chairman: Robert N. Giaimo (Dem., Conn.); Ranking Minority Member: Delbert L. Latta (Rep., Ohio)

Committee on Education and Labor: Chairman: Carl D. Perkins (Dem., Ky.); Ranking Minority Member: Albert H. Quie (Rep., Minn.)

Committee on Interior and Insular Affairs: Chairman: Morris K. Udall (Dem., Ariz.);

Ranking Minority Member: Joe Skubitz (Rep., Kans.)

Committee on International Relations: Chairman: Clement J. Zablocki (Dem., Wis.); Ranking Minority Member: William S. Broomfield (Rep., Mich.)

Committee on Interstate and Foreign Commerce: Chairman: Harley O. Staggers (Dem., W.Va.); Ranking Minority Member: Samuel L. Devine (Rep., Ohio)

Committee on the Judiciary: Chairman: Peter W. Rodino Jr. (Dem., N.J.); Ranking Minority Member: Robert McClory (Rep., Ill.)

Committee on Public Works and Transportation: Chairman: Harold T. Johnson (Dem., Calif.); Ranking Minority Member: William H. Harsha Jr. (Rep., Ohio)

Committee on Rules: Chairman: James J. Delaney (Dem., N.Y.) Ranking Minority Member: James H. Quillen (Rep., Tenn.)

Committee on Ways and Means: Chairman: Albert C. Ullman (Dem., Ore.); Ranking Minority Member: Barber B. Conable Jr. (Rep., N.Y.)

ORGANIZATION AND ADMINISTRATION

Several Senate committees were reorganized and given new names: On February 4, 1977, the Senate Committee on Agriculture and Forestry was renamed the Committee on Agriculture, Nutrition, and Forestry. On February 11, 1977, the Senate Committee on Commerce was renamed the Committee on Commerce, Science, and Transportation; the Senate Committee on Interior and Insular Affairs was renamed the Committee on Energy and Natural Resources; the Senate Committee on Public Works was renamed the Committee on Environment and Public Works; and the Senate Committee on Labor and Public Welfare was renamed the Committee on Human Resources. The Senate also reduced the number of committees and subcommittees that one senator could be the chairman of, and imposed a limit on the amount that a senator could earn from outside sources, such as giving speeches.

In the House, the name of the Committee on Banking, Currency, and Housing was changed to the Committee on Banking, Finance, and Urban Affairs effective January 4, 1977.

Both the House and the Senate enacted new ethics rules in 1977. The new ethics rules limited the value of gifts that members could accept from lobbyists, expanded the previous financial disclosure requirements, and placed caps on outside income. [See note 5, p. xxix]

MAJOR LEGISLATION PASSED

Airlines: In the Airline Deregulation Act of 1978, Congress freed the airline industry from a significant amount of federal regulation and protection in favor of free market competition.

Arms Exports: The Carter administration wanted to sell nearly $5 billion worth of fighter jets to Egypt, Israel, and Saudi Arabia. Applicable law stated that unless both chambers of Congress rejected the sale, the sale would go through. Thus, when the Senate voted to not block the sale, there was no vote in the House.

Department of Energy: In the Department of Energy Organization Act, Congress combined several agencies into a new Department of Energy with cabinet-level status.

Employment: In the Humphrey-Hawkins Full Employment and Balanced Growth Act of 1978, Congress enacted one of the most optimistic and unrealistic bills in American history. The act directed the government to achieve full employment, end the budget and trade deficits, control inflation, and increase wages. The act was a political gesture and was forgotten soon after its passage.

Environment: In the Clean Air Act Amendments of 1977, Congress ordered automobile manufacturers, other industrial polluters, and the nation's cities to comply with new air quality standards within certain deadlines.

Government Ethics: In the Ethics in Government Act of 1978, Congress set forth new financial disclosure rules applicable to Congress, the executive branch, and the federal judiciary.

Panama Canal: The Senate approved two treaties between the U.S. and Panama concerning the Panama Canal. The first, the Panama Canal Treaty, provided for the gradual transfer of control over the Canal from the U.S. to Panama, which would take until 1999 to complete. The second, the Treaty Concerning the Permanent

TABLE OF KEY VOTES

Senate

Subject of Vote	Date of Vote	For			Against		
		D	R	Total	D	R	Total
Department of Energy Established	May 18, 1977	51	23	74	1	9	10
Air Pollution Laws Strengthened	June 10, 1977	49	24	73	1	6	7
Government Ethics Legislation Passed	June 27, 1977	51	23	74	0	5	5
Panama Canal Treaty Approved	March 16, 1978	52	16	68	10	22	32
Panama Canal Neutrality Treaty Approved	April 18, 1978	52	16	68	10	22	32
Airlines deregulated	April 19, 1978	49	34	83	9	0	9
Blocking Mideast Jet Sale	May 15, 1978	33	11	44	28	26	54
D.C. Constitutional Amendment Approved	August 22, 1978	48	19	67	13	19	32
Tax Reforms Passed	October 10, 1978	54	32	86	3	1	4
Full Employment Bill Passed	October 13, 1978	53	17	70	4	15	19
Presidential Records Bill Passed	October 13, 1978	Passed by voice vote					

House

Subject of Vote	Date of Vote	For			Against		
		D	R	Total	D	R	Total
Air Pollution Laws Strengthened	May 26, 1977	218	108	326	39	10	49
Department of Energy Established	June 3, 1977	215	95	310	4	16	20
D.C. Constitutional Amendment Approved	March 2, 1978	228	61	289	48	79	127
Full Employment Bill Passed	March 16, 1978	233	24	257	41	111	152
Tax Reforms Passed	August 10, 1978	224	138	362	47	2	49
Airlines deregulated	September 21, 1978	245	118	363	5	3	8
Government Ethics Legislation Passed	September 27, 1978	248	120	368	17	13	30
Presidential Records Bill Passed	October 10, 1978	Passed by voice vote					

[See note 7, p. xxix]

Neutrality and Operation of the Panama Canal, gave Panama exclusive military control over the Canal after 1999, but guaranteed that the Canal would be neutral and forever open to all nations.

Presidential Records: In the Presidential Records Act of 1978, Congress stated that subject to certain exceptions, a president's records would become public property once the president left office. The act was a reaction to Watergate and President Nixon's assertion of executive privilege over his papers and tapes.

Taxation: In the Revenue Act of 1978, Congress enacted several tax cuts, including a one-time $100,000 income tax exclusion for people over the age of 55 selling their home at a profit.

FAILED LEGISLATION

Campaign Financing: Republicans and conservative Democrats successfully blocked a bill to make the Treasury pay for the costs of congressional campaigns instead of private donors and special interest groups.

Labor: The House rejected a proposal to create a subminimum wage for teenagers.

Neutron Bomb: The Senate rejected a proposal to end funding for development of the radiation weapon known as the neutron bomb, which was designed to kill people rather than destroy buildings.

RELATIONS WITH THE PRESIDENT

President Jimmy Carter generally was successful in getting his foreign policy initiatives approved by the Senate, particularly the Panama Canal treaties and Middle East arms exports. Carter's domestic legislative achievements were more modest, and he failed to get any comprehensive energy legislation passed. Many liberal Democrats in Congress regarded Carter as too conservative and gave at best lukewarm support for his legislative agenda.

Carter vetoed 19 bills during the 95th Congress. None of these vetoes was of lasting significance.

NOMINATIONS, APPOINTMENTS, AND CONFIRMATIONS

The Judiciary: There were no significant nominations, appointments or confirmations in the federal judiciary during the 95th Congress.

The Executive Branch: On January 20, 1977, President Jimmy Carter nominated his cabinet: Brock Adams to be secretary of transportation; Cecil D. Andrus to be secretary of the Interior; Griffin B. Bell to be attorney general; Robert S. Bergland to be secretary of agriculture; W. Michael Blumenthal to be secretary of the Treasury; Harold Brown to be secretary of defense; Joseph A. Califano Jr. to be secretary of health, education, and welfare; Patricia R. Harris to be secretary of housing and urban development; Juanita M. Kreps to be secretary of commerce; F. Ray Marshall to be secretary of labor; and Cyrus Vance to be secretary of state. That same day, the Senate confirmed Adams, Andrus, Bergland, Blumenthal, Brown, Harris, Kreps, and Vance by voice vote. On January 24, 1977, the Senate confirmed Califano by a vote of 95 to 1. On January 25, 1977, the Senate confirmed Bell by a vote of 75 to 21. On January 26, 1977, the Senate confirmed Marshall by a vote of 74 to 20. Finally, on August 4, 1977, Carter nominated James R. Schlesinger to be secretary of energy, a new cabinet-level position, and that same day the Senate confirmed him by voice vote.

IMPEACHMENTS

None.

CONSTITUTIONAL AMENDMENTS

Congress sent a proposed constitutional amendment concerning the District of Columbia to the states for ratification. As proposed, the amendment would have given the District equal representation in the House, Senate, and electoral college. The necessary three-fourths of the states never ratified this amendment.

FURTHER READING

Anderson, Patrick. *Electing Jimmy Carter: The Campaign of 1976*. Baton Rouge: Louisiana State University Press, 1994.

Carter, Jimmy. *Why Not The Best?* Nashville, Tenn.: Broadman Press, 1975.

Lewis, Finlay. *Mondale*. New York: Perennial Library, 1984.

O'Neill, Thomas P., with William Novak. *Man of the House; The Life and Political Memoirs of Speaker Tip O'Neill*. New York: Random House, 1987.

The Presidency and Domestic Policies of Jimmy Carter. Westport, Conn.: Greenwood Press, 1994.

The 96th Congress

JANUARY 3, 1979-JANUARY 3, 1981

First Session: January 15, 1979-January 3, 1980
Second Session: January 3, 1980-December 16, 1980

In the 1978 elections for the 96th Congress, the Democrats lost 3 seats in the Senate, reducing their majority from 61 to 58 of the 100 seats. The Republicans gained 3 seats, giving them a total of 41. One seat was held by an independent. In the House, the Democrats lost 16 seats, lowering their majority from 292 to 276 of the 435 seats. The Republicans gained 14 seats, giving them a total of 157. Of the 2 remaining vacant seats, 1 would ultimately be taken by a Democrat and 1 by a Republican. [See note 3, p. xxix]

BACKGROUND

According to the census of 1980, the population of the United States as of April 1, 1980, was 226,545,805, resulting in a population density of 64.0 persons for each of the country's 3,539,289 square miles. This was a population increase of 11.4 percent over the 1970 census.

On March 26, 1979, Israeli Prime Minister Menachem Begin and Egyptian President Anwar Sadat executed a peace treaty between their two nations in a ceremony hosted by President Carter at the White House. The signing of the peace treaty was the culmination of Carter's Camp David peace conference during the 95th Congress. Elsewhere in foreign affairs, however, events were going badly for the Carter administration. In Iran, the pro-Western and pro-economic development government of Shah Mohammed Reza Pahlavi was being threatened by an Islamic fundamentalist revolution. The United States considered Iran an important ally, both for its moderate position within the OPEC (Organization of Petroleum Exporting Countries) cartel on price increases and its presence as a military counterweight to the Soviets in the Middle East. The Shah left Iran shortly before his regime was overthrown by an Islamic religious leader, the Ayatollah Ruhollah Khomeini. On November 4 an armed mob stormed the U.S Embassy in Teheran, the Iranian capital, and took the Americans present there hostage. Mobs of anti-American demonstrators also attacked the U.S. embassy in Pakistan on November 21, and the embassy in Libya on December 2. Finally, in December 1979 the Soviet Union intervened militarily in the neighboring central Asian nation of Afghanistan in order to sustain the pro-Soviet Afghan government.

Also in 1979, the economic condition known as *stagflation* continued, as economic growth stayed low while interest rates and inflation remained high. At Three Mile Island in Pennsylvania, a nuclear power plant narrowly avoided a meltdown. The incident served to discredit the nuclear power industry, thus helping to keep the United States dependent on imported oil whose price was set by OPEC, and strengthen the antinuclear environmental movement. On July 15 Carter made a speech on national television in order to promote new conservation legislation, but Congress took no significant action on Carter's proposals. Finally, Congress created the Department of Education and authorized a $1.5 billion loan to the Chrysler Corporation in order to prevent Chrysler from going under.

In 1980 the American hostage situation in Iran became a serious embarrassment for the United States and the Carter administration. Despite several diplomatic initiatives and an unsuccessful military rescue operation, Carter could not convince the Iranians to free the hostages. The public began to view Carter as weak and ineffective, unable to preserve American prestige abroad. This perception was heightened by the Soviet invasion of Afghanistan. Carter responded by stopping American grain exports to the Soviets and withdrawing the United States from the 1980 Summer Olympics in Moscow, but he could do little else. Afghanistan was a poor, landlocked and mountainous country, where the neighboring Soviet Union had dominated the government for many years and American influence was minimal. Nevertheless, the appearance of impotence hurt Carter politically. The Republican Party's candidate in the 1980 presidential election, Ronald W. Reagan, ran a successful campaign that was critical of Carter and promised to increase military spending in order to reassert American strength in the world again. Riding Reagan's coattails, the GOP made large gains in the Senate. [See 97th Congress]

SENATE LEADERSHIP

Vice President: Walter F. Mondale. [See biographical note in 95th Congress]

President Pro Tempore: Warren Grant Magnuson (Dem., Wash.) first had been elected to Congress as a representative to the 75th Congress and had been elected to the Senate in 1944. He served as president pro tem in only the 96th Congress.

Majority Leader: Robert C. Byrd (Dem., W.Va.) [See biographical note in 95th Congress]

Majority Whip: Alan Cranston (Dem., Calif.)

Minority Leader: Howard H. Baker Jr. (Rep.,

Tenn.) [See biographical note in 95th Congress]

Minority Whip: Theodore F. Stevens (Rep., Alaska)

Chairman and Ranking Minority Members of Key Committees: [See also Organization and Administration, below]

Committee on Agriculture, Nutrition, and Forestry: Chairman: Herman E. Talmadge, (Dem., Ga.); Ranking Minority Member: Jesse A. Helms (Rep., N.C.)

Committee on Appropriations: Chairman: Warren G. Magnuson (Dem., Wash.); Ranking Minority Member: Milton R. Young (Rep., N.D.)

Committee on Armed Services: Chairman: John C. Stennis (Dem., Miss.); Ranking Minority Member: John G. Tower (Rep., Tex.)

Committee on Banking, Housing, and Urban Affairs: Chairman: William Proxmire (Dem., Wis.); Ranking Minority Member: Jake Garn (Rep., Utah)

Committee on the Budget: Chairman: Edmund S. Muskie (Dem., Maine), until he resigned effective May 7, 1980, to become the secretary of state. Ernest F. Hollings (Dem., S.C.) became the next chairman effective the same day. Ranking Minority Member: Henry Bellmon (Rep., Okla.)

Committee on Commerce, Science, and Transportation: Chairman: Howard W. Cannon (Dem., Nev.); Ranking Minority Member: Robert W. Packwood (Rep., Ore.)

Committee on Energy and Natural Resources: Chairman: Henry M. Jackson (Dem., Wash.); Ranking Minority Member: Mark O. Hatfield (Rep., Ore.)

Committee on Environment and Public Works: Chairman: Jennings Randolph (Dem., W.Va.); Ranking Minority Member: Robert T. Stafford (Rep., Vt.)

Committee on Finance: Chairman: Russell B. Long (Dem., La.); Ranking Minority Member: Robert J. Dole (Rep., Kans.)

Committee on Foreign Relations: Chairman:

Frank F. Church (Dem., Idaho); Ranking Minority Member: Jacob K. Javits (Rep., N.Y.)

Committee on Human Resources: Chairman: Harrison A. Williams Jr. (Dem., N.J.); Ranking Minority Member: Richard S. Schweiker (Rep., Pa.)

Committee on the Judiciary: Chairman: Edward M. Kennedy (Dem., Mass.); Ranking Minority Member: J. Strom Thurmond (Rep., S.C.)

Committee on Rules and Administration: Chairman: Claiborne D. Pell (Dem., R.I.); Ranking Minority Member: Mark O. Hatfield (Rep., Ore.)

HOUSE LEADERSHIP

Speaker of the House: Thomas Phillip "Tip" O'Neill Jr. (Dem., Mass.) [See biographical note in 95th Congress]

Majority Leader: James C. Wright (Dem., Tex.)

Majority Whip: John Brademas (Dem., Ind.)

Minority Leader: John J. Rhodes (Rep., Ariz.)

Minority Whip: Robert H. Michel (Rep., Ill.)

Chairman and Ranking Minority Members of Key Committees: [See also Organization and Administration, below]

Committee on Agriculture: Chairman: Thomas S. Foley (Dem., Wash.); Ranking Minority Member: William C. Wampler (Rep., Va.)

Committee on Appropriations: Chairman: Jamie L. Whitten (Dem., Miss.); Ranking Minority Member: Silvio O. Conte (Rep., Mass.)

Committee on Armed Services: Chairman: C. Melvin Price (Dem., Ill.); Ranking Minority Member: Robert C. Wilson (Rep., Calif.)

Committee on Banking, Finance, and Urban Affairs: Chairman: Henry S. Reuss (Dem., Wis.); Ranking Minority Member: J. William Stanton (Rep., Ohio)

Committee on the Budget: Chairman: Robert N. Giaimo (Dem., Conn.); Ranking Minority

Member: Delbert L. Latta (Rep., Ohio)

Committee on Education and Labor: Chairman: Carl D. Perkins (Dem., Ky.); Ranking Minority Member: John M. Ashbrook (Rep., Ohio)

Committee on Foreign Affairs: Chairman: Clement J. Zablocki (Dem., Wis.); Ranking Minority Member: William S. Broomfield (Rep., Mich.)

Committee on Interior and Insular Affairs: Chairman: Morris K. Udall (Dem., Ariz.); Ranking Minority Member: Don H. Clausen (Rep., Calif.)

Committee on Interstate and Foreign Commerce: Chairman: Harley O. Staggers (Dem., W.Va.); Ranking Minority Member: Samuel L. Devine (Rep., Ohio) until June 27, 1979, when he resigned. James T. Broyhill (Rep., N.C.) became the next ranking minority member effective the same day.

Committee on the Judiciary: Chairman: Peter W. Rodino Jr. (Dem., N.J.); Ranking Minority Member: Robert McClory (Rep., Ill.)

Committee on Public Works and Transportation: Chairman: Harold T. Johnson (Dem., Calif.); Ranking Minority Member: William H. Harsha Jr. (Rep., Ohio)

Committee on Rules: Chairman: Richard W. Bolling (Dem., Mo.) Ranking Minority Member: James H. Quillen (Rep., Tenn.)

Committee on Ways and Means: Chairman: Albert C. Ullman (Dem., Ore.); Ranking Minority Member: Barber B. Conable Jr. (Rep., N.Y.)

ORGANIZATION AND ADMINISTRATION

In the 94th Congress, the House Committee on Foreign Affairs was renamed the Committee on International Relations. On February 5, 1979, the name was changed back to the Committee on Foreign Affairs.

On March 7, 1979, the Senate Committee on

C H R O N O L O G Y

January 3, 1979:	The 96th Congress begins. During this Congress, President Carter made numerous changes to his cabinet. [See Nominations, Appointments, and Confirmations: The Executive Branch, below]
January 15, 1979:	The first session begins.
March 13, 1979:	Congress passes the Taiwan Relations Act.
May 30, 1979:	Congress passes Mideast assistance legislation.
July 11, 1979:	Congress passes legislation creating the Department of Education.
July 31, 1979:	The House censures Charles C. Diggs Jr. (Dem., Mich.)
December 17, 1979:	Congress passes the Crude Oil Windfall Profits Tax Act of 1980.
December 19, 1979:	Congress approves a financial bailout for the Chrysler Corporation.
January 3, 1980:	The first session ends, and the second session begins.
June 6, 1980:	Congress overrides President Carter's veto of a bill ending an oil import tax.
June 9, 1980:	Congress passes the Deep Seabed Hard Mineral Resources Act.
June 19, 1980:	Congress passes trucking deregulation legislation.
October 2, 1980:	The House expels Michael Myers (Dem., Pa.)
December 16, 1980:	The second session ends
January 3, 1981:	The 96th Congress ends.

[See note 6, p. xxix]

Human Resources was renamed the Committee on Labor and Human Resources. [See note 5, p. xxix]

MAJOR LEGISLATION PASSED

Chrysler: In the Chrysler Corporation Loan Guarantee Act of 1979, Congress extended federal assistance to the nation's third largest auto maker, which was in financial trouble and threatening hundreds of thousands of layoffs if it went out of business.

Department of Education: In the Department of Education Organization Act, Congess consolidated over 100 federal education programs into a new, cabinet-level Department of Education. Congress also renamed the Department of Health, Education, and Welfare the Department of Health and Human Services.

Energy: In the Crude Oil Windfall Profits Tax Act of 1980, Congress imposed a tax on the enormous profits to be made from rising oil prices after the government ended oil price controls. Portions of the tax revenues were earmarked for tax cuts and low income fuel assistance.

Middle East: As part of the effort to cement the Camp David peace process in the Middle East, Congress enacted the International Security Assistance Act of 1979. The act gave military and economic assistance to both Egypt and Israel.

Ocean Mining: In the Deep Seabed Hard Mineral Resources Act, Congress prepared the way for ocean mining in anticipation of the conclusion of a United Nations conference on a law of the sea treaty.

Taiwan: In the Taiwan Relations Act, Congress

TABLE OF KEY VOTES

Senate

Subject of Vote	Date of Vote	For			Against		
		D	R	Total	D	R	Total
Taiwan Relations Bill Passed	March 13, 1979	56	34	90	1	5	6
Department of Education Established	April 30, 1979	48	24	72	5	16	21
Middle East Aid Approved	May 14, 1979	42	31	73	6	5	11
Ocean Mining Bill Passed	December 14, 1979	Passed by voice vote					
Oil Windfall Profits Tax Passed	December 17, 1979	52	22	74	6	18	24
Chrysler Bailout Approved	December 19, 1979	41	12	53	17	27	44
Trucking deregulated	April 15, 1980	34	36	70	18	2	0
Oil Import Fee Veto Overridden	June 6, 1980	35	33	68	10	1	10

House

Subject of Vote	Date of Vote	For			Against		
		D	R	Total	D	R	Total
Taiwan Relations Bill Passed	March 13, 1979	241	104	345	14	41	55
Middle East Aid Approved	May 30, 1979	233	114	347	7	21	28
Oil Windfall Profits Tax Passed	June 28, 1979	Passed by voice vote					
Department of Education Established	July 11, 1979	175	35	210	89	117	206
Ocean Mining Bill Passed	June 9, 1980	Passed by voice vote					
Chrysler Bailout Approved	December 18, 1979	209	62	271	48	88	36
Oil Import Fee Veto Overridden	June 5, 1980	193	142	335	34	0	34
Trucking deregulated	June 19, 1980	228	139	367	12	1	13

[See note 7, p. xxix]

enacted a compromise between the U.S.'s desire to improve relations with the People's Republic of China (PRC) and continue existing ties with Taiwan. The act promised that the United States would continue its economic and military ties with Taiwan, but in a concession to the PRC the act demoted Taiwan diplomatically by providing that henceforth, relations would be conducted through a private foundation, the American Institute in Taiwan.

Trucking: In the Motor Carrier Act of 1980, Congress reduced the powers of the Interstate

Commerce Commission and began the process of deregulating the trucking industry.

FAILED LEGISLATION

Defense: On May 7, 1980, the Senate rejected a proposal to transfer $2 billion from defense spending to civilian programs. The military's failure to rescue the American hostages in Iran several weeks earlier on April 24 was influential.

Energy: On June 27, 1980, the House rejected President Carter's initiative to create an Energy Mobilization Board.

RELATIONS WITH THE PRESIDENT

President Jimmy Carter was damaged politically by events such as the Iranian hostage crisis and the Soviet invasion of Afghanistan. The public, and many members of Congress, viewed Carter as a weak president. This perception helped to defeat Carter's efforts in the area of energy legislation. Also, as a middle-of-the-road Democrat from the south, Carter was looked upon with suspicion by the liberal wing of his party, which controlled both Houses of Congress.

Carter vetoed 12 bills during the 96th Congress. A particularly signficant veto was Carter's veto of a bill that would end an oil import fee Carter supported. Congress overrode Carter's veto, because it considered the $4.62 per barrel tax to be too high. [See Table of Key Votes, above]

NOMINATIONS, APPOINTMENTS, AND CONFIRMATIONS

The Judiciary: There were no significant nominations, appointments, or confirmations in the federal judiciary during the 96th Congress.

The Executive Branch: On July 20, 1979, President Carter nominated Benjamin R. Civiletti to succeed Griffin B. Bell as attorney general; Patricia R. Harris to succeed Joseph A. Califano as secretary of health, education, and welfare (henceforth the Department of Health and Human Services); and G. William Miller to succeed W. Michael Blumenthal as secretary of the Treasury. On July 27, 1979, the Senate confirmed Harris by voice vote; on August 1, 1979, it confirmed Civiletti by a vote of 94 to 1; and on August 2, 1979, it confirmed Miller by a vote of 97 to 1. On July 21, 1979, Carter nominated Charles W. Duncan Jr. to succeed James R. Schlesinger as secretary of energy, and on July 31, 1979, the Senate confirmed Duncan by a vote of 95 to 1. On August 2, 1979, Carter nominated Moon Landrieu to fill Harris's former position as secretary of housing and urban development, and on September 12, 1979, the Senate confirmed Landrieu by a vote of 97 to 0. On September 10, 1979, Carter nominated Neil E. Goldschmidt to succeed Brock Adams as secretary of transportation, and on September 21, 1979, the Senate confirmed Goldschmidt by a vote of 83 to 0. On November 14, 1979, Carter nominated Shirley M. Hufstedler for secretary of education, a new cabinet-level position, and on November 30, 1979, the Senate confirmed Hufstedler by a vote of 81 to 2. On December 11, 1979, Carter nominated Philip M. Klutznick to succeed Juanita M. Kreps as secretary of commerce, and on December 20, 1979, the Senate confirmed Klutznick by a vote of 74 to 0. Finally, on May 5, 1980, Carter nominated Edmund S. Muskie to succeed Cyrus R. Vance as secretary of state, and on May 7, 1980, the Senate confirmed Muskie by a vote of 94 to 2.

IMPEACHMENTS

None.

CONSTITUTIONAL AMENDMENTS

None.

SCANDALS

It was during this Congress that the "Abscam" scandal broke. The FBI had been using agents to pose as rich Arabs looking to purchase political influence from members of Congress in matters ranging from securing gambling licenses to obtaining U.S. residency. Seven members of Congress were charged with accepting bribes: Senator Harrison A. Williams Jr. (Dem., N.J.) and Congressman John W. Jenrette Jr. (Dem., S.C.), Richard Kelly (Rep., Fla.), Raymond F. Lederer (Dem., Pa.), John M. Murphy (Dem., N.Y.), Michael J. Myers (Dem., Pa.) and Frank Thompson Jr. (Dem., N.J.). Although all seven would be convicted of criminal offenses, only Myers was expelled from Congress, by a House vote of 376 to 30 on October 2, 1980. The other five Representatives and Senator Williams [See also 97th Congress], resigned or were defeated for reelection before they faced disciplinary action.

Also, during this Congress, the House on July 31, 1979, voted 414 to 0 to censure Charles C. Diggs Jr. (Dem., Mich.) for misuse of funds.

FURTHER READING

Carter, Jimmy. *Why Not The Best?* Nashville, Tenn.: Broadman Press, 1975.

Lewis, Finlay. *Mondale*. New York: Perennial Library, 1984.

O'Neill, Thomas P., with William Novak. *Man of the House; The Life and Political Memoirs of Speaker Tip O'Neill*. New York: Random House, 1987.

The Presidency and Domestic Policies of Jimmy Carter. Westport, Conn.: Greenwood Press, 1994.

The 97th Congress

JANUARY 3, 1981-JANUARY 3, 1983

First Session: January 5, 1981-December 16, 1981
Second Session: January 25, 1982-December 23, 1982

In the 1980 elections for the 97th Congress, the Republicans gained 12 seats in the Senate to hold a new majority of 53 of the 100 seats. The Democrats lost 12 seats, leaving them with a total of 46. One seat was held by an independent. In the House, the Democrats lost 33 seats, reducing their majority from 276 to 243 of the 435 seats. The Republicans gained 35 seats, giving them a total of 192. [See note 3, p. xxix]

BACKGROUND

Ronald W. Reagan was inaugurated as the 40th president of the United States on January 20, 1981. That same day, Iran released the American hostages it had held since the U.S. Embassy was seized by an armed mob in November 1979. On March 30, 1981, John W. Hinckley shot Reagan outside a hotel in Washington, D.C., but the president survived the assassination attempt and recovered quickly.

The Reagan administration planned to revive the economy by reducing federal income taxes, which in theory would stimulate the economy and eventually create so much economic growth that personal incomes would increase and the resulting tax revenues would more than offset the loss from the tax cut. In effect, Reagan promised a painless means to grow the economy out of recession and the budget deficit. During the summer of 1981, Reagan won a major legislative victory when Congress enacted his income tax cut

proposals. Also that summer, Reagan faced his first major domestic political challenge when the Professional Air Traffic Controllers' Organization (PATCO) went on strike. Without air traffic controllers, most of the nation's airports would have to shut down and air traffic would be crippled. Despite PATCO's grievances, Reagan insisted that PATCO members abide by the terms of their previously negotiated contract and fired the air traffic controllers who refused to return to work. Reagan transferred many military air traffic controllers to temporary duty in civilian airports, where they assisted the controllers not on strike while the Federal Aviation Administration trained new controllers. The result was the destruction of PATCO and a victory for Reagan.

By the end of 1981 the Soviet Union successfully had pressured Poland into declaring martial law in order to suppress growing popular unrest. Reagan responded by placing more restrictions on the sale of American technology and equipment to the Soviets.

In 1982 unemployment neared 10 percent, and the economy was in a recession. Inflation dropped dramatically, however, from the double digit rates of the Carter administration to roughly six percent. Whether this turnaround was due to Reagan's tax cuts and other economic initiatives is uncertain, but the turnaround was politically positive for the Reagan administration, especially when the economy began to recover by year's end. Less positive were growing budget deficits, which for fiscal 1982 reached nearly $100 billion. Reagan had criticized former President Carter for the size of the budget deficit, but Reagan's tax cuts and sharp increases in military spending were creating an even larger budget deficit that would persist throughout the 1980s and result in year after year of record deficits.

Also during 1982, the Justice Department agreed to end its long-standing antitrust prosecution against American Telephone and Telegraph (AT&T) when AT&T agreed to divest itself of regional telephone companies, which then became known as the "Baby Bells." The AT&T breakup was a victory for the Justice Department, but antitrust activity generally declined under the probusiness Reagan administration.

SENATE LEADERSHIP

Vice President: Walter F. Mondale had been vice president until January 20, 1981, when George Herbert Walker Bush became the new vice president. Bush had served as a representative from Texas in the 90th and 91st Congresses and had held a variety of posts before being elected vice president, including being the chief liaison officer to Communist China and director of the CIA. [See note 8, p. xxix]

President Pro Tempore: J. Strom Thurmond (Rep., S.C.) first had been elected to the Senate in 1954. Before serving in the Senate, Thurmond had been governor of South Carolina from 1947 to 1951 and an unsuccessful third-party candidate for president in 1948. Thurmond was originally a Democrat, but became a Republican in 1964. He served as president pro tem in the 97th through the 99th Congresses.

Majority Leader: Howard H. Baker Jr. (Rep., Tenn.) was the son-in-law of former Senate Republican leader Everett Dirksen and first had been elected to the Senate in 1966. A moderate respected by members of both parties, Baker was the leader of the Senate Republicans in the 95th through the 98th Congresses.

Majority Whip: Theodore F. Stevens (Rep., Alaska)

Minority Leader: Robert C. Byrd (Dem., W.Va.) [See biographical note in 95th Congress]

Minority Whip: Alan Cranston (Dem., Calif.)

Chairman and Ranking Minority Members of Key Committees:

Committee on Agriculture, Nutrition, and Forestry: Chairman: Jesse A. Helms (Rep., N.C.); Ranking Minority Member: Walter D. Huddleston (Dem., Ky.)

Committee on Appropriations: Chairman: Mark O. Hatfield (Rep., Ore.); Ranking Minority Member: William Proxmire (Dem., Wis.)

Committee on Armed Services: Chairman: John G. Tower (Rep., Tex.); Ranking Minority Member: John C. Stennis (Dem., Miss.)

Committee on Banking, Housing, and Urban Affairs: Chairman: Jake Garn (Rep., Utah); Ranking Minority Member: Harrison A. Williams Jr. (Dem., N.J.), until March 11, 1982, when he resigned. On April 20, 1982, Donald W. Riegle Jr. became the next ranking minority member effective the same day.

Committee on the Budget: Chairman: Pete V. Domenici (Rep., N.M.); Ranking Minority Member: Ernest F. Hollings (Dem., S.C.)

Committee on Commerce, Science, and Transportation: Chairman: Robert W. Packwood (Rep., Ore.); Ranking Minority Member: Howard W. Cannon (Dem., Nev.)

Committee on Energy and Natural Resources: Chairman: James A. McClure (Rep., Idaho); Ranking Minority Member: Henry M. Jackson (Dem., Wash.)

Committee on Environment and Public Works: Chairman: Robert T. Stafford (Rep., Vt.); Ranking Minority Member: Jennings Randolph (Dem., W.Va.)

Committee on Finance: Chairman: Robert J. Dole (Rep., Kans.); Ranking Minority Member: Russell B. Long (Dem., La.)

Committee on Foreign Relations: Chairman:

C H R O N O L O G Y

January 3, 1981:   The 97th Congress begins.

January 5, 1981:   The first session begins.

January 20, 1981:   President Reagan nominates his cabinet members, all of whom are confirmed by the Senate by February 3, 1981.

May 1, 1981:   Senator Harrison ("Pete") Williams (Dem., N.J.) is convicted by a federal jury in New York of bribery and conspiracy charges in connection with the Abscam investigation.

July 3, 1981:   Supreme Court Justice Potter Stewart retires.

July 7, 1981:   President Reagan nominates Sandra Day O'Connor, the first woman named to the Supreme Court, to replace Stewart.

July 13, 1981:   Congress passes the fiscal 1982 budget bill.

July 31, 1981:   Congress passes the Economic Recovery Tax Act of 1981.

August 24, 1981:   Senate Ethics Committee unanimously recommends Senator Williams be expelled from the Senate.

September 21, 1981: The Senate confirms O'Connor.

October 28, 1981:   Congress fails to block an AWACS sale to Saudi Arabia.

December 4, 1981:   Congress passes fiscal 1982 defense appropriation legislation.

December 16, 1981:   The first session ends.

January 25, 1982:   The second session begins.

March 11, 1982:   Senator Williams, under threat of expulsion, resigns from the Senate.

June 18, 1982:   Congress extends civil rights legislation.

July 1, 1982:   President Reagan nominates George P. Shultz to succeed Alexander M. Haig Jr. as secretary of state.

July 15, 1982:   The Senate confirms Shultz.

July 22, 1982:   The House rejects funding for "binary" chemical weapons.

August 5, 1982:   The House rejects a nuclear freeze resolution.

August 28, 1982:   President Reagan vetoes a $14.2 billion spending bill.

September 9, 1982:   The House votes to override Reagan's veto.

September 10, 1982: The Senate votes to override Reagan's veto.

September 24, 1982: Congress passes savings and loan deregulation legislation.

October 1, 1982:   Congress fails to approve a proposed balanced budget amendment to the Constitution.

November 15, 1982:   President Reagan nominates Donald P. Hodel to succeed James B. Edwards as secretary of energy.

December 8, 1982:   The Senate confirms Hodel.

December 19, 1982:   Congress passes fiscal 1983 defense appropriation legislation.

December 23, 1982:   The second session ends.

January 3, 1983:   The 97th Congress ends.

[See note 6, p. xxix]

Charles H. Percy (Rep., Ill.); Ranking Minority Member: Claiborne D. Pell (Dem., R.I.)

Committee on the Judiciary: Chairman: J. Strom Thurmond (Rep., S.C.); Ranking Minority Member: Joseph R. Biden Jr. (Dem., Del.)

Committee on Labor and Human Resources: Chairman: Orrin G. Hatch (Rep., Utah); Ranking Minority Member: Edward M. Kennedy (Dem., Mass.)

Committee on Rules and Administration: Chairman: Charles M. Mathias Jr. (Rep., Md.); Ranking Minority Member: Wendell H. Ford (Dem., Ky.)

HOUSE LEADERSHIP

Speaker of the House: Thomas Phillip "Tip" O'Neill Jr. (Dem., Mass.) [See biographical note in 95th Congress] During the Reagan presidency, O'Neill became one of the senior statesmen for the Democrats and their viewpoints.

Majority Leader: James C. Wright (Dem., Tex.)

Majority Whip: Thomas S. Foley (Dem., Wash.)

Minority Leader: Robert H. Michel (Rep., Ill.)

Minority Whip: Trent Lott (Rep., Miss.)

Chairman and Ranking Minority Members of Key Committees: [See also Organization and Administration, below]

Committee on Agriculture: Chairman: Kika de la Garza (Dem., Tex.); Ranking Minority Member: William C. Wampler (Rep., Va.)

Committee on Appropriations: Chairman: Jamie L. Whitten (Dem., Miss.); Ranking Minority Member: Silvio O. Conte (Rep., Mass.)

Committee on Armed Services: Chairman: C. Melvin Price (Dem., Ill.); Ranking Minority Member: William L. Dickinson (Rep., Ala.)

Committee on Banking, Finance, and Urban Affairs: Chairman: Fernand J. St. Germain (Dem., R.I.); Ranking Minority Member: J. William Stanton (Rep., Ohio)

Committee on the Budget: Chairman: James R. Jones (Dem., Okla.); Ranking Minority Member: Delbert L. Latta (Rep., Ohio)

Committee on Education and Labor: Chairman: Carl D. Perkins (Dem., Ky.); Ranking Minority Member: John M. Ashbrook (Rep., Ohio), who died on April 24, 1982. John N. Erlenborn (Rep., Ill.) became the next ranking minority member effective the same day.

Committee on Energy and Commerce: Chairman: John D. Dingell Jr. (Dem., Mich.); Ranking Minority Member: James T. Broyhill (Rep., N.C.)

Committee on Foreign Affairs: Chairman: Clement J. Zablocki (Dem., Wis.); Ranking Minority Member: William S. Broomfield (Rep., Mich.)

Committee on Interior and Insular Affairs: Chairman: Morris K. Udall (Dem., Ariz.); Ranking Minority Member: Manuel Lujan Jr. (Rep., N.M.)

Committee on the Judiciary: Chairman: Peter W. Rodino Jr. (Dem., N.J.); Ranking Minority Member: Robert McClory (Rep., Ill.)

Committee on Public Works and Transportation: Chairman: James J. Howard (Dem., N.J.); Ranking Minority Member: Don H. Clausen (Rep., Calif.)

Committee on Rules: Chairman: Richard W. Bolling (Dem., Mo.); Ranking Minority Member: James H. Quillen (Rep., Tenn.)

Committee on Ways and Means: Chairman: Daniel D. Rostenkowski (Dem., Ill.); Ranking Minority Member: Barber B. Conable Jr. (Rep., N.Y.)

ORGANIZATION AND ADMINISTRATION

At the beginning of the 97th Congress the salaries for both senators and representatives was $60,662.50 a year. The 97th Congress raised the salaries for representatives to $69,800 but didn't give senators a raise. Unlike senators, however, representatives were limited in the amount of outside income they could earn. Senators could earn as much as they wished from giving speeches and other outside activities, but representatives could make no more than 30 percent over their House salaries.

The name of the House Committee on Interstate and Foreign Commerce was changed to the Committee on Energy and Commerce effective January 3, 1981. [See note 5, p. xxix]

MAJOR LEGISLATION PASSED

Budget: In the fiscal 1982 appropriations bill, Congress cut $35 billion worth of government spending. The spending cuts were exclusively in nondefense areas, such as welfare. [See Welfare, below]

Civil Rights: Congress extended the enforcement provisions of the 1965 Voting Rights Act, which give the federal government the power to supervise elections in areas with a history of racial discrimination, for another 25 years.

Defense: President Reagan succeeded in getting Congress to approve greatly increased defense spending. First, for fiscal 1982, Congress increased the defense budget from $196 billion in fiscal 1981 to $211.6 billion. There were several pieces of legislation involved, such as a bill for nuclear weapons programs and a bill for military construction projects, but the most significant was a massive $199.7 billion Pentagon funding bill. [See Table of Key Votes, below] Second, for fiscal 1983, Congress increased the defense budget to $232 billion and also raised the salaries of military personnel. Many Republicans voted against the 1983 defense bill, however, since they wanted even higher defense spending.

Savings and Loans: In the Net Worth Guarantee Act, Congress increased the ability of S&Ls to invest and lend money, lowered the amount of federal supervision, and permitted more competition between S&Ls and commercial banks. Although this deregulation was intended to help the financially troubled S&L industry, it may have encouraged the abuses and excessive spec-

ulation that led to the collapse of the S&Ls in the late 1980s.

Taxes: In the Economic Recovery Tax Act of 1981, Congress, going along with the Reagan administration's theory of supply side economics, enacted approximately $750 billion in tax cuts for businesses and individuals for fiscal 1982 through fiscal 1986. The theory was that these tax cuts would stimulate the economy, without adding to the budget deficit because the increased economic activity would generate more tax revenues. In fact, budget deficits rose in future years.

Welfare: Congress cut a variety of social programs in order to finance the Reagan budget cuts, tax cuts, and defense spending increases. One notable target, included in the fiscal 1982 budget bill [See Budget, above], was the program called Aid to Families with Dependent Children (AFDC). In this bill, Congress reduced payments to working parents by lowering the amount of permitted nonwelfare outside earned income.

FAILED LEGISLATION

Defense: There were two particularly significant developments in the House. First, on July 22, 1982, the House voted 225 to 192 to reject the Reagan administration's request for funding of a new program called "binary" chemical weapons. In such a weapon, there are two critical chemical elements, which are kept separate and harmless inside the weapon (such as an artillery shell) until a weapon is fired and the combined chemicals become lethal against the enemy. The idea was to reduce the perceived Soviet superiority in chemical weapons but not endanger the civilians living near where the weapons would be stored. Second, on August 5, 1982, the House narrowly defeated by a 204 to 202 vote a resolution that called for a nuclear weapons freeze in defiance of the Reagan military buildup.

Mideast: In 1981 President Reagan approved the sale of five AWACS (Airborne Warning and Control System) planes and other military hardware to Saudi Arabia. A major oil producer, Saudi Arabia was militarily weak and vulnerable if the

TABLE OF KEY VOTES

Senate

Subject of Vote	Date of Vote	For			Against		
		D	R	Total	D	R	Total
Budget Passed	July 13, 1981	Passed by voice vote					
Taxes Cut	July 31, 1981	Passed by voice vote					
Blocking AWACS Sale	October 28, 1981	36	12	48	11	41	52
1982 Defense Spending Bill Passed	December 4, 1981	37	47	84	4	1	5
Civil Rights Bill Passed	June 18, 1982	42	43	85	1	7	8
Balanced Budget Amendment Approved	August 4, 1982	22	47	69	24	7	31
Spending Bill Veto Overridden	September 10, 1982	39	21	60	4	26	30
Savings and Loans Bill Passed	September 24, 1982	Passed by voice vote					
1983 Defense Spending Bill Passed	December 19, 1982	26	37	63	16	15	31

House

Subject of Vote	Date of Vote	For			Against		
		D	R	Total	D	R	Total
Budget Passed	June 26, 1981	47	185	232	188	5	193
Taxes Cut	July 29, 1981	133	190	323	106	1	107
Civil Rights Bill Passed	October 5, 1981	229	160	389	7	17	24
Blocking AWACS Sale	October 14, 1981	193	108	301	33	78	111
1982 Defense Spending Bill Passed	November 18, 1981	163	172	335	54	7	61
Savings and Loans Bill Passed	May 20, 1982	188	84	272	16	75	91
Spending Bill Veto Overridden	September 9, 1982	220	81	301	13	104	117
Balance Budget Amendment Defeated (failed: two-thirds majority required)	October 1, 1982	69	167	236	167	20	187
1983 Defense Spending Bill Passed	December 14, 1982	191	13	204	36	164	200

[See note 7, p. xxix]

Soviet Union invaded the Mideast. The AWACS used highly advanced and secret technology to monitor enemy air movements. However, the AWACS sale was opposed strongly by a range of pro-Israel interests, who wanted Congress to block the arms sales. While the House passed a bill to cancel the sale, the Senate did not, so the AWACS sale went through. [See Table of Key Votes, above]

RELATIONS WITH THE PRESIDENT

President Ronald W. Reagan brought a new conservative agenda to Congress. This agenda always was not popular, either with Congress or the public. However, Reagan successfully projected the image of a determined leader, and was nicknamed the "great communicator." Although he quietly abandoned his pledge to balance the budget, most of his other legislative initiatives were ultimately passed by Congress.

Reagan vetoed 14 bills during the 97th Congress. One veto led to the first significant defeat of his presidency. On August 28, 1982, Reagan vetoed a bill providing for $14.2 billion in additional military and social spending because he thought the bill should give more to the military, but both Republicans and Democrats disagreed with his position and successfully overrode his veto. [See Table of Key Votes, above]

NOMINATIONS, APPOINTMENTS, AND CONFIRMATIONS

The Judiciary: On July 3, 1981, Supreme Court Justice Potter Stewart retired. President Ronald W. Reagan nominated Sandra Day O'Connor, the first female nominee to the Supreme Court, on July 7, 1981. The Senate confirmed O'Connor on September 21, 1981, by a 99 to 0 vote.

The Executive Branch: On January 20, 1981, President Reagan nominated his cabinet members, all of whom were confirmed by the Senate. Caspar W. Weinberger was confirmed as secretary of defense on January 20, 1981, by a 97 to 2 vote. The following nominations were confirmed

on January 21, 1981: Alexander M. Haig Jr. to be secretary of state by a 93 to 6 vote; Donald T. Regan to be secretary of the Treasury by a 98 to 0 vote; and Richard S. Schweiker to be secretary of health and human services by a 99 to 0 vote. The following nominations were confirmed on January 22, 1981: Malcolm Baldrige to be secretary of commerce by a 97 to 1 vote; Terrel H. Bell to be secretary of education by a 90 to 2 vote; John R. Block to be secretary of agriculture by a 98 to 0 vote; James B. Edwards to be secretary of energy by a 93 to 3 vote; Andrew L. Lewis Jr. to be secretary of transportation by a 98 to 0 vote; Samuel R. Pierce Jr. to be secretary of housing and urban development by a 98 to 0 vote; William French Smith to be attorney general by a 96 to 1 vote; and James G. Watt to be secretary of the Interior by an 83 to 12 vote. Raymond J. Donovan was confirmed as secretary of labor on February 3, 1981, by an 80 to 17 vote.

On July 1, 1982, Reagan nominated George P. Shultz to succeed Haig as secretary of state, and on July 15, 1982, the Senate confirmed Shultz by a vote of 97 to 0. On November 15, 1982, Reagan nominated Donald P. Hodel to succeed James B. Edwards as secretary of energy, and on December 8, 1982, the Senate confirmed Hodel by a vote of 86 to 8.

IMPEACHMENTS

None.

CONSTITUTIONAL AMENDMENTS

The Republican-dominated Senate voted in favor of a constitutional amendment requiring a balanced federal budget, but the Democrat-dominated House failed to approve the amendment by the necessary two-thirds majority. President Reagan supported the amendment.

SCANDALS

The Abscam scandal, which began in the 96th Congress [See Scandals in 96th Congress], played itself out in this Congress. The only senator implicated in the government's sting operation where FBI agents posed as wealthy Arabs looking to purchase influence, was Harrison A. Williams Jr. (Dem., N.J.). In one FBI videotape, Williams was seen refusing a cash bribe offered by the undercover agents, whereas the other Abscam defendants had willingly taken their bribes. Nevertheless, despite Williams' claim that the government had "manufactured" the evidence against him, he was convicted of promising to use his influence to get government contracts for a titanium mining venture in which the undercover "Arabs" would lend $100 million and in which Williams would get an 18 percent interest. Thus, on May 1, 1981 a federal jury in Brooklyn, New York convicted Williams of bribery and conspiracy offenses. On August 24, 1981, the Senate Ethics Committee held that Williams had acted in an "ethically repugnant" manner, recommending that he be expelled. Just hours before a near-certain Senate vote of expulsion, on March 11, 1982, Williams resigned from the Senate.

Further Reading

Langston, Thomas S. *Ideologues and Presidents: From the New Deal to the Reagan Revolution*. Baltimore: Johns Hopkins University Press, 1992.

Mann, Thomas E. and Ornstein, Norman J. *The American Elections of 1982*. Washington: American Enterprise Institute for Public Policy Research, 1983.

O'Neill, Thomas P., with William Novak. *Man of the House; The Life and Political Memoirs of Speaker Tip O'Neill*. New York: Random House, 1987.

Sick, Gary. *October Surprise: America's Hostages in Iran and the Election of Ronald Reagan*. New York: Times Books, 1992.

The 98th Congress

JANUARY 3, 1983 - JANUARY 3, 1985

First Session: January 3, 1983-November 18, 1983
Second Session: January 23, 1984-October 12, 1984

In the 1982 elections for the 98th Congress, the Republicans gained 2 seats in the Senate, increasing their majority from 53 to 55 of the 100 seats. The Democrats lost 1 seat, reducing their total to 45. In the House, the Democrats gained 25 seats, increasing their majority from 243 to 268 of the 435 seats. The Republicans lost 26 seats, leaving them with a total of 166. One seat was vacant, and would ultimately be taken by a Democrat before the end of this Congress. [See note 3, p. xxix]

BACKGROUND

In 1983 President Reagan committed American troops to their first full-scale military intervention in a foreign nation since the Vietnam War. In the Caribbean island nation of Grenada, Communist rebels had seized power, and were holding American students hostage at a local medical school. There also was evidence that the Communists had formed a military relationship with Cuba. Cuban troops disguised as work brigades were not only present on the island but were working on expanding an airfield that theoretically could be used by aircraft against shipping in Caribbean sea lanes. On October 25, 1983, American forces landed in Grenada, and after a few days freed the hostages and removed the Communists from power. In purely military terms, the outcome of the Grenada action was a foregone conclusion, given the massively superior resources available to the U.S. Politically, however, it was a victory for Reagan's effort to reassert American strength after Vietnam, and the success of the operation set a precedent for larger actions in Libya, Panama, and Iraq in coming years.

In addition to Grenada, Reagan took other actions during the 98th Congress against the perceived Communist threat in Central America. The U.S. sent aid to the government of El Salvador, which was fighting Communist guerrillas, despite El Salvador's questionable record on human rights. In nearby Nicaragua, however, the U.S. was supporting local rebels, since they were opposed to the leftist Sandinista government. Unlike their feelings concerning U.S. policy toward Grenada, Congress and the American public had reservations about Reagan's policy in Central America. The similarity to Vietnam was superficially present, in that the U.S. was becoming financially and militarily involved in suppressing a local Communist movement. Furthermore, the Reagan administration was in the position of supporting a government against rebels in one country, while turning around and supporting the rebels against the government in a neighboring country. At one point, polls indicated that approximately 70 percent of the American public had these two positions confused.

Elsewhere in the world, the American peacekeeping mission in Beirut, Lebanon, suffered a serious setback on October 23, 1983, when a vehicle loaded with explosives detonated outside of the U.S. Marine headquarters and killed 241 servicemen. Soon thereafter, Reagan quietly withdrew the remaining Marines. Although this was a tacit admission of defeat, it did not hurt Reagan politically as the Iran situation had hurt former President Carter. Finally, relations with the Soviet Union deteriorated. The Soviets shot down a South Korean airliner that they claimed was on a spy mission in Soviet airspace, killing all the passengers aboard, including some American citizens. In addition, the U.S. was adding hundreds of cruise missiles with nuclear warheads to its arsenal in Great Britain and Western Europe, in response to new Soviet SS-20 missile installations. The Soviets retaliated by cancelling negotiations over reducing intermediate range nuclear weapons in Europe.

On the domestic front, the American economy during the 98th Congress was making a strong recovery from the recession of the early 1980s, while inflation stayed at an annual rate of four percent or less. Industrial production, personal income, and new home construction showed strong increases in both 1983 and 1984. There were, however, problem areas in the economy that Reagan and Congress were content to ignore. The national trade deficit set new records in both years, $60 billion in 1983 and $107 billion in 1984. Further, the increase in personal incomes was largely for upper middle class and wealthy Americans. With respect to lower middle class and poor Americans, Reagan and his administration's economists adhered to a theory called "trickle-down economics," which held that the economic gains of the prosperous elements of American society eventually would trickle down and benefit less prosperous Americans.

SENATE LEADERSHIP

Vice President: George Herbert Walker Bush [See biographical note in 97th Congress]

President Pro Tempore: J. Strom Thurmond (Rep., S.C.) [See biographical note in 97th Congress]

Majority Leader: Howard H. Baker Jr. (Rep., Tenn.) [See biographical note in 95th Congress]

Majority Whip: Theodore F. Stevens (Rep., Alaska)

Minority Leader: Robert C. Byrd (Dem., W.Va.) [See biographical note in 95th Congress]

Minority Whip: Alan Cranston (Dem., Calif.)

Chairman and Ranking Minority Members of Key Committees:

Committee on Agriculture, Nutrition, and Forestry: Chairman: Jesse A. Helms (Rep., N.C.); Ranking Minority Member: Walter D. Huddleston (Dem., Ky.)

Committee on Appropriations: Chairman: Mark O. Hatfield (Rep., Ore.); Ranking Minority Member: John C. Stennis (Dem., Miss.)

Committee on Armed Services: Chairman: John G. Tower (Rep., Tex.); Ranking Minority Member: Henry M. Jackson (Dem., Wash.), until September 1, 1983, when he died in office. Samuel A. Nunn (Dem., Ga.) became the next ranking minority member effective the same day.

Committee on Banking, Housing, and Urban Affairs: Chairman: Jake Garn (Rep., Utah); Ranking Minority Member: William Proxmire (Dem., Wis.)

Committee on the Budget: Chairman: Pete V. Domenici (Rep., N.M.); Ranking Minority Member: Lawton M. Chiles Jr. (Dem., Fla.)

Committee on Commerce, Science, and Transportation: Chairman: Robert W. Packwood (Rep., Ore.); Ranking Minority Member: Ernest F. Hollings (Dem., S.C.)

Committee on Energy and Natural Resources: Chairman: James A. McClure (Rep., Idaho); Ranking Minority Member: J. Bennett Johnston Jr. (Dem., La.)

Committee on Environment and Public Works: Chairman: Robert T. Stafford (Rep., Vt.) Ranking Minority Member: Jennings Randolph (Dem., W.Va.)

CHRONOLOGY

January 3, 1983:	The 98th Congress and the first session begin.
January 25, 1983:	President Reagan nominates Elizabeth H. Dole to succeed Andrew L. Lewis Jr. as secretary of transportation.
February 1, 1983:	The Senate confirms Dole.
February 18, 1983:	President Reagan nominates Margaret M. Heckler to succeed Richard S. Schweiker as secretary of health and human services.
March 7, 1983:	The Senate confirms Heckler.
March 11, 1983:	The Senate fails to pass economic stimulus legislation.
March 23, 1983:	Congress passes a package of social legislation.
June 28, 1983:	The Senate fails to approve a proposed constitutional amendment concerning abortion.
October 19, 1983:	Congress approves a Martin Luther King Jr. holiday. President Reagan nominates William P. Clark to succeed James G. Watt as secretary of the Interior.
October 31, 1983:	A nuclear freeze resolution dies in the Senate.
November 8, 1983:	Congress approves funding for the MX missile.
November 15, 1983:	The House votes against reviving the Equal Rights Amendment.
November 18, 1983:	The Senate confirms Clark, and the first session ends.
January 23, 1984:	The second session begins.
March 20, 1984:	The Senate fails to approve a proposed constitutional amendment concerning school prayer.
May 10, 1984:	Congress approves funding for anti-Communist initiatives in El Salvador and Nicaragua.
June 26, 1984:	Congress passes legislation tying highway funds to an increase in state drinking ages.
October 11, 1984:	Congress finally passes fiscal 1985 appropriations legislation.
October 12, 1984:	The second session ends.
January 3, 1985:	The 98th Congress ends.

[See note 6, p. xxix]

Committee on Finance: Chairman: Robert J. Dole (Rep., Kans.); Ranking Minority Member: Russell B. Long (Dem., La.)

Committee on Foreign Relations: Chairman: Charles H. Percy (Rep., Ill.); Ranking Minority Member: Claiborne D. Pell (Dem., R.I.)

Committee on the Judiciary: Chairman: J. Strom Thurmond (Rep., S.C.); Ranking Minority Member: Joseph R. Biden Jr. (Dem., Del.)

Committee on Labor and Human Resources: Chairman: Orrin G. Hatch (Rep., Utah); Ranking Minority Member: Edward M. Kennedy (Dem., Mass.)

Committee on Rules and Administration: Chairman: Charles M. Mathias Jr. (Rep., Md.); Ranking Minority Member: Wendell H. Ford (Dem., Ky.)

HOUSE LEADERSHIP

Speaker of the House: Thomas Phillip "Tip" O'Neill Jr. (Dem., Mass.) [See biographical note in 95th Congress]

Majority Leader: James C. Wright (Dem., Tex.)

Majority Whip: Thomas S. Foley (Dem., Wash.)

Minority Leader: Robert H. Michel (Rep., Ill.)

Minority Whip: Trent Lott (Rep., Miss.)

Other Leaders:

Geraldine A. Ferraro (Dem., N.Y.): After three terms in Congress, where she was a close ally of Speaker Tip O'Neil, Ferraro was selected by the Democratic nominee for president, Walter F. Mondale, as his vice presidential running mate.

Chairman and Ranking Minority Members of Key Committees:

Committee on Agriculture: Chairman: Kika de la Garza (Dem., Tex.); Ranking Minority Member: Edward R. Madigan (Rep., Ill.)

Committee on Appropriations: Chairman: Jamie L. Whitten (Dem., Miss.); Ranking Minority Member: Silvio O. Conte (Rep., Mass.)

Committee on Armed Services: Chairman: C. Melvin Price (Dem., Ill.); Ranking Minority Member: William L. Dickinson (Rep., Ala.)

Committee on Banking, Finance, and Urban Affairs: Chairman: Fernand J. St. Germain (Dem., R.I.); Ranking Minority Member: Chalmers P. Wylie (Rep., Ohio)

Committee on the Budget: Chairman: James R. Jones (Dem., Okla.); Ranking Minority Member: Delbert L. Latta (Rep., Ohio)

Committee on Education and Labor: Chairman: Carl D. Perkins (Dem., Ky.), who died on August 3, 1984. Augustus F. Hawkins (Dem., Calif.)

became the next chairman effective the same day. Ranking Minority Member: John N. Erlenborn (Rep., Ill.)

Committee on Energy and Commerce: Chairman: John D. Dingell Jr. (Dem., Mich.); Ranking Minority Member: James T. Broyhill (Rep., N.C.)

Committee on Foreign Affairs: Chairman: Clement J. Zablocki (Dem., Wis.), who died on December 3, 1983. Dante B. Fascell (Dem., Fla.) became the next chairman effective January 25, 1984. Ranking Minority Member: William S. Broomfield (Rep., Mich.)

Committee on Interior and Insular Affairs: Chairman: Morris K. Udall (Dem., Ariz.); Ranking Minority Member: Manuel Lujan Jr. (Rep., N.M.)

Committee on the Judiciary: Chairman: Peter W. Rodino Jr. (Dem., N.J.); Ranking Minority Member: Hamilton Fish Jr. (Rep., N.Y.)

Committee on Public Works and Transportation: Chairman: James J. Howard (Dem., N.J.); Ranking Minority Member: Gene Snyder (Rep., Ky.)

Committee on Rules: Chairman: Claude D. Pepper (Dem., Fla.); Ranking Minority Member: James H. Quillen (Rep., Tenn.)

Committee on Ways and Means: Chairman: Daniel D. Rostenkowski (Dem., Ill.); Ranking Minority Member: Barber B. Conable Jr. (Rep., N.Y.)

ORGANIZATION AND ADMINISTRATION

The Senate gave its members a 15 percent pay raise, from $60,662.50 to $69,800, making salaries for members of the Senate equal to salaries for members of the House. Also like the House, the Senate imposed a 30 percent of salary ($20,940) cap on outside income from honoraria for speeches, etc. [See note 5, p. xxix]

MAJOR LEGISLATION PASSED

Appropriations for 1985: Through most of 1984, Congress found it impossible to agree on a variety of appropriations measures. The Democrats and Republicans in Congress could not reach a consensus with the Reagan administration on matters concerning agriculture, crime, the defense budget, the post office, and transportation. Without appropriations, the federal government itself could not operate. By October 1, 1984, the start of fiscal year 1985, Congress was forced to resort to a series of four interim funding bills in order to keep the government from shutting down. Even so, Reagan was forced to send 500,000 government workers home on October 4, since the government technically was broke. On October 11 Congress reached agreement on a massive $470 billion appropriations bill, which included $274.4 billion for the fiscal 1985 defense budget.

Drunk Driving: In response to public pressure for a crackdown on young people driving while intoxicated, Congress acted to withhold some federal highway funds from states that didn't raise the drinking age to 21 by 1987. The effectiveness of this measure was stalled for several months, however, due to the ongoing 1985 appropriations impasse. [See Appropriations for 1985, above]

El Salvador and Nicaragua: In an "urgent" supplemental appropriations bill, Congress authorized aid to El Salvador that would amount to $196,550,000 for measures designed to defeat the Communist rebels. In the same bill, Congress authorized approximately $21 million in aid to the Nicaraguan contras (anti-Communist rebels fighting the government of Nicaragua).

Martin Luther King Jr. Holiday: Congress made the third Monday in January a federal holiday to honor Rev. Martin Luther King Jr., the famous African American civil rights leader of the 1960s who fought for equal rights and believed in nonviolent change.

MX Missile: Congress approved $2.1 billion for the new and controversial MX Missile program. The MX was designed to carry 10 very precisely targeted nuclear warheads into Soviet territory. Such precisely targeted warheads could destroy Soviet missile silos and possibly destabilize the

superpower stalemate by giving the U.S. a perceived incentive to attack first. This funding was contained within the fiscal 1984 defense bill.

Social Security: Congress raised the age for receiving Social Security benefits from 65 to 67, to be phased in between 2000 and 2027. In the same act, Congress reformed the mechanism for Medicare reimbursements to hospitals, extended supplemental unemployment benefits for an additional six months, and increased Supplemental Security Income benefits.

Strategic Defense Initiative: In a speech on March 23, 1983, President Reagan called for an antimissile defense system known as SDI or "Star Wars" to be based on a space security system. Reagan promised to share any new technology with the Soviet Union in an effort to end the nuclear stalemate known as mutually assured destruction (MAD). Congress approved $1.4 billion for SDI as part of the defense budget in the 1985 appropriations vote. [See Appropriations for 1985, above]

FAILED LEGISLATION

Additional Economic Stimulus: Senate Democrats tried to increase the amount of federal spending aimed at creating 280,000 new jobs at a cost of $1.7 billion, but the Senate rejected their initiative. [See Table of Key Votes, below]

Nuclear Freeze: The House passed a resolution calling for a joint U.S.-Soviet freeze on the testing of nuclear weapons, but the resolution died in a motion to table, or kill, the bill in the Senate. [See Table of Key Votes, below]

RELATIONS WITH THE PRESIDENT

President Ronald W. Reagan pursued a conservative agenda with Congress, one that was not always popular either with Congress or the public. However, Reagan successfully projected the image of a determined leader, and was nicknamed the "great communicator." Although he failed to deliver his pledge to balance the budget, most of

TABLE OF KEY VOTES

Senate

Subject of Vote	Date of Vote	For			Against		
		D	R	Total	D	R	Total
Additional Economic Stimulus Defeated	March 11, 1983	32	2	34	46	7	53
Social Security Revised	March 23, 1983	41	47	88	3	6	9
Abortion Amendment Defeated	June 28, 1983	15	34	49	31	19	50
Martin Luther King Jr. Holiday Passed	October 19, 1983	41	37	78	4	18	22
Nuclear Freeze Resolution Killed (this was a motion to table, or kill, the bill)	October 31, 1983	12	46	58	33	7	0
MX Missile Approved	November 8, 1983	36	50	86	5	1	6
School Prayer Amendment Rejected (failed: two-thirds majority required)	March 20, 1984	19	37	56	26	18	44
El Salvador and Nicaragua Aid Passed	April 5, 1984	23	53	76	18	1	19
Drinking Age Raised	June 26, 1984	Passed by voice vote					
1985 Appropriations Passed	October 11, 1984	35	43	78	6	5	1

House

Subject of Vote	Date of Vote	For			Against		
		D	R	Total	D	R	Total
Social Security Revised	March 9, 1983	76	152	228	188	14	202
Nuclear Freeze Resolution Killed	May 4, 1983	218	60	278	43	106	149
Martin Luther King Holiday Passed	August 2, 1983	249	89	338	13	77	90
MX Missile Approved	November 2, 1983	176	152	328	86	11	97
Equal Rights Amendment Rejected (failed: two-thirds majority required)	November 15, 1983	225	53	278	38	109	147
El Salvador and Nicaragua Aid Passed	May 10, 1984	95	116	211	160	46	206
Drinking Age Raised	June 7, 1984	208	89	297	19	54	73
1985 Appropriations Passed	October 10, 1984	Standing vote*		252	Standing vote*		60

[See note 7, p. xxix]

*A standing vote is essentially a head count, not broken down by party. The for and against votes are tallied by having all the persons voting "yes" stand and be counted, and then all the persons voting "no" stand and be counted.

his other legislative initiatives were ultimately passed by Congress.

Reagan vetoed 24 bills during the 98th Congress. None of these vetoes was of historic significance.

NOMINATIONS, APPOINTMENTS, AND CONFIRMATIONS

The Judiciary: There were no significant nominations, appointments or confirmations in the federal judiciary during the 98th Congress.

The Executive Branch: On January 25, 1983, President Reagan nominated Elizabeth H. Dole to succeed Andrew L. Lewis Jr. as secretary of transportation, and on February 1, 1983, the Senate confirmed Dole by a vote of 97 to 0. On February 18, 1983, Reagan nominated Margaret M. Heckler to succeed Richard S. Schweiker as secretary of health and human services, and on March 7, 1983, the Senate confirmed Heckler by a vote of 82 to 3. Finally, on October 19, 1983, Reagan nominated William P. Clark to succeed James G. Watt as secretary of the Interior, and on November 18, 1983, the Senate confirmed Clark by a vote of 71 to 18.

IMPEACHMENTS

None.

CONSTITUTIONAL AMENDMENTS

None. In the Senate, there was a proposed constitutional amendment to permit antiabortion legislation and another to permit school prayer, but both failed to pass. In the House, Speaker Thomas P. "Tip" O'Neill Jr. tried to revive the long dormant Equal Rights Amendment for women, but it failed to pass.

FURTHER READING

Johnson, Haynes Bonner. *Sleepwalking Through History: America in the Reagan Years*. New York: Anchor Books, 1992.

O'Neill, Thomas P., with William Novak. *Man of the House; The Life and Political Memoirs of Speaker Tip O'Neill*. New York: Random House, 1987.

Schaller, Michael. *Reckoning With Reagan: America and its President in the 1980s*. New York: Oxford University Press, 1992.

The 99th Congress

JANUARY 3, 1985-JANUARY 3, 1987

First Session: January 3, 1985-December 20, 1985
Second Session: January 21, 1986-October 18, 1986

In the 1984 elections for the 99th Congress, the Republicans lost 2 seats in the Senate, reducing their majority from 55 to 53 of the 100 seats. The Democrats gained 2 seats, raising their total to 47. In the House, the Democrats lost 16 seats, reducing their majority from 268 to 252 of the 435 seats. The Republicans gained 16 seats, giving them a total of 182. One seat was vacant, and would ultimately be taken by a Democrat before the end of this Congress. [See note 3, p. xxix]

BACKGROUND

Ronald W. Reagan was inaugurated for his second term as the 40th president of the United States on January 20, 1985. During the presidential elections of 1984, Reagan had benefited from the recovery of the American economy after the recession of the early 1980s without a return of the high inflation of the 1970s. In 1985 the economy continued to grow, inflation remained below four percent, and unemployment dropped below seven percent. The national trade deficit, however, rose to a record $150 billion, due in large part to American industry's inability to compete with foreign exporters, particularly the Japanese. The U.S. became a debtor nation for the first time since World War I, owing more to foreign nations than foreign nations owed to the U.S. The federal budget deficit also reached a record level, rising over $200 billion. Reagan by now

largely had abandoned his promise to eliminate the federal budget deficit during his presidency, but he did sign the Gramm-Rudman-Hollings deficit reduction plan that Congress enacted on December 11, 1985. Gramm-Rudman-Hollings unsuccessfully attempted to eliminate the budget deficit by fiscal 1991 through a series of automatic spending cuts.

In foreign affairs, 1985 was a turnaround year in U.S.-Soviet relations. The Soviet Union's new leader, Communist Party General Secretary Mikhail Gorbachev, was committed to achieving better relations with the United States. Gorbachev initiated two major new policies known in Russian as *glasnost* and *perestroika*. Glasnost meant openness, an end to the Soviet repression of free expression and Western ideas. Perestroika meant restructuring, or reforming the stagnant Soviet economy, which included a decentralization of economic planning. Until Gorbachev's rise to power and his new policies, U.S.-Soviet relations during Reagan's presidency generally had been tense and hostile. One of the first moves toward the end of the cold war occurred on November 20, 1985, when Reagan and Gorbachev met in Geneva, Switzerland, in order to discuss arms reductions and set a schedule for future talks.

In 1986 economic growth was low but steady, unemployment continued to decline, and inflation was at its lowest level in over 20 years. The national trade deficit was nearly $170 billion, however, and the federal government went $220 billion deeper into debt. On April 3, 1986, the national debt of the federal government reached $2 trillion, double the national debt of just five years before. During 1986 Congress approved a comprehensive overhaul of the federal internal revenue code, whose rules and regulations determine the amount of tax revenue raised by the federal government. Personal income tax rates were lowered, but many loopholes and deductions were eliminated in order to offset the loss of revenue.

In foreign affairs, 1986 was generally a good year for the Reagan administration. On April 14 the U.S. launched air strikes against military installations in the North African nation of Libya. For some time, Libya had been supporting terrorist attacks against Americans abroad. Libya also had attacked American military operations in the international waters of the Gulf of Sidra, along the Libyan coast, which Libya claimed were its territorial waters. The air strike severely damaged Libya's military capability, temporarily ended Libya's anti-American provocations, and strengthened Reagan's political image as a strong leader.

SENATE LEADERSHIP

Vice President: George Herbert Walker Bush [See biographical note in 97th Congress]

President Pro Tempore: J. Strom Thurmond (Rep., S.C.) [See biographical note in 97th Congress]

Majority Leader: Robert Dole (Rep., Kans.) first had been elected to Congress as a representative to the 87th Congress and first had been elected to the Senate in 1968. He became the leader of the Senate Republicans in the 99th Congress. Dole was a tough and effective leader, and a prominent figure in Republican Party presidential politics.

Majority Whip: Alan K. Simpson (Rep., Wyo.)

Minority Leader: Robert C. Byrd (Dem., W.Va.) [See biographical note in 95th Congress]

Minority Whip: Alan Cranston (Dem., Calif.)

Chairman and Ranking Minority Members of Key Committees:

Committee on Agriculture, Nutrition, and Forestry: Chairman: Jesse A. Helms (Rep., N.C.); Ranking Minority Member: Edward Zorinsky (Dem., Neb.)

Committee on Appropriations: Chairman: Mark O. Hatfield (Rep., Ore.); Ranking Minority Member: John C. Stennis (Dem., Miss.)

Committee on Armed Services: Chairman: Barry M. Goldwater (Rep., Ariz.); Ranking Minority Member: Samuel A. Nunn (Dem., Ga.)

Committee on Banking, Housing, and Urban Affairs: Chairman: Jake Garn (Rep., Utah); Ranking Minority Member: William Proxmire (Dem., Wis.)

Committee on the Budget: Chairman: Pete V. Domenici (Rep., N.M.); Ranking Minority Member: Lawton M. Chiles Jr. (Dem., Fla.)

Committee on Commerce, Science, and Transportation: Chairman: John C. Danforth (Rep., Mo.); Ranking Minority Member: Ernest F. Hollings (Dem., S.C.)

Committee on Energy and Natural Resources: Chairman: James A. McClure (Rep., Idaho); Ranking Minority Member: J. Bennett Johnston Jr. (Dem., La.)

Committee on Environment and Public Works: Chairman: Robert T. Stafford (Rep., Vt.); Ranking Minority Member: Lloyd M. Bentsen Jr. (Dem., Tex.)

Committee on Finance: Chairman: Robert W. Packwood (Rep., Ore.); Ranking Minority Member: Russell B. Long (Dem., La.)

Committee on Foreign Relations: Chairman: Richard G. Lugar (Rep., Ind.); Ranking Minority Member: Claiborne D. Pell (Dem., R.I.)

Committee on the Judiciary: Chairman: J. Strom Thurmond (Rep., S.C.); Ranking Minority Member: Joseph R. Biden Jr. (Dem., Del.)

Committee on Labor and Human Resources:

C H R O N O L O G Y

January 3, 1985:	The 99th Congress and the first session begin. President Reagan nominates Edwin Meese III to succeed William French Smith as attorney general.
January 18, 1985:	President Reagan nominates James A. Baker III to succeed Donald T. Regan as secretary of the Treasury, William J. Bennett to succeed Terrel H. Bell as secretary of education, and John S. Herrington to succeed Donald P. Hodel as secretary of energy.
January 22, 1985:	President Reagan nominates Hodel to succeed William P. Clark as secretary of the Interior.
January 29, 1985:	The Senate confirms Baker.
February 6, 1985:	The Senate confirms Bennett, Herrington, and Hodel.
February 23, 1985:	The Senate confirms Meese.
March 6, 1985:	President Reagan vetoes an emergency farm credit bill.
April 17, 1985:	President Reagan nominates William E. Brock III to succeed Raymond J. Donovan as secretary of labor.
April 26, 1985:	The Senate confirms Brock.
July 11, 1985:	Congress lifts restrictions on covert operations in Angola. Congress passes legislation imposing economic sanctions on South Africa.
July 24, 1985:	A line-item veto initiative dies in the Senate.
September 10, 1985:	School prayer legislation dies in the Senate.
November 1, 1985:	Congress passes the Gramm-Rudman-Hollings budget controls.
December 4, 1985:	President Reagan nominates Otis R. Bowen to succeed Margaret M. Heckler as secretary of health and human services.
December 12, 1985:	The Senate confirms Bowen.

(Continued on p. 509)

Chairman: Orrin G. Hatch (Rep., Utah); Ranking Minority Member: Edward M. Kennedy (Dem., Mass.)

Committee on Rules and Administration: Chairman: Charles M. Mathias Jr. (Rep., Md.); Ranking Minority Member: Wendell H. Ford (Dem., Ky.)

HOUSE LEADERSHIP

Speaker of the House: Thomas Phillip "Tip" O'Neill Jr. (Dem., Mass.) [See biographical note in 95th Congress]

Majority Leader: James C. Wright (Dem., Tex.)

Majority Whip: Thomas S. Foley (Dem., Wash.)

Minority Leader: Robert H. Michel (Rep., Ill.)

Minority Whip: Trent Lott (Rep., Miss.)

Chairman and Ranking Minority Members of Key Committees:

Committee on Agriculture: Chairman: Kika de la Garza (Dem., Tex.); Ranking Minority Member: Edward R. Madigan (Rep., Ill.)

Committee on Appropriations: Chairman: Jamie L. Whitten (Dem., Miss.); Ranking Minority Member: Silvio O. Conte (Rep., Mass.)

Committee on Armed Services: Chairman: Le.

(Continued from p. 508)

C H R O N O L O G Y

December 20, 1985:	The first session ends.
January 21, 1986:	The second session begins.
February 24, 1986:	President Reagan nominates Richard E. Lyng to succeed John R. Block as secretary of agriculture.
March 6, 1986:	The Senate confirms Lyng.
March 25, 1986:	A proposed constitutional amendment requiring a balanced budget dies in the Senate.
April 10, 1986:	Congress acts to weaken existing gun control legislation.
May 7, 1986:	President Reagan vetoes legislation blocking an arms sale to Saudi Arabia.
June 5, 1986:	The Senate fails to override Reagan's veto.
June 17, 1986:	President Reagan nominates Supreme Court Justice William H. Rehnquist to be the new chief justice when Warren E. Burger retires and nominates Antonin Scalia to be a new justice.
June 24, 1986:	Congress passes tax reform legislation.
September 17, 1986:	The Senate confirms Rehnquist and Scalia.
September 24, 1986:	Congress passes legislation privatizing Conrail.
September 26, 1986:	Supreme Court Chief Justice Warren E. Burger retires.
October 9, 1986:	Congress passes immigration reforms.
October 18, 1986:	The second session ends.
January 3, 1987:	The 99th Congress ends.

[See note 6, p. xxix]

Aspin (Dem., Wis.); Ranking Minority Member: William L. Dickinson (Rep., Ala.)

Committee on Banking, Finance, and Urban Affairs: Chairman: Fernand J. St. Germain (Dem., R.I.); Ranking Minority Member: Chalmers P. Wylie (Rep., Ohio)

Committee on the Budget: Chairman: William H. Gray III (Dem., Pa.); Ranking Minority Member: Delbert L. Latta (Rep., Ohio)

Committee on Education and Labor: Chairman: Augustus F. Hawkins (Dem., Calif.); Ranking Minority Member: James M. Jeffords (Rep., Vt.)

Committee on Energy and Commerce: Chairman:

John D. Dingell Jr. (Dem., Mich.); Ranking Minority Member: James T. Broyhill (Rep., N.C.) until July 13, 1986, when he resigned. Norman F. Lent (Rep., N.Y.) became the next ranking minority member effective the same day.

Committee on Foreign Affairs: Chairman: Dante B. Fascell (Dem., Fla.); Ranking Minority Member: William S. Broomfield (Rep., Mich.)

Committee on Interior and Insular Affairs: Chairman: Morris K. Udall (Dem., Ariz.); Ranking Minority Member: Donald E. Young (Rep., Alaska)

Committee on the Judiciary: Chairman: Peter W. Rodino Jr. (Dem., N.J.); Ranking Minority

TABLE OF KEY VOTES

Senate

Subject of Vote	Date of Vote	For D	For R	For Total	Against D	Against R	Against Total
Angola Aid Passed	May 15, 1985	35	40	75	11	8	19
Gun Control Weakened	July 9, 1985	30	49	79	13	2	15
South Africa Sanctions Passed	July 11, 1985	44	36	80	0	12	12
Line-Item Veto Defeated (failed: 60 votes needed to cut off debate)	July 24, 1985	12	46	58	33	7	40
School Prayer Bill Killed (this was a motion to table, or kill, the bill)	September 10, 1985	38	24	62	8	28	36
Immigration Reform Passed	September 19, 1985	28	41	69	19	11	30
Budget Control Bill Passed	October 10, 1985	13	38	51	29	8	37
Balanced Budget Amendment Defeated (failed: two-thirds majority required)	March 25, 1986	23	43	66	24	10	34
Saudi Arabia Arms Veto Override Defeated (override failed: two-thirds majority required)	June 5, 1986	42	24	66	5	29	34
Tax Reform Passed	June 24, 1986	44	53	97	3	0	3
Conrail Privatized	September 19, 1986	38	50	88	7	0	7

House

Subject of Vote	Date of Vote	For D	For R	For Total	Against D	Against R	Against Total
South Africa Sanctions Passed	June 5, 1985	239	56	295	6	121	127
Angola Aid Passed	July 11, 1985	Passed by voice vote					
Budget Control Bill Passed	November 1, 1985	248	1	249	2	178	180
Tax Reform Passed	December 17, 1985	Passed by voice vote					
Gun Control Weakened	April 10, 1986	131	161	292	115	15	130
Conrail Privatized	September 24, 1986	210	99	309	35	71	106
Immigration Reform Passed	October 9, 1986	168	62	230	61	105	166

[See note 7, p. xxix]

Member: Hamilton Fish Jr. (Rep., N.Y.)

Committee on Public Works and Transportation: Chairman: James J. Howard (Dem., N.J.); Ranking Minority Member: Gene Snyder (Rep., Ky.)

Committee on Rules: Chairman: Claude D. Pepper (Dem., Fla.); Ranking Minority Member: James H. Quillen (Rep., Tenn.)

Committee on Ways and Means: Chairman: Daniel D. Rostenkowski (Dem., Ill.); Ranking Minority Member: John J. Duncan (Rep., Tenn.)

ORGANIZATION AND ADMINISTRATION

The Senate decided to permit TV and radio coverage of its floor proceedings, something that the House had permitted for several years but the Senate had been reluctant to allow. [See note 5, p. xxix]

MAJOR LEGISLATION PASSED

Angola: Congress lifted restrictions on covert CIA aid to the UNITA (Union for the Total Independence of Angola) rebels, who were fighting a pro-Soviet government. The lifting of restrictions was part of the fiscal 1986 foreign assistance authorization bill.

Budget Control: Increasing concern over the budget deficit led Congress to enact a novel form of budgetary control, known as Gramm-Rudman-Hollings after Senate sponsors Phil Gramm (Rep., Tex.), Warren B. Rudman (Rep., N.H.), and Ernest F. Hollings (Dem., S.C.). The budget deficit was supposed to be reduced step by step until fiscal 1991, when the budget would be balanced. If the required progress was not made according to a predetermined schedule, a series of automatic spending cuts would be triggered. Although Gramm-Rudman-Hollings was important and ground-breaking legislation, it was a failure. Due to loopholes in the law and problems with the constitutionality of the automatic spending cut process, the budget was not balanced by 1991.

Conrail: Congress decided to privatize Conrail, the federally owned and operated railroad formed from bankrupt railroads in the 1970s. The government was authorized to make a public offering of Conrail stock to the public. This measure was part of a fiscal 1987 budget reconciliation bill designed to lower the deficit by $11.7 billion.

Gun Control: In a victory for the NRA and congressional delegations from western states, Congress weakened the Gun Control Act of 1968's restrictions on the interstate sale of handguns, rifles, and shotguns.

Immigration: Congress substantially overhauled the immigration laws, imposing civil fines and criminal penalties on employers who knowingly hire illegal aliens. However, Congress authorized amnesty for illegal aliens who had continuously resided in the U.S. before January 1, 1982.

South Africa: Congress imposed economic sanctions on South Africa, which was becoming an international pariah for refusing to end the system of black and white segregation called *apartheid.*

Tax Reform: The 1986 tax reform act was the first complete overhaul of the federal tax code since 1954. Congress lowered and simplified the income tax brackets while simultaneously ending many loopholes and deductions.

FAILED LEGISLATION

Line-Item Veto: The veto power given to the president by the Constitution permits the president to veto an entire bill, but not specific items within an otherwise acceptable bill. The theory behind the line-item veto always has been that an all-or-nothing veto power forces a president to sign bills containing wasteful spending or pork-barrel projects that he or she doesn't have the power to veto separately. (Most state governors hve line-item veto powers.) Legislation giving the president the line-item veto died in the Senate when a vote to cut off debate, a moved called "invoking cloture," failed to get the necessary 60 votes. [See Table of Key Votes, above]

School Prayer: Congress has the power to say what types of cases may be heard by the federal courts. There was an initiative to prevent school prayer cases from going to federal court in order to allow localities to permit school prayer without fear of federal court intervention, but it died in the Senate when the Senate voted to table, or kill, the bill. [See Table of Key Votes, above]

RELATIONS WITH THE PRESIDENT

The increasingly prosperous domestic economy and Reagan's foreign policy victories made the first Congress of his second term a successful one, with the administration's legislative agenda getting through Congress largely as expected. The massive increase in the budget deficit and national debt were not yet significant political issues, and the failure of Gramm-Rudman-Hollings [See Major Legislation, Budget Control] was not yet a political liability for Reagan.

Reagan vetoed 18 bills during the 99th Congress. Two vetoes were particularly significant. First, on March 6, 1985, Reagan vetoed an emergency farm credit bill designed to help financially strapped farmers, on the grounds that it would add billions to the budget deficit. Neither the House nor the Senate attempted to override the veto. Second, when Reagan approved the sale of military equipment to Saudi Arabia, Congress passed legislation blocking the sale. On May 7, 1986, Reagan vetoed that legislation. On June 5, 1986, an initiative in the Senate to override the veto failed. [See Table of Key Votes, above]

NOMINATIONS, APPOINTMENTS, AND CONFIRMATIONS

The Judiciary: On September 26, 1986, Supreme Court Chief Justice Warren E. Burger retired. Aware of Burger's impending resignation, President Ronald W. Reagan had on June 17, 1986, nominated Supreme Court Justice William H. Rehnquist to be the new chief justice, and Antonin Scalia to fill the vacancy on the Court after Burger's retirement. On September 17, 1986, the Senate approved Rehnquist's promotion to

chief justice by a 65 to 33 vote, and confirmed Scalia by a 98 to 0 vote.

The Executive Branch: On January 3, 1985, President Reagan nominated Edwin Meese III to succeed William French Smith as attorney general, and on February 23, 1985, the Senate confirmed Meese by a vote of 63 to 31. On January 18, 1985, Reagan nominated James A. Baker III to succeed Donald T. Regan as secretary of the Treasury, William J. Bennett to succeed Terrel H. Bell as secretary of education, and John S. Herrington to succeed Donald P. Hodel as secretary of energy. On January 29, 1985, the Senate confirmed Baker by a vote of 95 to 0, and on February 6, 1985, the Senate confirmed Bennett by a vote of 93 to 0 and Herrington by a vote of 93 to 1. On January 22, 1985, Reagan nominated Hodel to succeed William P. Clark as secretary of the Interior, and on February 6, 1985, the Senate confirmed Hodel by a vote of 93 to 1. On April 17, 1985, Reagan nominated William E. Brock III to succeed Raymond J. Donovan as secretary of labor, and on April 26, 1985, the Senate confirmed Brock by voice vote. On December 4, 1985, Reagan nominated Otis R. Bowen to succeed Margaret M. Heckler as secretary of health and human services, and on December 12, 1985, the Senate confirmed Bowen by a vote of 93 to 2. Finally, on February 24, 1986, Reagan nominated Richard E. Lyng to succeed John R. Block as secretary of agriculture, and on March 6, 1986, the Senate confirmed Lyng by a vote of 95 to 2.

IMPEACHMENTS

On October 9, 1986, the Senate removed federal Judge Harry E. Claiborne from office. Claiborne had been convicted of tax fraud in 1984 and already was serving a prison sentence, but until Congress removed him from office he continued to collect his $78,700 annual salary while in jail.

CONSTITUTIONAL AMENDMENTS

None. The Senate narrowly rejected a proposed constitutional amendment requiring a balanced budget. [See Table of Key Votes, above]

FURTHER READING

Johnson, Haynes Bonner. *Sleepwalking Through History: America in the Reagan Years*. New York: Anchor Books, 1992.

O'Neill, Thomas P., with William Novak. *Man of the House: The Life and Political Memoirs of Speaker Tip O'Neill*. New York: Random House, 1987.

Schaller, Michael. *Reckoning With Reagan: America and its President in the 1980s*. New York: Oxford University Press, 1992.

The 100th Congress

JANUARY 3, 1987-JANUARY 3, 1989

First Session: *January 6, 1987-December 22, 1987*
Second Session: *January 25, 1988-October 22, 1988*

In the 1986 elections for the 100th Congress, the Democrats gained 8 seats in the Senate to create a new majority of 55 of the 100 seats. The Republicans lost 8 seats, reducing their total to 45. In the House, the Democrats gained 6 seats, increasing their majority from 252 to 258 of the 435 seats. The Republicans lost 5 seats, leaving them with a total of 177. [See note 3, p. xxix]

BACKGROUND

By the 100th Congress, President Reagan had established himself as a strong president. He was the first president to complete two full terms since Dwight D. Eisenhower (January 20, 1953-January 20, 1961). Reagan had succeeded in getting his principal legislative priorities through Congress, such as federal income tax cuts and tax code reforms, in addition to increasing military spending. Further, Reagan's military successes in Grenada and against Libya, and his now improved relations with reformist Soviet leader Mikhail Gorbachev, seemed to support his conservative "peace through strength" approach to foreign policy. This impression was reinforced by the situation in Afghanistan, a poor, mountainous and isolated country in Central Asia where the Soviet military was trying to prop up a puppet government friendly to the Soviet Union. Under Reagan, the U.S. had been financing Afghan rebels fighting the Soviets, and the

cost of the protracted guerrilla war finally was making the Soviets consider leaving Afghanistan. By the end of 1987, Reagan and Gorbachev had agreed upon the terms of a treaty [See Major Legislation, below] to reduce U.S. and Soviet nuclear stockpiles.

During 1987 the American economy continued to grow for the sixth consecutive year, unemployment was under six percent, and inflation was low. By the end of the year, however, some of the underlying problems of the American economy became apparent.

First, there had been over-speculation on Wall Street. Market indexes such as the Dow Jones Industrial Average, one of the most widely followed indexes, reached record highs. Moreover, financial markets were vulnerable, because advances in telecommunications and computer technology had linked Wall Street to stock markets around the world and made possible computerized stock trading. On Friday, October 16 the stock market declined after months of advances. The decline caused financial institutions and computer stock programs to initiate further sales, which caused a ripple effect throughout the world and gathered momentum while American stock markets were closed for the weekend. On Monday, October 19 orders to sell securities from throughout the U.S. and around the world hit Wall Street, which suffered its largest one-day loss in history. The Dow Jones declined

22.6 percent in one day, far exceeding the 12.8 percent drop on October 29, 1929, that had precipitated the Great Depression. The stock market recoverd quickly, and there was no new depression, but the crash had caused hundreds of billions of dollars in paper losses.

Second, the trade deficit was now nearly $200 billion a year, making it the fifth consecutive year that the value of imports had exceeded exports by a record level.

In 1988 relations with the Soviet Union steadily improved, and there was progress in arms reduction negotiations. Gorbachev's reforms were opening the Soviet system and helping to end the cold war, but now the people of Russia, other Soviet nationalities, and the countries of Eastern Europe were free to vent decades of discontent. The result was growing internal unrest with the Soviet Union, which was aggravated by the failure of Gorbachev's economic reforms. In domestic affairs, the U.S. was experiencing a new public health challenge. The Acquired Immune Deficiency Syndrome (AIDS), which spread primarily by sexual contact, was expanding rapidly and no longer was limited to intravenous drug users and homosexuals. Finally, the Iran-Contra affair, involving the covert sale of arms to Iran in order to woo Iranian "moderates" and also finance the anti-Communist (contra) rebels in Nicaragua, was becoming a significant executive branch embarrassment.

SENATE LEADERSHIP

Vice President: George Herbert Walker Bush [See biographical note in 99th Congress]

President Pro Tempore: John Cornelius Stennis (Dem., Miss.) first had been elected to the Senate in 1947. The 100th Congress was his only Congress as president pro tem.

Majority Leader: Robert C. Byrd (Dem., W.Va.) [See biographical note in 95th Congress]

Majority Whip: Alan Cranston (Dem., Calif.)

Minority Leader: Robert Dole (Rep., Kans.) [See biographical note in 99th Congress]

Minority Whip: Alan K. Simpson (Rep., Wyo.)

Chairman and Ranking Minority Members of Key Committees:

Committee on Agriculture, Nutrition, and Forestry: Chairman: Patrick J. Leahy (Dem., Vt.); Ranking Minority Member: Jesse A. Helms (Rep., N.C.), until January 20, 1987, when he became the ranking minority member on the Senate Foreign Relations Committee. Richard G. Lugar (Rep., Ind.) became the next ranking minority member effective the same day.

Committee on Appropriations: Chairman: John C. Stennis (Dem., Miss.); Ranking Minority Member: Mark O. Hatfield (Rep., Ore.)

Committee on Armed Services: Chairman: Samuel A. Nunn (Dem., Ga.); Ranking Minority Member: John W. Warner (Rep., Va.)

Committee on Banking, Housing, and Urban Affairs: Chairman: William Proxmire (Dem., Wis.); Ranking Minority Member: Jake Garn (Rep., Utah)

Committee on the Budget: Chairman: Lawton M. Chiles Jr. (Dem., Fla.); Ranking Minority Member: Pete V. Domenici (Rep., N.M.)

Committee on Commerce, Science, and Transportation: Chairman: Ernest F. Hollings (Dem., S.C.); Ranking Minority Member: John C. Danforth (Rep., Mo.)

Committee on Energy and Natural Resources: Chairman: J. Bennett Johnston Jr. (Dem., La.); Ranking Minority Member: James A. McClure (Rep., Idaho)

Committee on Environment and Public Works: Chairman: Quentin N. Burdick (Dem., N.D.); Ranking Minority Member: Robert T. Stafford (Rep., Vt.)

Committee on Finance: Chairman: Lloyd M. Bentsen Jr. (Dem., Tex.); Ranking Minority Member: Robert W. Packwood (Rep., Ore.)

Committee on Foreign Relations: Chairman: Claiborne D. Pell (Dem., R.I.); Ranking Minority

Member: Richard G. Lugar (Rep., Ind.) until January 20, 1987, when he became the ranking minority member on the Senate Agriculture, Nutrition, and Forestry Committee. Jesse A. Helms (Rep., N.C.) became the next ranking minority member effective the same day.

Committee on the Judiciary: Chairman: Joseph R. Biden Jr. (Dem., Del.); Ranking Minority Member: J. Strom Thurmond (Rep., S.C.)

Committee on Labor and Human Resources: Chairman: Edward M. Kennedy (Dem., Mass.); Ranking Minority Member: Orrin G. Hatch (Rep., Utah)

Committee on Rules and Administration: Chairman: Wendell H. Ford (Dem., Ky.); Ranking Minority Member: Theodore F. Stevens (Rep., Alaska)

HOUSE LEADERSHIP

Speaker of the House: James Claude Wright Jr. (Dem., Tex.) first had been elected to Congress in the 84th Congress and served as Speaker in the 100th and 101st Congresses. Scandals forced him to resign during the 101st Congress.

Majority Leader: Thomas S. Foley (Dem., Wash.)

Majority Whip: Tony Coelho (Dem., Calif.)

Minority Leader: Robert H. Michel (Rep., Ill.)

Minority Whip: Trent Lott (Rep., Miss.)

Chairman and Ranking Minority Members of Key Committees:

Committee on Agriculture: Chairman: Kika de la Garza (Dem., Tex.); Ranking Minority Member: Edward R. Madigan (Rep., Ill.)

Committee on Appropriations: Chairman: Jamie L. Whitten (Dem., Miss.); Ranking Minority Member: Silvio O. Conte (Rep., Mass.)

Committee on Armed Services: Chairman: Les Aspin (Dem., Wis.); Ranking Minority Member: William L. Dickinson (Rep., Ala.)

Committee on Banking, Finance, and Urban Affairs: Chairman: Fernand J. St. Germain (Dem., R.I.); Ranking Minority Member: Chalmers P. Wylie (Rep., Ohio)

Committee on the Budget: Chairman: William H. Gray III (Dem., Pa.); Ranking Minority Member: Delbert L. Latta (Rep., Ohio)

Committee on Education and Labor: Chairman: Augustus F. Hawkins (Dem., Calif.); Ranking Minority Member: James M. Jeffords (Rep., Vt.)

Committee on Energy and Commerce: Chairman: John D. Dingell Jr. (Dem., Mich.); Ranking Minority Member: Norman F. Lent (Rep., N.Y.)

Committee on Foreign Affairs: Chairman: Dante B. Fascell (Dem., Fla.); Ranking Minority Member: William S. Broomfield (Rep., Mich.)

Committee on Interior and Insular Affairs: Chairman: Morris K. Udall (Dem., Ariz.); Ranking Minority Member: Donald E. Young (Rep., Alaska)

Committee on the Judiciary: Chairman: Peter W. Rodino Jr. (Dem., N.J.); Ranking Minority Member: Hamilton Fish Jr. (Rep., N.Y.)

Committee on Public Works and Transportation: Chairman: James J. Howard (Dem., N.J.), who died on March 25, 1988. Glenn M. Anderson (Dem., Calif.) became the next chairman effective April 20, 1988. Ranking Minority Member: John Paul Hammerschmidt (Rep., Ark.)

Committee on Rules: Chairman: Claude D. Pepper (Dem., Fla.); Ranking Minority Member: James H. Quillen (Rep., Tenn.)

Committee on Ways and Means: Chairman: Daniel D. Rostenkowski (Dem., Ill.); Ranking Minority Member: John J. Duncan (Rep., Tenn.), who died on June 2, 1988. William R. Archer (Rep., Tex.) became the next ranking minority member effective the same day.

ORGANIZATION AND ADMINISTRATION

No developments of historical significance. [See note 5, p. xxix]

C H R O N O L O G Y

January 3, 1987:	The 100th Congress begins.
January 6, 1987:	The first session begins.
June 26, 1987:	Supreme Court Justice Lewis F. Powell Jr. retires.
July 21, 1987:	Congress passes tough new trade legislation.
September 9, 1987:	President Reagan nominates C. William Verity Jr. to succeed Malcolm Baldrige as secretary of commerce.
October 2, 1987:	Congress passes the fiscal 1988 defense bill, which contains a SALT II compliance requirement.
October 13, 1987:	The Senate confirms Verity.
October 27, 1987:	Congress expands Medicare to include catastrophic medical coverage.
November 2, 1987:	President Reagan nominates James H. Burnley to succeed Elizabeth H. Dole as secretary of transportation.
November 3, 1987:	Congress passes an extension of the independent counsel law.
November 5, 1987:	President Reagan nominates Frank C. Carlucci to succeed Caspar W. Weinberger as secretary of defense.
November 20, 1987:	The Senate confirms Carlucci.
November 24, 1987:	After two unsuccessful other nominations, President Reagan nominates Anthony M. Kennedy to replace Justice Powell.
November 30, 1987:	The Senate confirms Burnley.
December 1, 1987:	President Reagan nominates Ann D. McLaughlin to succeed William E. Brock III as secretary of labor.
December 11, 1987:	The Senate confirms McLaughlin.
December 22, 1987:	The first session ends.
January 25, 1988:	The second session begins.
February 3, 1988:	The Senate confirms Kennedy.
April 20, 1988:	Congress approves reparations to Japanese Americans interned during World War II.
May 27, 1988:	The Senate approves the INF Treaty.
July 25, 1988:	President Reagan nominates Richard L. Thornburgh to succeed Edwin Meese III as attorney general.
July 28, 1988:	Congress passes drought relief legislation.
August 10, 1988:	President Reagan nominates Nicholas F. Brady to succeed James A. Baker III as secretary of the Treasury and Lauro F. Cavazos to succeed William J. Bennett as secretary of education.
August 11, 1988:	The Senate confirms Thornburgh.
September 14, 1988:	The Senate confirms Brady.
September 20, 1988:	The Senate confirms Cavazos.
October 13, 1988:	Congress passes AIDS legislation.
October 22, 1988:	The second session ends.
January 3, 1989:	The 100th Congress ends.

[See note 6, p. xxix]

TABLE OF KEY VOTES

Senate

Subject of Vote	Date of Vote	For			Against		
		D	R	Total	D	R	Total
Trade Legislation Passed	July 21, 1987	52	19	71	0	27	27
SALT II Limits Approved	October 2, 1987	52	4	56	2	40	42
Medicare Expanded	October 27, 1987	50	36	86	1	10	11
Independent Counsel Extended	November 3, 1987	51	34	85	0	10	0
Japanese American Reparations Passed	April 20, 1988	44	25	69	7	20	27
INF Treaty Approved	May 27, 1988	51	42	93	1	4	5
Agriculture Aid Passed	July 28, 1988	49	45	94	0	0	0
AIDS Legislation Passed	October 13, 1988	Passed by voice vote					

House

Subject of Vote	Date of Vote	For			Against		
		D	R	Total	D	R	Total
Trade Legislation Passed	April 30, 1987	247	43	290	6	131	137
SALT II Limits Approved	May 20, 1987	227	12	239	18	159	177
Medicare Expanded	July 22, 1987	241	61	302	14	113	127
Japanese American Reparations Passed	September 17, 1987	180	63	243	43	98	141
Independent Counsel Extended	October 21, 1987	238	84	322	3	84	7
Agriculture Aid Passed	July 28, 1988	228	140	368	6	23	29
AIDS Legislation Passed	October 13, 1988	Passed by voice vote					

[See note 7, p. xxix]

MAJOR LEGISLATION PASSED

Agriculture: Congress authorized $3.9 billion in emergency drought relief for American farmers who had suffered from regional droughts in 1983, 1986, and 1988.

AIDS: Congress finally addressed the AIDS (Acquired Immune Deficiency Syndrome) epidemic with significant legislation. In one act, Congress appropriated funds for AIDS education, blood testing, counseling, research, community and home-based health services, and so forth. However, conservatives were determined to eliminate any perceived acceptance of homosexuality in the law and claimed that provisions keeping blood tests confidential infringed on the rights of coworkers and others to know of a potential health risk. When Senator Jesse Helms (Rep., N.C.) threatened to filibuster the bill in the Senate, the bill's sponsors feared a national conservative uproar and rewrote the bill in order to eliminate the controversial portions and secure passage.

Independent Counsel: Congress passed a five-year extension, until December 31, 1992, of the arrangement whereby independent counsel could be designated to investigate wrongdoing by high government officials. Without this law, such investigations would revert to the Justice Department, which is itself an executive branch agency and possibly subject to pressure from the White House.

INF Treaty: The Senate approved the INF (Intermediate range Nuclear Force) Treaty between the U.S. and the Soviet Union, which banned the manufacture and testing of ground-based nuclear missiles with a range of between 300 and 3,400 miles. The treaty also provided for the destruction of 1,752 existing Soviet missiles and 859 existing U.S. missiles.

Japanese-American Reparations: After more than 40 years, Congress enacted legislation making a formal apology to the Japanese Americans held in detention camps during World War II. Further, a $20,000 tax-free payment was authorized for each of the roughly 60,000 detainees still alive.

Medicare: Congress expanded the Medicare system, which served over 30 million people, in order to provide coverage for catastrophic medical expenses. This expanded Medicare coverage was to be financed by the beneficiaries, however, through increased premiums and a small surtax on high-income Medicare participants. These changes proved to be very unpopular with the elderly, and Congress repealed the catastrophic coverage measure in the 101st Congress.

SALT II: Despite President Reagan's opposition to the Strategic Arms Limitation Treaty, which had been negotiated in the late 1970s but never approved by the Senate, Congress required compliance with the SALT II missile-building limitations. This was accomplished by incorporating the limitations into the fiscal 1988 defense authorization bill.

Trade: The rising trade deficit, which reached $156.2 billion in 1986, led Congress to pass trade legislation requiring the government to retaliate against foreign countries for allegedly unfair trade practices.

FAILED LEGISLATION

Campaign Finance Reform: Majority Leader Robert C. Byrd (Dem., W.Va.) tried to get a campaign finance reform bill through the Senate. The Republicans opposed the bill's spending caps, and successfully filibustered the bill to death, defeating 15 votes to invoke cloture (cut off debate) throughout the 100th Congress.

RELATIONS WITH THE PRESIDENT

President Reagan closed out his presidency with yet another series of foreign policy successes and continued economic prosperity. He left office as a popular president, and there is a school of thought that his vice president, George Bush, was elected president in the 1988 elections primarily out of continuing support for Reagan. However, this last Congress of the Reagan Administration showed some weaknesses in Reagan's authority. Congress overrode two important vetoes [See below], approved SALT II and AIDS measures that Reagan and the Republicans did not support [See Major Legislation, above], and resisted several Reagan nominees to fill a vacancy on the Supreme Court.

Reagan vetoed 19 bills during the 100th Congress. Two bills were particularly significant. First, on January 21, 1987, Reagan vetoed a clean water bill providing funds for local sewage plant construction. The bill was very popular with both business and environmental organizations, and Congress overrode Reagan's veto. The House voted 401 to 26 to override on February 3, 1987, and the Senate voted 86 to 14 to override the next day. Second, on March 16, 1988, Reagan vetoed a bill designed to overcome the Supreme Court's 1984 decision in *Grove City College v. Bell*, where the Court adopted a very narrow interpretation of four major civil rights laws. The bill would restore the broader, pre-*Grove* coverage of those laws. The Senate voted 73 to 24 to override on March 22, 1988, and the same day the House voted 292 to 133 to override as well.

NOMINATIONS, APPOINTMENTS, AND CONFIRMATIONS

The Judiciary: On June 26, 1987, Supreme Court Justice Lewis F. Powell Jr. retired. It took President Ronald W. Reagan three attempts to replace Powell. First, Reagan nominated Robert H. Bork on July 1, 1987, but the Senate voted against Bork's confirmation on October 23, 1987, by a 58 to 42 vote. Second, Reagan nominated Douglas Ginsburg on October 29, 1987, but Ginsburg withdrew on November 7, 1987, after media reports about his prior use of marijuana made Senate confirmation unlikely. Finally, Reagan nominated Anthony M. Kennedy on November 24, 1987, and the Senate confirmed Kennedy on February 3, 1988, by a 97 to 0 vote.

The Executive Branch: On September 9, 1987, President Reagan nominated C. William Verity Jr. to succeed Malcolm Baldrige as secretary of commerce, and on October 13, 1987, the Senate confirmed Verity by a vote of 84 to 11. On November 5, 1987, Reagan nominated Frank C. Carlucci to succeed Caspar W. Weinberger as secretary of defense, and the Senate confirmed Carlucci by a vote of 91 to 1 on November 20, 1987. Reagan nominated James H. Burnley to succeed Elizabeth H. Dole as secretary of transportation on November 2, 1987, and on November 30, 1987, the Senate confirmed Burnley by a vote of 74 to 0. On December 1, 1987, Reagan nominated Ann D. McLaughlin to succeed William E. Brock III as secretary of labor, and on December 11, 1987, the Senate confirmed her by a vote of 94 to 0. On July 25, 1988, Reagan nominated Richard L. Thornburgh to succeed Edwin Meese

III as attorney general, and on August 11, 1988, the Senate confirmed Thornburgh by a vote of 85 to 0. On August 10, 1988, Reagan nominated Nicholas F. Brady to succeed James A. Baker III as secretary of the Treasury and Lauro F. Cavazos to succeed William J. Bennett as secretary of education. On September 14, 1988, the Senate confirmed Brady by a vote of 92 to 2, and on September 20, 1988, the Senate confirmed Cavazos by a vote of 94 to 0.

IMPEACHMENTS

None.

CONSTITUTIONAL AMENDMENTS

None.

FURTHER READING

Johnson, Haynes Bonner. *Sleepwalking Through History: America in the Reagan Years.* New York: Anchor Books, 1992.

Schaller, Michael. *Reckoning With Reagan: America and its President in the 1980s.* New York: Oxford University Press, 1992.

Simon, Paul. *Advice & Consent: Clarence Thomas, Robert Bork and the Intriguing History of the Supreme Court's Nomination Battles.* Washington: National Press Books, 1992

Wright, James C. *Reflections of a Public Man.* Fort Worth, Tex.: Madison Publishing Co., 1984.

The 101st Congress

JANUARY 3, 1989-JANUARY 3, 1991

First Session: January 3, 1989-November 22, 1989
Second Session: January 23, 1990-October 28, 1990

In the 1988 elections for the 101st Congress, the Democrats and the Republicans neither gained nor lost any seats in the Senate, the Democrats keeping their majority at 55 of the 100 seats and the Republicans retaining their 45 seats. In the House, the Democrats gained 1 seat, raising their majority from 258 to 259 of the 435 seats. The Republicans lost 3 seats, reducing their total to 174. Two seats were vacant, but both would ultimately be taken by Republicans before the end of this Congress. [See note 3, p. xxix]

BACKGROUND

According to the census of 1990, the population of the United States as of April 1, 1990, was 248,709,873, resulting in a population density of 70.3 persons for each of the country's 3,536,342 square miles. This was a population increase of 9.8 percent over the 1980 census.

George Herbert Walker Bush was inaugurated as the 41st President of the United States on January 20, 1989. Foreign policy and defense issues dominated most of the national agenda during the 101st Congress. In 1989 the Iron Curtain collapsed. While the Communist governments of Eastern Europe were overthrown, the Soviet Union was swept by political turmoil and nationalistic stirrings. Foreign aid proposals for America's former adversaries usually were overtaken by events before they could be decided by votes. In 1990 with Germany reunited and the cold war undoubtedly over, many in Congress began to press for cuts in defense spending. The B-2 stealth bomber program and the Strategic Defense Initiative came under attack. Congress also acted to cut military aid to El Salvador and to the Nicaraguan contras, both programs having been politically volatile from the start. Efforts to cut defense spending further were halted temporarily, however, after August 2, 1990, when Iraqi troops invaded the neighboring oil-rich country of Kuwait, an action that threatened Saudi Arabia's oil fields. Unwilling to see Iraq dominate the Persian Gulf region, President George Bush began to deploy American military units and rally the international community around the issue of forcing Iraq out of Kuwait.

Congress played only a minor role in shaping the nation's foreign policy. In domestic affairs, however, the Democrats used their solid majorities in both the House and the Senate to control the legislative agenda. Unlike his predecessor, Ronald Reagan, Bush had to face questions about the strength of his leadership. Many people believed that Bush won in 1988 due to Reagan's popularity and the weakness of the Democratic candidate, Michael Dukakis. Thus, Bush lacked a strong popular mandate. As a result, he frequently had to use his veto power to block legislative initiatives supported by the Democratic majorities in both chambers. [See Relations with the President, below]

The spiraling budget deficit was the chief domestic policy issue during the 101st Congress. From less than $1 trillion in 1980, the national debt had grown to $3 trillion by 1989, driven up by annual deficits running at more than $200 billion a year. Most of the Democrats in Congress blamed the tax cuts of the 1980s for exacerbating the budget deficit, but Bush promised "Read my lips, no new taxes" a phrase that came to represent his fiscal policy. In order to reach an agreement on a budget for the 1991 fiscal year, Bush and eight congressional leaders met early in 1990 to hammer out a budget deficit reduction program. Negotiations went on sporadically through the spring and summer of 1990. Even by October, they had produced no budget, and the government was forced to shut down for three days until stopgap funding could be arranged. An initial budget compromise was rejected by the House on October 5. Finally, an agreement was reached on the Budget Reconciliation Act of 1990, which was approved by both the House and the Senate on October 27, just one day before the second session of the Congress adjourned. The act projected more than $200 billion in deficit reduction over five years, with some spending cuts, but largely through new tax increases insisted upon by Democratic congressional leaders.

SENATE LEADERSHIP

Vice President: George Herbert Walker Bush had been vice president until January 20, 1989, when J. Danforth "Dan" Quayle became the new vice president. Quayle first had been elected to Congress as a representative from Indiana to the 95th Congress and to the Senate in 1980, where he served until he was elected vice president on Bush's ticket in the November 1988 election. [See note 8, p. xxix]

President Pro Tempore: Robert C. Byrd (Dem., W.Va.) [See biographical note in 95th Congress] first became president pro tem in this Congress.

Majority Leader: George J. Mitchell (Dem., Maine) first had entered Congress in 1980 after being appointed to the Senate by the governor of

Maine to fill the vacancy left by Edmund S. Muskie's (Dem., Maine) resignation. He subsequently won the election of 1982 and kept his seat. The 101st Congress was his first Congress as majority leader.

Majority Whip: Alan Cranston (Dem., Calif.)

Minority Leader: Robert Dole (Rep., Kans.) [See biographical note in 99th Congress]

Minority Whip: Alan K. Simpson (Rep., Wyo.)

Chairman and Ranking Minority Members of Key Committees:

Committee on Agriculture, Nutrition, and Forestry: Chairman: Patrick J. Leahy (Dem., Vt.); Ranking Minority Member: Richard G. Lugar (Rep., Ind.)

Committee on Appropriations: Chairman: Robert C. Byrd (Dem., W.Va.); Ranking Minority Member: Mark O. Hatfield (Rep., Ore.)

Committee on Armed Services: Samuel A. Nunn (Dem., Ga.); Ranking Minority Member: John W. Warner (Rep., Va.)

Committee on Banking, Housing, and Urban Affairs: Chairman: Donald W. Riegle Jr. (Dem., Mich.); Ranking Minority Member: Jake Garn (Rep., Utah)

Committee on the Budget: Chairman: James R. Sasser (Dem., Tenn.); Ranking Minority Member: Pete V. Domenici (Rep., N.M.)

Committee on Commerce, Science, and Transportation: Chairman: Ernest F. Hollings (Dem., S.C.); Ranking Minority Member: John C. Danforth (Rep., Mo.)

Committee on Energy and Natural Resources: Chairman: J. Bennett Johnston Jr. (Dem., La.); Ranking Minority Member: James A. McClure (Rep., Idaho)

Committee on Environment and Public Works: Chairman: Quentin N. Burdick (Dem., N.D.); Ranking Minority Member: John H. Chafee (Rep., R.I.)

C H R O N O L O G Y

January 3, 1989:	The 101st Congress and the first session begin.
January 20, 1989:	President Bush nominates his cabinet members, all of whom are confirmed by the Senate by March 2, 1989, except for John G. Tower, Bush's nominee to be secretary of defense.
March 9, 1989:	The Senate rejects Tower.
March 14, 1989:	President Bush nominates House Minority Whip Richard Cheney (Rep., Wyo.) to be secretary of defense.
March 17, 1989:	The Senate confirms Cheney.
April 13, 1989:	Congress ends military aid to the Nicaraguan contras.
May 31, 1989:	James Claude Wright Jr. (Dem., Tex.) resigns as Speaker of the House.
June 6, 1989:	Thomas S. Foley (Dem., Wash.) becomes the next Speaker.
June 14, 1989:	Richard A. Gephardt (Dem., Mo.) becomes the new House majority leader.
June 15, 1989:	Tony Coelho (Dem., Calif.) resigns from the Congress and is succeeded as Democratic majority whip by William H. Gray III (Dem., Pa.)
September 26, 1989:	Congress approves continued funding for the B-2 bomber program.
October 19, 1989:	A constitutional amendment banning flag burning fails to pass the Senate.
October 20, 1989:	The Senate impeaches Federal District Judge Alcee L. Hastings.
November 3, 1989:	The Senate impeaches Federal District Judge Walter L. Nixon Jr.
November 16-17, 1989:	The House and the Senate vote pay raises for their members.
November 22, 1989:	The first session ends.
January 23, 1990:	The second session begins.
June 11, 1990:	The Supreme Court in *U.S. v. Eichman* strikes down a congressional anti-flagburning law.
June 21, 1990:	A proposed constitutional amendment against flag burning fails to pass the House.
June 26, 1990:	Another proposed constitutional amendment against flag burning fails to pass the Senate.
July 13, 1990:	Congress passes the Americans With Disabilities Act.
July 20, 1990:	Supreme Court Justice William J. Brennan announces his retirement.
July 25, 1990:	President Bush nominates David H. Souter to replace Brennan.
October 2, 1990:	The Senate confirms Souter.
October 27, 1990:	Congress passes the Omnibus Budget Reconciliation Act of 1990.
October 28, 1990:	The second session ends.
December 17, 1990:	President Bush nominates Lamar Alexander to succeed Lauro F. Cavazos as secretary of education. Alexander would be confirmed during the 102nd Congress.
January 3, 1991:	The 101st Congress ends.

[See note 6, p. xxix]

Committee on Finance: Chairman: Lloyd M. Bentsen Jr. (Dem., Tex.); Ranking Minority Member: Robert W. Packwood (Rep., Ore.)

Committee on Foreign Relations: Chairman: Claiborne D. Pell (Dem., R.I.); Ranking Minority Member: Jesse A. Helms (Rep., N.C.)

Committee on the Judiciary: Chairman: Joseph R. Biden Jr. (Dem., Del.); Ranking Minority Member: J. Strom Thurmond (Rep., S.C.)

Committee on Labor and Human Resources: Chairman: Edward M. Kennedy (Dem., Mass.); Ranking Minority Member: Orrin G. Hatch (Rep., Utah)

Committee on Rules and Administration: Chairman: Wendell H. Ford (Dem., Ky.); Ranking Minority Member: Theodore F. Stevens (Rep., Alaska)

HOUSE LEADERSHIP

Speaker of the House: James Claude Wright Jr. (Dem., Tex.), who resigned effective May 31, 1989, first had been elected to Congress in the 84th Congress and served as Speaker in the 100th and 101st Congresses. Various scandals [See Scandals, below] forced him to resign. Thomas S. Foley (Dem., Wash.) became the next Speaker effective June 6, 1989. Foley first had been elected to Congress as a Representative to the 89th Congress and first served as Speaker in the 101st Congress.

Majority Leader: Thomas S. Foley (Dem., Wash.), who became Speaker of the House effective June 6, 1989. Richard A. Gephardt (Dem., Mo.) became the next majority leader effective June 14, 1989. Normally, the majority whip, which is the third-ranking position in the House hierarchy, takes over the second-ranked position of majority leader when the position becomes vacant. However, with Tony Coehlo's (Dem., Calif.) resignation [See Majority Whip, below], that position also was vacant when Majority Leader Foley became the Speaker. The Democrats chose Gephardt, who first had been elected to Congress as a representative to the 95th Congress,

as their new majority leader. Gephardt also had been a prominent candidate for the Democratic presidential nomination in 1988.

Majority Whip: Tony Coelho (Dem., Calif.), who resigned effective June 15,1989. William H. Gray III (Dem., Pa.) became the new majority whip effective June 15, 1989. Gray, who had served as chairman of the Budget Committee during the 99th and 100th Congresses, was the first African American to hold one of the top three House leadership posts.

Minority Leader: Robert H. Michel (Rep., Ill.)

Minority Whip: Richard Cheney (Rep., Wyo.), who resigned effective March 23, 1989, to become the secretary of defense. Newt Gingrich (Rep., Ga.) became the next minority whip. Gingrich was the leader of the conservative Republican faction of the House and would become Speaker in the 104th Congress.

Chairman and Ranking Minority Members of Key Committees:

Committee on Agriculture: Chairman: Kika de la Garza (Dem., Tex.); Ranking Minority Member: Edward R. Madigan (Rep., Ill.)

Committee on Appropriations: Chairman: Jamie L. Whitten (Dem., Miss.); Ranking Minority Member: Silvio O. Conte (Rep., Mass.)

Committee on Armed Services: Chairman: Les Aspin (Dem., Wis.); Ranking Minority Member: William L. Dickinson (Rep., Ala.)

Committee on Banking, Finance, and Urban Affairs: Chairman: Henry B. Gonzalez (Dem., Tex.); Ranking Minority Member: Chalmers P. Wylie (Rep., Ohio)

Committee on the Budget: Chairman: Leon E. Panetta (Dem., Calif.); Ranking Minority Member: William E. Frenzel (Rep., Minn.)

Committee on Education and Labor: Chairman: Augustus F. Hawkins (Dem., Calif.); Ranking Minority Member: William F. Goodling (Rep., Pa.)

Committee on Energy and Commerce: Chairman: John D. Dingell Jr. (Dem., Mich.); Ranking Minority Member: Norman F. Lent (Rep., N.Y.)

Committee on Foreign Affairs: Chairman: Dante B. Fascell (Dem., Fla.); Ranking Minority Member: William S. Broomfield (Rep., Mich.)

Committee on Interior and Insular Affairs: Chairman: Morris K. Udall (Dem., Ariz.); Ranking Minority Member: Donald E. Young (Rep., Alaska)

Committee on the Judiciary: Chairman: Jack B. Brooks (Dem., Tex.); Ranking Minority Member: Hamilton Fish Jr. (Rep., N.Y.)

Committee on Public Works and Transportation: Chairman: Glenn M. Anderson (Dem., Calif.); Ranking Minority Member: John Paul Hammerschmidt (Rep., Ark.)

Committee on Rules: Chairman: Claude D. Pepper (Dem., Fla.), who died on May 30, 1989. John J. Moakley (Dem., Mass.) became the next chairman effective June 7, 1989. Ranking Minority Member: James H. Quillen (Rep., Tenn.)

Committee on Ways and Means: Chairman: Daniel D. Rostenkowski (Dem., Ill.); Ranking Minority Member: William R. Archer (Rep., Tex.)

ORGANIZATION AND ADMINISTRATION

Congress ran into a storm of public protest when it considered taking a 51 percent pay raise for its members, a measure that was rejected on February 7, 1989. Several months later, however, lesser pay increases passed both the House and the Senate. The House voted 252 to 174 to give its members a 40 percent raise on November 16, 1989, and the Senate followed suit, voting 56 to 43 to give its members a 10 percent raise on November 17, 1989. [See note 5, p. xxix]

MAJOR LEGISLATION PASSED

Banking and Finance: Congress began the rescue of the savings-and-loan industry from the massive losses stemming from the failure of dereg-

ulation with the passage of the Financial Institutions Reform, Recovery, and Enforcement Act of 1989. This measure authorized $50 billion for the cleanup of approximately 250 S&Ls and enacted tough new net-worth requirements expected to affect an additional 800 S&Ls.

Budget and Taxes: After months of impasse and the near shutdown of the federal government, Congress enacted the Omnibus Budget Reconciliation Act of 1990 on October 27, 1990, which set forth deficit reduction measures that cut $28 billion from the projected budget deficit for fiscal 1991 and $236 billion over the next five years, largely as a result of tax increases.

Civil Rights: Congress passed the Americans With Disabilities Act, prohibiting employment discrimination on the basis of disabilities. The ADA also required more accommodations for the handicapped in public facilities.

Defense: In 1989 Congress challenged funding for the Strategic Defense Initiative (SDI), an antimissile defense system to be positioned in orbit around the Earth. President Bush had sought $4.9 billion for continued SDI funding, down $1 billion from former President Reagan's request. The House approved only $3.1 billion. The Senate wanted to appropriate $4.5 billion, and the House and Senate conferees eventually compromised on a figure of $3.8 billion.

There was also a congressional attack, led by Senator Patrick J. Leahy (Dem., Vt.), on the expensive Stealth bomber program. The Stealth bomber is actually a nickname for the B-2 bomber that was developed with modern composite materials and a unique body design in order to absorb or deflect enemy radar so that the B-2 could "stealthily" bomb enemy targets without being detected and risk being shot down. Leahy's attempt to end the $70 billion B-2 program was defeated when both Chambers of Congress voted to continue the project.

Environment: For the first time in more than a decade, Congress enacted new clean air legislation. In the Clean Air Act Amendments, Congress authorized funding to reduce acid-rain

T A B L E   O F   K E Y   V O T E S

Senate

Subject of Vote	Date of Vote	For			Against		
		D	R	Total	D	R	Total
Tower Nomination Defeated	March 9, 1989	3	44	47	52	1	53
Contra Military Aid Ended	April 13, 1989	50	39	89	4	5	9
Ending the B-2 Bomber	September 26, 1989	27	2	29	28	43	71
Congressional Pay Raise Approved	November 17, 1989	43	13	56	12	31	43
Medicare Catastrophic Coverage Act Repealed	November 21, 1989	54	45	99	0	0	0
Constitutional Amendment Against Flag Burning Rejected (failed: 2/3rds majority required)	June 26, 1990	20	38	58	35	7	42
Americans With Disabilities Act Passed	July 13, 1990	54	37	91	0	6	6
Military Aid to El Salvador Cut	October 19, 1990	55	19	74	0	25	25
Civil Rights Act Veto Override (failed: 2/3rds majority required)	October 24, 1990	55	11	66	0	34	34
Budget Reconciliation Act of 1990 Passed	October 27, 1990	31	23	54	24	22	46

(Continued on p. 527)

emissions, phase out chlorofluorocarbons, and curb industrial pollution.

Foreign Policy: Working with the White House, congressional leaders developed a compromise concerning aid to the Nicaraguan contras. Rather than cut off American support entirely, Congress agreed to continue funds for food, medicine, and other non-military supplies.

Health: Congress repealed the 1988 Medicare Catastrophic Coverage Act, which greatly had expanded the Medicare program, but was opposed strenuously by beneficiaries who did not like having to pay a small surtax for their new benefits. [See 100th Congress] Further, the AIDS crisis spurred Congress to authorize nearly a billion dollars in emergency funding in the Ryan White Comprehensive AIDS Resources Emergency Act. The money was designated for grant programs to help support organizations in the most hard hit areas.

Immigration: Under the Immigration Act of 1990, the categories and priorities of persons seeking legal entry into the United States were overhauled and the annual ceiling for legal immigrants was raised to 675,000 from 500,000.

Judiciary: In an attempt to relieve overcrowded court calendars, Congress created 85 new positions in the understaffed federal judiciary: 74 new district court and 11 new circuit court judgeships. The increase was the first since 1984.

Labor: Congress passed legislation raising the

(Continued from p. 526)

TABLE OF KEY VOTES

House

Subject of Vote	Date of Vote	For			Against		
		D	R	Total	D	R	Total
Contra Military Aid Ended	April 13, 1989	153	156	309	98	12	110
Ending the B-2 Bomber	July 26, 1989	116	28	144	135	144	279
Congressional Pay Raise Passed	November 16, 1989	168	84	252	85	89	174
Medicare Catastrophic Coverage Act Repealed	November 21, 1989	96	164	360	56	10	66
Military Aid to El Salvador Cut	May 22, 1990	219	31	250	28	135	163
Constitutional Amendment Against Flag Burning Rejected (failed: 2/3rds majority required)	June 21, 1990	95	159	254	160	17	177
Americans With Disabilities Act Passed	July 12, 1990	232	145	377	5	23	28
Family and Medical Leave Bill Veto Override (failed: 2/3rds majority required)	July 25, 1990	194	38	232	57	138	195
First Budget Summit Agreement Approved	October 5, 1990	108	71	179	149	105	54
Budget Reconciliation Act of 1990 Passed	October 27, 1990	239	34	273	15	139	154

[See note 7, p. xxix]

hourly minimum wage from $3.35 to $4.25 over a two-year period. The law also established a lower minimum wage rate for teenage employees.

Science and Technology: The Energy and Water Development Appropriations Act of 1990 included the appropriation of the first $225 million for the Superconducting Supercollider, the enormous particle accelerator that was estimated to cost $4 billion, but ultimately became much more expensive.

Securities: In a delayed reaction to the stock market's historic one-day decline on "Black Monday," October 19, 1987, Congress passed three new laws concerning securities regulation: (1) the Securities Acts Amendments of 1990; (2) the Securities and Exchange Commission Authorization Act of 1990; and (3) the Securities Enforcement Remedies and Penny Stock Reform Act of 1990. These laws gave the Securities and Exchange Commission new powers to restrict computerized program trading that could cause wide price swings, to halt trading altogether, to supervise the activities of large traders, and to impose greater civil penalties for securities violations.

FAILED LEGISLATION

Congress failed to approve a constitutional amendment against flag burning by the required two-thirds majority of each chamber.

RELATIONS WITH THE PRESIDENT

Although he had served as vice president for eight years under Ronald Reagan, a very successful president, George Bush was unable to dominate Congress as his predecessor had. He preferred to focus on foreign policy, an area in which he had considerable experience, and in which the president can act with fewer congressional limitations. However, tensions between the president and the Democrat-controlled Congress carried over to upset the traditional bipartisan support that a president usually enjoys when confronting a foreign crisis. Democrats, particularly in the Senate, often were critical of Bush's plans to use American troops to force Iraq to withdraw after that nation's invasion of Kuwait in August 1990.

Bush vetoed 21 bills during the 101st Congress. Two were particularly significant. First, Bush vetoed the Family and Medical Leave Bill, and a veto override attempt failed in the House. Second, Bush vetoed the Civil Rights Act of 1990, which would have implemented certain amendments to existing civil rights legislation. This time, the veto override failed in the Senate. [See Table of Key Votes, above]

NOMINATIONS, APPOINTMENTS, AND CONFIRMATIONS

The Judiciary: On July 20, 1990, Supreme Court Justice William J. Brennan announced his retirement. President Bush on July 25, 1990, nominated New Hampshire State Supreme Court Judge David H. Souter to succeed Brennan. During his confirmation hearings before the Senate Judiciary Committee, Souter consistently refused to set forth his position on such controversial issues as abortion, stating that he had never formulated any personal opinion that would influence his decision in a future case before the Supreme

Court. Despite some skepticism by the senators and the public, Souter's nomination was confirmed by the Senate on October 2, 1990, by a 90 to 9 vote.

The Executive Branch: On January 20, 1989, President Bush nominated his cabinet members, all of whom were confirmed by the Senate except for John G. Tower. James A. Baker was confirmed to be secretary of the state, and Elizabeth H. Dole was confirmed to be secretary of labor, both by 99 to 0 votes, on January 25, 1989. Robert A. Mosbacher was confirmed to be secretary of commerce, and Samuel K. Skinner was confirmed to be secretary of transportation, both by 100 to 0 votes, on January 31, 1989. Jack Kemp was confirmed to be secretary of housing and urban development, and Manuel Lujan Jr. was confirmed to be secretary of the Interior, both by 100 to 0 votes, on February 2, 1989. On February 8, 1989, Clayton Yeutter was confirmed to be secretary of agriculture by a 100 to 0 vote. On March 1, 1989, Louis W. Sullivan was confirmed to be secretary of health and human services by a vote of 98 to 1, while on the same day, James D. Watkins was confirmed to be secretary of energy by a 99 to 0 vote. On March 2, 1989, Edward J. Derwinski was confirmed to be secretary of veterans affairs by a vote of 94 to 0.

Bush did not replace several other cabinet-level officials from the Reagan administration, and no Senate confirmation vote was required for continuing those officials.

Also on January 20, 1989, President Bush nominated former Texas Republican Senator John G. Tower to be secretary of defense. Rumors arose, however, that Tower had a drinking problem. On March 9, 1989, the Senate rejected Tower's nomination (by a vote of 47 to 53), the first time in American history a nominee for secretary of defense had been rejected. On March 14, 1989, Bush nominated House Minority Whip Richard Cheney (Rep., Wyo.) for the post, and on March 17, 1989, the Senate confirmed Cheney by a vote of 92 to 0. Finally, on December 17, 1990, Bush nominated Lamar Alexander to succeed Lauro F. Cavazos (continued from the Reagan administration) as secretary of education. Alexander would be confirmed during the 102nd Congress.

IMPEACHMENTS

There were two significant judicial impeachments. A federal district judge in Florida, Alcee L. Hastings, was accused of accepting $150,000 from defendants in a criminal racketeering trial in exchange for light sentences. Although Hastings had been found not guilty when tried before a jury, the Senate on October 20, 1989, found him guilty of 8 out of 11 articles of impeachment relating to conspiracy to obtain a bribe and removed him from his office. Hastings was the first federal official to be impeached despite having been acquitted by a court. The other federal judge impeached, District Judge Walter L. Nixon Jr., of Mississippi, was accused of making false statements to federal investigators concerning his attempt to influence the drug prosecution of the son of a business associate. On February 9, 1986, a jury found Nixon guilty of perjury, and on November 3, 1989, the Senate removed him from office.

CONSTITUTIONAL AMENDMENTS

After the Supreme Court's June 21, 1989, decision in *Texas v. Johnson* that a Texas state anti-flag-burning law violated the First Amendment, Congress considered various constitutional amendments to ban flag burning and other forms of desecration. One such amendment failed to get the necessary two-thirds majority in the Senate on October 19, 1989. The Senate's vote effectively made the issue moot, and the House put off its vote. Only days before, both chambers of Congress had voted overwhelmingly in favor of a federal statute against flag burning, the 1989 Flag Protection Act. However, on June 11, 1990, the Supreme Court in *U.S. v. Eichman* struck it down by a narrow 5 to 4 majority, again on First Amendment grounds. Both the House and the Senate voted on another anti-flag burning amendment, but the initiative failed in both chambers. [See Table of Key Votes, above]

FURTHER READING

Jentleson, Bruce W. *With Friends Like These: Reagan, Bush, and Saddam, 1982-1990.* New York: W.W. Norton & Co., 1994.

Kolb, Charles. *White House Daze: The Unmaking of Domestic Policy in the Bush Years.* New York: Free Press, 1994.

Wright, James C. *Reflections of a Public Man.* Fort Worth, Tex.: Madison Publishing Company, 1984.

The 102nd Congress

JANUARY 3, 1991-JANUARY 3, 1993

First Session: *January 3, 1991-January 3, 1992*
Second Session: *January 3, 1992-October 9, 1992*

I n the 1990 elections for the 102nd Congress, the Democrats gained 1 seat in the Senate, increasing their majority from 55 to 56 of the 100 seats. The Republicans lost 1 seat, reducing their total to 44 seats. In the House, the Democrats gained 8 seats, increasing their majority from 259 to 267 of the 435 seats. The Republicans lost 7 seats, leaving them with a total of 167. One seat was held by an independent. [See note 3, p. xxix]

BACKGROUND

When the 102nd Congress convened, the United States was on the verge of war. On August 2, 1990, during the 101st Congress, Iraq had invaded and occupied the neighboring emirate of Kuwait. If Iraq and its dictator Saddam Hussein controlled Kuwait, which had considerable oil reserves, Hussein would be in a position to dominate the strategic Persian Gulf both militarily and economically. In response, President George Bush had mobilized the American military and even called up some reserve units. With few exceptions most of the world, including most Islamic nations, supported the United States. Saudi Arabia invited American forces to land and establish a base on its territory, and many other nations in the Islamic world and elsewhere sent military and/or financial assistance.

There were some concerns in Congress about Bush's emphasis on military preparation rather than diplomatic negotiation. In order to fend off a confrontation with Congress, Bush sent some peace feelers to the Iraqis, all of which were rejected. On January 12, 1991, Congress passed a resolution approving the use of force [See Major Legislation, below] as technically is required by the War Powers Act, although Bush, like all presidents before him, never conceded that he needed Congress's approval for military operations that are short of an all-out declaration of war. On January 15, 1991, the United States and its allies commenced Operation Desert Storm, the official name for the war to force Iraq out of Kuwait. The Iraqi troops entrenched in Kuwait numerically were superior to the Desert Storm forces, but technologically were inferior. The American forces used laser guided bombs, cruise missiles, night vision scopes, radar-invisible aircraft, and other advanced weapons to defeat the Iraqis. The allies also had better leadership. The Gulf War ended on February 27, 1991, much sooner and with far fewer casualties than most experts had predicted.

After the Gulf War victory, President Bush received historically high popular approval ratings. More than 90 percent of the American public believed that Bush was doing a good job as president. The high approval rating was deceptive, however. Americans traditionally have supported presidents in wartime, if the war is short and successful. Once the Gulf War was over, Americans became more concerned with the economy, which had slipped into a recession.

Bush took no substantive action to revive the economy, and his popularity began to decline.

After the Gulf War, the most significant foreign policy development was in the Soviet Union. Soviet leader Mikhail Gorbachev had initiated a political reform of the Soviet system, encouraging freedom of speech and popular participation in government. These reforms made Gorbachev popular in the U.S. and elsewhere in the free world, but encouraged domestic dissent. First, the various ethnic nationalities that had been suppressed by the Soviets were demanding independence. Second, Gorbachev's economic reforms had failed, and both Communism and Gorbachev were discredited. In Russia, the largest portion of the Soviet Union, Boris Yeltsin was elected president. Yeltsin had once been a Communist and a close ally of Gorbachev, but now he was the head of an independent Russia. In the summer of 1991, reactionaries in the Soviet leadership staged a coup, and overthrew Gorbachev. The reactionaries wanted to restore the repressive but stable order of the old Soviet Union. The Russian people and most of the military supported Yeltsin, and the coup collapsed. Yeltsin was committed to democracy, and independence for Russia and the other nations that comprised the old Soviet Union. On Christmas Day 1991 Gorbachev resigned in a speech that was televised throughout the world, and the Soviet Union ceased to exist.

During the final months of the Soviet Union, Bush and Gorbachev had agreed upon several significant nuclear arms reduction measures. Progress in arms reduction continued after the breakup of the Soviet Union. For Bush and the Republicans, however, the end of the cold war created a new political crisis. Ever since Reagan's victory in the 1980 presidential election, the Republicans had cast themselves as the party of American military strength against Communism and Soviet agression. Reagan had even characterized the Soviet Union as an "evil empire." The collapse of the Soviet Union, however, meant that the Republicans could no longer campaign on cold war issues.

As the American economy continued to suffer from a recession, Bush was unable to put together a credible domestic policy agenda. The Democrats were preparing for the 1992 presidential election and planned to attack Bush's record on the economy, but they were split among several contenders and moreover had been out of the White House for 12 years. Furthermore, the American public increasingly was dissatisfied with the partisan political feuding between Republicans and Democrats in Congress. The result was the sudden emergence of the most successful independent campaign for president since Robert LaFollette in 1924 and Theodore Roosevelt in 1912. Texas billionaire H. Ross Perot, one of America's richest men and a leader in the movement to free American prisoners of war in Vietnam, expressed an interest in running for president. Unlike the Democrats or the Republicans, Perot was willing to make the national debt and the federal budget deficit an issue and spoke out against deficit spending. Perot succeeded in making the deficit an important issue in the 1992 elections. Although Perot did not commit himself to running for president until October 1992, just a month before the election, his supporters already had put him on the ballot in all 50 states. Democrat William ("Bill") J. Clinton won the election, but nearly 20 percent of the electorate voted for Perot, the highest independent percentage since 1924.

Because he did not have a political party with representation in Congress, however, Perot's impact on the legislative agenda was limited to the response by the Democrats and Republicans in the next Congress to Perot's electoral success. President Clinton would quietly drop his campaign pledge to pass a middle-class tax cut, and went into the 103rd Congress with a budget deficit reduction plan, adopting Perot's position that spending cuts and tax increases desperately were needed to stem the red ink. Another Perot issue, namely that the North American Free Trade Agreement (NAFTA) would hurt rather than help American workers because businesses would relocate to low-wage Mexico, also would be a major issue in the 103rd Congress. Perot's success demonstrated the extent of the American public's discontent with the political status quo.

SENATE LEADERSHIP

Vice President: J. Danforth "Dan" Quayle [See biographical note in 101st Congress]

President Pro Tempore: Robert C. Byrd (Dem., W.Va.) first became president pro tem in the 101st Congress. [See biographical note in 95th Congress]

Majority Leader: George J. Mitchell (Dem., Maine) [See biographical note in 101st Congress]

Majority Whip: Wendell H. Ford (Dem., Ky.)

Minority Leader: Robert Dole (Rep., Kans.) [See biographical note in 99th Congress]

Minority Whip: Alan K. Simpson (Rep., Wyo.)

Chairman and Ranking Minority Members of Key Committees:

Committee on Agriculture, Nutrition, and Forestry: Chairman: Patrick J. Leahy (Dem., Vt.); Ranking Minority Member: Richard G. Lugar (Rep., Ind.)

Committee on Appropriations: Chairman: Robert C. Byrd (Dem., W.Va.); Ranking Minority Member: Mark O. Hatfield (Rep., Ore.)

Committee on Armed Services: Chairman: Samuel A. Nunn (Dem., Ga.); Ranking Minority Member: John W. Warner (Rep., Va.)

Committee on Banking, Housing, and Urban Affairs: Chairman: Donald W. Riegle Jr. (Dem., Mich.); Ranking Minority Member: Jake Garn (Rep., Utah)

Committee on the Budget: Chairman: James R. Sasser (Dem., Tenn.); Ranking Minority Member: Pete V. Domenici (Rep., N.M.)

Committee on Commerce, Science, and Transportation: Chairman: Ernest F. Hollings (Dem., S.C.); Ranking Minority Member: John C. Danforth (Rep., Mo.)

Committee on Energy and Natural Resources: Chairman: J. Bennett Johnston Jr. (Dem., La.); Ranking Minority Member: Malcolm Wallop (Rep., Wyo.)

Committee on Environment and Public Works: Chairman: Quentin N. Burdick (Dem., N.D.), who died on September 8, 1992. Daniel P. Moynihan (Dem., N.Y.) became the next chairman effective September 15, 1992. Ranking Minority Member: John H. Chafee (Rep., R.I.)

Committee on Finance: Chairman: Lloyd M. Bentsen Jr. (Dem., Tex.); Ranking Minority Member: Robert W. Packwood (Rep., Ore.)

Committee on Foreign Relations: Chairman: Claiborne D. Pell (Dem., R.I.); Ranking Minority Member: Jesse A. Helms (Rep., N.C.)

Committee on the Judiciary: Chairman: Joseph R. Biden Jr. (Dem., Del.); Ranking Minority Member: J. Strom Thurmond (Rep., S.C.)

Committee on Labor and Human Resources: Chairman: Edward M. Kennedy (Dem., Mass.); Ranking Minority Member: Orrin G. Hatch (Rep., Utah)

Committee on Rules and Administration: Chairman: Wendell H. Ford (Dem., Ky.); Ranking Minority Member: Theodore F. Stevens (Rep., Alaska)

HOUSE LEADERSHIP

Speaker of the House: Thomas Stephen Foley (Dem., Wash.) first had been elected to Congress as a Representative to the 89th Congress and first had served as Speaker in the 101st Congress. [See biographical note in 101st Congress]

Majority Leader: Richard A. Gephardt (Dem., Mo.) first had been elected to Congress as a representative to the 95th Congress and had been a prominent candidate for the Democratic presidential nomination in 1988.

Majority Whip: William H. Gray III (Dem., Pa.)

Minority Leader: Robert H. Michel (Rep., Ill.)

Minority Whip: Newt Gingrich (Rep., Ga.) was the leader of the conservative Republican faction of the House and would become Speaker in the 104th Congress.

C H R O N O L O G Y

January 3, 1991:	The 102nd Congress and the first session begin.
January 12, 1991:	Congress passes a Persian Gulf resolution.
January 22, 1991:	President Bush nominates Lynn Martin to succeed Elizabeth H. Dole as secretary of labor.
February 7, 1991:	The Senate confirms Martin.
February 19, 1991:	President Bush nominates Edward R. Madigan to succeed Clayton Yeutter as secretary of agriculture.
March 7, 1991:	The Senate confirms Madigan.
March 13, 1991:	Congress passes the first of two savings and loan bailout bills
March 14, 1991:	The Senate confirms Lamar Alexander, who was nominated during the 101st Congress, to succeed Lauro F. Cavazos as secretary of education.
June 27, 1991:	Supreme Court Justice Thurgood Marshall retires.
July 1, 1991:	President Bush nominates Clarence Thomas to replace Marshall.
October 15, 1991:	The Senate confirms Thomas.
October 25, 1991:	President Bush nominates William P. Barr to succeed Richard L. Thornburgh as attorney general.
November 20, 1991:	The Senate confirms Barr.
November 27, 1991:	Congress passes the second of two savings and loan bailout bills.
January 3, 1992:	The first session ends and the second session begins.
March 2, 1992:	President Bush vetoes a China trade bill.
March 11, 1992:	The House votes to override Bush's veto.
March 13, 1992:	The House votes to make information concerning the House bank scandal public.
March 18, 1992:	The Senate fails to override Bush's veto.
April 1, 1992:	The House Ethics Committee rebukes 22 past and present members of the House for abusing their banking privileges.
May 20, 1992:	Congress votes to approve the ratification and certification of the 27th Amendment, limiting congressional pay raises
August 6, 1992:	Congress passes the Freedom Support Act.
September 28, 1992:	President Bush vetoes a second China trade bill.
September 30, 1992:	The House votes to override Bush's veto.
October 1, 1992:	The Senate approves the START Treaty. The Senate fails to override Bush's veto of the China trade bill.
October 9, 1992:	The second session ends.
January 3, 1993:	The 102nd Congress ends.

[See note 6, p. xxix]

Chairman and Ranking Minority Members of Key Committees:

Committee on Agriculture: Chairman: Kika de la Garza (Dem., Tex.); Ranking Minority Member: Edward R. Madigan (Rep., Ill.), who resigned effective March 8, 1991, to become the secretary of agriculture. E. Thomas Coleman (Rep., Mo.) became the next ranking minority member effective the same day.

Committee on Appropriations: Chairman: Jamie L. Whitten (Dem., Miss.); Ranking Minority Member: Silvio O. Conte (Rep., Mass.), who died on February 8, 1991. Joseph M. McDade (Rep., Pa.) became the next ranking minority member effective the same day.

Committee on Armed Services: Chairman: Les Aspin (Dem., Wis.); Ranking Minority Member: William L. Dickinson (Rep., Ala.)

Committee on Banking, Finance, and Urban Affairs: Chairman: Henry B. Gonzalez (Dem., Tex.); Ranking Minority Member: Chalmers P. Wylie (Rep., Ohio)

Committee on the Budget: Chairman: Leon E. Panetta (Dem., Calif.); Ranking Minority Member: Willis D. Gradison Jr. (Rep., Ohio)

Committee on Education and Labor: Chairman: William D. Ford (Dem., Mich.); Ranking Minority Member: William F. Goodling (Rep., Pa.)

Committee on Energy and Commerce: Chairman: John D. Dingell Jr. (Dem., Mich.); Ranking Minority Member: Norman F. Lent (Rep., N.Y.)

Committee on Foreign Affairs: Chairman: Dante B. Fascell (Dem., Fla.); Ranking Minority Member: William S. Broomfield (Rep., Mich.)

Committee on Interior and Insular Affairs: Chairman: Morris K. Udall (Dem., Ariz.), who resigned effective May 4, 1991. George Miller (Dem., Calif.) became the next chairman effective May 9, 1991. Ranking Minority Member: Donald E. Young (Rep., Alaska)

Committee on the Judiciary: Chairman: Jack B. Brooks (Dem., Tex.); Ranking Minority Member: Hamilton Fish Jr. (Rep., N.Y.)

Committee on Public Works and Transportation: Chairman: Robert A. Roe (Dem., N.J.); Ranking Minority Member: John Paul Hammerschmidt (Rep., Ark.)

Committee on Rules: Chairman: John J. Moakley (Dem., Mass.); Ranking Minority Member: Gerald B. H. Solomon (Rep., N.Y.)

Committee on Ways and Means: Chairman: Daniel D. Rostenkowski (Dem., Ill.); Ranking Minority Member: William R. Archer (Rep., Tex.)

ORGANIZATION AND ADMINISTRATION

The Senate finally made it illegal for members to receive any honoraria, namely, payments to senators for speeches and public appearances that were often a cover for large gifts from special interest groups. Honoraria were already illegal in the House, but members of the House actually were receiving a larger salary ($125,100 a year) than senators ($101,900 a year). This discrepancy was due to the much larger salary raise that the House gave its members in the 101st Congress. [See Organization and Administration in the 101st Congress] Therefore, when the Senate ended honoraria, it simultaneously gave its members a $23,200 pay raise to bring senators' salaries into parity with representatives' salaries. Senator Robert C. Byrd (Dem., W.Va.), was the Senate president behind this change in senate policy because he became convinced that the bad publicity surrounding senate honoraria was damaging the institution's reputation. [See note 5, p. xxix]

MAJOR LEGISLATION PASSED

Aid to Ex-Soviet Republics: In the Freedom Support Act, Congress authorized one of the largest foreign assistance appropriations in U.S. history. The recipients would be Russia, the Ukraine, and the other nations formed when the Soviet Union collapsed at the end of 1991. The act gave $410 million in direct aid to the ex-Soviet republics; $12.3 billion to the International Monetary Fund (IMF), which supervised many of the international assistance programs to ex-Soviet states; and $3 billion to a currency stabilization fund for the Russian ruble.

Persian Gulf War: Congress narrowly passed a use of force resolution, giving its consent to President Bush's use of American military forces against Iraq to free Kuwait, provided that Bush exhaust all peaceful diplomatic options. Congress's resolution was pursuant to U.N. Resolution 678 of November 29, 1990, authorizing member nations to use "all necessary means" to free Kuwait.

Savings and Loan Bailout: Congress was forced to pass two appropriations bills to finance the bailout of the bankrupt savings-and-loan industry. The first bill provided $30 billion in funds and the second bill provided $25 billion in funds.

START Treaty: On July 31, 1991, President Bush and Soviet leader Mikhail Gorbachev executed the Strategic Arms Reduction Treaty (START), in which the U.S. and the Soviet Union agreed to reduce their nuclear bombers and long-range missiles by approximately one-third. However, the Soviet Union collapsed by the end of 1991. [See Background, above] On May 23, 1992, the ex-Soviet states with nuclear arsenals, namely, Russia, the Ukraine, Kazakhstan, and Belarus, agreed to abide by the START Treaty. Several months after this assurance, the Senate approved the treaty.

Unemployment Benefits: Despite resistance from the Bush administration, Congress acted three times to extend benefits for the unemployed, because the current recession was making it difficult for the jobless to find work. First, in 1991 Congress gave 13 to 20 weeks of extra benefits to recipients who had used up their standard 26 weeks of benefits. Second, as the recession continued, Congress added an extra 13 weeks of emergency benefits. Finally, when these emergency provisions were about to expire on July 4, 1992, Congress extended them to March 6, 1993.

FAILED LEGISLATION

Family Leave: Congress passed legislation guaranteeing up to 12 weeks of unpaid leave to employees who wished to take care of a newborn or a sick family member. President Bush vetoed the bill on September 22, 1992. On September 24, 1992, the Senate voted 68 to 31 to override, but on September 30, 1992, the House sustained the veto when it voted 258 to 169 to override, falling short of the required two-thirds majority.

Trade With China: Twice, Congress passed bills designed to restrict China's trade with the U.S. if China did not improve its human rights policies. Congress passed the first bill on July 23, 1991, and Bush vetoed it on March 2, 1992. Congress failed to override the veto. [See Table of Key Votes, below] Congress passed the second bill on September 14, 1992, and Bush vetoed it on September 28, 1992. Again, Congress failed to override the veto. [See Table of Key Votes, below]

RELATIONS WITH THE PRESIDENT

The successful outcome of Operation Desert Storm gave President Bush historically high approval ratings, but he completely failed to channel this popular support into any domestic legislative momentum with Congress. Bush made half-hearted initiatives to restore the capital gains tax break for wealthy investors, but otherwise continued to be preoccupied with foreign policy. In the foreign policy area, Bush was successful [See Major Legislation, above], but as the economy deepened into recession he took no action. The slogan "It's the economy, stupid" was often used in the 1992 presidential campaign by Clinton and Perot supporters [See Background, above] to describe Bush's apparent inability to perceive that it was his do-nothing approach to domestic economic matters with Congress that was destroying the support for his presidency.

Bush vetoed 25 bills during the 102nd Congress. He vetoed two bills affecting China's status as a trading partner, and those vetoes were not overriden. [See Failed Legislation, above] He also vetoed a family leave bill, which Congress also failed to override. [See Failed Legislation, above]

NOMINATIONS, APPOINTMENTS, AND CONFIRMATIONS

The Judiciary: Supreme Court Justice Thurgood Marshall retired on June 27, 1991. President George Bush nominated Clarence Thomas, an African American like Marshall and only the second to be nominated to the Court, on July 1, 1991, to replace Marshall. Thomas, a federal appellate judge and former head of the Equal Employment Opportunity Commission, went before the Senate Judiciary Committee for public hearings beginning on September 10, 1991. Thomas was criticized by the senators on the committee for his conservative views and belief in the principles of "natural law." The committee split on September 27, 1991, by a 7 to 7 vote over whether to recommend Thomas's confirmation to the Senate. The Committee voted 13 to 1 that same day to send Thomas's nomination before the full Senate without a recommendation. After that vote, however, a new development arose.

Anita Hill, a former employee of Thomas's when he was with the Department of Education and then when he headed the Equal Employment Opportunity Commission, and who was now a professor at the University of Oklahoma Law School, accused Thomas of sexually harassing her on the job. The Judiciary Committee recovened hearings, which due to the sensational publicity were nationally televised. Hill accused Thomas of various crude sexual overtures, and stood by her allegations even though former prosecutor Arlen Specter (Rep., Pa.) openly questioned her veracity since she had followed Thomas in Thomas's move to the EEOC. Thomas angrily accused the committee of conducting a "high-tech lynching" of him on account of his race, although Thomas's race was practically a non-issue in the hearings and Hill herself was African American. Women's rights organizations were vocal in their support for Hill and opposition to Thomas's appointment, but to no avail: the Senate confirmed Thomas

on October 15, 1991, by a 52 to 48 vote. Most senators were unwilling to vote against an African American nominee to the Supreme Court, and the evidence against Thomas rested primarily on Hill's personal and impossible-to-verify allegations.

The Executive Branch: During the 101st Congress, President Bush nominated Lamar Alexander to succeed Lauro F. Cavazos as secretary of education, and on March 14, 1991, the Senate confirmed Alexander by voice vote. On January 22, 1991, Bush nominated Lynn Martin to succeed Elizabeth H. Dole as secretary of labor, and on February 7, 1991, the Senate confirmed Martin by a vote of 94 to 0. On February 19, 1991, Bush nominated Edward R. Madigan to succeed Clayton Yeutter as secretary of agriculture, and on March 7, 1991, the Senate confirmed Madigan by a vote of 99 to 0. Bush nominated William P. Barr on October 25, 1991, to succeed Richard L. Thornburgh as attorney general, and on November 20, 1991, the Senate confirmed Barr by voice vote.

IMPEACHMENTS

None.

CONSTITUTIONAL AMENDMENTS

One of the initial package of proposed amendments to the Constitution in 1789 was a limit on congressional pay raises: "no law, varying the compensation for the services of the senators and representatives, shall take effect until an election of representatives shall have intervened." Unlike the first ten amendments in the Bill of Rights, the required three-fourths of the states did not ratify this amendment, and it faded into obscurity. In 1982 Gregory D. Watson, legislative aide to a Texas state legislator, learned about the amendment. Watson began a one-man campaign to revive the amendment, and successfully convinced state legislatures around the country to ratify the amendment. On May 7, 1992, the 38th state (Michigan) ratified it, thus achieving the necessary three-fourths total, but there was some

TABLE OF KEY VOTES

Senate

Subject of Vote	Date of Vote	For D	For R	For Total	Against D	Against R	Against Total
Persian Gulf Resolution Passed	January 12, 1991	10	42	52	45	2	47
S&L Bailout Bill #1 Passed	March 7, 1991	33	36	69	23	7	30
S&L Bailout Bill #2 Passed	November 27, 1991	23	21	44	23	10	33
First China Trade Bill Veto Override (failed: two-thirds majority required)	March 18, 1992	51	9	60	4	34	38
Freedom Support Act Passed	July 2, 1992	43	33	76	13	7	20
START Treaty Approved	October 1, 1992	55	38	93	1	5	6
Second China Trade Bill Veto Override	October 1, 1992	51	8	59	5	35	40

House

Subject of Vote	Date of Vote	For D	For R	For I	For Total	Against D	Against R	Against I	Against Total
Persian Gulf Resolution Passed	January 12, 1991	86	164	0	250	179	3	1	183
S&L Bailout Bill #1 Passed	March 13, 1991	89	103	0	192	141	39	1	181
S&L Bailout Bill #2 Passed	November 27, 1991	Standing vote*			112	Standing vote*			63
First China Trade Bill Veto Override	March 11, 1992	246	110	1	356	10	51	0	61
House Bank Scandal Information Released	March 13, 1992	260	165	1	426	0	0	0	0
Freedom Support Act Passed	August 6, 1992	161	94	0	255	95	68	1	164
Second China Trade Bill Veto Override	September 30, 1992	242	102	1	345	14	60	0	74

[See note 7, p. xxix]

*A standing vote is essentially a head count, not broken down by party. The for and against votes are tallied by having all the persons voting "yes" stand and be counted, and then all the persons voting "no" stand and be counted.

debate in Congress as to whether a ratification that took 203 years was valid. Nevertheless, on May 13, 1992, archivist Don W. Wilson of the National Archives announced that he would exercise his power to certify what was now the Twenty-seventh Amendment to the Constitution. Since congressional pay raises were politically unpopular anyway, the opposition to the Twenty-seventh Amendment in Congress faded. Although technically not necessary, on May 20, 1992, Congress voted to approve the ratification and certification of the Twenty-seventh Amendment.

SCANDALS

In the House of Representatives, many members found that they would have much to explain to their constituents when a scandal broke over the House bank and post office. For many years, members had been able to use these facilities for their private banking needs and were not penalized if they bounced checks and overdrew their accounts. On April 1, 1992, the House Committee on Standards of Official Conduct (the Ethics Committee) effectively rebuked 22 past and present members of the House for abusing their privileges, and named 303 other past and present members who had bounced checks. Tommy F. Robinson (Rep., Ark.) bounced a record 996 checks. Pursuant to a House vote [See Table of Key Votes, above], this information was made available to the public. The scandal fanned public distrust of Congress and was a contributing factor in the decision of many Congressmen to retire at the end of the 102nd Congress. Also, a number of representatives tainted by the affair were defeated in primaries or in the general elections of 1994.

In the Senate, the Senate Ethics Committee completed its investigation into the activities of the "Keating Five," the five senators who allegedly had used their influence to help Charles Keating, the infamous head of Lincoln Saving and Loan. [See 101st Congress] The five were Alan Cranston (Dem., Calif.), Dennis DeConcini (Dem., Ariz.), John Glenn (Dem., Ohio), John McCain (Rep., Ariz.), and Donald W. Riegle Jr. (Dem., Mich.). All five senators had used "poor judgment," as the Ethics Committee put it, in accepting campaign contributions from Keating and indirectly helping Keating evade federal regulators investigating Lincoln. Only Cranston's activities on behalf of Keating, however, were "substantially linked" to campaign funds received from Keating. On November 19, 1991 the Ethics Committee voted 5 to 0, with one abstention, to officially reprimand Cranston in the name of the Senate. A reprimand is one step below a censure, which is an official Senate rebuke. The other four senators received written letters of admonishment from the committee, but no other official action.

FURTHER READING

Kolb, Charles. *White House Daze: The Unmaking of Domestic Policy in the Bush Years*. New York: Free Press, 1994.

Matalin, Mary. *All's Fair: Love, War, and Running For President*. New York: Random House and Simon & Schuster, 1994.

Perot, H. Ross. *United We Stand: How We Can Take Back Our Country*. New York: Hyperion, 1992.

Simon, Paul. *Advice & Consent: Clarence Thomas, Robert Bork and the Intriguing History of the Supreme Court's Nomination Battles*. Washington: National Press Books, 1992.

The 103rd Congress

JANUARY 3, 1993-JANUARY 3, 1995

First Session: January 5, 1993-November 26, 1993
Second Session: January 25, 1994-October 7, 1994

In the 1992 elections for the 103rd Congress, the Democrats in the Senate neither gained nor lost any seats, keeping their majority at 56 of the 100 seats. The Republicans also kept their 44 seats. In the House, the Democrats lost 9 seats, reducing their majority from 267 to 258 of the 435 seats. The Republicans gained 7 seats giving them a total of 176. One seat was held by an independent. [See note 3, p. xxix]

BACKGROUND

William Jefferson Clinton was inaugurated as the 42nd president of the United States on January 20, 1993. Bill Clinton was the first Democratic president in over a decade, the last being Jimmy Carter (1977-1981), and won the 1992 election with only 43.29 percent of the popular vote thanks to the unusual three-way election of 1992 (incumbent President George H.W. Bush received 38 percent and independent H. Ross Perot received nearly 20 percent.) [See the 102nd Congress]

This low support base made Clinton vulnerable from the onset of his presidency to attacks from his political rivals. Clinton had other handicaps as well. As a student, he had protested against the Vietnam War like millions of other Americans, and had never served in the military. Nevertheless, many conservatives were critical, especially when, early in 1993, Clinton announced a new policy of tolerance for gays in the military. Further, his wife, First Lady Hilary Rodham Clinton, was a controversial figure to much of mainstream America. She had her own successful career as an attorney, having achieved partnership in a large law firm, and was a visible part of the Clinton administration from the outset. Many Americans still were uncomfortable with a woman in such a prominent role.

The result was a hardening of Clinton's political opposition early in his term. The Republicans could now muster a nearly unanimous voting bloc against legislation they opposed, such as Clinton's deficit reduction plan in the spring of 1993, which involved some higher taxes for wealthy—and predominantly Republican—Americans. Moreover, Ross Perot, capitalizing on his success in 1992, stayed in the political limelight, forming the United We Stand America group to organize his followers. One of Perot's primary targets was the North American Free Trade Agreement (NAFTA) involving the United States, Canada, and Mexico. NAFTA was originally a Reagan-Bush initiative, but now was backed by Clinton.

Despite this opposition, Clinton chalked up several successes in 1993. He was able to get the deficit reduction plan passed, although it took Vice President Gore's tie-breaking vote in the Senate to do it. Gore also was instrumental in getting NAFTA passed. In the fall of 1993, Gore debated Perot over the merits of NAFTA on national television, and Gore was widely perceived as the victor. This victory, and strong Republican support in Congress, resulted in the passage of NAFTA, despite the opposition of most Democrats and the trade union movement.

Also during 1993, as the recession waned, public attention turned from economic problems to the decades-old issue of how to reduce the nation's crime rate. Even though the U.S. had a higher percentage of its population in prison than all but a handful of other countries, most people favored the "get tough" approach to dealing with crime. In response, Congress passed a major crime control bill backed by the president.

Nineteen ninety-four, however, was a much tougher year for Clinton. His administration's health care reform initiative, led by the first lady, died in the face of Republican and health care industry opposition and public skepticism. The U.S. peacekeeping mission in Somalia had to be withdrawn after conflict with local warlords, and there were crises in Bosnia and Haiti. Scandals dating back to when Clinton was governor of Arkansas also reemerged to undermine his support. These included a questionable real estate deal known as "Whitewater" (named after a development site) and various alleged sexual infidelities. There were also embarrassments involving senior Clinton officials, such as when Surgeon General Jocelyn Elders made a public comment that seemed to support teaching masturbation in schools, which led to her removal. The Republicans skillfully exploited Clinton's weakness in the summer and fall of 1994, resulting in a Republican landslide in the November congressional elections. Nevertheless, Clinton was able to get the worldwide General Agreement on Trade and Tariffs (GATT) approved before the 103rd Congress ended.

SENATE LEADERSHIP

Vice President: Albert A. Gore Jr., was elected as vice president on Clinton's ticket in the November 1992 elections. Gore first had been elected to Congress as a Democratic representative from Tennessee to the 95th Congress, and served in the House until he was elected senator

in the November 1984 elections. Gore unsuccessfully sought the Democratic presidential nomination in 1988, and removed himself from contention early in the 1992 nomination process, when then President Bush appeared to be a certain winner. Gore claimed that he wanted to spend more time with his family. As Bush's popularity sank and the Democrats' chances improved, however, Gore joined the Clinton campaign and was elected vice president.

President Pro Tempore: Robert C. Byrd (Dem., W.Va.) [See biographical note in 95th Congress]

Majority Leader: George J. Mitchell (Dem., Maine) [See biographical note in 101st Congress]

Majority Whip: Wendell H. Ford (Dem., Ky.)

Minority Leader: Robert Dole (Rep., Kans.) [See biographical note in 99th Congress]

Minority Whip: Alan K. Simpson (Rep., Wyo.)

Chairman and Ranking Minority Members of Key Committees:

Committee on Agriculture, Nutrition, and Forestry: Chairman: Patrick J. Leahy (Dem., Vt.); Ranking Minority Member: Richard G. Lugar (Rep., Ind.)

Committee on Appropriations: Chairman: Robert C. Byrd (Dem., W.Va.); Ranking Minority Member: Mark O. Hatfield (Rep., Ore.)

Committee on Armed Services: Chairman: Samuel A. Nunn (Dem., Ga.); Ranking Minority Member: J. Strom Thurmond (Rep., S.C.)

Committee on Banking, Housing, and Urban Affairs: Chairman: Donald W. Riegle Jr. (Dem., Mich.); Ranking Minority Member: Alfonse M. D'Amato (Rep., N.Y.)

Committee on the Budget: Chairman: James R. Sasser (Dem., Tenn.); Ranking Minority Member: Pete V. Domenici (Rep., N.M.)

Committee on Commerce, Science, and Transportation: Chairman: Ernest F. Hollings (Dem., S.C.); Ranking Minority Member: John C. Danforth (Rep., Mo.)

Committee on Energy and Natural Resources: Chairman: J. Bennett Johnston Jr. (Dem., La.); Ranking Minority Member: Malcolm Wallop (Rep., Wyo.)

Committee on Environment and Public Works: Chairman: Max Baucus (Dem., Mont.); Ranking Minority Member: John H. Chafee (Rep., R.I.)

Committee on Finance: Chairman: Daniel P. Moynihan (Dem., N.Y.); Ranking Minority Member: Robert W. Packwood (Rep., Ore.)

Committee on Foreign Relations: Chairman: Claiborne D. Pell (Dem., R.I.); Ranking Minority Member: Jesse A. Helms (Rep., N.C.)

Committee on the Judiciary: Chairman: Joseph R. Biden Jr. (Dem., Del.); Ranking Minority Member: Orrin G. Hatch (Rep., Utah)

Committee on Labor and Human Resources: Chairman: Edward M. Kennedy (Dem., Mass.); Ranking Minority Member: Nancy Landon Kassebaum (Rep., Kans.)

Committee on Rules and Administration: Chairman: Wendell H. Ford (Dem., Ky.); Ranking Minority Member: Theodore F. Stevens (Rep., Alaska)

HOUSE LEADERSHIP

Speaker of the House: Thomas Stephen Foley (Dem., Wash.) [See biographical note in 101st Congress]

Majority Leader: Richard A. Gephardt (Dem., Mo.) first had been elected to Congress as a representative to the 95th Congress. He was a prominent candidate for the Democratic presidential nomination in 1988.

Majority Whip: David E. Bonior (Dem., Mich.)

Minority Leader: Robert H. Michel (Rep., Ill.) Michel did not seek reelection to the 104th Congress.

Minority Whip: Newt Gingrich (Rep., Ga.) was the leader of the conservative Republican faction of the House. He would become Speaker in

the 104th Congress when the Republicans won a majority in the House during the November 1994 elections and Gingrich was the senior House Republican since Minority Leader Michel had not sought reelection.

Chairman and Ranking Minority Members of Key Committees: [See also Organization and Administration, below]

Committee on Agriculture: Chairman: Kika de la Garza (Dem., Tex.); Ranking Minority Member: Pat Roberts (Rep., Kans.)

Committee on Appropriations: Chairman: William H. Natcher (Dem., Ky.); Ranking Minority Member: Joseph M. McDade (Rep., Pa.)

Committee on Armed Services: Chairman: Ronald V. Dellums (Dem., Calif.); Ranking Minority Member: Floyd D. Spence (Rep., S.C.)

Committee on Banking, Finance, and Urban Affairs: Chairman: Henry B. Gonzalez (Dem., Tex.); Ranking Minority Member: Jim Leach (Rep., Iowa)

Committee on the Budget: Chairman: Martin Olav Sabo (Dem., Minn.); Ranking Minority Member: John R. Kasich (Rep., Ohio)

Committee on Education and Labor: Chairman: William D. Ford (Dem., Mich.); Ranking Minority Member: William F. Goodling (Rep., Pa.)

Committee on Energy and Commerce: Chairman: John D. Dingell Jr. (Dem., Mich.); Ranking Minority Member: Carlos J. Moorhead (Rep., Calif.)

Committee on Foreign Affairs: Chairman: Lee H. Hamilton (Dem., Ind.); Ranking Minority Member: Benjamin A. Gilman (Rep., N.Y.)

Committee on the Judiciary: Chairman: Jack B. Brooks (Dem., Tex.); Ranking Minority Member: Hamilton Fish Jr. (Rep., N.Y.)

Committee on Natural Resources: Chairman: George Miller (Dem., Calif.); Ranking Minority Member: Donald E. Young (Rep., Alaska)

C H R O N O L O G Y

January 3, 1993:	The 103rd Congress begins.
January 5, 1993:	The first session begins.
January 20, 1993:	President Clinton nominates his cabinet.
January 21, 1993:	The Senate confirms all of Clinton's cabinet nominees with the exception of the attorney general position.
February 4, 1993:	Congress passes family and medical leave legislation.
March 11, 1993:	The Senate confirms Janet Reno as attorney general.
June 14, 1993:	President Clinton nominates Ruth Bader Ginsburg to succeed Supreme Court Justice Byron R. White.
June 25, 1993:	Congress passes a deficit reduction package.
August 3, 1993:	The Senate confirms Ginsburg.
September 23, 1993:	Congress approves aid for Russia.
October 6, 1993:	Congress sets forth a policy concerning gays in the military.
November 20, 1993:	Congress passes NAFTA and the Brady Bill.
November 26, 1993:	The first session ends.
December 16, 1993:	President Clinton nominates Bobby Ray Inman to succeed Les Aspin as secretary of defense.
January 18, 1994:	Defense Secretary nominee Inman withdraws.
January 24, 1994:	President Clinton nominates William J. Perry to be secretary of defense.
January 25, 1994:	The second session begins.
February 3, 1994:	The Senate confirms Perry.
March 17, 1994:	Congress rejects a constitutional amendment requiring a balanced budget.
April 15, 1994:	U.S. representatives sign the General Agreement on Trade and Tariffs (GATT).
April 21, 1994:	Congress passes crime control measures.
May 13, 1994:	President Clinton nominates Stephen G. Breyer to succeed Supreme Court Justice Harry A. Blackmun.
May 31, 1994:	Sam Gibbons (Dem., Fla.) becomes acting chairman of the Ways and Means Committee after former Chairman Dan Rostenkowski (Dem., Ill.) is indicted.
July 29, 1994:	The Senate confirms Breyer.
October 7, 1994:	The second session ends.
November 8, 1994:	In the 1994 congressional elections, the Republicans win both the House and the Senate for the first time since the early 1950s.
December 1, 1994:	In a special lame duck session, Congress passes legislation to implement GATT.
December 6, 1994:	President Clinton nominates Robert E. Rubin to succeed Treasury Secretary Lloyd Bentsen.
December 28, 1994:	President Clinton nominates Dan Glickman to succeed Agriculture Secretary Mike Espy.
January 3, 1995:	The 103rd Congress ends.

[See note 6, p. xxix]

Committee on Public Works and Transportation: Chairman: Norman Y. Mineta (Dem., Calif.); Ranking Minority Member: Bud Shuster (Rep., Pa.)

Committee on Rules: Chairman: John J. Moakley (Dem., Mass.); Ranking Minority Member: Gerald B. H. Solomon (Rep., N.Y.)

Committee on Ways and Means: Chairman: Daniel D. Rostenkowski (Dem., Ill.); until he was indicted. [See Scandals, below] Sam M. Gibbons (Dem., Fla.) became the acting chairman effective May 31, 1994. Ranking Minority Member: William R. Archer (Rep., Tex.)

ORGANIZATION AND ADMINISTRATION

In the House, the Committee on Interior and Insular Affairs was renamed the Committee on Natural Resources. Reform measures to streamline the committee system died in both the House and the Senate. [See note 5, p. xxix]

MAJOR LEGISLATION PASSED

Brady Bill: After many years of lobbying by gun control advocates, Congress acted to impose a background check and a five-day waiting requirement on handgun purchases. This legislation was known as the Brady Bill after Reagan press secretary Jim Brady, who had been wounded in 1981 during an assassination attempt on the president and whose wife became a leader in the gun control movement.

Crime Control: Congress passed a $30 billion package of crime control measures, including funds for more prison construction and hiring more police officers. The package also included increased penalties for a wide variety of offenses, several social programs, and a ban on certain types of automatic assault weapons. The passage of the latter was a defeat for the National Rifle Association.

Deficit Reduction: Congress enacted a package of tax increases and spending cuts in order to reduce the federal deficit. Unlike Gramm-Rudman-Hollings in the 99th Congress or the budget agreement of the 101st Congress, this leg-

islation targeted the tax increases almost exclusively against wealthy Americans, with most low-income taxpayers getting a tax decrease due to an expansion of a tax break called the Earned Income Tax Credit.

Family and Medical Leave: Unlike the Bush administration, which had opposed this legislation, President Clinton supported guaranteed family and medical leave time for employees. Under the measure passed by Congress, the leave time was without pay, but employees could not lose their jobs for taking it.

Gays in the Military: One of the first actions of the Clinton administration was to propose a new policy of tolerance for homosexuals in the armed services. The proposal was very controversial and unpopular with many segments of society, and ultimately Congress simply approved a policy of avoiding inquiry wherever possible, a policy nicknamed "don't ask, don't tell." This policy was included as part of the fiscal 1994 Defense Appropriations Bill.

GATT: In a special lame duck session after the November 1994 elections, Congress approved legislation implementing the General Agreement on Trade and Tariffs, a world-wide trade pact signed by the United States and 116 other countries on April 15, 1994.

NAFTA: Congress approved the North American Free Trade Agreement (NAFTA), which established a free trade zone between the United States, Canada, and Mexico. NAFTA had its origins in the Reagan-Bush years and was supported by the Clinton administration even though most Democrats and unions strongly opposed it. NAFTA's passage was only possible with strong Republican support.

Russian Aid: In a fiscal 1994 foreign aid bill, Congress approved $2.5 billion in aid to Russia and the other former Soviet republics.

FAILED LEGISLATION

Campaign Finance Reform: A campaign finance bill with limits on campaign spending was passed

TABLE OF KEY VOTES

Senate

Subject of Vote	Date of Vote	For			Against		
		D	R	Total	D	R	Total
Family and Medical Leave Bill Passed	February 4, 1993	55	16	71	2	25	27
Deficit Reduction Bill Passed	June 25, 1993	49	0	50*	6	43	49
Russian Aid Funded	September 23, 1993	52	36	88	3	7	10
Gays in the Military Legislation Passed	October 6, 1993	Passed by voice vote					
Crime Control Bill Passed	November 19, 1993	53	42	95	2	2	4
Brady Bill Passed	November 20, 1993	47	16	63	8	28	36
NAFTA Approved	November 20, 1993	27	34	61	28	10	38
Balanced Budget Amendment Defeated (rejected: two-thirds majority required)	March 1, 1994	22	41	63	34	3	37
GATT Approved	December 1, 1994	41	35	76	13	11	24

House

Subject of Vote	Date of Vote	For				Against			
		D	R	I	Total	D	R	I	Total
Family and Medical Leave Bill Passed	February 3, 1993	224	40	1	265	29	134	0	163
Deficit Reduction Bill Passed	May 27, 1993	218	0	0	218	38	175	1	214
Russian Aid Funded	June 17, 1993	202	107	0	309	47	63	1	111
Gays in the Military Legislation Passed	September 29, 1993	230	38	0	268	25	136	1	162
Brady Bill Passed	November 10, 1993	184	54	0	238	69	119	1	189
NAFTA Approved	November 17, 1993	102	132	0	234	156	43	1	200
Balanced Budget Amendment Defeated (rejected: two-thirds majority required)	March 17, 1994	99	172	0	271	151	1	1	153
Crime Control Bill Passed	April 21, 1994	219	65	1	285	34	107	0	141
GATT Approved	November 29, 1994	167	121	0	288	89	56	1	146

[See note 7, p. xxix]

*Since the vote was 49 to 49, Vice President Gore cast a tie-breaking 50th "yes" vote

by the House and Senate, but there were differences in the House and Senate versions, and Senate Republicans were able to prevent the bill from ever going to conference with the House to reconcile the differences.

Economic Stimulus: Early in 1993 Clinton proposed approximately $16 billion in new spending to help stimulate the economy out of the recession. The proposal died in the Senate.

Health Care Reform: Clinton placed his wife, First Lady Hilary Rodham Clinton, in charge of the effort to fashion the details of a complete national health care plan. Despite months of preparation and a vigorous effort by the Clinton administration to get the plan through Congress, opposition from the Republicans and much of the insurance industry, along with widespread public concern over the bureaucratic complexity of the bill, prevented the legislation from ever coming to a vote.

RELATIONS WITH THE PRESIDENT

As discussed in Background, above, Clinton's success began to fade as his political opposition hardened and he identified himself with such controversial matters as health care reform. His Republican opponents rejuvenated their party and won the battle for public support with proposals such as the Contract With America, a collection of conservative initiatives unveiled to unify the GOP for the 1994 mid-term elections.

Clinton vetoed no bills during the 103rd Congress.

NOMINATIONS, APPOINTMENTS, AND CONFIRMATIONS

The Judiciary: On June 14, 1993, President Clinton nominated Ruth Bader Ginsburg to succeed Supreme Court Justice Byron R. White, who wished to retire. The Senate confirmed Ginsburg on August 3, 1993, by a 96 to 3 vote. On May 13, 1994, Clinton nominated Stephen G. Breyer to succeed Supreme Court Justice Harry A.

Blackmun, who also wished to retire. The Senate confirmed Breyer on July 29, 1994, by an 87 to 9 vote.

The Executive Branch: On January 20, 1993, President Clinton formally submitted his cabinet nominees to the Senate, three of whom were confirmed by voice vote. The same day Les Aspin became secretary of defense, Lloyd Bentsen secretary of the Treasury, and Warren Christopher secretary of state. On January 21, 1993, Bruce Babbitt was confirmed as secretary of the Interior, Jesse Brown as secretary of veterans affairs, Ronald H. Brown as secretary of commerce, Henry G. Cisneros as secretary of housing and urban affairs, Mike Espy as secretary of agriculture, Hazel R. O'Leary as secretary of energy, Federico F. Pena as secretary of transportation, Robert B. Reich as secretary of labor, Richard W. Riley as secretary of education, and Donna E. Shalala as secretary of health and human services.

Clinton withdrew his nominee for attorney general, Zoe Baird, after negative publicity surfaced concerning her failure to pay the proper withholding taxes, and comply with other legal formalities in connection with employing a nanny. Clinton considered nominating federal Judge Kimba M. Wood, but she had experienced similar nanny problems and also had been a Playboy bunny in her youth. Finally, Clinton nominated Florida prosecutor Janet Reno, and on March 11, 1993, the Senate confirmed Reno by a vote of 98 to 0.

There were several changes in the cabinet during the remainder of this Congress. On December 16, 1993, Clinton nominated Bobby Ray Inman to succeed Les Aspin as secretary of defense, but Inman withdrew on January 18, 1994, out of a professed concern that the media was preparing to launch a personal attack campaign against him for reasons that were unclear. Clinton then nominated William J. Perry for the post on January 24, 1994, and on February 3, 1994, the Senate confirmed Perry by a vote of 97 to 0. After the November 1994 elections, Treasury Secretary Lloyd Bentsen indicated that he wished to resign, and on December 6, 1994, Clinton nominated

Robert E. Rubin as Bentsen's successor. Rubin would be confirmed during the 104th Congress.

Finally, there were charges that Secretary of Agriculture Mike Espy had improperly accepted gifts from agricultural business interests, and Espy indicated that he too wished to resign. On December 28, 1994, Clinton nominated Dan Glickman to succeed Espy, and Glickman would also be confirmed during the 104th Congress.

IMPEACHMENTS

None.

CONSTITUTIONAL AMENDMENTS

Both chambers of Congress rejected a rather mild balanced budget amendment to the Constitution, which would have required a three-fifths majority in both the House and Senate to approve deficit spending. [See Table of Key Votes, above]

SCANDALS

In the House, the powerful chairman of the Ways and Means Committee, Dan Rostenkowski (Dem., Ill.), was indicted by federal prosecutors on 17 felony counts. The charges concerned extensive financial irregularities. According to the prosecutors, Rostenkowski embezzled $688,000 in public funds and $56,267 in campaign funds and used most of this money ($529,200) to hire phony employees, mainly cronies, friends, and relatives who were paid for doing nothing. Under the rules of the House, the indictment automatically precluded Rostenkowski from continuing as Ways and Means chairman, and Sam M. Gibbons (Dem., Fla.) became the acting chairman effective May 31, 1994. Despite the indictment, Rostenkowski ran for reelection in his heavily Democratic Chicago district, but was defeated by Republican Michael P. Flanagan.

In the Senate, charges of sexual harassment against Senator Bob Packwood (Rep., Ore.) led to an Ethics Committee investigation. Approximately two dozen women, many of whom were former staffers or campaign workers, had given personal accounts to the press of incidents concerning improper touching, grabbing, and kissing by Packwood. Packwood issued a public apology, but refused to discuss specific conduct. The Ethics Committee had to go to court in order to enforce its request for Packwood's private diaries, which could substantiate the women's allegations. Senators from both parties called for Packwood's resignation, but he refused and stayed in office through this Congress. During the 104th Congress, the Ethics Committee unanimously recommended that Packwood be expelled from the Senate, and Packwood resigned faced with almost certain expulsion by the whole Senate.

FURTHER READING

Gore, Albert A. Jr. *Creating a Government That Works Better and Costs Less: The Report of the National Performance Review.* New York: Penguin Books, 1993.

Margolies-Mezvinsky, Marjorie. *A Woman's Place: The Freshmen Women Who Changed the Face of Congress.* New York: Crown Publishers, 1994.

McKenzie, Nancy F., Editor. *Beyond Crisis: Confronting Health Care in the United States.* New York: Penguin Books, 1994.

Oakley, Meredith L. *On the Make: The Rise of Bill Clinton.* Washington: Regnery Publishing, 1994.

Woodward, Bob. *The Agenda: Inside the Clinton White House.* New York: Pocket Books, 1994.

The 104th Congress

JANUARY 3, 1995 - JANUARY 3, 1997

First Session: January 4, 1995-January 3, 1996*
Second Session: Began January 3, 1996

In the 1994 elections for the 104th Congress, the Republicans in the Senate gained 8 seats, giving them a new majority of 52 seats out of the 100. The Democrats lost 8 seats, lowering their strength from 56 seats to 48 seats. During the first session of Congress, two senators with Republican sympathies (Ben Nighthorse Campbell of Colorado and Richard C. Shelby of Alabama) left the Democratic Party for the Republican Party, and Robert Packwood (Rep., Ore.) resigned [See Scandals, p. 556]. Therefore, by the end of the first session the Senate had 53 Republicans, 46 Democrats, and 1 vacancy.

In the House, the Republicans gained 54 seats, which gave them a new majority of 230 seats out of the 435, while the Democrats lost 54 seats, reducing their strength from 258 seats to 204 seats. One seat belonged to an independent. During the first session of Congress, five representatives with Republican sympathies (Nathan Deal of Georgia, James A. Hayes of Louisiana, Greg Laughlin of Texas, Michael Parker of Mississippi, and W.J. "Billy" Tauzin of Louisiana) left the Democratic Party for the Republican Party, and two more Democrats resigned, one of whom was succeeded by a Republican in a special election. Therefore, at the end of the first session there were 236 Republicans, 197 Democrats, 1 independent and 1 vacancy in the House. [See note 3, p. xxix]

BACKGROUND

The 1994 congressional elections resulted in a stunning victory for the Republican Party, which for the first time since the early 1950s achieved a majority in both the House and the Senate. In those four decades, the Senate had experienced a Republican majority only for six years in the 1980s, while the House Republicans never had been able to unseat the strongly entrenched Democratic majority.

As in most mid-term elections, turnout for the 1994 congressional elections was well below 50 percent of the eligible voters, yet the scope of the GOP victory was seen as evidence of widespread dissatisfaction with big government, career politicians, the growing federal budget deficit, the Democratic Party, and President Clinton. The Republicans also benefited from other factors. The party had done a remarkable job of organizing its supporters and recruiting and training young, ambitious candidates for office. Moreover, President Clinton's low standings in the polls, and a perception among moderates that he had drifted to the Left since winning the presidency as a centrist left his Democratic supporters vulnerable and dispirited.

The new Republican agenda was epitomized by the Contract With America, created by Newt Gingrich (Rep., Ga.) during the 1994 campaigns when he was the House minority whip. The

As this book was being prepared for press in January 1996, the first session of the 104th Congress ended. This chapter was added to keep this edition as up to date as possible. The second session of the 104th Congress and subsequent Congresses will be added in future editions.

Contract was a package of 10 broad reform proposals that supporters pledged to vote on within the first 100 days of the 104th Congress. Most congressional Republicans signed the Contract With America, and it became the focus of activity during the first session of the 104th Congress. The 10 provisions of the Contract With America, as they translated into specific legislative initiatives, concerned:

(1) Reforming the internal operations of Congress.

(2) Passing a balanced budget amendment, and giving the president the line-item veto.

(3) Shifting spending from crime prevention to law enforcement.

(4) Reforming the nation's welfare system.

(5) Providing family tax relief in the form of tax credits for child adoption and for care of the aged.

(6) Curbing the reduction in post-cold war military spending, and forbidding the use of American troops in U.N. missions under non-American commanders.

(7) Reducing the tax burden on Social Security recipients.

(8) Lowering the capital gains tax, and ending unfunded mandates (the practice of passing laws that impose new costs on the state and local governments without providing the funds to pay for those costs.)

(9) Reforming the nation's tort system by capping punitive damages awards in civil suits and restricting product liability litigation.

(10) Limiting the terms of senators and representatives.

Gingrich, who had been instrumental in bringing down Speaker Jim Wright in the 101st Congress, became the Speaker of the House in the 104th Congress. He energetically pursued the Contract during the early months of the first session, shepherding bills for nine of the ten Contract objectives through the House. (Only the term limits proposal died, largely because some House Republicans, now that they were in the majority, lost their enthusiasm for a measure aimed at forcing incumbents out of office.) In the end, however, only two Contract items — congressional reform and unfunded mandates — were enacted into law by the end of the first session. [See Legislation, p. 553; also see Organization and Administration, p. 552 with respect to changes in internal House operations] Most of the other bills stalled in the less conservative and more deliberative Senate, and even when the Senate managed to pass a welfare reform bill reflecting the Contract's goals, President Clinton vetoed it. While Clinton's fellow Democrats were in the minority in Congress, they still held enough seats to prevent the Republicans from obtaining the two-thirds majority necessary to override a veto.

By the fall of 1995, the three-way relationship of a conservative Republican House, a moderate Republican Senate, and a liberal Democratic White House gridlocked the legislative process with the annual government appropriations bills that fund the various departments of the federal government. [See Legislation, p. 553] The Republicans, especially the members of the conservative freshman class, were convinced they had an electoral mandate to achieve a balanced budget by checking the growth in government spending on social programs, such as Medicare and welfare, and turning control over these programs to the states. The Democrats charged that the Republicans were less interested in a balanced budget than they were in cutting social spending. As evidence of this, they pointed to the Republicans' proposed tax cuts, which they said favored the rich and required greater spending cuts to reach a balanced budget. Attempts to negotiate a compromise failed, and in November and December 1995 a number of federal agencies and programs shut down for lack of funding. As the second session began on January 3, 1996 many government agencies still were shut down and nearly 300,000 government workers were on paid furlough. The president and the Republican congressional leadership did manage to agree on stopgap legislation that reopened government

C H R O N O L O G Y

January 3, 1995:	The 104th Congress begins.
January 4, 1995:	The first session begins.
January 10, 1995:	The Senate confirms Robert E. Rubin as secretary of the Treasury.
January 11, 1995:	The House passes congressional reform legislation. [See Organization and Administration, p. 552]
February 1, 1995:	Congress passes legislation barring unfunded mandates legislation.
March 2, 1995:	The Senate rejects a constitutional amendment requiring a balanced budget.
March 30, 1995:	The Senate confirms Dan Glickman as secretary of agriculture.
August 11-13, 1995:	Ross Perot's United We Stand convention ends with the formation of the Reform Party.
September 8, 1995:	Senator Robert Packwood (Rep., Ore.) announces his resignation.
November 8, 1995:	Retired General Colin Powell announces that he will not run for president.
November 13, 1995:	The inability of the congressional Republicans and the White House to agree on the federal budget and the federal appropriations bills triggers a series of government shutdowns. The situation was not resolved when the first session ended.
December 6, 1995:	The House ethics committee dismisses all but three minor ethics charges against Speaker Newt Gingrich (Rep., Ga.).
January 3, 1996:	The first session ends and the second session begins.

[See note 6, p. xxix]

offices by mid-January.

Away from Washington, interest continued to grow in the possibility of a third political party that could overcome the partisanship that seemed to paralyze the Capitol by fielding an independent presidential candidate for the 1996 elections. Most of the interest focused on two moderates: retired General Colin Powell, the first African American to head the Joint Chiefs of Staff, and Ross Perot, the independent candidate for president in the 1992 elections. After much speculation, on November 8, 1995, Powell announced that he would not run for president and that he would not be an independent, but instead was joining the Republican Party. Perot and his supporters, however, decided to create the Reform Party, and began the process of qualifying the party for the ballot in all 50 states. By the end of the first session of the 104th Congress, the new Reform Party's chances of success or choice of a candidate still were unknown, although organizers already had succeeded in qualifying the party in California, the state with the most electoral votes.

Meanwhile, inside Washington, many members of Congress were tiring of the partisan bickering: by January of 1996, 12 senators and 33 representatives from both parties had decided not to seek reelection in the next election. Among those had who announced their retirement by the end of the first session were veteran senators Bill Bradley (Dem., N.J.), Sam Nunn (Dem., Ga.),

Alan K. Simpson (Rep., Wyo.), Nancy Kasselbaum (Rep., Kan.), J. Bennett Johnson Jr. (Dem., La.), William Cohen (Rep., Maine), and Mark Hatfield (Rep., Ore.)

SENATE LEADERSHIP

Vice President: Albert A. Gore Jr. [See biographical note in 103rd Congress] had been active during the 103rd Congress, leading the effort to pass NAFTA (the North American Free Trade Agreement) with the help of most Republicans and over the opposition of most congressional Democrats and independent leaders such as Ross Perot. Gore lost much of his prominence in the 104th Congress when the new Republican majority took the initiative in Congress.

President Pro Tempore: J. Strom Thurmond (Rep., S.C.) [See biographical note in 97th Congress]

Majority Leader: Robert Dole (Rep., Kan.) [See biographical note in 99th Congress] was a traditional, moderate, compromise-oriented politician, and thus the political and legislative agenda in the 104th Congress tended to be set by House Speaker Gingrich and the more conservative Republicans in the House. Still, Dole was the senior statesman of the Republican Party and its front-running candidate for the 1996 presidential nomination.

Majority Whip: C. Trent Lott (Rep., Miss.) The minority whip in the 103rd Congress had been Alan K. Simpson (Rep., Wyo.), but when the Republicans became the majority party in the 104th Congress, Simpson lost his position to the younger and more conservative Lott. Lott first had been elected to the House in the 93rd Congress, and first was elected to the Senate in 1988.

Minority Leader: Thomas A. Daschle (Dem., S.D.) After the retirement of George J. Mitchell (Dem., Maine), the Senate Democratic leader in the 103rd Congress, the Senate Democrats chose Daschle to be their new leader. He first had been elected to the House in the 96th Congress and first was elected to the Senate in 1986.

Minority Whip: Wendell H. Ford (Dem., Ky.)

Other Leaders:

Phil Gramm (Rep., Tex.): Like Bob Dole, Gramm was seeking the Republican presidential nomination for the 1996 elections. More conservative than Dole, Gramm frequently led the party's right-wing in criticizing Dole's willingness to compromise with the White House and the Democrats.

Chairman and Ranking Minority Members of Key Committees: [See also Organization and Administration, p. 552]

Committee on Agriculture, Nutrition, and Forestry: Chairman: Richard G. Lugar (Rep., Ind.); Ranking Minority Member: Patrick J. Leahy (Dem., Vt.)

Committee on Appropriations: Chairman: Mark O. Hatfield (Rep., Ore.); Ranking Minority Member: Robert C. Byrd (Dem., W.Va.)

Committee on Armed Services: Chairman: J. Strom Thurmond (Rep., S.C.); Ranking Minority Member: Samuel A. Nunn (Dem., Ga.)

Committee on Banking, Housing, and Urban Affairs: Chairman: Alfonse M. D'Amato (Rep., N.Y.); Ranking Minority Member: Paul Sarbanes (Dem., Md.)

Committee on the Budget: Chairman: Pete V. Domenici (Rep., N.M.); Ranking Minority Member: James Exon (Dem., Neb.)

Committee on Commerce, Science, and Transportation: Chairman: Larry Pressler (Rep., S.D.); Ranking Minority Member: Ernest F. Hollings (Dem., S.C.)

Committee on Energy and Natural Resources: Chairman: Frank H. Murkowski (Rep., Alaska); Ranking Minority Member: J. Bennett Johnson Jr. (Dem., La.)

Committee on Environment and Public Works: Chairman: John H. Chafee (Rep., R.I.); Ranking Minority Member: Max Baucus (Dem., Mont.)

Committee on Finance: Chairman: Robert W. Packwood (Rep., Ore.), who resigned as chairman September 8, 1995 [See Scandals, p. 5xx]. William V. Roth Jr. (Rep., Del.) became the next chairman. Ranking Minority Member: Daniel P. Moynihan (Dem., N.Y.)

Committee on Foreign Relations: Chairman: Jesse A. Helms (Rep., N.C.); Ranking Minority Member: Claiborne D. Pell (Dem., R.I.)

Committee on the Judiciary: Chairman: Orrin G. Hatch (Rep., Utah); Ranking Minority Member: Joseph R. Biden Jr. (Dem., Del.)

Committee on Labor and Human Resources: Chairman: Nancy Landon Kasselbaum (Rep., Kan.); Ranking Minority Member: Edward M. Kennedy (Dem., Mass.)

Committee on Rules and Administration: Chairman: Theodore F. Stevens (Rep., Alaska); Ranking Minority Member: Wendell H. Ford (Dem., Ky.)

HOUSE LEADERSHIP

Speaker of the House: Newton "Newt" L. Gingrich (Rep., Ga.). Before the 1994 elections, Gingrich was the House minority whip for the Republicans and a leader of the more partisan and conservative faction within the party. The Contract With America [See Background, p. 547] was Gingrich's creation. After the 1994 elections, Minority Leader Robert H. Michel (Rep., Ill.) did not seek reelection, so Gingrich, as the senior leader among House Republican, was elected Speaker without opposition in the Republican dominated 104th Congress. Gingrich aggressively pursued the Republican agenda, edging out the more senior Senate majority leader Bob Dole as the primary Republican spokesman on Capitol Hill. However, the fiery partisan rhetoric that had made Gingrich an effective minority whip now created negative impressions in the press and with the public, as did the $4.5-million cash advance Gingrich was to receive from publisher Rupert Murdoch for Gingrich's book *To Renew America.* Gingrich later declined the cash advance, but the negative publicity persisted. Through most of 1995 there was speculation that

Gingrich would run for the Republican nomination in the 1996 presidential election, but by the end of the first session Gingrich had disavowed any such ambition.

Majority Leader: Richard K. Armey (Rep., Tex.) With Gingrich's support, the House Republicans chose Armey to be their majority leader. Armey helped Gingrich get the Contract With America proposals through the House, and was a prominent figure in the budget negotiations with the White House during the government shutdown at the end of the first session. Armey first was elected to Congress as a representative to the 99th Congress.

Majority Whip: Thomas D. DeLay (Rep., Tex.) The House Republicans chose another Texan to serve as Armey's right hand man. DeLay first was elected to Congress as a representative to the 99th Congress, and this was his first Congress as majority whip.

Minority Leader: Richard A. Gephardt (Dem., Mo.) first had been elected to Congress as a representative to the 95th Congress. He was a prominent candidate for the Democratic presidential nomination in 1988. Normally, Thomas S. Foley (Dem., Wash.), the Democratic Speaker of the House in the 103rd Congress, would have become the minority leader in the 104th Congress, since that is the senior position for the minority party. However, Foley was defeated in the 1994 election, becoming the first Speaker of the House to lose a reelection campaign since William Pennington (Rep., N.J.), who was Speaker in the 36th Congress. In Foley's absence, Gephardt rose from the number two position in the House Democratic leadership to minority leader.

Minority Whip: David E. Bonior (Dem., Mich.) succeeded Gephardt as his party's whip. Bonier first had been elected as a representative to the 95th Congress. During the 104th Congress, he was particularly vocal in calling attention to Speaker Gingrich's personal eccentricities and some potential ethics concerns involving Gingrich's finances.

Chairman and Ranking Minority Members of Key Committees: The 104th House eliminated some committees and renamed others as part of its internal reform process. [See Organization and Administration, p. 552]

Committee on Agriculture: Chairman: Pat Roberts (Rep., Kan.); Ranking Minority Member: Kika de la Garza (Dem., Tex.)

Committee on Appropriations: Chairman: Robert L. Livingston (Rep., La.); Ranking Minority Member: David Obey (Dem., Wis.)

Committee on Banking and Financial Services: Chairman: Jim Leach (Rep., Iowa); Ranking Minority Member: Henry B. Gonzalez (Dem., Tex.)

Committee on the Budget: Chairman: John R. Kasich (Rep., Ohio); Ranking Minority Member: Martin Olav Sabo (Dem., Minn.)

Committee on Commerce: Chairman: Tom Bliley (Rep., Va.); Ranking Minority Member: John D. Dingell Jr. (Dem., Mich.)

Committee on Economic and Educational Opportunities: Chairman: William F. Goodling (Rep., Pa.); Ranking Minority Member: Bill Clay (Dem., Mo.)

Committee on International Relations: Chairman: Benjamin A. Gilman (Rep., N.Y.); Ranking Minority Member: Lee H. Hamilton (Dem., Ind.)

Committee on the Judiciary: Chairman: Henry Hyde (Rep., Ill.); Ranking Minority Member: John Conyers Jr. (Dem., Mich.)

Committee on National Security: Chairman: Floyd D. Spence (Rep., S.C.); Ranking Minority Member: Ronald V. Dellums (Dem., Calif.)

Committee on Resources: Chairman: Donald E. Young (Rep., Alaska); Ranking Minority Member: George Miller (Dem., Calif.)

Committee on Rules: Chairman: Gerald B. H. Solomon (Rep., N.Y.); Ranking Minority Member: John J. Moakley (Dem., Mass.)

Committee on Transportation and Infrastructure: Chairman: Bud Shuster (Rep., Pa.); Ranking Minority Member: Norman Y. Mineta (Dem., Calif.), who resigned as ranking minority member on September 11, 1995. James Oberstar (Dem., Minn.) became the next ranking minority member.

Committee on Ways and Means: Chairman: William R. Archer (Rep., Tex.); Ranking Minority Member: Sam M. Gibbons (Dem., Fla.)

Other Leaders:

Even before the 1994 elections, the Republicans had made a concerted effort to bring junior Republicans into important policy-making positions. For example, two young members, John Boehner (Rep., Ohio) and Susan Molinari (Rep., N.Y.), shared the chair of the House Republican Conference, an organization that helped set the party's congressional agenda.

ORGANIZATION AND ADMINISTRATION

While the Senate adopted no significant internal reforms during the first session of the 104th Congress, as part of the Contract With America [See Background, p. 547], the new Republican majority in the House extensively reformed that chamber's internal structure and procedures. [See note 5, p. xxix]. The changes included:

(1) Establishing a term limit for the Speaker of the House: no member would be allowed to serve as Speaker for more than four consecutive two-year terms.

(2) Imposing term limits for committee and subcommittee chairmen: chairmen would be limited to three consecutive two-year terms.

(3) Abolishing funding for legislative service organizations, popularly known as caucuses, which previously had operated from House-provided office facilities. (Dozens of such caucuses had been formed to represent the interests of various groups and special interests such as African Americans, oil-states, women, and major cities.

(4) Requiring a three-fifths majority (rather than the usual simple majority) of the House to approve any increase in income taxes and barring bills that included retroactive tax increases.

(5) Requiring that House proceedings be reported verbatim in the *Congressional Record*. Members of the House would no longer have the right to edit and revise the official record of their comments on the floor, and the public would know that the published record reflected the actual proceedings.

The House also consolidated its committee system, eliminating the committees devoted to the District of Columbia, Merchant Marine and Fisheries, Post Office, and Civil Service. In an economy move, committee staff personnel was cut by one-third. Finally, many committees were renamed: the Committee on Armed Services became the Committee on National Security; the Committee on Banking, Finance, and Urban Affairs became the Committee on Banking and Financial Services; the Committee on Education and Labor became the Committee on Economic and Educational Opportunities; the Committee on Energy and Commerce became the Committee on Commerce; the Committee on Foreign Affairs became the Committee on International Relations; the Committee on Natural Resources became the Committee on Resources; and the Committee on Public Works and Transportation became the Committee on Transportation and Infrastructure.

MAJOR LEGISLATION PASSED

By the end of the first session, only two significant Contract With America items had been passed into law [See Background, p. 547]. Both were measures that President Clinton agreed with, and so there was no real Democratic opposition.

Congressional Reform: The 104th Congress, spurred by its new Republican majority, passed legislation requiring congressional compliance with federal laws and regulations. For many years, congressional internal operations staff had been exempted from the very health, safety, labor, and other federal laws that Congress enacted for the nation at large. For example, because Congress did not want to submit to the bureaucratic compliance measures ordinary businesses and other government entities had to endure, congressional employees were not covered by the same workplace safety measures that protected employees in private sector businesses.

Unfunded Mandates: Congress acted to end the practice of passing federal laws and regulations that imposed costs on state and local governments without providing the funding to cover such costs.

FAILED AND PENDING LEGISLATION

Welfare Reform: Congress enacted legislation that would give the states a much greater degree of control over welfare programs currently administered by the federal government. The federal government would make financial contributions in the form of block grants, but the states would administer the programs and determine who was eligible for assistance. The federal school lunch program also would be farmed out to the states. This bill was vetoed by President Clinton, and as of the end of the first session there was no significant action in Congress to either pass a new bill or override Clinton's veto.

Budget Appropriations: At the end of the first session, the president and congressional Republicans still were deadlocked over many appropriations bills for the fiscal year that began on October 1, 1995. The chart on page 554 details the situation as of the beginning of the second session on January 3, 1996.

RELATIONS WITH THE PRESIDENT

Relations between President Clinton and the congressional Republicans had been tense since the beginning of his administration, but they deteriorated further once the Republicans gained control of the 104th Congress. For the first time, Clinton was forced to veto legislation that the

STATUS OF BUDGET APPROPRIATION BILL

for fiscal year 1996, as of January 3, 1996

Appropriations Bill	Congressional Status	Final Action by Clinton
Agriculture, Commerce, and Justice	Passed both chambers	Approved
State and Judiciary	Passed both chambers	Vetoed
Defense	Passed both chambers	Approved
District of Columbia	In conference	
Energy and Water	Passed both chambers	Approved
Foreign Affairs	In conference	
Interior	Passed both chambers	Vetoed
Labor, Health and Human Services, Education	Stalled in the Senate	
Legislative Branch (internal operations of Congress)	Passed both chambers	Approved
Military Construction	Passed both chambers	Approved
Transportation	Passed both chambers	Approved
Treasury, Postal Service, General Government	Passed both chambers	Approved
Veterans Affairs, Housing and Urban Development, Independent Agencies	Passed both chambers	Vetoed

Democratic minority could not prevent the Republicans from passing. On the other hand, while the Republicans held the majority, they did not have the two-thirds majority in both chambers necessary to override a veto. The Republicans stepped up the congressional investigation into Whitewater, a failed real estate development deal in Arkansas involving a savings and loan collapse and allegedly improper financial dealings by the President and First Lady Hillary Clinton while Clinton was the governor of Arkansas. Poor relations between congressional leaders and the president contributed to the government shutdown that took place toward the end of the first session. [See Background, p. 547]

NOMINATIONS, APPOINTMENTS, AND CONFIRMATIONS

The Judiciary: There were no significant nominations, appointments, or confirmations in the federal judiciary during the first session of the 104th Congress.

The Executive Branch: After the November 1994 elections, Treasury Secretary Lloyd Bentsen indicated his wish to resign. President Clinton nominated Robert E. Rubin as Bentsen's successor, and on January 10, 1995, the Senate confirmed Rubin as secretary of the Treasury by a 9 to 0 vote. Also during the 103rd Congress, secretary of agriculture Mike Espy, who had been

TABLE OF KEY VOTES

Senate

Subject of Vote	Date of Vote	For			Against		
		D	R	Total	D	R	Total
Congressional Reform	January 11, 1995	45	53	98	1	0	1
Unfunded Mandates	January 27, 1995	35	51	86	10	0	10
Constitutional Amendment: Balanced Budget (rejected: two-thirds majority required)	March 2, 1995	14	51	65	33	2	35
Welfare Reform	September 19, 1995	35	52	87	11	1	12

House

Subject of Vote	Date of Vote	For				Against			
		D	R	I	Total	D	R	I	Total
Congressional Reform	January 5, 1995	199	229	1	429	0	0	0	0
Constitutional Amendment: Balanced Budget	January 26, 1995	72	228	0	300	129	2	1	132
Unfunded Mandates	February 1, 1995	130	230	0	360	73	0	1	74
Welfare Reform	March 24, 1995	9	225	0	234	193	5	1	199
Constitutional Amendment: Term Limits (rejected: two-thirds majority required)	March 29, 1995	38	189	0	227	163	40	1	204

[See note 7, p. xxix]

charged with accepting improper gifts, indicated that he wished to resign, and on December 28, 1994, Clinton nominated Dan Glickman to succeed him. On March 30, 1995, the Senate confirmed Glickman by a 94 to 0 vote.

IMPEACHMENTS

None.

CONSTITUTIONAL AMENDMENTS

The House rejected a bill limiting members of both the House and the Senate to 12 years in office that would have sent a constitutional amendment on term limits to the states for ratification. Since the bill originated in the House but did not receive the necessary two-thirds majority, it died in the House and there was no vote in the Senate.

As part of the Contract With America [See Background, p. 547] the House approved a balanced budget amendment to the Constitution, but the Senate rejected it by a vote of 66 in favor and 34 against, one vote short of the necessary two-thirds majority. The one Republican vote against the amendment was Mark O. Hatfield (Rep., Ore.), who later announced his intention to retire from the Senate. The final vote as it appears in the Table of Key Votes above was recorded as 65 in favor and 35 against, because Robert Dole (Rep., Kans.) reversed his vote in favor to a vote against. (Under Senate procedures, only a senator voting against a bill can move to reconsider it at a later date. Therefore, Dole's switch was designed to enable him eventually to reintroduce the balanced budget amendment for another vote. He had not done so by the end of the first session.)

SCANDALS

In the Senate, the sexual harassment charges against Senator Bob Packwood (Rep., Ore.) [See 103rd Congress] led to ethics hearings. Senator Barbara Boxer (Dem., Calif.), a prominent advocate of women's issues, led the drive for Packwood's resignation or removal. The entire affair became an embarrassment for the Senate Republicans. On September 8, 1995, Packwood announced that he would leave the Senate effective October 1, 1995.

In the House, the Committee on Standards of Official Conduct investigated various alleged improprieties by Speaker Newt Gingrich (Rep., Ga.). On December 6, 1995, the committee dismissed charges of wrongdoing concerning Gingrich's book contract with a publishing firm owned by media magnate Rupert Murdoch [See the Speaker's biography under House Leadership], and charges that Gingrich improperly had accepted free cable TV time to broadcast a college course that he was teaching. The committee did find three minor ethics violations, but called for no punishment. The violations were that Gingrich (1) improperly promoted his college course in his floor speeches in the House, (2) improperly promoted events sponsored by GOPAC (a Republican political action committee) in his floor speeches, and (3) improperly employed Republican political consultant Joseph Gaylord to screen congressional staff candidates,

which violated the House rule against using private funds for congressional operations.

Also in the House, Representative Enid Waldholtz's (Rep., Utah) husband Joseph, who had been in charge of her 1994 campaign finances, disappeared for several days in November 1995 at the same time that millions of dollars of financial irregularities and improper contributions in the Waldholtz campaign fund were being revealed. When Joseph Waldholtz resurfaced, he turned himself in to the authorities claiming that he was not responsible for the financial problems. Representative Waldholtz filed for divorce, and on December 11, 1995, denied any wrongdoing during an emotional five-hour, televised press conference. At the end of the first session, the investigation into Waldholtz's finances was still pending.

FURTHER READING

Drew, Elizabeth. *On the Edge: The Clinton Presidency*. New York: Simon & Schuster, 1994.

Gingrich, Newt. *To Renew America*. New York: HarperCollins, 1995.

Perot, H. Ross. *Preparing Our Country for the 21st Century*. New York: HarperCollins, 1995.

Powell, Colin. *My American Journey*. New York: Random House, 1995.

Appendixes

APPENDIX A

CONSTITUTION OF THE UNITED STATES OF AMERICA

We the People of the United States, in Order to form a more perfect Union, establish Justice, insure domestic Tranquillity, provide for the common defence, promote the general Welfare, and secure the Blessings of Liberty to ourselves and our Posterity, do ordain and establish this Constitution for the United States of America.

ARTICLE I

Section 1. All legislative Powers herein granted shall be vested in a Congress of the United States, which shall consist of a Senate and House of Representatives.

Section 2. The House of Representatives shall be composed of Members chosen every second Year by the People of the several States, and the Electors in each State shall have the Qualifications requisite for Electors of the most numerous Branch of the State Legislature.

No Person shall be a Representative who shall not have attained to the age of twenty five Years, and been seven Years a Citizen of the United States, and who shall not, when elected, be an Inhabitant of that State in which he shall be chosen.

[Representatives and direct Taxes shall be apportioned among the several States which may be included within this Union, according to their respective Numbers, which shall be determined by adding to the whole Number of free Persons, including those bound to Service for a Term of Years, and excluding Indians not taxed, three fifths of all other Persons.][1] The actual Enumeration shall be made within three Years after the first Meeting of the Congress of the United States, and within every subsequent Term of ten Years, in such Manner as they shall by Law direct. The Number of Representatives shall not exceed one for every thirty Thousand, but each State shall have at Least one Representative; and until such enumeration shall be made, the State of New Hampshire shall be entitled to chuse three, Massachusetts eight, Rhode-Island and Providence Plantations one, Connecticut five, New-York six, New Jersey four, Pennsylvania eight, Delaware one, Maryland six, Virginia ten, North Carolina five, South Carolina five, and Georgia three.

When vacancies happen in the Representation from any State, the Executive Authority thereof shall issue Writs of Election to fill such Vacancies.

The House of Representatives shall chuse their Speaker and other Officers; and shall have the sole Power of Impeachment.

Section 3. The Senate of the United States shall be composed of two Senators from each State, [chosen by the Legislature thereof,][2] for six Years; and each Senator shall have one Vote.

Immediately after they shall be assembled in

---

[1] The part in brackets was changed by section 2 of the Fourteenth Amendment.
[2] The part in brackets was changed by the first paragraph of the Seventeenth Amendment.

Consequence of the first Election, they shall be divided as equally as may be into three Classes. The Seats of the Senators of the first Class shall be vacated at the Expiration of the second Year, of the second Class at the Expiration of the fourth Year, and of the third Class at the Expiration of the sixth Year, so that one third may be chosen every second Year; [and if Vacancies happen by Resignation, or otherwise, during the Recess of the Legislature of any State, the Executive thereof may make temporary Appointments until the next Meeting of the Legislature, which shall then fill such Vacancies.][3]

No Person shall be a Senator who shall not have attained to the Age of thirty Years, and been nine Years a Citizen of the United States, and who shall not, when elected, be an Inhabitant of that State for which he shall be chosen.

The Vice President of the United States shall be President of the Senate, but shall have no Vote, unless they be equally divided.

The Senate shall chuse their other Officers, and also a President pro tempore, in the Absence of the Vice President, or when he shall exercise the Office of President of the United States.

The Senate shall have the sole Power to try all Impeachments. When sitting for that Purpose, they shall be on Oath or Affirmation. When the President of the United States is tried, the Chief Justice shall preside: And no Person shall be convicted without the Concurrence of two thirds of the Members present.

Judgment in Cases of Impeachment shall not extend further than to removal from Office, and disqualification to hold and enjoy any Office of honor, Trust or Profit under the United States: but the Party convicted shall nevertheless be liable and subject to Indictment, Trial, Judgment and Punishment, according to Law.

Section 4. The Times, Places and Manner of holding Elections for Senators and Representatives, shall be prescribed in each State by the Legislature thereof; but the Congress may at any time by Law make or alter such Regulations, except as to the Places of chusing Senators.

The Congress shall assemble at least once in every Year, and such Meeting shall [be on the first Monday in December][4], unless they shall by Law appoint a different Day.

Section 5. Each House shall be the Judge of the Elections, Returns and Qualifications of its own Members, and a Majority of each shall constitute a Quorum to do Business; but a smaller Number may adjourn from day to day, and may be authorized to compel the Attendance of absent Members, in such Manner, and under such Penalties as each House may provide.

Each House may determine the Rules of its Proceedings, punish its Members for disorderly Behaviour, and, with the Concurrence of two thirds, expel a Member.

Each House shall keep a Journal of its Proceedings, and from time to time publish the same, excepting such Parts as may in their Judgment require Secrecy; and the Yeas and Nays of the Members of either House on any question shall, at the Desire of one fifth of those Present, be entered on the Journal.

Neither House, during the Session of Congress, shall, without the Consent of the other, adjourn for more than three days, nor to any other Place than that in which the two Houses shall be sitting.

Section 6. The Senators and Representatives shall receive a Compensation for their Services, to be ascertained by Law, and paid out of the Treasury of the United States. They shall in all Cases, except Treason, Felony and Breach of the Peace, be privileged from Arrest during their Attendance at the Session of their respective Houses, and in going to and returning from the same; and for any Speech or Debate in either House, they shall not be questioned in any other Place.

No Senator or Representative shall, during the Time for which he was elected, be appointed to any civil Office under the Authority of the United States, which shall have been created, or the Emoluments whereof shall have been encreased during such time; and no Person holding any Office under the United States, shall be a Member of either House during his Continuance in Office.

Section 7. All Bills for raising Revenue shall

---

[3] The part in brackets was changed by the second paragraph of the Seventeenth Amendment.
[4] The part in brackets was changed by section 2 of the Twentieth Amendment.

originate in the House of Representatives; but the Senate may propose or concur with Amendments as on other Bills. Every Bill which shall have passed the House of Representatives and the Senate, shall, before it become a Law, be presented to the President of the United States; If he approve he shall sign it, but if not he shall return it, with his Objections to that House in which it shall have originated, who shall enter the Objections at large on their Journal, and proceed to reconsider it. If after such Reconsideration two thirds of that House shall agree to pass the Bill, it shall be sent, together with the Objections, to the other House, by which it shall likewise be reconsidered, and if approved by two thirds of that House, it shall become a Law. But in all such Cases the Votes of both Houses shall be determined by yeas and Nays, and the names of the Persons voting for and against the Bill shall be entered on the Journal of each House respectively. If any Bill shall not be returned by the President within ten Days (Sundays excepted) after it shall have been presented to him, the Same shall be a Law, in like Manner as if he had signed it, unless the Congress by their Adjournment prevent its Return, in which Case it shall not be a Law.

Every Order, Resolution, or Vote to which the Concurrence of the Senate and House of Representatives may be necessary (except on a question of Adjournment) shall be presented to the President of the United States; and before the Same shall take Effect, shall be approved by him, or being disapproved by him, shall be repassed by two thirds of the Senate and House of Representatives, according to the Rules and Limitations prescribed in the Case of a Bill.

Section 8. The Congress shall have Power To lay and collect Taxes, Duties, Imposts and Excises, to pay the Debts and provide for the common Defence and general Welfare of the United States; but all Duties, Imposts and Excises shall be uniform throughout the United States;

To borrow Money on the credit of the United States;

To regulate Commerce with foreign Nations, and among the several States, and with the Indian Tribes;

To establish an uniform Rule of Naturalization, and uniform Laws on the subject of Bankruptcies throughout the United States;

To coin Money, regulate the Value thereof, and of foreign Coin, and fix the Standard of Weights and Measures;

To provide for the Punishment of counterfeiting the Securities and current Coin of the United States;

To establish Post Offices and post Roads;

To promote the Progress of Science and useful Arts, by securing for limited Times to Authors and Inventors the exclusive Right to their respective Writings and Discoveries;

To constitute Tribunals inferior to the supreme Court;

To define and punish Piracies and Felonies committed on the high Seas, and Offences against the Law of Nations;

To declare War, grant Letters of Marque and Reprisal, and make Rules concerning Captures on Land and Water;

To raise and support Armies, but no Appropriation of Money to that Use shall be for a longer Term than two Years;

To provide and maintain a Navy;

To make Rules for the Government and Regulation of the land and naval Forces;

To provide for calling forth the Militia to execute the Laws of the Union, suppress Insurrections and repel Invasions;

To provide for organizing, arming, and disciplining, the Militia, and for governing such Part of them as may be employed in the Service of the United States, reserving to the States respectively, the Appointment of the Officers, and the Authority of training the Militia according to the discipline prescribed by Congress;

To exercise exclusive Legislation in all Cases whatsoever, over such District (not exceeding ten Miles square) as may, by Cession of particular States, and the Acceptance of Congress, become the Seat of the Government of the United States, and to exercise like Authority over all Places purchased by the Consent of the

Legislature of the State in which the Same shall be, for the Erection of Forts, Magazines, Arsenals, dock-Yards, and other needful Buildings;—And

To make all Laws which shall be necessary and proper for carrying into Execution the foregoing Powers, and all other Powers vested by this Constitution in the Government of the United States, or in any Department or Officer thereof.

Section 9. The Migration or Importation of such Persons as any of the States now existing shall think proper to admit, shall not be prohibited by the Congress prior to the Year one thousand eight hundred and eight, but a Tax or duty may be imposed on such Importation, not exceeding ten dollars for each Person.

The Privilege of the Writ of Habeas Corpus shall not be suspended, unless when in Cases of Rebellion or Invasion the public Safety may require it.

No Bill of Attainder or ex post facto Law shall be passed.

[No Capitation, or other direct, Tax shall be laid, unless in Proportion to the Census or Enumeration herein before directed to be taken.[5]]

No Tax or Duty shall be laid on Articles exported from any State.

No Preference shall be given by any Regulation of Commerce or Revenue to the Ports of one State over those of another; nor shall Vessels bound to, or from, one State, be obliged to enter, clear, or pay Duties in another.

No Money shall be drawn from the Treasury, but in Consequence of Appropriations made by Law; and a regular Statement and Account of the Receipts and Expenditures of all public Money shall be published from time to time.

No Title of Nobility shall be granted by the United States: And no Person holding any Office of Profit or Trust under them, shall, without the Consent of the Congress, accept of any present, Emolument, Office, or Title, of any kind whatever, from any King, Prince, or foreign State.

Section 10. No State shall enter into any Treaty, Alliance, or Confederation; grant Letters of Marque and Reprisal; coin Money; emit Bills of Credit; make any Thing but gold and silver Coin a Tender in Payment of Debts; pass any Bill of Attainder, ex post facto Law, or Law impairing the Obligation of Contracts, or grant any Title of Nobility.

No State shall, without the Consent of the Congress, lay any Imposts or Duties on Imports or Exports, except what may be absolutely necessary for executing itís inspection Laws: and the net Produce of all Duties and Imposts, laid by any State on Imports or Exports, shall be for the Use of the Treasury of the United States; and all such Laws shall be subject to the Revision and Controul of the Congress.

No State shall, without the Consent of Congress, lay any Duty of Tonnage, keep Troops, or Ships of War in time of Peace, enter into any Agreement or Compact with another State, or with a foreign Power, or engage in War, unless actually invaded, or in such imminent Danger as will not admit of delay.

ARTICLE II

Section 1. The executive Power shall be vested in a President of the United States of America. He shall hold his Office during the Term of four Years, and, together with the Vice President, chosen for the same Term, be elected, as follows:

Each State shall appoint, in such Manner as the Legislature thereof may direct, a Number of Electors, equal to the whole Number of Senators and Representatives to which the State may be entitled in the Congress: but no Senator or Representative, or Person holding an Office of Trust or Profit under the United States, shall be appointed an Elector.

[The Electors shall meet in their respective States, and vote by Ballot for two Persons, of whom one at least shall not be an Inhabitant of the same State with themselves. And they shall make a List of all the Persons voted for, and of the Number of Votes for each; which List they shall sign and certify, and transmit sealed to the Seat of the Government of the United States, directed to the President of the Senate. The President of the Senate shall, in the Presence of the Senate and House of Representatives, open all the Certificates,

---

[5] The Sixteenth Amendment gave Congress the power to tax incomes.

and the Votes shall then be counted. The Person having the greatest Number of Votes shall be the President, if such Number be a Majority of the whole Number of Electors appointed; and if there be more than one who have such Majority, and have an equal Number of Votes, then the House of Representatives shall immediately chuse by Ballot one of them for President; and if no Person have a Majority, then from the five highest on the list the said House shall in like Manner chuse the President. But in chusing the President, the Votes shall be taken by States, the Representation from each State having one Vote; a quorum for this Purpose shall consist of a Member or Members from two thirds of the States, and a Majority of all the States shall be necessary to a Choice. In every Case, after the Choice of the President, the Person having the greatest Number of Votes of the Electors shall be the Vice President. But if there should remain two or more who have equal Votes, the Senate shall chuse from them by Ballot the Vice President.][6]

The Congress may determine the Time of chusing the Electors, and the Day on which they shall give their Votes; which Day shall be the same throughout the United States.

No Person except a natural born Citizen, or a Citizen of the United States, at the time of the Adoption of this Constitution, shall be eligible to the Office of President; neither shall any Person be eligible to that Office who shall not have attained to the Age of thirty five Years, and been fourteen Years a Resident within the United States.

In Case of the Removal of the President from Office, or of his Death, Resignation, or Inability to discharge the Powers and Duties of the said Office,[7] the Same shall devolve on the Vice President, and the Congress may by Law provide for the Case of Removal, Death, Resignation or Inability, both of the President and Vice President, declaring what Officer shall then act as President, and such Officer shall act accordingly, until the Disability be removed, or a President shall be elected.

The President shall, at stated Times, receive for his Services, a Compensation, which shall neither be encreased nor diminished during the Period for which he shall have been elected, and he shall not receive within that Period any other Emolument from the United States, or any of them.

Before he enter on the Execution of his Office, he shall take the following Oath or Affirmation:[7] "I do solemnly swear (or affirm) that I will faithfully execute the Office of President of the United States, and will to the best of my Ability, preserve, protect and defend the Constitution of the United States."

Section 2. The President shall be Commander in Chief of the Army and Navy of the United States, and of the Militia of the several States, when called into the actual Service of the United States; he may require the Opinion, in writing, of the principal Officer in each of the executive Departments, upon any Subject relating to the Duties of their respective Offices, and he shall have Power to grant Reprieves and Pardons for Offences against the United States, except in Cases of Impeachment.

He shall have Power, by and with the Advice and Consent of the Senate, to make Treaties, provided two thirds of the Senators present concur; and he shall nominate, and by and with the Advice and Consent of the Senate, shall appoint Ambassadors, other public Ministers and Consuls, Judges of the supreme Court, and all other Officers of the United States, whose Appointments are not herein otherwise provided for, and which shall be established by Law: but the Congress may by Law vest the Appointment of such inferior Officers, as they think proper, in the President alone, in the Courts of Law, or in the Heads of Departments.

The President shall have Power to fill up all Vacancies that may happen during the Recess of the Senate, by granting Commissions which shall expire at the End of their next Session.

Section 3. He shall from time to time give to the Congress Information of the State of the Union, and recommend to their Consideration such Measures as he shall judge necessary and expedient; he may, on extraordinary Occasions, convene both Houses, or either of them, and in Case of Disagreement between them, with Respect to the Time of Adjournment, he may adjourn them

---

[6] The material in brackets has been changed by the Twelfth Amendment.
[7] This provision has been affected by the Tweny-fifth Amendment.

to such Time as he shall think proper; he shall receive Ambassadors and other public Ministers; he shall take Care that the Laws be faithfully executed, and shall Commission all the Officers of the United States.

Section 4. The President, Vice President and all civil Officers of the United States, shall be removed from Office on Impeachment for, and Conviction of, Treason, Bribery, or other high Crimes and Misdemeanors.

ARTICLE III

Section 1. The judicial Power of the United States shall be vested in one supreme Court, and in such inferior Courts as the Congress may from time to time ordain and establish. The Judges, both of the supreme and inferior Courts, shall hold their Offices during good Behaviour, and shall, at stated Times, receive for their Services, a Compensation, which shall not be diminished during their Continuance in Office.

Section 2. The judicial Power shall extend to all Cases, in Law and Equity, arising under this Constitution, the Laws of the United States, and Treaties made, or which shall be made, under their Authority;—to all Cases affecting Ambassadors, other public Ministers and Consuls;—to all Cases of admiralty and maritime Jurisdiction;—to Controversies to which the United States shall be a Party;—to Controversies between two or more States;—between a State and Citizens of another State;[8]—between Citizens of different States;—between Citizens of the same State claiming Lands under Grants of different States, and between a State, or the Citizens thereof, and foreign States, Citizens or Subjects.[8]

In all Cases affecting Ambassadors, other public Ministers and Consuls, and those in which a State shall be Party, the supreme Court shall have original Jurisdiction. In all the other Cases before mentioned, the supreme Court shall have appellate Jurisdiction, both as to Law and Fact, with such Exceptions, and under such Regulations as the Congress shall make.

The Trial of all Crimes, except in Cases of Impeachment, shall be by Jury; and such Trial shall be held in the State where the said Crimes shall have been committed; but when not committed within any State, the Trial shall be at such Place or Places as the Congress may by Law have directed.

Section 3. Treason against the United States, shall consist only in levying War against them, or in adhering to their Enemies, giving them Aid and Comfort. No Person shall be convicted of Treason unless on the Testimony of two Witnesses to the same overt Act, or on Confession in open Court.

The Congress shall have Power to declare the Punishment of Treason, but no Attainder of Treason shall work Corruption of Blood, or Forfeiture except during the Life of the Person attained.

ARTICLE IV

Section 1. Full Faith and Credit shall be given in each State to the public Acts, Records, and judicial Proceedings of every other State. And the Congress may by general Laws prescribe the Manner in which such Acts, Records and Proceedings shall be proved, and the Effect thereof.

Section 2. The Citizens of each State shall be entitled to all Privileges and Immunities of Citizens in the several States.

A Person charged in any State with Treason, Felony, or other Crime, who shall flee from Justice, and be found in another State, shall on Demand of the executive Authority of the State from which he fled, be delivered up, to be removed to the State having Jurisdiction of the Crime.

[No Person held to Service or Labour in one State, under the Laws thereof, escaping into another, shall, in Consequence of any Law or Regulation therein, be discharged from such Service or Labour, but shall be delivered up on Claim of the Party to whom such Service or Labour may be due.][9]

Section 3. New States may be admitted by the Congress into this Union; but no new State shall be formed or erected within the Jurisdiction of any other State; nor any State be formed by the

---

[8] The Eleventh Amendment limited federal jurisdiction over civil litigation involving the states.
[9] This paragraph refers to slavery, abolished by the Thirteenth Amendment.

Junction of two or more States, or Parts of States, without the Consent of the Legislatures of the States concerned as well as of the Congress.

The Congress shall have Power to dispose of and make all needful Rules and Regulations respecting the Territory or other Property belonging to the United States; and nothing in this Constitution shall be so construed as to Prejudice any Claims of the United States, or of any particular State.

Section 4. The United States shall guarantee to every State in this Union a Republican Form of Government, and shall protect each of them against Invasion; and on Application of the Legislature, or of the Executive (when the Legislature cannot be convened) against domestic Violence.

ARTICLE V

The Congress, whenever two thirds of both Houses shall deem it necessary, shall propose Amendments to this Constitution, or, on the Application of the Legislatures of two thirds of the several States, shall call a Convention for proposing Amendments, which, in either Case, shall be valid to all Intents and Purposes, as Part of this Constitution, when ratified by the Legislatures of three fourths of the several States, or by Conventions in three fourths thereof, as the one or the other Mode of Ratification may be proposed by the Congress; Provided that no Amendment which may be made prior to the Year One thousand eight hundred and eight shall in any Manner affect the first and fourth Clauses in the Ninth Section of the first Article; and that no State, without its Consent, shall be deprived of its equal Suffrage in the Senate.

ARTICLE VI

All Debts contracted and Engagements entered into, before the Adoption of this Constitution, shall be as valid against the United States under this Constitution, as under the Confederation.

This Constitution, and the Laws of the United States which shall be made in Pursuance thereof; and all Treaties made, or which shall be made,

under the Authority of the United States, shall be the supreme Law of the Land; and the Judges in every State shall be bound thereby, any Thing in the Constitution or Laws of any State to the Contrary notwithstanding.

The Senators and Representatives before mentioned, and the Members of the several State Legislatures, and all executive and judicial Officers, both of the United States and of the several States, shall be bound by Oath or Affirmation, to support this Constitution; but no religious Test shall ever be required as a Qualification to any Office or public Trust under the United States.

ARTICLE VII

The Ratification of the Conventions of nine States, shall be sufficient for the Establishment of this Constitution between the States so ratifying the Same.

Done in Convention by the Unanimous Consent of the States present the seventeenth Day of September in the Year of our Lord one thousand seven hundred and Eighty seven and of the Independence of the United States of America the Twelfth. IN WITNESS whereof We have hereunto subscribed our Names,
George Washington,
President and deputy from Virginia.
New Hampshire:
John Langdon,
Nicholas Gilman.
Massachusetts:
Nathaniel Gorham,
Rufus King.
Connecticut:
William Samuel Johnson,
Roger Sherman.
New York:
Alexander Hamilton.
New Jersey:
William Livingston,
David Brearley,
William Paterson,
Jonathan Dayton.
Pennsylvania:
Benjamin Franklin,

Thomas Mifflin,
Robert Morris,
George Clymer,
Thomas FitzSimons,
Jared Ingersoll,
James Wilson,
Gouverneur Morris.
Delaware:
George Read,
Gunning Bedford Jr.,
John Dickinson,
Richard Bassett,
Jacob Broom.
Maryland:
James McHenry,
Daniel of St. Thomas Jenifer,
Daniel Carroll.
Virginia:
John Blair,
James Madison Jr.
North Carolina:
William Blount,
Richard Dobbs Spaight,
Hugh Williamson.
South Carolina:
John Rutledge,
Charles Cotesworth Pinckney,
Pierce Butler.
Georgia:
William Few,
Abraham Baldwin.
(Ratification of the Constitution was completed on June 21, 1788)

AMENDMENTS

AMENDMENT I

(First ten admendments ratified December 15, 1791.)
Congress shall make no law respecting an establishment of religion, or prohibiting the free exercise thereof; or abridging the freedom of speech, or of the press; or the right of the people peaceably to assemble, and to petition the Government for a redress of grievances.

AMENDMENT II

A well regulated Militia, being necessary to the security of a free State, the right of the people to keep and bear Arms, shall not be infringed.

AMENDMENT III

No Soldier shall, in time of peace be quartered in any house, without the consent of the Owner, nor in time of war, but in a manner to be prescribed by law.

AMENDMENT IV

The right of the people to be secure in their persons, houses, papers, and effects, against unreasonable searches and seizures, shall not be violated, and no Warrants shall issue, but upon probable cause, supported by Oath or affirmation, and particularly describing the place to be searched, and the persons or things to be seized.

AMENDMENT V

No person shall be held to answer for a capital, or otherwise infamous crime, unless on a presentment or indictment of a Grand Jury, except in cases arising in the land or naval forces, or in the Militia, when in actual service in time of War or public danger; nor shall any person be subject for the same offences to be twice put in jeopardy of life or limb; nor shall be compelled in any criminal case to be a witness against himself, nor be deprived of life, liberty, or property, without due process of law; nor shall private property be taken for public use, without just compensation.

AMENDMENT VI

In all criminal prosecutions, the accused shall enjoy the right to a speedy and public trial, by an impartial jury of the State and district wherein the crime shall have been committed, which district shall have been previously ascertained by law, and to be informed of the nature and cause of the accusation; to be confronted with the witnesses against him; to have compulsory process for obtaining witnesses in his favor, and to have the Assistance of Counsel for his defence.

AMENDMENT VII

In Suits at common law, where the value in controversy shall exceed twenty dollars, the right of trial by jury shall be preserved, and no fact tried by a jury, shall be otherwise re-examined in any Court of the United States, than according to the rules of the common law.

AMENDMENT VIII

Excessive bail shall not be required, nor excessive fines imposed, nor cruel and unusual punishments inflicted.

AMENDMENT IX

The enumeration in the Constitution, of certain rights, shall not be construed to deny or disparage others retained by the people.

AMENDMENT X

The powers not delegated to the United States by the Constitution, nor prohibited by it to the States, are reserved to the States respectively, or to the people.

AMENDMENT XI

(Ratified February 7, 1795)

The Judicial power of the United States shall not be construed to extend to any suit in law or equity, commenced or prosecuted against one of the United States by Citizens of another State, or by Citizens or Subjects of any Foreign State.

AMENDMENT XII

(Ratified June 15, 1804)

The Electors shall meet in their respective states, and vote by ballot for President and Vice–President, one of whom, at least, shall not be an inhabitant of the same state with themselves; they shall name in their ballots the person voted for as President, and in distinct ballots the person voted for as Vice–President, and they shall make distinct lists of all persons voted for as President, and of all persons voted for as Vice–President, and of the number of votes for each, which lists they shall sign and certify, and transmit sealed to the seat of the government of the United States, directed to the President of the Senate;—The President of the Senate shall, in the presence of the Senate and House of Representatives, open all the certificates and the

votes shall then be counted;—The person having the greatest number of votes for President, shall be the President, if such number be a majority of the whole number of Electors appointed; and if no person have such majority, then from the persons having the highest numbers not exceeding three on the list of those voted for as President, the House of Representatives shall choose immediately, by ballot, the President. But in choosing the President, the votes shall be taken by states, the representation from each state having one vote; a quorum for this purpose shall consist of a member or members from two-thirds of the states, and a majority of all the states shall be necessary to a choice. [And if the House of Representatives shall not choose a President whenever the right of choice shall devolve upon them, before the fourth day of March next following, then the Vice–President shall act as President, as in the case of the death or other constitutional disability of the President.—][10] The person having the greatest number of votes as Vice–President, shall be the Vice–President, if such number be a majority of the whole number of Electors appointed, and if no person have a majority, then from the two highest numbers on the list, the Senate shall choose the Vice–President; a quorum for the purpose shall consist of two–thirds of the whole number of Senators, and a majority of the whole number shall be necessary to a choice. But no person constitutionally ineligible to the office of President shall be eligible to that of Vice–President of the United States.

AMENDMENT XIII

(Ratified December 6, 1865)

Section 1. Neither slavery nor involuntary servitude, except as a punishment for crime whereof the party shall have been duly convicted, shall exist within the United States, or any place subject to their jurisdiction.

Section 2. Congress shall have power to enforce this article by appropriate legislation.

AMENDMENT XIV

(Ratified July 9, 1868)

Section 1. All persons born or naturalized in

---

[10] The section in brackets was superceded by section 3 of the Twentieth Amendment.

the United States, and subject to the jurisdiction thereof, are citizens of the United States and of the State wherein they reside. No State shall make or enforce any law which shall abridge the privileges or immunities of citizens of the United States; nor shall any State deprive any person of life, liberty, or property, without due process of law; nor deny to any person within its jurisdiction the equal protection of the laws.

Section 2. Representatives shall be apportioned among the several States according to their respective numbers, counting the whole number of persons in each State, excluding Indians not taxed. But when the right to vote at any election for the choice of electors for President and Vice President of the United States, Representatives in Congress, the Executive and Judicial officers of a State, or the members of the Legislature thereof, is denied to any of the male inhabitants of such State, being twenty–one years of age,[11] and citizens of the United States, or in any way abridged, except for participation in rebellion, or other crime, the basis of representation therein shall be reduced in the proportion which the number of such male citizens shall bear to the whole number of male citizens twenty–one years of age in such State.

Section 3. No person shall be a Senator or Representative in Congress, or elector of President and Vice President, or hold any office, civil or military, under the United States, or under any State, who, having previously taken an oath, as a member of Congress, or as an officer of the United States, or as a member of any State legislature, or as an executive or judicial officer of any State, to support the Constitution of the United States, shall have engaged in insurrection or rebellion against the same, or given aid or comfort to the enemies thereof. But Congress may by a vote of two–thirds of each House, remove such disability.

Section 4. The validity of the public debt of the United States, authorized by law, including debts incurred for payment of pensions and bounties for services in suppressing insurrection or rebellion, shall not be questioned. But neither the United States nor any State shall assume or pay

any debt or obligation incurred in aid of insurrection or rebellion against the United States, or any claim for the loss or emancipation of any slave; but all such debts, obligations and claims shall be held illegal and void.

Section 5. The Congress shall have power to enforce, by appropriate legislation, the provisions of this article.

AMENDMENT XV
(Ratified February 3, 1870)

Section 1. The right of citizens of the United States to vote shall not be denied or abridged by the United States or by any State on account of race, color, or previous condition of servitude.

Section 2. The Congress shall have power to enforce this article by appropriate legislation.

AMENDMENT XVI
(Ratified February 3, 1913)

The Congress shall have power to lay and collect taxes on incomes, from whatever source derived, without apportionment among the several States, and without regard to any census or enumeration.

AMENDMENT XVII
(Ratified April 8, 1913)

The Senate of the United States shall be composed of two Senators from each State, elected by the people thereof, for six years; and each Senator shall have one vote. The electors in each State shall have the qualifications requisite for electors of the most numerous branch of the State legislatures.

When vacancies happen in the representation of any State in the Senate, the executive authority of such State shall issue writs of election to fill such vacancies: *Provided,* That the legislature of any State may empower the executive thereof to make temporary appointments until the people fill the vacancies by election as the legislature may direct.

This amendment shall not be so construed as to affect the election or term of any Senator chosen before it becomes valid as part of the Constitution.

---

[11] See the Ninteenth and Twenty-sixth Amendments.

AMENDMENT XVIII

(Ratified January 16, 1919)

[Section 1. After one year from the ratification of this article the manufacture, sale, or transportation of intoxicating liquors within, the importation thereof into, or the exportation thereof from the United States and all territory subject to the jurisdiction thereof for beverage purposes is hereby prohibited.

Section 2. The Congress and the several States shall have concurrent power to enforce this article by appropriate legislation.

Section 3. This article shall be inoperative unless it shall have been ratified as an amendment to the Constitution by the legislatures of the several States, as provided in the Constitution, within seven years from the date of the submission hereof to the States by the Congress.][12]

AMENDMENT XIX

(Ratified August 18, 1920)

The right of citizens of the United States to vote shall not be denied or abridged by the United States or by any State on account of sex.

Congress shall have power to enforce this article by appropriate legislation.

AMENDMENT XX

(Ratified January 23, 1933)

Section 1. The terms of the President and Vice President shall end at noon on the 20th day of January, and the terms of Senators and Representatives at noon on the 3d day of January, of the years in which such terms would have ended if this article had not been ratified; and the terms of their successors shall then begin.

Section 2. The Congress shall assemble at least once in every year, and such meeting shall begin at noon on the 3d day of January, unless they shall by law appoint a different day.

Section 3.[13] If, at the time fixed for the beginning of the term of the President, the President elect shall have died, the Vice President elect shall become President. If a President shall not have been chosen before the time fixed for the beginning of his term, or if the President elect shall have failed to qualified, then the Vice President

elect shall act as President until a President shall have qualified; and the Congress may by law provide for the case wherein neither a President elect nor a Vice President elect shall have qualified, declaring who shall then act as President, or the manner in which one who is to act shall be selected, and such person shall act accordingly until a President or Vice President shall have qualified.

Section 4. The Congress may by law provide for the case of the death of any of the persons from whom the House of Representatives may choose a President whenever the right of choice shall have devolved upon them, and for the case of the death of any of the persons from whom the Senate may choose a Vice President whenever the right of choice shall have devolved upon them.

Section 5. Sections 1 and 2 shall take effect on the 15th day of October following the ratification of this article.

Section 6. This article shall be inoperative unless it shall have been ratified as an amendment to the Constitution by the legislatures of three–fourths of the several States within seven years from the date of its submission.

AMENDMENT XXI

(Ratified December 5, 1933)

Section 1. The eighteenth article of amendment to the Constitution of the United States is hereby repealed.

Section 2. The transportation or importation into any State, Territory, or possession of the United States for delivery or use therein of intoxicating liquors, in violation of the laws thereof, is hereby prohibited.

Section 3. This article shall be inoperative unless it shall have been ratified as an amendment to the Constitution by conventions in the several States, as provided in the Constitution, within seven years from the date of the submission hereof to the States by the Congress.

AMENDMENT XXII

(Ratified February 27, 1951)

Section 1. No person shall be elected to the office

---

[12] The Eighteenth Amendment was repealed by section 1 of the Twenty-first Amendment.

[13] See the Twenty-fifth Amendment.

of the President more than twice, and no person who has held the office of President, or acted as President, for more than two years of a term to which some other person was elected President shall be elected to the office of the President more than once. But this Article shall not apply to any person holding the office of President when this Article was proposed by the Congress, and shall not prevent any person who may be holding the office of President, or acting as President, during the term within which this Article becomes operative from holding the office of President or acting as President during the remainder of such term.

Section 2. This article shall be inoperative unless it shall have been ratified as an amendment to the Constitution by the legislatures of three–fourths of the several States within seven years from the date of its submission to the States by the Congress.

AMENDMENT XXIII
(Ratified March 29, 1961)

Section 1. The District constituting the seat of Government of the United States shall appoint in such manner as the Congress may direct:

A number of electors of President and Vice President equal to the whole number of Senators and Representatives in Congress to which the District would be entitled if it were a State, but in no event more than the least populous State; they shall be in addition to those appointed by the States, but they shall be considered, for the purposes of the election of President and Vice President, to be electors appointed by a State; and they shall meet in the District and perform such duties as provided by the twelfth article of amendment.

Section 2. The Congress shall have power to enforce this article by appropriate legislation.

AMENDMENT XXIV
(Ratified January 23, 1964)

Section 1. The right of citizens of the United States to vote in any primary or other election for President or Vice President, for electors for President or Vice President, or for Senator or

Representative in Congress, shall not be denied or abridged by the United States or any State by reason of failure to pay any poll tax or other tax.

Section 2. The Congress shall have power to enforce this article by appropriate legislation.

AMENDMENT XXV
(Ratified February 10, 1967)

Section 1. In case of the removal of the President from office or of his death or resignation, the Vice President shall become President.

Section 2. Whenever there is a vacancy in the office of the Vice President, the President shall nominate a Vice President who shall take office upon confirmation by a majority vote of both Houses of Congress.

Section 3. Whenever the President transmits to the President pro tempore of the Senate and the Speaker of the House of Representatives his written declaration that he is unable to discharge the powers and duties of his office, and until he transmits to them a written declaration to the contrary, such powers and duties shall be discharged by the Vice President as Acting President.

Section 4. Whenever the Vice President and a majority of either the principal officers of the executive departments or of such other body as Congress may by law provide, transmit to the President pro tempore of the Senate and the Speaker of the House of Representatives their written declaration that the President is unable to discharge the powers and duties of his office, the Vice President shall immediately assume the powers and duties of the office as Acting President.

Thereafter, when the President transmits to the President pro tempore of the Senate and the Speaker of the House of Representatives his written declaration that no inability exists, he shall resume the powers and duties of his office unless the Vice President and a majority of either the principal officers of the executive department or of such other body as Congress may by law provide, transmit within four days to the President pro tempore of the Senate and the Speaker of the House of Representatives their written declaration that the President is unable to discharge the powers and duties of his office. Thereupon Congress shall decide the issue, assembling within forty–eight hours for that purpose if not in session. If the Congress, within twenty–one days after receipt of the latter written declaration, or, if Congress is not in session, within twenty–one days after Congress is required to assemble, determines by two–thirds vote of both Houses that the President is unable to discharge the powers and duties of his office, the Vice President shall continue to discharge the same as Acting President; otherwise, the President shall resume the powers and duties of his office.

AMENDMENT XXVI
(Ratified July 1, 1971)
Section 1. The right of citizens of the United States, who are eighteen years of age or older, to vote shall not be denied or abridged by the United States or by any State on account of age.
Section 2. The Congress shall have power to enforce this article by appropriate legislation.

AMENDMENT XXVII
(Ratified May 7, 1992)
No law varying the compensation for the services of the Senators and Representatives shall take effect, until an election of Representives shall have intervened.

APPENDIX B

PRESIDENTS AND VICE PRESIDENTS OF THE UNITED STATES

President	Dates of Presidency	Vice President
George Washington, Fed (1732-1799)	April 30, 1789-March 4, 1793	John Adams
Washington	March 4, 1793-March 4, 1797	Adams
John Adams, Fed (1735-1826)	March 4, 1797-March 4, 1801	Thomas Jefferson
Thomas Jefferson, Dem-Rep (1743-1826)	March 4, 1801-March 4, 1805	Aaron Burr
Jefferson	March 4, 1805-March 4, 1809	George Clinton
James Madison, Dem-Rep (1751-1836)	March 4, 1809-March 4, 1813	Clinton
Madison	March 4, 1813-March 4, 1817	Elbridge Gerry
James Monroe, Dem-Rep (1758-1831)	March 4, 1817-March 4, 1821	Daniel D. Tompkins
Monroe	March 4, 1821-March 4, 1825	Tompkins
John Q. Adams, Dem-Rep (1767-1848)	March 4, 1825-March 4, 1829	John C. Calhoun
Andrew Jackson, Dem-Rep (1767-1845)	March 4, 1829-March 4, 1833	Calhoun
Jackson, Dem	March 4, 1833-March 4, 1837	Martin Van Buren
Martin Van Buren, Dem (1782-1862)	March 4, 1837-March 4, 1841	Richard M. Johnson
W.H. Harrison, Whig (1773-1841)	March 4, 1841-April 4, 1841	John Tyler
John Tyler, Whig (1790-1862)	April 6, 1841-March 4, 1845	
James K. Polk, Dem (1795-1849)	March 4, 1845-March 4, 1849	George M. Dallas
Zachary Taylor, Whig (1784-1850)	March 4, 1849-July 9, 1850	Millard Fillmore
Millard Fillmore, Whig (1800-1874)	July 10, 1850-March 4, 1853	
Franklin Pierce, Dem (1804-1869)	March 4, 1853-March 4, 1857	William R. King
James Buchanan, Dem (1791-1868)	March 4, 1857-March 4, 1861	John C. Breckinridge
Abraham Lincoln, Rep (1809-1865)	March 4, 1861-March 4, 1865	Hannibal Hamlin
Lincoln	March 4, 1865-April 15, 1865	Andrew Johnson
Andrew Johnson, Rep (1808-1875)	April 15, 1865-March 4, 1869	
Ulysses S. Grant, Rep (1822-1885)	March 4, 1869-March 4, 1873	Schuyler Colfax
Grant	March 4, 1873-March 4, 1877	Henry Wilson
Rutherford B. Hayes, Rep (1822-1893)	March 4, 1877-March 4, 1881	William A. Wheeler
James A. Garfield, Rep (1831-1881)	March 4, 1881-Sept. 19, 1881	Chester A. Arthur
Chester A. Arthur, Rep (1830-1886)	Sept. 20, 1881-March 4, 1885	
Grover Cleveland, Dem (1837-1908)	March 4, 1885-March 4, 1889	Thomas A. Hendricks
Benjamin Harrison, Rep (1833-1901)	March 4, 1889-March 4, 1893	Levi P. Morton
Grover Cleveland, Dem (1837-1908)	March 4, 1893-March 4, 1897	Adlai Stevenson
William McKinley, Rep (1843-1901)	March 4, 1897-March 4, 1901	Garret A. Hobart
McKinley	March 4, 1901-Sept. 14, 1901	Theodore Roosevelt

President	Years of Presidency	Vice President
Theodore Roosevelt, Rep (1858-1919)	Sept. 14, 1901-March 4, 1905	
Roosevelt	March 4, 1905-March 4, 1909	Charles W. Fairbanks
William H. Taft, Rep (1857-1930)	March 4, 1909-March 4, 1913	James S. Sherman
Woodrow Wilson, Dem (1856-1924)	March 4, 1913-March 4, 1917	Thomas R. Marshall
Wilson	March 4, 1917-March 4, 1921	Marshall
Warren G. Harding, Rep (1865-1923)	March 4, 1921-Aug. 2, 1923	Calvin Coolidge
Calvin Coolidge, Rep (1872-1933)	Aug. 3, 1923-March 4, 1925	
Coolidge	March 4, 1925-March 4, 1929	Charles G. Dawes
Herbert Hoover, Rep (1874-1964)	March 4, 1929-March 4, 1933	Charles Curtis
Franklin D. Roosevelt, Dem (1882-1945)	March 4, 1933-Jan. 20, 1937	John N. Garner
Roosevelt	Jan. 20, 1937-Jan. 20, 1941	Garner
Roosevelt	Jan. 20, 1941-Jan. 20, 1945	Henry A. Wallace
Roosevelt	Jan. 20, 1945-April 12, 1945	Harry S. Truman
Harry S. Truman, Dem (1884-1972)	April 12, 1945-Jan. 20, 1949	
Truman	Jan. 20, 1949-Jan.20, 1953	Alben W. Barkley
Dwight D. Eisenhower, Rep (1890-1969)	Jan. 20, 1953-Jan. 20, 1957	Richard Nixon
Eisenhower	Jan. 20, 1957-Jan. 20, 1961	Nixon
John F. Kennedy, Dem (1917-1963)	Jan. 20, 1961-Nov. 22, 1963	Lyndon B. Johnson
Lyndon B. Johnson, Dem (1908-1973)	Nov. 22, 1963-Jan. 20, 1965	
Johnson	Jan. 20, 1965-Jan. 20, 1969	Hubert H. Humphrey
Richard Nixon, Rep (1913-1994)	Jan. 20, 1969-Jan. 20, 1973	Spiro T. Agnew
Nixon	Jan. 20 1973-Aug. 9, 1974	Agnew
		Gerald R. Ford
Gerald R. Ford, Rep (1913-)	Aug. 9, 1974-Jan. 20, 1977	Nelson A. Rockefeller
Jimmy Carter, Dem (1924-)	Jan. 20, 1977-Jan. 20, 1981	Walter F. Mondale
Ronald Reagan, Rep (1911-)	Jan. 20, 1981-Jan. 20, 1985	George Bush
Reagan	Jan. 20, 1985- Jan. 20, 1989	Bush
George Bush, Rep (1924-)	Jan. 20 1989-Jan. 20, 1993	Dan Quayle
Bill Clinton, Dem (1946-)	Jan. 20, 1993-	Al Gore

Abbreviations: (Dem) Democrat, (Dem-Rep) Democratic-Republican, (Fed) Federalist, (Rep) Republican

APPENDIX C

SPEAKERS OF THE HOUSE OF REPRESENTATIVES
1789–1995

Congress		Speaker
1st	(1789-1791)	Frederick A. C. Muhlenberg, Admin-Pa.
2nd	(1791-1793)	Jonathan Trumbull, Fed-Conn.
3rd	(1793-1795)	Muhlenberg
4th	(1795-1797)	Jonathan Dayton, Fed-N J.
5th	(1797-1799)	Dayton
6th	(1799-1801)	Theodore Sedwick, Fed-Mass.
7th	(1801-1803)	Nathaniel Macon, Dem-Rep-N.C.
8th	(1803-1805)	Macon
9th	(1805-1807)	Macon
10th	(1807-1809)	Joseph B. Varnum, Dem-Rep-Mass.
11th	(1809-1811)	Varnum
12th	(1811-1813)	Henry Clay, Dem-Rep-Ky.
13th	(1813-1814)	Clay
	(1814-1815)	Langdon Cheves, Dem-Rep-S.C.
14th	(1815-1817)	Clay
15th	(1817-1819)	Clay
16th	(1819-1820)	Clay
	(1820-1821)	John W. Taylor, Dem-N.Y.
17th	(1821-1823)	Philip P. Barbour, Dem-Rep Va.
18th	(1823-1825)	Clay
19th	(1825-1827)	Taylor
20th	(1827-1829)	Andrew Stevenson, Dem-Rep Va.
21st	(1829-1831)	Stevenson
22nd	(1831-1833)	Stevenson
23rd	(1833-1834)	Stevenson
	(1834-1835)	John Bell, Whig-Tenn.
24th	(1835-1837)	James K. Polk, Dem-Tenn.
25th	(1837-1839)	Polk
26th	(1839-1841)	Robert M. T. Hunter, Dem-Va.
27th	(1841-1843)	John White, Whig-Ky.
28th	(1843-1845)	John W. Jones, Dem-Va.
29th	(1845-1847)	John W. Davis, Dem-Ind.
30th	(1847-1849)	Robert C. Winthrop, Whig-Mass.

Congress		Speaker
31st	(1849-1851)	Howell Cobb, Dem-Ga.
32nd	(1851-1853)	Linn Boyd, Dem-Ky.
33rd	(1853-1855)	Boyd
34th	(1855-1857)	Nathaniel P. Banks, Rep-Mass.
35th	(1857-1859)	James L. Orr, Dem-S.C.
36th	(1859-1861)	William Pennington, Rep-N.J.
37th	(1861-1863)	Galusha A. Grow, Rep-Pa.
38th	(1863-1865)	Schuyler Colfax, Rep-Ind.
39th	(1865-1867)	Colfax
40th	(1867-1868)	Colfax
	(1868-1869)	Theodore M. Pomeroy, Rep-N.Y.
41st	(1869-1871)	James G. Blaine, Rep-Maine
42nd	(1871-1873)	Blaine
43rd	(1873-1875)	Blaine
44th	(1875-1876)	Michael C. Kerr, Dem-Ind.
	(1876-1877)	Samuel J. Randall, Dem-Pa.
45th	(1877-1879)	Randall
46th	(1879-1881)	Randall
47th	(1881-1883)	Joseph Warren Keifer, Rep-Ohio
48th	(1883-1885)	John G. Carlisle, Dem-Ky.
49th	(1885-1887)	Carlisle
50th	(1887-1889)	Carlisle
51st	(1889-1891)	Thomas Brackett Reed, Rep-Maine
52nd	(1881-1893)	Charles F. Crisp, Dem Ga.
53rd	(1893-1895)	Crisp
54th	(1895-1897)	Reed
55th	(1897-1899)	Reed
56th	(1899-1901)	David B. Hendersen, Rep-Iowa
57th	(1901-1903)	Hendersen
58th	(1903-1905)	Joseph G. Cannon, Rep-Ill.
59th	(1905-1907)	Cannon
60th	(1907-1909)	Cannon
61st	(1909-1911)	Cannon
62nd	(1911-1913)	James B. "Champ" Clark, Dem-Mo.
63rd	(1913-1915)	Clark
64th	(1915-1917)	Clark

Congress		Speaker	Congress		Speaker
65th	(1917-1919)	Clark	85th	(1957-1959)	Rayburn
66th	(1919-1921)	Frederick H. Gillett, Rep-Mass.	86th	(1959-1961)	Rayburn
			87th	(1961)	Rayburn
67th	(1921-1923)	Gillett		(1962-1963)	John W. McCormack, Dem-Mass.
68th	(1923-1925)	Gillett			
69th	(1925-1927)	Nicholas Longworth, Rep-Ohio	88th	(1963-1965)	McCormack
			89th	(1965-1967)	McCormack
70th	(1927-1929)	Longworth	90th	(1967-1969)	McCormack
71st	(1929-1931)	Longworth	91st	(1969-1971)	McCormack
72nd	(1931-1933)	John Nance Garner, Dem-Tex.	92nd	(1971-1973)	Carl Albert, Dem-Okla.
			93rd	(1973-1975)	Albert
73rd	(1933-1935)	Henry T. Rainey, Dem-Ill.[1]	94th	(1975-1977)	Albert
74th	(1935-1936)	Joseph W. Byrns, Dem-Tenn.	95th	(1977-1979)	Thomas P. O'Neill Jr., Dem-Mass.
75th	(1937-1939)	Bankhead			
76th	(1939-1940)	Bankhead	96th	(1979-1981)	O'Neill
	(1940-1941)	Sam Rayburn, Dem-Tex.	97th	(1981-1983)	O'Neill
77th	(1941-1943)	Rayburn	98th	(1983-1985)	O'Neill
78th	(1943-1945)	Rayburn	99th	(1985-1987)	O'Neill
79th	(1945-1947)	Rayburn	100th	(1987-1989)	Jim Wright, Dem-Tex.
80th	(1947-1949)	Joseph W. Martin Jr., Rep-Mass.	101st	(1989)	Wright[2]
				(1989-1991)	Thomas S. Foley, Dem-Wash.
81st	(1949-1951)	Rayburn			
82nd	(1951-1953)	Rayburn	102nd	(1991-1993)	Foley
83rd	(1953-1955)	Martin	103rd	(1993-1995)	Foley
84th	(1955-1957)	Rayburn	104th	(1995-)	Newt Gingrich, Rep-Ga.

Abbreviations: (Admin) Administration; (Dem) Democrat; (Dem-Rep) Democratic-Republican; (Fed) Federalist; (Rep) Republican.

[1] Rainey died in 1934, but was not replaced until the next Congress.

[2] Wright resigned and Foley became the Speaker on June 6, 1989.

APPENDIX D

LEADERS OF THE HOUSE SINCE 1899

Although there has been a Speaker of the House since the first Congress, because the Speakership was created by the Constitution, the positions of House majority leader, majority whip, minority leader, and minority whip are not Constitutional offices but political ones. They became formal political positions in the 56th Congress. See that Congress for more information.

Congress	House Floor Leaders Majority	Minority	House Whips Majority	Minority
56th (1899-1901)	Sereno E. Payne (Rep. N.Y.)	James D. Richardson (Dem. Tenn.)	James A. Tawney (Rep. Minn.)	Oscar W. Underwood [1] (Dem. Ala.)
57th (1901-1903)	Payne	Richardson	Tawney	James T. Lloyd (Dem. Mo.)
58th (1903-1905)	Payne	John Sharp Williams (Dem. Miss.)	Tawney	Lloyd
59th (1905-1907)	Payne	Williams	James E. Watson (Rep. Ind.)	Lloyd
60th (1907-1909)	Payne	Williams/Champ Clark [2] (Dem. Mo.)	Watson	Lloyd[3]
61st (1909-1911)	Payne	Clark	John W. Dwight (Rep. N.Y.)	None
62nd (1911-1913)	Oscar W. Underwood (Dem. Ala.)	James R. Mann (Rep. Ill.)	None	John W. Dwight (Rep. N.Y.)
63rd (1913-1915)	Underwood	Mann	Thomas M. Bell (Dem. Ga.)	Charles H. Burke (Rep. S.D.)
64th (1915-1917)	Claude Kitchin (Dem. N.C.)	Mann	None	Charles M. Hamilton (Rep. N.Y.)
65th (1917-1919)	Kitchin	Mann	None	Hamilton
66th (1919-1921)	Franklin W. Mondell (Rep. Wyo.)	Clark	Harold Knutson (Rep. Minn.)	None
67th (1921-1923)	Mondell	Claude Kitchin (Dem. N.C.)	Knutson	William A. Oldfield (Dem. Ark.)
68th (1923-1925)	Nicholas Longworth (Rep. Ohio)	Finis J. Garrett (Dem. Tenn.)	Albert H. Vestal (Rep. Ind.)	Oldfield
69th (1925-1927)	John Q. Tilson (Rep. Conn.)	Garrett	Vestal	Oldfield
70th (1927-1929)	Tilson	Garrett	Vestal	Oldfield/ John McDuffie (Dem. Ala.)[4]
71st (1929-1931)	Tilson	John N. Garner (Dem. Texas)	Vestal	McDuffie
72nd (1931-1933)	Henry T. Rainey (Dem. Ill.)	Bertrand H. Snell (Rep. N.Y.)	John McDuffie (Dem. Ala.)	Carl G. Bachmann (Rep. W.Va.)
73rd (1933-1935)	Joseph W. Byrns (Dem. Tenn.)	Snell	Arthur H. Greenwood (Dem. Ind.)	Harry L. Englebright (Rep. Cal.)
74th (1935-1937)	William B. Bankhead (Dem. Ala.)[5]	Snell	Patrick J. Boland (Dem. Pa.)	Englebright
75th (1937-1939)	Sam Rayburn (Dem. Texas)	Snell	Boland	Englebright
76th (1939-1941)	Rayburn/ John W. McCormack	Joseph W. Martin Jr. (Rep. Mass.) (Dem. Mass.)[6]	Boland	Englebright

[1] Underwood became minority whip in 1901.
[2] Clark became minority leader in 1908.
[3] In 1908 Lloyd resigned to become chairman of the Democratic Congressional Campaign Committee, leaving the post of minority whip vacant until the 62nd Congress.
[4] McDuffie became minority whip after Oldfield died on Nov. 19, 1928.
[5] Bankhead became Speaker of the House on June 4, 1936, leaving the post of majority leader vacant until the 75th Congress.
[6] Rayburn was elevated to the Speaker of the House on Sept. 16, 1940 and McCormack became majority leader on September 26, 1940.

Congress	House Floor Leaders		House Whips	
	Majority	Minority	Majority	Minority
77th (1941-1943)	McCormack	Martin	Boland/ Robert Ramsspeck (Dem. Ga.)[7]	Englebright
78th (1943-1945)	McCormack	Martin	Ramspeck	Leslie C. Arends (Rep. Ill.)
79th (1945-1947)	McCormack	Martin (Dem. Ala.)	Ramspeck/ John J. Sparkman[8]	Arends
80th (1847-1949)	Charles A. Halleck (Rep. Ind.)	Sam Rayburn (Dem. Texas)	Leslie C. Arends (Rep. Ill.)	John W. McCormack (Dem. Mass.)
81st (1949-1951)	McCormack	Martin	J. Percy Priest (Dem. Tenn.)	Arends
82nd (1951-1953)	McCormack	Martin	Priest	Arends
83rd (1953-1955)	Halleck	Rayburn	Arends	McCormack
84th (1955-1957)	McCormack	Martin	Carl Albert (Dem. Okla.)	Arends
85th (1957-1959)	McCormack	Martin	Albert	Arends
86th (1959-1961)	McCormack	Charles A. Halleck (Rep. Ind.)	Albert	Arends
87th (1961-1963)	McCormack/ Carl Albert (D Okla.)[9]	Halleck	Albert/Hale Boggs (Dem. La.)[10]	Arends
88th (1963-1965)	Albert	Halleck	Boggs	Arends
89th (1965-1967)	Albert	Gerald R. Ford (Rep. Mich.)	Boggs	Arends
90th (1967-1969)	Albert	Ford	Boggs	Arends
91st (1969-1971)	Albert	Ford	Boggs	Arends
92nd (1971-1973)	Hale Boggs (Dem. La.)	Ford	Thomas P. O'Neill Jr. (Dem. Mass.)	Arends
93rd (1973-1975)	Thomas P. O'Neill Jr. (Dem. Mass.)	Ford/ John J. Rhodes (Rep. Ariz.)[11]	John J. McFall (Dem. Calif.)	Arends
94th (1975-1977)	O'Neill	Rhodes	McFall	Robert H. Michel (Rep. Ill.)
95th (1977-1979)	Jim Wright (Dem. Tex.)	Rhodes	John Brademas (Dem. Ind.)	Michel
96th (1979-1981)	Wright	Rhodes	Brademas	Michel
97th (1981-1983)	Wright	Robert H. Michel (Rep. Ill.)	Thomas S. Foley (Dem. Wash.)	Trent Lott (Rep. Miss.)
98th (1983-1985)	Wright	Michel	Foley	Lott
99th (1985-1987)	Wright	Michel	Foley	Lott
100th (1987-1989)	Thomas S. Foley (Dem. Wash.)	Michel	Tony Coelho (Dem. Calif.)	Lott
101st (1989-1991)	Foley/ Richard A. Gephardt (Dem. Mo.)[12]	Michel	Coelho/ William H. Gray III (Dem. Pa.)[13]	Dick Cheney (Rep. Wyo.)/ Newt Gingrich (Rep. Ga.)[14]
102nd (1991-1993)	Gephardt	Michel	Gray/David E. Bonior (Dem. Mich.)[15]	Gingrich
103rd (1993-1995)	Gephardt	Michel	Bonior	Gingrich
104th (1995-)	Gingrich	Gephardt	Richard Armey (Rep. Tex.)	Bonior

[7] Boland died on May 18, 1942 and Ramspeck became majority whip on June 8, 1942.

[8] Ramspeck resigned on Dec. 31, 1945 and Sparkman became majority whip on Jan. 14, 1946.

[9] Albert became majority leader when McCormack was elevated to the Speaker of the House on Jan. 10, 1962.

[10] Boggs became majority whip on Jan. 10, 1962 and filled the vacancy caused by the elevation of Albert to majority leader.

[11] Ford became vice president on Dec. 6, 1973 and Rhodes became minority leader on Dec. 7, 1973.

[12] Foley succeeded Wright as Speaker of the House on June 6, 1989 and Gephardt became majority leader on June 14, 1989.

[13] Gray became majority whip on June 14, 1989, filling the vacancy resulting from Coehlo resignation from Congress on June 15, 1989.

[14] Cheney resigned on March 17, 1989 to become secretary of defense and Gingrich became minority whip on March 23, 1989.

[15] Gray resigned from Congress on Sept. 11, 1991 and Bonior became majority whip.

APPENDIX E

LEADERS OF THE SENATE SINCE 1911

The offices of Senate majority leader and minority leader did not become formal until the 62nd Congress. See that Congress for further information. Similarly, the Senate majority whip became a formal office in the 63rd Congress and the minority whip in the 64th Congress. All of these offices are political offices, which evolved over time and were not created by the Constitution.

Congress	Senate Floor Leaders Majority	Minority	Senate Whips Majority	Minority
62nd (1911-1913)	Shelby M. Cullom (Rep. Ill.)	Thomas S. Martin (Dem. Va.)	None	None
63rd (1913-1915)	John W. Kern (Dem. Ind.)	Jacob H. Gallinger (Rep. N.H.)	J. Hamilton Lewis (Dem. Ill.)	None
64th (1915-1917)	Kern	Gallinger	Lewis	James W. Wadsworth Jr. (Rep. N.Y.)/ Charles Curtis (Rep. Kan.)[1]
65th (1917-1919)	Thomas S. Martin (Dem. Va.)	Gallinger/ Henry Cabot Lodge (Rep. Mass.)[2]	Lewis	Curtis
66th (1919-1921)	Henry Cabot Lodge (Rep. Mass.)	Martin/ Oscar W. Underwood (Dem. Ala.)[3]	Charles Curtis (Rep. Kan.)	Peter G. Gerry (Dem. R.I.)
67th (1921-1923)	Lodge	Underwood	Curtis	Gerry
68th (1923-1925)	Lodge/Charles Curtis (Rep. Kan.)[4]	Joseph T. Robinson (Dem. Ark.)	Curtis/Wesley L. Jones (Rep. Wash.)[5]	Gerry
69th (1925-1927)	Curtis	Robinson	Jones	Gerry
70th (1927-1929)	Curtis	Robinson	Jones	Gerry
71st (1929-1931)	James E. Watson (Rep. Ind.)	Robinson	Simeon D. Fess (Rep. Ohio)	Morris Sheppard (Dem. Tex.)
72nd (1931-1933)	Watson	Robinson	Fess	Sheppard
73rd (1933-1935)	Joseph T. Robinson (Dem. Ark.)	Charles L. McNary (Rep. Ore.)	Lewis	Felix Hebert (Rep. R.I.)
74th (1935-1937)	Robinson	McNary	Lewis	None
75th (1937-1939)	Robinson/ Alben W. Barkley (Dem. Ky.)[6]	McNary	Lewis	None
76th (1939-1941)	Barkley	McNary	Sherman Minton (Dem. Ind.)	None
77th (1941-1943)	Barkley	McNary	Lister Hill (Dem. Ala.)	None
78th (1943-1945)	Barkley	McNary	Hill	Kenneth Wherry (Rep. Neb.)
79th (1945-1947)	Barkley	Wallace H. White Jr. (Rep. Maine)	Hill	Wherry
80th (1947-1949)	Wallace H. White Jr. (Rep. Maine)	Alben W. Barkley (Dem. Ky.)	Kenneth Wherry (Rep. Neb.)	Scott Lucas (Dem. Ill.)

[1] Wadsworth served as minority whip for just one week, from Dec. 6 to Dec. 13, 1915.
[2] Gallinger died on Aug. 17, 1918 and Lodge became minority leader on August 24, 1918.
[3] Martin died on Nov. 12, 1919 and Underwood became minority leader on April 27, 1920. Gilbert M. Hitchcock (Dem., Neb.) acted as minority leader in the interim.
[4] Lodge died on Nov. 9, 1924 and Curtis became majority leader on Nov. 28, 1924.
[5] Jones became majority whip, filling the vacancy resulting from the elevation of Curtis to majority leader.
[6] Robinson died on July 14, 1937 and Barkley became majority leader on July 22, 1937.

Congress	Senate Floor Leaders Majority	Senate Floor Leaders Minority	Senate Whips Majority	Senate Whips Minority
81st (1949-1951)	Scott W. Lucas (Dem. Ill.)	Kenneth S. Wherry (Rep. Neb.)	Francis Myers (Dem. Pa.)	Leverett Saltonstall (Rep. Mass.)
82nd (1951-1953)	Ernest W. McFarland (Dem. Ariz.)	Wherry/Styles Bridges (Rep. N.H.)[7]	Lyndon B. Johnson (Dem. Tex.)	Saltonstall
83rd (1953-1955)	Robert A. Taft (Rep. Ohio)/ William F. Knowland (Rep. Calif.)[8]	Lyndon B. Johnson (Dem. Tex.)	Leverett Saltonstall (Rep. Mass.)	Earle Clements (Dem. Ky.)
84th (1955-1957)	Lyndon B. Johnson (Dem. Texas)	William F. Knowland (Rep. Calif.)	Earle Clements (Dem. Ky.)	Saltonstall
85th (1957-1959)	Johnson (Dem. Mont.)	Knowland Dirksen (Rep. Ill.)	Mike Mansfield	Everett McKinley
86th (1959-1961)	Johnson (Rep. Ill.)	Everett McKinley Dirksen (Rep. Calif.)	Mansfield	Thomas H. Kuchel
87th (1961-1963)	Mike Mansfield (Dem. Mont.)	Dirksen (Dem. Minn.)	Hubert H. Humphrey	Kuchel
88th (1963-1965)	Mansfield	Dirksen	Humphrey	Kuchel
89th (1965-1967)	Mansfield	Dirksen (Dem. La.)	Russel Long	Kuchel
90th (1967-1969)	Mansfield	Dirksen	Long	Kuchel
91st (1969-1971)	Mansfield	Dirksen/ Hugh Scott (Rep. Pa.)[9]	Edward M. Kennedy (Dem. Mass) (Rep. Mich.)[10]	Hugh Scott (Rep. Pa.)/ Robert P. Griffin
92nd (1971-1973)	Mansfield	Scott (Dem. W.Va.)	Robert C. Byrd	Griffin
93rd (1973-1975)	Mansfield	Scott	Byrd	Griffin
94th (1975-1977)	Mansfield	Scott	Byrd	Griffin
95th (1977-1979)	Robert C. Byrd (Dem. W.Va.)	Howard H. Baker Jr. (Rep. Tenn.)	Alan Cranston (Dem. Calif.)	Ted Stevens (Rep. Alaska)
96th (1979-1981)	Byrd	Baker	Cranston	Stevens
97th (1981-1983)	Howard H. Baker Jr. (Rep. Tenn.)	Robert C. Byrd (Dem. W.Va.)	Ted Stevens (Rep. Alaska)	Alan Cranston (Dem. Calif.)
98th (1983-1985)	Baker	Byrd	Stevens	Cranston
99th (1985-1987)	Bob Dole (Rep. Kan.)	Byrd	Alan K. Simpson (Rep. Wyo.)	Cranston
100th (1987-1989)	Byrd	Bob Dole (Rep. Kan.)	Cranston	Alan K. Simpson (Rep. Wyo.)
101st (1989-1991)	George J. Mitchell (Dem. Maine)	Dole	Cranston	Simpson
102nd (1991-1993)	Mitchell	Dole	Wendell H. Ford (Dem. Ky.)	Simpson
103rd (1993-1995)	Mitchell	Dole	Ford	Simpson
104th (1995-1996)	Dole	Thomas Dasche (Dem. S.D.)	Trent Lott (Rep., Miss.)	Wendell H. Ford (Dem., Ky.)

[7] Wherry died on Nov. 29, 1951 and Bridges became minority leader on Jan. 8, 1952.

[8] Taft died on July 31, 1953 and Knowland became majority leader on Aug. 4, 1953. Taft's Senate seat was filled by a Democrat, Thomas Burke, on Nov. 10, 1953. The makeup of the Senate changed to 48 Democrats, 47 Republicans, and 1 Independent, thus giving control of the Senate to the Democrats. Knowland remained majority leader until the end of the 83rd Congress.

[9] Dirksen died on Sept. 7, 1969 and Scott became minority leader on Sept. 24, 1969.

[10] Griffin became minority whip on Sept. 24, 1969 and filled the vacancy resulting from the elevation of Scott to minority leader.

APPENDIX F

REPRESENTATIVES UNDER EACH APPORTIONMENT

See Article 1, section 2 of the Constitution, page 559.

States	1788[1]	1st census 1790	2d census 1800	3d census 1810	4th census 1820	5th census 1830	6th census 1840	7th census 1850	8th census 1870	9th census 1880	10th census 1890	11th census 1900	12th census 1910	13th census 1920[7]	15th census 1930	16th census 1940	17th census 1950	18th census 1960	19th census 1970	20th census 1980	21st census 1990
Alabama				1[3]	3	5	7	7	6	8	8	9	9	10	9	9	9	8	7	7	7
Alaska																	1[5]	1	1	1	1
Arizona												1[3]	1	2	2	3	4	5	6		
Arkansas						1[3]	1	2	3	4	5	6	7	7	7	7	6	4	4	4	4
California							2[3]	2	3	4	6	7	8	11	20	23	30	38	43	45	52
Colorado									1[3]	1	2	3	4	4	4	4	4	4	5	6	6
Connecticut	5	7	7	7	6	6	4	4	4	4	4	4	5	5	6	6	6	6	6	6	6
Delaware	1	1	1	2	1	1	1	1	1	1	1	1	1	1	1	1	1	1	1	1	1
Florida							1[3]	1	1	2	2	2	3	4	5	6	8	12	15	19	23
Georgia	3	2	4	6	7	9	8	8	7	9	10	11	11	12	10	10	10	10	10	10	11
Hawaii																	1[5]	2	2	2	2
Idaho											1[3]	1	1	2	2	2	2	2	2	2	2
Illinois				1[3]	1	3	7	9	14	19	20	22	25	27	27	26	25	24	24	22	20
Indiana				1[3]	3	7	10	11	11	13	13	13	13	13	12	11	11	11	11	10	10
Iowa							2[3]	2	6	9	11	11	11	11	9	8	8	7	6	6	5
Kansas								1	3	7	8	8	8	8	7	6	6	5	5	5	4
Kentucky		2	6	10	12	13	10	10	9	10	11	11	11	11	9	9	8	7	7	7	6
Louisiana				1[3]	3	3	4	4	5	6	6	6	7	8	8	8	8	8	8	8	7
Maine				7[4]	7	8	7	6	5	5	4	4	4	4	3	3	3	2	2	2	2
Maryland	6	8	9	9	9	8	6	6	5	6	6	6	6	6	6	6	7	8	8	8	8
Massachusetts	8	14	17	13[4]	13	12	10	11	10	11	12	13	14	16	15	14	14	12	12	11	10
Michigan						1[3]	3	4	6	9	11	12	12	13	17	17	18	19	19	18	16
Minnesota								2[3]	2	3	5	7	9	10	9	9	9	8	8	8	8
Mississippi				1[3]	1	2	4	5	5	6	7	7	8	8	7	7	6	5	5	5	5
Missouri					1	2	5	7	9	13	14	15	16	16	13	13	11	10	10	9	9
Montana											1[3]	1	1	2	2	2	2	2	2	2	1
Nebraska									1[3]	1	3	6	6	6	5	4	4	3	3	3	3
Nevada									1[3]	1	1	1	1	1	1	1	1	1	1	2	2
New Hampshire	3	4	5	6	6	5	4	3	3	3	2	2	2	2	2	2	2	2	2	2	2
New Jersey	4	5	6	6	6	6	5	5	5	7	7	8	10	12	14	14	14	15	15	14	13
New Mexico												1[3]	1	2	2	2	2	2	3	3	
New York	6	10	17	27	34	40	34	33	31	33	34	34	37	43	45	45	43	41	39	34	31
North Carolina	5	10	12	13	13	13	9	8	7	8	9	9	10	10	11	12	12	11	11	11	12
North Dakota											1[3]	1	2	3	2	2	2	2	1	1	1

States	1788[1]	1st census 1790	2d census 1800	3d census 1810	4th census 1820	5th census 1830	6th census 1840	7th census 1850	8th census 1870	9th census 1880	10th census 1890	11th census 1900	12th census 1910	13th census 1920[2]	15th census 1930	16th census 1940	17th census 1950	18th census 1960	19th census 1970	20th census 1980	21st census 1990
Ohio			1[3]	6	14	19	21	21	19	20	21	21	21	22	24	23	23	24	23	21	19
Oklahoma													5[3]	8	9	8	6	6	6	6	8
Oregon								1[3]	1	1	1	2	2	3	3	4	4	4	4	5	5
Pennsylvania	8	13	18	23	26	28	24	25	24	27	28	28	30	32	36	33	30	27	25	23	21
Rhode Island	1	2	2	2	2	2	2	2	2	2	2	2	2	3	2	2	2	2	2	2	2
South Carolina	5	6	8	9	9	9	7	6	4	5	7	7	7	7	6	6	6	6	6	6	6
South Dakota											2[3]	2	2	3	2	2	2	2	2	1	1
Tennessee		1[3]	3	6	9	13	11	10	8	10	10	10	10	10	9	10	9	9	8	9	9
Texas							2[3]	2	4	6	11	13	16	18	21	21	22	23	24	27	30
Utah												1[3]	1	2	2	2	2	2	2	3	3
Vermont		2	4	6	5	5	4	3	3	3	2	2	2	2	1	1	1	1	1	1	1
Virginia	10	19	22	23	22	21	15	13	11	9	10	10	10	10	9	9	10	10	10	10	11
Washington											1[3]	2	3	5	6	6	7	7	7	8	9
West Virginia									3	4	4	5	6	6	6	6	6	5	4	4	3
Wisconsin							2[3]	3	6	8	9	10	11	11	10	10	10	10	9	9	9
Wyoming											1[3]	1	1	1	1	1	1	1	1	1	1
Total	65	106	142	186	213	242	232	237	143	293	332	357	391	435	435	435	437	435	435	435	435

[1] Apportionment was mandated by article I, section 2 of the Federal Constitution, and remained in effect until the first census in 1790.

[2] No apportionment was made in 1920.

[3] On several occasions, new states were admitted to the Union after a particular census, and Congress would provide for a certain number of representatives in the House until the next census and apportionment. For example, Congress gave Tennessee one representative after the first census, Ohio one after the second census, etc.

FIRST Tennessee, 1
SECOND Ohio, 1
THIRD Alabama, 1; Illinois, 1; Indiana, 1; Louisiana, 1; Mississippi, 1
FIFTH Arkansas, 1; Michigan, 1
SIXTH California, 2; Florida, 1; Iowa, 2; Texas, 2; Wisconsin, 2
SEVENTH Minnesota, 2; Oregon, 1
EIGHTH Nebraska, 1; Nevada, 1
NINTH Colorado, 1
TENTH Idaho, 1; Montana, 1; North Dakota, 1; South Dakota, 2; Washington, 1; Wyoming, 1
ELEVENTH Utah, 1
TWELFTH Oklahoma, 5
THIRTEENTH Arizona, 1; New Mexico, 1
SEVENTEENTH Alaska, 1; Hawaii, 1

[4] Twenty Representatives were apportioned to Massachusetts, but 7 of them were subsequently credited to Maine when that area became a State in 1823.

[5] Apportionment was temporarily increased to 437 from 435 by Public Laws 85-508 and 86-3 due to the admission of Alaska and Hawaii as States.

APPENDIX G

CONGRESSIONAL PAY RATES

Years	Salary	President Pro Tempore Majority/Minority Leaders[1]
1789-1815	$6.00 per diem[2]	-
1815-1817	$1,500 per annum	-
1817-1855	$8.00 per diem	-
1855-1865	$3,000 per annum	-
1865-1871	$5,000 per annum	-
1871-1873	$7,500 per annum	-
1873-1907	$5,000 per annum	-
1907-1925	$7,500 per annum	-
1925-1932	$10,000 per annum	-
1932-1933	$9,000 per annum	-
1933-1935	$8,500 per annum	-
1935-1947	$10,000 per annum	-
1947-1955	$12,500 per annum	-
1955-1965	$22,500 per annum	-
1965-1969	$30,000 per annum	$35,000 per annum
1969-1975	$42,500 per annum	$49,500 per annum
1975-1977	$44,600 per annum	$52,000 per annum
1977-1978	$57,500 per annum	$65,000 per annum
1979-1983	$60,662.50 per annum[3]	$68,575 per annum
1983	$69,800 per annum	$69,800 per annum
1984	$72,600 per annum	$72,600 per annum
1985-1986	$75,100 per annum	$85,000 per annum
1987 (Jan. 1-Feb 3)	$77,400 per annum	$87,600 per annum
1987 (Feb. 4)	$89,500 per annum	$99,500 per annum
1990	$98,400 per annum[4]	$109,500 per annum
1991	$101,900 per annum	$113,400 per annum
1991 (Aug. 15)	$125,100 per annum[5]	$138,900 per annum
1992	$129,500 per annum[6]	$143,800 per annum

[1] House and Senate majority and minority leaders received the same salary as other members until October 1, 1965. Prior to 1969, the president pro tempore was compensated at the same rate as other senators, except when there was no vice president. On those occasions, he was paid at the vice president's rate. On October 1, 1969, his salary was tied to that of the majority and minority leaders.

[2] Senators received $7.00 per diem during the 4th Congress (1795-1796).

[3] Effective January 3, 1983, House members' salaries increased to $69,800 per year. Senators' salaries increased to the House rate on July 1, 1983.

[4] In November 1989, the Senate and House approved a pay raise and ethics bill setting different salaries and regulations on honoraria for the two bodies. For House members, it provided a 7.9-percent pay increase in February 1990 and a 25-percent raise a year later to $120,750. A House ban on receiving honoraria took effect in 1991 at the same time as the 25-percent pay hike. Also in November of 1989, the Senate adopted a 9.7-percent increase (to $98,400) to take effect on February 1, 1990, and turned down the 25-percent raise for 1991. Instead, it permitted senators to receive some honoraria, although reducing the amount somewhat, from $35,800 to $26,568 in 1990. In 1991 both houses received a 3.6-percent cost-of-living increase.

[5] In August 1991, the Senate voted to raise senators' salaries to $125,100—the same level as the House—and adopted a ban on honoraria.

[6] This increase resulted from an automatic cost-of-living adjustment under a provision of the 1989 salary law.

APPENDIX H

CONGRESSIONAL BUILDINGS

Senate Buildings:

   Russell Senate Office Building - Delaware & Constitution Aves. N.E., 20510
   Dirksen Senate Office Building - 1st St. & Constitution Ave. N.E., 20510
   Hart Senate Office Building - 2nd St. & Constitution Ave. N.E., 20510

House Buildings:

   Cannon House Office Building - 1st St. & Independence Ave. S.E., 20515
   Longworth House Office Building - Independence & N.J. Aves. S.E., 20515
   Rayburn House Office Building - Independence Ave. & S. Cap. St. S.W., 20515
   O'Neill House Office Building - New Jersey Ave. & C St. S.E., 20515
   Ford House Office Building - 2nd & D Sts. S.W., 20515
   House Office Building Annex No. 3 - 501 1st St. S.E., 20515

Other Buildings:

   Library of Congress (Thomas Jefferson Building) - 10 First St. S.E., 20540
   John Adams Building (Library of Congress) - 110 2nd St. S.E., 20540
   James Madison Memorial Building (Library of Congress Annex) - 101
   Independence Ave. S.E., 20540

GLOSSARY

Act: A bill that has become law by being passed by both the House and the Senate and subsequently signed by the president (or passed over his *veto*).

Advice and Consent: The phrase (in Article II, section 2 of the Constitution) that describes the Senate's approval of treaties and the confirmation of presidential *nominations*. Unlike nominations, which only require a simple majority, treaties must be approved by a two-thirds vote of those present when the vote is taken. Under the Constitution, the House does not participate in either the approval of treaties or the confirmation of presidential nominations.

Amendment: A change or revision to an existing law or to a pending *bill*. To be distinguished from a *Constitutional Amendment*.

Bill: Any piece of legislation before it becomes law, after which it is called an *act*.

Bipartisan: Mutual cooperation and compromise between Democrats and Republicans in Congress.

Cloture: A procedure in the Senate for ending debate on a bill so it can be brought to a vote. (see also *filibuster*). It takes three-fifths of the Senate membership, which now means 60 out of 100 senators, to invoke cloture. There is no cloture procedure in the House, because

the rules allow the majority leadership to set strict limits on the time for debating any action on the floor.

Committee: A group of senators or representatives that drafts legislation and conducts hearings on matters within its jurisdiction. For example, a bill concerning agriculture introduced in the House would typically go first to the House Agriculture Committee for hearings and revisions before the House would vote on the bill. The head of the committee is the chairman, who is a member of the political party with a majority in that chamber of Congress; the senior member of the minority party is the ranking minority member. Both the House and the Senate have committees that handle the bulk of their internal administrative work.

Conference Committee: A joint group of representatives and senators designated by the leadership to reconcile differences between the House and the Senate versions of the same bill. The conference committee resolves the differences and sends the conference version of the bill to both chambers for their approval.

Congress: The legislature of the federal government composed of two branches, the *Senate* and the *House of Representatives*. The Congress has existed since 1789, but since there is a *congressional election* every two years, each and every two-year period since 1789 is known by a number. For example, the Congress which first met in 1789 was the First Congress, elected in November of 1788, the Congress that met in 1791 was the Second Congress, elected in November of 1790, and the Congress that met in 1995 was the 104th Congress, elected in November of 1994.

Congressional elections: Every two years the entire *House of Representatives* and approximately one-third of the *Senate* are up for re-election. The first congressional election was held in November of 1788 for the first Congress which began in 1789, and there have been congressional elections every two years since, with the most recent as of the date of this writing being in 1994 for the 104th Congress which began in 1995.

Congressional Record: The official transcript of daily proceedings in the House and Senate. The Congressional Record is not always an exact record of speeches and remarks, however, since members can edit and revise their comments.

Congressman/Congresswoman: Although technically any member of Congress, whether a senator or a representative, is a "Congressman" or a "Congresswoman," the terms are most commonly used for representatives, while senators are called senators.

Constitutional Amendment: A change or addition to the U.S. Constitution. The Constitution may be amended if two-thirds of the House and two-thirds of the Senate present when the vote is taken vote in favor of a proposed amendment, and then three-fourths of the states ratify that amendment. Since there are now 50 states, an amendment thus becomes effective when 38 states have ratified it. (The Constitution also provides for amendments by a convention called by the states, but this procedure has never been used.) The president's signature is not required, and he cannot *veto* a constitutional amendment. The Constitution currently has 27 amendments, on subjects ranging from basic protections of individual rights to technical matters such as pay raises for members of Congress.

Filibuster: An attempt by a minority senator to prevent a bill from coming to a vote by making a prolonged speech on the Senate floor. During the 1960s, senators from the South filibustered for days when they tried to block civil rights legislation, sometimes simply reading from phone books in an effort to take up time. Ending a filibuster, a procedure known as *cloture*, requires a three-fifths vote of the whole membership of the Senate. This means that if there is a filibuster, even if a majority of the senators favor passing the bill targeted by the filibuster, that majority needs 60 votes to shut off debate and then take a vote on the legislation.

House Leadership: The leader of the House of Representatives is the Speaker of the House, who is elected at the beginning of each new Congress by the members of the majority political party in the House. There is also a House majority leader, who works with the Speaker and is considered the second most powerful member of the House. In addition to the House majority leader there is a House majority whip, who is responsible for making sure that party members vote consistently with the party agenda. The leader of the political party in the minority is the House minority leader, and there is also a House minority whip.

House Majority Leader, Majority Whip, Minority Leader, Minority Whip: See *House Leadership*.

House of Representatives: One of the two branches of Congress, the other being the *Senate*. Currently, there are 435 representatives in the House, each of whom serves a two-year term. The entire House is up for re-election in every *congressional election*.

The House is intended to be the branch that is most responsive to the voters, which is why representatives are elected for short terms: in effect, representatives are constantly running for re-election and must constantly prove themselves to their voters. When Congress first met in 1789, there was one representative for every 30,000 people, these 30,000 people constituting a "congressional district." Since the U.S. population has grown so rapidly, today a congressional district contains over 600,000 people. The size of the House was capped at 435 in the early 20th century so that the House wouldn't become too large to be efficient. States with large populations get many representatives: California, the most populous state, has over 50. States with small populations are guaranteed at least one representative by the Constitution: Wyoming, which has the lowest population of all the states and contains approximately 450,000 people, has only one representative and its single congressional district covers the whole state. Representatives must be at least 25 years old.

Since the House is supposed to be the branch that is most in touch with the voters, it gets certain powers that the Senate does not: all tax legislation must originate in the House, and if there is no clear winner in a presidential election the House chooses the next president.

Impeachment: The process of removing certain federal officials from office. Congress has the sole power to remove federal officials, such as judges, justices of the Supreme Court, and even the president of the United States, through the impeachment process. First, a simple majority of the House must vote in favor of impeaching someone. Then, there is an impeachment trial, conducted solely by the Senate, where there must be a two-thirds majority of those present when the vote is taken in order to convict the impeached official. If the president is being impeached, the chief justice of the Supreme Court presides over the Senate impeachment trial. If convicted, the impeached person is removed from office, but the Senate cannot impose any criminal sentence.

Lame Duck Session: The portion of a congressional session that occurs between the biennial November election for the next Congress and the end of the congressional session, usually in December. Since members of Congress who lost in the November elections or are otherwise not returning to Congress in January can still vote on pending bills, they can vote without having to face any political repercussions. Therefore, lame duck sessions may be the time when controversial or unpopular measures come up for a vote.

Majority Leader and Majority Whip: See *House Leadership* and *Senate Leadership*.

Minority Leader and Minority Whip: See *House Leadership* and *Senate Leadership*.

Nomination: The naming by the president of a person to fill a senior federal office, such as a cabinet position or an ambassadorship. Under the Constitution, nominations must be confirmed by a simple majority of the Senate.

Pocket Veto: A presidential *veto* that is accomplished by holding on to a bill after Congress adjourned its final session. Normally, a president has to veto a bill within ten days (excluding Sundays) after receiving it or the bill automatically becomes law. However, if the final session of Congress ends before the ten days are up, the president can hold onto a bill without vetoing it and the bill will not automatically become a law. A pocket veto thus avoids the political confrontation of a regular veto.

Quorum: The number of members required to be present in order to transact business or take votes in the House or the Senate. In both the House and the Senate, a quorum is a simple majority of the entire membership, not just of the members present.

Recess: A short break within a congressional *session*, during which no business is conducted. Although Congress is still technically in session, members can go home for holidays, visit their constituents, etc.

Select Committee: A committee established for a special purpose and a limited time period. For example, in 1973 the Senate created the

Senate Select Committee on Presidential Campaign Activities, nicknamed the Watergate Committee, to investigate the Watergate affair. At the conclusion of the committee's activities, it was dissolved.

Senate: One of the two branches of Congress, the other being the *House of Representatives*. There are two senators for every state, regardless of its population or size, and since there are now 50 states there are 100 senators. Senators are elected for six-year terms, and approximately one-third of the senators must run for re-election in every *congressional election*. Senators serve six-year terms so that they can make decisions they believe are in the best interests of the country, even if politically unpopular, with less concern about the immediate impacts on their chances for re-election. Senators must be at least 30 years old.

Since the Senate is supposed to be less vulnerable to political mood swings, the Senate enjoys certain powers that the House does not: the Senate alone approves treaties, confirms presidential *nominations*, and conducts *impeachment* trials.

Senate Leadership: The Senate leadership is more complicated than the *House Leadership*. First, the Constitution provides that the vice president of the United States also serves as the president of the Senate, although in practice the vice president rarely exercises the right to preside over the Senate unless there is a tie vote on an important matter, in which case the vice president gets to cast the tie-breaking vote. Under the Constitution, the Senate president pro tempore presides over the Senate in the vice president's absence. Effectively, however, the Senate majority leader, who is elected by the political party with the most senators, is the leader of the Senate. His second in command is the Senate majority whip, who is responsible for making sure that party members vote consistently for the party's agenda. There is also a Senate minority leader, who leads the minority political party in the Senate, and a Senate minority whip.

Senate Majority Leader, Majority Whip, Minority Leader, Minority Whip: See *Senate Leadership*.

Senate President Pro Tem: See *Senate Leadership*.

Session: A set period during which Congress is scheduled to meet and conduct business. It is rare for a single Congress to have more than two sessions.

Speaker of the House: See House Leadership.

Special Session: A session of Congress held in addition to its regular sessions. The president has the authority under Article II, section 3 of the Constitution (see Appendix A) to convene either the Senate and/or the House "on extraordinary occasions." These occasions are called special sessions. Before the Twentieth Amendment in 1933, a new president was inaugurated in March, but Congress frequently did not convene until months later. Therefore, special sessions were fairly common before 1933 in order to conduct business without having to wait for Congress's next regular session to convene. Many such special sessions of the Senate were called to confirm the president's cabinet nominees. After the Twentieth Amendment, which synchronizes the timing of Congress's regular sessions with the presidential inauguration and places both in the month of January, special sessions have become much less frequent.

Standing Committee: A permanent committee that exists from Congress to Congress in either the House or the Senate unless it is abolished. The committees listed in the tables of key committees for each Congress are (or were) standing committees.

State of the Union Address: The annual address made by the president of the United States to Congress, usually in January, which typically sets forth the president's political agenda for the upcoming year. Today, the State of the Union Address is a nationally televised speech, but before television the address was often just a written message that the president sent to Congress.

Subcommittee: Internal subdivisions of committees, which typically review a bill and hold hearings on it before the matter is considered by the full committee.

Veto: The formal rejection by the president of a bill passed by the House and the Senate. The president must veto a bill within ten days (excluding Sundays) after receiving it or the bill automatically becomes law. If the president vetoes a bill, Congress can override the veto and pass the bill into law without the president's signature, but two-thirds of the House and two-thirds of the Senate must vote in favor of a veto override. See also *Pocket Veto*.

Voice Vote: A vote in either the House or the Senate, conducted by simply asking the members in favor to say "yea" and the members against to say "nay." If a bill is passed or rejected by voice vote, there is no record of which members or how many voted in favor or against the bill. In either chamber, if one-fifth of the members present so request, the voice vote procedure is dispensed with and the vote of every member is taken and recorded. Voice votes were very common until the 20th century, when it became routine to request recorded votes for all but the most noncontroversial matters.

SOURCES FOR FURTHER STUDY

Set forth below are general reference sources concerning Congress. For more specific sources on particular topics and/or historical periods, see the Further Reading section of the Congress and/or Congresses concerned.

American Landmark Legislation. 6 Vols. Dobbs Ferry, N.Y.: Oceana Publications, 1976.

Baker, Richard A. *The Senate of the United States: A Bicentennial History*. Malabar, Fla.: R.E. Krieger, 1988.

Baker, Richard A. and Davidson, Roger H. *First Among Equals: Outstanding Senate Leaders of the 20th Century*. Washington, D.C.: Congressional Quarterly, 1991.

The Bicentennial Almanac: 200 Years of America 1776-1976. Nashville, Tenn.: T. Nelson, 1975.

Byrd, Senator Robert C. *The Senate, 1789-1989*. 4 Vols. Washington, D.C.: U.S. Government Printing Office, 1988-1994.

Carruth, Gorton. *The Encyclopedia of American Facts and Dates*. New York: HarperCollins, 1993.

Congressional Quarterly. *American Leaders, 1789-1991: A Biographical Summary*. Washington, D.C.: Congressional Quarterly, 1991.

Congressional Quarterly. *Congress A to Z: A Ready Reference Encyclopedia*. Washington, D.C.: Congressional Quarterly, 1993.

Congressional Quarterly. *Congress and the Nation, 1945-1992*. 8 Vols. Washington, D.C.: Congressional Quarterly, 1993.

Dole, Senator Robert J. *Historical Almanac of the United States Senate*. Washington, D.C.: U.S Government Printing Office, 1989.

The Economic Regulation of Business and Industry: A Legislative History of U.S. Regulatory Agencies. New York: Chelsea House, 1973.

Encyclopedia of American History. New York: Harper & Row, 1982.

Encyclopedia of the American Legislative System. 3 Vols. New York: Charles Scribner's Sons and Maxwell Macmillan International, 1994.

Encyclopedia of the American Presidency. 4 Vols. New York: Simon & Schuster, 1994.

Encyclopedia of the United States Congress. New York: Simon & Schuster, 1995.

Goodwin, George. *The Little Legislatures; Committees of Congress*. Amherst, Mass.: University of Massachusetts Press, 1970.

Hall, Kermit L. *The Oxford Companion to the Supreme Court*. New York: Oxford University Press, 1992.

Harness, Gregory. *Presidential Vetoes, 1789-1988*. Washington, D.C.: U.S. Government Printing Office, 1992.

Hutchinson, E.P. *Legislative History of American Immigration Policy, 1798-1965*. Philadelphia: University of Pennsylvania Press, 1981.

Johnson, Nancy P. *Sources of Compiled Legislative Histories: A Bibliography of Government Documents, Periodical Articles, and Books 1st Congress-101st Congress*. Littleton, Colorado: Fred B. Rothman & Co., 1993.

Kane, Joseph Nathan. *Facts About the Presidents*. New York: H.W. Wilson, 1993.

Kravitz, Walter. *Congressional Quarterly's American Congressional Dictionary*. Washington, D.C.: Congressional Quarterly, 1993.

The Legislative History of the Federal Antitrust Laws and Related Statutes. New York: Chelsea House, 1978.

Martis, Kenneth C. *The Historical Atlas of Political Parties in the United States Congress, 1789-1989*. New York: Macmillan, 1989.

Martis, Kenneth C. and Elmes, Gregory A. *The Historical Atlas of State Power in Congress, 1790-1990*. Washington, D.C.: Congressional Quarterly, 1993.

Miller, William Lee. *Arguing About Slavery: The Great Battle in the United States Congress*. New York: Alfred A. Knopf, 1996.

Nelson, Garrison. *Committees in the U.S. Congress, 1947-1992*. Washington, D.C.: Congressional Quarterly, 1993.

Oleszek, Walter J. *Congressional Procedures and the Policy Process*. Washington, D.C.: Congressional Quarterly, 1988.

Peters, Ronald M., Jr. *The Speaker: Leadership in the U.S. House of Representatives*. Washington, D.C.: Congressional Quarterly, 1994.

Peters, Ronald M., Jr. *The American Speakership: The Office in Historical Perspective*. Baltimore: Johns Hopkins University Press, 1990.

Reams, Bernard D. and Haworth, Charles R. *Congress and the Courts: A Legislative History, 1787-1977*. 30 Vols. Buffalo, N.Y.: Hein, 1978.

Reams, Bernard D. *Congress and the Courts: A Legislative History, Second Series, 1978-1984*. 22 Vols. Buffalo, N.Y.: Hein, 1985.

Schlesinger, Arthur M. Jr. *History of U.S. Political Parties, 1789-1972*. New York: Chelsea House Publishers, 1973.

Silbey, Joel H. *The Congress of the United States, 1789-1989*. 23 Vols. Brooklyn, N.Y.: Carlson Publishers, 1991.

Smith, Solomon. *Legislative History: Draft and Selective Service Acts (1863-1967)*. New Haven, Conn.: Yale University Law Library, 1968.

U.S. Government. *Biographical Directory of the United States Congress, 1774-1989*. Washington, D.C.: U.S. Government Printing Office, 1989.

U.S. Government. *Black Americans in Congress, 1870-1989*. Washington, D.C.: U.S. Government Printing Office, 1989.

U.S. Government. *To Make All Laws: The Congress of the United States, 1789-1989*. Washington, D.C.: U.S. Government Printing Office, 1989.

U.S. Government. *Women in Congress, 1917-1990*. Washington, D.C.: U.S. Government Printing Office, 1991.

INDEX

N

U